SALVADOR DALI & ANDY WARHOL

SALVADOR DALI & ANDY WARHOL

Encounters in New York and Beyond

by Torsten Otte

Scheidegger & Spiess

**This book is dedicated to
the memory of my father,
Hubert Otte**

Salvador Dalí (1904–1989) and Andy Warhol (1928–1987), who was a generation younger, are among the most famous artists of the twentieth century. Contemporaries often called them "art celebrities" and mentioned them in the same breath as Picasso.[1] Their fame was the result of accomplished self-staging, along with the skillful marketing of their work and their person. Both artists succeeded in drawing public and media attention to themselves in their own special way. The artists themselves were also aware that this, in itself, was a significant accomplishment. Salvador Dalí remarks in his *Diary of a Genius,* published in the mid-1960s: "It is difficult to hold the world's interest for more than half an hour at a time. I myself have done so successfully for twenty years, and every day. My motto has been: 'Let them speak of Dalí, even if it is favorably.'"[2] Indeed, scarcely a day went by from the 1940s to the 1960s that his name was not mentioned publicly. It was similar from the mid-1960s with regard to Andy Warhol, who once stated: "Publicity is like eating peanuts. Once you start you can't stop,"[3] and emphasized that "*any* publicity was good publicity."[4] On the occasion of the "Surrealism in Art" exhibition shown at Knoedler Gallery in New York in early 1975, one commentator quite rightly opined that Warhol occupied the spot in public awareness that Dalí had paved the way for with Surrealism.[5] At the time Warhol had already become a notorious party-goer who declared provocatively that he went "to the opening of anything, including a toilet seat."[6] Owing to his persistent presence in the public spotlight, he was assured a place in the tabloid press, which also liked to report on Dalí's eccentric appearances. Art critics reacted to this with horror and promptly denied both the status of a serious artist. Their commercial success was also a thorn in the side of many people.

Is their media presence reason enough to compare these two artists whose works seem quite different at first glance and who would appear to have nothing in common? Salvador Dalí and Andy Warhol were representatives of different art movements. Dalí, born in 1904 in Figueres, Spain, became one of the major and most well-known representatives of Surrealism as early as the 1930s, while Warhol, born in 1928 in Pittsburgh in the United States, rose to become one of the most important and famous representatives of Pop Art in the 1960s. In 1966, Warhol was asked in an interview whether Pop Art had anything to do with Surrealism and he replied, "Not for me."[7] While Dalí created modern art using the techniques of the old masters, Warhol discovered silkscreen printing, with which he produced serial art without expending too much time or effort. Both artists therefore succeeded in creating art icons of the twentieth century using quite different techniques—Dalí with his painting *The Persistence of Memory,* better known by the title *The Soft Watches,* and Warhol with his proverbial *Campbell's Soup Can* series.[8]

Dalí and Warhol have other points in common. Both are famous for a signature feature: Dalí for his upward twirling mustache, Warhol for his conspicuous wig. Less well known is that they were in contact with each other on a regular basis in the 1960s and 1970s.

There are an extraordinary number of publications dealing with the life and works of Dalí. The same applies to Warhol. However, no work thus far has compared the two artists and provided a detailed exploration of their

1
According to Solomon 1966 and Tomkins in Coplans 1970, p. 13. In 1971 Robert Hughes wrote in *TIME* magazine: "Next to Picasso and that camping St. John of the Cheque, Salvador Dalí, Warhol is the supreme example of the artist-as-celebrity." Cf. Hughes 1971, p. 42.

2
Dalí 1965, p. 175.

3
Warhol/Colacello 1979, p. 176. *Cosmopolitan* spoke in 1966 of an "overnight success": "Andy Warhol painted his Campbell's soup cans and Brillo boxes and became one of the most talked-about artists since Dalí." Cf. James 1966, pp.14f.

4
Warhol/Hackett 1980, p. 124. In *Andy Warhol's Exposures* Warhol writes: "All the scandals help business because there's no publicity like bad publicity." Cf. Warhol/Colacello 1979, p. 53.

5
André 1975, p. 91.

6
Warhol/Colacello 1979, p. 19.

7
In Goldsmith 2004, pp. 4f.

8
Insofar as they exist, the English working titles are used; otherwise the French, Spanish, or Catalan titles are used.

relationship to each other and their encounters. Until now the relationship between the two artists has been addressed, for the most part, only peripherally. When Patrick S. Smith interviewed the art critic David Bourdon—author of a major Warhol biography in 1989—for his book *Andy Warhol's Art and Films* and asked him "Do you think that Salvador Dalí had any influence on Andy, as either an artist or as a lifestyle?" he simply answered, "I have no idea. It's conceivable that he had a big influence as a model ... for what a successful publicity-oriented artist could be."[9] The first to address the relationship between Dalí and Warhol in a book was Warhol himself, together with his employee Bob Colacello. In the work *Andy Warhol's Exposures* compiled by Colacello for Warhol in 1979, an entire chapter is dedicated to Dalí, which tells of Warhol's relationship with his older colleague.[10] Since the 1980s a whole string of people from the entourage of the two artists have written their memoirs and mentioned their relationship to each other peripherally.[11] The memoirs *Famous For 15 Minutes*, published in 1988 by Isabelle Collin Dufresne, who initially belonged to Dalí's entourage before featuring in Warhol's movies as Ultra Violet, can be highlighted.[12] The Warhol biography by Victor Bockris published a year later also touches on the relationship between the two artists. Here the reader learns, for example, that both Dalí and Warhol created window displays for the New York department store Bonwit Teller and that Dalí was announced as a member of Warhol's show ensemble in 1966, with the title *Andy Warhol Up-Tight* (later: *Exploding Plastic Inevitable*), which caused quite a stir.[13]

In 1998 the Salvador Dalí Museum in St. Petersburg, Florida, held the exhibition "Andy Warhol at the Dalí," showing central works by Warhol. In the exhibition guide, curator William Jeffett took up the links between Warhol and Dalí mentioned by Victor Bockris and wrote: "Andy Warhol and Salvador Dalí's careers were deeply intertwined, from Warhol's own use of Dalí as a role model to his later friendship with Dalí. ... Warhol, much as Dalí, would create a publicity machine in the pursuit of fame."[14] At the beginning of 2014 the same museum presented another Warhol exhibition, bearing the title "Warhol: Art. Fame. Mortality." This display also concentrated exclusively on Warhol's work, showing his paintings, drawings, prints, photographs, videos, and movies, including a *Screen Test* that Warhol had produced of Dalí in 1966. William Jeffett, as the chief curator of the museum, points out in the catalogue that it was not the purpose of the exhibition to present differences and similarities between the two artists: "Arguably the younger Warhol looked to the older Dalí as a model for what it was to be an artist. Both existed in a social world of other artists. Both also experimented with what were the new media of photography and film. These media in part played into the construction of an artistic and public self."[15] Hank Hine, director of the Dalí Museum, adds:

Warhol took the same stage Dalí had before him, that of the celebrity defining the style of the art of his moment, denizen of TIME magazine covers, ever-visible while never knowable, a compelling and mysterious persona misdirecting an over-curious audience away from the secretive core of his productive self.

9
In Smith 1986, p. 230.

10
Warhol/Colacello 1979, pp. 127ff.

11
Lear 1985, pp. 113, 268; Lear 2009, pp. 65ff.; Colacello 1990, pp. 172ff., 286f.; Makos 1988, p. 74; Finkelstein 1989 (n.p.); Tusquets Blanca 2003, p. 162; Bond, unpublished autobiography; Pitxot 2014, pp. 87f., 149.

12
Cf. Ultra Violet 1988, pp. 78f., 90, 121f.

13
Bockris 1989, pp. 71f., 247.

14
In *Andy Warhol at the Dalí* (n.p.).

15
In *Warhol: Art. Fame. Mortality.*, p. 11.

... In a sense he accomplished a cinematic dream that Dalí once professed—that the camera should be nailed to the floor like Christ to the cross to record what was in its field and what was not.[16]

At the opening of the exhibition, Hine remarked, in addition to the press: "Dalí and Warhol are very strange brothers. Maybe uncle and nephew. Certainly not father and son."[17]

Apart from these two Warhol exhibitions, there were interesting Dalí exhibitions in which the relationship of the Spaniard to his younger colleague from the United States was touched on in passing.[18] The retrospective held in 2004 in Venice and Philadelphia on the occasion of Dalí's 100th birthday is worthy of special mention. The catalogue contains an "Encyclopedia" with parallels between Dalí and Warhol listed under the heading "Andy Warhol (1928–87)." Apart from the mentioned similarities, attention is drawn to the fact that both artists were fascinated by the phenomenon of Mao Zedong and that both adopted the painting of the Italian Renaissance.[19] Michael R. Taylor also states here:

Dalí's earlier efforts to blur the line between high and low culture opened the door to Warhol's subsequent exploration of the media-saturated culture of the post-Second World War era, where fame had become increasingly attainable, but also increasingly transitory. There can be no doubt that Dalí's paintings, films, and even his hilarious newspaper, the Dalí News, *informed Warhol's own efforts in this vein, such as* Interview *magazine, which began production in 1969, as well as his films, screen tests, and television programs.*[20]

Under the heading "Prints," dedicated to Dalí's extensive print production, Juliette Murphy adds: "Here, Dalí subversively manipulates consumerism ... by compelling the spectator to unveil his own knowledge through challenging his taste. In this sense he can be placed at the heart of twentieth-century art, in line with Andy Warhol, whose use of print both mirrors and reflects the society that it satisfies, and by which it is sustained."[21] A further remarkable exhibition took place at the end of 2009 entitled "Dalí Dalí featuring Francesco Vezzoli" at the Moderna Museet in Stockholm, which had already held one of the first major exhibitions about Warhol at the beginning of 1968. An advertisement for the Drexel Burnham Lambert investment bank with a photo of Warhol is reproduced in the catalogue, as well as his famous quote, "Good business is the best art."[22] In the catalogue, the curator John Peter Nilsson writes: "As a phenomenon, Salvador Dalí is highly interesting today. In many ways, he presages Andy Warhol, who also became aware at an early stage of how the image of art or the artist is filtered through the mass media before the actual encounter with the object or person takes place."[23]

Apart from the already mentioned books and catalogues, other publications emerged over the years that touched on the relationship between Dalí and Warhol or dealt with it more extensively, reporting on their encounters.[24] The photographs by David McCabe taken in 1964/65 were published in *A Year in the Life of Andy Warhol* in 2003. One of the photo series had been captured in Dalí's studio at the St. Regis Hotel in New York.[25] The Dalí biography by Edmond Baudoin compiled in 2012 for the major retrospective

16
In ibid., pp. 7f.

17
Quoted according to Bradshaw 2013.

18
Cf. Aguer/Fanés in *Salvador Dalí: Àlbum de família,* pp. 73f.; Mas in *El ojo invisible,* pp. 145f. Fanés and Diego in Guldemond 2005, pp. 387ff., 453f.; Jeffett in *Pollock to Pop,* p. 41; Fanés and King in Gale 2007, pp. 49, 223f.; King in Gott 2009, p. 297; King in King/Brenneman 2010, pp. 41f.; Fetz in Matt 2011, pp. 220ff.; Pacquement, Dufrêne and Martin in Martin/Aguer/Bouhours/Dufrêne 2012, pp. 12, 25, 41, 45; Bouhours 2012, pp. 76ff.

19
Taylor in Ades 2004, pp. 461, 463, and in Taylor 2008, pp. 23ff.

20
Taylor in Ades 2004, p. 463.

21
Murphy in Ades 2004, p. 454.

22
Nilsson/Olof-Ors 2009, pp. CCXXXIIIf.

23
Nilsson in ibid., p. XIII.

→ **41/42** [pp. 390/391]

24
Carol 1990, p. 97; Etherington-Smith 1993, pp. 272, 378; Diego 1999, pp. 22ff.; Nuridsany 2001, pp. 324f.; Diego 2003, pp. 207ff.; +

25
McCabe/Dalton 2003, pp. 38ff.

at the Centre Georges Pompidou in Paris is also worth special mention. The French illustrator and comic-book artist wrote it in the form of a comic strip that also includes the description of an imagined encounter between Dalí and Warhol at the Guggenheim Museum dated as 1978, the year the first stereoscopic painting by Dalí was exhibited there. In the fictitious dialogue, Warhol admits to Dalí that he is intimidated by his masterful artistic career, to which Dalí gives the friendly reply that Warhol has no reason to feel intimidated, as his own style was also very good.[26] Also revealing is a text from 1998 in which the Spanish artist Víctor Mira explains in an artistic and ironic manner, under the title *The two most clever sons of Salvador Dalí*, why Andy Warhol and Joseph Beuys are the two cleverest sons of Salvador Dalí: the latter had given himself an unmistakable signature feature with his mustache and Warhol and Beuys had emulated him congenially with a wig and hat.[27] Mira also points out that Warhol—like Dalí before him—chose money as a theme for his artwork, that all three artists were Catholic, and that all three had death or near-death experiences: Dalí saw himself as a reincarnation of his deceased brother, Beuys survived the downing of his plane in the Crimea during World War II, and Warhol was reborn in a New York hospital after a failed attempt on his life.[28]

In Beuys's homeland, Germany, the view of Warhol's work was different than it was in the United States until way into the 1980s. After the catastrophe of World War II and liberation from the Nazi regime, new values were being sought in art, and the work by the American fell on fertile ground. It was therefore no coincidence that the first Warhol monograph was published in 1970, authored by the art historian Rainer Crone. The art dealer and curator Heiner Bastian even referred to Warhol's art as one of "the greatest things we had ever seen."[29] In 1968 Warhol exhibited his works in Kassel at *documenta 4*, which at the time was much influenced by Pop Art. Further participation in *documenta* followed in 1977 and 1982. What is remarkable in this regard is that for years, the *documenta* art directors had disregarded Dalí.[30] It was not until 2012, more than two decades after Dalí's death, that his paintings *The Great Paranoiac* (1936) and *Spain* (1938) were also exhibited in Kassel.[31] The reasons for turning Dalí down were his negative attitude towards abstract art and his ambiguous political statements in those years. Dalí's enormous commercial success and his public popularity was apparently also a thorn in the side of the critics. Interestingly, Warhol's comparable success, owing in particular to the many commissioned portraits, was not so contentious. His presence in the American tabloids was not detrimental to the high regard accorded to Warhol in Germany. This was an interesting dynamic. In his Warhol biography, Victor Bockris quotes an unnamed author with the words: "And even if Andy wasn't an intellectual they always saw him there [in Germany] in an intellectual way."[32] Warhol cultivated verbal indifference, as shown by his famous quote: "If you want to know all about Andy Warhol, just look at the surface: of my paintings and films and me, and there I am. There's nothing behind it."[33] "This supposed indifference," according to Paolo Bianchi and Christoph Oswald, "opened the doors to reception; Warhol's works serve viewers as a mirror of their own projections up until today."[34]

13

+
Pérez Andújar 2003, pp. 237, 242; Ross 2003, pp. 116f.; Argillet 2004, pp. 133f.; San Martín 2004, pp. 20f., 23, 122f.; Nuridsany 2004, pp. 21, 444f.; Argillet 2004, pp. 133f.; Sáez-Mateu in Maurer Queipo/Rißler-Pipka 2007, pp. 26, 34, 36; Millet 2008, pp. 31ff.; King 2007, pp. 143, 171f.; Joseph-Lowery in *Ray Johnson...Dalí/Warhol and others...*, p. 43; Guilbert 2008, p. 24; Grenier 2011, pp. 233f.; Dufrêne 2012, pp. 244f.; Ingram 2014, *This is Dalí*, p. 64; Ingram 2014, *This is Warhol*, pp. 48f.; Montua 2015, pp. 265ff., 307f., 333, 375ff., 419.

26
Baudoin 2012 (n.p.).

→ 1 [p. 361]

27
Mira 1988 (n.p.). The photographs reinforce the text's irony. As an opening photo, Mira chose a shot by Philippe Halsman from the year 1954, showing Salvador Dalí with a vertical moustache reaching way over his eyebrows. Cf. Dalí/Halsman 1954, p. 17. Mira copied this moustache onto photos of Warhol and Beuys, making the two artists into "the two most clever sons of Salvador Dalí."

28
Mira 1988 (n.p.). With regard to this it should be mentioned that Warhol knew Beuys personally. However, the two artists only met briefly in passing. Cf. Bianchi/Doswald 2000, p. 108.

29
Bockris 1989, p. 171.

30
It was only in 1967 as part of *documenta III* that he was represented with a small body study from the year 1934. It also seems remarkable that the catalogue at the time indicated Dalí's place of birth as "Figueras (California)." Cf. *documenta III, Handzeichnungen*, p. 44.

31
In *dOCUMENTA (13): Das Begleitbuch / The Guidebook* it says: "Arguably, the very notion of contemporary art owes a great deal to Salvador Dalí: his signature style, his commercial success, and his instinct for controversy made him a household name in his lifetime." Cf. p. 58.

32
Bockris 1989, p. 341.

33
Warhol (1966) in Goldsmith 2004, p. 90. For the extend of editing of Warhol's original brief comments, cf. Wrbican in Meyer-Hermann 2008, p. 00:57:00.

34
Bianchi/Doswald 2000, p. 106 (translated from the German).

This was indeed the case, but not only in Germany. In other countries the reception of Warhol's art also involved an intellectualization by critics. Gerard Malanga, Warhol's most important assistant in the 1960s, once stated: "I was with Andy twenty-four hours a day at that time, and I know that he would never choose an image for the kinds of reasons critics dug up."[35] It becomes obvious that Warhol was no intellectual when one takes the time to study his path through life and become acquainted with his personality and creative work. Studying the biography, personality, and artistic work of Dalí, on the other hand, reveals that he can truly be regarded as an intellectual. Sigmund Freud's psychoanalysis, discoveries in natural science, and an intensive dialogue with the history of art are at the foundations of his art.

Understanding both Dalí and Warhol also requires knowledge of their written work. However, great caution must be exercised when using it, as both artists pursued the aim of veiling and mystifying concrete aspects of their lives in their writing. Dalí once remarked in an interview that lying was "a natural gift" for him. "I can never tell the truth, even in dreams. I manage to transform my fantasies into real things, to everyone's benefit. I must invent everything, constantly."[36] For example, he glorified his deceased brother, who also bore the name Salvador, as a young genius.[37] Warhol expressed himself similarly in this respect and declared once in an interview, "I'd prefer to remain a mystery, I never like to give my background away and, anyway, I make it all up differently every time I'm asked."[38] Warhol particularly liked, for example, to foster confusion about the date and place of his birth, at times claiming to have been born in 1929 and at others stating 1930 as his year of birth. He also left his place of birth uncertain and only named the state of Pennsylvania.[39] It is therefore a systematic part of this publication to take a critical view of the legends woven by the two artists: The study of the written works by Dalí and Warhol merely forms a starting point. Of course the comprehensive research material on the artists is also analyzed. For the reasons stated, the present work does not focus on the existing art theory related to the motives and intentions of the two artists.

The many integrated comments and statements by contemporary witnesses who knew either Dalí or Warhol or both and provided valuable information in interviews or written correspondence are a key structural element of this study. The memories of these contemporary witnesses, in addition to the literature, form the backbone of the study. These memories are particularly valuable because some of those questioned speak for the first time about their experiences with either Dalí or Warhol or both. Most had also never been interviewed about the relationship between the two artists and their dealings with one another. Since the interviews deal with events that in some cases go back over fifty years, it is understandable that precise memories have often faded. Some of the witnesses also stated openly that they could no longer recall certain details. However, in many cases it was by all means possible to verify the statements made by those interviewed through comments by other contemporary witnesses and research. The evaluation of all the interviews that other authors held with contemporary witnesses (in some cases already deceased) also contributed to accomplishing this task.

35 Bockris 1989, p. 171.

36 In Mercouri/Dalí 1965, p. 92.

37 Gibson 1997, pp. 22f.

38 Warhol (1966) in Goldsmith 2004, p. 87; Warhol also goes on to say, "It's not just that it's part of my image not to tell everything, it's just that I forget what I said the day before and I have to make it all up over again." See also fn. 33.

39 Bourdon 1989, p. 14.

Examples of this are the material in the Dalí biography by Ian Gibson and the Warhol biography by Victor Bockris. The aim of this study is to provide a major platform for the statements by contemporary witnesses and to relate these to the personal testimonials by Dalí and Warhol, which are also often included verbatim. As both Dalí and Warhol are famous for their overtly eccentric lives, the reader of this study is faced with numerous anecdotes in this regard. This not only serves as entertainment, but also always enables a systematic comparison of the two artists. The aim is to present readers with a wide spectrum of personal experiences and impressions, enabling as intimate a look as possible at the work and complex personalities of the two artists.

The publication is organized in six parts. The first is dedicated to the biographies of Salvador Dalí and Andy Warhol, the second presents biographical parallels and comparisons between the two artists' personalities. The third section is dedicated to the wide entourage of the two artists. The fourth gives the reader an overview of the scope of the artistic activities of the two protagonists, with a special emphasis on the parallels while also exploring the extent to which Dalí and Warhol served as mutual inspiration for one another.[40] The fifth part of the study is dedicated to the encounters between Dalí and Warhol, addressing first of all the question of their first meeting followed by an attempt to systematically reconstruct the encounters in subsequent years, which took place mainly in New York. The sixth and last section investigates how the one artist felt about the work and personality of the other, inquiring the extent to which Dalí and Warhol were bound by a true artist friendship, or whether competition and envy played a role.

40
It must be pointed out at this point that it is not the task of the study to illuminate Dalí's and Warhol's complete artistic oeuvres. Both artists were exceptionally productive and left a very rich legacy that has not yet been fully catalogued.

Salvador Dalí

Salvador Dalí was born on May 11, 1904, in the Catalan town of Figueres, not far from the French border. He was the second child of the notary Don Salvador Dalí Cusí and his wife Doña Felipa Domènech Ferrés. The first child—also a son, named Salvador Galo Anselmo—had been born on October 12, 1901 and died of a gastrointestinal infection just twenty-two months after his birth. This blow led the parents to wish for another child. Nine months and ten days after the death of their first son, the future painter was born, christened Salvador Felipe Jacinto on May 20, 1904. Dalí's lifelong obsession comprised convincing himself that he was a "reborn Salvador," which he used to justify his eccentric behavior, meant initially to prove to his parents and later to the whole world who the living Salvador was. His spirited, but moody father, who tended towards fits of rage, and especially his sensitive mother, anxiously shielded their son and spoiled him. Dalí's sister Ana María was born in January 1908, but her brother still contrived to draw the family's attention. This family also included the mother-in-law of the notary, María Anna Ferrés, and his sister-in-law, who both moved into the Dalí household in 1910, along with the nanny Llùcia Gispert de Montcanut.

In the year his sister was born, Salvador Dalí was enrolled in the Escuela Pública de Párvulo elementary school in town. Esteban Trayter Colomer, his teacher there, was interested in art and enjoyed a good reputation in town. Since he lived very close to the Dalí family, he often invited Salvador to his home to show him his collection of art objects.

Dalí's father had spent the first nine years of his life in Cadaqués, on the coast not far from Figueres. He began dreaming of owning a property in the picturesque fishing village on the Costa Brava. The notary rented a converted barn from his friend Josep ("Pepito") Pichot, which he later bought from him. From then on, the Dalí family spent their summer months in Cadaqués. The village and Cap de Creus to the north-east—a bizarrely shaped rocky landscape—held a great fascination for the young Salvador and later provided an inspiration for his works of art.

In 1910 his father decided to enroll him at the Collège Hispano-Français de l'Immaculée Conception Béziers, a school that had been opened by the Christian Brothers in Figueres. As the language of instruction was exclusively French, Salvador Dalí soon learned French, which would become his first language. This was not the only influence the school had on him: a copy of the painting *The Angelus* by Jean-François Millet hung in the corridor to the classroom, which impressed him and was to become a further obsession, as well as a source of inspiration for his later life as an artist.

In July 1912 the Dalí family moved into a house at Carrer Monturiol no. 24 (now no. 10), with rooms that were more spacious than those in the previous house. The roof terrace of the new house became one of the most important childhood haunts for Dalí. It had two washrooms that were no longer used, one of which the young painter was allowed to convert into his atelier. Among the studio's inventory was a complete collection of Gowan's Art Books. Dalí's father had bought these books, which had been published since 1905, and they introduced Dalí from a young age to almost all the masters of European painting.

As the school did not prepare the students for the final secondary school exams, Salvador Dalí—following his father's ambitious plans—had to take an entrance exam for the state-run Instituto of Figueres in June 1916. After passing the exam, he spent the vacation with Pepito Pichot, who ran the finca "Molí de la Torre" (Tower Mill) near Figueres, owned by his sister María, a wealthy opera singer. The stay at Molí de la Torre was to be a revelation for the young artist, as it was there that he first saw the impressionist paintings by María and Pepito Pichot's brother Ramón. Ramón Pichot was a friend of the young Picasso and had already established himself as an impressionist painter in Paris. Salvador Dalí now dedicated himself energetically to painting, and wanted to become an impressionist, too.

After Dalí had been admitted to the state-run Instituto, his father also enrolled him at a private school, the Marist College. Dual attendance of both state and private schools was common in families who intended to send their children to university later on. Much to his parents' delight, the young Dalí achieved excellent academic results. As Don Salvador Dalí had not failed to notice his son's artistic talent, he also enrolled him at the drawing school in Figueres in the fall of the same year. The director of this school was the Andalusian Juan Núñez Fernández, an excellent artist and copperplate engraver, who also taught at the Instituto. Núñez recognized his student's exceptional talent. He was young Salvador's art teacher for six years, fostering his long-term development. As the two got on brilliantly, Núñez also invited his protégé to his home. Dalí made such great progress that he was awarded a special mention (diploma de honor) at the end of his first year at the state drawing school. Don Salvador Dalí was so delighted with his now thirteen-year-old son's artistic progress that he exhibited his latest works in their own home. In December 1918, Salvador Dalí went on to display his works, together with two other painters from Figueres, at the Teatre Principal (municipal theater). The local press showered him with praise.

During the period between January and June 1919, the little magazine *Studium* was published at the Instituto, edited by Dalí and other students. Apart from illustrations, texts, and poems, every month Dalí contributed a piece about a famous painter, "Los grandes maestros de la pintura."[1] That same year, he started writing a diary in his school exercise books; seven of at least twelve of these diaries have since been rediscovered, covering the period from November 1919 to December 1920.[2]

In early February 1921, Doña Felipa died of uterine cancer; she was only forty-seven years old. This was a heavy blow for Dalí, as he had always had a stronger bond with his mother than with his authoritarian father. After the death of Doña Felipa, Dalí's father married his sister-in-law Catalina in December 1922.

In January 1922, Dalí's works were shown at an exhibition in Barcelona. The display at the prestigious gallery belonging to Josep Dalmau was initiated by the Catalan Student Union. Dalí contributed eight works, all of which were sold. Barcelona's newspapers reported very reverentially about

1
These were about the painters Goya, El Greco, Dürer, Leonardo da Vinci, Michelangelo, and Velázquez. See Guillamet/Ferrerós/Pascuet 2003, pp. 15ff.

2
Fanés in Dalí 2004, pp. 7f.

the works by the notary's son. He was also awarded a painting prize by the principal of the University of Barcelona. This great success was repeated when Dalí participated half a year later in an exhibition in his hometown of artists from the Empordà region.

After Dalí passed his final exam at the Instituto in Figueres in June 1922, there was nothing stopping him from studying at the San Fernando Royal Academy of Fine Arts in Madrid. He arrived in the Spanish capital in September, accompanied by his father and his sister. On September 11, 1922, Dalí applied to be admitted to the entrance exam at the School of Painting, Sculpture and Graphics—a faculty within the Royal Academy. His exam task was to draw a replica of Jacopo Sansovino's *Bacchus*. Although Dalí's drawing did not meet the scale requirements and turned out too small, due to its perfection he was accepted as a student. Dalí enrolled in courses in perspective, anatomy, art history (ancient and medieval), and sculptural drawing. He lived in Madrid at the Residencia de Estudiantes, a modern student residence financed by private sponsors and therefore free of state or church influence. During the first months at the "Resi," he dedicated himself fully to his studies. He visited the Prado on Sunday mornings and during the rest of his free time the shy Dalí shut himself up in his room and painted. The medical student José ("Pepín") Bello was the first to take note of Dalí's painting, which was still influenced by cubism at the time. The discovery spread throughout the "Resi" like wildfire and gave Dalí access to a sophisticated and dandyish circle of friends in the dorm. The circle of friends surrounding Pepín Bello included Luis Buñuel, who had moved into the "Resi" in 1917. The sociable Buñuel, brimming with self-confidence, had started his academic career at the Faculty of Agricultural Mechanical Engineering, then switched to industrial mechanical engineering and finally decided to study entomology. The circle of friends also included Federico García Lorca, who came to the "Resi" in 1919 and studied law. The newly acquired friends introduced Dalí to Madrid's nightlife. They also gathered in cafés during the day to discuss politics, contemporary art, and new books, such as the works of Sigmund Freud. The first two volumes of Freud's *Collected Works* had been published in Spanish in September 1922 and later on Dalí referred to Freud's *Interpretation of Dreams* as "one of the capital discoveries" in his life.[3] For the second year at the academy in Madrid, Dalí enrolled in preparatory color studies, art history (modern and contemporary), still life, and copper engraving. However, he had to interrupt his studies on account of an incident: in the fall of 1923, elections were being held for a new professor of painting. When the students' preferred candidate Daniel Vázquez Díaz was not awarded the post, it led to vehement protests. As rumors were circulating that Dalí was one of the main instigators of the unrest, he was summoned to appear before a disciplinary committee. Dalí, who made no secret of his support for Vázquez Díaz and refused to denounce those participating in the protest, was excluded from studying for a year and was therefore forced to return to Figueres.

There was also an incident in his hometown in mid-May 1924. King Alfonso XIII, paying an official visit to Girona, decided spontaneously to also inspect the garrison in nearby Figueres. As Alfonso XIII had never been

3
Dalí 1942,
note p. 167.

very popular in the town, potential trouble makers were detained, in order to prevent the anticipated riots. Dalí was among them and spent May 21 in solitary confinement in Figueres, was later transferred to the prison in Girona on May 30, and was released on June 11. Presumably the reason for the detainment was an attempt to intimidate Dalí's father, who in April 1923 had appealed for legal action against the rightists for election fraud, a few months before Primo de Rivera's coup.

In October 1924 Dalí resumed his studies in Madrid. Over the years that followed, he and Federico García Lorca developed a deep personal relationship. The poet was a guest in Cadaqués twice. On his first visit during the Holy Week of the year 1925, Lorca dazzled Dalí's family with his charm and Ana María also became friends with him. Dalí dedicated the summer of 1925 entirely to painting and for this, took a break from his studies in Madrid. Furthermore, the gallery owner Josep Dalmau had invited him to Barcelona for a solo exhibition. The November 1925 exhibition displayed seventeen paintings and five drawings—including eight portraits of Ana María, who was Dalí's preferred model at the time. The exhibition was a resounding success. Since the young artist wanted to travel to Paris, Dalmau wrote a letter of recommendation to Max Jacob and another to André Breton.

Dalí embarked on his first journey to Paris in April 1926. Because he was not at all practically inclined, Don Salvador Dalí instructed his wife and Ana María to accompany him. Dalí considered getting to know Picasso as the purpose of his journey. Buñuel, who had been residing in the French capital since 1925, met the traveling party on the railway platform and introduced Dalí to the painter Manuel Ángeles Ortiz, one of Lorca's friends, who also knew Picasso. When Dalí went to see Picasso at Rue de la Boétie, he had his painting *Girl from Figueres* with him. According to Dalí, Picasso contemplated the work for fifteen minutes without making a comment, before going on to show his compatriot his own paintings for two hours.[4]

The April 1926 edition of José Ortega y Gasset's journal *Revista de Occidente* published Lorca's "Ode to Salvador Dalí," which the poet had been working on since his first visit to Cadaqués. The painter felt flattered and it is generally understood that the following month Lorca also attempted to make sexual advances towards him. In June 1926 Dalí had his final exams at the School of Painting, Sculpture and Graphics at the Royal Academy. He was invited for an oral exam on June 14. However, the young painter refuted the competence of the professors present and as a consequence he was definitively expelled from the Academy. Back in Figueres, Dalí dedicated himself to painting, through which he processed his relationship with Lorca. Works from that time were shown at Dalí's second solo exhibition at the Dalmau Gallery, held in early January 1927 and once again meeting with great success.

In the July 1927 edition of the Catalan art magazine *L'Amic de les Arts*, Dalí published the text "Saint Sebastian," which he dedicated to his friend Federico García Lorca. It propagated an "aesthetics of objectivity" and rejected any form of sentimentality. Lorca must have understood this as confirmation of Dalí's resolve to refuse him sexually. However, in summer 1927

4
See ibid., p. 206. According to another source, Dalí also showed Picasso the painting *Departure (Homage to Fox Newsreel)*. See Aguer in Ades 2004, p. 473.

the poet did in fact attempt once again to seduce the painter. As it was to no avail, the friendship spiraled into a crisis.

In September 1927, Joan Miró and the Parisian art dealer Pierre Loeb visited Dalí in Figueres. Miró had never met Dalí before, but valued his works. As they were passionate Catalans, it followed that Miró took Dalí under his wing and promoted his compatriot in Paris, where Luis Buñuel was involved in preparations for a movie in the fall of 1928, which was to be based on Ramón Gómez de la Serna's short stories about life in the city. Buñuel had persuaded his mother to fund the movie, but Gómez de la Serna failed to deliver the promised script. Buñuel subsequently contacted Dalí to propose working together on the project. In January 1929, the moviemaker traveled to Figueres, where the two friends collaborated on the script for the movie *Un Chien andalou,* which they completed in less than a week. Buñuel started shooting the movie back in Paris in April 1929. Dalí followed his friend shortly thereafter to help with the realization. The premiere was held on June 6, 1929, in front of a selected audience in the Studio des Ursulines, and became a smashing success.

During Dalí's second stay in Paris, Joan Miró introduced him to the social life of the French capital and to André Breton and the group of surrealists, as well as to the Belgian art dealer Camille Goemans. Goemans liked Dalí's works and he signed a contract with him in May 1929, giving the gallery owner exclusive sales rights to the Catalan's works for six months. In early August 1929, Camille Goemans visited Dalí in Cadaqués, accompanied by his girlfriend, as well as René Magritte and his wife. A couple of days later, Paul Éluard and his wife Gala also arrived with their daughter Cécile, along with Luis Buñuel. Dalí was fascinated by Gala. For him it was love at first sight, and she also felt drawn towards him. Gala was born in Kazan in 1894 as Elena Ivanovna Diakonova. She had been given the nickname Gala in Russia, which she kept. She became Dalí's most important figure of attachment and took on the role of not only wife and muse, but also mother and manager. She also tried, as an experienced woman, to release Dalí from his fear of the sexual act—albeit without success. While Paul Éluard and the other guests returned to Paris in September 1929, she stayed with Dalí in Cadaqués a few weeks longer.

Un Chien andalou was screened in Paris from October 1929. The movie provoked a scandal and vehement reactions in the press. However, the surrealists received it enthusiastically and the script was published in the final edition of the journal *La Révolution surréaliste* on December 15, 1929. As the journal was the mouthpiece of the surrealist movement, the publication of this edition marked Dalí's and Buñuel's official acceptance into surrealist circles. At the same time, Galerie Goemans showed Dalí's first solo exhibition in Paris, which was once again a financial success. Some of the exhibited works were on the theme of Dalí's "heterosexual turmoil," in which masturbation plays a central role. The painting *The Sacred Heart* caused a particular stir, as it bears the inscription: "parfois je crache par plaisir sur le portrait de ma mère" ("sometimes I spit for pleasure on the portrait of my mother"). The painter insisted later that this title was merely of psychoanalytical significance. Even so, his father was angered by the work of art, which he regarded as an outrageous defilement of the memory of his deceased wife. It culminated in a quarrel between father and son in Figueres, which led to a breaking off of relations that was to last until 1935. Dalí's relationship with Gala had already caused the notary to disinherit his son. The break with his father also resulted in Dalí moving to Port Lligat, not far from Cadaqués. Lídia Nogués, decried in the village as "half mad," with whom the artist was utterly fascinated, sold him a half-dilapidated fishing cottage in the Port Lligat bay. During the following years, Dalí bought further cottages close by, and after World War II he joined them with the first cottage to make an interwoven house with extensions.

At the turn of 1929/1930, Dalí and Buñuel worked together on the script for their second movie, which was to bear the title *L'Âge d'or*. Dalí's love for Gala caused delays. The movie had its premiere on November 28, 1930 at Studio 28 in Paris. Owing to its stance against religion and against bourgeois society, shortly afterwards there was an attack by two extremist groups, who intimidated the viewers, smeared the screen and destroyed the exhibits displayed in the foyer of the movie theater, including a painting by Dalí. The movie *L'Âge d'or* became the talk of the town until it was censored due to a press campaign, and later banned totally.

In summer 1930 Dalí developed his "paranoiac-critical" method, which plays a central role in his art. Dalí combined his paranoia-like visions and dreams in double images, opening up alternative perceptions for the viewer. In his text "The Visible Woman," he explains, "It is by a distinctly paranoiac process that it has been possible to obtain a double image: in other words, a representation of an object that is also, without the slightest pictorial or anatomical modification, the representation of another entirely different object, this one being equally devoid of any deformation or abnormality disclosing some adjustment."[5] Although, in the years that followed, the artist provided many further explanations of his "paranoiac-critical" method and thereby made the term famous, it ultimately defied definition.[6]

Dalí exhibited at the Galerie Pierre Colle in Paris in early June 1931. The sixteen works presented included the painting *The Persistence of Memory (The Soft Watches)*, which was to later become his most famous work. The gallery owner Julien Levy purchased the painting for 250 dollars and agreed with Dalí to exhibit his works at his newly opened gallery in New York, the first American art dealer to do so. Two months prior to Levy presenting his first surrealist exhibition in January 1932 in New York, the first exhibition of surrealist art in the U.S. took place at the Wadsworth Atheneum in Hartford, Connecticut, entitled "Newer Super-Realism." The American public received Surrealism with great enthusiasm. The press reported effusively about the new art movement and journalists were especially taken with Dalí's *Soft Watches*. The second solo exhibition followed just a few months later at the Galerie Pierre Colle in Paris. Despite his growing fame, Dalí still had financial problems. Help came in the form of a group of twelve financially strong art lovers that formed as a group called "Zodiac" in January 1933. For a year, Dalí received a monthly sum from one of the patrons, in return for which he could choose a painting.

5
In Finkelstein
1998, p. 224.

6
In 1979 the artist remarked in the Spanish TV program *Imágenes*, "I don't know what it consists of but ... it works very well!" Quoted according to Gibson 1997, p. 255.

Dalí's first solo exhibition comprising twenty-five works took place at the end of 1933 at the New York gallery owned by Julien Levy. It was met with great enthusiasm by the public and the press. Dalí was in high spirits when he heard of its success. His good mood was lifted even further by the civil wedding ceremony with Gala, which took place on January 30, 1934 at the city hall in Paris. Gala had divorced Paul Éluard in July 1932.

In early 1934, André Breton wrote a long letter to Dalí, insinuating that some of his views were detrimental to the surrealist movement. Breton criticized in particular that Hitler featured in Dalí's work, as well as a representation of Lenin with a grotesquely elongated posterior in the painting *The Enigma of William Tell*. Spurred by Breton, it was suggested to exclude Dalí from the movement. On February 5, 1934, a special surrealist conference took place, which Dalí also turned up at, with a severe cold. Due to a spectacular appearance with several layers of pullovers, which he constantly took on and off, and a thermometer in his mouth, Dalí was just able to stave off exclusion.

At the beginning of November 1934, Dalí and Gala boarded a ship in Le Havre for their first crossing to America. Caresse Crosby was also on board, a friend of the couple and a member of the "Zodiac" group. Crosby, the inventor of the modern brassiere, had founded the publishing house Black Sun Press in Paris in 1927, together with her husband Harry. After arrival in the United States, she acted as Dalí's interpreter for his first contact with the press, as he did not speak any English at this point. Dalí's new exhibition opened in the Julien Levy Gallery a few days later. The next exhibition followed in the Wadsworth Atheneum in Hartford, Connecticut, where he gave a talk on the occasion of the opening in December 1934. He made another address in January 1935 before returning to Europe, this time at the New York Museum of Modern Art. On the day before departure, Caresse Crosby and Joella Levy, the wife of the gallery owner Julien Levy, held a farewell ball at the "Coq Rouge," in honor of Dalí, which was to go down in art history as the "Bal Onirique," because of the bizarre costumes worn by the guests.

Back in Europe, Dalí gave a talk at the "International Surrealist Exhibition" on July 1, 1936 at the London New Burlington Galleries, wearing a diving suit, symbolizing immersing oneself in the subconscious. The artist was in danger of suffocating, but was freed from the diving suit just in time by a frantically sought screwdriver.

The Dalís arrived in New York once again in December 1936. On December 9, the exhibition "Fantastic Art, Dada and Surrealism" opened at the Museum of Modern Art, which was a great success among the viewing public. This was followed the very next day by a private presentation of Dalí's new works at the Julien Levy Gallery. On December 14, the evening before the public opening, the artist was awarded a high accolade: he appeared on the title page of *TIME* magazine, which reported not only on the exhibition at the Museum of Modern Art, but also in detail about his artistic career. Before their departure to Europe, Dalí and Gala visited Hollywood in late January 1937.

On July 19, 1938, Dalí visited Sigmund Freud, who was living in exile in London. Stefan Zweig had arranged the meeting and accompanied him with Edward James, an English patron and a friend of Dalí, to Hampstead in the north of London. Dalí showed Freud his painting *Metamorphosis of Narcissus* painted the previous year and he sketched the founder of psychoanalysis during his visit.

In February 1939, Dalí and his muse traveled once again to the United States, where he was appointed by the Bonwit Teller department store in New York to decorate two display windows. Back in December 1936 he had already designed a display for the department store that had caused a stir, on the occasion of the "Fantastic Art, Dada and Surrealism" exhibition, but it was this new assignment that really triggered a flood of press reports. As the management of the department store had altered the decoration without Dalí's consent, the Spaniard accidentally destroyed the display window in a fit of rage, was then arrested and had to spend a couple of hours in a prison cell. He could not have wished for better publicity for his exhibition, which was due to open a few days later at Julien Levy's gallery. Following from the Levy exhibition, Dalí designed a surrealist pavilion for the World's Fair in New York, *Dream of Venus*. However, this assignment also saw an infringement of his artistic freedom—the fair management and an investor did not allow him to set up a reproduction of Botticelli's Venus with the head of a fish. As a reaction to this prohibition, Dalí had hundreds of flyers scattered from a plane circling over New York, proclaiming a "Declaration of the Independence of the Imagination and the Rights of Man to His Own Madness."

When the artist returned to Paris in June 1939, an article by André Breton, "The Most Recent Tendencies in Surrealist Painting" was published in *Minotaure*, the new magazine of the surrealist movement, in which Breton stipulated that Dalí's influence was rapidly declining and that, due to his wish to refine his "paranoiac-critical" method, his art suffered from an over-indulgence of entertainment. The article marked the definitive split between Dalí and the surrealist movement. Later on Breton turned Dalí's name into the anagram "Avida Dollars," basically meaning "greedy for dollars."

After the Germans occupied France, Dalí and Gala traveled to Lisbon and boarded the *Excambion*, sailing to New York in August 1940. After their arrival in New York, the couple traveled on to Virginia and settled at Hampton Manor, which belonged to their friend Caresse Crosby, who had invited them. There, Dalí completed his autobiography *The Secret Life of Salvador Dalí*, which was published in New York in October 1942 and was a great success. Dalí and Gala lived exclusively in the United States until 1948. During this time, the artist built up his fame and dedicated himself increasingly to commercial assignments.

In November 1941, the Museum of Modern Art opened a Dalí retrospective, which was presented alongside a Miró retrospective. The exhibition subsequently toured eight cities in the U.S. until May 1943. In Cleveland, the exhibition was visited by the twenty-eight-year-old businessman A. Reynolds Morse, accompanied by his fiancée and later wife Eleanor.

They were fascinated by Dalí's art and, barely a year later, they purchased their first painting from him, which was to form the start of the most significant private Dalí collection, now housed by the Salvador Dalí Museum in St. Petersburg, Florida. Dalí paid another visit to Hollywood in September 1945. Alfred Hitchcock had asked him to create the dream sequence for his movie *Spellbound*. A while later Walt Disney suggested that they venture to do an animated cartoon together, by the name of *Destino*. However, the project was soon abandoned and only a few seconds of movie material were shot.

After the U.S. Air Force dropped the atomic bomb on Hiroshima on August 6, 1945, Dalí's "nuclear" or "atomic" period began. Upon returning to his homeland, which was still under Franco's totalitarian rule, he declared himself in July 1948 to be a mystic and pursued "Nuclear Mysticism." Many works with a religious content were created in the years that followed, such as the painting *The Madonna of Port Lligat*, which Dalí presented to Pope Pius XII during a private audience on November 23, 1949. When Dalí started to paint in large format in the mid-1950s, he employed the set designer Isidor Bea, who prepared the canvases in the ensuing years and completed secondary details on the paintings. The first work Bea assisted with was *The Last Supper* in 1955. As business was flourishing, Dalí also employed other assistants. At the end of 1959 the artist decided to employ a secretary. His choice was Peter Moore, born in London in 1919 and awarded the honorary rank of captain upon his departure from the military. Dalí agreed with Moore that instead of a salary, he would receive a commission of ten percent on all contracts he negotiated. However, Gala continued to handle the sales of the oil paintings and drawings. In 1974, the Catalan Enrique Sabater replaced Moore. Sabater—unlike his predecessor—also negotiated the contracts for Dalí's oil paintings and drawings. In 1980 followed a brief intermezzo with the French Jean-Claude Du Barry, director of a modeling agency in Barcelona, until the French photographer Robert Descharnes entered into Dalí's service in the same year as his last secretary.

After World War II, Dalí typically spent most of the year in his Spanish homeland and the winter months in Paris and New York. In Paris, he and Gala always resided at Hôtel Le Meurice and in New York at the St. Regis Hotel. Over the years, the artist gathered an entourage of models, aristocrats, transvestites, transsexuals, and dwarfs. Apart from Gala, the Spaniard Nanita Kalaschnikoff became a close confidante, given the nickname "Louis XIV." Amanda Lear, who later became famous as a disco queen, and the American artist Pandora also gained his trust.

From the mid-1960s, Dalí dedicated himself increasingly to prints, which he recognized as a welcome source of income. He initially created book illustrations, but soon print editions were published in increasingly greater print runs. Over the course of the many lucrative assignments, Dalí took a dangerous step: he started signing blank print sheets. The situation escalated in 1974 when French customs officers discovered 40,000 blank print sheets with signatures in a truck at the entrance to Andorra and the press covered the story.

Although Dalí had stopped signing in December 1980 for health reasons, countless newly signed prints by the artist appeared in the years that followed. The art market was well and truly flooded with forgeries and Dalí had become one of the most widely plagiarized artists.

During the last two and a half decades of his life, Dalí was still honored with major exhibitions. A retrospective was opened at Huntington Hartford's Gallery of Modern Art in New York in December 1965, with 366 exhibits. A major exhibition of 236 works was displayed from November 1971 at the Museum Boymans-van-Beuningen in Rotterdam, and from December 1979 the Centre Georges Pompidou in Paris showed a retrospective comprising 168 paintings, 219 drawings, as well as prints and objects.

Public interest in Dalí's art continued unabated. On September 28, 1974, the Teatre-Museu Dalí was opened in the town where the artist had been born. The museum building had originally housed the municipal theater, where Dalí's paintings were first exhibited. The building had been destroyed during the Spanish Civil War and remained a ruin until it was rebuilt and converted. The work on the museum, designed by Dalí personally, took almost four years. Today, the Dalí Museum houses many paintings, prints, sculptures, and installations, and became one of Spain's major attractions within just a few years.

Gala had already withdrawn to Púbol in the Baix Empordà region in 1971, where Dalí had bought a fourteenth-century castle that he refurbished and decorated for her. The artist did not seem to mind Gala's love affairs with young men, for which his muse liked to withdraw to Púbol. Although their relationship suffered greatly in later years, Gala's death on June 10, 1982, was a heavy blow for Dalí. The artist's health had been deteriorating since the end of the 1970s. After the death of his muse, he withdrew completely to Púbol. The now bedridden Dalí suffered severe burns there at the end of August, when his bed caught fire due to a short-circuit in the constantly activated bell-push system, which Dalí used when he needed something. Two months later, Torre Galatea, a wing of the Teatre-Museu Dalí in Figueres, became the artist's last abode. During the final years of Dalí's life, his friend and painter colleague Antoni Pitxot, whose uncle was Ramón Pichot, took care of the surrealist.

Salvador Dalí died on January 23, 1989 of heart failure and a lung infection. His body was embalmed and he lay in state in a hall at his museum. As many as 15,000 people came to pay the painter their last respects, before he was laid to rest after a short funeral service under the dome of his Teatre-Museu Dalí in Figueres on January 26, 1989.

Andy Warhol

Andy Warhol was born as Andrew Warhola in Pittsburgh on August 6, 1928. His parents Ondrej and Julia Warhola were from farming families from Miková, a village in the northeast of Slovakia, near the Polish border. They were members of the Ruthene church of the Byzantine-Slavic Rite, which was united with the Roman-Catholic Church in the sixteenth century. The Warholas' first child was born in 1911, a daughter, Josephine. The child fell ill just a few months after her birth; a severe cold eventually led to her death, as the village did not have any medical services. Ondrej Warhola's family owned a large farm and was well-off by regional standards. Ondrej had already visited America a few times. In 1912 he immigrated to the United States permanently, in order to avoid military service. At first he left his wife behind on his parents' farm, until she was able to join him in the U.S. after World War I.

Julia Warhola gave birth to three sons in Pittsburgh: Paul on June 26, 1922; John on May 31, 1925; and Andrew on August 6, 1928. In the 1920s, Pittsburgh was the sixth largest city in the U.S. and a center of the American coal and steel industry. Ondrej Warhola worked as an industrial systems installer at the Eichleay Corporation. The family lived in a two-room apartment in Soho, the poor district. The Warholas were deeply religious and firmly integrated into the local Ruthenian community. However, they spoke poor English. Julia Warhola refused to speak the local language for a long time, so her children did not learn English until they started school. During the Great Depression, Ondrej Warhola temporarily lost his job. In order to improve the family income, Julia Warhola made flower creations out of old cans and colorful crepe paper, which she sold door-to-door for twenty-five cents apiece. The three sons also took on odd jobs in an attempt to contribute to the family income. In 1934 the family was able to move into their own home—a one-story brick house—in South Oakland on the other side of the city. As Ondrej and his wife lived frugally, they paid the purchase price of $3,200 in cash.

Andrew Warhola started school at Soho Elementary School when he was four years old. However, as he was beaten up on his very first day of school by a girl, he refused to attend anymore. When he transferred into second grade at Holmes Elementary School in 1934, this single school day was counted as his first school year. Andrew's great talent for drawing was noticed during class, so his art teacher recommended that he take the free art classes held on Saturday afternoons at the Carnegie Museum of Art. Andrew attended these regularly until 1941 and they not only taught him drawing and painting techniques, but also introduced him to art history.

During his first year at Holmes Elementary School, Andrew came down with scarlet fever and two years later he contracted chorea. He remained bedridden for the whole summer of 1936. His mother took care of him and supplied him with painting books, comics, and movie magazines. It was around this time that a pigmentation deficiency affected his skin and thereafter he was often taken to be an albino. Andrew became a movie fan during the 1930s. At the time he was especially enthusiastic about Shirley Temple. An autographed photo with a personal dedication from the child star was to become the basis of his autograph collection. In the years that followed, he became an avid moviegoer and he also read movie magazines regularly.

His father Ondrej Warhola contracted jaundice while working for a company in a mine in West Virginia. After his return to Pittsburgh, his health deteriorated rapidly and after a protracted illness he died of peritonitis on

1

May 15, 1942—five days after being admitted to hospital. After the death of their father, Paul and John ensured the family's livelihood.

From 1942 Andrew Warhola started to attend the Schenley High School, which he graduated from a few months before his seventeenth birthday in the spring of 1945. In September he enrolled at Carnegie Institute of Technology—the present-day Carnegie Mellon University—in Pittsburgh as a student in the Department of Painting and Design, with the major "Pictorial Design." He chose drawing, pictorial representation, decorative art, color theory, and thought and expression as courses. Between the first and second years at university he worked for his brother Paul, who transported groceries by truck in Pittsburgh and the area. However, Andrew sold not only fruit and vegetables, but also some drawings—especially milieu studies and portraits—which he created in his free time. These works brought him a scholarship. He also successfully earned scholarships repeatedly in subsequent years. During summer vacations he worked at Joseph Horne's Department Store in Pittsburgh, where he decorated display windows for about fifty cents an hour.

During the second year of his studies, Andrew Warhola became friends with Philip Pearlstein. His fellow student, who was four years older, was also from Pittsburgh and Warhol was impressed by his knowledge of art history and by the fact that *LIFE* magazine had published one of his paintings in 1941. In summer 1947 they shared a shack on an old industrial site, which they used as a studio, with their fellow students Dorothy Cantor and Arthur Elias. During that summer the two friends also traveled to New York, followed in the spring vacation of 1948 by another stay together in the metropolis.

At that time Andrew took up the position of art director for the student magazine *Cano*. For his contributions—including the cover design for the November 1948 edition—he used the "blotted line" technique, a monotype technique in which a pencil drawing on water-repellent paper is traced with ink and then the still-wet ink is pressed onto a second sheet.

In January 1949, Warhola submitted his painting *The Lord Gave Me My Face, But I Can Pick My Own Nose*[1] for the annual exhibition of the Associated Artists of Pittsburgh—a regional artists' group. After controversial discussions, the jury rejected the painting because of its repulsive motif—a young man picking his nose. However, the work was praised by one of the jury members, George Grosz, and it was finally displayed in June 1949 in an alternative exhibition at the Arts and Crafts Center in Pittsburgh.

In mid-June 1949, Andrew Warhola graduated from his studies as a Bachelor of Fine Arts in Pictorial Design. In the summer of the same year he moved to New York, where he shared an apartment at St. Mark's Place, near Avenue A, a run-down district of the city, with Philip Pearlstein for two months. The friends moved again in September and became tenants of the dance therapist Francesca Boas, daughter of the anthropologist Franz Boas, who lived in Chelsea on West Twenty-First Street. In his search for work, Warhola contacted the picture editors of major magazines in New York. Tina S. Fredericks, the art director of *Glamour*, was taken with his work and accorded him one of his first assignments. The September issue of the year 1949 published Warhola's illustrations for a series of articles on the subject of "What

1
At some point the painting gained the title of *The Broad Gave Me My Face, But I Can Pick My Own Nose.* This is not the correct title. See Cueff 2009, p. 71. Leonard Kessler confirmed this to the author in a letter in August 2011, "Andy's title was *The Lord Gave Me My Face But I Can Pick My Own Nose.* … Andy would never have used the words … 'The broad' … He had the most respect for his mother."

Is Success?" depicting young women and shoes on ladders. Warhola used the "blotted line" technique for his designs, which he was to apply often from then on for his assignments. During this time he experimented with his name and signed his works as "André Warhol." For the work assigned by Fredericks, he decided to drop the "a" from his surname definitively. When he was given an assignment for the February 1950 edition of the magazine *Mademoiselle* shortly afterwards, Warhol changed his first name "Andrew" to "Andy." From then on he signed his works exclusively as "Andy Warhol."

Over the course of his career as a commercial artist, Warhol worked for many magazines, including *Vogue, Seventeen, The New Yorker,* and *Harper's Bazaar.* Between 1953 and 1960 he produced various promotional books as advertising gifts for potential customers. During these years Warhol designed postcards, letter paper, book covers, album covers, and placemats. In the mid-1950s he once again created window displays, this time for the New York department store Bonwit Teller.

Warhol was a guest at the wedding of Philip Pearlstein and their former fellow student Dorothy Cantor in August 1950. The two friends then went separate ways. At the time Warhol was already living on the west side of 103rd Street and shared his apartment with dancers, actors, and authors. He moved several times that same year. In the fall of 1950 he lived in a humble apartment at 216 East Seventy-Fifth Street. There was no hot water, but there were mice, which Warhol combated with a Siamese cat. Later on he acquired a second Siamese cat and it did not take long for the pair to reproduce. His mother, who was concerned about her son's wellbeing, moved in with him in 1952 and lived with him until 1971. In 1953 Warhol was given the opportunity to move into an apartment at Lexington Avenue 242 in the middle-class district of Manhattan, which he rented from Leonard Kessler, who had been a fellow student at Carnegie Tech.

Warhol's enthusiasm for Truman Capote began in 1949; the author had just published his novel *Other Voices, Other Rooms.* The photo of Capote on the rear cover impressed Warhol so much that he bombarded the author with fan mail and calls, until Capote's mother asked him vociferously to stop. After this harsh rejection, Warhol approached his idol by creating illustrations inspired by his works. In summer 1952 these works were shown at Alexander Iolas's Hugo Gallery in New York. Although this was Warhol's first solo exhibition, it attracted little interest. Capote, accompanied by his mother, went to view the pictures and Warhol had the opportunity to speak to Capote for half an hour. Years later a friendship developed between them, which lasted until the author's death. In 1954 Warhol received an offer to exhibit works at the Loft Gallery, run by the advertising designer Jack Wolfgang Beck and his assistant Vito Giallo. After a group exhibition with seven other artists, Warhol held a solo exhibition showing a series of marbled paper sculptures with little figures depicted on them, and a second solo display with drawings of the dancer John Butler.

In those years Warhol had regularly received assignments from the shoe company I. Miller. In 1955 the then art director, Peter Palazzo, conceived a new advertising campaign: A company advertisement was to appear weekly in the *New York Times* with an illustration by Warhol, in a modern, graphic, black and white style. Over a number of years, the young commercial artist received an annual remuneration of $20,000, as well as a bonus if a certain number of illustrations were exceeded. Warhol's drawing brought him several awards within the advertising sector. Spurred by this success, he published the portfolio *À la Recherche du Shoe Perdu*, in which extravagant ladies' shoes are presented.

Warhol was swamped with assignments, which led him to take on two assistants in 1955. While Vito Giallo only worked for him for a few months, Nathan Gluck worked alongside him until 1964. From 1957 to the early 1960s, he also employed Ted Carey. Some years previously, Warhol had already found another important colleague in his mother. She inscribed texts onto her son's drawings in her curlicue handwriting and signed them with his name. Warhol was also able to rely on the help of friends. He organized "coloring parties" where every guest was assigned a particular color. They gathered in a restaurant-grocery shop called Serendipity 3, a trendy venue opened by Stephen Bruce, Calvin Holt and Patch Harrington on East Fifty-Eighth Street in 1954.[2] Warhol's drawings sold well there and exhibitions of his works were held. At that time, Warhol was making sketchbooks with drawings of young men. Stephen Bruce posed as a model for the artist, as did Warhol's partner at the time, Charles Lisanby. Some of the portraits of Lisanby were exhibited at the beginning of 1956 at the Bodley Gallery in New York. In June 1956 the two of them embarked on a journey around the world that took them to Honolulu, Tokyo, Hong Kong, Manila, Singapore, Bangkok, Calcutta, Kathmandu, New Delhi, Agra, Cairo, and Rome.

From the end of April to the beginning of August 1956, the Museum of Modern Art exhibited "Recent Drawings U.S.A.," a major retrospective that Warhol participated in with a shoe drawing. Shoes were also the theme of his second solo exhibition, which opened at the Bodley Gallery in December 1956. It displayed sheets with extravagant footwear, inscribed with the names of famous personalities. When Warhol founded Andy Warhol Enterprises, Inc. in 1957, with branches in Philadelphia and Chicago, he had worked his way up to become one of the most famous and well-paid commercial artists in the U.S. In 1959 he bought the house at 1342 Lexington Avenue for $60,000, which he moved into with his mother. During that year he published *Wild Raspberries*, together with the interior decorator Suzie Frankfurt, which was one of his last promotional books: a humorous cookery book. The original drawings were exhibited in December 1959 at the Bodley Gallery.

In 1960, under the influence of the emerging art movement surrounding Robert Rauschenberg and Jasper Johns, Warhol created his first paintings with advertising motifs from newspaper adverts. Alongside this, Warhol produced pictures with comic strip figures, such as Batman, Dick Tracy, Popeye, and Superman. He used templates for these works, which he projected enlarged onto a canvas, in order to trace the contours and inscriptions. He let the generously applied paint drip down visibly. In April 1961 Warhol displayed some of these works in the display window at the Bonwit Teller department store—albeit without attracting any interest from the art

2
The term "serendipity" was coined by Horace Walpole, meaning the gift of making fortunate and unanticipated, chance discoveries.

world. He had also attempted to break into the art world when he visited the Leo Castelli Gallery and saw paintings by Roy Lichtenstein, which were also based on comic strips. Castelli decided against representing Warhol, as he was afraid his works were too similar to Lichtenstein's. As a result, Warhol decided to abandon this subject. He nonetheless invited Castelli's assistant, Ivan C. Karp, to his studio to show him works. Karp criticized the careless application of color that led to drip marks. Consequently, the artist decided on a painting technique in which the motifs were painted uniformly and were more stylized. Apart from his work for Leo Castelli, Ivan C. Karp acted as Warhol's private agent for one and a half years and brought customers to the artist's studio, receiving a commission on any sales. Karp introduced Warhol to Henry Geldzahler, the new young assistant curator of American twentieth-century art at the Metropolitan Museum of Art in New York. This encounter evolved into a friendship. Geldzahler advised Warhol in art and social matters, introducing him to influential people, including Irving Blum, who directed the Ferus Gallery in Los Angeles. Blum was the first art dealer who had the courage to exhibit Warhol's new works and in July 1962 he opened the "Campbell's Soup Cans" exhibition at his gallery, with thirty-two small pictures of realistically represented Campbell's soup cans.[3] Warhol had started painting soup cans towards the end of 1961. When searching for new subjects, he had asked friends and acquaintances for suggestions. It was recommended to him to paint what people saw every day and what everybody recognized. He was also advised to paint money. Taking up these subjects went hand in hand with the search for a new method of pictorial representation. As serial repetition had become a signature feature of Warhol's art, the artist initially experimented with stamps, stencils, and templates, until he discovered silkscreen printing in the spring of 1962, which was to define his further work.

3 At the time the company produced thirty-two different ready-made soups, so Warhol's depictions differ only through the flavor indicated on the label.

On May 11, 1962, *TIME* magazine published an article, "The Slice-of-Cake School," about the new Pop Art artists, in which Warhol was the only one presented with a photograph. In October 1962 the Sidney Janis Gallery in New York opened the group exhibition "The New Realists," showing over fifty works by twenty-nine European and American artists of the "younger generation." Warhol, represented with five works, had achieved the transition from commercial artist to Pop Art artist.

On August 5, 1962—one day after the end of Warhol's "Campbell's Soup Cans" exhibition in Los Angeles—Marilyn Monroe died. The news of the untimely death of the actress, which was reported on in detail by the media, was taken up by Warhol as his new subject. Just a few days after Monroe's death, Warhol acquired a publicity shot of the actress, removed the lower part and had a silkscreen template made. He used it to produce a silkscreen series that was to become his most famous. Several early *Marilyn* portraits were shown at the Stable Gallery in New York in November 1962. Shortly thereafter, Warhol produced a large *Death and Disaster* series composed of *Car Crash, Electric Chair,* and *Suicide* paintings.

As the scope and scale of his work made it increasingly difficult to paint at home, in June 1963 Warhol started renting an old fire station on

East Eighty-Seventh Street for $150 a month. He also took on the poet Gerard Malanga as his new assistant. Malanga was from the Bronx, was studying at Wagner College and was only twenty years old when Warhol first employed him for one dollar and twenty-five cents an hour—the legal minimum wage at the time. His first task consisted of assisting Warhol with printing some portraits of Elizabeth Taylor. They were displayed in October 1963 together with portraits of Elvis Presley at the Ferus Gallery in Los Angeles.

A few months later, the Factory, as Warhol now called his studio, moved to an industrial floor at 331 East Forty-Seventh Street in the shade of the Empire State Building. Warhol's new residence measured over 400 square meters. It had two toilets, a pay phone, and an open freight elevator. The new Factory soon became the hub of New York pop culture. The visitors gradually developed into an entourage around Warhol, including the high-society Brigid Berlin, who was given the name Brigid Polk and became one of the artist's closest confidantes, and Billy Linich, a twenty-one-year-old lighting technician from the Off-Broadway scene, who later called himself Billy Name and lived with several friends in an apartment painted and wallpapered in silver. Warhol asked Name whether he could also adorn the new Factory in silver, whereupon Name decorated the concrete walls and columns with aluminum foil, painted the floors with aluminum paint, and sprayed objects with silver metallic paint. The Silver Factory soon became New York's trendy hangout.

In summer 1963 Warhol purchased a Bolex 16mm movie camera and started shooting movies with it. He called his first movie *Sleep*. The black-and-white silent movie lasting five hours and twenty-one minutes shows the performance artist and poet John Giorno, who was then Warhol's life partner, in various sleeping positions, and it caused a stir because of its lack of action. Soon after completing *Sleep*, other movies followed—all silent movies characterized by a rigid camera perspective and the absence of editing and montage. From the end of 1964 Warhol started producing sound movies and he shot his first color movie in March 1965. Warhol started incorporating all visitors to the Factory into the production of his movies and pictures. Jane Holzer had been a regular visitor to the Factory since the beginning of 1964. The attractive young woman married to a wealthy businessman became one of the first "superstars" to appear in Warhol's movies, as Baby Jane Holzer. The first *Screen Tests* were also created at this time, in which everyone could prove their star qualities by posing in front of the running camera as motionlessly and rigidly as possible.

In 1964 Warhol's works were shown in three exhibitions. In January the Galerie Ileana Sonnabend in Paris showed several *Death and Disaster* paintings, which left a deep impression in Europe. Warhol's second exhibition opened in April at the Stable Gallery in New York, in which the artist succeeded in disturbing the critics. It featured exclusively sculptures, *Brillo, Campbell's, Del Monte, Kellogg's,* and *Heinz Boxes*, which were wooden replicas of detergent and food cartons. Due to this exhibition's lack of financial success, Warhol switched to Leo Castelli, who presented the more appealing *Flowers* paintings from November and was able to sell all the exhibited works.

In 1964 Warhol received the assignment to create a mural for the New York State Pavilion at the World's Fair in New York. The artist delivered a mural of 20 × 20 feet consisting of twenty-five panels, *Thirteen Most Wanted Men*, whose templates were photos of wanted men. When the work was revealed just a few days before the start of the World's Fair, there was an outcry because the depicted criminals were exclusively Italians, some of whom were no longer being pursued by the law. Warhol was asked to contribute a different work, or else to withdraw, whereupon he decided to cover the work with silver paint.

At the beginning of 1965, Warhol met the twenty-two-year-old Edith "Edie" Minturn Sedgwick, who came from a wealthy family. The artist sensed that the young lady would be a special asset for his movie production and he used her as a new superstar. This was the beginning of an exceptionally fruitful collaboration—Edie Sedgwick became Warhol's most well-known superstar and together with her he built up his presence in the media even further. Sedgwick was also at Warhol's side in May 1965 when, during the opening of his "Flowers" exhibition at the Galerie Ileana Sonnabend, he explained that he was giving up painting in favor of film. Warhol did in fact dedicate himself increasingly to the medium of film in the years that followed. In 1965 he met the moviemaker Paul Morrissey, who was to play an important role in movie production at the Factory and take over as film director three years later. Until the 1970s, new superstars were regularly discovered for Warhol's movies, including Nico, Viva, and Joe Dallesandro as the most famous, along with Edie Sedgwick. Warhol chose the German model Nico to be the singer for the band The Velvet Underground, which he supported and produced from the mid-1960s onwards. Under the title *Andy Warhol, Up-Tight*, which was changed later to *Exploding Plastic Inevitable*, Warhol presented a multimedia show that initially caused a stir in New York, and later while on tour throughout the U.S.

Nonetheless, he also continued to produce paintings that were exhibited with great success. About 4,000 viewers showed up for the opening of a retrospective at the Institute of Contemporary Art at the University of Pennsylvania in Philadelphia. For an exhibition at the Leo Castelli Gallery in April 1966, the artist had a room decorated with a curious *Cow Wallpaper* printed in garish colors, with *Silver Clouds*, big silver balloons filled with helium, floating through the gallery. The exhibition space was otherwise empty.

In summer 1967 Warhol met Frederick W. Hughes. Hughes had studied art history and had worked at the Boston Museum of Fine Arts, until the influential de Menil family—the biggest art collectors in the U.S.—became his patrons. He had excellent contacts and soon became president of Andy Warhol Films Inc., as well as Warhol's manager and close friend. In February 1968 the Factory was relocated to a floor in the 33 Union Square West building. It was no longer a party venue, but more like an office. Frederick Hughes hired Jed Johnson, who took over Gerard Malanga's duties and was to play an important role not only at the Factory, but also in the artist's private life. He was Warhol's life partner until the beginning of the 1980s.

Frederick Hughes, Jed Johnson, and Paul Morrissey were present when Valerie Solanas entered the Factory on June 3, 1968, and fired shots at

Warhol and the art critic Mario Amaya without warning. Warhol was critically injured. An operation lasting several hours saved his life. The artist spent eight weeks in hospital. In March 1969 he had to have another operation because of his injuries. Valerie Solanas had previously been a guest at the Silver Factory and had even played a role in the movie *I, a Man*. The radical feminist was the founder and only member of the militant "Society for Cutting Up Men (S.C.U.M.)." In her manifesto she propagated the elimination of the male gender. Solanas gave herself up to the police on the very day of the assault and explained that she had shot at Warhol as revenge for the degradation of women in his movies. After being sentenced she was admitted to a psychiatric ward.

In the fall of 1969, the first edition of *Interview* magazine was published, edited by Warhol together with Gerard Malanga, Paul Morrissey, and John Wilcock. *Interview* was originally a pure movie magazine, which was intended to serve as an entrance ticket to movie festivals and performances for Warhol and Morrissey. However, the monthly magazine was soon extended to include other subjects, such as fashion and lifestyle. In 1970 Warhol and Morrissey took on Bob Colacello, who as chief editor succeeded in turning *Interview* into a glamorous magazine and reaching an ever-wider readership. Colacello was soon involved in all social and business matters at the Factory.

With the *Mao* portraits created in the year 1972, Warhol again began dedicating himself increasingly to painting, which he had never fully given up. During this phase he favored hand-painted, expressive pictorial backgrounds. In 1974 the artist bought a townhouse on East Sixty-Sixth Street, which he moved into with Jed Johnson. During the same year, the Factory was relocated to Broadway 860 and its activities operated officially under the name Andy Warhol Enterprises, Inc. Vincent Fremont, who had started at the Factory three years previously and who soon gained Warhol's special trust, became vice president of the company. At the end of the 1970s the Factory was a flourishing enterprise: commissioned portraits, for which Warhol used his own Polaroid photos as templates, represented the main source of income. His international clients included industrialists, fashion designers, politicians, heads of state, and stars from the entertainment scene.

In spring 1977, the legendary Studio 54 opened in New York. The disco soon achieved cult status as a meeting place for the glitterati and the famous. Warhol became a regular guest there, along with Truman Capote, Bianca Jagger, Liza Minnelli, and the fashion designer Halston, thereby cementing his image as a notorious partygoer. At this time the artist started capturing his surroundings in snapshots, some of which were published in *Andy Warhol's Exposures* in 1979. One year later Warhol followed this with his memoirs from the 1960s, *POPism*, which had been compiled by his assistant Pat Hackett.

In the 1970s Vincent Fremont realized video productions for Warhol. From 1979 to 1983 he produced the shows *Fashion* and *Andy Warhol's TV* for the artist, broadcast on cable channels, with guests from the art, entertainment, and fashion worlds. A similar show followed in 1985, *Andy Warhol's Fifteen Minutes*, which was broadcast on MTV.

In 1984 Warhol bought a five-story building in midtown for $1.2 million, and relocated his business activities there. In the same year he started to work with Jean-Michel Basquiat and Francesco Clemente on collaborative paintings. Later on he continued the cooperation with Basquiat only. Warhol contributed hand-painted trademarks and captions to these *Collaboration Works*.

Although Warhol had suffered from bilious attacks for some time and had to cancel business appointments for the first time in January 1987, during that same month he flew to attend the opening of his "Last Supper" exhibition in the Palazzo delle Stelline in Milan, where he presented his interpretations of Leonardo da Vinci's famous mural painting. Back in New York, the artist was forced to undergo a gall bladder operation, which was successful. However, one day later there were unexpected complications and as a consequence Warhol died in his sleep of cardiac arrest on the morning of February 22, 1987. Andy Warhol was buried next to his mother in Pittsburgh, attended by his family and a few friends. A memorial service was held on April 1, 1987 in St. Patrick's Cathedral in New York, attended by more than 2,000 people.

2

Salvador Dalí and Andy Warhol had quite different journeys through life
starting from birth: Dalí was born into wealthy circumstances, while Warhol
was the youngest child of poor immigrants. They also belonged to different
generations and therefore established themselves as artists in different eras
within the art scenes of their times. Dalí gained fame as early as the 1930s,
while Warhol did not achieve his artistic breakthrough until the 1960s. Even
so, there are interesting biographical parallels and similarities with regard
to the artists' personalities.

European Roots

Andy Warhol's parents came from Miková, a small village in Slovakia, which together with the Czech Republic formed Czechoslovakia from
1918 to 1939 and again from 1945 to 1992. Warhol, however, was born in the
United States. Julia Warhola had followed her husband to America a few
years before the birth of her three sons Paul, John, and Andrew. Warhol's
parents' European origins became an important factor for him as a child.
Julia Warhola remained true to her roots her whole life and did not become
very "Americanized." At home, the family spoke Carpatho-Russian in the
local dialect of the Prešov area. English was difficult for Mrs. Warhola and
the grammar of the new language remained alien to her.[1] Shortly before his
mother's death, Warhol remarked in an interview that he did not speak the
native language of his parents.[2] However, he had no difficulty in understanding it. Paul Warhola recalled:

*I was the oldest boy and we spoke our language, Carpatho-Russian at
home, I mean most of the time. I knew it fluently. In fact when I went to Europe
one time, after about three days I sounded like a native. I knew the language
pretty well. ... Andy understood ... he and Mum spoke it all the time. She preferred speaking it whenever they were together. As a kid growing up I had to
learn English first in school. Then I brought it home and used it with everyone.
Yeah, I was the first one to learn English.[3]*

Julia Warhola remarked in 1966 in an interview, "Andy no talk Slovak,
but he understands. I no speak English so good. Andy very good for school.
He keep school nice. He says, 'I like school.'"[4] Having said that, Warhol also
had problems in school; when he went to school, he spoke English that was
scarcely comprehensible grammatically.[5] Contrary to Dalí, he recounted
very few details about his childhood, but in his book *THE Philosophy of Andy
Warhol* he refers to his childhood as "growing up Czechoslovak."[6] He also
states therein that he encouraged his mother to read English comics to him,
"My father was away a lot on business trips to the coal mines, so I never saw
him very much. My mother would read to me in her thick Czechoslovakian
accent as best as she could and I would always say 'Thanks, Mom,' after she
finished with Dick Tracy, even if I hadn't understood a word. She'd give me
a Hershey Bar every time I finished a page in my coloring book."[7] Even when
he started his studies, Warhol still had problems with the English language
due to his "hunkie" accent and said, for example, "ats" instead of "that is,"
"jeetjet" instead of "did you eat yet," or "yunz" instead of "all of you." One

1
See Bourdon
1989, pp. 16f.,
and Guiles
1989, p. 13, who
writes that
Mrs. Warhola
spoke Czech.

2
Warhol (1973) in
Goldsmith 2004,
p. 208.

3
Paul Warhola
in a conversation
with the author
on November 27,
2012 in Pitts-
burgh.

4
In Weinraub
1966, p. 101.

5
Bockris 1989,
p. 36.

6
Warhol 1975,
Philosophy,
Contents.

7
Ibid., pp. 21f.

37

of his teachers recalled later that Warhol had driven a course director to despair with his "mutilations" of the English language.[8]

Dalí was also confronted with more than one language in his childhood. When he was six years old, his father enrolled him in the Collège Hispano-Français de l'Immaculée Conception Béziers in Figueres. The language of instruction at this school, which Dalí attended for six years, was exclusively French, so he soon spoke perfect French, albeit with a strong Catalan accent. While Dalí was growing up, Catalan—in addition to Spanish—was an official language of the Catalonian region—with its capital, Barcelona. It was only during the time of the Franco dictatorship that public use of Catalan was suppressed. Dalí consequently also learned Spanish and grew up with three languages. As a result, he was at a loss with spelling and developed the habit of writing according to how things sounded.[9] In 1951 he remarked in an interview:

I have never been good at spelling. During the third year of my baccalaureate, my father hired a teacher especially for spelling. I came to know it so well that the teacher would purposefully give me some real puzzles which I solved perfectly. I became a master in spelling. Then after six months of not seeing the professor I was as in the beginning. People think I misspell words so much on purpose, and it is not true; when I have to write a letter to a minister or someone of importance, I ask a friend to write it.[10]

There is no strong evidence as to whether this private teacher actually existed. However, it is a fact that Dalí, like most Spanish children, had difficulty with the letters B and V, which are pronounced the same in Spanish, as well as with H.[11] Another difficulty for him was that in Catalan—contrary to Spanish—the written O is pronounced as U and the written E as A. In 1965 the artist remarked in conversations with Alain Bosquet that he had started to write in Castilian (Spanish). It was only later when he joined the surrealist group that he switched to French.[12] Even so, Dalí used all three languages in public, although by his own account, he favored French, "Now, when I want to speak Castilian or Catalonian, I have to translate my thoughts from French. I've grown accustomed to the nuances and the etymology in French. Sometimes when I want to express certain niceties in Spanish, I can't find the right words."[13] Jonathan Guinness, 3rd Baron Moyne, who knew Dalí well, reports, "The language I spoke always with Dalí was French, as did my wife. ... I once talked to Dalí about languages because he wrote his books in French and this rather puzzled me. And he said, '*Je pense en français.*' I think he really did because through the accent you could sort of realize that this was really good French."[14] However, Dalí was evidently also perfectly capable of discarding his Catalan accent. The French flacon designer Pierre Dinand recalls, "He spoke French fluently, very well, sometimes without an accent. When he was doing business, I remember, one day he was speaking about the price of a license ... I was surprised that I heard Salvador Dalí suddenly with no accent at all. But when he was speaking to the people and was making his show, he had the very strongest accent, whenever he spoke about '*la gare de Perpignan, le centre du monde.*' ... It was incredible."[15]

8
Bockris 1989,
p. 60.

9
Gibson 1997,
p. 38.

10
In Arco 1984,
p. 57.

11
Gibson 1997,
p. 38.

12
In Bosquet 1969,
p. 105.

13
Ibid.

14
Lord Moyne in a
conversation
with the author
on December 17,
2014 in London.

15
Pierre Dinand in
a conversation
with the author
on March 1, 2013
in Paris.

2

When Dalí traveled with Gala to the United States for the first time in 1934, he did not speak a word of English and Gala spoke only a little English.[16] Caresse Crosby, who accompanied the two on the crossing, acted as an interpreter when the artist faced the American press for the first time.[17]

In time Dalí learned to speak English, too, as he and Gala lived exclusively in the U.S. from 1940 to 1948. However, even after all the years in America he still seemed to have problems with the language. Irene Halsman, who posed with Dalí in 1949 before her father Philippe's camera, recalls:

Sometimes my father used me and my sister in photo shoots ... On these occasions, when I met Dalí, I was very impressed by him. I was small, and thought he was very tall and handsome. His black hair was always slicked back, and he was often in the same navy blue pinstriped suit. I was very impressed how dapper and elegant he was. Entering the room, in a deep voice he'd say "Bonjour! Bonjour!" And when he would leave, he would again say "Bonjour! Bonjour!" He didn't seem to know English well, so he would combine it with other languages like French and Catalan. He never said a sentence in one language. It was a combination, like, "Give me le book." He was also surreal when he wrote letters to my father. He didn't really know how to write in English or in French—his spelling was always his own.[18]

Until the winter of 1979/80, Dalí spent several months a year in New York. Warhol's assistant Gerard Malanga, who met him in 1965 at the opening of the major Dalí retrospective at Huntington Hartford's Gallery of Modern Art in New York, remembers Dalí's English as follows: "He would sometimes make the remark in the third person singular, like, 'Dalí says ...' or 'Dalí does this' or 'Dalí does that.' But come to think of it, Dalí's English was not very perfect and so this was his personal way of expressing himself."[19] Dalí reserved good English for moments that were not public, when he was interested in a true conversation. The mathematics professor Thomas Banchoff, who met the artist for the first time in 1975, recalls, "He acted rather outrageously in public ... But if he wanted to find out something in particular he didn't sound crazy at all, or at least if you spoke to him in private he was very precise, really, about asking questions that he was interested in. ... He really spoke English quite well—not without an accent, certainly, not perfectly, but he didn't care. He was interested in communicating."[20] Pandora, Dalí's muse and confidante in the 1970s, also confirms that the artist's language level was dependent on the situation and reports, "He didn't really talk to others too much, unless he knew them. He spoke his broken Dalínian—his style of English. He didn't want people to know he spoke perfect English, really, which he did. He wasn't into trivial small talk—any of that."[21] His "Dalínian" mentioned by Pandora, or "Dalínian English," is explained by Dalí as follows in conversations with Alain Bosquet:

... now, English no longer bothers me. Evidently, I've fashioned a special way of pronouncing English. I've even made some records with Dalían intonations in a freakish English. I roll my r's as in Spanish, and I exaggerate my French pronunciation. I also inject some Catalonian into my French way of pronouncing English. Very often, neither Americans nor Englishmen

16
Man Ray 1988, p. 92.

17
Crosby 1953, p. 321.

18
Irene Halsman in a telephone conversation with the author on February 9, 2015.

19
Gerard Malanga in an e-mail to the author on September 24, 2009.

20
Prof. Thomas Banchoff in a telephone conversation with the author on May 26, 2010.

21
In Michaud 1991, Summer, p. 5.

understand what I'm saying, but if they manage to grasp a small detail, the result is a deafening applause. The phenomenon is extraordinary: basically, they're applauding themselves for having understood me. Instead of saying "butterfly" I say "booterrrrflaaaaaaaaeeeeee."[22]

This also explains why Warhol had difficulty following "Dalínian English." In *Andy Warhol's Exposures,* he says, "Dalí makes long winding speeches in Spanish, French, and English—all at once. I never understand a word he says. Except 'Dalí' and 'Gala.'"[23]

Creative Motherly Care

Salvador Dalí and Andy Warhol were both very attached to their mothers. Dalí referred to his mother as the "angel" of his "Dalínian Olympus": "Her breast, after her blood, brought life to me. Her sweet voice rocked my dreams."[1] Dalí was only sixteen years old when Doña Felipa Domènech died of uterine cancer at the age of forty-seven. As he reports in his autobiography *The Secret Life of Salvador Dalí,* her early death was the "greatest blow" he had experienced in his life. "She adored me with a love so whole and so proud that she could not be wrong—my wickedness, too, must be something marvelous!"[2]

Andy Warhol openly admitted later on that he was a mama's boy:

I think I'm missing some chemicals and that's why I have this tendency to be more of a—mama's boy. A—sissy. No, a mama's boy. A "butterboy." I think I'm missing some responsibility chemicals and some reproductive chemicals. If I had them I would probably think more about aging the right way and being married four times and having a family—wives and children and dogs. I'm immature, but maybe something could happen to my chemicals and I could get mature. I could start getting wrinkles and stop wearing my wings.[3]

What is remarkable is that the artist was in his mid-forties when he put this down on paper. Warhol never had the opportunity to develop a close relationship to his father. As he reported later, his father was mostly away on business trips to the coal mines.[4] Furthermore, Ondrej Warhola died when Warhol was just thirteen, so his mother became his most important attachment figure.

Both artists were thus half-orphaned at a young age, leaving the role of the missing parent to be filled by other family members. In the Warhola family, the eldest son Paul became the head of the family, and in Dalí's case it was the sister of the deceased Doña Felipa who took on the role of mother. Don Salvador Dalí even later married his sister-in-law Catalina. Dalí and his sister Ana María got on exceptionally well with their aunt Catalina and accepted her in her new role.[5] Dalí had also had a very close relationship with his mother because of his father's authoritarian character: He was moody and tended to burst out in anger. The artist later wrote, "To the manchild I was, my father was a giant of strength, violence, authority, and imperious love. Moses plus Jupiter."[6] His mother was the exact opposite, with a quiet and sensitive nature. In an interview, Dalí remarked, "I loved her, but I admired my father."[7]

22
In Bosquet 1969, p. 105. The recordings mentioned here really exist. In 1960 *Echo Magazine,* Vol. I, No. 4, was published in New York with a documentation of Dalí's language, with the title *Dalílinguistics* on a flexi record. See Altaió 2004, p. 237.

23
Warhol/Colacello 1979, p. 127.

1
Dalí 1976, p. 31.

2
Dalí 1942, pp. 152f.

3
Warhol 1975, *Philosophy,* p. 111.

4
Ibid., p. 21.

5
In his early diaries Dalí wrote about his aunt, "She is very intelligent, and we get on very well … we joke a lot." See Dalí 2004, p. 140 (translated from the German).

6
Dalí 1976, p. 23.

7
In Arco 1984, p. 57.

Dalí's parents' first child was a son, whom they had already christened with the name Salvador. However, the child died of a gastrointestinal infection just twenty-two months after his birth. Warhol's parents also had to mourn the death of their first child. Their daughter Josephine died after just a few months of a severe cold, as there were no medical services at the time in Miková. Andrew was born seventeen years later, while Dalí was born just nine months after the death of his brother. Because of the early death of her first son and the fear of losing another son, Dalí's mother was overprotective and he was mollycoddled as a child. Doña Felipa could not refuse especially her son anything and showered him with gifts. Dalí recalled, "For some time my mother had been asking me, 'Sweetheart, what do you wish? Sweetheart, what do you want?'"[8] Dalí wanted his mother to fetch the movie projector:

I can still hear the regular noise of the crank on the projector my mother turned by hand as she showed us little films. I remember a documentary, The Taking of Port Arthur, *reporting [on] the Russo-Japanese War, in which generals saluted like automatons, and another picture,* The Schoolboy in Love. *My mother is behind me, in the dark. My sister and my friends and I strain our eyes towards the moving screen. She is the picture angel.*[9]

Andy Warhol also wished for a movie projector as a child. However, as the Warhola family was far from wealthy, Julia Warhola worked as a domestic aid for a dollar a day until she had saved the twenty dollars for a movie projector. Warhol's brother John recalled later:

Money was real hard to get and Andy wanted things that we just couldn't afford. When he was seven, for instance, he wanted a movie projector. We didn't have the money to buy the screen but we could show the pictures right on the wall. It was just black and white. He'd watch Mickey Mouse or Little Orphan Annie and he got ideas and then he would draw a lot. My mother bought that without my father knowing about it.[10]

When Warhol was diagnosed with chorea in 1936, the doctor in charge prescribed rest and care. His mother was overprotective and moved her son's sickbed into the dining room and devoted herself to his care. In *THE Philosophy of Andy Warhol* the disease is dramatized a little, "I had three nervous breakdowns when I was a child, spaced a year apart. One when I was eight, one at nine, and one at ten. The attacks—St. Vitus Dance—always started on the first day of summer vacation. I don't know what this meant. I would spend all summer listening to the radio and lying in bed with my Charlie McCarthy doll and my un-cut-out cut-out paper dolls all over the spread and under the pillow."[11]

Dalí's mother also supplied material to stimulate the child's imagination and fantasy, and to console him. In *The Secret Life* he states, "My mother, who was always of an angelic tenderness, consoled me as best as she could, then bought me a sumptuous album in which we pasted hundreds of transfer pictures ... ."[12] Of course Dalí also soon realized that sick children receive greater attention from their parents. In his *Unspeakable Confessions* he reports that his father, "... spent the night sitting up with me when I was sick. The next day, a Sunday, he instructed that he not be disturbed. ... I also

8
Dalí 1942, p. 70.

9
Dalí 1976, p. 32.

10
In Bockris 1989, p. 36.

11
Warhol 1975, *Philosophy,* p. 21.

12
Dalí 1942, p. 48.

often pretended to be sick, just to worry my parents, and then peed in bed with pristine pleasure."[13]

Dalí and Warhol undoubtedly inherited their creativity from their mothers. The ancestors on Doña Felipa Domenèch Ferrés's side had a creative vein. Her father Jaume Ferrés was a renowned craftsman, said to be the first in Catalonia to work with tortoiseshell.[14] He ran an old family enterprise in Barcelona specialized in art objects, which his daughter, María Anna Ferrés—Dalí's grandmother—later took over. María Anna's firstborn, Dalí's mother, helped in the workshop and showed considerable skill.[15] The grandmother and mother delighted Salvador and his sister Ana María later with their artistic creativity. The grandmother made paper cuts and the mother formed delicate wax figurines out of colored candle wax. Dalí's mother was also good at drawing.[16] In his *Secret Life*, the artist recalls, "Later my mother drew astonishing pictures of fantastic animals on a long strip of paper with colored pencils. She then carefully folded this strip where each picture stopped, so that the whole could be reduced to a small book which unfolded like an accordion."[17]

Warhol's mother, Julia Warhola, also had an exceptional talent for drawing, which she passed on to her three sons—her son Andrew was undoubtedly the most talented.[18] Andrew and his mother portrayed each other or they drew the cat. Mrs. Warhola recalled later, "I drew pictures so Andy made pictures when he was a little boy. He liked to do that, sure, he made very nice pictures. We made pictures together. I like to draw cats. I'm really a cat woman."[19] So Julia Warhola encouraged her son's artistic talent from a young age. However, she did not show her creative vein only at home, but also within the Ruthene immigrant community that the family was part of. She painted Easter eggs there.[20] Her talent also helped to improve the family's financial situation, as she made imaginative flower creations out of old tins and crepe paper. As the works were unsalable in the Pittsburgh district that the Warhola family lived in, she went to the affluent Oakland neighborhood and peddled her flower creations door-to-door for twenty-five cents apiece.[21]

When Warhol was working as a commercial artist in the 1950s, his mother made a significant contribution to her son's success by inscribing his drawings with her ornate, old-fashioned calligraphy and writing his signature. This calligraphy soon became his trademark. Nathan Gluck, Warhol's assistant from 1955 to the mid-1960s, recalled later, "Because Andy liked his mother's penmanship he one day asked her to sign his name on a drawing. This became a regular routine except when Mrs. Warhola did not feel well or was asleep, in which case I was asked to fake her writing! If the drawing needed a caption, Mrs. Warhola would painstakingly copy it out letter-by-letter, but sometimes she mistook one letter for another and would write Marlyn Monore for Marilyn Monroe, for example. Andy loved those errors."[22]

Warhol also found another solution for making his mother's handwriting available for his work without her active involvement. As his assistant Gerard Malanga explains:

There was a place in the 1960s you'd go to, an art supply store, Art Brown & Brothers. It doesn't exist anymore. ... There was a company that

---

13
Dalí 1976,
pp. 24, 28.

14
Dalí 1949, p. 86.

15
Gibson 1997,
p. 17.

16
Dalí 1949,
p. 36; Gibson
1997, p. 17.

17
Dalí 1942, p. 48.

18
Guiles 1989,
pp. 13f.

19
Quoted
according to
Bockris 1989,
p. 30.

20
Francis in
Francis/Koepplin
1999, p. 9.

21
Bourdon 1989,
p. 17.

22
In McShine 1989,
p. 425.

made a sheet called Letraset. ... when you wanted to do a letter if you were spelling out a word, you'd take a coin and rub it across the sheet and the letter would then adhere to the paper. ... That's how I used to make the posters for the flyers. I designed all those flyers for the Warhol movies with Letraset. Andy had a Letraset made of his mother's handwriting from A to Z and the numbers and some of the designs like the stars, the snake, the turtle. ... Letraset would make custom-made sheets. And he had a sheet made. ... If you used one letter you could connect it to the next letter so actually it looked like it was handwriting.[23]

In the 1950s, Warhol not only worked on his own career, but also promoted his mother as a naive artist. In 1957, Julia Warhola's unique calligraphy gave the famous graphic artist and designer Reid Miles the idea to commission her with the record cover design for *The Story of Moondog* by the blind New York street musician and composer Moondog, released by Prestige Records.[24] Her design consisted of sixteen handwritten lines that represented the prose poem "The Story of Moondog" by Stewart Preston. However, she had difficulty completing it. Mrs. Warhola spent the entire evening writing the words over and over again on a piece of paper, as her writing tended to slant upwards and to get ever bigger. Nathan Gluck later recollected: "She also did a record album, and she would misspell words and start over again, and the writing would start small and get bigger and slant upwards. And finally, Andy told her just to do it; then he cut the whole thing apart and pasted it up so that it made some bit of sense. *She* got an Art Directors Club award for it."[25] In addition to the Art Director's Club award, Mrs. Warhola also received an award for the record cover design from the American Institute of the Arts.[26] Curiously, on the Art Directors Club award, "Andy Worhol's mother" was inscribed with exactly the same mistake that appears on the record cover.[27]

Owing to this great success, Warhol encouraged his mother to draw what she enjoyed drawing: cats. It is said that Mrs. Warhola complained later that her son was a "harsh taskmaster," who always insisted, even when she was tired, "You have to get up and do another pussycat."[28] In 1960 Warhol published some of her cat drawings in the promotional book *Holy Cats by Andy Warhol's Mother.*[29] He had the works reproduced on colored paper of different textures and thicknesses and made them into a little book bound by thread. It tells the story of the deceased Hester, who meets many of her fellow species in cat heaven. Warhol had given the cat to a friend who wanted to have her sterilized, but she died on the operating table. Many years later Warhol confided to his diaries, "My darling Hester. She went to pussy heaven. And I've felt guilty ever since. That's how we should have started *POPism.*"[30]

TIME **Magazine Reports**

On December 14, 1936, Salvador Dalí was awarded a special honor: his photo appeared on the cover of *TIME* magazine. The photo shows the artist full face with a narrow little mustache that looks painted on, and wearing an

23
Gerard Malanga in a conversation with the author on July 2, 2012 in Hudson, NY.

24
Maréchal 2008, no. 22.

25
In O'Connor/Liu 1996, p. 32.

26
The Andy Warhol Museum, p. 173.

27
Maréchal 2008, no. 22.

28
Quoted according to Bourdon 1989, p. 58.

29
The latest research has shown that the book was not published until 1960, and not in 1957 or 1958 as previously assumed. Details by Schleif in Schleif 2013, pp. 124ff.

30
Hackett 1989, p. 325, September 16, 1980.

elegant suit. The shot is part of a series of photo portraits that Man Ray took between the end of the 1920s and the beginning of the 1930s.[1] The magazine included an article entitled "Marvelous & Fantastic" about the exhibition "Fantastic Art, Dada and Surrealism," which was on view at the New York Museum of Modern Art from December 1936 to January 1937. The exhibition brought together over 700 works and reproductions by nearly 100 artists. The "Dada and Surrealism" section, which was the centerpiece of the exhibition, included works by Dalí, as well as by Hans Arp, Max Ernst, Alberto Giacometti, René Magritte, André Masson, Joan Miró, Francis Picabia, Man Ray, Yves Tanguy, and other artists.[2] It is worth remarking that about a quarter of the *TIME* article was dedicated to Dalí, reporting on his development until that time. It stated, "But surrealism would not have attracted its present attention in the U.S. were it not for a handsome 32-year-old Catalan with a soft voice and a clipped cinemactor's mustache, Salvador Dalí. … Artist Dalí who wears a knitted Catalan liberty cap whenever possible, takes surrealism in dead earnest, but has a faculty for publicity which should turn any circus press agent green with envy."[3] The *TIME* magazine edition of December 14, 1936 is documentation, that of all the surrealists, Dalí attracted the greatest attention. In 1954, Dalí was photographed by Philippe Halsman with this now famous cover page in his hands, for the photography edition *Dali's Mustache*. Halsman succeeded in capturing the same atmosphere as Man Ray had done: Dalí is standing in front of a black background, which makes his protruding ears stand out, and he is looking steadfastly into the camera. The artist is once again wearing a black suit. The most noticeable difference, however, is the mustache that now twirls up as far as the artist's ears. When the photo was taken, Dalí was sporting the longest mustache of his life—his "antennae" at the time were twenty-five centimeters long.[4] The photo was used in the preface to *Dali's Mustache*, where the painter explains, "At the age of 29, I undertook my first American Campaign. On the day I disembarked in New York, my photograph appeared on the cover of *TIME* magazine. It showed me wearing the smallest mustache in the world. Since then the world has shrunk considerably while my mustache, like the power of my imagination, continued to grow."[5]

Some years later, on Salvador Dalí's fifty-eighth birthday (May 11, 1962), *TIME* magazine reported on the newly emerging Pop Art and introduced the new art movement in an article entitled "The Slice-of-Cake School," "Unknown to one another, a group of painters have come to the common conclusion that the most banal and even vulgar trappings of modern civilization can, when transposed literally to canvas, become Art."[6] A small section of the text was dedicated to the artists Wayne Thiebaud, Roy Lichtenstein, Andy Warhol, and James Rosenquist. It mentioned that Warhol earned a living with advertisements for women's magazines, but that his "serious work" also comprised realistic paintings of everyday objects. The magazine quoted Warhol as follows: "I just paint things I always thought were beautiful, things you use every day and never think about it. I'm working on soups, and I've been doing some paintings of money. I just do it because I like it."[7] Warhol is the only artist in the article accorded a photograph, showing him in front

1
See Chéroux 2010, p. 114.

2
Jean 1961, pp. 271ff.

3
"Marvelous & Fantastic," pp. 60, 62.

4
Mas Peinado 2004, p. 251. See also the chapter **Mustache, Wig, and Other Signature Features** in this part.

5
Dalí/Halsman 1954, p. 1.

6
"The Slice-of-Cake School," p. 52.

7
In ibid.

of the 72 × 52 inch painting *Big Campbell's Soup Can with Can Opener (Vegetable)*. Behind him one can also spot the works *Telephone [3]* and *200 One Dollar Bills*. He is holding a spoon in his hand, alluding to eating out of an opened can of Campbell's Soup, but he is holding it the wrong way round. The dominance of Warhol in this article is surprising, considering that at this point in time, contrary to the other artists presented, he was not yet represented by any gallery.

Avida Dollars and Drella

When Salvador Dalí came to Madrid in September 1922 to commence his studies at the San Fernando Royal Academy of Fine Arts, he attracted attention with his eccentric appearance. In his autobiography *The Secret Life of Salvador Dalí,* the artist states that he bought himself a large black felt hat and a pipe, which he never lit, but always had hanging from the corner of his mouth. He wore short pants with stockings and sometimes puttees, with a waterproof cape that nearly reached the ground, completing his attire on rainy days.[1] Due to Dalí's "fantastic" appearance, his fellow students soon gave him a nickname. "These knew me by sight, and I was even the butt of their caustic humor. They called me 'the musician,' or 'the artist,' or 'the Pole.' My anti-European way of dressing had made them judge me unfavorably, as a rather commonplace, more or less hairy romantic residue."[2] Dalí learned that he could use extravagant clothing as a distraction from his shyness.[3] Luis Buñuel reports in his memoirs: "... we used to call him the 'Czechoslovakian painter,' although for the life of me I can't remember why. I do remember, however, passing his room one morning when the door was open and, glancing inside, seeing him putting the finishing touches on a superb portrait. 'The painter from Czechoslovakia's done an incredible painting,' I rushed to tell Lorca."[4] The nickname mentioned by Buñuel would also have been fitting for Andy Warhol. His parents came from Miková, located in what is now Slovakia, which from 1918 to 1939 and again from 1945 to 1992 was part of Czechoslovakia. Years later, Dalí would be given a further, significantly more original nickname.

The article "The Most Recent Tendencies in Surrealist Painting," in which André Breton wrote about Salvador Dalí, appeared in the final edition of the surrealist magazine *Minotaure* from May 1939: "Dalí's painting is already being eroded by profound and absolute monotony. His determination to rarefy his paranoiac-critical method still further has reduced him to concocting entertainment on the level of *crossword puzzles*."[5] This article marked Dalí's exclusion from the surrealist movement. One year later, Breton once again attacked Dalí's hunger for publicity and wealth and formed the anagram "Avida Dollars" from the letters of his name, and from then on, used it when referring to him.[6] This new coinage, which basically means "greedy for dollars," became famous no least because Dalí himself repeatedly commented on it. In *The Unspeakable Confessions*, he wrote about Breton, "All he achieved was to compose a talisman that saw me through the doors of banks and safes. America recognized me as its prodigal son and threw

1
Dalí 1942, p. 160.
See also Dalí 1949, p. 82;
Buñuel 1984, p. 64.

2
Dalí 1942, p. 175.

3
Etherington-Smith 1993, p. 39.

4
Buñuel 1984, p. 64.

5
Breton 2002, p. 147.

6
Polizzotti 1996, pp. 679f.;
Aguer in Ades 2004, p. 498.

dollars at my head like handfuls of confetti. Breton is responsible for my financial success. I have every reason to thank him for inventing that beneficent distinguished image."[7] Dalí's biographer Ian Gibson points out that the female adjective "avida" was, ironically, more appropriate for Gala than for Dalí. It was she who spent large sums of money for her own pleasure.[8] Ultra Violet confirmed, "Gala was Avida Dollars. It was *not* Dalí. Gala used to gamble, she was very superstitious, she needed money. Gala is responsible for Dalí's success, and his failure, though I don't like to use that word."[9]

Andy Warhol was also given a nickname by his entourage, which led to an array of interpretations and comments. In the mid-1960s, he was given the nickname "Drella" at the Factory, which he explains in *POPism* as follows: "'Drella' was a nickname somebody had given me that stuck more than I wanted it to. Ondine and a character named Dorothy Dyke used it all the time—they said it came from combining Dracula and Cinderella."[10] Gerard Malanga later recalled that it was Ondine who had come up with the name.[11] Ondine himself, however, who had gained fame through his role in Warhol's film *Chelsea Girls*, explained that "Drella" had been the name of a cat belonging to Debbie Cane, whose father Herbert Cane wrote the gossip column of the *San Francisco Chronicle*. He had always known Warhol as "Andy" and hardly ever called him "Drella."[12] The author Ronald Tavel, who came to the Factory at the end of 1964 and wrote film scripts there, later reported,

I just remember asking Ondine, and he said, "Well, it sounds good that way because his real name is 'Warhola,' right? So, Drella Warhola sounds right." And I said, "Yes, it does. No arguing with poetry." And, so, the hangers-on—the shirt-tail people—were called "The Drella Drellas," and they always referred to that: "Drella showed up with The Drella Drellas." Or, that, "The Drella Drellas at this party or that event." I don't know. It might be traced to Ondine, for all I know, who would be the type to give everyone [Laughs] ... and "Drella!" There's something very ironic about "Drella" because it sounds like "dowager." Your mother hen kind of [thing], which was his image then. He was, sort of, to us like a clucking mother hen.[13]

Evidently Warhol also recognized the "literary qualities" of his nickname and in his book *a – a novel*, published in 1968, he referred to himself throughout as "Drella." With the album *Songs for Drella*, Lou Reed and John Cale paid homage to Warhol. In "Small Town," a piece about the artist's origins, there is a line, "I'm no Dalí coming from Pittsburgh."[14]

Both nicknames, "Drella" and "Avida Dollars," have negative connotations. Gerard Malanga once interpreted Warhol's nickname as follows: "It's like fairy tales. It's like 'Vicious Heidi's.' You know, that kind of thing. 'Drella' is just sort of a homosexual ... sort of a campy name like 'The Witch': 'The Wicked Witch of the North.' That kind of thing, and it had an association kind of meaning. It had nothing specifically to do with Andy. Like instead of 'Here comes Andy,' 'Here comes Drella.' That kind of thing: watch out or be on your guard."[15] The nickname "Drella," as a combination of "*Dracula*" and "Cinder*ella*" can be a reference to some of Warhol's characteristics: "Cinderella" stands for the shy and unprepossessing artist who succeeded in rising to be one of the most famous names of his time. "Dracula" refers to

7
Dalí 1976, p. 162. Similarly, in Pauwels/Dalí 1985, pp. 82f.

8
Gibson 1997, p. 453.

9
In "Reminiscences of Dalí: A Conversation with Amanda Lear and Ultra Violet," moderated by Dawn Ades, in Taylor 2008, p. 207. Regarding Gala's gambling addiction see also Moore 2009, pp. 186f.

10
Warhol/Hackett 1980, p. 153.

11
In Smith 1986, p. 404.

12
In ibid., pp. 427f.

13
In ibid., pp. 489f.

14
Reed 2006, p. 332.

15
In Smith 1986, p. 411. Similarly, also in Bockris 1989, p. 200.

Warhol's ingenious talent in appropriating alien ideas, in order to enhance his own fame. Warhol's superstar Holly Woodlawn writes in her memoirs, "I think a lot of the Warhol entourage thought Andy was taking from them, living vicariously through them. Sucking from them what he wanted and then casting their drained souls aside."[16] Woodlawn reports that Warhol also bore the nickname "Grandma," because of his "snow-white hair."[17] Dalí also referred to himself once as a kind of Dracula. He remarked to the Spanish director José Montes-Baquer, who shot the TV movie *Impressions de la Haute Mongolie* with him, "Dalí is a universal genius. For this reason, hundreds of people approach him daily to enrich themselves. But what they do not know is that Dalí, as well as being a universal genius, is also an intellectual vampire who enriches himself with all the people who come close to him."[18]

Experience of Death

On October 12, 1901, Salvador Dalí's mother gave birth to a son who was christened Salvador Galo Anselmo Dalí. However, the child died just twenty-two months later on August 1, 1903, as the result of "an infectious gastro-enteritic cold,"[1] according to the death certificate. Nine months and ten days after this tragic stroke of fate, the parents had a second son, whom they called Salvador Felipe Jacinto Dalí. As Dalí reports in his *Secret Life*, the death of the first Salvador plunged his parents into deep despair and they found solace only after he came into the world.[2] It might be surprising that the painter repeatedly claimed in his autobiographical writing that his brother had died three years before his birth at the age of seven as a result of meningitis. In his *Unspeakable Confessions* he says:

As is known, three years after the death of my seven-year-old elder brother, my father and my mother at my birth gave me the same name, Salvador, which was also my father's. This subconscious crime was aggravated by the fact that in my parents' bedroom—an attractive, mysterious, redoubtable place, full of ambivalences and taboos—there was a majestic picture of Salvador, my dead brother, next to a reproduction of Christ crucified as painted by Velázquez; and this image of the cadaver of the Savior whom Salvador had without question gone to in his angelic ascension conditioned in me an archetype born of four Salvadors who cadaverized me. The more so as I turned into a mirror image of my dead brother.[3]

The art historian and art critic Ricard Mas Peinado from Catalonia points out that it was by all means usual at that time in the rural homeland of the artist to keep a picture of a child who had died and to give the next child the name of the deceased.[4] In view of local traditions, it is hardly tenable to speak of a "subconscious crime."

Dalí was very adept at including all the details of the tragic event in the myth of the two Salvadors that he created. Despite their strong physical resemblance, as Dalí writes in his *Secret Life*, the two Salvadors had fundamental differences:

My brother and I resembled each other like two drops of water, but we had different reflections. Like myself he had the unmistakable facial morphology

16
Woodlawn/
Copeland 1991,
p. 163.

17
Ibid., p. 163.

18
Quoted according to José
Montes-Baquer,
http://u2r2h-
documents.
blogspot.de/
2007/07/
download-
impression-de-
la-haute.html
(last accessed
on April 6, 2016).

1
Gibson 1997,
p. 21.

2
Dalí 1942, p. 2.

3
Dalí 1976, p. 241.

4
Mas Peinado
2004, p. 43.

of a genius. He gave signs of alarming precocity, but his glance was veiled by the melancholy characterizing insurmountable intelligence. I, on the other hand, was much less intelligent, but I reflected everything. I was to become the prototype par excellence *of the phenomenally retarded "polymorphous perverse".... My brother was probably a first version of myself, but conceived too much in the absolute.*[5]

In fact the two brothers were scarcely alike. Two photos exist of the first Salvador, showing an exceptionally pretty child with "almost angelic" features,[6] whose physiognomy was quite different from that of the second Salvador.[7]

If Dalí is to be believed, then his childhood was overshadowed by the presence of the first Salvador, whom he was constantly measured against and whom he therefore had to assert himself against within his family. In *The Unspeakable Confessions* he says,

Many is the time I have relived the life and death of this elder brother, whose traces were everywhere when I achieved awareness—in clothes, pictures, games—and who remained always in my parents' memories through indelible affective recollections. I deeply experienced the persistence of his presence as both a trauma—a kind of alienation of affections—and a sense of being outdone. All my efforts thereafter were to strain toward winning back my rights to life, first and foremost by attracting the constant attention and interest of those close to me by a kind of perpetual aggressiveness.[8]

It remains doubtful whether the behavior of the young Dalí was really characterized by a "perpetual aggressiveness." The artist's childhood diaries contain no indication of this. There is no mention of the dead brother in the writings. It is therefore hardly surprising that Dalí only reluctantly consented to the publication of part of his diaries by the American collector A. Reynolds Morse in 1962, and only under the specific condition that the publication should not be released on the market.[9] The artist displayed a similar reaction when his sister Ana María published her book *Salvador Dalí visto por su hermana* in 1949, in which she portrays quite a different Salvador: "My brother was affable and cordial, with a great sense of humor. It was only when an abnormal desire to attract attention dominated him that he became capable of the most absurd things."[10] Dalí was less than delighted when he learned of the book's publication. The painter residing in New York reacted angrily to his sister's portrayal and complained to A. Reynolds Morse, "My sister has destroyed my image, I have worked all these years to prove what a monster I was and she has ruined my legend, she has proved I am just a nice little boy."[11] The artist, already world-renowned, reacted immediately and penned a memorandum in January 1950, which he then printed on cards and distributed widely: "... my sister could not resist speculating materially, and pseudo-sentimentally, with my name, selling paintings of mine without my permission and publishing absolutely false accounts of verifiable facts of my life. For which reasons I feel it my duty to warn collectors and biographers."[12] Dalí was thinking only of his reputation when he wrote these lines. He was afraid that after the publication of his sister's book, the public would no longer believe his version of his childhood and the two Salvadors.

[5] Dalí 1942, p. 2.

[6] Gibson 1997, p. 23.

[7] The photos are in Gibson 1997, as no.1 and no. 2 reproduced following p. 164.

[8] Dalí 1976, p. 12.

[9] Fanés in Dalí 2004, p. 7.

[10] Quoted according to Gibson 1997, p. 454.

[11] Quoted according to Etherington-Smith 1993, p. 320.

[12] Quoted according to Gibson 1997, p. 456.

2

Andy Warhol's experience of death was far more dramatic than Salvador Dalí's. Warhol did not arrive at the Factory until late afternoon on June 3, 1968. His taxi drove up at 4:15 p.m.; Valerie Solanas, who had already asked after him in the morning, had been waiting in front of the building for several hours. The artist was disgruntled when he saw her.[13] As a radical feminist and founder of the organization "S.C.U.M." ("Society for Cutting Up Men"), Solanas propagated world peace through the annihilation of the male gender. She had given Warhol a film manuscript to read, *Up Your Ass*. When she asked for it back, he claimed to have lost it. After this, she came to the Factory regularly and demanded money from Warhol. He finally relented and let her participate in a scene for the film *I, a Man*, for which she received a payment of twenty-five dollars.[14] Solanas left a positive impression on Warhol, and she also seemed to have enjoyed the filming. However, shortly afterward she berated him as a vulture and a thief. She remarked to the publisher Maurice Girodias, "Talking to him is like talking to a chair."[15] Although Valerie Solanas had been harassing Warhol again by telephone for a while, the artist took her und his then life companion Jed Johnson, who was also present, with him into the lift on that very June 3, 1968, to go to the Factory where the critic and curator Mario Amaya was waiting for him. After arriving at the fifth floor, Jed Johnson went into Warhol's office. Fred Hughes and Paul Morrissey were also present, sitting at their desks. Morrissey was on the telephone and gave Warhol the receiver, before leaving the room. Viva was on the line, calling from Kenneth's beauty salon, where she was having her hair done for a scene in the film *Midnight Cowboy*, which she was acting in under the direction of John Schlesinger, together with other Warhol superstars. When Warhol started to get bored with the conversation, he asked Hughes to take over—at least that is what it says in *POPism* and in the majority of Warhol literature.[16] However, as Viva remembers it, the film shooting had not yet begun at this point, and furthermore she had not yet spoken to Warhol, who had only just taken over the receiver from Fred Hughes[17] when a dramatic event happened, reported as follows in *POPism*:

... I heard a loud exploding noise and whirled around: I saw Valerie pointing a gun at me and I realized she'd just fired it.

I said, "No! No, Valerie! Don't do it!" and she shot at me again. I dropped down to the floor as if I'd been hit—I didn't know if I actually was or not. I tried to crawl under the desk. She moved in closer, fired again, and then I felt horrible, horrible pain, like a cherry bomb exploding inside me.

As I lay there, I watched the blood come through my shirt and I heard more shooting and yelling. (Later—a long time later—they told me that the two bullets from a .32-caliber gun had gone through my stomach, liver, spleen, esophagus, left lung, and right lung.) Then I saw Fred standing over me and I gasped, "I can't breathe." He kneeled down and tried to give me artificial respiration but I told him no, no, that it hurt too much. He got up from the floor and rushed to the phone to call an ambulance and the police.

Then suddenly Billy was leaning over me. He hadn't been there during the shooting, he'd just come in. I looked up and I thought he was laughing, and that made me start to laugh, too, I can't explain why. But it hurt so much,

---

13 Bourdon 1989, p. 284.

14 Bockris 1989, p. 272; Warhol/Hackett 1980, p. 271.

15 Bockris 1989, p. 273.

16 See Warhol/Hackett 1980, p. 272; Bockris 1989, p. 298; Bourdon 1989, p. 284.

17 Viva in an e-mail to the author on April 18, 2012.

*and I told him, "Don't laugh, oh, please don't make me laugh." But he wasn't
laughing, it turned out, he was crying.*

*It was almost a half hour before the ambulance got there. I just stayed
still on the floor, bleeding.*[18]

After Solanas shot at Warhol, she turned her attention to the others
present and shot first of all at Amaya, hitting him in the hip. However, he
was able to flee to the back room and slam the big double doors shut. Morrissey, who had gone to the bathroom, had not heard the shots at all and
saw the blood-covered Amaya holding the door shut. Jed Johnson braced
himself against the door to Warhol's office. When Solanas tried to open it she
thought it was locked. When she finally pointed her weapon at Fred Hughes
and claimed that she had to shoot him, Hughes kneeled on the floor and
begged "*Please!* Don't shoot me! Just *leave!*" He succeeded in persuading the
confused and indecisive Solanas to flee.[19]

At 4:45 p.m., Warhol was taken to the Columbus Hospital on East Nineteenth Street between Second and Third Avenue and shortly afterwards was
declared clinically dead.[20] In *POPism* it says that during the first minutes in
the operating room, the artist heard the doctors saying words like "forget it"
and "no chance."[21] Amaya, who was lying on another operating table and had
suffered a penetrating gunshot wound, sat up and cried, "Don't you know
who this is? It's Andy Warhol. He's famous. And he's rich. He can afford to
pay for an operation. For Christ's sake, do something!"[22] Warhol was operated on for over five hours by a medical team under the direction of Dr.
Giuseppe Rossi. His life was hanging on a thread, but he pulled through.[23]
Warhol had to stay at the hospital for nearly two and a half months and was
first released in late July 1968.[24] During this time, his nephew Paul C. Warhola looked after him. He spent almost every day at his uncle's side, slept in
his room and was a kind of "errand boy" for him, taking care of his mail and
his contact with the outside world.[25]

Valerie Solanas gave herself up to the police on the afternoon of June
3, 1968.[26] She was charged with two cases of attempted murder and with the
illegal possession of firearms. She defended her actions before the examining
magistrate, "I was right in what I did. I have nothing to regret." She rejected
a court-appointed defense lawyer and shouted, "Warhol deserved what he
got! He is a goddamned liar and a cheat. All that comes out of his mouth is
lies." The judge had her committed to a psychiatric hospital.[27]

Paul C. Warhola reveals how deeply the events affected the artist's life,
"Whenever I would visit him he'd say 'Paulie, now look, when you go out,
when you see a crowd on a corner or somewhere, always go to the other side,'
in other words, 'don't get involved.'"[28] Friends and staff could hardly overlook
that Warhol had changed. The actress Sally Kirkland, who had made her
film debut in a Warhol film in 1964, remarks: "He was almost spiritual. My
observation was that he was just so incredibly loving and gentle and frag-
ile."[29] The playwright Robert Heide, who had worked on several projects with
Warhol, comments, "He thought that he had died and come back. And there
was always a ghostly feeling after that. He was not so sure of himself and he
was always a little nervous. ... I think he got more confidence when he came

18
Warhol/Hackett
1980, pp. 272f.

19
Ibid., pp. 273f.

20
Bockris 1989,
pp. 301f.;
Warhol/Hackett
1980, p. 274.

21
Warhol/Hackett
1980, p. 274.

22
Quoted accord-
ing to Bockris
1989, pp. 301f.

23
Bourdon 1989,
p. 286; Bockris
1989, pp. 301f.

24
Bourdon 1989,
p. 290.

25
Paul C. Warhola
in a telephone
conversation
with the author
on June 28, 2013.

26
Warhol/Hackett
1980, p. 277.

27
Bourdon 1989,
p. 286.

28
Paul C. Warhola
in a telephone
conversation
with the author
on June 28, 2013.

29
Sally Kirkland in
a telephone
conversation with
the author on
December 16,
2012.

to business. He knew that he couldn't trust everyone."[30] While according to Viva, Warhol had been shy towards women before the event, he was "deeply afraid" of them afterwards.[31] Brigid Berlin, Warhol's closest confidante, says about his fears,

When he came back to the Factory after being shot he really believed that when he was shot he died. ... And he would get very afraid to go to the Factory on a Saturday to paint sometimes because he always thought that he was gonna get stuck in the elevator, that somebody, I guess, was gonna come in and he'd call you and say "Will you come over and babysit?" And when you'd say "Oh God, Andy, I don't feel like going over there now. I've got other things to do," he'd bribe you and say "Well, you can go to the pastry store and buy anything you want." ... He checked the bathrooms, the toilet, every inch of the place, the garbage pails everything. "Is something burning?"[32]

The incident also had a tremendous publicity effect. Many collectors and museums first became aware of Warhol and the prices of his works went up. The Pop Art artist had reached lofty heights in the public eye through the attempted murder—"the same level as Picasso and Dalí."[33]

Working on Their Own Myths

Salvador Dalí and Andy Warhol are among the few twentieth-century artists who became myths during their own lifetimes. The basis for the Dalí myth is the autobiography *The Secret Life of Salvador Dalí*. In his life story published in New York in 1942, which sold very successfully, the Spaniard knitted together fiction and reality in a very deliberate way. The paradoxical title, which promised the reader a glimpse into the secrets of his eccentric artist existence, had the desired effect on the public.[1] In 1948 Dalí returned to his Spanish homeland and his fame spread rapidly in Europe, too. An important testimony to these early years is a conversation that the journalist Manuel del Arco had with the artist in the summer of 1948, which was published in *Diario de Barcelona*.[2] Del Arco also asked Dalí specifically about the image that the world had of him.

— Do you consider yourself well-judged?
—Very few people know my painting. They know the unusual themes but they are not concerned about the technique: they know the myth Dalí.
— And haven't you encouraged the "myth Dalí"?
— In any case I have done nothing to destroy it; and only my painted work will be able to enlighten it, to give it another sense.
— We are before a dual personality: the painter and the myth. Which one of the two makes you happier?
— Painting, because one must paint an important work of art almost in secret; but contrary to public opinion, the myth protects my painting.[3]

Something similar also applies to Warhol. An interview entitled "Modern *Myths:* Andy Warhol" was published in 1981 in the magazine *Arts* that also inquired about the relationship between his work and the myth. The discussion was prompted by the publication of the portfolio "Myths," which contains portraits of the American celebrities and icons of popular culture

30 Robert Heide in a conversation with the author on December 6, 2012 in New York.

31 Quoted according to Brown 1996, p. 38.

32 Brigid Berlin in a conversation with the author on December 4, 2012 in New York.

33 Bourdon 1989 (German ed.), p. 290.

1 See the chapter **Autobiographies Written "With Four Hands"** in Part 4.

2 Arco 1984, p. 15.

3 Ibid., p. 17.

The Star (Greta Garbo), *Uncle Sam, Superman, The Witch, Mammy, Howdy Doody, Dracula, Mickey Mouse, Santa Claus,* and *The Shadow*.[4] The idea of letting Warhol take on the role of one of the figures came up very early on.[5] At the beginning of the 1980s he was already world-famous and enjoyed his myth status. Warhol's publisher Ronald Feldman recalled later, "We had fun making up the list of myths. Andy was clear who he wanted. I wanted him to become a myth. I said, 'You're already a myth, but wouldn't you like to become another kind of myth? Like the tooth fairy?' He called me one day, and said, 'I'm going to be a shadow.' He'd already done abstract shadows, of light, of floors … . Andy wanted to be the shadow from the radio program, Lamont Cranston."[6] The popular radio crime series *The Shadow* was broadcast from 1930 to 1954. In 1937/38 Orson Welles lent him his voice. Owing to his great popularity, *The Shadow* was soon going on manhunts in comics, novellas, and movies and can therefore be regarded as a pioneering figure for modern superheroes, such as Batman or Superman. His distinguishing features were a black cloak, a dark floppy hat, a red cape half covering his face, and two pistols. Warhol's *The Shadow* was accorded particular attention, because it was not only a representation of the popular hero, but also a self-portrait of the artist. The introduction to the said interview states:

In a certain sense Warhol himself is a myth. He has come to symbolize success and stardom in the arts, yet still somehow remains an elusive figure. The mystification surrounding his public image renders it difficult for some to see his art for what it really is—powerful, persistent images that have never failed to capture the spirit of the time. It is no wonder that The Shadow *print is a self-portrait. A red-tinted photo-silkscreened image of the artist's face casts a distorted shadow haloed by the application of diamond dust. We see man and myth, artist and stardust, portrayed side by side.[7]*

For the silkscreen, Warhol avoided all of the hero's well-known attributes, but the colors nonetheless evoked his red cape and the black cloak and hat. The decision to include such a self-portrait in the "Myths" portfolio was well thought out by Warhol. For Warhol as an artist and a person, *The Shadow* was an ideal identification figure, a strong and anonymous character behind a mask.[8] It was one way of approaching his own myth in a pointedly ironic manner. Dalí, on the other hand, evidently enjoyed commenting on his myth in public.

Dalí and Warhol did not cultivate an identical image, but there were many parallels in the way they stage-managed their fame, in particular, giving a striking signature feature to their outer appearance, especially since an unmistakable appearance is a prerequisite in the media world for the creation of a myth.

Mustache, Wig, and Other Signature Features

Salvador Dalí had an unusual physical appearance. His personal stylist, Lluís Llongueras,[1] referred to the artist's image as "attractive, unusual, sometimes elegant, always original," highlighting the "antenna mustache"

4
See Feldman/ Schellmann 2003, II.258–267.

5
See Hackett 1989, p. 358, February 16, 1981.

6
In *Warhol Myths*, p. 83. Susan Yung, who interviewed Ronald Feldman, kindly provided the author with the English original of the interview.

7
Blinderman in Goldsmith 2004, p. 291.

8
Although Warhol claimed in the interview that he hadn't understood *The Shadow*, such statements are part of the self-camouflaging of the artist. See in Goldsmith 2004, p. 292.

1
Dalí met him in September 1961 at the opening
+

as a signature feature,[2] which the painter himself commented on with the words: "Like two erect sentries, my mustache defends the entrance to my real self."[3]

Dalí grew his mustache from the end of the 1920s. In early November 1928 he wrote in a letter to his fellow student Pepín Bello, "Now I'm sporting a wonderfully thin little mustache!"[4] During these years, Dalí's mustache was short and thin and looked as if it had been painted on. Man Ray describes the painter as follows in his autobiography: "He was a slim young man with a timid little mustache like a penciled eyebrow but which later took on the more menacing proportions of a bull's horns."[5] It was also Man Ray who created the most well-known images of Dalí from this time, a series of photographic portraits showing the artist in an elegant suit.[6] One of these photos shows his face from the front, drawing attention not only to his mustache, but also to his protruding ears. The photo became famous by gracing the cover of *TIME* magazine in December 1936.[7] In the meantime Dalí had achieved great fame in the U.S. and his mustache grew along with his success. The public was enraptured with his appearance. In 1939 Dalí decided, most surprisingly, to shave his mustache off and to pose for the photographer Serge Lido without what was to become his signature feature.[8] Lido's photos are an important testimony to the fact that, at that time, the artist did not attribute the significance to his mustache that it was accorded in subsequent years.

In the 1940s Dalí then grew a mustache that curved slightly upwards, which he documented impressively in the painting *Soft Self-Portrait with Fried Bacon* created in 1941. The mustache becomes a distinctive feature in this self-portrait through the empty eye sockets and the gently melting likeness. Four years later, Dalí analyzed his mustache in the first edition of his newspaper *Dalí News*, which was published on November 20, 1945 in New York, tracing the development phases over the latter years.[9]

In 1954 Dalí wore the longest mustache of his life, with twenty-five centimeter-long "antennae."[10] This length could not be attributed to natural growth only. His secretary Captain Peter Moore reports in his memoirs that the artist lengthened his mustache using hair from his head that he attached with wax.[11] In the same year Dalí published, together with Philippe Halsman, the photo volume *Dalí's Mustache*. Halsmann writes in the postface:

... [L]ast November, I saw that Dalí's mustache had suddenly reached his eyebrows, I realized that Dalí had stepped into this vacuum. This great painter had become the great mustache of our times.

As a photographer I saw my duty. I switched on my lights and for three hours I photographed the play and interplay of his mustache. Like two worms, its two branches could twist and turn in any direction. So could the conversation of its owner ... .[12]

After the first shots, Halsman decided to make a book out of it. He tentatively told Dalí about his plan, as he could scarcely imagine that anyone would even buy such a book. Dalí replied, "Nobody realizes the commercial possibilities of my mustache. Only yesterday a TV network offered me $500 for the right to televise it for 10 minutes."[13] After several months, the result was the volume *Dalí's Mustache*. Some of the ideas for the shots came from

---

2 Llongueras 2003, p. 122.

3 Dali/Halsman 1954, p. 17.

4 Quoted according to Mas Peinado 2004, p. 124 (translated from the German).

5 Man Ray 1988, p. 197.

6 Chéroux 2010, p. 114.

7 See the chapter **TIME Magazine Reports** in this part.

8 See Otte 2006, Ill. 25, 39, 73.

→ **23** [p. 377]

9 *Dalí News*, November 20, 1945, p. 4, reproduced in Abadie 1980, p. 119.

10 Mas Peinado 2004, p. 251.

11 Moore 2009, p. 158.

12 Dali/Halsman 1954, p. 118.

13 Ibid., p. 119.

+ of Llongueras's hairdressing salon in the Avenida del General Goded (today Pau Casals) in Barcelona. Llongueras 1989, p. 7.

Dalí, others from Halsman, but most of them—as well as the captions—from both of them.[14] For the majority of the shots Dalí treated his mustache with Hungarian mustache wax.[15] This trick enabled the photo *A gentleman never discusses figures*, where he formed his mustache to a number eight,[16] or the one where he stuck blossoms on the tips to celebrate Mother's Day.[17] Halsman reported that Dalí had displayed "surprising patience and a capacity for suffering" during the shared project.[18] There is a remarkable photo for which Dalí pushed the tips of his mustache through the holes of a piece of Swiss cheese.[19] In order to realize this shot, two assistants had to pull the tips of the mustache through the holes in the cheese, while Dalí looked through a third hole with one eye. It took an hour to complete the shot, with Dalí losing half of his eyelashes and a third of his mustache.[20]

Dalí cultivated the fact that he was able to draw the attention of the public with his mustache. In *Dalí's Mustache*, he remarks ironically, "Many American tourists visited me this summer in Spain. Did they want to see my paintings? Not at all! They were only interested in my mustache. The public does not need great painting. What it needs is a better mustache."[21] Dalí stylized his signature feature into a cult object, also by claiming to use his mustache for painting.[22] He started to spread this legend with *Dalí's Mustache*. In answer to the question of how he managed to represent fine details in his paintings, he said: "Nature gave me my best tools." Dalí and Halsman illustrated this with a photograph that shows the Spaniard with his head close to the easel, while tugging on the left end of his mustache with his right hand, in order to use it as a paintbrush.[23] The claim that he used the hair of his mustache for painting even had celebrities fooled. Carlos Lozano, who belonged to Dalí's entourage, reported that George Harrison had told him over lunch that the Beatles had paid $5,000 for "a single whisker from the Divine's mustache."[24] Amanda Lear also recounted this extraordinary transaction.[25] Years later, Dalí's muse recalled this peculiarity once again:

He liked to say that he used a hair of his mustache to paint, which was not true. But Yoko Ono and the Beatles heard this, and they wanted to buy one hair of this mustache. And Dalí asked me, "Well, should I sell it to them?' I said, 'Are you crazy?'" So we went into the garden and found a small herb that looked a bit like a human hair—just a bit of grass or something. And Dalí sold it to the Beatles for, I think, $8,000 or $10,000.[26]

There is doubt as to whether this really happened. Yoko Ono refutes the story, saying that neither she nor John Lennon ever bought anything from Dalí.[27]

Apart from the mustache, a walking cane became another one of Dalí's signature features. Amanda Lear and many other contemporaries reported that the artist reinforced each sentence by gesturing with his cane.[28] Pandora observed that the cane also served practical purposes for him: "He carried a cane to protect himself from rushing fans. He waved it furiously at any intruder."[29] There was not only the one cane. Over the years Dalí gathered quite a collection of various walking canes, which will be discussed elsewhere.[30]

In his later years, Dalí's appearance was striking, in general. Ultra Violet describes this in her memoirs:

14
Ibid.

15
Ibid., p. 123.

16
Ibid., p. 37.

17
Ibid., p. 85.

18
Ibid., p. 119.

19
Ibid., p. 89.

20
Ibid., p. 119.

21
Ibid., p. 118.

22
Amanda Lear in "Reminiscences of Dalí: A Conversation with Amanda Lear and Ultra Violet," moderated by Dawn Ades, in Taylor 2008, p. 217.

23
Dali/Halsman 1954, p. 49.

24
Thurlow 2000, p. 166.

25
Lear 1985, p. 84. In this version, it is said to have been Ringo Starr who purchased a mustache hair from Dalí for $5,000.

26
In "Reminiscences of Dalí: A Conversation with Amanda Lear and Ultra Violet," moderated by Dawn Ades, in Taylor 2008, p. 217. Ultra Violet added that Dalí added his signature (ibid.).

27
Yoko Ono in an e-mail from Amanda Season Keeley to the author on September 1, 2010.

28
Lear 1985, p. 11.

29
Michaud 1991, Summer, p. 5.

30
See the chapter **A Passion for Collecting** in this part.

I am dazzled by the elegance of Dalí's suits, the drama of his cape, the symbolism of his Fabergé gold-knobbed cane, which he holds up in a pontifical gesture. My ear delights in the way he over pronounces every vowel, adding a few of his own on top, so that the word "limousine" comes out "li-moi-ri-si-ne."

When Dalí enters the room, every head turns to take in his famed mustache and his luxuriant dark hair, falling to a tie patterned in gold brocade. His tawny leashed ocelot prances ahead of him.[31]

In the 1960s Dalí often appeared in public with a tamed ocelot on a leash.[32] He had purchased the creature in 1960 in New York under unusual circumstances, as Catherine Moore, the wife of Dalí's secretary Peter Moore, reports. Dalí and Gala spotted the creature when they were visiting a movie theater near the St. Regis Hotel one evening. While they were waiting by the box office, they noticed a vagrant sitting on the floor, who had an ocelot. The couple bought the animal from him for $100 and kept it in Moore's room. Moore was surprised when he discovered the wild cat during the night, but did not let it show and later christened the ocelot "Babou," which means "gentleman" in Hindi.[33] Dalí took the animal back with him to his Spanish homeland. In order to be able to travel in and out of the country without any difficulties, Dalí apparently declared a fictitious type of animal to the customs authorities. As it was not on any list, there were no regulations preventing it from being granted entry into Spain.[34] In order not to be a danger to people, the ocelot's carnassials were filed down and the claws were surgically removed.[35] In fact it was not Dalí, but Moore who kept the ocelot and even adorned the animal with a jeweled collar around its neck. When Moore got married in 1971, he gave his wife a second ocelot as a gift, which the couple named "Bouba."[36] Amanda Lear reports that Dalí continued to show himself proudly in public with the animals and liked to be photographed with them.[37] Of course this was also the case in New York. Andy Warhol reports in *Andy Warhol's Exposures* that Dalí liked going around there in the 1960s with two ocelots on leashes.[38] The surrealist later admitted that he had only shown himself with the ocelots for publicity reasons:

I like neither animals nor children. They move. Movement around me causes anxiety. I tolerate the tame ocelot belonging to my secretary, Captain Moore, because Gala loves it, and because such an animal furnishes an excellent subject for mundane conversation. Note that this damnable little beast, with trimmed teeth and claws and jeweled collar, has already succeeded in cuckolding me. One day, in the elevator of the St. Regis Hotel, I was going back to my suite with him. Two ladies exclaimed: "Why it's Dalí's ocelot!" And they did not even notice that the divine Dalí himself was there![39]

Contrary to Dalí, Warhol was fond of animals. In his book *America* he writes, "I never met an animal I didn't like."[40] Warhol kept a couple of Siamese cats in the early 1950s, which he called Hester and Sam, who soon reproduced. When portrayed in 1976 by his artist colleague Jamie Wyeth, Warhol posed with his dachshund Archie in his arms. Wyeth later remarked, "Andy had two dachshunds, Amos and Archie. He often carried Archie about in his arms, he was very fond of them, he adored them. So that's why I

---

31 Ultra Violet 1988, p. 72.

32 Argillet 2004, p. 66; Thurlow 2000, p. 92; Lear 1985, p. 152.

33 Moore 2009, pp. 42ff.

34 Hans Mayer in a conversation with the author on March 11, 2011 in Düsseldorf.

35 Manuel Donato Díez in a conversation with the author on March 20, 2013 in Nordstemmen.

36 Moore 2009, p. 42.

37 Lear 1985, p. 152.

38 Warhol/Colacello 1979, p. 129.

39 Pauwels/Dalí 1985, p. 154; similarly, in Mercouri/Dalí 1965, p. 92.

40 Warhol 1985, p. 191.

41
In Prekop/Cihlář 2011, p. 240.

42
Colacello 1990, p. 150.

43
Geneviève Waïte in a telephone conversation with the author on March 2, 2012.

44
Ibid.

45
Mas Peinado 2004, p. 252.

46
Llongueras 1989, p. 9.

47
Llongueras 2003, p. XXXIII; Llongueras 1989, p. 9.

→
41/42
[p. 390/391]

49
See the chapter **The 1960s** in Part 5.

50
McCabe/Dalton 2003, pp. 39ff.

51
David McCabe in a telephone conversation with the author on June 14, 2010.

48
In the short movie *Dalí's Fantastic Voyage* produced in 1965 by Albert and David Maysles, Dalí appears wearing a black wig. Philippe Halsman took photos of him during the production. Cf. *Dalí by Halsman* 2011, pp. 56ff. Also in the 1966 TV movie *Soft Self-Portrait of Salvador Dalí* by Jean-Christophe Averty, the artist is wearing a wig in some scenes.

52
James Warhola in a conversation with the author on December 2, 2012 in New York.

wanted to paint him like that."[41] Bob Colacello adds in his memoirs: "Archie went everywhere with Andy, to work, to dinner, to parties, and to Europe. He had already crossed the Atlantic ten times, on Andy's lap, never in the hold. (Later, Andy got a second dachshund, named Amos, and Archie stayed home.)"[42] Warhol liked to share his love for his dogs with others. The actress and singer Geneviève Waïte, who came to New York in 1968 to present her movie *Joanna* and was a frequent guest at the Factory, recalls: "He had this little dog, a dachshund, called Archie. And then he got me a dog, the same breed—Archie's wife. And then that dog bit my son, who was four years old, and he bit his eye. So now he has a shapeless scar under his eye. Then I had to give the dog away. I gave it back to Andy and Andy gave it to someone else. Dachshunds really don't like little children."[43]

At the beginning of 1968 Waïte also met Dalí in Paris, when he held a party at the Gare de Lyon featuring magicians and a man who played Chopin with his feet.[44] Since Dalí's hair had meanwhile gone very thin, he started wearing hats, such as a Catalan barretina.[45] He also wore conspicuous wigs when he appeared in public. At the end of 1974 Dalí instructed Lluís Llongueras to design various wigs for him and they met in Port Lligat to discuss the details.[46] One year later, Llongueras handed over the requested wigs to Dalí at his Parisian salon on Rue Saint Honoré, which the artist tried on for the first time in the presence of the press. Dalí presented himself quite ceremoniously; first with one wig that looked like Charles Baudelaire's hairstyle, then with another that was reminiscent of Velázquez.[47] Dalí had high regard for Baudelaire and referred to Velázquez as one of his favorite painters. However, photographic and filmed recordings from the 1960s show that Dalí was already wearing wigs earlier on.[48] In early 1965, Warhol and the British photographer David McCabe visited Dalí at his studio at the St. Regis Hotel in New York.[49] The photographs that resulted from this encounter show Dalí with a shaggy black wig.[50] It is possible that the encounter encouraged Warhol to wear "those crazy fright wigs" himself later on.[51] In the years that followed Warhol did indeed start to wear ever more striking wigs. His nephew James Warhola, however, refutes the correlation that was often made between Warhol's wigs and Dalí's mustache:

A lot of people say Dalí had his mustache and so Andy needed a trademark. ... Dalí's mustache hadn't anything to do with Uncle Andy's hair because his hair was just one of those things that developed naturally. ... He kept his wigs very neat in the late 1950s and early 1960s. But then after that the wigs became more unkempt with a lot of different types of wigs. He had morning wigs, party wigs, dinner wigs. He had them for different times of the day. ... And I think, slowly, it became more obvious that he was wearing wigs. In the beginning it wasn't so obvious. ... I would say in '64 it started to become obvious. But even then people would say "I never knew he had a wig on."[52]

Warhol's relatives knew that he wore a wig, as the artist liked to give discarded models to his brother Paul as a gift. Paul later recalled, "He gave me all the wigs and, you know, I was bald, so I put them on. Sometimes I had fun with them. I had about fifteen of them—different kinds. I got all the old ones. Andy didn't want them and so I took them. Some of them suited me pretty good at that time."[53]

Wigs also really suited Dalí, so he often let himself be photographed with his artificial head of hair. In 1964 he declared in an interview in *Playboy* that he wanted to shave his mustache off and wear a wig instead:

In two years I plan a tremendous agony: to cut off my mustache. I will do this because my hair [has] collapse[d] on top, and I wish to wear a wig. But it is not possible to have both a mustache and a wig—this is too much. So I must cut off my mustache. The ceremony will take place in Venice, and there will be television and everybody will come—a completely liturgical scene. I will then have not one but two wigs made—one gray for daytime, one black for night; and with this gesture, the monarchy will arrive back in Europe. General Franco will decide to re-establish the monarchy in Spain, and in this moment of the return of the monarchy, everybody will wear wigs again, and there will be a renaissance of ornamentation and plumes and tremendous quantities of little cakes and candies. Art and painting will flourish. And so will Dalí.[54]

The announcement that he wanted to wear wigs instead of a mustache was inspired by the hairstyles of the time. In the 1960s the Beatles were causing quite a stir and were called "mushroom heads" because of their hairdos. In the aforementioned interview, Dalí remarked on this: "Since the sexes of the Beatles are so ambiguous—nobody knows if it is boy or girl with the hair so long ... ."[55] However, in the end the painter decided not to make wigs his new signature feature and he only wore them occasionally when he appeared in public. This raises the question of the extent to which Warhol influenced Dalí in this matter. Lluís Llongueras does not see any connection:

Dalí's were much more varied, and he used them to respond to promotional requirements: the Baudelaire one ... to inspire himself to write ... the Velázquez one for painting ... or other similar ideas. Warhol used them more out of necessity and coquetry with practically no variation of style or color, similar to his own. It was his "wig" for every day. This defines the difference between a good artist (Warhol) and Dalí, an authentic genius.[56]

Warhol had an inferiority complex because of his—in his view—not very attractive appearance. He suffered, in particular, on account of his pale skin, which was caused by a pigment disorder, as well as his unusually red nose, which formed a conspicuous contrast to it.[57] Photos from the early 1950s, which Warhol manipulated, document that he was unhappy with his face. He touched up his hair on a passport photo with a pencil so that it would look fuller, as well as his nose, to make it narrower.[58] He did something similar with a portrait photo, retouching a nostril subtly with a pencil.[59] On another photo, which shows him with a black cap in front of a mirror, he outlined his profile with a black pen and colored over part of his nose, to make it look smaller.[60] In 1957 Warhol had his nose corrected and also underwent exfoliation, but he was not satisfied with the result. At least that is what he reported in *THE Philosophy of Andy Warhol*, where it also says that even within his family he bore the nickname "Andy the Red-Nosed Warhola," after the popular Christmas song *Rudolph, the Red-Nosed Reindeer*.[61] Warhol's fellow student Leonard Kessler remarks on this, "I never heard anyone refer

---

53
Paul Warhola in a conversation with the author on November 27, 2012 in Pittsburgh.

54
Dalí 1964, p. 48. Similarly, also in Mercouri/Dalí 1965, p. 94.

55
Dalí 1964, p. 48.

56
Lluís Llongueras in an e-mail to the author on February 2, 2010 (translated from the Spanish).

57
Bourdon 1989, p. 18.

58
Ill. in *Andy Warhol: "Giant" Size*, p. 47.

59
Ill. in ibid., p. 20.

60
Ill. in ibid., p. 46.

61
Warhol 1975, *Philosophy*, pp. 63f.

62
Leonard Kessler
in a letter to the
author in August
2011.

63
Paul Warhola
in a conversation
with the author
on November 27,
2012 in
Pittsburgh.

64
In Bourdon 1989,
p. 39.

66
Guiles 1989,
p. 63; Bourdon
1989, p. 39.

65
Fred Lawrence
Guiles dates
this purchase to
1951. Cf. Guiles
1989, p. 63.
Victor Bockris
reports on the
other hand that
Willers did not
meet Warhol
until 1953. Cf.
Bockris 1989,
p. 105.

67
Robert Heide
in a conversation
with the author
on December 6,
2012 in New York.

68
Giorno 1994,
p. 144.

69
Ibid.

70
In Hahn 1966,
p. 7.

71
In Wilcock 2010,
p. 106.

to Andy as 'Andy the Red-Nosed Warhola.' Andy was our 'kid'... One of three young men, seventeen years old in our freshman class of World War 2 veterans .... He was painfully shy ... very non verbal. But he was an original."[62] Warhol's brother Paul confirmed that he had heard of the nickname "Andy the Red-Nosed Warhola," but nobody in the family had called his brother that: "It was just Andy all the time."[63]

At the beginning of the 1950s Warhol was increasingly concerned about his loss of hair. While Dalí was already over sixty years old when he started to wear hats and wigs, Warhol was a young man of twenty. Alfred Carlton Willers, who got to know Warhol in 1953 in the photographic department of the New York Public Library, became friendly with him and later reported, "He had absolutely no hair on the top of his head and he was extremely self-conscious about this. He took to wearing a hat everywhere, indoors and out, in theaters and at dinner parties. I told him 'Andy, this is insane. Other people are confused by this. They think it's either phony or rude. Why don't you buy a wig?'"[64] Warhol heeded this advice and bought himself a toupee.[65] It had a natural color tone and was rather inconspicuous.[66] However, he soon switched to a gray hairpiece, which he wore long, smooth, and with a parting on the left side. Warhol's inspiration for his hairdo was a photo of Truman Capote, which had made a great impression on him. "Andy was obsessed with Truman Capote," according to the playwright Robert Heide, "He fashioned his wig after the photo from 'Other Voices, Other Rooms' on the back cover, where the hair is falling into the eyes and you push your hair back. That was why he had that style of wig made."[67] John Giorno, who was Warhol's partner in the 1960s, later delivered a detailed description of his partner's artificial head of hair: "Around the back of his neck, where the silver hair piece rose up from his real hair, there were five little quarter-inch bands of dyed color. First there was a thin band of blond, then a thin band of grey, then a thin band of brown, then a thin band of silver, and then a thin band of black nearest the skin, on top of which sat the wig."[68] Giorno also remarks that he knew that Warhol wore a wig, but he never touched it or even mentioned it to him.[69]

At the beginning of the 1960s it was not yet common knowledge that Warhol wore a wig, but many people suspected it. Marcel Duchamp remarked in an interview in 1966, "Does he dye his hair? He looks like a Merino, a white rabbit with pink eyes ... it's very strange, that grey-white hair which doesn't manage to be blond, or the other way around."[70] For Naomi Levine, who had met the artist three years previously and became his first superstar, it was clear that he wore a wig. She later recalled, "I tried to pull it off in California, and it made him very mad."[71] At the end of September 1963, Warhol traveled to Los Angeles for the opening of his exhibition of *Elvis* portraits at the Ferus Gallery. After that he shot the movie *Tarzan and Jane Regained ... Sort of* in California, with Taylor Mead and Naomi Levine in the leading roles. However, Levine did not carry out the "assault" on his wig until after the movie had been shot. The artist and his star spent the day together in Disneyland, where the feisty Levine made a pass at him. When Warhol resisted, she tried to pull his wig off. She did not succeed, but Warhol started shouting loudly. Levine abandoned her advances and traveled back to New York.[72]

Over two decades later, Warhol was to find himself in a similar, but much more unpleasant situation. The incident, which he committed to his diaries on October 30, 1985, was like a nightmare for him. He wrote:

I guess I can't put off talking about it any longer.

Okay, let's get it over with. Wednesday. The day my biggest nightmare came true.

... I'm just going to talk through this quickly because otherwise I can't face it.

Nobody from the office would go with me to the Rizzoli Bookstore in Soho, but Rupert's old assistant Bernard had stopped by to visit and he said he would. Rupert dropped us off. The store is long and the signing was on the second floor in the balcony.

I'd been signing America books for an hour or so when this girl in line handed me hers to sign and then she—did what she did. The Diary can write itself here.

[She pulled Andy's wig off and threw it over the balcony to a male who ran out of the store with it. Bernard held the female while the store called the police but Andy declined to press charges. The staff at Rizzoli asked him if he'd like to stop, but there were people with books still waiting so he said no, that he would finish. The Calvin Klein coat he was wearing had a hood, so he pulled it up over his head and kept signing.]

I don't know what held me back from pushing her over the balcony. She was so pretty and well-dressed. I guess I called her a bitch or something and asked how she could do it. But it's okay, I don't care—if a picture gets published, it does. There were so many people with cameras. ...

... So I was too nerve-racked, it was like in a movie. I signed for one and a half hours more I guess, pretending that it didn't mean anything, and eventually it doesn't. You have to live with it. It was like getting shot again, it wasn't real.[73]

There are no reports of a similar incident regarding Dalí and his mustache. However, it is known that out of fear of potential assaults on his signature feature, he ordered replacement mustaches from Lluís Llongueras as a precaution.[74]

Warhol never thought of growing a mustache, as he remarked in an interview with Glenn O'Brien in 1977.[75] At this point the wig had long since become his signature feature. His nephew James, however, wore a mustache in the 1980s that Warhol refers to in his diaries as a "Salvador Dalí mustache."[76] James Warhola says about this: "I guess he found my 'Dalí' mustache amusing to recognize it. He has never said much to me about it."[77]

Over the years Warhol acquired some 400 wigs.[78] The colors ranged from gray tones and whitish-gray to light silver.[79] While they were "fairly naturalistic" in the 1950s, they became "increasingly sleek and platinum" during the 1960s and "suggested mops of fuzzy plastic yarn" in the 1980s.[80] Gigi Williams, who became the makeup artist for portrait assignments at the Factory towards the end of the 1970s and sometimes did Warhol's makeup

---

72 Bockris 1989, p. 184; Levine in Wilcock 2010, p. 106. According to John Giorno, Warhol got into a similar situation in November 1963 at Lita Hornick's annual party, when the poet Willard Maas touched his hair, to find out if it was a wig. Cf. Giorno 1994, pp. 142f.

73 Hackett 1989, p. 689.

74 Mas Peinado 2004, p. 252.

75 In Goldsmith 2004, p. 260.

76 Hackett 1989, p. 574, May 17, 1984.

77 James Warhola in an e-mail to the author on September 13, 2011.

78 Bockris 1989, p. 475.

79 Bourdon 1989, pp. 12, 39.

80 Ibid., p. 12.

for photo shoots, adds, "He would have different lengths, so it looks like he needed a haircut and then he would come in the next day with a short one and say, 'You know, I had a hair cut.'"[81]

Warhol sometimes regarded his appearance as a suit and he once stated, "It's so great to get home and take off my Andy suit."[82] The "Andy suit" consisted not only of a wig, but also of his clothes, which—as David Bourdon puts it—were "a study in casual eccentricity."[83] In *POPism* Warhol describes his dress style in the 1960s as follows: "In those days I didn't have a real fashion look yet. I just wore black stretch jeans, pointed black boots that were usually all splattered with paint, and button-down-oxford cloth shirts under a Wagner College sweatshirt that Gerard had given me. Eventually I picked up some style from Wynn, who was one of the first to go in for the S & M leather look."[84] Looking back, Wynn Chamberlain remarked about his "S & M leather look" at the time: "Somebody gave me a black leather jacket and I used to wear it but I wasn't into that sort of thing ... But I wore it and everybody thought that I was. There was a bar in New York called The Wagon Wheel, which is the first S & M bar. But it was also a very glamorous bar. ... It was like café society meets hookers. (laughs) I mean everybody was there from Dalí to lots of countesses, foreign heirs, Eurotrash, you name it."[85] Robert Heide speaks of Warhol's great fashion sense: "Andy liked fashion a lot. He was running around at one time dressed in black jeans. He was the person that would wear torn jeans, which still are popular now ... He could be very elegant. He could also go to an opening with a tie and a black jacket. Andy was much more focused and aware than people thought when they met him."[86] Udo Kier, who played the leading role in the Factory movies *Flesh for Frankenstein* and *Blood for Dracula* directed by Paul Morrissey, even points out that it was thanks to Warhol that blue jeans became socially acceptable:

Later on we only met on social occasions, in Paris or in other places. Andy then took me with him to Maxim's Restaurant, where he kept making little waving movements, as the Fürstenbergs, or such and such, were sitting on the next table and he knew them all. Andy was someone who actually made blue jeans socially acceptable. No matter where he went, he always wore blue jeans, a jacket, and a tie, and had a plastic bag with him with a Polaroid camera and a tape recorder. ... He was also accepted—even when a tuxedo was mandatory. He didn't conform to that.[87]

Bob Colacello adds that it was Fred Hughes who was the first to combine jeans with suit jackets. To a certain extent Warhol copied this outfit, which then became known as "the Warhol look."[88] Ingeborg Princess zu Schleswig-Holstein, who came to the Factory in 1980, remarks with regard to this: "He was always masked, to be honest. ... He always looked like Andy Warhol with his wig and the right glasses and the jeans that had to be just right and that were freshly washed and ironed every day. The jeans always had to be ironed. He always appeared as Andy Warhol. He would never have deigned to appear exposed without a wig, never without makeup."[89]

The tape recorder mentioned by Udo Kier was Warhol's most important "companion," along with a camera. The artist explains the role it played in his life in his *Philosophy*:

81
Gigi Williams in a telephone conversation with the author on May 5, 2014.

82
Quoted according to Makos 1988, p. 50.

83
Bourdon 1989, p. 12.

84
Warhol/Hackett 1980, p. 28.

85
Wynn Chamberlain in a telephone conversation with the author on August 26, 2011.

86
Robert Heide in a conversation with the author on December 6, 2012 in New York.

87
Udo Kier in a telephone conversation with the author on January 7, 2011 (translated from the German).

88
Colacello 1990, p. 92.

89
Ingeborg Princess zu Schleswig-Holstein in a conversation with the author on June 30, 2011 in Hamburg (translated from the German).

But I didn't get married until 1964 when I got my first tape recorder. My wife. My tape recorder and I have been married for ten years now. When I say "we," I mean my tape recorder and me. A lot of people don't understand that.

The acquisition of my tape recorder really finished whatever emotional life I might have had, but I was glad to see it go. Nothing was ever a problem again, because a problem just meant a good tape, and when a problem transforms itself into a good tape it's not a problem anymore. An interesting problem was an interesting tape. Everybody knew that and performed for the tape. You couldn't tell which problems were real and which problems were exaggerated for the tape. Better yet, the people telling you the problems couldn't decide any more if they were really having the problems or if they were just performing.[90]

In order to make good recordings, Warhol developed a refined technique. According to Udo Kier again: "He did not say much. He spoke very quietly, which was very interesting. For example, when we went out to eat with Mick Jagger and Bianca Jagger, he placed a tape recorder on the table and spoke very quietly. This made all the others talk much louder than normal and everything was recorded."[91] Jonathan Guinness, 3rd Baron Moyne, whose daughter Catherine became editor at *Interview* in 1975, reports something similar: "His characteristic to me was that he always spoke in a whisper. He was intelligent and amusing and I am not playing him down. But one of the results of his talking or whisper was that one moved very close to him and felt that it was all very confidential."[92]

Warhol especially liked to record prominent personalities—including Dalí, of course, which will be elaborated on elsewhere.[93] When he was with big stars, he took every opportunity to switch his tape recorder on. Yoko Ono recalls, "When I came back to New York accompanied by John, Andy took us to Serendipity the first day. He was always recording us, and photographing us. Even on the short trip in the car to Serendipity. Well, he was like that."[94] Monique van Vooren, who played the leading female role in *Flesh for Frankenstein*, reports that she had introduced Warhol to Elizabeth Taylor and that his tape recorder caused trouble:

I had been in a film in which she starred called Ash Wednesday *directed by Larry Peerce ... Dominick Dunne was the producer and he became a great writer, but afterwards. Elizabeth and Richard [Burton] were at the Grand Hotel and I had an apartment in Rome ... just at the Piazza di Spagna. And she asked me for dinner and they came to pick me up. And Andy was with me and Andy came and we went to one of her favorite restaurants in Rome and Andy started ... he had a tape recorder on the table, and when she saw it she got very, very upset and she wanted him to stop that immediately. He really didn't do well but subsequently they became good friends.*[95]

For Warhol, the tape recorder was also a kind of "weapon," which he could use at parties to encourage others to comment on something, instead of having to talk himself. The singer and actress Asha Puthli reports that she met Warhol in 1970 at a book party at the Gotham Book Mart given by Gerard Malanga and recounts, "Andy was carrying around a tape recorder with a microphone which he held up to people while asking them some question

90
Warhol 1975, *Philosophy*, pp. 26f.

91
Udo Kier in a telephone conversation with the author on January 7, 2011 (translated from the German).

92
Lord Moyne in a conversation with the author on December 17, 2014 in London.

93
See the chapter **The 1970s** in Part 5.

94
Yoko Ono in an e-mail from Amanda Season Keeley to the author on September 1, 2010.

95
Monique van Vooren in a telephone conversation with the author on June 8, 2012.

about the evening, trying to be as shocking as possible. I said to Andy that I don't like to have phallic looking objects shoved in front of my face and the only time I will bear with it is when I'm in a recording studio. Andy had a wonderful sense of humor and that was the start of our friendship."[96]

Warhol also loved recording telephone calls on tape. With great enthusiasm, he recorded conversations with his close friend Brigid Berlin, who also had her own tape recorder running at the same time. In *POPism* the artist reports that this was common practice at that time:

Everyone, absolutely everyone, was tape-recording everyone else. Machinery had already taken over people's sex lives—dildos and all kinds of vibrators—and now it was taking over their social lives, too, with tape recorders and Polaroids. The running joke between Brigid and me was that all our phone calls started with whoever'd been called by the other saying, "Hello, wait a minute," and running to plug in and hook up. I'd provoke any kind of hysteria I could think of on the phone just to get myself a good tape.[97]

Vincent Fremont, who helped Berlin catalogue her tape recordings, calls Warhol's recording habit an obsession: "Andy loved recording and documenting the world as he lived it with audiotapes, Polaroid film, videotape, point and shoot cameras."[98]

The camera became one of Warhol's further signature features in the 1970s. Polaroid and compact cameras made it possible for the artist to capture his surroundings in countless images, which he made extensive use of. This also applies to his encounters with Dalí, which is reported on in another chapter.[99] Along with the tape recorder, the camera became Warhol's second "weapon." The author Albert Goldman reported about a dinner together: "Andy would come with his Polaroid and sit there at the table. Everybody was carrying on and he'd say nothing, but periodically he goes brrr with the machine and then this long thing comes out eeeee. I always thought it was just like sticking his tongue out at the company. Puking on them in a way. Now I ogle you ... Now I puke on you."[100]

According to his friend, the photographer Christopher Makos, Warhol looked his best during the last year of his life. He dressed fashionably, wore big black glasses, and a "huge, jutting out wildly" wig.[101] At the beginning of the 1980s the artist had started to attend fitness classes with Sharon Hammond (Countess Sondes), who ran a studio in her apartment at 555 Park Avenue. There, Warhol occasionally met Leslie Curtis, a close friend of Hammond and wife of the actor Tony Curtis.[102] Leslie Curtis recalls, "Andy would come there in the very early morning, maybe seven, eight o'clock ... when I visited her I would be up already, I'm an early riser and he would be sneaking into the gym. (laughs) He had the key, because they were good friends. And he would do his exercise and give me a little sort of wave and off he would go back to his home."[103] Warhol's diaries reveal that he frequented the fitness studio regularly and with perseverance.[104] The fitness classes at Park Avenue ended in April 1982 when neighbors complained about the noise.[105] After that Lidija Cenjic, the founder of SoHo Fitness, who had already worked with Warhol at Sharon Hammond's studio, became his personal trainer.[106] The regular visits to the studio show that even in the 1980s Warhol was concerned

---

96
Asha Puthli in an e-mail to the author on January 2, 2012.

97
Warhol/Hackett 1980, p. 291.

98
Vincent Fremont in a conversation with the author on June 28, 2012 in New York.

99
See the chapter **Warhol Photographs Dali** in Part 4.

100
Quoted according to Bockris 1989, p. 422.

101
Makos 1988, pp. 13f.

102
Hackett 1989, p. 288, May 21, 1980.

103
Leslie Curtis in a telephone conversation with the author on April 27, 2013.

104
Hackett 1989, p. 417, November 24, 1981.

105
Ibid., p. 438, April 9, 1982 and April 12, 1982.

106
Makos 2006, June 1982.

with his appearance. In 1981, he became a model at the Zoli Agency and four years later he switched to the Ford Agency.[107] According to Christopher Makos, who did test shots for the agencies,[108] Warhol entered the fashion business because he was tired of constantly being asked to pose for a photo just because he was famous.[109] Sam Bolton, who was taken on as Fred Hughes' assistant in September 1985, said that it was his most ambitious project and that he loved being a model more than anything else.[110] Chris Royer, who was one of the fashion designer Halston's model elite, recalls how proud Warhol was to have his own Zed card and recounts: "Andy told me that he was starting to model with Zoli Model Agency. He gave me what was called his model Zed card and inscribed it with 'I love you Chris.' The Zed card consisted of a head shot of Andy on top and then three smaller pictures below. This was a standard layout used for all professional models and they were sent out to the fashion trade. Andy loved being a professional model!"[111] Cornelia Guest, who was one of Warhol's close friends, adds, "Nobody looked like him, he was a great model. He had a ball doing it. ... I mean, oh my God, if you wanted someone to look like Andy Warhol, you couldn't get anybody else to look like that. Andy was incredibly smart. He had a wonderful face, he was in great shape, he took good care of himself and he looked the way he looked. He also loved to make money. So I'm sure he was thrilled when he got paid lots of money to model."[112] Benjamin Liu, who was Warhol's assistant at the time and had worked as a model himself, points out that today all agencies have a group of "celebrity models" and that Warhol was also a trendsetter in this respect.[113] Ingeborg Princess zu Schleswig-Holstein recalls that Warhol pursued his model career with great earnest and discipline: "During the 1980s he was always—quite regrettably—'on a diet' and got thinner and thinner, because he believed that as a model he had to be ever thinner, ever thinner."[114] Vincent Fremont reports that other people often mentioned Warhol's weight loss to him and recounts:

When Andy lost a noticeable amount of weight around 1980 people would ask me "What is wrong with Andy, he has lost a lot of weight, is he sick?" My answer was "No, he is a male model now." It was true Andy joined the Zoli Modeling Agency. Andy cut his wigs shorter at that time as well. Andy loved being around young people and always encouraged them to be creative and to work hard. Andy told friends that he became a male model so that he could meet new young people so that he could put them into his magazine Interview. *Andy wanted to be one of the boys, like the other male models at the Zoli Agency but that just could not happen, he was Andy Warhol, older and more peculiar looking. On the head sheet with pictures of all the Zoli models it read "for special bookings only" next to Andy's picture.*[115]

Warhol's career as a model did not meet with acceptance from all those working at the Factory. The artist recorded in his diaries: "Have I told the Diary I've decided to become a male model? So then Fred got so overwrought—he thinks I'm crazy to start modeling. But it's something I want to do so I ignored him. Chris [Makos] said Fred's just jealous. ... And then Bob told me that I look like a fool on the runway doing my modeling jobs. I told him I didn't care, and he said that *he* cared, that it made his job harder if I looked like a fool."[116]

107
Cf. *The Andy Warhol Museum*, pp. 189, 191.

108
Makos 2006, March 1983; Colacello 1990, p. 442.

109
Makos 1988, p. 14.

110
Colacello 1990, p. 489.

111
Chris Royer in a telephone conversation with the author on October 7, 2013.

112
Cornelia Guest in a telephone conversation with the author on January 3, 2013.

113
Benjamin Liu in a conversation with the author on November 30, 2012 in New York.

114
Ingeborg Princess zu Schleswig-Holstein in a conversation with the author on June 30, 2011 in Hamburg (translated from the German).

115
Vincent Fremont in a conversation with the author on June 28, 2012 in New York.

116
Hackett 1989, p. 370, April 9, 1981 and p. 412, October 14, 1981.

2
The Extroverted Dalí and the Introverted Warhol

Both Salvador Dalí and Andy Warhol were shy in their younger years. Warhol's eldest brother Paul reported, "Andy was shy in a way. ... Like myself, I couldn't get up and speak before an audience. Maybe it was something we inherited from the family."[1] Later on, Warhol cultivated his shyness and exaggerated it by fostering the taciturn artist image. Dalí chose the opposite extreme: "As a child I was shy, especially with society people who belonged to a higher class than mine. I always blushed terribly whenever I doffed my hat. ... Now, the reverse is true: it's I who intimidate others."[2] What was intimidating was Dalí's extreme exhibitionism, about which he once remarked, "... my exhibitionism masks my true personality. I escape observation while attracting it, and, under cover of the most provocative dandyism, I retire into the farthest corner of my palace to fondle my gold all alone."[3] Dalí's "provocative dandyism" was accompanied by downright clownery. The author and lyricist Claire Goll explains, "Dalí was like a clown who never wants to take his makeup off, because he needs the circus to live. With his breathtaking sense of the absurd he had no choice but to act."[4] The Spaniard admitted that it was his wish to be perceived as a clown, "I want people to think that I am a clown, or a showman, rather than a serious painter."[5] Dalí's clownery apparently went too far even for close friends. Nanita Kalaschnikoff, who was the most important woman in the artist's life after Gala and whom he called "Louis XIV," later recalled that she often raised the issue of his eccentric behavior with him: "He tried to explain to me, probably trying to explain it to himself, trying to discover why he was like that and telling me about his childhood and his youth, which made all that he was, like all of us. He said he was quite shy and he didn't want to perform like that at all. And he knew I didn't like the whole surreal .... He said 'You didn't like me this afternoon, but I have to because if I wasn't, I'd be the real little Dalí, shy, and be nothing.' It was his curtain."[6] The artist justified his insistence on proving himself with the myth of the two Salvadors, which has been reported about elsewhere.[7] Benedetta Barzini, who was a photo model in the 1960s and was given the accolade of one of the "100 Great Beauties of the World" by *Harper's Bazaar*,[8] recalls:

I remember his attempts to drag me around with his court—but I wouldn't go—I remember talking with him in the St. Regis Hotel quite often —but I was sort of allergic to his eccentric behavior. With me he was more "normal" so on one of our encounters I asked him why he needed to put on a show always. He told me about his dead brother Salvador and his birth with parents that called him like his dead brother and anything he did his brother had done it better—so at an early age he sought attitudes that his brother couldn't have had.[9]

The Austrian artist Ernst Fuchs recognized that Dalí's eccentric exhibitionism was coupled with self-irony: "Salvador Dalí's appearances were always grand gestures. However, for friends and those who knew him, the gleaming spark of self-irony drunken with knowledge was always evident. This earned him the respect that he deserved for his deep modesty, which

---

1 Paul Warhola in a conversation with the author on November 27, 2012 in Pittsburgh.

2 In Bosquet 1969, p. 70.

3 Pauwels/Dalí 1985, p. 77.

4 Goll 1976, p. 245 (translated from the French).

5 Mercouri/Dalí 1965, p. 94.

6 Nanita Kalaschnikoff in the documentary *The Fame and Shame of Salvador Dalí*.

7 See the chapter **Experience of Death** in this part.

8 Angell 2006, ST17.

9 Benedetta Barzini in an e-mail to the author on May 23, 2011.

he concealed shamefully when triumphantly proclaiming, 'I am a genius.' He knew neither rage and remorse, nor an outward display of modesty."[10] Fuchs also saw in Dalí a fellow artist who attempted to conceal his intellectuality behind his eccentric behavior:

It was always a great performance—there's no doubt about it—and it had a depth of which most people were not even aware. They saw the great showman placing himself in the spotlight, without pausing to ask if there was more behind it. And I don't think that he would have wanted them to, anyway, because he was a very shy person who wanted to avoid people sensing the depth of his intellectuality. ... He found a particular self-affirmation in these kinds of provocations, knowing beforehand what the reaction would be. ... For example, he had a bowel movement and let one rip, so to speak, filling the entire room with the stink. Then he even went on to speak of it proudly and said, "Yes, yes, let everyone smell how I reek." That was remarkable, because what he meant was: that is also Dalí. That's me in the truest sense of the word. That was what he meant, I think. He always had great fun putting on such performances.[11]

Dalí cultivated a monarchic and pompous persona, but the self-irony remained evident. Bob Colacello sees a parallel with Warhol in this respect:

Dalí was an unabashed monarchist and he himself was like a royal figure, he had his scepter with the golden knob. (laughs) When he would introduce people, he gave everyone titles. He called me "Count Valpolicella." He would introduce this Spanish socialite as "Louis XIV." I never knew her real name. Dalí was a surrealist. What he was doing was Surrealism. It wasn't realism. (laughs) To understand Dalí as a personality you have to understand that, I think, he saw himself and his public appearances as part of his art. You could say that Dalí was one of the first performance artists. In fact, he did do performances. ... I took him seriously as an artist but his mode of expression was not "serious." He was campy. I mean he was high camp before Susan Sontag wrote about such things. And I think that's why he annoyed a lot of the official art world because he kind of made fun of the whole idea of being intellectual and being art critical, and his writings were like parodies of intellectual writing about painting and art. ... He was like Andy in creating this bizarre atmosphere that was also very glamorous. ... And I think both Dalí and Andy were attracted to glamour. And that was part of their attraction to high society and to beautiful young people. This was all glamorous. That's what Interview magazine was about. We thought everybody in the magazine should be glamorous in some way. ... And I think that a lot of the kind of ironic attitude that you find in Dalí's work and in Dalí's way of being you also find in Andy's, this very high sense of irony, which a lot of people didn't get. ... It's something people might not want to say, but there is a connection between this ironic and campy kind of way of thinking and being homosexual. And I think Dalí's sexuality was certainly ambiguous.[12]

Dalí's pompous and eccentric behavior sometimes led to him being regarded as "mad." However, Carlos Lozano, a member of his entourage, also reports in his memoirs that it was just a ploy by the Spaniard to play

10
Fuchs 2001, p. 435 (translated from the German).

11
Prof. Ernst Fuchs in conversation with the author on May 14, 2010 in Klagenfurt (translated from the German).

12
Bob Colacello in a conversation with the author on June 26, 2012 in New York.

the madman, to then simply stun people with his brilliance.[13] Dalí's "first motto," which became the "theme of his life" as he put it, was to become famous: "The only difference between a madman and myself is that I am not mad!"[14] He used this phrase for the first time in a lecture that he gave during the opening of his exhibition at the Wadsworth Atheneum in Hartford, Connecticut, on December 18, 1934.[15] He never tired of repeating it.[16]

Demonstrations of his "madness" were reserved for public appearances. The German artist Heiner Meyer, who was "chief cook and bottle washer" in the Dalí household in the early 1970s, recalls:

In my experience, as soon as a camera was present a switch flipped and the man was totally different. … I asked him why he presented himself differently to the media, as I had also seen another side of him. He said because that was precisely what people expected of him. Then he cited an example: there is a movie that Renoir made about Picasso and it has a scene where he paints a picture onto a sheet of glass, but in reality the picture is already sketched out in advance. That is, he did not want to make the blunder of a wrong stroke.[17]

The actor William Rothlein, who met Dalí in 1964 and was supported by him, reports:

In public, with me, Dalí was always sort of "on show." He would always seem to be on stage, performing. And yet he would look at me in the middle of his performances so to speak, with people around. And there was this little glimpse in his eye and he smiled. It was like an in-thing, an in-joke between him and me. And I knew he was performing and he was showing me that he was performing. … But in private, just him and me, he was totally different. He'd let all that go. He so to speak let his guard down. He wasn't protecting himself anymore with a show, with an act for people. He was really more himself of course—quiet and more calm and thoughtful. He would think and we would talk sometimes about certain things, about his past, about his experiences with certain people who would come up in his mind and he would tell me about them. I can remember many times that I would be in that kind of situation in Spain. In New York it was almost impossible to ever be in that relaxed situation with him because there were too many people around. It was always difficult. There were always photographers. He loved to have photographers around, taking photos and reporters or journalists, someone interviewing him or other famous people like movie actors, movie people, or directors.[18]

Many contemporary witnesses report that Dalí also presented himself as completely "normal" within more intimate circles. Jonathan Guinness, 3rd Baron Moyne, who regularly spent the summer in Cadaqués with his family and owned a property there, reports, "I went to one of his parties, where nobody except really locals from Cadaqués, which I was included in, were there. And he was different. He was much more like a conventional civilized Catalan person. He did not show off in front of the other Catalans. He showed off for foreigners, I think."[19] Leslie Curtis, who married Tony Curtis in 1968 and became acquainted with Dalí, recalls that the artist could even be very sensitive:

13
Thurlow 2000,
p. 15.

14
Dalí 1965, p. 7.

15
Aguer in Ades
2004, p. 489.

16
Gibson 1997,
p. 341.

17
Heiner Meyer in
a conversation
with the author
on February 16,
2011 in Bielefeld
(translated from
the German).

18
William Rothlein
in a telephone
conversation
with the author
on February 3,
2015.

19
Lord Moyne in a
conversation
with the author
on December 17,
2014 in London.

One of the evenings that we had dinner, we walked from the St. Regis Hotel where we all liked to stay at that time. We went to have dinner at La Grenouille, which was a very fine French restaurant not far from the St. Regis, because we could walk. And so we walked there, Dalí and Tony, myself, Gala, and her then lover, whom, I guess, Dalí accepted as a friend. We also had with us a man named Gene Shacove. And Gene Shacove was the hairdresser from Beverly Hills upon whom the film Shampoo was supposedly based. He was a very charming, gregarious gentleman who I think, just from the beginning of the evening, was very nervous to go out to dinner with Dalí and these elegant people in this very fine, rather formal restaurant. And I was aware of his nervousness. I think Tony was, too. We went to the dinner and, of course, everybody at the restaurant, you know, "Dalí, Dalí!" they were rushing around, and Tony and they were excited ... and this beautiful table, laden with flowers and beautiful crystal and so on. Dalí ordered the wine—I think it was Château Lafite 59, which was very expensive—and the wine was poured and we were making a toast to the evening. And Gene Shacove, the hairdresser, spilled his wine. He knocked his glass over in his nervousness. And everybody stopped. There were probably a dozen of us at the table. And even the wait staff, they were, like, open-mouthed. And Dalí took his glass of wine and he lifted it and poured it on the table and said to Gene Shacove, "It is only wine." The manner in which he spoke was quiet and not at all critical. And that to me was the essence of this man who had a public persona and a private persona. And immediately the staff came and whisked away everything just like in the movies, before you knew, the linen, the crystal, the flowers, everything was replaced. And we resumed our dinner. And I thought it was such a wonderful, compassionate gesture.[20]

While Dalí compensated for his shyness through extroverted behavior, Warhol adopted the strategy of introverted reticence, as already mentioned. Despite the difference in the outward behavior of the two artists, Vera von Lehndorff, better known as Veruschka, sees a direct parallel:

Dalí mixed different languages, got somehow caught up in a word, and then it got out of hand. Then nobody had a clue what he was on about. ... However, I also had conversations with him and understood what he was talking about. ... Dalí may have been complicated, but he had absolutely no arrogance. You can't say that he was a man who exuded warmth, but he was very friendly and obliging. ... Warhol was, of course, also a difficult one—and you couldn't have a normal conversation with him. He had a curious, squeaky little voice, "Oh, hi! Hi Veruschka! You're so beautiful," (laughs) he always said. We chatted a little, then he snapped a picture and he was gone again. He had built up a kind of protective shield—always evasive: "I don't know," "Oh, you're so beautiful," "Oh, how great."[21]

The "snaps" mentioned by Vera von Lehndorff were another one of Warhol's strategies for not having to engage in conversations. The camera therefore soon became one of the artist's signature features, along with the tape recorder and the wig.[22] Marc Balet, who took over as art director at *Interview* in 1975, reports that the magazine also helped Warhol to keep his distance: "Andy would go around the city with a bunch of *Interviews* under

20
Leslie Curtis in a telephone conversation with the author on April 27, 2013.

21
Vera von Lehndorff in a telephone conversation with the author on January 6, 2012 (translated from the German).

22
See the chapter **Mustache, Wig, and Other Signature Features** in this part.

his arm and sign them and give them out. It allowed him to be the third party basically—like him photographing at a party. He didn't have to be part of the party, he could just photograph the party."[23] At parties and other social events Warhol often stood in the corner, as Nicholas Haslam recalls, "You didn't see him in the middle of the room and talking, you'd see him sit in the corner and watch. ... He just didn't really have small talk and he didn't want to get involved in conversations. ... He was very self-contained."[24] The Munich gallery owner Bernd Klüser, who realized graphic editions with Warhol in the 1980s, is of the opinion that this attitude helped the artist to not have to engage with all people, who were mostly obtrusive:

It was an avoidance strategy, as it were. It allowed him to clam up without a reaction and play the "sphinx." In reality he was taking in a lot of details. Once you reached a certain level of familiarity and intimacy, the conversations were a lot more open. I recall a big party at our home, Warhol and Beuys were there. The occasion was the opening of the exhibition with the Beuys portraits, with lots of guests from the museum and art scene. Warhol chatted casually and in a good mood with some people, while with others he adopted his famous attitude. If he didn't like someone, he was capable of completely ignoring them without a hint of politeness, which understandably made some guests uncomfortable. At breakfast the next morning, however, he would ask further questions about these people: "Who was that? What does he do for a living? Why was he invited?" In any case, I was amazed by the curiosity with which he had stored every piece of information behind his closed curtain. In interactions with people he did not know, he was highly sensitive and vulnerable, but he also had no qualms when it came to offending others by ignoring them.[25]

Another of the artist's strategies for parties and public events was to appear alongside friends and employees. Vito Giallo, Warhol's assistant in the mid-1950s, says, "He had to be near his friends constantly. I mean we often went to parties and he would never ever go alone. I don't think he ever showed up at a party alone in his life. ... I think it was just he felt more sure of himself if somebody was there next to him that knew him or maybe he could even speak for him."[26] Wynn Chamberlain, who met Warhol in 1954, explained, "He knew that the best thing for him to do was to shut up because he had no training to be in New York with the people he wanted to meet. He was a Czechoslovakian bumpkin from Pittsburgh."[27] Warhol let himself be quoted later as follows in *POPism*: "I always took a group of superstars with me to the colleges where I had 'speaking engagements' because I was too shy and scared to talk myself—the superstars would do all the talking and answer all the questions from the audience and I would just be sitting quietly up there onstage like a good mystique."[28] Warhol cultivated his reticence in public as his signature feature. However, he could not deny that he was not eloquent. With reference to a lunch with the foreign press at the New York Biltmore Hotel, which he attended together with Bob Colacello and Fran Lebowitz, he noted in his diaries in December 1976:

Bob had told them weeks ago when they invited me that I would come and just be present but that he would give the talk on Interview *and they said*

23
Marc Balet in a conversation with the author on December 3, 2012 in New York.

24
Nicholas Haslam in a conversation with the author on July 20, 2012 in London.

25
Bernd Klüser in a conversation with the author on April 30, 2010 in Munich (translated from the German).

26
Vito Giallo in a telephone conversation with the author on May 25, 2010.

27
Wynn Chamberlain in a telephone conversation with the author on August 26, 2011.

28
Warhol/Hackett 1980, p. 247.

fine. After Bob's speech, though, they asked questions all directed at me—and I wasn't prepared so I just said yes and no. But afterwards I regretted doing my same old shy act, when I should have used the situation for practice—I'd love to be able to talk more and give little speeches. I want to work on that.[29]

This also explains why he preferred to present himself to the press with assistants and staff. Marc Balet also experienced such an occasion, which took place at the beginning of October 1983 during a stay in Milan.[30]

Andy sat in the Hotel de Milan in the middle of Milan for a series of interviews I organized for him. It was a big deal. Journalists from all over Europe came to do quick fifteen minutes interviews with him. I speak Italian, so I translated for Andy. I had to stay there all day while these journalists arrived for their fifteen-minutes interviews with him. Some of them spoke English but many of them did not. In those cases, I would translate from Italian to English for Andy. I was sitting there in the salon and heard someone say, "Next to speak to Andy is the Walter Cronkite of Italy." And I said, "Oh, okay..." Andy asked, "Who is this?" and I said, "This is the Italian Walter Cronkite." Then I overheard the Cronkite guy talking in Italian to his assistant saying that he already knew Andy. Of course, Andy had no idea who this person was. His question to Andy was, "How does Andy Warhol see the world?" and I said to Andy in English, "He wants to know how you see the world, Andy." Andy replied, "Oh, gee, I don't know what to say." And I turned to the journalist and said, "Oh, Andy just said, that he sees the world through rose-tinted spectacles." And the guy started yelling to his assistant, "You see! You see! Only a genius like Andy Warhol would come up with a phrase like that." Then Andy asked me, "What did he say? What did he say?" and I said, "Oh, he thinks you're a genius, Andy." "Oh, thanks," he replied.[31]

Contemporary witnesses observed that Warhol—similar to Dalí— could flip a switch when he was out in public. The photographer Paul Weiss, who photographed him in 1979 and supplied *Interview* magazine with photos of the Washington party world, reports: "When we were in a smaller room before we went out into the party, he was talkative. I found him to be very gracious and very nice. ... He would be a ... let's say 'normal person' and as soon as he walked out of the room into the public ... then you would see the transformation come over him of being the shy eccentric artist."[32] Nick Rhodes of Duran Duran, who was friends with Warhol, adds:

He was actually incredibly charming and funny with a very dry sense of humor. And I don't think a lot of people got to see that, because it wasn't so much part of this public persona which was more of a shy, withdrawn thing. ... But I think with Andy I learned to understand that this could be switched on and switched off when he felt like it because he was obviously highly intelligent and really very good at reading situations, too. So, if he felt uncomfortable sometimes, it was like a mechanism that he used to certainly withdraw and appear to become rather more shy. Whereas when he was excited by something he wanted to know about it and he was perfectly happy to integrate and chat.[33]

Jamie Wyeth, another of Warhol's friends, confirms that his uncommunicative attitude was dependent on the situation. "When you were alone

29
Hackett 1989, p. 6, December 7, 1976.

30
Ibid., p. 534.

31
Marc Balet in a conversation with the author on December 3, 2012 in New York.

32
Paul Weiss in a telephone conversation with the author on March 30, 2015.

33
Nick Rhodes in a conversation with the author on December 15, 2014 in London.

with him, he would talk his head off. ... I always loved the idea that he hid behind this mask called Andy Warhol with this sort of non-talking kind of non-smiling visage when in fact he was ... curious about things and had a wonderful sense of humor."[34] Warhol was therefore quite talkative in the company of friends. The diamond dealer and designer John Reinhold reports that he could talk to Warhol about everything and that he was not at all shy in his presence.[35] The painter Peter Wise remarks on their shared activities:

In one way there was no difference between the public persona and the private persona of Andy. They were the same person, he didn't really change. The one thing he did change, though, is that in public he was very guarded, he didn't say much. In private you couldn't shut him up. If he felt you had his confidence, he'd call you at night and say, "Oh, it's so good to get out of my Andy suit. Let me tell you what happened tonight." And then you'd be on the phone for an hour. And the same thing if we [Andy, Christopher Makos, and I] were sharing a house together, it would just be, "What we gonna do? Let's bla bla bla bla bla bla bla" in this non-stop talking, which is very different. The same personality, if you understand, he wasn't ... acting differently, being like a whole different personality. But the difference between not saying anything and being like a cipher that's inscrutable in public, that was just the opposite in private. He couldn't be more forthcoming.[36]

Bob Colacello hit the nail on the head ironically once, by comparing Warhol's verbosity in his "inner circle" with that of a "decadent fishwife."[37] Warhol's "inner circle" of course also included his relatives. "My uncle was very talkative," said Paul C. Warhola, "He was always asking questions about us, what we were doing, what we were involved with. ... My uncle was very inquisitive. He shared a lot of different things with me during my visits and also within the hospital. There was a real separation between the Andy Warhol at home with my grandmother and the family and the public arena."[38]

When dealing with the press, the "public Warhol" perfected his monosyllabic taciturnity over the years and always answered journalists' questions reticently with a quiet voice, interspersed with pauses for reflection. He was able to use few words to say even less. Vincent Fremont sees in this a parallel to Dalí's handling of the media.

Andy was soft-spoken but at the same time was a powerful force even if he was just standing in a room and not speaking to anyone. Andy knew how to play or use the media to his advantage, not unlike Dalí. Andy gave short answers to the press when questioned, sound bites as they would call them now, and the press loved it. When Ron Galella, the most notorious paparazzi in New York in the 1970s, was hated and banned from movie premiers, society events, etc., Andy would never turn him away from a party or opening that Andy was involved in, and he realized Ron was recording life just like Andy liked to do. Andy and Dalí understood the power of a photograph and controlling one's image.[39]

By giving so little of himself away, Warhol reversed the situation—it was the interviewer who had to open up, rather than Warhol.[40] Brigid Berlin says about this:

34
Jamie Wyeth in a telephone conversation with the author on April 3, 2013.

35
John Reinhold in a telephone conversation with the author on May 26, 2010.

36
Peter Wise in a conversation with the author on June 28, 2012 in New York.

37
Quoted according to Bockris 1989, p. 382.

38
Paul C. Warhola in a telephone conversation with the author on June 28, 2013.

39
Vincent Fremont in a conversation with the author on June 28, 2012 in New York.

40
Nemeczek 2007, p. 79.

Sometimes when somebody would interview him he did this so well that after one sentence the person that was interviewing him really lost control and had no idea in the world that he was interviewing Andy because Andy was interviewing him. "Gee, you don't think he is cute?" (laughs) Andy turned it around, he was doing the interview. And when anybody says that Andy was quiet and so shy that's the biggest joke of the century.[41]

Catherine Hesketh, who became editor at *Interview* in 1975 and was a close friend of Warhol, concurs with Brigid Berlin when she says, "He wasn't at all shy, really. I don't know why people would say he was shy."[42]

Warhol coupled the image of the introverted and taciturn artist with seeming naivety. Henry Geldzahler referred to it as a "dumb blonde" image.[43] Many fell for it. Ultra Violet reports in her memoirs, "Andy loves to play dumb—the village idiot, the global idiot. When he first uses this technique on me, I naively explain, on and on. Then I realize it's part of his flattery. He wants you to think he's learning from you. Later, I see he takes it a step further—he actually learns many things that way."[44] Warhol therefore proceeded on a similar principle to Dalí, who played the "mad" eccentric, only to confound people with his keen wit. The surrealist was clever enough to recognize that Warhol's naivety was also just put on. Antoni Pitxot recalled that Dalí once remarked to him, "Warhol is the most intelligent person from New York."[45]

Addiction to Fame

Both Salvador Dalí and Andy Warhol were addicted to fame. Dalí dedicated an entire chapter to the subject of fame in his book *The Passions According to Dalí*, published in 1968. Warhol followed his example when he published *THE Philosophy of Andy Warhol (From A to B and Back Again)* in 1975. What is noticeable is that the two artists had different approaches to the topic of fame, which can be explained by their public images. While Dalí made no secret of his addiction to fame, Warhol commented on his interest in prominence with wit and irony. In his *Passions*, Dalí says, "I satisfy my exhibitionism at will. I enjoy the glory that has been granted me and that the growing methods of collective cretinization have amplified."[1] Dalí's addiction to fame and his exhibitionism were therefore closely intertwined. He stated in an interview with Melina Mercouri, "... I love publicity in all its forms. I am an exhibitionist. I like it when everybody is talking about Dalí, even when it is in good terms. But when it is in bad terms, it is marvelous! I love it when everybody is busy with Dalí. ... I don't think I like publicity in itself. What I like is to prove to me that I exist, symbolically. ..."[2] The wish to prove his own existence can be explained by Dalí's shyness, which he covered up cleverly with his eccentric behavior.[3] Amanda Lear reports that his craving for fame sometimes went too far even for Gala. "Gala was very upset sometimes, because Dalí was *so* crazy about publicity, and being written about in papers, and putting on a show. And she said, 'One day, with all these eccentricities, you're going to end up in jail!'"[4] Dalí was not averse to even the most outlandish behavior, as he confirmed in conversations with Alain Bosquet in 1966:

41
Brigid Berlin in a conversation with the author on December 4, 2012 in New York.

42
Catherine Hesketh in a telephone conversation with the author on August 27, 2012.

43
Feldman/ Schellmann 1989, p. VII.

44
Ultra Violet 1988, p. 93.

45
Antoni Pitxot in a telephone conversation with the author on August 5, 2009 (translated from the Spanish).

1
Pauwels/Dalí 1985, p. 57.

2
In Mercouri/Dalí 1965, p. 93.

3
See the chapter **The Extroverted Dalí and the Introverted Warhol** in this part.

4
In "Reminiscences of Dalí: A Conversation with Amanda Lear and Ultra Violet," moderated by Dawn Ades, in Taylor 2008, p. 218.

2

It's like money, if someone opens the door and brings in a mountain of gold, I'll accept it without flinching; and the same holds true for popularity, I accept it just as easily. I'm not always as well-known as I should be. Last Christmas, I received a tiny bell. I walked around in the streets of New York and whenever I felt that people weren't paying enough attention to the Divine Dalí, I jingled the bell. I simply couldn't stand the thought that someone might not recognize me.[5]

When reading Dalí's remarks, one gets the impression that fame and money had the same value for him. His secretary Peter Moore emphasized, however, that Dalí was not driven by money, but by fame alone.[6]

Fame was also a driving force for Andy Warhol. It was clear to Philip Pearlstein, who had studied with Warhol at the Carnegie Institute of Technology in Pittsburgh from 1945, that he had been fascinated by fame from a young age:

I knew him as a young man, what he became later I'm not sure. But when I knew him, he was just a very pleasant, intelligent young man who was ambitious to be successful as an artist, because when we came to New York we had no money, no resources of any kind, and survival was the main thing. His work was so charming, the portfolio that he showed to the art directors of the time, that he got work immediately—but not as a serious artist and he had ten years as a very prominent illustrator. And it came out of poverty—he had no money, I had no money—that there was desperation, it was not to be famous but to survive. He was fascinated with fame. In fact that's why he seems to have been attracted to me because when I was in high school—before I got drafted into World War II—I won some big prizes and had paintings reproduced in LIFE magazine. And when he met me, after I came back as a veteran of World War II on the G.I. Bill—I went back to college, and so we were classmates—he asked me, how it was to be famous, how it feels to be famous, so I said "Well, you know, it only lasted five minutes." That's the beginning of that joke.[7]

The painter Harold Stevenson, who was friends with Warhol and had also come to New York in 1949, remarks, "Andy was a very modest person but he saw the opportunity to become famous and it kind of went to his head. ... So he proceeded of course to take every opportunity that came his way. ... Andy didn't care where the fame came from. He just wanted to be famous."[8] Warhol himself put it in a nutshell in the famous "Andy Warhol: My True Story" interview in 1966: "I never wanted to be a painter; I wanted to be a tap-dancer."[9]

Contrary to Dalí, Warhol had little self-confidence with regard to his appearance. According to some contemporary witnesses, Warhol's craving for fame was, therefore, compensation for this. Stephen Bruce recalls that he was always surrounded by attractive people at Serendipity 3: "He enjoyed his own celebrity and this was his access to meet all those pretty young men. ... His celebrity made him feel more secure so that he could be seen around attractive people. I think attractive people valued his work and his sense of being."[10] Warhol, according to John Giorno, wanted to be famous to be able to have any boyfriend he wanted and he also saw fame as a basis for being

5
In Bosquet 1969, p. 80.

6
Peter Moore in the documentary *The Fame and Shame of Salvador Dalí.*

7
Philip Pearlstein in a telephone conversation with the author on April 13, 2010.

8
Harold Stevenson in a telephone conversation with the author on February 8, 2011.

9
In Goldsmith 2004, p. 89. For the extend of editing of Warhol's original brief comments, cf. Wrbican in Meyer-Hermann 2008, p. 00:57:00.

10
Stephen Bruce in a telephone conversation with the author on July 6, 2011.

accepted as a successful artist.[11] Warhol himself acknowledged this aspect in his *Philosophy*: "The people who have the best fame are those who have their name on stores. The people with very big stores named after them are the ones I'm really jealous of. Like Marshall Field. ... A good reason to be famous ... is so you can read all the big magazines and know everybody in all the stories. Page after page, it's just all the people you've met. I love that kind of reading experience and that's the best reason to be famous."[12] In order to be able to read about himself in the major magazines, Warhol immersed himself in New York nightlife. He was a regular guest at Studio 54. In *Andy Warhol's Exposures* the artist referred to the desire to go out as a "social disease," with symptoms listed as follows:

You want to go out every night because you're afraid if you stay home you might miss something. You choose your friends according to whether or not they have a limousine. You prefer exhilaration to conversation unless the subject is gossip. You judge a party by how many celebrities are there—if they serve caviar they don't have to have celebrities. When you wake up in the morning, the first thing you do is read the society columns. If your name is actually mentioned your day is made. Publicity is the ultimate symptom of Social Disease.[13]

The photographer Santi Visalli, who often photographed Warhol beginning in the 1960s, has the following explanation for his constant presence on the New York nightlife scene: "To me it seemed that he was creating *tableaux vivants*. He could do that every night because most nights he encountered different people. He could create for each group fifteen minutes of fame—as he liked to say ... and I think that was one of his trademarks in New York. Beside his movies and his paintings I personally think that every night he was making a new *tableau vivant*."[14] With this, Visalli is alluding to Warhol's perhaps most famous dictum: "In the future everybody will be world-famous for fifteen minutes."[15] Lady Anne Lambton, who came to work at the Factory in the early 1970s, has a similar view of Warhol's extensive participation in New York nightlife:

He didn't want to miss that fifteen minutes, so he was obsessed with celebrity and fame, but he was also obsessed with youth and beauty and older and interesting ... What I'm saying is he went out and hungrily found the next thing, the next fifteen minutes, all the time ... he was utterly obsessed with celebrity ... utterly. But, he was also utterly obsessed with the ordinary celebrity of life. ... If he saw a star ... any star ... who wasn't a star yet, but just an obvious star of life ... he was obsessed. He was obsessed with the next fifteen minutes.[16]

A Passion for Collecting

Michael Ward Stout, who became Salvador Dalí's American lawyer at the end of 1974 and often saw Andy Warhol in Dalí's presence, remembers both artists as avid collectors: "Dalí and Warhol were collectors of various kinds of things. Dalí had unusual collections of jewels, gems, and paintings, of course, and Warhol was also a big collector. Most important, they both

11
John Giorno in a conversation with the author on March 13, 2011 in Besançon.

12
Warhol 1975, *Philosophy*, pp. 77f.

13
Warhol/Colacello 1979, p. 19.

14
Santi Visalli in a Skype conversation with the author on July 9, 2012.

15
In Warhol/ König/Hultén/ Granath 1968 (n.p.).

16
Lady Anne Lambton in a telephone conversation with the author on August 11, 2012.

1
Michael Ward Stout in a telephone conversation with the author on June 9, 2010.

2
Pierre Dinand in an e-mail to the author on April 20, 2012.

3
Quoted according to Lear 1985, p. 36.

4
Lear continues: "I say 'apparently' because, to seduce the Divine Maestro, his followers would embellish their gifts with some kind of historical aura, which was not always authentic. But Dalí always pretended to believe everything he was told. He adored lies and exaggerations." Ibid., p. 37.

→
30 [p. 382]

5
See the chapter **Mustache, Wig, and Other Signature Features** in this part.

6
Pitxot/Aguer/Puig 2008, pp. 68f.

7
The portrait of Philip IV is a black and white reproduction of the painting *Philip IV* by Velázquez, painted between 1652 and 1655. See López-Rey/Delenda 2014, p. 385, no. 115.

8
Pitxot/Aguer 1998, p. 34.

9
See the chapter **Mona Lisa in New York** in Part 4.

10
Photo printed in Pitxot/Aguer 1998, p. 34.

11
Depicted in Descharnes/Néret 1993, no. 272.

12
Lord Moyne in a conversation with the author on December 17, 2014 in London.

collected interesting people."[1] The French flacon designer Pierre Dinand, who had regular contact with Dalí in the 1970s, reports that the Spaniard had a particular affinity for collecting medals and badges, "I remember one day after lunch his velvet jacket was dirty, full of sauce and falling pieces of food. I suggested asking for some hot water to help to clean it, he answered, certainly not; 'I want to keep the traces of my last meals, yesterday's breakfast, yesterday's dinner; they are my military medals and decorations.' There were traces of eggs, ketchup, or sauce on the velvet. He loved it."[2] Amanda Lear adds in her memoirs that Dalí's vests were the dirtiest of all. The artist explained to her, "Gala makes me change my vest from time to time. I should like to organize an exhibition of them. They look like maps—pictures of remarkable natural beauty."[3] As Lear goes on to report, Dalí had an extensive collection of canes, "Every one of them had been a present: the one with the handle carved by Fabergé, the one which had belonged to Victor Hugo and the one which Montesquieu had brandished so elegantly in the portrait by Boldini. His most recent cane had, apparently, previously belonged to Sarah Bernhardt."[4] Since Dalí always carried a cane with him, it was to become one of his important signature features, along with his famous mustache.[5] Part of the artist's extensive collection can be seen today at his house in Port Lligat, the Casa-Museu Salvador Dalí.[6] In addition to the many other exhibited objects are three eye-catching pictures in the house's so-called "model's room": portraits of Philip IV of Spain, Stalin, and the German emperor Wilhelm II.[7] All three historical personalities wore a mustache, which for Dalí was the deciding criterion for hanging the pictures in his house. The artist claimed to collect famous mustaches.[8] A photo taken in the mid-1950s shows him together with the three portraits, as well as a reproduction of the *Mona Lisa* by Philippe Halsman, with Dalí's face and hands, which was created for the book *Dalí's Mustache*.[9] A copper engraving from Dalí's parental home of the officer and local politician Josep Margarit, who was the basis for Dalí's "mustache collection," hangs in the middle, behind the pictures arranged in a row.[10] The engraving shows Margarit with a very bushy mustache, which strikingly twirls upward at the ends.[11]

Apart from the artist's cane and mustache collection, many other objects are collected at Dalí's house; valuable antiques as well as kitschy mass-produced goods. Jonathan Guinness, 3rd Baron Moyne, characterizes Dalí's astounding aesthetic taste as follows: "He had the most amazing aesthetic taste. I think that house was so beautiful—in quite a mad way, but it really was a certain *haute* taste they had, the two of them. I mean more Dalí than Gala, but Gala too, obviously. ... Of course he was a voyeur. I think it was part of his aestheticism. He liked beautiful people like he liked beautiful objects."[12] The artist and moviemaker Steven Arnold, who visited Port Lligat for the first time in 1972, calls the style of the house "a magnificent combination of Ludwig of Bavaria meets Woolworth's" and he reports in his unpublished autobiography, "In room after room—cut-outs of rock, connected by tiny stairways—there were superb antiques with vases of plastic flowers, rock crystal busts, masks, gifts from Coco Chanel, chairs he'd made out of driftwood, Tiffany lamps, an exquisite collection of Fabergé eggs, mummies, skeletons, stuffed animals, religious statuary, geodes, crystal balls, occult books in huge armoires, and vulgar horn chairs upholstered in leopard print."[13] All these objects were an expression of and the result of Dalí's passion for collecting.[14]

Andy Warhol's career as a collector began rather conventionally. Even before his tenth birthday he was a movie fan and collected autographs. He stuck the signed photos of stars, such as Errol Flynn, Glenn Ford, Veronica Lake, Carmen Miranda, Jane Russell, and Mae West into a special photo album.[15] He especially cherished an autograph by the child star Shirley Temple, which he received in 1941 and was his most prized possession, as his brother Paul Warhola recalled.[16]

As Warhol's income improved over the course of the 1950s, due to his success as a commercial artist, he started to collect avidly. His biographer David Bourdon reports that all of his abodes were a mess. His apartment always looked like a "scavenger's pleasure palace," a style that could have been called "Victorian surrealist."[17] The living room was decorated with an "eclectic mix of period furniture, American folk art, and kitsch curios." The most spectacular objects included two carved, painted, and gilded English carousel figures in the form of a military centaur from the time around 1915, a seventy-two-inch-tall painted wood statue of Punch, and a "Perfume Your Handkerchief" device that could spray four different scents.[18] There was also a brass, four-poster bed with cupids and a stuffed peacock, which Warhol had discovered at a taxidermist's. Later on he gave the peacock away,[19] but the collection shows that Warhol's and Dalí's penchant for decorations was similar. Dalí decorated his library with a stuffed eagle, as well as three stuffed swans. He had let the latter swim in Port Lligat Bay and even fitted them with helmets that he could affix candles to, so that he could illuminate them at dusk.[20] Warhol also had other stuffed animals: the head of a mouse, a penguin, an owl, a lion, and a Great Dane. The latter three adorned the Factory.[21] The Great Dane, called Cecil, stood by the front door of Warhol's studio for almost twenty years, from about 1968. Warhol's associates said that the animal had belonged to Hollywood director Cecil B. DeMille.[22]

In 1959 Warhol purchased a four-story townhouse on the Upper East Side, which gave him more space for his collection. Later on, Henry Geldzahler remembered the house at 1342 Lexington Avenue as follows: "It was very crowded. We were never allowed off the first floor. The living quarters were upstairs; his mother was downstairs. I never went anywhere but upstairs in the big room where he was painting, and he had a collection of some Surrealist stuff ... Frank Stella—small paintings of squares ... a John Chamberlain crushed car sculpture ... Carmen Miranda's shoes, which were four-inch shoes and three-inch room for feet."[23] Warhol's manager, Fred Hughes, who came to the Factory in 1966, was a significant influence on Warhol the collector. Hughes recalled later that the artist was unstoppable whenever he discovered a new potential collection:

I suspect that Andy was a collector all his life; film magazines—he was mesmerized by Hollywood—were an early enthusiasm. He often talked about his collections with me, and one of the chief sources of our friendship and

13
Arnold, unpublished autobiography.

14
Dalí's friend Nanita Kalaschnikoff described it by stating, "He loved collecting oddities." See Gibson 1997, p. 529.

15
Ill. in Francis/King 1997, p. 34.

16
Paul Warhola in a conversation with the author on November 27, 2012 in Pittsburgh. Depicted in Baldwin/Keller 1999, p. 134.

17
Bourdon 1989, p. 60.

18
Ibid., p. 68.

19
Ibid., p. 60.

20
Pitxot/Aguer/Puig 2008, pp. 39ff.

21
The Andy Warhol Museum 2004, no. 157; Colacello 1990, p. 236.

22
The Andy Warhol Museum 2004, no. 157.

23
In Smith 1986, pp. 306f.

collaboration was that he enjoyed sharing the little bit of expertise that I had in various fields. Indeed, when he discovered a new area of interest, he would become extremely eager and covetous, forcing us to intercede in an attempt to dampen his frenzy. Then again, Andy had no pretentions to connoisseurship, and if American Indian baskets attracted him, he suddenly wanted lots of them. To him it was all so much fun, and he would act like an excited child.[24]

Around 1970, Warhol established himself as one of the most well-known collectors of French Art Deco and contributed significantly to making the style fashionable again. It was also predominant in the Factory at that time. The artist explained ironically that it was quite easy to recognize good pieces: "Oh, I just love Art Deco. It's so easy. Everything has a signature."[25] In the "Art Déco" exhibition shown in October 1970 at the Finch College Museum of Art, many of the objects were from Warhol's collection. However, as the artist wanted to avoid making his predilections public, the catalogue attributes most of the items to Fred Hughes.[26] Even so, seven years later Warhol provided good insight into his purchasing and collecting habits when the exhibition "Andy Warhol's 'Folk and Funk'" was shown at the New York Museum of American Folk Art. The artist was one of the museum curators and provided about seventy-five folk art objects, including store signs, weather vanes, wind turbines, wooden Indians and tin cans. His favorite item was a light blue door with a frame from a classicistic, eighteenth-century villa, which he was also photographed with for the catalogue cover.[27] This exhibition was the first introduction to Andy Warhol the collector. The catalogue states,

Warhol is unique as a collector. He buys the widest variety of objects from kitschy plastic jewelry to museum-quality primitive sculpture. Concentrating solely on what appeals to him instinctively, he has collected without any traditions, avoided what is popular or fashionable. Art dealer Ivan Karp calls this "a creative kind of collecting; his collecting is as much an invention as his art is." In that sense, Warhol's collection is an extension of his strongly individualistic and eccentric personality. Thus, it is Andy's eye that is the focus of this exhibition.[28]

Fifteen years after Warhol's death, the Andy Warhol Museum in Pittsburgh opened the exhibition "Possession Obsession," which provided even more extensive insight into Warhol's activities as a collector. The catalogue also includes interior photos of Warhol's house at 57 East, Sixty-Sixth Street, which Robert Mapplethorpe had shot for the magazine *House & Garden* at the end of 1987—Warhol died on February 22 of that year.[29] The artist had bought the six-story 1911 Gregorian style house at the heart of the Upper Eastside in 1974 for $310,000. As one of his visitors put it, the generous stairs and light, open rooms conveyed "the traditional old money look" that Warhol had always sought.[30] His life partner at the time, Jed Johnson, who until then had never had anything to do with interior design, began looking for new pieces of furniture and gathered a remarkable furniture collection in the Federal and Empire styles. This was the start of Johnson's highly successful career as an interior designer.[31] Warhol avoided decorating his abodes with his own works. For example, one of the photos by Mapplethorpe shows that

---

24 In Sotheby's 1988, Preface.

25 Quoted according to Coblentz 1977, p. 8.

26 Bourdon 1989, p. 326.

27 Ibid., p. 365. Warhol said: "You can go in and out of it and still go nowhere." Quoted according to Colacello 1990, p. 236.

28 Coblentz 1977, p. 7.

29 Smith 2002, pp. 126ff.

30 Bockris 1989, p. 392.

31 Bourdon 1989, p. 352.

at the house on Sixty-Sixth Street there is only a little *Mao* portrait standing on a dresser in the bedroom.[32]

In Dalí's house in Port Lligat, Spain, on the other hand, one could admire several of his own works. The library, for example, was adorned with the two cubist paintings *Cadaqués* (ca. 1923) and *Port Alguer* (1924), as well as the "apocalyptic pomegranate," a special bomb that had been used to engrave some illustrations for the monumental book *L'Apocalypse de Saint Jean* published by Joseph Forêt in 1960.[33] Furthermore, the painting *Leda Atomica* (1949) was hung up in the hallway of the house, and on the wall in the yellow room, which owes its name to a yellow bench, were a *Self Portrait* that Dalí had painted at the age of sixteen, and a study for the painting *Galatea of the Spheres* from 1952.[34]

Both Dalí and Warhol collected works of art. Warhol owned quite a colorful selection of works from a variety of artists from the sixteenth to the twentieth centuries. The paintings included some works by so-called salon painters of the nineteenth century, such as Sir Lawrence Alma-Tadema, William Adolphe Bouguereau, Jules Breton, and Georges Jules Victor Clairin.[35] This is remarkable insofar as it was none other than Dalí who also defended salon painting, of which little notice was taken during either of the artists' lifetimes. Fred Hughes remarked about Warhol's interest in nineteenth-century salon painting:

There were two sides to him. One side of him loved modern American things, but in his everyday life he was turning to older, more classical art. He thought that classical antiques were too expensive, but he loved Egyptian jars, American classical furniture and silver and got these things at bargain prices. He loved Alma-Tadema, Bouguereau, and the Vienna Secession. At the same time, grandeur made him nervous. He was nervous too that his whole life was a bubble that would burst.[36]

The Bouguereau painting in Warhol's collection, *Mignon Pensive*, shows a contemplative girl in a mountain landscape.[37] Bouguereau was also represented in Dalí's art collection with two female nudes. The paintings were kept at the Teatre-Museu Dalí even during the artist's lifetime. One work is housed in the Masterpiece Room on the third floor, which also has further works by other artists that Dalí collected over the years. The Spaniard referred to the works as "timeless masterpieces." These include a painting by El Greco and two paintings each by Gerard Dou, Marià Fortuny, Ernest Meissonier, and Modest Urgell.[38] Also exhibited is *The Box in a Valise* by Marcel Duchamp, one of the few modern artists whom Dalí appreciated greatly and was on friendly terms with. The *Box in a Valise*, often called a "portable museum," which Duchamp published as a limited edition, is a cardboard box that fits into a handy suitcase and contains a total of sixty-nine miniature replicas, models, and reproductions of his works. Editions were published in various formats between 1941 and 1968.[39] Dalí owned a copy of the 1958 edition.[40] Warhol even owned two copies, one of the original 1941 edition and one of the 1961 edition.[41] Otherwise, however, Dalí's collection included very little modern art, which can be explained by his reserved attitude towards it, although he did own a few works by Warhol.[42] Warhol's colorful art collection included also modern

32
Depicted in Aronson 1987, pp. 190f.

33
Pitxot/Aguer/Puig 2008, pp. 38ff.

34
Ibid., p. 70.

35
Sotheby's 1988, vol. V, cat. 2808ff.

36
In Bockris 1989, p. 338.

37
Sotheby's 1988, vol. V, cat. 2813.

38
Pitxot/Aguer/Puig 2005, pp. 102ff.

39
Bonk 1998, pp. 298ff.

40
Pitxot/Aguer/Puig 2005, p. 104.

41
Sotheby's 1988, vol. V., cat. 2847, 2864.

42
See the chapter **Exchange of Gifts** in Part 6.

artists. Almost every big name was represented—of course, also Dalí.[43] Given the many artists and styles that Warhol collected, it is nearly impossible to identify any direction or concept. There was one twentieth-century artist revered by both Warhol and Dalí. In 1966, Warhol remarked in the famous interview "Andy Warhol: My True Story" that Andrew Wyeth and John Sloan were among his favorite American artists.[44] In *Andy Warhol's Exposures*, he says about Dalí, "He worships Andrew Wyeth and so do I."[45] Dalí's veneration for Wyeth is reported about by Wyeth's son Jamie Wyeth, who had his first solo exhibition at the Knoedler Gallery in New York in 1966:[46]

I met Dalí with my father at Knoedler's when I had my exhibition. … He was more excited about meeting my father Andrew Wyeth. He fell onto the floor and sort of acted as if he were a child with my father. He'd admired my father's work. And then later, this is a number of years later, I went into the St. Regis bookstore at the Hotel St. Regis in New York, where Sr. Dalí lived in the winter, and there was a book of Dalí's that I bought and when I went to pay for the book the man at the counter said, "Would you like Sr. Dalí to sign the book?" and I said, "Yes, that would be nice to sign it for my father Andrew Wyeth." And when I came back a week later he had not only signed it, but he'd done a drawing of himself as a baby being led by my father (laughs) and then wrote all over the book.[47]

Jamie Wyeth also remembers well how Warhol expressed his admiration for his father:

He was interested in all forms of painting insofar, but he was particularly interested in my father. And so he would come down and visit me at Chadds Ford, my farm, and of course my father would come down, and we had fascinating times. The interesting thing, when Warhol died, I was so sad and I didn't wanna go to the big auction at Sotheby's. But then several people told me, "Well, there are a lot of paintings that he collected that you might be interested in." So I bought a number of paintings that people didn't think looked like Warhol, but he had a fascinating collection. He was very eclectic … I knew him pretty well, but I was only in his house twice in my life and he lived just down the street on Sixty-Sixth Street. His house was just stacked to the ceiling with objects. … Oh my God, he was a pack rat.[48]

Warhol's significant other, Jed Johnson, later remarked that Warhol had confided to him that antiques made him feel rich.[49] However, the artist avoided showing others his collection. While the door to the Factory was open to everyone, Warhol was selective with guests as far as his private house was concerned. He only received family members there, for example, his nephew Paul C. Warhola and a couple of his friends. Paul, who was studying theology at the time and later became a priest, reports:

My uncle was very appreciative of the fact that I was going to become a Byzantine Catholic priest. And looking back on it now, I think that that was one of the reasons why he opened the doors to allow myself and my friends to stay there. I think he had a regard for my training and my theological background and I don't think he would have done it for anybody else. His home was really off limits. … During all the visits that we made over the years to visit him and my grandmother I can hardly remember any visitors.[50]

43
See ibid.

44
In Goldsmith 2004, p. 87.

45
Warhol/Colacello 1979, p. 129.

46
Factory Work, p. 32.

47
Jamie Wyeth in a telephone conversation with the author on April 3, 2013.

48
Ibid.

49
Aronson 1987, p. 194.

50
Paul C. Warhola in a telephone conversation +

Warhol let only a few of his friends set foot in his house. Nick Rhodes of Duran Duran, who got to know him in 1981, recalls, "I dropped him off there several times. He always said that he was embarrassed because of the amount of things he had and he said you couldn't move in there."[51] Steven M. L. Aronson thinks that Warhol let less than one percent of his good friends enter his house, including Diana Vreeland and Truman Capote.[52] Therefore, the artist was by no means seeking to show off his antiques and his collection. It seems that he, too, only got a certain amount of pleasure out of them. Fred Hughes said, "Andy was not one to enjoy the *display* of his collection. Rather, he felt comfortable in the knowledge that it was safely put away in storerooms, and in this very Byzantine way, he enjoyed it immensely."[53] Jed Johnson later reported that Warhol had developed a unique routine for enjoying his collection, "He kept most of the rooms locked. ... He'd walk through the house every morning before he left, open the door of each room with a key, peer in, then relock it. Then at night when he came home he would unlock each door, turn the light on, peer in, lock up, and go to bed."[54] For Warhol, it was not about living with his collection: The feeling of owning it was enough for him. However, he was not concerned with preserving his many possessions. He once remarked, "I don't believe in restoration. I really don't. I think things should look just *as they are*."[55] Jed Johnson added later, "I think that when a person buys something there's an obligation he takes on to conserve it. But once Andy bought something, he was on to the next thing—his buying was a conquest, not an adoption."[56] Johnson also reports that for years Warhol went shopping for two or three hours every day.[57] So it is hardly surprising that after the artist's death many boxes and bags were discovered that were still unpacked.[58] When Johnson left Warhol at the end of 1980, the artist's collecting turned manic. During their partnership he had kept his promise to deposit his purchases on the top floor only. After Johnson moved out, he started distributing the purchases he had made out of frustration throughout all the rooms. The house was soon so full that there was hardly room to move.[59] Warhol went on habitual shopping tours in the morning. Brigid Berlin, who often accompanied him, recalls:

We'd take these walks and we'd go down to these crummy antique shops which I called "junk shops" and Andy would go in and we'd see this woman, her name was Bee and she had upswept blond hair, she must have been seventy something then, and she was selling these hideous-looking plastic bracelets. And I said, "Andy, why are you buying this crap for? It's so ugly." Well, every one of them was a bakelite bracelet and nobody had ever heard of them then. And I mean, he was buying them for a dollar fifty. And when he went to buy cookie jars we'd go down these three little steps. He'd see a cookie jar, he'd buy the cookie jar for fifteen dollars. They'd wrap it up in a piece of newspaper, stick it in an old plastic shopping bag. We'd walk out of there, with all these shopping bags, shopping bags, and shopping bags.[60]

During his morning tours in the 1980s, Warhol always stopped off at the antique shop that his former assistant Vito Giallo had opened in 1979 on Madison Avenue.[61] He also called in to see his friend, the diamond dealer and designer John Reinhold, who explains:

+ with the author on June 28, 2013.

51 Nick Rhodes in a conversation with the author on December 15, 2014 in London.

52 Aronson 1987, p. 186.

53 Sotheby's 1988, Preface.

54 Quoted according to Aronson 1987, p. 194.

55 Quoted according to Coblentz 1977, p. 13.

56 Quoted according to Aronson 1987, p. 196.

57 Bockris 1989, p. 393.

58 Bourdon 1989, pp. 415f.

59 Bockris 1989, pp. 439f.

60 Brigid Berlin in a conversation with the author on December 4, 2012 in New York.

61 Giallo in O'Connor/Liu 1996, pp. 24f.

2

Andy collected almost everything. He was totally fascinated with jewelry and especially with diamonds. He lived on East Sixty-Sixth Street and my office at that time was on East Forty-Sixth Street. Almost every day he was in town he would leave his house at a certain moment around 11 a.m. and he would walk down Madison Avenue, shopping along the way. There were a few jewelry shops on his route that he often stopped at and then he would meet me in my office and we would go across the street to a coffee shop and have something that we called "nervous coffee" because I always worked best when I was nervous on coffee and so did he. I would go back to my office and he would continue downtown to the Factory. He had a fascination for antiques, and he had a fascination for diamonds, and he had a fascination for jewelry. He would often wear necklaces under his shirt, but nobody knew that he was wearing them.[62]

At that time Warhol struck up friendly relations with the chemist Stuart Pivar from Brooklyn. Pivar, also a passionate collector, reported later that they went shopping virtually every day together for a couple of hours. On Sundays he picked up the artist from church and went to a flea market with him.[63] "He didn't like compartments in his life," according to Pivar, "and he didn't like compartments in his collecting. He just responded to things individually, not because they belonged to this or that category. He didn't collect like an interior decorator either, because he had a niche or a shelf that was empty. He never collected Chinese art. 'Once I start,' he said, 'I'll never be able to stop.'"[64]

The full extent of Warhol's collecting mania came to light after his death when his possessions were auctioned at Sotheby's in New York at the end of April and beginning of May 1988, initiated by the executor of his estate, Fred Hughes. The auction house summarized the objects into more than 3,400 lots, divided into six categories: Art Nouveau and Art Deco; Collectibles, Jewelry, Furniture, Decorations and Paintings; Jewelry and Watches; American Indian Art, Americana; Paintings, Drawings and Prints; and Contemporary Art. When evaluating the objects, the auction house did not take Warhol's fame into account. With the exception of the American Indian Art, all the lots achieved at least double the estimated price. Warhol's giant cookie jar collection from the 1940s and 1950s, which he had rarely spent more than twenty-five dollars apiece on, brought in between $1,980 and $23,100 in groups of two to five. The total proceeds of the auction amounted to over $25 million. Furthermore, in June, a filing cabinet was discovered in a storage room in Warhol's house that had a double base, concealing a further 273 pieces of jewelry, including 72 diamonds, dozens of sapphires and a 300-carat emerald gem. These items were also auctioned at Sotheby's on December 4, 1988, bringing in a further $1.64 million.[65]

Warhol was also an avid collector of mundane objects. He instructed his staff not to throw anything away. Every snippet had to be kept, whether it was postmarked stamps on incoming mail, or flat tape recorder batteries. He placed most of his mail—with the exception of bills and checks—into big cardboard boxes, which he sealed up when they were full, dated and stored on shelves. This was the birth of the so-called *Time Capsules*.[66] The first *Time*

62
John Reinhold in a telephone conversation with the author on May 26, 2010.

63
Pivar in Sotheby's 1988, vol. V (n.p.).

64
Quoted according to Bockris 1989, p. 440.

65
Bourdon 1989, pp. 416f.

66
Ibid., pp. 347f.

Capsules were created by Warhol in 1974 on the occasion of the relocation of his Factory from 33 Union Square to new rooms in the 860 Broadway building.[67] Vincent Fremont was there and reported retrospectively:

In the back he had big, big boxes where he threw everything. They were huge. We started thinking about moving out of that little floor. I said, why don't we call them "time capsules" and make them smaller so we can carry them? So I found the F-42 box, which was about the right size, and we had shelving made that Ronnie Cutrone measured out to that specification. It was the right box, you could carry it. He could increase his volume and make it neat. He liked it neat and labeled. Andy, Ronnie, and I would label all those boxes. He liked volume.[68]

Up until his death in 1987, Warhol put together 615 *Time Capsules*.[69] The cardboard boxes he used measured 10 ¼ × 17 ⅞ × 14 ¼ inches. He placed up to 280 items into the boxes and when they were full, they were sealed, labeled, and not opened again during Warhol's lifetime.[70] It was only after the death of the artist that the Andy Warhol Museum in Pittsburgh started to open the *Time Capsules* and make an inventory of their contents.[71] The contents confirm that Warhol kept everything: source material and testimonies for his art, items of clothing and objects belonging to his mother, early children's books from the 1930s, objects belonging to celebrities (Clark Gable's shoes, a velvet dress belonging to Jean Harlow), the previously mentioned autograph from Shirley Temple, newspaper and magazine extracts—including reports about Dalí[72]—as well as everyday documents such as bills, receipts, telephone notes, letters, and much more.[73] THE Philosophy of Andy Warhol says about the *Time Capsules*:

… now I just drop everything into the same-size brown cardboard boxes that have a color patch on the side for the month of the year. I really hate nostalgia, though, so deep down I hope they all get lost and I never have to look at them again. That's another conflict. I want to throw things right out the window as they're handed to me, but instead I say thank you and drop them into the box-of-the-month. But my other outlook is that I really do want to save things so they can be used again someday.[74]

Sterile Love and Voyeurism

Salvador Dalí and Federico García Lorca became close friends during their studies in Madrid. Lorca visited Dalí in the summers of 1925 and 1927 in Cadaqués and was welcomed very cordially by the painter's family. A deep bond formed between the two over the years. In April 1926 the poet published his "Ode to Salvador Dalí," a tribute to his friend, who was flattered. One month later Lorca apparently made sexual advances towards Dalí. Many years later the painter reported in discussion with Alain Bosquet:

He was homosexual, as everyone knows, and madly in love with me. He tried to screw me twice … I was extremely annoyed, because I wasn't homosexual, and I wasn't interested in giving in. Besides, it hurts. So nothing came of it. But I felt awfully flattered vis-à-vis the prestige. Deep down, I felt that he was a great poet and that I did owe him a tiny bit of the Divine Dalí's

---

67
Andy Warhol's Time Capsule 21, p. 11.

68
In McShine 1989, pp. 439, 441.

69
Andy Warhol's Time Capsule 21, p. 12.

70
Ibid., p. 286.

71
Ibid., p. 15.

72
The article "Dilly Dalí," published in *TIME* magazine on December 6, 1963 was found in *Time Capsule 30*, while the *New York Post* of August 30, 1984 with the headline "SALVADOR DALÍ FLEES DEATH IN FIERY CASTLE" was discovered in *Time Capsule 533*.

73
Andy Warhol's Time Capsule 21, pp. 14ff.

74
Warhol, 1975, *Philosophy*, p. 145.

asshole. He eventually bagged a young girl, and she replaced me in the sacrifice. Failing to get me to put my ass at his disposal, he swore that the girl's sacrifice was matched by his own: it was the first time he had ever slept with a woman.[1]

Dalí remarked about artists in general, "We have a certain compensation, we've got long hair, we're slightly homosexual, we assume the feminine role ourselves, which allows us to resist women more effectively and for a longer time."[2] In later years Dalí admitted also feeling drawn towards androgynous young men. In *The Passions According to Dalí* he recalls, "When García Lorca tried to seduce me, I refused with distaste. But, now that I am growing older, I am a little more attracted to men. My voyeurism has extended to include them even with satisfaction. On the condition that they have no beards, that they are very young, that they look like girls, and have long hair and angelic faces. To see a penis rise on a very supple, almost feminine body, is a delight to my eyes."[3]

It was not until shortly before his death that Dalí was prepared to talk about his feelings for García Lorca. Ian Gibson had already repeatedly requested an interview with Dalí when writing his biography about García Lorca. However, Dalí first granted Gibson an interview when the writer was working on his biography about him. In January 1986 Gibson received a call from Antoni Pitxot, who informed him that Dalí would see him. The encounter took place the same day in the Torre Galatea of the Teatre-Museu Dalí in Figueres. Dalí was in bad shape at the time and had difficulty expressing himself, but his mind was sharp.[4] Ian Gibson reports:

Once my ear became accustomed to Dalí's voice, I realized, with Pitxot's help, that he was telling me how much Federico García Lorca had loved him. The poet's love for him had been intensely physical, he said. No question of mere affection. Dalí had tried to return the passion but was unable to. Instead Lorca had made love in Dalí's presence, as we saw earlier, to the skinny but powerfully seductive Margarita Manso. He went on to recall the poet's obsession with death and his famous, stage-by-stage enactments of his death, burial and putrefaction in Granada. Gala was hardly mentioned: it was Lorca who was on Dalí's mind. I came away with the clear impression that Dalí's friendship with the poet was perceived by him as one of the fundamental experiences in his life.[5]

Dalí and Lorca met for the last time in the fall of 1935. A poetry and music evening was held at the end of September in Barcelona in honor of the poet, which he was also expected to attend. However, Lorca did not appear, paving the way for a scandal. The public was informed that the poet had just met Dalí, whom he had not seen for seven years, and had driven with him to Tarragona, fifty miles from Barcelona.[6] Lorca explained to the journalist Josep Palau i Fabre, "We are twin spirits. Here's the proof: seven years without seeing each other and yet we agree on everything as if we'd never stopped talking since then. Salvador Dalí is a genius, a genius."[7] Lorca remained astounded at Dalí's total obsession with Gala. He confided to the poet Rafael Alberti that he did not understand how a woman could satisfy his friend sexually, he who hated breasts and vulvae, was afraid of venereal

1
In Bosquet 1969,
p. 36.

2
Ibid., pp. 94f.

3
Pauwels / Dalí
1985, p. 155.

4
Gibson 1997,
p. 610.

5
Ibid., p. 611.

6
Gibson 1989,
p. 414.

7
Quoted
according to
Gibson 1989,
p. 415.

diseases, had potency problems, and had an anal obsession.[8] He cried, "It's impossible! He can only get an erection when someone sticks a finger up his anus!"[9]

Edward James, who was Dalí's main patron at the time, witnessed the reunion of the two friends. James was born into a wealthy family in Scotland in 1907. His financial independence allowed him to dedicate himself to art early on. At the age of nineteen, he bought his first Bruegel, then at twenty-one he inherited a million pounds, which made it possible for him to acquire works by Picasso and the surrealists.[10] James, who also wrote poetry, encountered the world of ballet and music in Paris and started commissioning young composers. In 1931 he married the Austrian dancer and actress Tilly Losch, who divorced him just three years later, however. She explained before the court that James was homosexual. James's alleged homosexuality has often been the subject of research. George Melly, who published James's autobiography, once stated, "Edward was and *wasn't* homosexual," imitating his squeaky voice.[11] After the divorce, James went on long journeys through Europe, spending a lot of time in France in particular. As he wrote in his autobiography, he was introduced to Dalí's art at the house of Charles and Marie-Laure de Noailles in Hyères.[12] Over time he gathered more than 250 surrealist works, of which more than 180 were by Dalí.[13] Dalí and Gala were charmed by James. They traveled in Italy together and forged a special relationship, which is reflected in their correspondence. Dalí wrote to James that he was fascinated by his "extraordinary poetic-critical spirit" and was delighted that they got on so well. The painter assured him that he and Gala were really fond of him and that his absence left a hole similar to the one in the nanny's back in his painting *The Weaning of Furniture-Nutrition*.[14] In their correspondence, the painter and his muse fondly called their friend "Petitou."[15] Dalí never spoke of the depth of his friendship with James. However, writings were found in James's legacy that indicated that the painter and his patron had been very close. In an undated piece of writing, James remarks, "Gala more than guessed how close Dalí and I were to each other—and now [in about 1936] accepted it as workable, even after she did once create a scene of jealousy one night in a hotel in Modena, which erupted into a scandal—with Dalí coming to my room in tears wearing only the top of his pyjamas. … He stood protesting outside the door how he could not stand her nagging about Lorca and now about me any longer."[16] James went on to write that a couple of expensive evening dresses by Elsa Schiaparelli, jeweled ear clips by Boivin, and a rare seventeenth-century golden and enamel snake bracelet decorated with emeralds were necessary to appease Gala's jealousy.[17] Regarding Dalí's sexual orientation, James concludes:

His real interests were instinctively far more homosexual than heterosexual; Gala tried to believe that she had cured him of his homosexuality, but she knew in her heart that she had not really at all. She had, however, managed to keep it "sublimated" (if you can call it that) by channeling it into erotic drawings and some obscene pictures which are owned by private collectors who buy pornography. Pierre Colle … offered me one small, brilliantly painted oil painting which was sheer pornography.[18]

8 Ibid., p. 414.

9 Gibson 1997, p. 268.

10 Secrest 1986, p. 165.

11 Gibson 1997, p. 328.

12 James 1982, pp. 135f.

13 Michi-Kusunoki in Ades 2004, p. 439.

14 Gibson 1997, p. 352.

15 Ibid., p. 353.

16 Quoted according to Etherington-Smith 1993, p. 217.

17 Ibid.

18 Quoted according to Etherington-Smith, p. 218.

2

Ian Gibson assumes probably rightly that the friendship between Dalí and James never found a "physical outlet." He refers to other biographers who report that the patron was inhibited towards both women and men. According to Gibson, Dalí, too, panicked at any form of touching or caressing unless it was by Gala.[19]

Dalí had homosexual interests—at least when it came to his curiosity and voyeurism. Carlos Lozano, who was openly gay and a member of the artist's entourage, had absolutely no doubts about this: Dalí preferred men's bodies to women's.[20] Nanita Kalaschnikoff also had no doubts about this: "He loved the body of a man. He was always surrounded by beautiful boys and beautiful bodies. But he didn't like men … . He would have been with García Lorca if he were homosexual because García Lorca adored him and he loved García Lorca."[21]

In the mid-1960s, Dalí described New York as a "paradise of eroticism"[22] and remarked about his regular stays in the metropolis, "I see a large number of bankers, interesting homosexuals that I've never come across in other countries, and enthusiastic Dalíists."[23] The Italian photographer Santi Visalli, an eyewitness, confirms:

Whenever Dalí came to New York, he was crazy about going to all those nightclubs for homosexuals. He liked to see all sorts of crazy things. He wanted to go to this one particular nightclub. I don't remember the name but in the sixties, it was a rare rare thing. I accompanied him, but I couldn't photograph inside there because they wouldn't let me. He was very curious, you know, he was always looking. I think he was there as an observer because it was really a curiosity for him—for me too. We are talking about the sixties.[24]

Although Andy Warhol never denied his homosexuality, he never discussed it publicly. Ultra Violet writes in her memoirs, "Even though Andy is open in his own circles about his homosexuality, he tries to keep it secret from the public."[25] The word "gay" was avoided at the Factory, in the sense of homosexuality. Warhol preferred to talk of people who "have a problem."[26] Bob Colacello remarks, "… he didn't like to say he was gay. He wouldn't commit to journalists. He wouldn't say, 'I'm gay' or 'I'm part of the gay movement.' His standard line was 'Sex is such hard work.' And the only cause he really believed in was the Warhol cause, the Andy movement."[27] Vito Giallo, who was Warhol's assistant in 1955, reports that the artist was very interested in finding out details of the lives of people who "have a problem," "Very often he would like two people—two gay boys—to know each other and then after they got together he wanted to know all the details. I mean, that for him was very exciting, rather than be there himself. He would rather hear it from one of the partners. And that he would often do. He would get me to know somebody or somebody to get to know me and then after he would want to know all about it."[28] Warhol himself had "a problem" in two respects. On the one hand he wished for a romantic love affair with a man, but on the other hand, his complexes with regard to his appearance meant that he was extremely restrained when it came to forging sexual relations.[29] On August 28, 1981, he confided in his diaries, "I look *better* thin. I guess I should try not to think so much about looks but I'm *not* thinking too much about looks.

19
Gibson 1997,
p. 376.

20
Ibid., p. 534.

21
Nanita
Kalaschnikoff in
the documentary
*The Fame and
Shame of
Salvador Dalí.*

22
Pauwels/Dalí
1985, p. 101.

23
In Bosquet 1969,
p. 14.

24
Santi Visalli in a
Skype conversation with the
author on July 9,
2012.

25
Ultra Violet 1988,
p. 155.

26
Colacello 1990,
p. 99.

27
Bob Colacello
in a telephone
conversation
with the author
on September
22, 2010.

28
Vito Giallo
in a telephone
conversation
with the author
on May 25, 2010.

29
Bockris 1989,
p. 89.

I never do. I *don't*. I like ugly people. I *do*. And anyway, ugly people are just as hard to get as pretty people—they don't want you, either."[30] Warhol was expressing here that he had difficulties in finding a suitable partner. Already in 1975, in *THE Philosophy of Andy Warhol*, he had allowed similar details of his sex life to be published:

After being alive, the next hardest work is having sex. Of course, for some people it isn't work because they need the exercise and they've got the energy for the sex and the sex gives them even more energy. Some people get energy from sex and some people lose energy from sex. I have found that it's too much work. But if you have the time for it, and if you need that exercise— then you should do it. But you could really save yourself a lot of trouble either way by first figuring out whether you're an energy-getter or an energy-loser. As I said, I'm an energy-loser. But I can understand it when I see people running around trying to get some.

It's just as much work for attractive people not *to have sex as for un- attractive people to have sex, so it's helpful if the attractive people happen to get energy from sex and if the unattractive people happen to lose energy from sex, because then their wants will fit in with the direction that people are pushing them in.*[31]

Elsewhere Warhol comes to the conclusion, "Fantasy love is much better than reality love. Never doing it is very exciting. The most exciting attractions are between two opposites that never meet."[32] Ultra Violet cites the phrase in her memoirs, "'Sex is an illusion. The most exciting thing is not doing it.' I've heard Dalí say the same thing. Is Warhol copying Dalí? Or does Warhol think like Dalí?"[33]

Indeed, Dalí also identified with the particular kind of attraction mentioned by Warhol, with two opposites not getting together, and in his novel *Hidden Faces*, published in 1944, he called it "cledalism." The Spaniard saw cledalism as the completion of the "passional trilogy" started by the Marquis de Sade in the eighteenth century, "Sadism may be defined as pleasure experienced through pain inflicted on the object; masochism, as pleasure experienced through pain submitted to by the object. Cledalism is pleasure and pain sublimated in an all-transcending identification with the object."[34] Many years later Dalí explained to Carlos Lozano that cledalism contained a system that was the key (French "clé") to his person,[35] which also lends meaning to the term "CléDalísm." It is evident in the preface to *Hidden Faces* that he identified with cledalism, as he states, "It is on the contrary a strict-ly Dalínian book and those who have read my 'Secret Life' attentively will readily discover beneath the novel's structure the continual and vigorous familiar presence of the essential myths of my own life and of my mytholo-gy."[36] Ian Gibson concludes that Lorca's "largely undeclared presence" runs through the novel *Hidden Faces*.[37] Dalí speaks of his friendship with Lorca in the preface and points out that in 1922 the poet had foreseen a literary career for him.[38] His decision to stay away from Lorca and later also from Gala, at least from a sexual point of view, is projected onto the hero and the heroine of the novel. In the key scene they are bound by hands and feet to trees, so that they are completely immobile and out of each others' reach,

30
Hackett 1989,
p. 403.

31
Warhol 1975,
Philosophy,
pp. 97f.

32
Ibid., p. 44.

33
Ultra Violet 1988,
p. 164.

34
Dalí 1944,
pp. xvif.

35
Gibson 1997,
p. 425.

36
Dalí 1944, p. xvii.

37
At the same time Gibson points out that cledalism develops the "theory of erotic self-denial or sublimation" that Dalí had already formulated in 1927 in his prose piece "Saint Sebastian." See Gibson 1997, pp. 425ff.

38
Dalí 1944,
pp. xv, xviif.

in order to attain the desired climax in this pose without physical contact or movement.

While in the novel *Hidden Faces* Dalí only hints at his attitude towards sexuality, in later years he revealed honest details about his sexual proclivities, "I am as miserly with my sperm as with my gold. Besides I have never found great pleasure in orgasm. What counts is everything that precedes it, less even, in the act than in the mind. When I was very young, an ejaculation delighted me sexually, but now is something which, without being positively disagreeable, is nearly so. What I am looking for is not an orgasm but the vision that would be capable of producing an orgasm."[39] The working title of the painting *The Great Masturbator* created in 1929 sheds unambiguous light on Dalí's preferred form of sexual fulfillment. In the *Playboy* interview "El pincel erótico de Dalí," published fifty years later, the artist explains that the said painting reflected "the guilt of a face completely extinguished vitally by so much masturbation: the nose touches the ground and has a horrible boil. Every time I lose a bit of sperm I have the conviction that I've wasted it. I feel guilty."[40] Dalí did not feel guilty, however, about repeatedly mentioning his proclivity for masturbation. Jonathan Guinness, 3rd Baron Moyne, who spent roughly one month a year in Cadaqués beginning in 1962, recalls that the artist said to several people, "*Je suis le plus grand masturbateur du monde.*"[41] Furthermore, Dalí asked his models to pose naked for him while he masturbated behind his easel. Susi Wyss, who got to know Dalí in 1964 and modelled regularly for him in the following years, recalls, "I often posed for him, and then he drew me. I was paid for it—it was easily earned money. We had so much fun. … Then Dalí also masturbated. If people were present who he didn't know, then he put something in front or went under his djellaba that he often wore. I also sewed him a couple, which he loved. And afterwards he made a cross on my forehead with his sperm."[42] In the mid-1960s, the Warhol superstar Ivy Nicholson also posed for Dalí. She reports that Dalí had had Peter Moore, his secretary at the time, track her down. She was three months pregnant with her twins when the artist completed a nude sketch of her in May 1965.

I heard that he used to tell people that he was going to paint their portrait so he would get a canvas and have them strip and do it to himself and then, after the pose, they'd expect to see the painting and they'd see nothing. This would be totally humiliating. So I tricked him. I called Milton Gunne to photograph me being painted which forced him to do my portrait because he was nuts about publicity. He actually did a beautiful portrait in charcoal.[43]

More often than not, the artist succeeded in upsetting or even shocking his models. The actress and author Constance Webb, who posed for Dalí at the beginning of the 1940s in his suite at the Beverly Hills Hotel, reports such an incident in her memoirs *Not Without Love*:

He was dressed in formal black trousers with a pinstripe, a starched ruffled shirt, and a velvet jacket. In those days, men did not wear ruffled shirts. He had a gardenia in his buttonhole, but his little brown feet were bare. …

… On his easel his drawing board was so large that nothing could be seen of him except his small brown feet. Every once in a while he would suddenly poke his head around the side of the board and stare intently. His dark brown

eyes reflected the light and glittered until they looked almost black. His mustache quivered at the curled-up ends. ...

Toward the end of my assignment with Dalí on a day little different from any other he showed me some of the sketches he had made of me. These were to be sylph-like in the backgrounds of other paintings. We then worked for about an hour and I took my usual break, lying back on the sofa. I wasn't paying much attention to Dalí, who usually studied his work or sharpened pencils or went out of the room. Suddenly he leaped onto the couch, penis erect, and after a few quick motions ejaculated all over my breasts. Then to my shock, disgust, and horror he proceeded to lick off the sperm. I couldn't wait to get to the bathroom, where I showered and tried to control my shaking body. Although married twice, I'd only known the "missionary position" as the sexual act. When I came out, Dalí darted into the bathroom and I heard the sound of the shower; I dressed as fast as I could and ran out of the suite.[44]

Dalí's "sterile sexuality" can be traced to his father's efforts to warn him of the dangers of venereal diseases by opening out on the piano a medical encyclopedia with photos of the devastating consequences. In the aforementioned *Playboy* interview, Dalí confessed that the book had scared the wits out of him.[45] The unforeseen consequence was that Dalí avoided all forms of physical closeness his entire life. "I, personally, never touch anybody, that's become proverbial. It's probably due to inhibitions that I received in earliest childhood. ... Perhaps you'll understand why touching anyone gives me the shivers."[46]

Dalí was indeed the "Great Masturbator," and he liked to ask others to masturbate in front of him. Carlos Lozano reports in his memoirs that it gave the surrealist great pleasure to persuade boys "to drop their pants" and to then watch them masturbate.[47] When the British photographer Robert Whitaker introduced Dalí to his pretty wife Susan in the spring of 1972, the artist also made clear advances towards her. Susan Whitaker recalls, "I walked in with my husband Bob and he had some friends and some other artists there. He asked me if I like to masturbate and threw a vibrator at me. I was a bit taken aback because I hadn't met him before, I knew nothing about him. ... I think he was just doing it for the shock value, just to make people laugh."[48] But also in the seclusion of his studio the subject of masturbation was always (subliminally) present. Elsa Peretti, who posed for Dalí in the 1960s and had to dress like a nun, recalls:

I was working as a model and I knew, through my agency, that Dalí needed one. His choice, between a few pictures, was one of me dressed in a body and with a blond wig, taken by Oriol Maspons but in person, I was totally different, with pony tail and glasses; I was finally booked.

I had to take a cab from Barcelona to Port Lligat and when I finally arrived, two hours late, he looked at me and said, "It's not the girl! It's not the girl! It's not the girl!"

I had to sleep in his house because the hotel he had booked for me, was already closed. Next day, we started working. Dalí was very professional. He drew me three hours in the morning and three hours in the afternoon. It was

[44]
Webb 2003,
pp. 97ff.

[45]
Calvo Serraller,
2006, p. 1535.

[46]
In Bosquet 1969,
pp. 71f.

[47]
Thurlow 2000,
p. 180.

[48]
Susan Whitaker
in a telephone
conversation
with the author
on April 18, 2012.
→ **12** [p. 371]

a pleasure working with him even though I couldn't move. It was very interesting to listen to him and to hear the sound of the pencil he was using on the paper. I could not really see him well because I was very short-sighted and also because I was sitting under a kind of arch.

During my free time, I went to sunbathe. Dalí would tell me, "Nuns don't sunbathe." While posing, I was sitting on a little box. Oriol told me that in general the box was connected to a kind of pump, linked to a spoon that had to hit "the right spot"; masturbation with a spoon? I don't know, and I never did.

I stayed in Cadaqués a week, one of the best of my life.

From that time on, I saw him in New York many times ... He used to invite me and other young people to top restaurants.[49]

Elsa Peretti arrived in New York in 1968 and soon became part of fashion's in-crowd. Of course she met Warhol, who, like Dalí, also sought to avoid physical contact wherever possible in his daily interactions with people. Robert Heide, who worked on different projects with Warhol in the 1960s, explains, "He wasn't like a person you would hug or grab on the arm or anything like that. He had sometimes an invisible wall ... for keeping that distance."[50] Santi Visalli, who had started to photograph the Pop Art artist at the time, remembers:

He had a complex personality. Also, I very rarely saw him make physical contact with a person, you know, like shaking hands or embracing somebody. In the sixties everybody was hugging everybody else. Personally I never saw him doing that. I have only one picture, taken when he was shooting the movie Chelsea Girls, *which shows Mario Montez, the female impersonator, sitting on his lap; this is a rare picture because I never saw him physically touching anyone. I don't know about his sexuality, but I don't think he had any.*[51]

Viva observed the following: "And yet if you so much as tried to touch Andy, he would actually shrink away. Shrink. I mean shrink backwards and whine. Many times I used to make a grab at Andy, kiddingly, or touch him, and he would cringe. Whine, 'Aw, Viva, awww.' We were all always touching Andy just to watch him turn red and shrink. Like the proverbial shrinking violet."[52] After the attempt on his life, Warhol reacted even more sensitively to being touched. Again Viva: "After Andy was shot he became really terrified of women. He was very much changed towards me, much cooler. He was sexually afraid of women before, I mean you couldn't touch him, he would cringe. That could have been an act, but afterwards he seemed to be deeply afraid."[53] Vincent Fremont reports that Warhol's aversion to being touched lasted well into the 1970s.

Andy could be considered a germaphobe and he did not like people touching him though he did shake hands with people. Later in the 1980s Andy was more relaxed about being touched or embraced when greeted. Andy did not like it when someone would get too close to him and start an intense conversation. Andy would back up slightly and look to me, Fred Hughes or Bob Colacello or anyone who was with him at the time and say, "Oh, you should talk to ..." Then he could slip away. We were very conscious of keeping Andy safe since in 1968 Andy was shot and almost killed by an assassination attempt

49
Elsa Peretti in a telephone conversation with the author on October 2, 2015.

50
Robert Heide in a conversation with the author on December 6, 2012 in New York.

51
Santi Visalli in a Skype conversation with the author on July 9, 2012.

52
In Stein/Plimpton 1982, p. 226.

53
Quoted according to Bockris 1989, pp. 315f.

by a deranged woman. Andy never traveled with bodyguards; his friends and people who worked with him protected him.[54]

It appears that the only one allowed to touch Dalí was Gala. The surrealist emphasized repeatedly that in his whole life he had only slept with Gala, that he owed it to her that he had overcome his fear of the sexual act.[55] In *The Passions According to Dalí*, the artist reiterates, "I swear that I have never made love with anyone but Gala. People refuse to believe me, because I spend a lot of time thinking up and arranging erotic games."[56] Susi Wyss, who was not only one of Dalí's models, but also took part in his erotic games and nevertheless had a good relationship with Gala, reports that they had both revealed to her that they had never slept together.[57] However, since Gala lived out her sexuality, she always had many lovers. Dalí tolerated this, and it can be assumed that he even forced the affairs of his wife. Wyss remarks, "Dalí was very sexual—*mais pas pratiquant.* ... He liked every form of sex, as long as he didn't have to practice it. ... He wanted to watch his wife when she had her young lovers. I wasn't present, but he undoubtedly watched, that's for sure."[58] The actor William Rothlein, who was Gala's great love in the 1960s, cannot confirm this: "Dalí was perfectly comfortable with us together and there was trust. He was very pleased all the time about my relationship with Gala. ... But he never watched us in any intimate situation. No, no, no! Not at all. That's all stories. Dalí may have been a voyeur and he may have liked to watch people having sex, but not his wife!"[59]

Indeed, Dalí enjoyed watching people having sex. For this purpose he liked staging the aforementioned erotic games, which he offers insight into in his *Passions* in the chapter dedicated to eroticism:

Eroticism starts with a third party. Thus I like to see a couple, heterosexual or not, reach ecstasy. I direct, I command the positions even to the most infinitesimal details: the movement of the feet, the way the hair falls, the direction of a glance or smile. To satisfy me they must be filled with passion or they must simulate it perfectly.

Not long ago, I attended a marvelous experiment. I was able to convince a young woman, who was pretty but of common origin, to allow herself to be sodomized by the boy she loved. She had resisted up to then because the idea was not to her taste. At last, I had convinced her: "For you, for you, I accept." I came with an American lady friend: as always my worry about being accompanied by a notary. We were seated on a sofa, they on the bed, like quadrupeds trying to mount, she like a tender little animal, he like a bull full of passion, suddenly forced, she exclaimed in Spanish: "For the Divine One! I am doing this for the Divine Dalí!"[60]

Elsewhere in the book Dalí clarifies that he remained true to his role as voyeur and masturbator in the erotic games he staged, "Personally, I avoid actual contact by accompanying the pleasures of voyeurism with a little masturbation."[61] Susi Wyss and other witnesses at the time confirm that these erotic games actually took place. Suzannah Fleming, who often posed for Dalí in the early 1970s, recalls:

Actually, there was the soiree and then the "orgy" to follow which was much more selective. I was sometimes, but not always, invited to these

54
Vincent Fremont in a conversation with the author on June 28, 2012 in New York.

55
Dalí 1986, p. 88.

56
Pauwels/Dalí 1985, p. 33.

57
Susi Wyss in a conversation with the author on October 25, 2013 in Paris (translated from the German).

58
Ibid.

59
William Rothlein in a telephone conversation with the author on February 3, 2015.

60
Pauwels/Dalí 1985, pp. 102f.

61
Ibid., p. 99.

receptions and banquets, but when I was I would inevitably be invited to the orgy that would take place afterwards. Dalí seemed to like to corrupt people by getting them to have sex with me—as though they were taking part in some Divine Dalían ritual (which it was in a sense). Of course it was mainly that he liked directing and watching the action—he would never touch me in a sexual way himself though—and I only once glimpsed his penis by accident. Often the people he selected for the orgy part were quite "buttoned up"—and it was as if he was orchestrating a type of initiation or "right of passage" for them. I used to think to myself that these people would wake up the next morning and wonder what had happened to them—was it a dream?![62]

Dalí never tired of recruiting attractive young people as protagonists for his erotic games. The star astrologer Elizabeth Teissier, who met Dalí in the 1960s when she was a successful model, reports,

I was in Paris at Catherine Harlé's model agency and Amanda Lear was there, too. One day she said she would like to take me with her to a lunch at Berkeley, to which Dalí had invited some friends. I replied, "Yes, of course. I'm interested in getting to know Dalí." ... Then we went to Berkeley and I must say, I was fascinated by him because he was really someone very special, as we know. ... He kept talking about rhinoceros powder. He said it was a substance that stimulated the libido and that it was very important to take this powder, etc. etc. ... Then he invited me to the Hôtel Le Meurice. As I found him very eccentric and his reactions were always very unexpected, I dragged my brother along with me, who was also very pleased to get to know Dalí.

We arrived at the hotel and Dalí did not want to believe that my brother was my brother. He said, "You have the green eyes of Stalin. Your brother's eyes are so blue. Surely he can't be your brother." And I said, "But he is my brother. Do you want my brother to show you his passport?" I was a bit offended—Stalin was very shocking for me. And then he said, "Okay, I want you two to make love." I said, "What?" I thought I was dreaming and laughed out loud. ... "If you don't want to do it today ..." said Dalí. "We will never do it as brother and sister!" I answered. Then we spoke of all kinds of other things and finally he said, "I'm throwing a big party next Sunday outside of Paris. I'm inviting you, if you like." And I thought okay, then I'm coming with my brother.

... Then we arrived there. It was quite far outside of Paris ... in the middle of a forest, and it was a house with a roof like a turtle. ... In the underground part there was a swimming pool. It was quite mad. Two naked women were swimming there. And when we arrived one floor lower—I had never seen anything like it before, it was actually "Sodom and Gomorrah"—there were all these people that you could hear shouting and breathing loudly ... men and women were running back and forth, naked, with towels, with chains, and were queuing for the shower. And then I saw Dalí. He was there with a very young girl with long, blonde pigtails like a fourteen-year-old girl. I saw the girl from behind. She kneeled in front of Dalí and he sat in front of her. I didn't see what she was really doing. It is quite possible that she was doing nothing at all and was just looking at him. ... I was quite shocked. Then I went back up and left all these people. I was rather disgusted. ... By the swimming pool there was Amanda Lear with her legs in the water and there were a few others, including

the singer Richard Anthony. ... I asked Amanda, "Are you not interested in what is going on down there?" and she said, "No, no, I'm not very interested in it." ... I waited, waited, and waited until my brother came back up again smiling. He said mysteriously that he had made an interesting encounter. ... And then we drove back.[63]

Andy Warhol had several serious relationships during his life. Cécile Guilbert lists the following "boyfriends" of his in her book *Warhol Spirit*: Charles Lisanby, Alfred Carlton Willers, Ed Wallowitch, Philip Fagan, Danny Williams, Victor Reilly, Rod La Rod, John Giorno, Sam Bolton, Jed Johnson, and Jon Gould.[64] Recalling the artist's relationships in the 1960s, Gerard Malanga explains:

Whenever Andy had a boyfriend my personal reaction was I could never treat it seriously because I could never think that Andy would have a relationship. (laughs) He had Rod La Rod, he had Richard Rheem, who is the nephew of George Rheem, the air-conditioning heir, and he had Philip Fagan. I could never visualize Andy having a relationship with anyone of these characters. (laughs) But in fact he did. ... Andy was so passive. ... And Jed Johnson, at that point Andy was no longer Mr. Passive, I mean he was a little more outgoing. ... This is a theory but it's actually true: There was something about Andy that was not virtually gay. Andy was a "boy" and he behaved like a boy, not a homosexual, but a boy. And adults love to give children gifts and it was like Andy was always, like, being showered with something. Somebody would give him a gift or whatever. He was a Peter Pan. He was a boy. And so because of that idea I had of Andy I could never think of him as an adult homosexual.[65]

Warhol's longest relationship was with the attractive Jed Johnson, which lasted from 1968 to 1980. Johnson moved in with him after the assassination attempt. He neither denied having a relationship with the artist, nor boasted about it. Many years later, describing his status he said, "I guess you could just call me the housekeeper."[66] After twelve years, Johnson suddenly moved out in January 1980. Although Warhol felt rejected, he reacted in his typically cool and distanced way.[67] However, some people did not fail to notice that he was affected by the separation. The author Raymond Foye later recalled that Warhol once called him late at night to complain that he had found one of Jed's socks in a drawer and that the relationship did indeed appear to be over.[68] Horst Weber von Beeren, who worked for Warhol's printer Rupert Jasen Smith for many years, also remembers very well that Warhol had a broken heart and that he even expressed it in his art.

On a trip through Germany Warhol put this odd doodle underneath his signature. Finally I asked him what that was supposed to be and he answered: "A broken heart." This was the time when Jed Johnson, who lived with Warhol in his Sixty-Sixth Street house, moved out, after terrible scenes, as I was told. Andy could spit fire. But why he bought Jed this gorgeous apartment, to run his interior design business from, I still don't understand. ... Andy and his broken-heart-doodles were at the time when Andy made a move on me: "Come on up to my room, but don't bring anybody!" Of course I did not go and he never forgave me for that. His narcissism was deeply hurt.[69]

63
Dr. Elizabeth Teissier-Hynek in a telephone conversation with the author on October 21, 2015 (translated from the German).

64
Guilbert 2008, p. 215.

65
Gerard Malanga in a conversation with the author on July 2, 2012 in Hudson, NY.

66
Quoted according to Bourdon 1989, p. 292.

67
Ibid., p. 387; Bockris 1989, p. 437.

68
Bockris 1989, p. 438.

69
Horst Weber von Beeren in a conversation with the author
+

2

+
on December 7,
2012 in New York.

70
Hackett 1989,
p. 344,
November 19,
1980.

71
Bourdon 1989,
p. 387.

72
Hackett 1989,
p. 377, April 30,
1981.

73
Bockris 1989,
p. 197.

74
Colacello 1990,
pp. 343, 437.

75
Warhol (1977) in
Goldsmith 2004,
p. 264.

76
Giorno 1994,
pp. 131f., 143f.

77
John Giorno
in a conversation
with the author
on March 13, 2011
in Besançon.

78
Quoted
according to
Colacello 1990,
p. 437.

79
Warhol/Hackett
1980, p. 294.

80
Quoted accord-
ing to Bockris
1989, p. 315.

In November 1980 Warhol met Jon Gould.[70] Gould was just twenty-seven, practically half the artist's age, and was a good-looking young man, tall, slim, athletic, with dark eyes and a brilliant smile. He was vice president of Paramount Pictures and Warhol found him attractive not least because of his connection to the film studio.[71] Warhol wrote in his diaries, "I love going out with Jon because it's like being on a real date—he's tall and strong and I feel that he can take care of me. And it's exciting because he acts straight so I'm sure people think he *is*."[72]

Warhol's love life was frequently the subject of speculation. The painter Ruth Kligman, who became known as Jackson Pollock's and Willem de Kooning's muse, and spent time with Warhol in the early 1960s, believed that he was increasingly becoming a voyeur because of his repressed sexuality.[73] Bob Colacello suspects that the combination of masturbation and voyeurism went hand in hand with an "abstract" love life. Indeed, Warhol often stated that "sex is so abstract." Colacello emphasizes that his boss had always been very precise in his choice of words.[74] When asked what he thought of masturbation, Warhol once replied laconically, "It helps."[75] From this point of view, his sexuality was comparable to Dalí's. Warhol's partner in the 1960s, John Giorno, confirmed that Warhol was a voyeur, who "generally speaking" did not have sex with anyone during these years. Their sexual moments together, whereby Warhol satisfied him orally, were therefore "unusual."[76] Giorno explains that Warhol's inferiority complexes set a fatal mechanism in motion:

Back then, Andy had a really beautiful body and a relatively big dick. When you looked at him you'd say this guy is gorgeous. He had a sort of classical Greek or Roman boy's body: firm muscles, well-shaped, hairless—like a marble sculpture—and then the Andy Warhol head on top. Andy was so young and he actually had a very smooth, unwrinkled, kind of really beautiful face. He himself didn't think it was beautiful, so he wasn't happy with it. I mean, he looked in the mirror and he thought his face was ugly with this wig-head. And when it looked at its body, it thought its body was ugly, you know, the face looked at the body and said "Oh it's as ugly as my head and as my face."[77]

Bob Colacello later pointed out the almost tragic contradiction that in the late 1970s Warhol had tried almost desperately to have "*real* sex," whereas the attractive young men he desired were only interested in going out with the famous artist and basking in his limelight, and not in getting to know the private person. This tension led Warhol to develop a "psychological defense mechanism" that no longer allowed anyone near him emotionally. His motto was, "I don't want to have sex, because I don't want to be involved."[78] In Viva's opinion, Warhol made movies because of the insights they afforded into the life of "normal people." In October 1968 he shot the film *Blue Movie*, in which Viva has sex with Louis Waldon. The movie was originally meant to have the title *Fuck*.[79] Viva explained, "Because Andy was so shy and had complexes about his looks, he had no private life. In filming as in 'hanging out' he merely wanted to find out how 'normal people' acted with each other. And I think my own idea about *Blue Movie* wasn't, as I believed at the time, to teach the world about 'real love' or 'real sex' but to teach Andy."[80] However

Benjamin Liu, Warhol's personal assistant in the 1980s, questions the voyeurism hypothesis.

I don't know exactly if it's a substitution for the lack of sex, although he and I have talked about that subject. But the way he says it to me is more juvenile: "Hey, Benjamin, all that sex. The body on the top of the other one, you know, that sweat and all that." … And I was imagining he and I are like two high school kids … (laughs) That's the way he talked to me and I go "Aha. Aha." And then he would ask me questions about my sex life a little bit. He was curious about that. … You know why? Because that means the subject of sex is still alive in him. …. Maybe he's looking for a direction, how to handle himself and Jon Gould. I don't know. Although everybody has a comment on their supposed sex life or lack thereof. … They go, "I don't think he ever had sex with Jon Gould." How do they know? Even Victor [Hugo (mutual friend and Halston's boyfriend)], who might know, said "I think Andy sometimes gets so heated from taking photographs of naked people that he might have gone to a corner and masturbated." I said, "How do you know?" Nobody really knows what goes on.[81]

Warhol liked to coquet in public with regard to his alleged asexuality. In the January 1981 edition of *Forum*, an interview with him was published in which he was evidently keen to describe himself as if he only needed sexual energy to work, but not sexuality as such.

—What makes you horny?

—Warhol: I never feel horny.

—Where does your sexual energy go, if not into sex?

—Warhol: I put it into work.

…

—You're still a virgin?

—Warhol: Yeah, I'm still a virgin.

—And you're fifty-two?

—Warhol: Yeah.[82]

The Child within the Man

Gerard Malanga compares Andy Warhol to Peter Pan and describes the artist as an eternal boy.[1] However, he is not the only one who thinks of Warhol as a boy. Vera von Lehndorff, better known as Veruschka, says that the artist "was rather like a lost child. He was always surrounded by people from the Factory."[2] His assistant in the early 1980s, Ingeborg Princess zu Schleswig-Holstein, "always had the feeling that somewhere deep inside sat a little Andrew, riding this Warhol spaceship."[3] Lady Anne Lambton, who came to the Factory in 1973 as a seventeen-year-old,[4] summarizes her experience with Warhol:

He was like a child … interested … forever interested in everything. I mean, in the things he was interested in. … I don't know any other humans you can really equate him to. It wasn't an act. That's all I can say. … and I was a child, too, so we converged at exactly the right moment … Well, we were both so interested in silly things. With Leo Castelli he would have been interested

81 Benjamin Liu in a conversation with the author on November 30, 2012 in New York.

82 In Cohen/Warhol 1981, p. 23. A section of the interview with Scott Cohen that remained unpublished is documented in Colacello 1990, p. 437: "SC: With all these beautiful people hanging around, don't you ever get turned on? AW: Well, I think only kids who are very young should have sex, and people who aren't young should never get excited. After twenty-five, you should look, but never touch." See also Hackett 1989, p. 358, February 17, 1981.

1 See the chapter **Sterile Love and Voyeurism** in this part.

2 Vera von Lehndorff in a telephone conversation with the author on January 6, 2012 (translated from the German).

3 Ingeborg Princess zu Schleswig-Holstein in a conversation with the author on June 30, 2011 in Hamburg (translated from the German).

4 See the chapter **Assistants, Employees, Secretaries, and Managers** in Part 3.

in serious things. The part of his character I knew was the part of a seventeen-year-old, really. He can't have always been like that ... or maybe he was and ... so Fred dealt with him, Vincent dealt with him, Bob dealt with him. ... And he just stayed true, knowing what he wanted in a pure way. It's delegation he was brilliant at.[5]

Jamie Wyeth also comes to similar conclusions as Lady Lambton. He and Warhol portrayed each other in 1976. Afterwards, Wyeth, who was eighteen years younger, stayed at the Factory for a while and was able to witness how Warhol occasionally acted out the "child within the man":

We'd go to toy stores and buy toys. He was very childlike and I'm rather childlike anyway. So we bought a train set together, which I still have and we got very excited over that and carried it back to his house one night. (laughs) ... That, I think, is what a lot of people miss when they talk about Warhol. He had such curiosity, almost like a little boy's curiosity about things. And his pose was to be sort of disinterested when in fact he was fascinated by things. And he had a sense of wonder, which was, I think, the most important thing.[6]

Once Warhol's curiosity had been sparked it could quickly turn into enthusiasm. When the actress Sally Kirkland asked the artist to promote her movie *Anna* in his TV show *Famous For Fifteen Minutes*, he showed immediate enthusiasm: "He was terribly generous with helping me get my movie off the ground, *Anna*. ... I think he was blown away that I introduced him to Paulina Porizkova, who was the number one model in the world at that time. He was very childlike in his enthusiasm, just very excited and enthusiastic about my movie."[7] Gigi Williams, who came to New York in 1973 and later became a make-up artist for portrait assignments at the Factory, adds that Warhol was not only able to show childlike enthusiasm, but also loved getting up to mischief like a little boy: "He was like a little kid. ... He would say things that would instigate behaviors so that he could watch. ... He would always try to start trouble. He would gossip in a way that he hoped would make a flare up, so he could laugh—'Oh, look what happened here!' He was a big gossip. I mean *Interview* was a perfect thing for him because he wanted gossip."[8]

Salvador Dalí also often showed the "child within the man." He even liked to refer to himself as the "newborn baby" and "child" of his wife Gala.[9] Outsiders could scarcely overlook this unusual mother-child relationship. The advertising professional Herbert Cerwin, who met Dalí and Gala in 1941 in California during their stay at the Del Monte Lodge Hotel in Pebble Beach, explains, "He was Dalí and he never forgot it. Or, perhaps Gala didn't permit it. Sometimes I thought he was a pathetically unhappy small boy with great talent under the domination and protective care of his mother."[10] However, most of the time Dalí was like a happy little boy. He took true childish delight in decorating the patio of his house with unusual accessories. Susan Whitaker, who traveled to Cadaqués in the spring of 1972 with her husband, the British photographer Robert Whitaker, recalls, "He showed me things that he liked. He had like a child's musical box by the *Lips Sofa* on the side .... He said 'Listen to this.' Then he pulled the cord and music was coming out of it. There were the eggs, and there was a camel [sculpture] ... He would just say, 'Look at this!' and 'Look at this!' but he wouldn't give an

5
Lady Anne Lambton in a telephone conversation with the author on August 11, 2012.

6
Jamie Wyeth in a telephone conversation with the author on April 3, 2013.

7
Sally Kirkland in a telephone conversation with the author on December 16, 2012.

8
Gigi Williams in a telephone conversation with the author on May 5, 2014.

9
Dalí 1976, p. 91.

10
Cerwin 1966, pp. 159f.

opinion."[11] It is hardly surprising that the artist and moviemaker Steven Arnold ascribes "childlike sweetness" to the private Dalí: "Underneath the outrageous showmanship of his public persona was a childlike sweetness and a naive, gentle, warm man of astonishing intelligence."[12] As was the case with Warhol, Dalí's childishness went hand in hand with an unusual sense of humor. Pandora reports on a "Sunday night dinner at the Plaza Hotel (one of many), where Dalí played musical chairs with twelve humans. Everyone had to move one chair over, all evening long, sitting in front of someone else's dinner and passing their meal back and forth. Dalí and I, who were only dining on soup, did not participate."[13] The Halston model Chris Royer remembers such shenanigans by the Spaniard well and remarks, "Dalí would get very inspired by watching the interaction of people at the table. He would then break it up and move them around again ... There was never a dull minute."[14] Royer adds that both artists had a "boyish sense of humor":

Dalí and Andy both had this amazing sense of humor that was very quirky. They loved to create mischief which produced excitement and inspiration. You really had to pay attention, because some people wouldn't get it and other people would go, "Oh oh, I can't believe you did this." They loved it when you understood and laughed at it. It was very subtle, they would plant it and then watch to see how people would react. Very, very funny! If you understood it you had a great time![15]

Dalí especially enjoyed playing his tricks when he was among high society. Jonathan Guinness, 3rd Baron Moyne, reports how the daughter of a Spanish lady was introduced to important personalities from Cadaqués: "There they came in, this Spanish lady and her daughter, and Dalí pulled out of a drawer a condom, a special condom with sort of lumps on it, and he said, 'Oh so funny, I bought this in Barcelona!' It rather horrified the mother and she and the daughter ran away quite quickly. (laughs) ... Remember that in those days Spain was much more Catholic and much more shocked."[16] Susi Wyss, who frequently posed as a model for Dalí beginning in 1964, recalls a similar situation in Paris, in which Dalí displayed his particular sense of humor and caused a stir:

At that point I was no longer shy. And when Dalí said to me, "Show me your tits" then I showed my tits. A lady fell unconscious once at the Hôtel Le Meurice. We were having tea ... He wanted to see the lady's face when she saw my tits—to shock, to provoke. But who were these ladies? Perhaps his customers. I have no idea. ... Dalí had a kind of prism—he was always discovering such things—and looked through it at the people sitting there. He was like a child, had always remained childlike. ... Dalí was a "naughty boy." He also liked to feel guilty when he had done something silly, had not done his work or whatever.[17]

Large Limousines

Salvador Dalí and Andy Warhol liked to provoke and shock others with sexual innuendoes. Ondine, a regular guest at Warhol's Factory in the 1960s, later stated: "Andy was always so provocative sexually. I think he knew that

11
Susan Whitaker in a telephone conversation with the author on April 18, 2012.

12
Arnold, unpublished autobiography.

13
Pandora in a letter to the author on August 15, 2010.

14
Chris Royer in a telephone conversation with the author on October 7, 2013.

15
Ibid.

16
Lord Moyne in a conversation with the author on December 17, 2014 in London.

17
Susi Wyss in a conversation with the author on October 25, 2013 in Paris (translated from the German).

everybody was really thinking about big cocks and he exposed that, too. When people came to see him at the Factory, like foreign journalists or art dealers, he would say quite blandly, 'Check him out, see how big his cock is,' and these people would be horrified."[1] Warhol loved talking about the male sex organ with his superstar Viva: "Actually, what Andy really liked to talk about was men's penises. I would say 20 per cent of his conversation with me was about penis size."[2] As Viva remarked on another occasion, there was also a reason: "Andy would try to pick out men for me. He'd say, 'Now go with this one, go with that one.' All these men in whom I had no interest whatsoever. He was always coming up with these guys I think he was interested in. He would try to get *me* to go off with them. He'd say 'Big cock, big dick. He's got a big cock, go with him.'"[3]

In the 1950s, Warhol started to draw young men. He was extremely successful in getting attractive young men to strip for him under the pretext of creating a book of "cock" drawings.[4] Warhol created a large series of body studies. Many of these works show penises.[5] In the late 1970s he started a comprehensive documentation of male genitalia with his Polaroid camera. Walter Steding, who was his assistant at that time, later remarked about the artist's interest in penis size: "Someone came by saying they had a really big dick. Andy said, 'Well, let's take a picture of it' ...."[6] Steding had to put the photos in a box, which he labeled "Sex Parts."[7] Warhol produced a whole series of Polaroids showing not only (erect) penises but also men engaging in sexual activities. Halston's boyfriend, the artist and window dresser Victor Hugo, recruited the young men from gay bath houses, bars, and the streets.[8] Ronnie Cutrone later stated that "hundreds of photo sessions" had been held at the Factory resulting in "hundreds and hundreds and hundreds of photographs. The ones that actually got done were mostly cocks and asses and things."[9] He recalled, "The choreography was basically strip and make yourself comfortable. Andy was a very shy, coy voyeur. He was like, 'Oh, oh, oh, that's so great. Oh, what can it do? Oh, what a big one. Boy, I wonder how it would look stuck in there?'"[10] Warhol selected several of the least openly sexual shots from his comprehensive collection of Polaroids as templates for his series of *Torso* paintings created in 1977. He liked to refer to the works as "landscapes."[11]

Many contemporary witnesses report that Dalí was also obsessed with male sex organs. Constance Webb, who posed for him in the 1940s, writes the following in her memoirs:

One morning Dalí invited me into his bedroom to see some more artwork. He walked over to a low, long chest of drawers in his bedroom and pointed dramatically at the drawings. There were about a dozen, all of penises. Dalí's mastery of his craft enabled him to make a drop of water look so real that one wanted to touch it to see if it was wet. The penises, carefully drawn in ink, represented every stage of activity from flaccid to vigorously erect. And they were as realistic as the drops of water he painted.[12]

Like Warhol, Dalí, too, was curious about penises in real life—especially large ones. Furthermore, he also liked to play matchmaker. The artist and moviemaker Steven Arnold reports in his autobiography: "He tried to fix me

1
Bockris 1989, p. 195.

2
In Brown 1996, p. 37.

3
In Stein/Plimpton 1982, p. 226.

4
Bourdon 1989, pp. 55f.

5
A funny work shows a red-colored erect penis with pinks hearts on it. Ill. in Francis/Koepplin 1999, cat. 82. More drawings in Cheim 1995, cat. 1ff.

6
In Bockris 1989, p. 418.

7
Ibid. Warhol produced a portfolio of prints entitled *Sex Parts* showing two men engaged in sexual activities. See Feldman/Schellmann 2003, II.172-177.

8
Cutrone in O'Connor/Liu 1996, p. 68, and in Smith 1986, p. 281.

9
In ibid. Ill. in Heymer/Garnatz 2003, cat. 180ff.

10
In O'Connor/Liu 1996, p. 68. Victor Hugo later remarked, "Andy was jerkin' off in the bathroom between taking the pictures." Quoted according to Bockris 1989, p. 418.

11
Bourdon 1989, p. 361; Colacello 1990, p. 337.

12
Webb 2003, p. 98.

up with a handsome bullfighter from Spain, whom he said had enormous genitalia … ."[13] Dalí's entourage included the Italian prince and occasional actor Alessandro "Dado" Ruspoli, who is said to have been the inspiration for Federico Fellini's famous film *La Dolce Vita*. Ruspoli reputedly had a large penis,[14] which Dalí did not hesitate to boast about to others.[15] When introducing Ruspoli to Carlos Lozano, another member of his entourage, the artist allegedly proudly remarked, "The Prince has the largest limousine ever. The biggest *polla* in history."[16] The term "limousine" was part of Dalí's special secret code.[17] Amanda Lear cites the artist as follows: "You know that members of the Court have their own vocabulary for describing certain things. Thus, instead of saying 'cock,' which is too vulgar, we talk about the 'limousine,' which is much more elegant; and instead of 'making love' we talk about the 'sewing machine,' because of the up and down jerking, just like a sewing machine."[18]

Transvestites and preoperative transsexuals were the *ne plus ultra* for Dalí.[19] The French flacon designer Pierre Dinand, who often accompanied the artist in the 1970s together with the Italian-American perfume executive Carlo Bilotti, recalls:

We were invited one evening for dinner at the cabaret L'Ange Bleu, where a splendid woman would make a musical striptease, at the end the creature would take everything off, and surprise it was not a woman but a man with an enormous dick. Dalí was very excited and immediately said to Carlo 'I want this creature to come to my room for a painting,' but Carlo didn't want to give Dalí's room number, instead he gave my room number without telling me.

The following evening, I had this tall transvestite knocking on my door to see Dalí. I took him to Dalí's room, and I did not stay further.[20]

Dalí's fascination with large male genitalia may have stemmed from the fact that he himself, according to Carlos Lozano, had a complex because of the size of his penis.[21] Elsa Peretti, who started her career as a model and posed for the artist in the 1960s in Port Lligat, recalls: "Dalí once said: 'I have a *titola* like a cigarette.' '*Titola*' is the word for penis in Catalan. … Of course I could never forget that because a cigarette is really small. But it was just between him and me. … To tell a girl that she should not be interested in him because he had a thing of such a small size I think is funny, but in a profound way."[22] Dalí even alluded to his complex himself in an interview for the Spanish *Playboy* in 1979. It came about through the Spanish author José María Carretero, who under the pseudonym El Caballero Audaz, penned semi-pornographic novels, which were sold in large quantities in Spain in the 1920s and 1930s and which Dalí had read in secret at his parents' home.[23] He got to know the author's daughter, Nanita Kalaschnikoff, in New York in 1955 and she became a close friend.[24] In the interview, Dalí commented on her father's literature:

I recall reading a book by El Caballero Audaz, which described how her body made a noise when fucking, as if piercing a watermelon with a fork. And I said to myself, "With one as small as mine it will be absolutely impossible for me to open a watermelon." But later I found out that it was about butt sex. It

---

13 Arnold, unpublished autobiography.

14 Gibson 1997, p. 530.

15 Lear 1985, p. 20.

16 Thurlow 2000, p. 61.

17 Rohwer/ Lehndorff 2011, p. 129.

18 Quoted according to Lear 1985, p. 51.

19 See the chapter **Companions, Courtiers, and Superstars** in Part 3.

20 Pierre Dinand in an e-mail to the author on April 18, 2012.

21 Thurlow 2000, p. 61; Gibson 1997, p. 534.

22 Elsa Peretti in a telephone conversation with the author on October 2, 2015.

23 Gibson 1997, p. 483.

24 Ibid. See the chapter **Companions, Courtiers, and Superstars** in Part 3.

was easier, although one must have a strong erection to be able to penetrate. And my problem is that I have always suffered from premature ejaculation. So merely the thought of it is enough to reach an orgasm.[25]

Illness Phobia

Salvador Dalí and Andy Warhol were both hypochondriacs. For Dalí, it was undoubtedly rooted in his childhood as his father had put a medical encyclopedia on the piano with photos showing the effects of venereal diseases. The artist later reported on how the pictures had horrified him: "My father spoke at length about venereal diseases, and I was terror-stricken. Whenever I went to a brothel after coming to Paris, I always kept a distance of two yards between myself and the prostitute. I thought you could get the clap through the air. Perhaps you'll understand why touching anyone gives me the shivers."[1] In later years, Dalí was also nearly hysterical in dealing with much less harmful illnesses. Pandora recalls that simply having ill people close-by repulsed him. He did not even want to talk about illnesses.[2] Amanda Lear reports from a visit to Dalí and Gala in Cadaqués,

Gala was leaving the following day with her latest companion, a young student from Aix-en-Provence. She was charming and begged me to take good care of Dalí. She was very concerned, however, about the outbreak of scabies in Avignon:

"Are you quite sure you were properly disinfected? You mustn't bring any disease here!"

Dalí had already stepped back several paces, he was so terrified at the merest allusion to germs.

"Don't worry," I assured them. "Anyway, you have enough potions here to protect you against anything."

The year before, when I had scratched myself slightly on the rocks, Rosa [the maid] had opened up their medicine cabinet.

"There is nothing we cannot cure here, except for appendicitis, and perhaps even that, I'm not sure! The Señora stocks up the medicine cabinet each time she comes back from New York."[3]

Gala also had an illness phobia. When she and Dalí spent time in Port Lligat, they employed the services of their personal doctor, Dr. Manuel Vergara, who had moved to Cadaqués in 1960. They ultimately agreed on an annual flat rate of 1,000 pesetas, which was a very small sum. The doctor was given no additional remuneration, such as a drawing or a small painting. He received only an illustrated dedication in a book. Dr. Vergara reported that Dalí and Gala expected him to be on call around the clock and that they made use of this. They called even for a harmless cold.[4] The American artist Howard R. Carr, who came to Cadaqués in 1969 and was part of Dalí's entourage for a number of years, tells of an incident that happened in winter 1972/73 in New York. Together with Warhol's employee Bob Colacello and Chris Murray, who had also already met Dalí in Cadaqués,[5] he went to visit the Spaniard at the St. Regis, "That was when Bob Colacello just about first met Dalí … . Chris said 'You know, Howard, that's a foot note in art history that from taking Bob

---

25
In Calvo Serraller 2006, pp. 1534f. (translated from the Spanish).

1
In Bosquet 1969, pp. 71f. See also the chapter **Sterile Love and Voyeurism** in this part.

2
Pandora in a conversation with the author on November 21, 2011 in Mariposa, California.

3
Lear 1985, pp. 92f.

4
Gibson 1997, p. 511.

5
Howard R. Carr, Chris Murray, and his wife Kim, were a musical trio; they played together in Washington for a few years and
+

up there, Dalí and Warhol had some meetings.' ... Gala was there with Dalí in New York at the St. Regis. And I had to use the toilet and so I asked, 'May I use the bathroom facilities?' and she was very unhappy about that."[6] Chris Murray, who opened the Govinda Gallery in 1975 in Washington and regularly exhibited Warhol there, adds,

I did invite Bob to come visit Dalí with me and Howard at the St. Regis Hotel where he lived in New York. I introduced Bob to Dalí that evening .... I do know that introduction that evening led to Bob getting Andy and Dalí together again .... Dalí and Andy had previously met. I think Dalí ended up editing an issue of Interview *as a result of that evening. Gala was there ... it was the first time I had met her. She had an imperious presence. ... I'll never forget when Howard asked to use the bathroom. Dalí said of course yes, but Gala turned to Howard and said: "What! ... You want to give me your VD?" That was an intense reaction to someone simply wanting to use her bathroom, especially a beautiful young gentleman like Howard.*[7]

Interestingly, Warhol includes a very similar anecdote in his book *Andy Warhol's Exposures*, however, he attributes it to the French author and photographer François-Marie Banier, who supposedly visited the Dalís in their suite at the St. Regis with Warhol and his entourage.[8] As Warhol always propagated a "just make it up" philosophy, it is quite possible that the people involved were swapped about in *Exposures*, which was written by Bob Colacello. Horst Weber von Beeren, who worked in the studio of Warhol's printer Rupert Jasen Smith and assisted Dalí in the winter of 1979 with the realization of a stereoscopic painting, also reports a very similar situation:

Dalí was wearing a floor-length jaguar fur coat and these very thick glasses, like Coca-Cola-bottoms. His language was intelligible somehow, heavily French-accented English. I felt he was from a different era and had long outlived the moment of the zeitgeist. I thought he and Gala were senile and hard of hearing. They were in a different galaxy. I was not allowed to use the bathroom in the suite where they were staying, but had to run down to the public toilet in the basement, racing past them, while they were waiting on a little banquette for the sledge to arrive for their last sledge ride though a snowy Central Park. Gala had a paranoid fear of germs.[9]

Gala's hypochondria can undoubtedly be explained by the fact that she had suffered poor health ever since childhood and had "something wrong with her neck glands." Consequently, she spent a large portion of her childhood in Moscow sanatoria.[10] When Gala was suffering from a lung infection and doctors feared she might contract tuberculosis, they recommended a visit to the Clavadel Sanatorium in Davos, Switzerland. She met and fell in love with the French poet Paul Éluard during her stay there from 1912 to 1914.[11] Given that at the time there was no vaccination or promising medical treatment for tuberculosis, Gala's fear of death began when she was young. Although doctors told her that her condition was only in the early stages, the stay in Davos traumatized her.[12]

Andy Warhol's hypochondria can be traced back to his becoming ill with chorea (St. Vitus's Dance) at the age of eight. In his *Philosophy*, published in 1975, he exaggerates, claiming that the attacks coincided with the start of

---

6 Howard R. Carr in a telephone conversation with the author on January 10, 2013.

+ performed for Dalí in the summer of 1972. Murray reports: "Howard played a pair of Moroccan bongos, I played a Kentucky mountain dulcimer, and Kim played bells. ... The music was a mix of far eastern melodies, folk music, and jazz. .... Dalí clearly enjoyed his little hippie/artist trio as we returned virtually every evening during cocktails. Chris Murray in e-mails to the author on November 15, 2012, and October 2, 2013.

7 Chris Murray in e-mails to the author on September 19, 2013 and October 2, 2013. Howard R. Carr relates the key scene as follows: "So they said yes and okay, so I went off and relieved myself. And when we left Chris said 'Oh, you know, Gala said he probably has VD' (laughs)." Howard R. Carr in a telephone conversation with the author on January 10, 2013.

8 Warhol/Colacello 1979, p. 128.

9 Horst Weber von Beeren in a conversation with the author on September 16, 2011 in Düsseldorf.

10 McGirk 1989, pp. 12, 14f.

11 Gibson 1997, p. 221.

12 Bona 1995, p. 20; Lacroix in *Dalí Lacroix Gala*, p. 116. See also the chapter **Muse and Mother** in Part 3.

his summer vacation when he was eight, nine, and ten.[13] Valerie Solanas's attempt to murder him in June 1968, which left him fighting for his life, had even greater repercussions. Warhol was subsequently hospitalized for nearly two and a half months.[14] In March 1969 he had to have a follow-up operation to remove bullet splinters that had been overlooked during the first operation. Since the doctors failed to sew his stomach muscles back together again properly, he had to wear a supporting brace for the rest of his life so that his stomach would not inflate like a balloon when he ate. In answer to the question of whether he was in pain, Warhol once said, "It slows you up some. I can't do the things I want to do, and I'm so scarred I look like a Dior dress. It's sort of awful, looking into the mirror and seeing all the scars. But it doesn't look that bad. The scars look pretty in a funny way. It's just that they are a reminder that I'm still sick and I don't know if I will ever be well again."[15] For Warhol, the scars left by the operations were also a great mental burden. His biographer Victor Bockris presumes that Warhol developed a phobia of hospitals due to the slip-up during the second operation and quotes the artist as saying, "I never want to go in again because I'll never come out alive."[16]

This illness phobia is often an issue in Warhol's diaries. Pat Hackett writes in the introduction that Warhol was particularly frightened of getting cancer. Every time he had a headache, he suspected a brain tumor. However, when he had genuine health concerns he hardly said a word about it.[17] The artist reports in his diaries in August 1983:

I just stepped in dog shit. In my hall. And I'm usually wearing slippers, but this time I wasn't. And usually you can smell it a mile away, but it just didn't smell, so I just finished cleaning it up. And I'm all flea-bitten. When you know there's fleas, you keep feeling them all the time whether they're there or not. So I just took a shower to get the shit off my foot and now I'm thinking what disease I can pick up from the whole episode.[18]

On May 22, 1984, his diary entry reads, "Then in the afternoon I went to Doc Cox's (cab $7) and I protested over the thermometer that they used, because it just sits there in water and everybody uses it; it's not right."[19] When reading this, it is evident that Warhol was a hypochondriac. Pat Hackett says, "Mentally he was hypochondriac. I mean it is not like he took a million medicines, but he was always worried about his health. And his other big fear was getting arrested for something and being put in jail. ... Those two things scared him most—getting cancer or being arrested."[20] In order to avoid illness, Warhol led a very health-conscious life, as Christopher Makos, the photographer and friend of the artist, states:

Andy had a masseur who got him interested in eating raw garlic, which, besides being a health fad, also reminded him of his Czechoslovakian ancestors, who used garlic as a cure for everything. The smell got pretty unbearable at times, and if it hadn't been for the heavy perfumes he wore, even Andy couldn't have got away with it. Then he got hooked on crystals and he wore them, carried them and put them in the pot when he boiled water for his herbal teas. He was searching for spirituality.[21]

Warhol's faith in the power of crystals can be attributed to the influence of his partner Jon Gould. He regularly visited two "crystal doctors" and spent

13
Warhol 1975,
Philosophy,
p. 21

14
See the chapter
**Experience
of Death**
in this part.

15
Quoted
according to
Bockris 1989,
p. 311.

16
Quoted
according to
ibid., p. 351.

17
Hackett 1989,
p. xviii.

18
Ibid., p. 524,
August 29, 1983.

19
Hackett 1989,
p. 576.

20
Pat Hackett in a
conversation
with the author
on December 4,
2012 in New York.

21
Makos 1988,
pp. 53f.

large sums on crystals.[22] When his gall bladder problems became worse, however, he stopped believing in their healing power.[23]

Warhol's health program also included regular telephone calls with his close friend and confidante Brigid Berlin. Pat Hackett explains, "He had a wide circle of friends of different types, types of people who helped him in different ways. ... A lot of people cared very much for Andy."[24] Warhol could talk to Berlin about his fears. In the documentary *Pie in the Sky*, which Vincent and Shelly Fremont made about Berlin's life, she recalls her friend as follows: "He used to call me up in the morning. He always talked about his health with me. I think I was the health person. There were other people he used for different topics. And he'd say all of a sudden out of the clear blue, 'Bridge, my balls are sore.' 'Oh God, Andy, come on, I don't know anything about sore balls.'"[25]

Warhol was diagnosed with a gall bladder problem as early as 1973. In the years that followed he did not experience any great discomfort. He first felt a stabbing pain in the stomach region in early February 1987. Since he was subjected to pain repeatedly over the next several weeks, he had an ultrasound scan done by his internist Dr. Cox, which revealed that his gall bladder was seriously inflamed and filled with liquid. An operation was unavoidable.[26] Brigid Berlin encouraged Warhol repeatedly to go ahead with the operation; she was amazed that her friend was able to endure the severe pain for so long. She herself had already had her gall bladder removed in 1979 and says that she had to show him her very inconspicuous scar "a million times."[27] "I went to the hospital, I had my gall bladder out and two days later I went over to the Factory. Andy couldn't believe that I'd had it out. I said: 'Andy, I had to. You've been having these gall bladder attacks. I've told you for so long, just get the thing out.' And he was scared to death because he'd already been shot and died and was panicked. And that is why he died, his damned gall bladder."[28] Benjamin Liu, Warhol's assistant and bodyguard in the 1980s, reports that before his operation the artist would panic when near a hospital, "Whenever we would pass a hospital, he would cover his eyes or block his view. And he'd get mad at me if we passed the Columbus-Mother Cabrini Hospital."[29] However, when the pain became unbearable, Warhol finally declared that he was ready to undergo the gall bladder operation. Pat Hackett writes, "He told me he had seen Dr. Cox and that he was going to 'the place' to have 'it' done (Andy's fear of hospitals and operations was so great that he couldn't bring himself to say these specific words) because 'they told me I'll die if I don't.' He said he would resume doing the Diary after 'it' was over, that he would call me from 'the place.'"[30] On February 20, 1987, Warhol was admitted to the New York Hospital as an "ambulatory emergency patient." Hackett later learned from the hospital staff member who registered Warhol's personal details that in her whole working life, Warhol was the only patient who knew the numbers of his Blue Cross card and his health insurance by heart.[31] Warhol chose to enter the hospital under the pseudonym Bob Robert and forbade all visits. Despite all the tension, he took the opportunity to enquire whether any big stars were currently at the hospital, upon which he was told, "You're the biggest."[32] Before his stay at the hospital, Warhol had

22
Bourdon 1989,
p. 390.

23
Vincent Fremont
in a conversation
with the author
on June 28, 2012
in New York.

24
Pat Hackett in a
conversation
with the author
on December 4,
2012 in New York.

25
Brigid Berlin
in the documentary *Pie in the Sky: The Brigid Berlin Story*.

26
Bourdon 1989,
p. 407.

27
Colacello 1990,
p. 489.

28
Brigid Berlin in a
conversation
with the author
on December 4,
2012 in New York.

29
Quoted
according to
Colacello 1990,
p. 489.

30
Hackett 1989,
pp. 806f.,
February 17, 1987.

31
Ibid., p. 807.

32
Bourdon 1989,
pp. 407f.

told all the doctors that he would not make it. When they tried to reassure him, he just kept insisting that he would never make it out of the hospital. [33]

Warhol was operated on, on the morning of February 21, 1987. There were no complications. His condition was stable and he was taken to his private room in the afternoon. The artist appeared well; he watched TV and made telephone calls. However, during the night his health deteriorated rapidly. Exactly what happened is not known. It is not documented whether the doctors and nurses on duty monitored the patient regularly and checked his readings; or if the private nurse, who was hired based on a recommendation by Warhol's personal doctor, was actually present. At 5:45 a.m. she noticed that Warhol had cyanosis. She alerted the ward nurse who then called for help. Resuscitation attempts failed and they were not able to insert an air tube into Warhol's airway. Rigor mortis had already set in. At 6:31 a.m. Andy Warhol was declared dead. It is assumed that the artist suffered a heart attack or a cardiac arrest during his sleep. [34]

At this time, Dalí was also already under the shadow of death and knew that his time had come. His dire health also meant that he could scarcely communicate with the outside world; he was dependent on the assistance of his close friend and confidant Antoni Pitxot. Nevertheless, he followed what was happening in the world. As Pitxot told the author, Dalí learned of Warhol's death through the media. [35] Dalí died on January 23, 1989. He outlived Andy Warhol by one year, eleven months, and a day.

33
Bockris 1989,
p. 487.

34
Bourdon 1989,
p. 409; Bockris
1989, p. 488.

35
Antoni Pitxot in a
letter to the
author on August
30, 2012.

Andy Warhol's public image includes the many superstars who belonged to his Factory, and also numerous staff and assistants. Less well known is that Salvador Dalí also employed several assistants in addition to his secretaries. For both artists, however, there was a woman who was by far the most important figure. Dalí often used pathetic phrasing to emphasize his wife Gala's special significance in his life. In *The Unspeakable Confessions* he writes, "Gala heard me. She adopted me. I became her newborn baby, her child, her son, her lover—the man to make love to—she opened heaven to me and we both sat down on its clouds, far from the world. She took unto herself the power to be my protectress, my divine mother, my queen."[1] Andy Warhol's mother, Julia Warhola, played a similarly important role in her son's life.

The question of whether the two artists mutually inspired one another with regards to their entourage is difficult to answer. On February 8, 1967, the *New York Post* reported, "Salvador Dalí has become the East Side Andy Warhol, traveling with a pack that includes at least three bizarre looking girls and one other man."[2] A decade later, *Andy Warhol's Exposures* stated, "Dalí surrounds himself with people who change their real names to brand names, just like my superstars in the sixties."[3] Was it Warhol who showed Dalí how to gather an entourage around him, or the other way around? Ultra Violet, who entered Dalí's circles in 1960 and became a Warhol superstar five years later, and knew both artists well, said at "The Dalí Renaissance" symposium at the Philadelphia Museum of Art in 2005, "Warhol copied everything from Dalí, meaning an entourage. Of course, he had a different entourage, the Factory."[4]

The following chapters provide a more detailed look at the two artists' entourages. Presented first are portraits of Gala Dalí and Julia Warhola, followed by introductions to other people who were close to Dalí or Warhol. Some of the latter were even a part of both artists' circles. Finally, insight is provided on their assistants, employees, secretaries, and managers, whose significance with regard to the work and impact of Dalí and Warhol is also not to be underestimated.

Muse and Mother

In *Andy Warhol's Exposures*, published in 1979, Warhol dedicates a chapter specifically to his fellow artist Dalí. It is noticeable that it contains more about Gala than about Dalí, stating:

The best and worst thing about Dalí is his wife Gala. She's the most beautiful, the most fascinating, the most imaginative wife an artist like Dalí could have. But on the other hand she's tough as nails, totally impossible, and scares me to death.

She's the only person I know, besides Ethel Merman, who absolutely refuses to let me take her picture, let alone tape-record her. ...

Gala always calls herself "Gala" and Dalí always calls himself "Dalí." They never say "I." So they use their names a lot. In fact, "Gala" is almost the only word Gala ever uses because she's the strong silent type. ...

1
Dalí 1976, p. 91.

2
Lilly 1967.

3
Warhol/Colacello 1979, p. 129.

4
In "Reminiscences of Dalí: A Conversation with Amanda Lear and Ultra Violet," moderated by Dawn Ades, in Taylor 2008, p. 212.

3

Gala is not too tall, but she walks erectly. She has strong handsome features and her thick black hair is rolled back in a thirties style. She's pushing ninety but looks like Greta Garbo in her prime.[1]

It is mentioned several times in the text that Warhol wanted to paint a portrait of Gala, but this was in vain. Bob Colacello, who authored *Andy Warhol's Exposures*, explains, "Andy wanted to trade portraits, the idea being that he would do the portrait of Gala and Dalí would do his portrait. And Gala would always say 'Dalí no do this. You a photographer, Dalí a painter. No trade oil painting for photograph.' And Andy would say, 'I hate her. I hate her.' After we laughed. ... Gala was very insulting to Andy, but she was insulting to everyone. That was her way of communicating."[2]

Gala, ten years older than Dalí, was born on August 26, 1894 as Elena Ivanovna Diakonova in Kazan, Russia. After the death of her father, her mother Antonia married the wealthy Moscow lawyer Dimitry Ilyitsch Gomberg. Gala grew up in Moscow with her two elder brothers Vadim and Nicolai and her younger sister Lidia. She had a good relationship with her stepfather, who favored her over her siblings.[3] She even took his name and called herself Elena Dimitrijevna Diakonova.[4] Furthermore, she apparently introduced herself as "Gala" from a very young age.[5] During her younger years Gala had a weak constitution.[6] A stay at the Clavadel sanatorium in Davos was recommended when she was diagnosed with tuberculosis. During this time, between the end of 1912 and April 1914, she met the seventeen-year-old Eugène Émile Paul Grindel, who later became a significant poet by the name of Paul Éluard. Shortly before the outbreak of World War I, in April 1914, Gala and Paul returned to their families. They already considered themselves to be engaged.[7] During the period that followed they exchanged letters, which continued until Paul Éluard's death in 1952.[8] In December 1914, Éluard was called up for military service. Gala suffered from constant worry about him and in August 1916 she traveled to join his family in Paris. On February 21, 1917, the couple married in the French capital during one of Éluard's furloughs from the front. Their daughter Cécile was born in May 1918. Gala knew early on that she was not made for the role of housewife and mother and soon entrusted her daughter to her mother-in-law's care. Cécile was only with her parents on special occasions and during the holidays.[9] After the war Éluard stumbled upon André Breton's circle in Paris. Breton had founded the Dadaist journal *Littérature* in March 1919 with Philippe Soupault and Louis Aragon. Éluard joined them, so Gala also gained access to the Dadaists' get-togethers and later the surrealists. Paul Éluard soon became enthusiastic about the works of Max Ernst, whom he had met in 1921 in the "Salon Dada."[10] At the beginning of November of the same year, he and Gala paid a visit to the painter and his wife Louise Straus in Cologne. This meeting marked the start of a love triangle. A male friendship developed between Éluard and Ernst, and Gala also felt drawn towards the German painter. In 1922 Max Ernst left his wife and moved in with the Éluards in Saint-Brice-sous-Forêt, a suburb of Paris, and later into their house in Eaubonne. However, the relationship with Gala and Ernst became an increasing burden for Paul Éluard. In 1924 he set off precipitately on a

1
Warhol/Colacello 1979, pp. 127f.

2
Bob Colacello in a telephone conversation with the author on September 22, 2010.

3
Bona 1995, p. 16; McGirk 1989, p. 13.

4
Bona 1995, p. 15.

5
Ibid., p. 18. Gateau writes that she had been called "Gala" since 1908. Cf. Gateau 1994, p. 32. It is said that it was Éluard who gave her the name, according to Carrière in Éluard 1989, p. vii.

6
See the chapter **Illness Phobia** in Part 2.

7
Gateau 1994, p. 33.

8
Paul Éluard's letters to Gala were published in English in 1989. Cf. Éluard 1989, pp. 3ff.

9
Gateau remarks that the grandmother supported Cécile financially. Cf. Gateau 1994, p. 162.

10
In detail ibid., pp. 72ff.

journey to Oceania. Ernst and Gala followed him and they aired their differences. Afterwards the painter stayed on for a while in Indochina, while the Éluards journeyed back.[11]

At the end of July 1929 René Magritte and his wife Georgette, the gallery owner Camille Goemans and his girlfriend Yvonne Bernard, along with Luis Buñuel, traveled to Cadaqués. A little while later Paul Éluard, Gala, and Cécile also arrived there. As Gala and Paul led a liberal marriage and allowed each other to have love affairs, it was to become their second fateful encounter with a young painter, after Max Ernst. Gala remarked later, "Éluard kept telling me about his handsome Dalí. I felt he was almost pushing me into his arms before I even saw him."[12] Dalí himself described the encounter in detail. One can only speculate about the degree of truth in his description of the courtship.[13] In his *Secret Life* he maintains that all he could think about thereafter was Gala.[14] Luis Buñuel was of the opinion that Dalí appeared transformed: "It was a complete metamorphosis. All he could talk about was Gala; he echoed every word she uttered."[15]

The encounter with Gala was not only a private, but also a professional turning point for Dalí. Following from this, his talent soon led to success. In February 1977, he admitted in an interview for the Spanish magazine *Guadalimar*, "It's reality. She transformed me. Without Gala, Dalí would be as much of a genius as he is, but he would be living in a hovel full of lice and candle drippings. He would be a disaster, half mad, half an illuminate. It was she who brought me out, introduced me to a life of triumph."[16] Dalí was grateful to Gala for her attention and eternalized her in many paintings. As early as the 1930s, he started signing many of his paintings with "Gala Salvador Dalí," remarking, "In signing my paintings Gala-Dalí, all I did was to give a name to an existential truth, since without my twin Gala I would no longer exist."[17]

Dalí and Gala married on January 30, 1934, in Paris. One of the witnesses was Yves Tanguy.[18] Six years after the death of Éluard, the couple also decided to have a church wedding. The ceremony took place on August 8, 1958, without photographers at the Sanctuary dels Àngels in the municipal district of Sant Martí Vell near Girona. Dalí remarked later that the religious ceremony left a deep impression on him and that he wanted to marry Gala again according to Coptic rituals, although this was never realized.[19] In the spring of 1966 another opportunity presented itself to walk down the aisle.[20] The Italian model Benedetta Barzini, who was part of the Dalí and Warhol circles in the 1960s, stepped into the role of bride. Barzini recalls the unusual occasion:

One day he told me that I resembled Gala when he first met her and asked me if he could re-live his wedding with her. He gave me a Gala dress and in the hotel we had this "wedding"—just the three of us—his secretary was standing behind with an ocelot. ...

Dalí only wanted me to resemble as much as possible his memory of the celebration (the dress, the hair, no make-up) but the wedding cake is really out of context if you consider the look of the "bride" and the period ... Gala wasn't there—she was never present in Dalí's "happenings" or excursions or outings. She seemed totally uninterested in the "public" Dalí.[21]

---

11 In detail ibid., pp. 88ff.

12 Gala quoted according to McGirk 1989, pp. 1f.

13 Cf. Dalí 1942, pp. 226ff.; Dalí 1976, pp. 88ff.

14 Dalí 1942, p. 230.

15 Buñuel 1984, p. 96.

16 In Gómez de la Serna 1988, p. 223.

17 Dalí 1976, p. 243.

18 Gibson 1997, p. 323.

19 In Bosquet 1969, pp. 93f.

20 Benedetta Barzini in an e-mail to the author on June 16, 2012.

21 Benedetta Barzini in e-mails to the author on May 23, 2011 and May 24, 2011.

The star astrologer Elizabeth Teissier, who says she advised the French president François Mitterand and the Spanish king Juan Carlos I, among others, has a similar view on this. She was also a model when she met Dalí and Gala in the 1960s:

Dalí was Taurus, ascendant Pisces, and Gala was Virgo. From an astrological point of view that is a perfect match. They were really made for each other and he could not do or decide anything without her. ... But she was very possessive. ... She watched over everything with her dark eyes, but she did leave him alone with his friends and his court. She didn't seem very interested. It is paradoxical, she was possessive, but at the same time independent.[22]

Although Dalí and Gala appeared to the outside world as the perfect couple, their private life was a different story. Dalí, the "Great Masturbator," preferred "sterile sexuality."[23] Gala, on the other hand, wanted to enjoy her sexuality to the full and had many lovers, which Dalí tolerated. Edward James, who was close to them both around 1936, recorded later: "As for Dalí's sex life with his wife, far from being jealous of her sexual infidelities, he actually facilitated them; one day he confessed to me: *'Je laisse Gala prendre des amants quand elle veut. Actuellement, je l'encourage et je l'aide, parce que cela m'excite.'*"[24] Gala's love affairs were hardly cheap. It is reported that her running expenses for a "gigolo" amounted to $10,000.[25] The Italian collector Mara Albaretto confirms that "Gala's boys cost a fortune." A significant proportion of the money that she and her husband gave Gala for works by Dalí is said to have gone towards her lovers.[26] Susi Wyss, acquainted with Dalí from 1964 on, reports:

Gala liked me because I made her laugh and because I knew fortune tellers. I also consulted an oracle for her and was never wrong. ... Gala wanted to know sometimes whether she would get a certain boy—and most of the time she did. They were all boys who also wanted money. They were paid—Captain Moore always arranged it. ... But she herself also gave the boys money. ... Dalí wanted to make his wife happy, so I had to bring all the pretty boys. Some didn't stay with Gala, because I didn't ask them straight away "Could you have it off with Gala?" But if it happened—I experienced it two or three times with little slave types—then they got something.[27]

As a rule the young men were in their mid-twenties. Gala mothered her lovers, but also displayed "girlish coquetry" towards them, in order to please them.[28] She also loved flirting. Horst Weber von Beeren, who worked for Warhol's printer Rupert Jasen Smith for many years and assisted Dalí in 1979, remembers a New Year's dinner together with Gala, Dalí, and his entourage at the St. Regis Hotel in New York: "Gala was sitting across from me, domed by her wig with a big black 'Minnie Mouse'-bow. She pulled the soft part of the bread out of the Baguette, rolled it into little balls and threw them at me. Unfortunately, she was already so weakened by age that they landed halfway on the table."[29] The jewelry designer Lee Brooks from San Francisco, who presented his and his partner Alex Maté's joint creations at the opening of the Teatre-Museu Dalí in Figueres, was astounded when Gala chose him as her companion for the evening by announcing, "You are my date." "She starts out the conversation by saying, 'Would you like a polite conversation or an

22
Dr. Elizabeth Teissier-Hynek in a telephone conversation with the author on October 21, 2015. (translated from the German).

23
See the chapter **Sterile Love and Voyeurism** in Part 2.

24
Quoted according to Etherington-Smith 1993, p. 218.

25
McGirk 1989, p. 130.

26
Gibson 1997, p. 509.

27
Susi Wyss in a conversation with the author on October 25, 2013 in Paris (translated from the German).

28
Bona 1995, p. 412.

29
Horst Weber von Beeren in a telephone conversation with the author on June 22, 2011.

30
Lee Brooks in a
conversation
with the author
on November 13,
2011 in
San Francisco.

31
Pierre Dinand in
e-mails to the
author on April
18, 2012 and
April 20, 2012.

32
William Rothlein
in telephone
conversations
with the author
on October 23,
2011 and
February 3, 2015.

33
Ibid.

34
Rohwer/Lehndorff
2011, pp. 127f.

35
Wynn Chamber-
lain in a telephone
conversation with
the author on
August 26, 2011.

interesting conversation?' And I said 'Oh, interesting.' She says 'What do you do in bed?'"[30] The flacon designer Pierre Dinand reports that Gala made even more blatant advances towards him: "At dinner at La Grenouille, I was sitting next to Gala and she kept touching my leg and more all dinner, telling me to come to her room later, with the obvious approbation of her husband. ... Gala was always chasing me. She had a strong Russian accent, always saying 'Karacho' for OK. ... She was making passes at every man nearby, in front of Dalí, even at eighty years old."[31]

At first glance, Gala's affairs and flirting may have appeared superficial. However, two cases are known in which Gala was very much in love. Furthermore, this affection was requited. In 1964 in New York she met the twenty-one-year-old William Rothlein, who lived in the loft belonging to the painter, moviemaker, and author Wynn Chamberlain. He had become acquainted with Warhol through Chamberlain the year before. Rothlein reports that Warhol had asked him to feature in his movies but he turned him down. He considered the artist's productions too amateurish at the time; he was interested in taking part in mainstream productions.[32] The opportunity to do so soon presented itself through Dalí. Rothlein recalls that he saw the Spaniard for the first time at The Blue Angel in New York. He was there with a couple of friends. Among them was Nico, who was then a successful model and shortly afterwards gained fame as a Warhol superstar and singer.

And Dalí saw her and came over to the table that I was at with her and some other people and said hello and then he walked on. ... The actual meeting with him was in March of 1964. I was out for the evening with a couple of friends of mine. ... Wynn, who was a painter, and Ruth Kligman, who was a friend of his. I met her through him. She was an artist herself. And we were going to see a movie at the Apollo Theater on Forty-Second Street. It was a film with Sophia Loren—Two Nights with Cleopatra—I remember that. We arrived and got out of the cab. Dalí and his wife Gala were buying tickets and I was standing there right behind them. And that's how I met them. They just looked at me and Dalí said "Bonjour" and "I would like to paint you" and I said "Yes." ... Gala asked me if I would give her my telephone number so that she could call me and I said "Yes, of course."[33]

Vera von Lehndorff, better known as Veruschka, who was in a relationship with William Rothlein at the time, reports that Dalí was fascinated by him straight away. Because they resembled each other, he was of the opinion that Rothlein was his reincarnation and called him "Adil," an anagram of Dalí. Rothlein received money and was sent to drama school. He played Dalí very well, according to von Lehndorff; and Gala, who was after him, was in seventh heaven. From now on the young version of Dalí sat to her left, and the original to her right.[34] Wynn Chamberlain also remembered that Rothlein's similarity to the young Dalí was astounding and attracted the attention of the painter and his muse. "Gala said 'Oh my God, this is ... Dalí! Dalí!' and she said 'Ah, Mr. Zanuck will love you.' ... She just fell madly in love with Adil. They were staying at the St. Regis and she used to send this limousine down to get him. He was so scared of her that he would go into the bathroom if he saw the limousine down below and take a razor and slash his face."[35] Gala's remark that the Hollywood producer Daryl F. Zanuck would love Rothlein indicates that already at this point in time there was the idea of shooting a movie about Dalí's life. This project is also mentioned in Charlton Lake's book *In Quest of Dalí*. Lake reports here of a discussion that Dalí held with two men in which Rothlein was mentioned: "For the purpose of your film there is—one much better than I. ... One of the handsomest boys I've ever seen. Everyone thinks so. Even Fellini. ... We'll have this boy play me as a young man. ... Then I'll come in later, wearing a wig, to play myself now. That way you get two Dalís for the price of one. But first I want to ask you one question: Do you have plenty of money? These things always cost much more than one plans on."[36] The movie was not realized.

In summer 1964 William Rothlein traveled to Spain with Dalí and Gala. The young actor soon settled in Port Lligat. He posed as a model for Dalí.[37] According to his own account, he soon saw the painter as a kind of father figure.[38] Meanwhile Gala traveled with him to Italy in the fall. In Verona she had Rothlein promise eternal love at the grave of Romeo and Juliet—a vow she regularly had her lovers make.[39] After that they visited the Italian doctor couple Mara and Giuseppe Albaretto in Turin. Gala confided her feelings for William to Mara Albaretto,[40] that she loved him like nobody else since Éluard—not even Dalí.[41] Looking back, Rothlein provides a sensitive insight into his relationship to Dalí's muse:

Gala and I became close—closer than old summer friends. ... She was very maternal. She was very gentle with me and very tender, very nice, very agreeable all the time. ... We liked each other. ... I was twenty-one years old and attracted to girls. ... Gala was jealous of women around me ... with me she became possessive and that was difficult. ...

As the months went on we finally got away from Spain, Gala and I alone. We traveled to Italy together. Dalí wanted us to go to Italy to see Federico Fellini. ... Fellini shot a screen test of me then. ... We drove from Spain to Italy and we took six weeks on this trip. And then when we were alone together and that is when we became intimate. ... I felt a lot of guilt because of my relationship with Dalí. ... I was under the impression that Dalí didn't know anything, but of course he knew everything. ... Then of course it got a little bit too much. It got out of hand and then he became very nervous about it. ... And I felt the only way that I could continue this situation and make something good come from it was to get that out of the way—the sexuality. And the only way to get that out of the way was to just get it over with. And then of course the relationship ended.[42]

Rothlein returned to the United States, married shortly afterwards and pursued his acting career. Although he saw Dalí and Gala again in Spain and New York, the relationship was not the same as before: "Once my relationship with Gala was pretty much over my relationship with Dalí ended as well. She ran interference between us. She was the one who really was in control. ... She liked to have power over people. I saw it in her dealings with various people that were around Dalí. She had control all the time of the situation and kept people away from him very often."[43]

The relationship between the painter and his muse was strained by the liaison with William Rothlein.[44] In 1971 Gala withdrew to the Castle of

36
In Lake 1969, p. 223.

37
He posed as a model for Dalí for the figure in the foreground of the painting *Tuna Fishing* (1966–1967). Cf. Gómez de Liaño 2004, p. 153.

38
William Rothlein in a telephone conversation with the author on October 23, 2011.

39
Gibson 1997, p. 509.

40
Ibid.

41
McGirk 1989, p. 129.

42
William Rothlein in telephone conversations with the author on October 23, 2011 and February 3, 2015. Photos of Rothlein with a Dalí mustache and with Federico Fellini in Aguer/Mattarella 2012, pp. 53, 253.

43
William Rothlein in telephone conversations with the author on October 23, 2011 and February 3, 2015.

44
Gibson 1997, p. 541.

45
Details of the history of the castle in Pitxot/Playà, 1998 pp. 9ff.

46
Pitxot/Aguer/Puig 2011, pp. 36ff.

47
See the chapter **Mao Marilyn** in Part 4.

Púbol. This was a fourteenth-century castle about eighty kilometers from Cadaqués.[45] After comprehensive restoration work, Dalí started to decorate the property according to his muse's wishes, also creating an impressive ceiling painting for the coat of arms room.[46] He introduced the castle to the public in the special edition of the French *Vogue* issued in December 1971 that he had designed.[47] Here he wrote:

Three months later on the way back to New York, in the middle of the ocean at five o'clock tea time, Gala took my hand and said to me suddenly: "Thank you once again. I accept the Castle of Púbol, but only under one condition: that you will only come and visit me at the castle upon written invitation." This condition, which was especially flattering to my masochist sensibilities, delighted me, as Gala was becoming the unassailable castle that she had never ceased to be. Intimacy and especially familiarity are detrimental to all passion. Sentimental austerity and distance, as displayed by the neurotic ceremony of courtly love, increase passion.[48]

48
Dalí 1971, pp. 173, 175 (translated from the French).

It was a clever move by Dalí to convey the impression that the love between him and his muse was unbroken. However, the couple had long been going their separate ways. According to Suzanne Guinness, Lady Moyne, who regularly spent the summer in Cadaqués with her family, Gala's move to Púbol was the "split" that Dalí upset most.[49] Her husband Jonathan Guinness, 3rd Baron Moyne, recalls:

49
Lady Moyne in the documentary *Salvador Dalí.*

Gala was astonishing—horrible in a way and marvelous in a way because she was very very bright and very very obstinate. ... She used to take up young men and she tried to take up my son Valentine who was far younger than her. And she said to him, "Viens à mon chateau. J'ai un chateau. Et Dalí ne peut pas venir sans permission écrite." So Valentine didn't go. He said, "No, thank you." We all said, "Now, Valentine that was very unenterprising of you." "All very well for you, Dad!" Valentine said (laughs). [50]

50
Lord Moyne in a conversation with the author on December 17, 2014 in London.

A frequent guest at the Castle of Púbol was the musician Jeff Fenholt, who met the nearly eighty-year-old Gala in 1973. He was to be her last big love. She came to life when Fenholt took her with him to New York rock clubs, as he remembered later: "I took Gala when we were in New York to all the Acid Rock Clubs and it was hilarious. She'd go to these places. She loved my friends—Rock guys—at that time we had long hair and we were skinny. She loved that. She said 'That is life.'"[51] Fenholt also later reported that he felt true love for Gala: "And I even thought, why in the hell, why can't I be born fifty years earlier or Gala born fifty years later or something."[52] As a token of her love, Gala showered Jeff with gifts. Once she showed the American collector A. Reynolds Morse a telegram from her beloved. It said, "Must have $38,000 or will die." Gala asked Morse to take the cash for Fenholt to the United States with him. However, he refused, because it was illegal.[53] Fenholt received not only paintings from Dalí, but also a house on Long Island worth $1.25 million.[54] As Gala's companion, Fenholt enjoyed a special status in the Dalí court. In *Andy Warhol's Exposures* it says: "Gala is always the last one to arrive at dinner. She makes a dramatic entrance on the arm of a teenage boy with long blond hair who played the lead in *Jesus Christ Superstar* somewhere, once. ... When Gala enters the room, Dalí stands up, snaps his

51
Jeff Fenholt in the documentary *Gala.*

52
Ibid.

53
Gibson 1997, p. 551.

54
McGirk 1989, p. 145.

fingers, calls for silence, waves his gold scepter and announces 'Gala! Y Jesús Cristu Superstar!' Everybody claps."[55]

As Dalí was anything other than practically inclined, Gala soon recognized the need to take care of the business and everyday matters. *Look* magazine referred to Dalí maliciously in the June 1947 edition as "one of the most highly paid and publicized painters in the world today," who lets his "petite, hawk-faced Russian wife" manage finances.[56] The magazine *LIFE* wrote about Gala, "She is self-effacing, shrewd and practical. ... She pays the bills, signs the contracts and otherwise acts as a buffer between Dalí and the world of reality."[57] Gala was notorious for unconventional business practices. She apparently used a simple telephone trick at times, accepting a spoken offer by telephone in Spanish pesetas and claiming later that they were talking about dollars.[58] When Dalí's productivity declined in the 1970s, Gala was faced with a new challenge. The art historian Sir John Richardson recalls:

Dalí wasn't doing any work at all, I mean except signing his name on large sheets of paper. Dalí would sign endless sheets of paper. The prices went up for signatures and they could be bought by anybody and you could dump some shit on it, it was still signed Dalí. And people would do it. He wasn't drawing, he wasn't painting. His eye had gone, he couldn't see very well and his hand was shaking. So, the time I knew him, he had really basically stopped painting and drawing. ...

I was briefly his dealer. He had a contract with Knoedler's and the contract included a show every two years. But there was no work being produced. I would say to Dalí "Look, come on, they're having a show, we gotta have something to show—old work or something." And then Gala would give me a huge dig with her very sharp elbows "Dalí need more money!" I said, "Well, we need the paintings." I'd go to Port Lligat and again I'd come back sore from Gala's picking away. And I'll never forget the lunches in Port Lligat, which took place at about five or six o'clock in the evening in this broiling sun, out in the open on the terrace and on a table with masses of gilt plate and candelabra. One really spooky thing I remember about those lunches was that all the candles in the candelabras were lit but the sun was still so intense that you couldn't see the flames—it cancelled out the flames. The only way you could see that the candles were lit was that the wax was dripping by the side of the candles, which was a very Dalí-ish thing. We would have lobsters in chocolate sauce. It was all of a piece. And Gala, who I really took such dislike to, was such a fucking nightmare—always "money, money." Money was all she wanted. And we went through this absurd situation, where, whenever Dalí appeared in New York and we'd go out to dinner or lunch rather, I'd be sitting next to Gala and my ribs would constantly be black and blue from her elbow, trying to get money for nothing, to spend on these boy hustlers she liked. And I would go down to the basement of Knoedler's with Dalí and we would try to find some bits of sculpture— nineteenth century corny sculptures of people, which were unsalable, bring them up and then Dalí would get somebody in to paint ants on them or whatever it was and turn them into a Dalí cliché. And they sold, which was so shocking to me. I mean, I put on this show and there was nothing in there that was really by the artist's hand.[59]

55
Warhol/Colacello 1979, pp. 127f.

56
"Dalí – Crazy," pp. 95, 97.

57
Quoted according to McGirk 1989, p. 109; unfortunately no source indication.

58
McGirk 1989, p. 146.

59
Sir John Richardson in a conversation with the author on July 3, 2012 in New York.

60
Quoted according to McGirk 1989, pp. 151f; unfortunately no source indication.

61
Gibson 1997, p. 585.

62
Cf. Rogerson 1987, p. 94; Mas Peinado 2004, pp. 267f.

63
Quoted according to Gibson 1997, p. 549.

64
In "Reminiscences of Dalí: A Conversation with Amanda Lear and Ultra Violet," moderated by Dawn Ades, in Taylor 2008, p. 207.

65
Carol/Navarro Arisa/Busquets 1985, pp. 78ff.

66
Gibson 1997, p. 588.

67
Puignau 1995, p. 174.

68
Gibson 1997, p. 589.

69
Gibson 1997, p. 454; McGirk 1989, p. 160.

70
Gibson 1997, pp. 589f.

3

By the beginning of the 1980s, Dalí and Gala no longer made any effort to propagate the myth of their marriage. In her last interview Gala remarked, "Being loved matters little to me. Personally, I don't love anyone. ... As for my relations with Dalí, they are what they are. We don't have these ordinary types of problems; we live in freedom [from each other] despite everything. We are not a couple."[60] There was an incident when the painter and his muse were staying at Hôtel Le Meurice in Paris in February 1981. During the early hours Dalí, with a black eye, knocked on the door of the suite where his secretary Enrique Sabater was staying. When Sabater stepped into the Dalís' suite he found Gala lying on the floor next to the bed. The doctors diagnosed two broken ribs and contusions on her arms and legs. Dalí admitted to Sabater that they had had a hefty quarrel that had ended in violence. The reasons for the argument had been brewing for a while: Gala was spending a fortune on Jeff Fenholt and threatened Dalí that she would leave him for her lover. Furthermore, the artist's right hand was shaking more and more, which made it impossible for him to paint and to earn enough money.[61] In light of this situation, she entered into business with shady dealers.[62] When she was asked about one of these dealers she exclaimed, "They are ALL crooks! Who cares! They pay us cash, so what difference does it make? Dalí painted the work. He can sell the rights to anyone he wishes, and as many times he wants."[63] Ultra Violet viewed Gala's greed for money as the reason for the whole situation situation and recalled, "... Dalí was the star, obviously, and though Gala was the muse and the model, and is in so many paintings, I think somehow she might have been frustrated."[64]

At the end of 1981 Gala's health deteriorated. She suffered from gall bladder complaints and had to be operated on at the Platón Clinic in Barcelona. After she recovered she was able to return to Port Lligat, where she fell down the stairs on February 24, 1982, and injured her leg. Because of the frequently aggressive disputes between her and Dalí, it was rumored that the painter had pushed her down the stairs during an argument. Two days later Gala slipped in the bath and suffered a comminuted fracture of the thighbone and was admitted to a private clinic in Figueres. There it was recommended that the necessary operation be carried out at the Platón Clinic in Barcelona again. There were serious complications during the procedure. For a while Gala's condition was life threatening, but she recovered again and was able to return to Port Lligat at the end of April,[65] where she refused to eat.[66] Cécile Éluard had learned from newspapers that Gala was on her death bed. She came to see her mother for the last time. However, Gala and Dalí had informed her that they did not wish to see her and that she could go.[67] Gala died on June 10, 1982 at about six o'clock in the morning. It had been her last wish to die at the Castle of Púbol and to be buried there.[68] In order to avoid bureaucratic obstacles, the body was taken secretly by car to Púbol, driven by Arturo Caminada, who had served the Dalís for forty-seven years, had been on pleasure trips at sea with the deceased, and had also been one of Gala's lovers.[69] A doctor confirmed that Gala had died there. The corpse was embalmed at Púbol. It was Dalí's wish that the body of his muse should resist decay for as long as possible.[70] The funeral service and the laying to rest in the crypt at the Castle of Púbol took place on June 11, 1982 to the exclusion of the public. Dalí did not attend, staying instead in Gala's room. He had asked his friend Antoni Pitxot to keep him company as a distraction. Dalí's cousin Gonzalo Serraclara, who attended the funeral service, reported later that the artist visited the crypt a couple of hours after the inhumation; Dalí seemed to be unmoved and even said to him, "Look, I'm not crying." Serraclara ascribed this behavior to the fact that the painter and his muse had been quarreling for months and that Gala's death was to a certain extent a release for Dalí. A couple of days later, Dalí, who was also ailing, struggled to the crypt in the morning, where he was found shaking in agitation. It emerged later that he had stumbled over the rubble that the masons had left lying around and had fallen over. It is said to have been his last visit to his muse's grave.[71]

When Gala Dalí died, Julia Warhola had already been dead about ten years. She had lived in New York with her son Andy Warhol for almost twenty years. Julia Warhola was born on November 17, 1892, as Julia Zavacky in Miková, in the northeast of Slovakia, near the Polish border. She had eight siblings. She met her husband-to-be Ondrej Warhola in 1908 or 1909. He had already been to America several times for long periods and had built up financial reserves. Ondrej and Julia married in 1909. Their daughter Josephine was born two years later. However, the child lived for only a few months. She had caught a severe cold and there was no doctor in the village. Ondrej went to America again in 1912 with about $160 in his pocket; he thus avoided being called up for the army. His youngest brother Joseph had already settled in Western Pennsylvania. In order to bring his wife out to join him as soon as possible, Ondrej worked as a miner in a coal pit. However, it was not possible for him to send his savings back to his homeland, so the war years were difficult for Julia. She lived on her husband's family's farm and worked in the fields. When her father-in-law died she worked in the household of the village priest. She borrowed money from him later to sail to America.[72] Julia Warhola gave birth to three sons in Pittsburgh: Paul on June 26, 1922; John on May 31, 1925; and Andrew on August 6, 1928.

After completing his studies at the Carnegie Institute of Technology in Pittsburgh, Andrew went to New York in the summer of 1949. During his initial years in the city he wrote a postcard to his mother every day that said, "I am fine and I will write again tomorrow."[73] In 1952 he moved into an apartment in the building next door, 216 East Seventy-Fifth Street. This was one of the few years in the artist's life that he lived alone.[74] The apartment was dilapidated. There was no hot water, but there were plenty of mice. Warhol tried to get rid of them with a Siamese cat, which kept him company and was named Sam. When Julia Warhola visited one day with her son Paul she was horrified. She saw it as her duty to clean the house, to take care of her son's laundry, and to cook him a decent meal, as his diet consisted mainly of cake and confectionery. She thought of moving to New York permanently to take care of Andrew,[75] which is what happened after another visit in the spring of 1952. John Warhola, who accompanied his mother, recalled later: "Andy had a hole in the sole of his shoes as big as a silver dollar. So I left him my best

71
Ibid., p. 591.

72
Bourdon 1989,
pp. 14, 16.

73
Bockris 1989,
p. 82.

74
Bourdon 1989,
pp. 30f.

75
Bockris 1989,
p. 96.

pair of shoes. I think when mother saw that she decided to move up there at once to look after Andy."[76] Practical considerations prompted Julia to move in with her son—he was the only one of her children who was not married. "She was close to all of us," according to Paul Warhola,

I mean, if you had asked her "Who is your favorite son?" she would say "They are all my favorites." ... She was a wonderful person. When my brother John decided to get married she decided to leave Pittsburgh and go up and take care of Andy's place. She said: "I wanna go up and spend time with my son Andy." ... She liked New York. She said: "I have the grocery store. It's right across the street." When she wanted gifts, she went down several blocks where the commercial district was with a lot of stores.[77]

Mother and son slept next to each other on mattresses in the apartment. The kitchen also served as Warhol's studio. They brought in a second Siamese cat that was christened Hester. The cats soon had offspring, all named Sam.[78] One year later Warhol was given the opportunity to rent the top floor of a five-story building on Lexington Avenue from Leonard Kessler, a former classmate who became an author and illustrator. Kessler, whose wife Ethel was pregnant at the time and had difficulty climbing stairs, recalls,

... Andy, Julia and twenty-five Siamese cats all named Sam moved to 242 Lexington. I kept one room for my studio and traveled each day from the suburbs ... Andy and his mother had a wonderful relationship. She took care of the cats ... and she knew each one of the cats ... "That's the good Sam ... and that's the fat Sam ..." naming each one. Andy created a little paperback book about the "25 Cats Name Sam" (Julia did the calligraphy). Spelling the word NAME was Julia's contribution ...

Julia cooked ... cleaned ... took care of Andy. She was our inspirational leader ... "Andy Vork ... Kessler Vork ..." she greeted us each working day ... "and then we eat Kapusta ..." her special soup.

Every Sunday Andy and Julia attended Church together.[79]

During the early years of living together Warhol gave his mother a tape recorder so she could send taped letters to her relatives in Pittsburgh. Julia not only sent recorded tapes, but also used the appliance to record Slovakian folk songs and then to sing them with herself as a duet.[80] Later on Warhol also proved to be generous towards his mother. Julia was delighted with her son's gifts, but also saw them as quite a waste and was convinced that her son would die one day as a poor man.[81] Furthermore, Warhol gave her $500 a week that she spent on parcels sent to her relations in Pittsburgh and Miková, or hoarded in a canning jar, where her son Paul discovered over $6,000 at one point.[82]

In 1960, when Warhol was able to purchase a four-story townhouse on the Upper East Side of Manhattan, 1342 Lexington Avenue, his mother moved in with him again.[83] She had the lower part of the house to herself, while he occupied the upper floors and worked on the first floor.[84] It is said that Warhol's intention behind the move was to ease the close relationship with his mother.[85] The size of the house alone made it possible to give each of them a whole floor. Warhol's nephew, James, who was a frequent guest, recalls:

76
In ibid.

77
Paul Warhola in a conversation with the author on November 27, 2012 in Pittsburgh.

78
Bourdon 1989, p. 33.

79
Leonard Kessler in a letter to the author in August 2011.

80
Gluck in O'Connor/Liu 1996, p. 32.

81
Bourdon 1989, p. 61.

82
Bockris 1989, p. 147.

83
Bourdon 1989, p. 68.

84
Warhol/Hackett 1980, p. 5.

85
Bockris 1989, p. 146.

My uncle, he really loved his mother. And he knew that he would miss her when she got too old and we had to take care of her in Pittsburgh. But she took care of him for let's say almost twenty years in New York and he kept it quiet. He was pampered by her: orange juice in the morning all the time, she cooked for him downstairs, did his laundry, and she would go grocery shopping. She did a lot. My uncle loved her for that. He prayed with her in the morning before he went out. … She lived on the ground floor but in the front it was a little bit lower than the sidewalk. In the back there was a garden, a little area where you can have a garden, so it was technically called a "garden apartment." So she had windows in the back and windows in the front, but there were only half windows in the front. And you'd see people walk by. So there was a basement underneath her floor that was low-ceilinged and creepy. But that was underneath—on another floor.[86]

The movie *Mrs. Warhola*, which Warhol shot in November 1966, gives an insight into Julia Warhola's domestic situation. His mother plays a peroxide blonde movie diva with many husbands. The artist commented on the movie with the words: "We're trying to bring back old people."[87] The color movie shows Mrs. Warhola doing household chores, talking incessantly with an incomprehensibly strong accent. Warhol's life partner Richard Rheem, who lived with him at the time, plays the role of her husband, who teases her fondly. She prepares scrambled eggs for him and shows him how to iron.[88] At the beginning of the 1970s, Julia stood in front of the camera once again. Warhol shot a total of three video tapes of his mother in her rooms. One tape shows her in bed just before falling asleep. Warhol's voice can be heard faintly in the background.[89] It might seem surprising that Warhol made his mother a star of some of his movies. Ted Carey, the artist's assistant from 1957 to the early 1960s, later recalled:

… she had a very strong accent, and Andy, I think, would have liked to have thought of his mother as very glamorous. And Mrs. Warhola was not glamorous, and I think he felt a little bit ashamed of her. In fact, Andy was very timid about people coming to his house, unless he knew you very well. And even more timid about letting you meet his mother. If you got to meet Andy's mother, then you knew that Andy liked you very much. And I can remember Andy taking his mother to the show at Serendipity. And I remember that he was so nervous. He was afraid to take her. Should he take her? She wanted to go. And, finally, I think she did go to the show, and Andy was, I think, very uncomfortable about it.[90]

It is not surprising that Julia was so keen on visiting the exhibition at Serendipity. After all, her curlicue handwriting had contributed to the success of her son's early drawings, which he had also let her sign with his name.[91] Mrs. Warhola identified with her son's works. When mother and son had an argument once, she packed her bags and went to Pittsburgh. Warhol had to admit to himself that he could not do without her and could not work anymore, so he asked her to come back. The painter and art director Joseph Giordano, who was friends with Julia and Andy, later stated:

I think he expected me to get in there and function, but it was just too much of a household to run. So he finally called her back. She insisted that I be there that night. She came in and slammed her suitcase on the ground and

86
James Warhola in a conversation with the author on December 2, 2012 in New York.

87
Quoted according to Bockris 1989, p. 263.

88
Meyer-Hermann 2008, p. 01:56:00.

89
Ibid., p. 01:26:00.

90
In Smith 1986, pp. 252f.

91
See the chapter **Creative Motherly Care** in Part 2.

turned around. She looked at him and said, "I am Andy Warhol." And there was a big discussion about why she was Andy Warhol. But I guess she convinced him that he was. She was exactly like Andy: she was a mythmaker. I think this is the basis of his whole character. He is a mythmaker. He knows how to perpetuate the myth.[92]

Sir John Richardson also confirms that Warhol and his mother had a lot in common, "Julia was the source of the tenacity and gentleness and down-to-earth resilience which were at the core of Andy's character. Narrow and uneducated she may have been, but Julia struck those who met her as humorous, mischievous, and shrewd—like her son."[93] Victor Bockris writes that Julia Warhola, despite her naive character, was the only person in Warhol's life who was just as difficult, manipulative, and strong as he was. Therefore the two of them were a good team, but also "prisoners of each others' needs and compulsions."[94] The playwright Robert Heide described the mother-son relationship as follows: "His mother was a very important, almost spooky presence—'My Andy can do no wrong. He's a good boy'—and Andy would retreat into that four- or five-year-old."[95] Gerard Malanga also remembers that Warhol reverted to being a little boy in his mother's presence.[96] It was reported that Julia called him her "little Andek" throughout her life.[97] Another nickname that she liked to use was "Andy Candy."[98] She treated him like a boy, encouraging him to do the right thing, nagging him about his clothes, or criticizing him because he had not married a nice girl.[99] Suzie Frankfurt, who published the parody cookbook *Wild Raspberries* together with Warhol, came out later with the following negative words:

She was very talented in some mad way, but she was so manipulative. When we were doing Wild Raspberries *Andy had to chain her to the lightbox to get all the calligraphy done. She said she'd copy it over and she didn't. He gave her too much bloody credit. I mean, she was like Miss Prima Donna. She wasn't really a very nice person. I never liked her. She was too much of a force in Andy's life. He adored her too much. She was omnipresent. She was too weird for me, too ill-kempt, too much of a Czechoslovakian peasant.*[100]

Joseph Giordano also pointed out her negative influence on Warhol: "She saw the possibilities in him, but she resented the package. I really adored Missy. But the ambivalence used to shock me. ... The crux of Andy Warhol is that he felt so unloved, so unloved. I know it came from his mother. I knew she was doing something wrong. She made him feel insignificant. She made him feel that he was the ugliest creature that God put on his earth."[101]

There are reports that Warhol's friends sometimes saw Julia Warhola downing a big glass of Scotch. Andy also claimed she was an alcoholic and consumed a case of Cutty Sark scotch a week.[102] There is no proof of this. It is said that Mrs. Warhola soon felt lonely, as her son was very busy and she did not participate in his public life.[103] However, in an interview published in 1966 in *Esquire* she said, "I like New York. You never lonesome. People nice. And the air ... air better than Pennsylvania. Here I have my church, big church on Fifteenth Street and Second Avenue. I go to ten-thirty Mass. Brand new church."[104] Therefore, as regards his mother's alcohol consumption, Warhol may have exaggerated greatly. Vito Giallo, who was his assistant in

---

92
In Bockris 1989, p. 133.

93
Quoted according to ibid., p. 98.

94
Ibid.

95
In ibid., pp. 126f.

96
Ibid., p. 165.

97
Ibid., p. 353.

98
Watson 2003, p. 228.

99
Bockris 1989, p. 98.

100
In ibid., p. 130.

101
In ibid., p. 133.

102
Bourdon in Wilcock 2010, p. 43; Bourdon 1989, p. 68.

103
Bockris 1989, pp. 107, 132.

104
In Weinraub 1966, p. 101.

the mid-1950s, remarks, "He was always emphasizing the fact that if you lied a little and made the story more interesting that it was okay. So sometimes you really couldn't believe everything he said."[105]

In *POPism* it says that towards the end of the 1960s Warhol's mother was somewhat confused and could no longer be left alone, as she let anyone into the house who claimed to know her son.[106] Andy forbade her to answer calls for him and installed her own telephone.[107] This also meant avoiding her overhearing his telephone calls. Warhol then shouted to his mother over the phone, "Hey, Mom, get off the phone!"[108]

In 1971 Julia Warhola had visibly aged. She suffered from arteriosclerosis and Alzheimer's.[109] Warhol's long-standing partner Jed Johnson, who took care of mother and son, recalled later:

She got really senile and she would just go out and leave the door open, forget where she went. ... We were just afraid that she would get lost. Once the police came. ... She really needed full-time attention and Andy couldn't do that. ...

She was really difficult. She needed medication which she didn't remember to take, and then she made a lot of demands but she didn't know what she was doing. I mean, she was like a bag lady. She had things stuffed in shopping bags and her whole bed was surrounded by shopping bags and she had things safety-pinned to her clothing. It was unbelievable. Little notes, money, and lost buttons. And she didn't sleep, she'd be up and she had a hard time walking around the house. She didn't make sense. Sometimes she'd get emotional but you didn't really know what she wanted. It was hard.[110]

In February 1971 Julia Warhola suffered a stroke and was admitted to a New York hospital. She was taken back to Pittsburgh, where she lived for a short while with her son John and then at her son Paul's house. There she suffered a second stroke and was in a coma for a few weeks. She was then taken in by a nursing home in the Squirrel Hill suburb. Warhol called his mother almost every day, but never visited her.[111] Many years later he recorded in his diaries: "And at Christmas time I really think about my mother and if I did the right thing sending her back to Pittsburgh. I still feel so guilty."[112]

Julia Warhola died on November 28, 1972, at the age of eighty. Andy received the message from his brother John: "I talked to him on the phone. I told him, 'I have some bad news.' I guess I was broken up. As close as he was he took death pretty good. He says, 'Uh,' he says 'Aaahhh,' he says, 'Well, don't cry,' he says. Still, you know, maybe he was the type he didn't want to let me know how bad he felt."[113] Warhol covered the costs of his mother's funeral, but did not attend. Paul Warhola later said, "I covered up for him a lot. I told relatives he happened to be out of the country. Andy didn't want to see nobody dead. He was deathly afraid. He explained to me one time, he says, 'You know, Paul,' he says, 'I don't want you to feel bad that I didn't come in, but, uh, you know, I want to remember Mother as she was.'"[114] Paul Warhola's son George, who lived with his uncle in New York for a month after Julia's death, reported that he was going through a difficult time then: "He almost had a nervous breakdown. He started saying, 'Why's everybody bothering me? I'm tired of everybody calling me.' He was real nervous for like

105
Vito Giallo in a telephone conversation with the author on May 25, 2010.

106
Warhol/Hackett 1980, p. 275.

107
Bockris 1989, p. 262.

108
Quoted according to ibid.

109
Ibid., p. 350.

110
In ibid., pp. 351f.

111
Ibid., pp. 352f.; Bourdon 1989, pp. 308, 322.

112
Hackett 1989, p. 704, December 27, 1985.

113
In Bockris 1989, pp. 361f.

114
In ibid, p. 362.

a week and a half. It was like he was tired of all this crap and just wanted to escape it all. I remember my uncle used to always keep that handkerchief of hers. He didn't want anybody to see him but he'd take off his wig and put the handkerchief on his head."[115] Warhol did not say a word about his mother's death to his friends and employees at the Factory. Fred Hughes and Jed Johnson only found out about it many weeks later by coincidence, and Vincent Fremont not until several years later.[116] In September 1974—two years after his mother's death—Warhol painted nine portraits of her.[117] Two years later friends asked how his mother was and he answered, "Oh, she's great. But she doesn't get out of bed much."[118]

Companions, Courtiers, and Superstars

One of the first to be admitted to Salvador Dalí's entourage was María Fernanda ("Nanita") Kalaschnikoff. Dalí met Kalaschnikoff, a Spanish woman married to a Russian and the mother of three daughters, in February 1955 at a charity ball in New York. He could not take his eyes off the tall blonde in a red evening dress and introduced himself to her, "I am Da-lí. I want to see you every day for the rest of my life. Who are you?"[1] This was the start of a lasting friendship. Nanita was always there for Dalí when he needed her.[2] For Dalí's biographer Ian Gibson there is no doubt that the painter also grew to love his friend, whom he called "Louis XIV" or "el Rey," because of her regal demeanor. Since he avoided physical closeness throughout his life, his relationship with her was platonic, but contained a "degree of erotic complicity," which he never achieved with Gala. Nanita, who was not only very sociable and easy to get along with, was also sexually uninhibited and gladly posed nude as a model for Dalí.[3] His secretary Peter Moore emphasized later: "She played an important part, she was the woman Dalí would really have liked to marry."[4]

In 1965 Amanda Lear came into Dalí's life. In her memoirs *My Life with Dalí,* she reports that she met him in the fall of 1965 at Castel's in Paris. She was an art student at the time, working as a model.[5] Some sources state that Amanda Lear was born as Alain Tapp and later performed in cabarets, such as the famous Le Carrousel in Paris, under the stage name Peki d'Oslo.[6] Lear herself emphasized that the media had avidly perpetuated rumors about her transsexuality when she recorded her first album in 1977 and launched her career as singer and disco queen in Europe.[7] Dalí's new female companion beguiled him. He revealed to the artist and moviemaker Steven Arnold: "She is very special to Dalí and most intelligent."[8] Ernst Fuchs, the Austrian artist, said that Dalí referred to his bond with Lear as a relationship of angels and he was very much in love with her.[9] Lear reports in her memoirs that Dalí's affection for her culminated in a marriage proposal.[10] According to her further accounts, even Gala had asked her later on to take care of Dalí and to marry him if anything should happen to her.[11] It never came to marriage.

In 1971, while arranging a screening of the movie *Luminous Procuress* by Steven Arnold in New York, Dalí met the American artist Pandora who

115 In ibid.

116 Bourdon 1989, p. 322; Bockris 1989, p. 362.

117 Cf. Printz/King-Nero 2010, no. 2799ff.

118 Quoted according to Bourdon 1989, p. 322.

1 Quoted according to Gibson 1997, p. 483.

2 Cf. Moore 2009, p. 238; Llongueras 2003, pp. 205f.; Gibson 1997, p. 572.

3 Ibid., p. 485.

4 Quoted according to ibid.

5 Lear 1985, p. 9.

6 Gibson 1997, pp. 527ff.; Fallowell/Ashley 1982, p. 69; Ashley/Thompson 2006, pp. 106f.; Haag 1999, p. 206.

7 Lear 1985, p. 267.

8 Arnold, unpublished autobiography.

9 Prof. Ernst Fuchs in a conversation with the author on May 13, 2010 in Klagenfurt.

10 Lear 1985, p. 213.

11 Ibid., p. 275.

played the leading role.[12] Arnold reports that it was love at first sight. Dalí took Pandora's head in his hands and "erupted like a volcano": "Look, look, *le* most fantastiueke amazing creature that Dalí has ever seen, one amazing cranium, one profile like Dalí paints in 'The Great Masturbator,' *la* profile, *la* profile, bravo dis es *le* most fantastic creature Dalí has ever seen. One living work of art."[13] The former Halston model Chris Royer, who was often invited to Dalí's dinners, describes Pandora as "a very tall, statuesque woman who was about six foot two [inches]. She wore a pale blue silk cocktail dress and her head was completely shaved. She had a very distinct profile with a beak-like nose and a porcelain white complexion. Her pale skin against the blue dress was amazing and striking to behold. In the dim light at Trader Vic's she looked almost mystical. Dalí was mesmerized by her."[14] From the first encounter, Dalí and Pandora communicated with one another in their own personal language, "Balk."[15] Pandora explains, "Dalí and I invented this language which is a sound vibration language, similar to the trill sounds in the Quechua language of Peru, which I had the greatest pleasure to hear in the Andes. With the usage of high and low tones, sometimes sounding as birds, we could communicate and know exactly what the other was expressing."[16] Steven Arnold describes a conversation between Dalí and Pandora: "They would say the word, 'Balk' to each other for hours, or the word, 'Butterfly.' Dalí would say, 'Buuuuttteeerrrfflyyyyeee,' and Pandora would answer, 'Bbbbaaaaaalllllkkkkkkk bbbbbaaaaalllllkkkkk,' to the astonishment of all the other guests at dinner, who would often be titled or rich. They would go on all evening, ignoring everybody else, speaking in balks."[17] Pandora became Dalí's companion. "Dalí loved Pandora and Pandora was a wonderful friend to Dalí and Gala," says the screenwriter and producer Jeremiah Newton: "She was so unusual-looking; she wore these wonderful hats by Mr. John, the designer, and she had such a great sense of style. ... Dalí liked that very much. He liked people who were interesting-looking and not run-of-the-mill."[18]

The first category also included the Indian singer and actress Asha Puthli, who met Dalí in 1970. She reports:

My meeting Dalí was totally unexpected. It happened across from the St. Regis Hotel (Fifty-fifth Street just off Fifth Avenue). I was headed to a shop called Sona (which was set up by the All India Handicrafts and Handlooms Export Corporation) when I heard indiscernible shouts and as the voice got closer I realized it was someone shouting "Arrête, arrête" in a very strident and demanding tone so I turned around and there was Salvador Dalí—couldn't mistake him with that moustache. ... I had been granted a Dance Scholarship by the famous Martha Graham. As a student I did not have much money to buy designer clothes so I did the best with what I had. It was the unconventional way that I dressed that initially drew the attention of several creative people at that time. Dalí was one. ... So I guess wearing a mirrored bolster pillow case with one end of it cut so that I could slip into it like a skirt or carrying a walking stick with a 1930s neck wrap with fox heads purchased in a thrift shop helped in getting attention from creative and imaginative people. At that first startling encounter I was equally intrigued and accepted his invitation for a drink at the St. Regis, just across the street from where he and Gala lived.[19]

12
See the chapter
The 1970s
in Part 5.

13
Arnold, unpublished autobiography.

14
Chris Royer in a telephone conversation with the author on October 7, 2013.

15
Pandora in an e-mail to the author on May 31, 2011.

16
Pandora in a letter to the author in August 2009.

17
Arnold, unpublished autobiography.

18
Jeremiah Newton in a telephone conversation with the author on August 8, 2010.

19
Asha Puthli in an e-mail to the author in January 2, 2012.

Asha Puthli soon realized that Dalí loved surrounding himself with "pretty young things." He invited her to meet him again the following week at the King Cole Bar at the St. Regis.

When I got there, already seated was a pale ethereal looking young writer I had already met at the Warhol Factory. He looked paler and even more frail this time. Again, shortly after I had arrived, Dalí, who, as I had observed in the earlier meeting, was not at all interested in knowing the people he invited or even communicating with them unless it served his purpose, left the two of us at the table and said he was going up to check on Gala, returned and took the young man upstairs. I had no patience for any megalomaniac who did not respect my time or the presence of a guest. The first time I had excused his behavior thinking it was a language problem but now I thought of Dalí as more of a butterfly catcher who pins down butterflies to observe them. I had no intention of staying there or spending any more time at Dalí's table in future, as I was leaving Dalí was back from checking on Gala and in an irate tone and my bad French, I said—"Je suis tres faché avec vous"—not that it would have mattered to him but it did to me to have the last word.[20]

Apart from extravagant clothing, it was the particular physiognomy of a person that tended to attract Dalí's attention. Amanda Lear reports in an interview that was published in March 1978 in Andy Warhol's *Interview*: "I remember Dalí told me that the first time he met me, that he fell in love with my skeleton. It's like the good foundation of a house. If a house doesn't have a good foundation, it will collapse. So, I suppose that when all else fails, I can always fall back on my bones."[21] The model Vera von Lehndorff, better known as Veruschka, had a similar experience. She had met Dalí at the beginning of the 1960s in New York through Peter Beard and his girlfiend at the time, Ali MacGraw. MacGraw, who was already a successful photo model, had invited Veruschka to accompany her to one of Dalí's dinners. "And then we met at the St. Regis Hotel, we waited in the foyer, and then at some point Dalí appeared," reports von Lehndorff.

Many other guests came whom he had also invited—loads of "crazy figures" who were difficult to make sense of at first. … I was incredibly young and shy at the time and just observed the events. Dalí was quite interested straight away, because I was so tall. … For Dalí there was always something he was particularly interested in: the look or the movement or the bones … And Dalí then said it as well and made others aware of this person and what he had found – in a very pronounced and also rather dramatic manner.[22]

Time and time again, models attracted Dalí's attention. In the case of Nena von Schlebrügge, the mother of the actress Uma Thurman, it was the eyes that he admired,[23] and with Ali MacGraw it was her "marvellously long and white feet."[24] On the evening of December 17, 1965, Dalí met the model Bettina Cirone at the opening of his retrospective at Huntington Hartford's Gallery of Modern Art in New York. This was the start of a new friendship. Cirone later became a successful photojournalist and also met and became friends with Andy Warhol. She recalls:

Dalí actually wanted me to pose for him naked. I didn't want to offend him but I didn't want to do it either. So, I told him I'm nothing but bones. I wasn't,

---

[20] Ibid.

[21] In Tinkerbelle 1978, p. 32.

[22] Vera von Lehndorff in a telephone conversation with the author on January 6, 2012 (translated from the German).

[23] Rohwer/Lehndorff 2011, p. 129.

[24] MacGraw reports in her autobiography that she let Dalí convince her to pose for him naked. Then he purportedly started to suck her toes. Cf. MacGraw 1991, pp. 65f. Dalí was also intrigued by Veruschka's and Amanda Lear's big feet.
+

but I wanted to tell him that to discourage him without offending him. Most art-ists like models who are fleshy. So, I figured that would make him lose interest. Instead, he took my hand in his, looked into my eyes and air kissed my hand and said "J'adore les os," which means "I love bones." I then proposed that if I did, I would want him to pose for me. I was an amateur photographer then and never had I considered a career in photography. It was a hobby. He agreed to, yet he never pressured me. Instead, he invited me to dinner with his wife Gala, mostly across the street from the St. Regis Hotel, to a restaurant called La Côte Basque, I think. He also invited me to parties at the hotel. ... Every year when he returned for the summer season to Cadaqués, Spain, Dali invited me to join him there but I never went because I had so many catalogue bookings during the summer season here in New York I never left. It was like two years or so later that I agreed to pose nude for Dali because I felt I could trust him. At that point, he was almost like a father figure to me. Gala was always very pleasant to me, too. She was attentive and always smiled and she seemed happy to see me. In my experiences with her, she didn't make me feel that she was demanding in any way.[25]

Male photo models also attracted Dalí's interest. An advertisement drew his attention to Jon Stevens in 1967 and he sought him out via his model agency. Dalí liked his striking male face and he had him pose for a series of drawings and paintings.[26] Towards the end of the 1960s Dalí's entourage in-cluded Jean-Claude du Barry, who had also worked as a model. The French-man claimed to be a descendent of the Comtesse du Barry, the lover of Louis XV. As he came from the Gascogne, where people did not mince their words, Dalí and Gala had given him the nickname "Vérité" ("Truth").[27] Du Barry was running a model agency in Barcelona, which enabled him to offer the painter and his muse beautiful young people.[28] While Gala's needs were more "overtly physical," Dalí's interests were "artistic and voyeuristic."[29] Du Barry remarked about him later:

I saw him as a figure out of the Italian Renaissance. He wanted to be sur-rounded by scientists, philosophers or beautiful people, actors and models. As Teilhard de Chardin tried to make the connection between science and religion, Dalí was looking for the connection between science and esthetics. I used to or-ganize the dinners, I'd bring girls and help him put on a show. My importance is that it was my models who inspired him. After a year I understood what kind of girl Dalí wanted. Above all, he wanted perfectly beautiful girls, tall and blonde with long legs and very regular features.[30]

Dalí thanked Du Barry for his services by declaring him his *"officier de culs"* ("officer of asses").[31]

Attractive young people could regularly be found in Dalí's company. Catherine Hesketh, née Guinness, who met the artist towards the end of the 1960s in Cadaqués, recalls, "He invited various people, any cute young people in the village for tea, for rosé champagne and to look around his garden and chat."[32] It was not difficult to be invited by Dalí. The American painter Robert Venosa, who came to Cadaqués in the summer of 1972, writes that when one was on the phone with him, he started by asking a question,

...[W]hich was always, "Are you beautiful"? If your reply was a confident "Yes!" you would be invited to show up at his Port Lligat home at 7 p.m. to sit

+
Lear writes that he once kneeled before her to kiss her feet. Cf. Lear 1985, p. 160.

25
Bettina Cirone in a telephone conversation with the author on August 11, 2014.

26
Jon Stevens in a telephone con-versation with the author on December 16, 2011.

27
Secrest 1986, pp. 202, 204.

28
By his own ac-count, Du Barry met Dalí in 1968 at the Hotel Ritz in Barcelona. Cf. Gibson 1997, p. 550. Accord-ing to other sources, the en-counter did not take place until November 1969. Cf. Llongueras 2003, p. 216; Secrest 1986, p. 202.

29
Gibson 1997, p. 550.

30
Quoted accord-ing to Secrest 1986, p. 203.

31
Carol/Navarro Arisa/Busquets 1985, p. 104.

32
Catherine Hesketh in a telephone conversation with the author on August 27, 2012.

beside his phallic-shaped swimming pool and drink pink champagne with aristocrats, vagabonds and some of the most interesting people you'd ever hope to meet. This was Dalí's ever-changing nightly court, which, of course, always included entertainment: gypsy flamenco dancers and singers; a group of lithe and lovely ballerinas, who, at Dalí's suggestion, would disrobe and dance in the nude; jugglers, magicians and ranting prophets; courageous but misguided fools; and always the itinerant troubadour inspired to peak performance by the presence of the great Dalí.[33]

If a young person had found his way to Dalí, he or she was often asked to bring their friends. The French interior designer Baron Roger de Cabrol, who had met Dalí in the 1970s, reports: "Dalí always wanted me to bring my friends. So I would always bring a group of people of my age. He loved that. He was very happy because he really wanted to be accepted by them."[34] It was not unusal for Dalí to encourage the young people he knew to keep an eye out for others like themselves. Susi Wyss, the self-appointed Swiss "glamour girl who likes to cook" often posed for him as a model and recalls: "He wanted me to come to Cadaqués, because I'm very gregarious. He tasked me with bringing the most beautiful girls and the prettiest boys to the house. I had a talent for it."[35] It was similar for the American painter Howard R. Carr, who met Dalí in 1969 through Jon Stevens: "Every time I went to Dalí to visit with him there were always like forty ballet dancers from Paris, there was a nuclear physicist with some princess. It was always an intriguing mix. … He would always say to me: 'Please bring me some beautiful people.' And I'd send off all sorts of glamorous young types."[36]

Amanda Lear is harsh in her retrospective judgement of Dalí's entourage:

Personally I was sickened by the parade of professional "virgins," false princesses, fake millionaires and would-be actresses who filled the salon of his suite at the Meurice every afternoon between five and eight. I would have liked to open his eyes to these impostors, telling him that he deserved better than this. But Dalí enjoyed it. It was quantity which counted. The more there were of these parasites, the more he felt like the Sun King surrounded by his servile subjects. Dalí liked to say that all these people came to him with the express purpose of being "cretinized," as he used to put it.[37]

Lear also reports that many of them just wanted to be wined and dined at the artist's expense or pose as a model for him in order to brag about it in public.[38] Michael Ward Stout, who became Dalí's New York lawyer in 1975, also made such an observation.[39] He remarked later that Dalí had few real friends and had to make do with "his transvestites, seedy models and his $3,000 Sunday dinners at Trader Vic's with his queers and odd costumed freaks, paid companions and other free-loaders, all vacuous in the extreme, but hungry."[40] Peter Moore also confirms in his memoirs *Flagrant Dalí* that Dalí tended to favor superficial acquaintances and once said to him after a dinner at Maxim's in Paris, "You see Captain, Dalí's system is infallible. After this evening, Dalí will never see his friends again! No greeting cards, no funerals, no jealousy. And during his next stay in Paris, Dalí will have a whole new group of friends and no problems!"[41]

Another insider report is provided by the memoirs of Carlos Lozano, bearing the title *Sex, Surrealism, Dalí and Me*. At the age of nine years, Lozano

33
Venosa 1991,
pp. 11f.

34
Baron Roger
Cabrol in a con-
versation with
the author
on December 5,
2012 in New York.

35
Susi Wyss in a
conversation
with the author
on October 25,
2013 in Paris
(translated from
the German).

36
Howard R. Carr
in a telephone
conversation with
the author on
January 10, 2013.

37
Lear 1985, p. 37.

38
Ibid., p. 62.

39
Gibson 1997,
p. 564.

40
Quoted
according to
ibid., p. 572.

41
Quoted accord-
ing to Moore
2009, pp. 239f.
(translated from
the French).

moved with his mother from Columbia to the United States and grew up initially on the West Coast. He travelled to New York with the Living Theater Company, who employed him later, and then on to Paris in April 1969.[42] A few days after his arrival there, two actors took him along to Dalí at Hôtel Le Meurice, where there were "Princes and Paupers' Tea" gatherings.[43] According to Lozano, everyone who appeared at tea with Dalí was "young and pretty." If someone was "old and crumbling," then it could only be about business.[44] The present Spanish ambassador bid farewell from the longhaired Lozano with the words: "*Au revoir, Mademoiselle*" and kissed his hand.[45] Howard R. Carr reports that Dalí was evidently fascinated by Lozano: "He was absolutely in love with him …. There was a certain handfull of people … they were muses. They were really wonderful individuals. He was one of them."[46]

Carlos Lozano reports in his memoirs that there was a hierarchy within Dalí's court: "There was a private kingdom, the confidential cosmos of Dalí and Gala; an outer court of hangers-on; the inner court, the fun court, inhabited by Louis XIV and Amanda Lear …."[47] In addition to this, Gala herself entertained a small entourage. Chris Royer recalls, "Gala was never one to be forgotten. She always had beautiful young men around her and instead of a handshake when seated she would offer her foot instead of her hand."[48] The jewelry designer Lee Brooks, who accompanied Gala one evening in Paris, reports: "I fell into the wrong category, because I'd been told previously by people that had been in social and other situations with Gala and Dalí: avoid Gala. Because they're very territorial about who is in their little group. And if you're in Gala's group, then Dalí doesn't pay much attention to you and Gala doesn't pay much attention to Dalí's group."[49]

Dalí's court was not only hierarchical, but was composed differently in New York, Paris, and Cadaqués. Amanda Lear concludes that there were qualitative differences: "In America, everything is larger than life. Dalí's court was too large to be held in his private salon, so here the daily rendezvous was in the bar of the hotel. The crowd at the Meurice seemed positively refined compared to the people Dalí received here: outrageous hippies, black dancers, carefully made-up models, dubious scientists as well as more credible philosophers."[50]

Furthermore, the constellation of Dalí's entourage was continuously changing. Many members were "all the rage" for a couple of weeks, but then disappeared again just as quickly from the artist's life, or reappeared a couple of years later.[51] "… [H]e could also be sadistic," according to Carlos Lozano, "For instance when he first gets you, he puts you on a silver platter, but then he drops you. At night, he will look around and point to certain people to go out to dinner with him, 'You, you, you, and you, but not you.' It's a court and you are not on the list anymore. He is tired of you; you don't count."[52] The American artist Louis Markoya, who became Dalí's assistant in the winter of 1970/71, observed:

Dalí's court changed from minute to minute, never mind day to day. I would say the total number ranged from one to around fifteen or as many as twenty. A good guess at the average would be around ten or twelve people. This changed constantly, as Dalí and/or the court members got bored or new, more

42
Thurlow 2000, pp. 20ff.

43
Ibid., pp. 11, 16.

44
Ibid., p. 38.

45
Ibid., p. 11.

46
Howard R. Carr in a telephone conversation with the author on January 10, 2013. Susi Wyss confirms that Lozano was very beautiful, but also subordinate. Dalí liked "slaves." Susi Wyss in a conversation with the author on October 25, 2013 in Paris.

47
Thurlow 2000, p. 29.

48
Chris Royer in a telephone conversation with the author on October 7, 2013.

49
Lee Brooks in a conversation with the author on November 13, 2011 in San Francisco.

50
Lear 1985, p. 113.

51
Gibson 1997, p. 516.

52
In Secrest 1986, p. 203.

interesting people showed up. Dalí loved the rich, famous, and the bizarre. Transvestites and transsexuals were around often, many also associated with Warhol. ... The normal court "happening" was in the cocktail lounge of the St. Regis, now gone. The hotel would close the lounge for Sunday evenings and Dalí would have it for court from 6 p.m. on, usually breaking with the four to ten most important (for that moment) members between 8 and 9 p.m. to go to Trader Vic's at the Plaza Hotel for dinner. ...

Dalí's entourage always included hangers-on that would be attractive to Warhol (freaks, homosexuals, transvestites and arrivistes [Dalí's word for climbers]). These climbers, who Dalí would rate as the world's best, would swap camps in a second if they saw any personal gain, or glimmer of fame in it. ...

Warhol was taking pictures of everything including the kitchen sink with his Poloroid SX–70 ... when he took my picture he stopped to say, "Dalí is not where it is happening," and extended an invitation to me to the Factory, where he would "show me around and I can really feel at home." I was pretty afraid of the crossdressers that usually accompanied Andy, and I know they were totally stoned many times, so I was afraid of being drugged at the Factory.[53]

Ultra Violet also reported that Warhol tried to win her over: "And I did spend more and more time with Warhol, who used to say, 'Dalí is too old, you should leave him.' But I didn't."[54] Ultra Violet was born in 1935 as Isabelle Collin Dufresne in La Tronche near Grenoble, the daughter of a wealthy glove manufacturer. As a rebellious youth, her parents sent her to America.[55] She lived with family friends in Bronxville for a while and later moved into an apartment on the Upper East Side of Manhattan. In New York, art became her entrée for getting to know important people.[56] Interestingly, Ultra Violet was not the only Warhol superstar who had contact to Dalí. Ivy Nicholson, a famous model in the 1950s who worked especially in Europe, could also occasionally be found in Dalí's company. Nicholson met Dalí in 1964 and he asked her to model for him. In the same year she also met Warhol and played in some of his movies.[57] Nicholson recalls her time at the Factory as follows: "I was madly in love with Andy during those years but he never fully reciprocated. ... Andy said to me once that the reason he loved me is that I was more masculine than all his boyfriends. I think that's so cute. ... I was there from '62 to '69. I said you marry me or I'm leaving."[58] After the attempt on Warhol's life in June 1968, Ivy went back to Paris.[59] While he was lying in hospital she proved her love once again. She was hysterical and screamed on the telephone that she would kill herself if Andy did not survive. She asked every ten minutes whether he had died and threatened to throw herself out of the window.[60]

At the time Nicholson went to Paris, Viva had already entered the Factory scene and rose to become one of the most famous Warhol superstars. Viva was born in 1938 in Thousand Islands, New York, as Janet Susan Mary Hoffmann and grew up in nearby Syracuse. She was the oldest of nine children. Her father was a well-known criminal defense lawyer and her parents were conservative. She later liked to say that it was the courtroom that had provided her acting lessons. After high school, Hoffmann attended the Catholic Marymount College in Tarrytown, New York. In her junior year she

53
Louis Markoya
in an e-mail
to the author on
May 17, 2010.

54
In "Reminis-
cences of Dalí:
A Conversation
with Amanda
Lear and Ultra
Violet," moder-
ated by Dawn
Ades, in Taylor
2008, p. 215.

55
Ultra Violet 1988,
pp. 48ff.

56
Ibid., pp. 61f.

57
Cf. Angell 2006,
pp. 14ff.

58
In "Ivy Nicholson:
Warhol's
Superstar."

59
Angell 2006,
p. 141.

60
Bockris 1989,
pp. 302, 304.

went to Paris to study art at the Sorbonne.[61] Warhol's movie *I, a Man* had made a positive impression on her. When she met the artist at a party she approached him about a role in his next movie. He replied, "O.K., you can be in the one we're shooting tomorrow, if you take off your blouse. If you won't, you can be in the one we're shooting the next day."[62] Hoffmann decided to go for the "blouse-off movie" before Warhol changed his mind, and appeared on the set the next day. When she had to take her blouse off there was a surprise: she had taped over her nipples with band-aids.[63] As a new Factory member, Hoffmann was given the name Viva by Paul Morrissey.[64] "We all loved Viva;" it says in *POPism*, "we'd never seen anything like her, and from then on, it was just taken for granted that she'd be in whatever movie we did."[65] In 1977 Warhol remarked in an interview that Viva was his "favorite person" and that she could make it in Hollywood.[66] Viva herself comments on this remark: "I didn't know about that, but I'm not surprised. He kept telling me my mind was 'a gold mine.'"[67] After a journey to the Warhol retrospective in Stockholm, Viva suggested to the artist that they marry. However, Warhol turned her down and she collapsed in a crying fit that lasted for days.[68] Viva also confirms retrospectively that she wanted to marry Warhol, but that sometimes her dream husband was also Paul Morrissey—depending on her mood.[69] She remarked about another Warhol superstar: "How could she have gotten any closer? I would say it was the longest running marriage in New York. She was the wife figure in his life."[70] The "wife figure" in Warhol's life was Brigid Berlin.

Brigid Berlin was born into high society in 1939. Her father was Richard E. Berlin, who led the Hearst media empire for half a century. Warhol liked to refer to Brigid as the "heiress" and romanticized her extravagance. He loved telling others that she had spent a fortune by holding parties on Fire Island and hiring a helicopter to fly to town for her post.[71] Already at the age of fourteen, Brigid was dependent on amphetamines, which a family doctor had used to treat her obesity. Her mother tried to turn her into a high society lady. Instead Brigid became, as she once put it herself, an "overweight troublemaker."[72] Warhol met her already in 1964. She was known as "the Duchess" or "the doctor," as she gave others a poke of amphetamine through the seat of their pants on request. At the Factory she soon gained the nickname "Brigid Polk."[73] Brigid was one of the first superstars and played a role in several of Warhol's movies. Her performance in the movie *Chelsea Girls* is impressive, in which she gives herself and her colleague Ingrid Superstar injections. Ingrid asks her in passing: "Aren't you in love with Andy?" Warhol and Berlin did not go out often together. Their shared time was spent talking on the telephone and while doing so, recording each other on tape.[74]

Brigid Berlin also met Salvador Dalí in February 1974. She recalls, "The first time I met Dalí was not with Andy, but with the Princess Nina Mdivani Harwood. ... she would carry on about Dalí saying 'You've got to meet my friend Dalí.' So, we go to the St. Regis where of course Dalí was staying and he comes down to the King Cole Bar. And everybody that walks in is all over him. And I didn't understand, you know, he's hard to understand. So, all I can say is I spent that time with him kind of with my mind wondering."[75]

61
Bourdon 1989, p. 260. Viva received a "Certificate of the French Language" from the Sorbonne. Viva in an e-mail to the author on April 18, 2012.

62
Quoted according to Bourdon 1989, p. 260.

63
Ibid. Viva reported in an e-mail to the author on April 18, 2012: "... Caroline de Bendern, a model from an old Aristocratic English family, who was staying at my place, suggested the band-aid."

64
Viva says: "Paul Morrissey thought it up on the spur of the moment and it had nothing to do with the paper towel, something that came out later. But I claimed during a talk show I took my name from the Viva paper towel just to be funny and shortly thereafter the Viva paper towel CEO sent me a carton of the Viva paper towels and a pink dress for my new baby, Alexandra." Ibid.

65
Warhol/Hackett 1980, p. 231.

66
In Goldsmith 2004, p. 250.

67
Viva in an e-mail to the author on April 18, 2012.

68
Bockris 1989, p. 289.

69
Viva in an e-mail to the author on April 18, 2012.

70
In Bockris, p. 317.

71
Warhol/Hackett 1980, p. 103.

72
Brigid Berlin in the documentary *Pie in the Sky: The Brigid Berlin Story*.

73
Bockris 1989, p. 193.

74
Brigid Berlin in the documentary *Pie in the Sky: The Brigid Berlin Story*. See also the chapter **Mustache, Wig, and other Signature Features** in Part 2.

75
Brigid Berlin in a conversation with the author on December 4, 2012 in New York.

Nena Thurman, who regularly attended these five o'clock receptions, recalls that another member of Warhol's Factory occasionally popped in: Edie Sedgwick.[76] Edie Sedgwick was perhaps the greatest and most famous Warhol superstar. In November 1971, Warhol commented on her early death in the *New York Post*: "She was immediately somebody you really cared about. I thought she was just magic and very imaginative."[77] Sedgwick was born in 1943 as Edith Minturn Sedgwick. She came from a wealthy, traditional family with a lot of children, who owned an enormous cattle farm in Santa Ynez Valley in California.[78] In the 1950s, crude oil was discovered on the ranch, which multiplied the wealth of the family.[79] Despite this, Sedgwick did not experience an easy youth. She suffered from anorexia during puberty, and also from violent abuse by her father. The family committed her to a psychiatric hospital. In 1963 she went to Cambridge, Massachusetts to study art, where she met the Harvard graduate Chuck Wein, who had participated in the psychologist Timothy Leary's LSD experiments.[80] Wein became Sedgwick's mentor and manager. He was determined to help her make it in the theater and movie worlds. At the time she also began taking LSD. After just a year she left Cambridge and went to Manhattan with Wein.[81] In New York, Segwick became a sought-after party girl who could afford to throw money away due to an inheritance.[82] In March 1965 she had her premiere in the Factory movie *Vinyl*, playing a minor role. Her presence stole the show from all the other performers. Edie Sedgwick died of drug abuse as a young woman in 1971.

Drug-taking was nothing unusual at the time and of course it also happened at the Factory, mostly amphetamines and marihuana. It was not unusual to see someone at the Factory injecting. Warhol may not have been present, but he did not make an issue of it.[83] The artist and moviemaker Wynn Chamberlain reported on his visits to the Factory: "He was like a lot of great artists and great film directors and so on: a voyeur. ... Andy was sitting there and he loved to watch people freaking out and he provided a place for people to do whatever they wanted to do. I always thought it would end in disaster."[84] Warhol had already started to take amphetamines in 1962, because of their appetite-suppressing effects, thinking he had to be super slim to correspond to his image of a star. At the beginning of 1963 he even got a prescription for Obetrol, an especially powerful appetite suppressant.[85] In *POPism* it says: "... but even that much was enough to give you that wired, happy go-go-go feeling in your stomach that you want to work-work-work, so I could just imagine how incredibly high people who took the straight stuff felt."[86] Warhol paid great attention not to take any prohibited substances, because he was aware that he was under constant media scrutiny.[87] In the late 1960s, Paul Morrissey, who was deeply averse to drug use, made sure that people focused on work at the Factory, and stopped the "hanging out."[88] The attempt on Warhol's life by Valerie Solanas in July 1968 also made Warhol more cautious when it came to accepting new members into his entourage.[89] In *POPism* he reports: "Crazy people had always fascinated me because they were so creative—they were incapable of doing things normally. Usually they would never hurt anybody, they were just disturbed themselves;

76
Nena Thurman in a telephone conversation with the author on July 11, 2012.

77
Quoted in Bourdon 1989, p. 316.

78
Ibid., p. 201.

79
Jonathan Sedgwick in Stein/Plimpton 1982, p. 75.

80
Wein in ibid., p. 450.

81
Bourdon 1989, p. 201.

82
In the summer of 1964 Edie inherited $80,000 from her grandmother. She had spent the money after six months. Cf. Sherman/Dalton 2009, p. 248.

83
Bourdon 1989, p. 208.

84
Wynn Chamberlain in a telephone conversation with the author on August 26, 2011.

85
Bockris 1989, pp. 175f.

86
Warhol/Hackett 1980, p. 33.

87
Bockris 1989, p. 175.

88
Bourdon 1989, p. 208.

89
See the chapter **Experience of Death** in Part 2.

but how would I ever know again which was which?"[90] After the attempted assassination, many of the initial members left the Factory and drug use was prohibited. Owing to the new members, the Factory was transformed from a glitzy gathering place into an office that soon became a flourishing business. However, even in the 1970s Warhol had some involvement with drugs. The main drug at Studio 54 was cocaine. Catherine Hesketh, who became editor at *Interview* in 1975, recalls that Warhol was often slipped little packages, but he threw them away.[91] She explains Warhol's reticence as follows: "He didn't really take drugs. He thought it was rude to refuse, so he accepted. And people were longing to give them to him. At Studio 54, everyone who was giving them to him was on drugs, and I think they longed to say that they had given drugs to Andy Warhol."[92]

Dalí, who was also often a guest at Studio 54, said about drugs: "Timothy Leary, the prophet of LSD, said: 'Dalí is the only painter of LSD without LSD.' ... I have never taken drugs, since I am the drug."[93] Dalí evidently adhered to this rule. Vera von Lehndorff retrospectively explains: "He always thought something up—and it was fascinating. Such a performance is typical of people who are perhaps on drugs, who suddenly simply drift off and lose themselves in some story. I thought this was kind of great with Dalí. I never thought that it might have anything to do with drugs—and indeed it didn't at all. He was completely 'clean' and didn't even drink wine."[94] Peter Beard, who realized happenings with Dalí, recalls a particular occasion:

One of our extravagances uptown is we would go around in a limo with Dalí and do these things. The limo delivered us back to the King Cole Bar and two or three people got out and then Dalí got out and I was the last person to get out. And he turned to me in the limo and said, "Mr. Beard, one thing, if you ever do any drugs, don't tell anybody." I had no idea what he meant but I could sort of figure it out because we did some extremely exciting and dynamic filming. And I guess he thought that I had done some coke. I had no idea what coke was. I had no idea what Dalí was talking about. And obviously Dalí ... he was giving me a secret there. He had experienced LSD of course and he had experienced things that would, in some people's eyes, lessen his accomplishment in painting because they would say he cheated, he did drugs, it wasn't his idea. And he never told anybody that he did drugs.[95]

The voyeurism of Dalí and Warhol also extended to twins, who exerted a particular fascination on both artists. With the relocation of the Factory to Union Square, the twins Jed and Jay Johnson appeared in Warhol's life. Jed came by one day to deliver a telegram and his quiet demeanor and good manners made an impression on Morrissey, who started a conversation with him. It emerged that Jed had come to New York just recently from Sacramento with his brother Jay. Morrissey took him on as an assistant.[96] Jed also came to play an important role in Warhol's private life, becoming the artist's life partner.[97]

At the end of the 1970s Warhol met another pair of twins: Richard and Robert Lasko. They came from Westport, Connecticut, and New York's Studio 54 became their second home. When Robert saw a sign for the Du Pont corporation one day, he thought that this would be the right name for him

90
Warhol/Hackett 1980, p. 279.

91
In Bockris 1989, p. 403.

92
Catherine Hesketh in a telephone conversation with the author on August 27, 2012.

93
Dalí 1970, pp. 96f.

94
Vera von Lehndorff in a telephone conversation with the author on January 6, 2012 (translated from the German).

95
Peter Beard in a Skype conversation with the author on September 24, 2010.

96
Warhol/Hackett 1980, p. 264.

97
See the chapter **Sterile Love and Voyeurism** in Part 2.

98
Du Pont in Gross
2007.

99
Hackett 1989,
p. 203,
February 10,
1979.

100
Colacello 1990,
pp. 354f.

and his brother.[98] Warhol knew that the twins were not Du Pont heirs,[99] but according to Bob Colacello their false statements about their own origins made them even more interesting to him. They were also always full of the latest gossip, even if it was as dubious as their name.[100] Richard Du Pont also recently reported about his encounters with Dalí:

Andy brought us to dinner one Sunday with Salvador Dalí at the Versailles Room at the St. Regis. Dalí always had these dinners, and there were always a lot of drag queens. One named Potassa would be wearing a beautiful gown from Oscar de la Renta or Halston, and she would run around with a big bottle of Champagne and say, "Cham-pan-ya!" After we met her, she would always let us know when Dalí was in town and invite us for these dinners. Sometimes Andy wouldn't be invited, which would make him upset.

...

Sometimes we'd be in the back of the limo, and Dalí and Potassa would say, "Pull it out, pull it out!" Dalí had a word for orgasm—I don't remember it, but he would say it and I would do it. I don't know why. Maybe I felt like I had to in order to get invited to dinner or something. I remember doing it for Andy in the balcony at Studio, and in the back at the Factory.

One time I did it for Andy and Dalí together. We were in a black limousine, going uptown on Park Avenue South. Potassa and Dalí's wife, Gala, were there, too. I don't know why Andy grabbed me; maybe he was trying to get Dalí turned on, or maybe he just wanted to show that he had control. At first I was scared. But Potassa was pouring her champagne and saying, "Cham-pan-ya!," and Andy was saying, "Do it, do it!" so I just did. Gala was laughing, and Potassa was clapping. It was like theater for them, I guess.[101]

101
In Gross 2007.

In Dalí's entourage was a pair of male twins whom he called Castor and Pollux: the twins John and Dennis Myers from England, who had settled in Cadaqués.[102] Owing to their looks they were predestined to keep Dalí company. "Dalí was in love with the twins," according to Susi Wyss, "but he never touched them. They posed naked for him—I was there. And they went with him to all the parties in Paris, to Helène Rochas, and other rich people."[103] In Carlos Lozano's memoirs he says about John and Dennis Myers:

102
Gibson 1997,
p. 530.

103
Susi Wyss in a
conversation
with the author
on October 25,
2013 in Paris
(translated from
the German).

The Twins were a vaudeville turn. Each finished the other's sentence on those rare occasions when they deigned to speak in company and, with each other, their sequence of sounds in staccato were more motes of dust in the beam of their extraordinary telepathy. They were exotically handsome. Dark and carved. Cecil Beaton had photographed them and Ken Russell had put them in The Music Lovers *as the sons of the contessa who became Tchaikovsky's patron."*[104]

104
Thurlow 2000,
pp. 59f. Photos
of the Myers
twins by Cecil
Beaton in
Garner/Mellor
2012, pp. 269,
284, 287.

April Ashley, whose exceptional beauty held a particular fascination for the artist, is very clear when she looks back on Dalí's enthusiasm for twins: "Dalí had a thing about twins, fornicating with twins and he also had a great fascination with preoperative transsexuals."[105]

105
April Ashley in
a telephone con-
versation with
the author
on July 30, 2011.

Dalí and Warhol were both fascinated by transsexuals and transvestites. In *Andy Warhol's Exposures* it says: "I'm never sure whether Dalí copied transvestites from me or I copied transvestites from Dalí."[106] Dalí's early diaries reveal that evidently, already as a sixteen-year-old, he was fascinated by androgynous people. After a visit to Can Gardia,[107] the first

106
Warhol/Colacello
1979, p. 127.

107
"Can Harida" is
the local name for
+

cinema in Figueres, which held varieté events, as well as movie screenings, he wrote: "The movie was, as usual, absolute trash, but at the end there was a great woman, a gypsy type, quite masculine, graceful, elegant. She danced tastefully and with exceptional style."[108]

Towards the end of the 1950s, Dalí started to frequent the Cabaret Le Carrousel in Paris.[109] It was April Ashley, in particular, who attracted his attention. She was born in 1935 in Liverpool as George Jamieson and had come to Paris in the 1950s. According to her report, she met Dalí in 1958:

He came to the Carrousel somewhere between three weeks to six weeks every night with chocolates and flowers and presents and everything like that begging to paint me. ... He was fascinated because in those days I was very beautiful. He couldn't believe what he was looking at. ... When he would come up to me and put his face close to me he would say "Oh, you're so beautiful. You're so beautiful." And with those mad eyes and that turned-up mustache he used to frighten the hell out of me when I was young. I was very shy in those days and he rather frightened me. So I said no. I did not want to be painted by him.[110]

In her autobiography *The First Lady* Ashley writes that she met the Spaniard before her sex reassignment surgery: "... he was excited by me. Put simply, Dalí, the Great Masturbator, liked chicks with dicks. (And the masturbation of and by them)."[111] The artist himself put it in a nutshell in *The Passions According to Dalí*: "To see a penis rise on a very supple, almost feminine body, is a delight to my eyes."[112] He added in an interview, "Quite frankly: I don't like cunts."[113]

In 1972 Suzannah Fleming came into Dalí's life. Fleming, who posed as a model for him, recalls that Dalí gave her the feeling that she was "the most beautiful, desirable, and perfectly androgynous being on earth."[114] She reports for the first time about her time at Dalí's side as follows:

I had run away from my family home in the distant suburbs of Chicago to live as one of the androgynous Flower Children of San Francisco when I was barely sixteen ...

I first met Dalí in New York at the St. Regis Hotel in the small lounge directly opposite the entrance. It was in 1972 when I was only seventeen and I had only arrived in the city from California a few days before. ... I was brought to see Dalí by a friend of mine—a gay Parisian man who was working for Air France in the Public Relations department at the time ...

With the help of my friend I spent the entire day preparing myself for my first meeting with Dalí that evening. We agreed I was to wear white see-through robes and we bought from a florist in Greenwich Village seven gardenias and some small rustic twigs, which we formed into a kind of sacrificial headpiece or crown. I remember saying to my friend that I felt like a lamb being prepared for a ritual slaughter! I also wore lots of jingle-jangle bracelets and little bells on my wrists and ankles and as I moved I sounded like an elaborate wind chime!

The idea was that we would leave early and go first to the Plaza Hotel to have a drink and relax before we went to meet Dalí at the St. Regis. Because I was completely naked under my see-through robes I had speculated that the Plaza would eject us the second we walked in. My friend assured me that if

+
"Gran Teatro del Jardín." Cf. Dalí, 2004, p. 218, fn. 30.

108
Dalí, 2004, pp. 43f. (translated from the German).

109
Gibson 1997, p. 527.

110
April Ashley in a telephone conversation with the author on July 30, 2011.

111
Ashley/ Thompson 2006, p. 107.

112
Pauwels/Dalí 1985, p. 155.

113
Dalí (1979) in Calvo Serraller 2006, p. 1532 (translated from the Spanish).

114
Suzannah Fleming in an e-mail to the author on November 25, 2011.

there was a problem he would tell them I was Dalí's "New Muse." He said both the Plaza and the St. Regis were accustomed to the outrageous "comings and goings" of Dalí and his entourage—he told me they would treat us like "royalty," because they benefited greatly from the association. We got in a taxi in plenty of time, but on the way there we were in a big collision with another cab and as a result my friend was injured when his head hit the partition. He was bleeding very badly from a gash that extended diagonally across his forehead and I tried to get him to the nearest hospital but he insisted that it was vitally important that we carried on to meet Dalí on foot up Fifth Avenue. By the time we arrived at the St. Regis we were late and my friend was awash with blood and I was profusely splattered and smeared through trying to attend him. Both Dalí and Gala were waiting for us in the lounge. Dalí rose gallantly to greet me and he kissed my hand and seemed completely mesmerized with me. I recall saying to Dalí nervously something to the effect of: "So sorry, the ritual sacrifice has already begun!" He seemed completely oblivious to my friend and when Gala protested to her husband about this Dalí became animated and asked someone to remove him into the lobby so we didn't have to see his suffering. Out in the lobby my friend apparently started to pass out and Gala instructed the staff to call an ambulance despite his desperate protests—and he was soon afterwards taken away to receive medical attention. Gala came back into the lounge and sat across from me and stared intensely—she said nothing for a long time and then left. Amanda Lear arrived and we were introduced to one another and Dalí asked me to stand up to show my body off, which was visible through my robe. He spoke alternately in French and English to Lear and I could decipher something about "one marvelous hermaphrodite" and "appearing one mysterious angel for Dalí." He asked me to turn my head and they consulted each other and agreed that I had the profile of Greta Garbo.

Many people would look at me and they would think of me as a tall, thin, attractive hippy girl, but I was always self-conscious about revealing my body, which was totally androgynous at the time. When I was in his suite and he was drawing me Dalí seemed to take great care to make me feel as though I was the most beautiful person to ever inhabit the world—and he showered me with expressions of adoration, presents, money, etc. He would start by singing to me very softly and as he would work he would become louder and more frenzied in his movements. He insisted that I never look his way as he was drawing me—I obeyed his instructions, but I got the impression he was probably masturbating as he drew. On one occasion after our session I told him I wanted to have a sex-change operation and I remember that he looked at me in such horror— and he made me promise I would never consider it again. He said "Please, from this precise moment you will only dream of Dalí and of being one marvelous Angel." Many times afterwards he would repeat this or different versions of it—I think he was terrified of the notion that I would alter the very thing that made me special to him.

The sessions were often quite bizarre—he would prepare elaborate sets for me and one of the most consistent features was a giant prop in the shape of scissors that he laid at my feet. He asked me to place my toe in the eye of the open scissors in a particular way. He would fuss greatly about getting the pose exactly right. Once he surrounded me with hundreds of gardenias and thorns—seemingly in homage to the "sacrificial headpiece" I wore when I first met him. When he was working on designs for Carlos Alemany he would have me wearing some of the jewels and sometimes things like fried eggs on my shoulders or breasts and when he was working on the designs for the angel figures for the dome of the Teatro Dalí he would have me wear some magnificent angel wings he'd had made especially. Once he ordered the bathtub in his suite filled with lychees in syrup and he had me submerge myself in the tub. He said they were like viewing "One Million Mysterious Angels at One Perfect Moment"!

On the few occasions I was permitted to look at what Dalí had been drawing, I was always amazed that he never included any of the elaborate props in the image. It occurred to me that these were more symbolic for Dalí and helped to engage him, rather than being part of the scene.

Sometimes, when Amanda Lear was in town, she would wander in and out—occasionally she would comment on the setting or on Dalí's drawing. On a few occasions Gala would come in. She never said anything to me—she would just glare. This made me really nervous because I didn't know if she was jealous of me and of all the attention Dalí paid me. I tried to pretend she wasn't in the room, but one day Dalí left the room momentarily and she began to mutter something at me—it seemed like a curse or a low growl—and I could just see her out of the corner of my eye pick something up off the table and I had a sense she was about to hurl it at me. As I instinctively ducked my head down I heard something whizz past me and shatter on the wall behind. Gala left the suite and slammed the door behind her and then Dalí came back in—oblivious to what had just occurred!

In one sense it was a business relationship insofar as I was being paid for modeling for him, which was an important aspect initially, but for me it soon became so much more than that. I would sit for him frequently, sometimes every evening of the week for several weeks in a row. It was fantastic money—at the time it was $300 per session (a great deal of money then for somebody like myself!)—and in the first season I was working three to four evenings a week on average.

Beyond the business relationship I realized I was becoming very attached to Dalí and certainly for the first time in my life I felt adored and appreciated and my self-esteem grew accordingly. I felt that as long as Dalí continued to shower me with his adoration I could keep my promise to him not to change myself through surgical intervention. What had seemed so pressing to me before I met Dalí was becoming less essential to my outlook on life. At the end of the season in New York he promised he would phone me from Paris and he kept to his promise at least once a week. He would often ring and would ask: "You are remembering Dalí, my Angel?"—he seemed to love it when I would tell him I had been dreaming of him. When he returned to New York the next year I felt especially close to him—and by then the business aspect seemed quite secondary somehow. What I loved was the way he would sometimes promenade me slowly through the lobby of the St. Regis or the Plaza, where he held his dinner parties on Sunday evenings …. It was always a great exhibition and I tried to wear something wonderful (and sometimes a little eccentric) for him in order to make a spectacle. It was as though he was so proud of possessing me completely—and I think he also liked to shock if he could.

I saw quite a lot of Dalí in the second season and toward the end of it he promised he would arrange to bring me to Paris, but in the event Gala opposed this move and Mr. Sabater called to explain to me that Gala had started to complain that I was occupying Dalí's thoughts too much and moreover that she felt I had become too greedy with the money. As a form of consolation he told me that several of his other models fell under the same general complaint, so I shouldn't feel too bad. It was this that started me thinking that however much I might be attached to Dalí emotionally he probably treated his other models in a similar way—with all-consuming adoration. I started to understand that my experience with him was probably not unique. Also, I knew his wife was the most important determining factor in everything. After this I noticed Dalí started to phone less from Paris and I was feeling quite insecure about whether or not he still loved me. I began to worry that I would never again find someone like Dalí who could make me feel so beautiful and loved. I started to contemplate breaking my promise to him and returning to my planned course of having a sex-change operation. Through modeling for Dalí and selling a drawing he'd given me in the first season I had more than enough money to go ahead with this plan—still, I fretted that it would hurt Dalí and end our relationship if I broke this one single promise to him.

By the time I was recovered from the surgery I had moved back to Chicago, having reconciled with my family, and soon Dalí started calling me from New York upon his return there. He wanted to arrange for me to fly to New York, but I kept making excuses because I was so afraid of having to tell him what I'd done—I was quite certain he would be crushed and never forgive me. He sent me presents and Mr. Sabater was on the phone weekly to offer to compensate me for travelling expenses, etc. Toward the end of Dalí's New York season I finally worked up enough courage to take Sabater up on the offer—as it included accommodation in the St. Regis and all expenses paid—and I knew I must finally face Dalí with the news that I was now a woman.

The first couple of days in New York I couldn't face the prospect and I made my excuses, saying that I didn't feel well and couldn't model for him. Finally I told Dalí while we were sitting in the King Cole Room and he immediately stormed out—he then suddenly returned just as quickly and pulled me up roughly—"You are showing Dalí." He marched me up to his suite grasping my arm as if I was a naughty child that needed to be brought to justice. Inside he ordered me to undress immediately and when he saw what I had done he snatched up his cane and jabbed me violently with it between my legs and shouted "Imposteur" and strode angrily out of the room.

Totally humiliated (but not altogether shocked) I got dressed and left quickly. While I was waiting for the lift I started to cry uncontrollably and Dalí came out and he started to beg me to come back inside the suite and he said he was very sorry. As he was walking me back we passed the staircase and he suddenly grasped me by the shoulders and pushed me down the stairs! I think I hit my head because the next thing I knew some hotel staff were standing over me asking me what happened and they helped me back to my room. That evening

Mr. Sabater came and organized my return to Chicago and some cash—we didn't talk about what happened, and I'm not sure he knew exactly what had transpired between Dalí and I. ...

Amazingly, that was not the last time I saw Dalí. In the following season I came to see him at the St. Regis and brought with me a beautiful girlfriend who had not yet had her surgery—it was a sort of peace offering. I saw it as the only way of reconciling with Dalí, and I got a strong sense at the time that he appreciated the gesture.[115]

Suzannah Fleming's report shows that Dalí was accustomed to dictating people and situations. If something did not go his way he could be unpredictable.[116] Warhol, on the other hand, preferred the role of the silent observer. Walter Steding, who became his assistant at the end of the 1970s, remarks: "He allowed good things to happen, anything to happen. He wasn't judgmental."[117]

In his book *Andy Warhol's Exposures* Warhol presents "Dalí's favorite transvestite high fashion model from Santo Domingo" Potassa de la Fayette with a full-page photo, showing her bare-breasted.[118] There are also Polaroid photos that he took in early 1977 at the Factory, showing Potassa in a "homemade black and gold fantasy dress."[119] The photo shooting was witnessed by Jamie Wyeth, who was working on a portrait of Arnold Schwarzenegger, and had already painted a portrait of Warhol:

There was Victor Hugo, who was in and out of the Factory a lot, brought Potassa de la Fayette down one afternoon. And Andy brought her into where I was working. ... And of course Schwarzenegger, who at that point barely spoke English, thought she was a beautiful girl and sort of started to make a move on her and Andy kept telling me, "Why don't you draw her?" So I started with the drawing and he took a lot of photographs and Victor kept speaking to her in Spanish. And then finally she raised her dress and there was this erect cock. Poor Arnold thought it was a woman of course. He was completely in a state of shock. ... Andy got a great deal of satisfaction out of it. ... I thought Potassa was extraordinary looking but I was equally astounded when she raised her dress. I had no idea that it was a man. And of course Andy kept saying "Oh, you're so pretty as a girl."[120]

The April 1978 issue of Warhol's *Interview* published an interview with Potassa de la Fayette, in which she talks about her life. One learns that she came to the United States with her parents when she was of school age. In the beginning Potassa only dressed up as a woman for parties, but then she became a "woman twenty-four hours a day" and started modeling. Potassa also mentions her relationship with Dalí, who saw in her "the reincarnation of Rubén Darío" and called her neck "one of the most beautiful in the world": "Every time I do a job for Dalí he pays me very well and the next day I buy clothes, flowers, champagne, things for the house. ... I modelled for him; I modelled a diamond tiara with two big wings and feathers while he sketched and then he painted."[121]

Apart from Potassa de la Fayette, there were other transvestites who were part of Dalí's entourage in the 1970s. Michael Ward Stout, who often helped to organize the artist's Sunday dinners, reports:

---

115 Suzannah Fleming in e-mails to the author on December 22, 23 and 28, 2011.

116 In 1965 during the shooting of Jack Bond's documentary *Dalí in New York*, when a severe dispute broke out with Jane Arden, Dalí cried, "You are my slave! ... Everybody is my slave. ... This lady says she is not my slave! Finish filming." Cf. Bond, unpublished autobiography, and the documentary *Dalí in New York*.

117 Walter Steding in a telephone conversation with the author on January 12, 2013.

118 Warhol/Colacello 1979, pp. 126f.

119 Hackett 1989, p. 15, January 12, 1977. Depictions of the Polaroids in Heymer/Garnatz 2003, no. 149–159.

120 Jamie Wyeth in a telephone conversation with the author on April 3, 2013.

121 In Reynolds 1977, p. 32.

Dalí was a very visual person. The transvestites he knew were always providing a sideshow. They were constantly fixing their make-up and their jewelry or crawling under the table or going to the ladies' room in elegant restaurants and causing disruptions. There was always drama, which Dalí liked. He was very fond of a talented transgender singer named International Chrysis. She was very intelligent and amusing.[122]

International Chrysis was born in 1951 as William Schumacher and grew up in the Bronx. At a young age she discovered her passion for cross-dressing and became a member of the New York drag queen troupe Hot Peaches. In the 1970s she performed in clubs, sang, danced, and stripped. International Chrysis was proud of her large fake breasts, which she jokingly christened "Johnson & Johnson." She made a conscious decision not to have sex-change surgery. She was often in Dalí's company and posed as a model for him.[123] She claimed to others that she was his mistress.[124]

When Andy Warhol discovered film as a means of artistic expression, it was also the start of the era of his underground superstars. One of the first stars was René Rivera, who was born in Puerto Rico and had grown up in the New York district of Harlem. He was a slim, dark-skinned young man, who appeared in Warhol's movies as a transvestite.[125] His stage name was Mario Montez—a homage to María Montez, who starred in many Hollywood movies in the 1940s.[126] It was only on stage and in movies that Montez appeared as a woman. His family and his professional circles were not to know of his inclination and as a devout Catholic he was plagued by qualms about committing a sin.[127] This explains why Montez later stated that his relationship with Warhol was strictly professional and that he was not part of his scene.[128] The most interesting movies with him include those in which he evokes the glamor of Hollywood divas, presenting a parody of old movie stars, as a cheap version with smeared lipstick and runs in their stockings. Montez was able to put the public under his spell and soon became a cult figure. In February 1966 the *New York Post* referred to him as "Manhattan's best known transvestite," and the *New York Times* highlighted his performance in *Chelsea Girls*.[129]

Towards the end of the 1960s the transvestites Jackie Curtis, Candy Darling, and Holly Woodlawn, whom Lou Reed sang about in his famous song "Walk on the Wild Side," became the last great Warhol superstars. Jackie Curtis was born in 1947 in New York as John Curtis Holder and chose the "androgynous" stage name Jackie Curtis, with which he upheld his identity.[130] Curtis had felt a vocation to be an actor ever since his youth. He was also a playwright and director of his own plays. In 1965 Jackie Curtis wrote his first theater piece and appeared on stage at the La Mama Experimental Theater Club.[131] Out of devotion to Warhol, he had the artist's first name tattooed onto his left shoulder in 1968.[132] As a transvestite, Jackie Curtis had a quirky style. Joe Dallesandro, who became one of the most famous Warhol superstars in the 1970s, remembered his colleague later as "really horrible-looking, because he didn't look right dressed as a woman. He looked like a man dressed as a woman, and it was just—not right."[133] Curtis himself referred to his style as "slatternly," appearing both "trampy and classy."[134]

---

122 Michael Ward Stout in a telephone conversation with the author on June 9, 2010.

123 International Chrysis in the documentary *Split*. Dalí had noticed her at the New York cabaret The Blue Angel.

124 Justin Davis in the documentary *Split*.

125 Bourdon 1989, p. 196.

126 Angell 2006, p. 134.

127 Warhol/Hackett 1980, p. 91.

128 Mario Montez in an e-mail from Marc Siegel to the author on February 13, 2010.

129 Angell 2006, p. 134.

130 Watson 2003, p. 267.

131 Highberger 2005, p. 6.

132 Curtis in Smith 1986, p. 273. The tattoo consisted of a large A, enclosing the other three letters. See the photo by Fred McDarrah in Francis/King 1997, p. 201.

133 In Highberger 2005, p. 120.

134 Bourdon 1989, p. 296.

The star, who had been addicted to drugs for years, died in 1985 of a heroin overdose at the age of just thirty-eight.

In contrast to Jackie Curtis, Candy Darling cultivated a completely different style and became the most glamorous Warhol superstar. Candy wanted to be a woman, with all the problems that a woman can have. She even borrowed tampons and made it seem very urgent.[135] Her biggest problem was her penis, which she referred to as "my flaw."[136] Candy Darling was born in 1944 as James Lawrence Slattery and came from Massapequa, Long Island. He was taken to be a girl already as a child.[137] After he had seen the movie *The Prodigal* at age nine, he wanted to be Lana Turner, who played the main role. Jimmy poured blue food coloring into the bath to turn the water into a vibrant "Technicolor blue," wore his mother's clothes, used her makeup, and wound a yellow towel around his head to imitate Lana Turner's blonde hair. Later on he adulated Kim Novak.[138] The playwright Robert Heide recalls that it was the particular blend of movie star imitation and natural beauty that fascinated Warhol:

I think he liked Candy Darling because Candy was very witty, very beautiful like Kim Novak. And you felt like you were really with her. She would always do these imitations like of Joan Bennett … (imitating Candy Darling) "An actress needs a thousand dollars just for a decent wardrobe. Why, these producers won't give me a second look." She would do it in the exact voice of Joan Bennett. Or Kim Novak (imitating Candy Darling) "I don't want to go to the picnic, Mom." Things like that. We [my partner John Gilman and I] were around everywhere; we were good friends with her. She would come over and we would take pictures. And she would dress up and go to the Russian Tearoom. People like Zsa Zsa Gabor said she was one of the most beautiful women they had ever seen. Zsa Zsa probably didn't know that she wasn't a woman. … Candy had a real style and could be funny and amusing.[139]

Owing to her beauty and presence, Candy Darling became the most prominent transvestite in Warhol's entourage. It was difficult to imagine that she was really a man. Dalí was also fascinated by Candy Darling and called her the "Queen of the North," while for him Potassa de la Fayette was the "Queen of the South."[140] Gigi Williams, who was married at the time to Warhol's assistant Ronnie Cutrone and liked to go to gay bars with him,[141] compares the two "Queens" as follows:

Potassa de la Fayette was wonderful. She was bigger than life. She was sexy and graceful and it was hard to imagine that she actually had a penis. … Candy Darling was totally different. Candy was white and when I say white I mean like an angel white. She was so beautiful, so lovely, insecure, and sweet. She wore a lot of white. She had blond hair. She was very Monroe-like, whereas Potassa was dark and exotic and flamboyant. … Potassa was more like an instigator. She pushed the boundaries, so to speak. She wanted to shock. She wanted that kind of attention whereas Candy didn't.[142]

Candy Darling died in 1974 at the age of just twenty-nine, of leukemia. Hundreds of people—including Gloria Swanson—expressed their grief at the funeral.[143] Dalí not only sent flowers,[144] but also attended the funeral personally. Candy Darling's friend Jeremiah Newton recalls:

135
Warhol/Hackett 1980, p. 227.

136
Ibid., p. 224.

137
Newton/ Passalacqua/ Hardy 1997, p. 11.

138
Bourdon 1989, p. 296.

139
Robert Heide in a conversation with the author on December 6, 2012 in New York.

140
Colacello 1990, p. 174.

141
Cutrone in O'Connor/Liu 1996, p. 68; Gigi Williams in a telephone conversation with the author on May 5, 2014.

142
Ibid.

143
Newton/ Passalacqua/ Hardy 1997, p. 15.

144
Lear 1985, p. 268; Jeremiah Newton in a telephone conversation with the author on August 8, 2010.

He [Dalí] adored her. He thought she was wonderful. When she died he did a wonderful drawing that he gave to the mother of how he felt. It is a very very small drawing of a strange bug. And he came to her funeral, which is unusual because he didn't like funerals. He came in and sat for a while but he left. ... After Candy died I went to interview Dalí. He wouldn't let me use a tape recorder. He said I had to write everything down by hand and it was hard because he spoke in several languages. ... But one thing I did write down was: He appreciated her luminosity and that she had this quality which was very bright and glowing all the time and her sincerity.[145]

The last transvestite in the circle of Warhol superstars was Holly Woodlawn. She was born in Puerto Rico in 1946 as Harold Ajzenberg, the son of a Puerto-Rican mother and an American soldier of German descent. He grew up in Florida.[146] Long before he met Warhol, Harold knew that he was different. As a boy he wore his mother's clothes and performed shows for his friends. At the age of fifteen he hitchhiked to New York and paid his way with prostitution. Then he met a man who he fell in love with. Harold moved to Brooklyn and started to take hormones, but he rejected the sex change that his partner wanted.[147] In 1969 he made his debut as a showgirl in a piece by Jackie Curtis and was discovered by Warhol and Paul Morrissey.[148] At the time he was performing under the name of "Holly"—his stage name evoked the figure of Holly Golightly from Truman Capote's *Breakfast at Tiffany's*.[149] When Holly appeared in the Factory movie *Trash* (1970), she had already gained the name "Woodlawn," derived from Woodlawn Cemetery in the Bronx.[150] In her autobiography she reports how she met numerous celebrities during the period that followed, such as Bette Davis, Mick Jagger, John Lennon and Yoko Ono, Jean Shrimpton, Roger Vadim, Alice Cooper, as well as Salvador Dalí and Gala.[151] She remembered the encounter with Dalí and Gala during a lunch as disconcerting:

I was one of the guests at a lunch party at Trader Vic's, which used to be at the Plaza Hotel. It was set up at a big table, there were about twenty of us. I sat between Tinkerbelle on my right side and to my left was movie star Sylvia Miles (who played the trashy whore in Midnight Cowboy*) with her eighteen-year-old boyfriend. It was like the "Last Supper" with Dalí at one end of the table and his crazy wife Gala at the other.*

When Dalí entered the restaurant he had a gold-handled, gold-tipped walking stick in his right hand, and held Gala's hand in his left. It was like a hush fell suddenly over the entire room. He descended and sat down regally, like God has arrived—you lucky person! As soon as they sat down the room exploded into chit-chat.

We all were served Spanish style Piña Coladas made with sixteen kinds of rum and served in coconuts with a gardenia flower floating on top, and I had at least five or six. I remember after lunch I could hardly stand up, let alone walk normally!

Dalí sat there at the table drinking and eating in silence, watching everyone like a hawk. He never spoke a word to me, ever. I avoided his piercing glare. I remember seeing his paintings when I was maybe fifteen or sixteen, crazy scary stuff like burning giraffes and melting clocks—and I thought this artist must be insane, or painting on drugs, his pictures look like a bad LSD trip!

145
Ibid.; Jeremiah Newton in an e-mail to the author on September 23, 2013.

146
Woodlawn/Copeland 1991, p. 29.

147
Woodlawn in Brown 1996, p. 41.

148
Bourdon 1989, p. 304.

149
Woodlawn/Copeland 1991, p. 3.

150
Ibid., pp. 3, 119.

151
Ibid., pp. 172ff.

At some point I got up go to the ladies room and I'll never forget, when I walked past Gala I went up to her and said "Oh Gala your dress is FABULOUS!" and bent down to give her a European kiss on the cheek, and she pushed me away with her hand!! Pushed me away, saying, "NOBODY kisses Gala! Not even Dalí!" I was just stunned and embarrassed![152]

Holly Woodlawn wrote that Andy Warhol loved transvestites because they put on a façade to conceal their true self, which was very "Warhol-esque."[153] There was also another aspect, which Benjamin Liu, Warhol's assistant in the 1980s, and also a drag queen performer at the time, describes as follows: "You have to remember what Andy was a fan of—the Hollywood star system and the stars, whether it's the glamor part of it or everything else that's attached to it. ... The drag queens also have their own system in a certain way. ... I think he likes the exaggeration of it."[154]

Suzannah Fleming reports that she met Holly Woodlawn and Jackie Curtis together at a party. In the conversation between the three of them it became clear why Dalí and Warhol were so very fascinated by their personalities:

They [Holly and Jackie] had obviously both met Dalí, and knew others like Candy Darling, who had, too. They were really interested that I was so close to Dalí, but I got the impression from them that it was sort of a cliché or a standing joke that if you were a young, attractive, pre-op "tranny" in New York and you met Dalí he was going to want to get a look at what you had between your legs—and if he thought you were naive enough he would mold you into a full-on muse that was his and his alone. I remember I talked to them about Warhol in this regard and of course it seemed they were saying that with Warhol he was not in any way interested in the sexual aspect—but he was interested in the face, and what came out of the face. It was as though Warhol was interested in the contrivance and theatricality of transexuals, but little more. He wasn't interested in their day-to-day problems—or the problems they could cause in his life if encouraged. For Dalí, he seemed to see transsexuality as more of a natural phenomenon—along the lines of a hermaphroditism—which he was fascinated with. This is how he saw me.[155]

Contrary to the members of Dalí's entourage, the Warhol superstars were in the public limelight from the beginning because of their roles in the artist's movies and achieved a degree of fame themselves. "The one thing that united us all at the Factory," wrote Ultra Violet, "is our urgent, overwhelming need to be noticed. Fame is the goal, rebellion the style, narcissism the aura for the superstars ... ."[156] The actress, singer, and dancer Monique van Vooren, who took on the main female role in the movie *Flesh for Frankenstein* directed by Paul Morrissey, also observed this: "Andy gave birthday parties for me, went to openings with me and we were fervent telephone pals. ... I wasn't really part of the group that he had with him all the time, because I had a life and a career besides Andy. ... I think, all the people around him were attracted to him and his fame hoping that some of his fame would reflect on them, which in many cases it did."[157] Nobody from Dalí's entourage achieved any notable fame, with the exception of Amanda Lear. This can be explained by the different attitudes of the two artists to

152
Holly Woodlawn in an e-mail from Craig Highberger to the author on March 9, 2010.

153
Woodlawn/ Copeland 1991, p. 2.

154
Benjamin Liu in a conversation with the author on November 30, 2012 in New York. Bob Colacello formulates it similarly: "Andy was attracted to anybody who had a lot of glamour ... Andy was attracted to exhibitionists. And I think most drag queens were exhibitionists. And drag queens were campy and Andy liked that." Bob Colacello in a telephone conversation with the author on September 22, 2010.

155
Suzannah Fleming in an e-mail to the author on December 25, 2011.

156
Ultra Violet 1988, p. 30.

157
Monique van Vooren in a telephone conversation with the author on June 8, 2012 and in an e-mail to the author on July 23, 2015.

their companions, courtiers, and superstars. Asha Puthli compares the two artists as follows:

Both were curious and drawn to people who defined a spirit of independence—people who dared to be different, beautiful or quirky-looking people, sort of the extremes …. Like his work, Dalí was manipulative, a little twisted; Andy was straightforward and simple. Dalí was only about Dalí. … Dalí, grandiose, seemed to want people around him for self-aggrandizement. While Andy, quiet and humble, also usually had an entourage, but these were friends and people he worked with.[158]

Ronnie Cutrone, whom Dalí designated in 1973 to photograph him at a party,[159] also commented on how the two artists behaved towards their entourage:

You have one over the top shy artist, who can hardly say one word in public, which is Andy, and then you have Dalí, who doesn't say anything but gives quiet commands from his hands to his entourage and they become a human being for him. And they use their hands to do it. … Andy in a way did that too with his assistants—but not like Dalí. I mean Dalí probably has them wipe his ass. That's the difference! And I don't mean that in a rude sense. I mean it in a funny sense. … Andy is the type of boss who would say "Give me a hand!" and Dalí would be the type of boss that'd say "Give me both arms and a leg too!" … Dalí needed a lot from any assistant he had. But then he had that wife and she was, I guess, so domineering. From what I hear on the grapevine, she was very controlling and crazy … and so was he. They found each other—bingo![160]

Warhol helped his superstars to gain considerable fame, but he was often accused of systematically exploiting the people around him. John Giorno, the superstar of the movie *Sleep* and the artist's life partner in the 1960s, counters this with the following:

He listened to people's crazy ideas and picked an idea out. And then he realized it. Picasso did the same. It was a kind of collaboration. He loved his superstars. Edie Sedgwick, me, Ondine, and all the others. Each of them had a limited time with him, then he looked for someone else. And those that he left complained and said they had been taken advantage of. Nobody was taken advantage of! It was a fair deal. They wanted to become superstars, he enabled this and in return he made use of their ideas.[161]

Warhol had a special talent for helping people discover their creativity and letting it blossom. "He would find talent in other people and he would use it," says Gigi Williams, "And all the people that really didn't like Andy thought he should be paying them. When you were actually around Andy he opened every door in the world. You could do whatever you wanted. He opened the door and it was up to you to take the next step. He was very generous in that way."[162] Catherine Hesketh adds:

He just had a way about him, some charisma, really. It's difficult to put your finger on why people want to open up for someone else. But he did have that extraordinary effect on people. And when people say that he's a bad influence, it's not really true. He didn't directly encourage people to do shocking things. They just wanted to do it because they wanted to have an effect on him. They wanted him to notice them.[163]

158
Asha Puthli in an e-mail to the author on January 2, 2012.

159
See the chapter ***Dalí News and Andy Warhol's Interview*** in Part 4.

160
Ronnie Cutrone in a telephone conversation with the author on July 8, 2012.

161
In Liebs/Schmidt 2011, p. 68 (translated from the German).

162
Gigi Williams in a telephone conversation with the author on May 5, 2014. The artist Neke Carson said about Warhol with regard to this: "The artists that he met, he was very encouraging to them. … And he'd always say, 'I want you to see so and so.' +

163
Catherine Hesketh in a telephone conversation with the author on August 27, 2012.

Joe Dallesandro emphasizes the same point when he says that many of those who came to the Factory expected too much:

See, these people, they'd done one film or something and they thought Andy was to take care of them for the rest of their lives. They were hitting him up every time they came in, and Andy never knew how to say no to anything. Andy was very docile; he was very frightened of everything. ...

... See, the only concept that Andy Warhol created that I liked was the one where everyone was a star. The trouble that Andy ran into with that concept was that the people who came to him were so insane. Very ill people. And when you allow them to be the star you seem to be exploiting them. But Andy wasn't exploiting them.[164]

Benjamin Liu also arrives at a similar conclusion:

There is that theory that has been going around for the longest time. ... Sometimes I think people liked the idea that they were being manipulated because it also gave them a sense of their own individual power. I do remember one time, I forgot who said that in an interview, one of the 1960s crew: when Andy became successful we were all hoping that we would become successful. ... So maybe that theory came out later when a lot of them actually did not. And a lot of them actually, tragically, wound up gone, dead, disappeared, drugged out, jumped out of the window, whatever they all did. Maybe they felt like, okay, the devil made me do it. ... And then it becomes more like a myth. It's a theory and a myth. I like to think of it that way. ... Maybe it's because I belong to the last decade [the 1980s]. I think we think a little bit differently.[165]

Most of the Factory members adopted a stage name or were given one by others. Billy Linich became Billy Name, Robert Olivo was Ondine, Jane Holzer was called Baby Jane Holzer, Brigid Berlin was given the name Brigid Polk, Susan Hoffmann became Viva, Isabelle Collin Dufresne was Ultra Violet, Susan Bottomly became International Velvet, Christa Päffgen called herself Nico, Ingrid von Schefflin was called Ingrid Superstar, and James Lawrence Slattery was known as Candy Darling. Dalí also gave his courtiers nicknames. Amanda Lear reveals in her memoirs that he named them systematically. He found the actual names either too prosaic or too difficult to pronounce.[166] Louis Markoya confirms this:

Dalí would always make excuses about forgetting the name Markoya, even though he could easily remember the Spanish flamenco guitarist Carlos Montoya, so this was obviously selective memory. So the first nickname came from me being an apprentice, mixing painting mediums, mostly copal and oils for Dalí. It was doing this mixing that Dalí came to call me "Mark Oil." "Karl Marx" came on the occasion of me preparing some very large panels with charcoal for the master. He left me in a room with the panels and took a book that I brought to be signed saying he would do a drawing for me. After three to four hours he returned to carefully inspect the panels, which he insisted had to be covered with perfectly uniform charcoal. He proudly showed me the drawing, which was of Karl Marx, who he said, I would be known as from then on. That name lasted about a week or two.[167]

Dalí called his friend Nanita Kalaschnikoff "Louis XIV" or "el Rey" and he called her daughters "the Peach" and "the Dauphin."[168] He liked to

+
And he would give his recommendation. In a funny way he gave his recommendation so much that it had no meaning in New York (laughs)." Neke Carson in a conversation with the author on December 6, 2012 in New York.

164
In Brown 1996, p. 35.

165
Benjamin Liu in a conversation with the author on November 30, 2012 in New York.

166
Lear 1985, p. 11.

167
Louis Markoya in an e-mail to the author on May 17, 2010.

168
Lear 1985, p. 13.

169
Ultra Violet 1988,
pp. 79, 81.

170
Secrest 1986,
p. 203.

171
William Rothlein
in a telephone
conversation
with the author
on October 23,
2011. Federico
García Lorca
had previously
called Dalí "Adil."

172
Howard R. Carr
reported in a
telephone call
to the author on
January 10,
2013 that this is
what Dalí had
called him and
Jon Stevens.

173
Lear 1985,
pp. 11f.

174
Ibid., p. 257.

175
Pauwels/Dalí
1985, p. 95.

176
In Steiner 1970,
"Salvador Dalí,"
as well as Steiner
1970, "Magical
Meeting."

177
Chris Royer in a
telephone con-
versation with
the author on
October 7, 2013.

178
Pandora in a
conversation with
the author on
November 20,
2011 in Mariposa,
California.
Pandora adds
that Gala invited
Purple Aluminum
to Púbol castle,
but it did not
happen. Ibid.

179
Colacello 1990,
p. 48.

180
Ibid., p. 47.

181
Angell 2006,
p. 213.

182
Woronov 2000,
p. 33.

183
Angell 2006,
p. 213.

call Ultra Violet "Isabeau de Bavière."[169] Dalí named Carlos Lozano "La Violetera" after a famous zarzuela,[170] and he called his younger doppelgänger William Rothlein "Adil," an anagram of his own name.[171] Dalí's entourage also included the Dioscuri Castor and Pollux (John and Dennis Myers), a unicorn, and a cardinal. All blondes were called "Ginesta" (Spanish for gorse), blond men were often named "El Dorado."[172] Dalí called slim people "Saint Sebastian," Chinese women "Red Guards," and rich prigs "Fillets of Sole."[173] A young man who once posed as a model for him sitting on a motorbike was named "Motorcycle."[174] Dalí also liked to give religious nicknames. In *The Passions According to Dalí* he explains, "I had found a young woman, extraordinarily beautiful, very mystical and very pure. I had baptized her 'the Christ,' because of the limpidity of her soul, because of a certain facial resemblance and because it was during Holy Week."[175] Dalí christened his friend, the actress Mia Farrow, as "Lilith," which he explained as follows: "Because she is a black moon child, like Lilith. ... the Lilith that was before Eve. Read up on her in the Bible."[176] For Chris Royer he chose the name "The Angel." She recalls, "I asked Dalí, 'Why am I The Angel'? He replied, 'Because I like to see your blue eyes watching people.' ... We would go around the St. Regis and I would look into the mirrors to watch what was happening in the room. He sketched me in that way and once the drawing was done, Dalí would call The Captain to take them to his Studio."[177] Pandora reports that Dalí also displayed humor with regard to nicknames: "One of my partners was named 'Purple Aluminum.' Dalí seated Purple Aluminum next to Ultra Violet at a dinner party. Ultra Violet did not know Purple Aluminum. She wondered who this gentleman was, and Dalí said, 'That is Purple Aluminum and he sit next to Ultra Violet.' That was really funny—Purple Aluminum and Ultra Violet together."[178]

At Dalí's absolutist court there was no resistance against the nicknames, whereas in Warhol's circle, there was. Bob Colacello reports that he was encouraged by Warhol to change his name to "Bob Cola." At the time he was still using his birth name "Robert Colaciello."[179] Warhol was of the opinion, however, that if he wanted to become famous he had to change his name as it was difficult to pronounce: "Look, Bob, newspapers only have a certain amount of space to put people's name, right? And if your name is too long it doesn't fit in that space and then they use somebody else's name and that person becomes famous instead of you."[180] Warhol's employee went on to delete the "i" from his surname, but was unwilling to go further. Mary Woronov, who came to the Factory in 1965, appeared in some movies and performed as a dancer in Warhol's *Exploding Plastic Inevitable* shows,[181] put up somewhat more resistance. In her memoirs she writes that the artist tried to call her "Mary Might." However, she rejected this name instinctively and did not answer to it.[182]

It is said that Mary Woronov was also the only superstar at the Factory to insist rigorously on receiving a fee from Warhol.[183] Years later the artist was still complaining in his diaries: "... I never have anything to say to Mary. I can't ever really forgive her for being such a creep about *Chelsea Girls* in the sixties, for demanding money—saying she wouldn't sign a release until she got it. She squeezed around \$1,000 out of us."[184] Ondine, an early superstar, who fascinated Warhol with his eloquence, also reported later that he had asked the artist for money at the time: "*Constantly, I asked for money. Constantly, people asked him for money. He NEVER paid anyone! He NEVER did anything to anybody! I mean, only when he was asked to pay – when they put the screws to him—did he really pay!*"[185] Jeremiah Newton is convinced that it was a better tactic not to ask Warhol for money:

He liked sincerity and he didn't like to be hassled for money all the time like a lot of people would hassle him. ... I didn't demand money and Candy didn't demand money. None of us had any money but we never asked him for anything. But he was generous. He gave money sometimes to us. ... I mean he didn't give us thousands of dollars or anything but twenty or forty dollars went a long way in those days.[186]

Warhol's devotees and followers were not aware that in the 1960s, despite the media hype surrounding him, the artist did not yet have the commercial success that he enjoyed later during the 1970s. "Andy was as famous as you could get in the 1960s," says Gerard Malanga, "He was getting a lot of press which may have created the illusion that he was successful financially. All the movies were financed not from the sale of his art but from the money he made on Madison Avenue as a commercial artist."[187] There is also another aspect, which Benjamin Liu points out: "You have to look at it in two ways. One is his background. He's a saver, like meaning to save everything. That includes money. So, some people use that word 'penny pincher.' I think he is very frugal. Among all the famous people he never actually hired a limousine that he paid for. It was always someone else's limousine. He'd never call for a limousine and say 'Hey, take me to the party.' It was always a taxi."[188] Pat Hackett, who met the artist in fall 1968 and worked for him until his death, states: "He could be generous. He could be generous and he could be cheap. Sometimes it depended on how his prices at auction were—like if there was an auction and somebody who collected his work was selling it, that really upset him."[189] The jewelry dealer and designer John Reinhold, who met Warhol in 1978 and became a close friend, recalls particular occasions when the artist showed generosity:

I can remember going home many nights, a zillion times, let's say we were in a taxi together with some younger person, and when they dropped Andy off he would always give them the money for the taxi. He always thought of that and he always did that. I mean, I never saw him not do it. It could have been two in the morning, three in the morning, he would always think to give the person the money for the cab. It wasn't only that he was generous, but he was always thinking of the other person.[190]

Another example of Warhol's generosity is revealed in his diaries, when he reports on May 27, 1977 about meeting his superstar Nico again at a Parisian gallery: "Nico looked older and fatter and sadder. She was crying, she said because of the beauty of the show. I wanted to give her some money but not directly so I signed a 500 franc note (\$100) and handed it to her and she got even more sentimental and said, 'I must frame *this*, can you give me another one, unsigned, to *spend*?'"[191]

184
Hackett 1989, p. 638, March 30, 1985.

185
In Smith 1986, p. 433.

186
Jeremiah Newton in a telephone conversation with the author on August 8, 2010.

187
Gerard Malanga in a conversation with the author on July 2, 2012 in Hudson.

188
Benjamin Liu in a conversation with the author on November 30, 2012 in New York.

189
Pat Hackett in a conversation with the author on December 4, 2012 in New York.

190
John Reinhold in a telephone conversation with the author on May 26, 2010.

191
Hackett 1989, p. 46.

Nico was born in Cologne in 1938 as Christa Päffgen and grew up near Berlin. When she was sixteen she was discovered by the photographer Herbert Tobias, who employed her for fashion shoots and gave her the name Nico. In 1955 she moved to Paris where Tobias' teacher, Willy Maywald, helped her to make an international breakthrough. Four years later she met Federico Fellini, who gave her a guest appearance in his movie *La Dolce Vita*. In 1964 Nico met Bob Dylan in Paris, who encouraged her musical ambitions. She recorded her first single the following year.[192] This was also the year that she met Andy Warhol.[193] Not least because of her beauty, the artist decided to let her appear in his movies. Not long afterwards Nico also caused a stir as the singer in the band produced by Warhol, The Velvet Underground. In *POPism* he says, "She had straight shoulder-length blond hair with bangs, blue eyes, full lips, wide cheekbones—the works. And she had this very strange way of speaking. People described her voice as everything from eery, to bland and smooth, to slow and hollow, to a 'wind in a drainpipe,' to an 'IBM computer with a Garbo accent.' She sounded the same strange way when she sang, too."[194]

Salvador Dalí always displayed great generosity as a host in his Spanish homeland. Peter Beard, who visited Dalí together with Vera von Lehndorff in Port Lligat, emphasizes: "We had a lot of fun in Port Lligat and we had a lot of amazing meals and Dalí was such a generous person. He was an incredibly generous person. That's the thing I'd really like to say about Dalí. I know he enjoyed us but he was so generous with us."[195] Susi Wyss also starts rhapsodizing when she recalls this hospitality:

I was allowed to stay with the notary at Cadaqués … . We were two girls—I took a friend with me. Everything was free—Captain Moore gave me money to live on. I was very spoilt. And we often went out to eat with Dalí, Amanda and the twins or with other people. It was very private and fun. Dalí liked to eat épaule d'agneau—but he did not eat much. Nor did he drink any champagne—it was only ever served to others. … Dalí was very generous, but not towards people who wanted money from him.[196]

Pandora adds that in this respect Gala was very protective of Dalí, "Many people just wanted to take from Dalí, and had nothing to give. It took three years for her to realize that the relationship was one that I did not want anything material from Dalí."[197] Elsa Peretti, who posed for Dalí in the 1960s,[198] had the same experience, "I think that Gala had a kind of sympathy for me because I was a normal person in a way and not trying to get a lot from him. She liked me and I think for this reason Dalí also liked me."[199]

Like Warhol, Dalí was only ever generous when he was not being asked for money. It is well known that this was also the case in New York. He regularly held his "$3,000 Sunday dinners," to which he invited many guests. Warhol was a frequent guest. In his diaries he reports about a dinner at Laurent, which took place in spring 1979 and to which Dalí had invited "about 40 persons": "He's really generous with these kids."[200] A particular token of Dalí's hospitality was his famous "Last Supper," which he held every year in New York. Pandora recalls:

Each year, as Dalí prepared to return to Europe, he would arrange a special dinner. Dalí called it, 'The Last Supper.' Twelve people would be chosen

---

192
Husslein 2008 (n.p.).

193
Angell 2006, p. 145.

194
Warhol/Hackett 1980, p. 145.

195
Peter Beard in a Skype conversation with the author on September 24, 2010.

196
Susi Wyss in a conversation with the author on October 25, 2013 in Paris (translated from the German).

197
Pandora in a conversation with the author on November 20, 2011 in Mariposa, California. She recalls, "Dalí offered gifts to me, but I would not accept them. He tried to give me his Sarah Bernardt cane, but I would not accept it. When Gala witnessed that, she said, 'Oh, Pandora is not here to take.'" Ibid.

198
See the chapter **Sterile Love and Voyeurism** in Part 2.

199
Elsa Peretti in a telephone conversation with the author on October 2, 2015.

200
Hackett 1989, p. 209, March 4, 1979. See also the chapter **The 1970s** in Part 5.

to attend. Scores of people would come to the St. Regis in the hope of being selected. How do you select just twelve from among so many famous people and celebrities? Sometimes it would be too difficult for Dalí to choose, so he would ask me to do it for him. Naturally, if Louis XIV was in New York, she was always invited. For me to choose from all these people was very difficult. Those who were not invited were unhappy; unhappy with me, not with Dalí. Therefore, Dalí was free from seeing their disappointment.

I knew some of the people that Dalí would want to invite. At other times, I just chose extraordinary thinkers, for instance, a scientist or a philosopher, so Dalí would not be bored. Dalí knew a lot of scientists, and I knew four-dimensional-thinkers and we would try to find a common language. ...

I always sat to Dalí's left when we dined. If Gala was attending, and on most occasions she did, she sat opposite Dalí. Once, when Gala did not attend, Dalí asked me to sit in Gala's place.[201]

An interesting insight into the "Last Supper" in spring 1973 is provided by a report that was published in the May issue of *Andy Warhol's Interview* in the same year:

DALÍ'S LAST SUPPER: Salvador DALÍ left town for spring in Paris, summer in Spain, but not before pouring out enough Taitinger Blanc et Blanc to start another run on the dollar. The twelve invited to his bubbly last supper, staged, appropriately, in a red-and-gilt, LUDWIG-like dining room at the St. Regis, including: HALSTON, in a pale blue brand new Big Shirt; PANDORA the star of LUMINOUS PROCURESS and a dead ringer for EDITH SITWELL; FRANCESCO SCAVULLO, looking great after a bout of pneumonia; a beautiful model named LISETTE; a mysterious ash-blonde who described herself as "a businesswoman from Beverly Hills"; a prominent Spanish journalist; a languid favorite of Dalí's named JUAN DE JESUS, whose mother is the Dominican consul in New York; and, at Dalí's right, "EL REY LOUIS QUATORZE," an extremely elegant Spanish lady who may be Bourbon but that's as far as the semblance with the Sun King goes. Midway through dinner Dalí's grander-than-grand wife GALA breezed in with a favorite of her own—a pale young blond whom she introduced as JESUS CHRIST SUPERSTAR—kissed her hubby on the cheek, snubbed the King, and breezed out. Highlight of the evening came when a very young fashion stylist named SEAN BYRNES asked Dalí: "What would we do without artists? Where would the magic come from?" El Maestro responded with a flawless gesture: first he spilled a glass of wine—red wine—across the table towards Sean, then he slipped a gold phallus underneath the table cloth, pushing it into the boy's wine-soaked hands. After dinner Dalí swept everyone up to see the COUNT BASIE at the Maisonette. "Leave your champagne here," he ordered, "there is mucho more next door!"[202]

Assistants, Employees, Secretaries, and Managers

Even as a commercial artist, Andy Warhol was good at involving others in his production. His mother contributed greatly at the time.[1] He also liked letting friends help him. He organized "coloring parties" for this purpose at

201
Pandora in a conversation with the author on November 20, 2011 in Mariposa, California.

202
"Small Talk," p. 46.

1
See the chapter **Creative Motherly Care** in Part 2.

2
Bourdon 1989,
p. 46.

Serendipity 3.[2] Stephen Bruce, who founded the restaurant together with Calvin Holt and Patch Harrington, describes these as follows:

He used to come in after doing what they called the rounds, taking his artwork to advertising agencies because Madison Avenue is around the corner from here. ... He would come in for a cappuccino and hot chocolate. ... He very rarely came alone, unless he came alone to converse with me. So he would bring five or six people and ... printed matter that he had drawn and printed already, and he would have them coloring special butterflies or shoes or different objects ... They would do all the work for him, as far as coloring with India ink, because that was very popular in the 1960s.[3]

3
Stephen Bruce
in a telephone
conversation
with the author
on July 6, 2011.

It did not take long for Warhol to become a recognized commercial artist and he was literally overwhelmed with assignments. He soon took on Vito Giallo as assistant. Giallo had been Jack Wolfgang Beck's assistant and now wanted to work freelance. Since he got on well with Warhol, he became his assistant for a few months in 1955. He came to Warhol's apartment at about ten or eleven o'clock and worked until the early afternoon.[4] The two of them enjoyed a friendly relationship and also spent their leisure time together, until this came to an end, which Giallo describes as follows:

4
Giallo in Bockris
1989, pp. 113f.

He had a habit of dropping people for strange reasons. He dropped me overnight because every Wednesday night he took sex lessons from this boy and girl and wanted me to join him. I refused to go. Andy was so disappointed. I didn't hear from him again until twenty-one years later when I opened my shop on Madison Avenue. Andy was so impressed that I was on Madison Avenue. We became friends again and the last eight years of his life, he visited me every morning until the day he died.[5]

5
Vito Giallo in
a telephone con-
versation with
the author on
May 25, 2010.

Vito Giallo was replaced by Nathan Gluck, who remained Warhol's assistant for almost ten years. Giallo himself had suggested Gluck as a successor.[6] Gluck was working for the George Kahn advertising agency and met Warhol in 1950.[7] He was talented, original, and had a positive influence on Warhol's career. Many friends later believed that Gluck was "one of Warhol's first victims," as the artist purportedly "used and abused" his assistants. Gluck later refuted this insinuation and emphasized that he had been Warhol's assistant and not his collaborator.[8] He worked for him between three and five hours a day and his task was to complete detailed and accurate drawings of shoes, jewels, perfume vials, hosiery, and other fashion accessories, and sometimes he had to arrange a layout with these. Warhol then corrected details or altered the composition.[9] As Warhol's situation was constantly improving in terms of assignments, he not only founded Andy Warhol Enterprises, Inc., but also decided to employ Ted Carey as a further assistant. Carey worked alongside Warhol up until the early 1960s.[10]

6
Gluck in
McShine 1989,
p. 425.

7
Gluck in
O'Connor/Liu
1996, p. 28.

8
Bockris 1989,
p. 118.

9
Gluck in Crone
1976, p. 18.

Even into the 1950s, Warhol did not want to mention the existence of his assistants. He preferred to let his clients believe that he was exceptionally diligent.[11] Warhol later made no secret of the fact that he was employing help. In the famous interview "Andy Warhol: My True Story" in 1966, he even declared that he had his paintings produced by others:

10
Smith 1986,
p. 246.

11
Bourdon 1989,
p. 43.

I'm not the exhibitionist the articles try to make me out as, but I'm not that much of a hard-working man, either: it looks like I'm working harder than I am here because all the paintings are copied from my one original by my assistants, like a factory would do it, because we're turning out a painting every day and a sculpture every day and a movie every day. Several people could do the work that I do just as well because it's very simple to do: the pattern's right there. After all, there are a lot of painters and draughtsmen who just paint and draw a little and give it to someone else to finish.[12]

In the early 1970s, Warhol went a little too far when he claimed in the documentary *Painters Painting* by Emile de Antonio, "Brigid [Polk] does all my paintings, but she doesn't know anything about them. ... Brigid has been doing my paintings for the last three years."[13] Speaking in retrospect, Brigid Berlin herself says, "We got in trouble ... . And the next day it's in *TIME* magazine that I did all the *Campbell's Soup Can* paintings. Well, he thought it was funny, but there were a lot of people that had bought *Campbell's Soup Cans* that didn't think that was funny. So, there had to be a retraction."[14] In *POPism* Warhol commented on the matter later as follows: "... I'd only been kidding. At that point I think I finally learned once and for all that the wrong flip remark in the press can cause just as many problems as a broken contract."[15]

Despite the public's image of Warhol, he was, in fact, personally involved in his art production. He produced the photographic templates for his paintings, painted the canvases, and also determined selections. Jamie Wyeth remarks on this, "He was an extremely hard worker, but if you'd asked him whether he painted, he would say, he didn't even paint these things. The kids did them, when in fact he was the one that did them."[16] One of these kids was Ronnie Cutrone, who was a regular guest at the Factory in the 1960s and Warhol's assistant from 1972 to 1982.[17] In 1978 he described his tasks as follows:

I started helping him out with the prints mostly, not the paintings. ... basically what I do is photograph anything that's not people ... .

Well, there's the general assumption that other people do his paintings, of course, which is bullshit. I['d] like to make that clear right now. I don't really touch the paintings at all. ... we work on it together, we talk about it ... and things like that, but nobody really ... touches the work except Andy.[18]

Early on Warhol stated that he wanted to be a machine.[19] Walter Steding, who started as his assistant in 1978, comments on this:

He wasn't so machine-like. He really needed to get his hands on each project. Another time I was helping, there was tape on the paint. In order to get a hard edge, he used tape. And I was helping to put the tape on and I was putting on a line and he said, no, he wanted to do that. It's just a mechanical thing, but he wanted to make sure it was his painting, his grid. ... And he would say, "Mix up a pretty blue!" Whatever pretty means. I think I knew and I made the blue for him that I believed he wanted. And I'd slide that down to him and dig the mop in it and then he'd swish that mop all around the canvas. ... He did all that swishing himself. He wouldn't let someone else come in and put the paint on.[20]

Warhol also used assistants and employees in the development of new ideas. The painter Ingeborg Princess zu Schleswig-Holstein, who came to the Factory in 1980, was initially assigned to *Interview* and helped later on with the production of paintings:

12
In Goldsmith 2004, p. 89.

13
In Antonio/ Tuchman 1984, pp. 120f.

14
Brigid Berlin in a conversation with the author on December 4, 2012 in New York.

15
Warhol/Hackett 1980, p. 249.

16
Jamie Wyeth in a telephone conversation with the author on April 3, 2013.

17
O'Connor/Liu 1996, p. 55.

18
In Smith 1986, pp. 277, 284.

19
In 1963 he remarked in an interview, "The reason I'm painting this way is that I want to be a machine, and I feel that whatever I do and do machine-like is what I want to do." In Goldsmith 2004, p. 18.

20
Walter Steding in a telephone conversation with the author on January 12, 2013.

3

We often had to fan out and find some objects that were then photographed and depicted later. We had to find interesting objects or think of something that might be suitable at that moment. It felt rather like being in an advertising agency ... And there were also phases where, for some reason, there wasn't much to do at the Factory. Then Andy would say: "Oh, why don't you go out and come back and tell me what to do?" or "Why don't you get inspired in town?"[21]

In 1963 Gerard Malanga came to the Factory and soon became Warhol's most important assistant. He was successful in guiding the special atmosphere that reigned at the Factory at the time onto a creative path. The actress Sally Kirkland, who was a frequent guest there in the 1960s, sees his abstinence as a reason for this: "He was by far the most normal person around Andy. ... There was this incredible amount of drugs going around. And he always seemed to be very straight and sober ... you could communicate at any time to him and he would be grounded and be able to tell you what was going on whereas with most people around Andy that wasn't the case."[22] Gerard Malanga was born in 1943 in the Bronx and felt drawn to art very early on. In high school he discovered his love of poetic literature. In the fall of 1962 he met Warhol at a party held by his mentors, the moviemakers Willard Maas and Marie Menken. A couple of months later, in June 1963, the poet Charles Henri Ford brought about another encounter between him and Warhol, as he knew that the artist was looking for an assistant for his silkscreen production. Gerard Malanga started working at the Factory just two days later.[23] In *POPism* it says: "The great thing, though, was that he really did seem to know about silkscreening. He started working for me right away—for $1.25 an hour, which he always reminds me was the New York State minimum wage at the time."[24]

In the same summer, Warhol also decided to make movies. He could not have chosen a better moment, as his new assistant also had expertise in this field.[25] Malanga helped on the technical front, but also stood in front of the camera himself for numerous movies.[26] He played a central role when the production of the *Screen Tests* started the following year, for which visitors to the Factory—including Salvador Dalí—were asked to gaze motionlessly into the camera.[27] Gerard Malanga left the Factory in September 1967 and spent a lengthy period of time in Rome, but he was back in New York when Valerie Solanas made the attempt on Warhol's life in June 1968. In September he helped him once again with silkscreen production,[28] and a year later he became co-editor of *Interview*. However, there were tensions within the Factory and Malanga felt, as he put it himself, "so much resistance" that he left the Factory for good in November 1970.[29]

In early 1964, William ("Billy") Linich entered the Factory scene and became a further important assistant. Linich was born in 1940 in Poughkeepsie, New York. After high school, in 1958 he went to New York City. In early 1960 he worked as a waiter at Serendipity 3[30] and soon afterwards found work as a lighting technician on the off-Broadway scene.[31] At that time he held "haircutting parties" at his apartment, where there was marijuana and amphetamines and he offered haircuts to his guests. He had learned this skill from his great-uncle, who had a hairdressing salon. At the end of December

21
Ingeborg Princess zu Schleswig-Holstein in a conversation with the author on June 30, 2011 in Hamburg (translated from the German).

22
Sally Kirkland in a telephone conversation with the author on December 16, 2012.

23
Malanga 2002, p. 139.

24
Warhol/Hackett 1980, pp. 26f.

25
Malanga 2002, p. 106.

26
Cf. Angell 2006, pp. 121f.

27
See the chapter **Warhol's Screen Tests of Dalí** in Part 4.

28
Gerard Malanga in a conversation with the author on July 2, 2012 in Hudson, New York.

29
Bourdon 1989, p. 307.

30
Stephen Bruce in a telephone conversation with the author on July 6, 2011.

31
Bourdon 1989, p. 170.

1963 Warhol was a guest at one of these parties and was able to take a look at Linich's apartment, which was adorned with silver foil and in which all objects were painted in silver.[32] Warhol asked Linich to coat his new studio, a big attic room on the fourth floor of the house on 231 East Forty-Seventh Street, in silver in a similar manner. Linich, who later called himself Billy Name, transformed Warhol's new studio between January and April 1964 into what was to become the legendary Silver Factory.[33] He furnished it with found objects, including a giant, curved, red couch. He covered the walls and piping with silver foil. Then he sprayed everything with silver bronze—even the toilet bowls. Billy loved reflecting surfaces and he fitted mirrors and little mirror shards everywhere.[34] He became one of the artist's most influential helpers and took on not only the role of decorator at the Factory, but also that of supervisor: "Andy was just starting to become famous, so it was necessary for him to have a buffer of some kind," according to Name, "If people would come on to Andy and want something from him, he would always say, 'Well, no, it's Billy's Factory'—people would want to have parties there all the time—'You have to see what Billy says.' I'd say, 'Oh no, because we're working.'"[35] The artist Neke Carson, who came to the Factory upon invitation by Warhol and was given a role in the movie ★★★★ *(Four Stars)* reports that there were rules at the Factory:

And then we all went out to some party or something that night. But I didn't have a place to stay and the thing was you couldn't stay in the Factory, otherwise it would just be people with sleeping bags all over the place. So the rule was, you could hang out there during the day but eventually Billy Name, the enforcer, would put you out. … Billy took pity on me and just let me stay there and then I went back to Providence the next day. … Then I started coming in like once a month and then it was just a gradual thing of just basically showing Andy what I was doing. … He would just be enthusiastic—he was doing that for a lot of people, which I don't think people understand, how much he like encouraged other people to do their work.[36]

Because of his experience, Billy Name did the lighting for the movie production and, like Gerard Malanga, stood in front of the camera for some of the movies.[37] He also documented the work at Warhol's studio in numerous photographs. He soon had his own darkroom at the Factory to which he withdrew more and more frequently in 1968, and finally did not emerge at all. In the spring of 1970 the door was opened. A bestial stench emanated from the darkroom. Cigarette butts were lying around everywhere and the walls were covered with astrological diagrams. A note was stuck to one of the walls that said: "Andy—I am not here anymore but I am fine. Love, Billy."[38]

In the later summer of 1965, Warhol met the young moviemaker Paul Morrissey, whom Gerard Malanga had invited to a movie screening. Warhol suggested that he come to the Factory the next day, to watch the work on a movie. Due to his technical expertise and business sense, Morrissey became an important member of the Factory and Warhol's right hand in movie production.[39] He was born in 1938, came from a Catholic family from Yonkers, New York, and received a Jesuit education at Fordham University in the Bronx. Later on he referred to his Catholic upbringing as "the best

32
Watson 2003,
p. 119.

33
Bockris 1989,
p. 192.

34
Warhol/Hackett
1980, pp. 63ff.

35
In: Shore/Tillman
1995, pp. 37f.

36
Neke Carson in
a conversation
with the author
on December 6,
2012 in New York.

37
Cf. Angell 2006,
pp. 117f.

38
Warhol/Hackett
1980, pp. 299f.

39
Bourdon 1989,
p. 208.

thing that ever happened to me."[40] After studying literature and completing his military service, he worked for a brief period at an insurance company and then as a social worker at New York City's Department of Social Services in Spanish Harlem.[41] When he met Warhol, Morrissey had already been familiar with the underground movie scene for a few years. He also rejected drugs and ensured that the Factory was gradually transformed into a drugs-free zone. This also meant that the days of those visitors who just hung out were numbered.[42] Morrissey had a significant influence on Warhol's movie production. Overall, the movies became more commercial, as well as more conventional. He himself showed little interest in formal and expressive experiments.[43] Morrissey assumed direction of *Flesh* (1968), and of most of the further productions. He also supported the actor Joe Dallesandro, who had been discovered during the shooting of *The Loves of Ondine*.[44]

In 1967 Frederick W. Hughes appeared on the Factory scene and became Warhol's agent and business manager. Hughes, originally from Houston, was the son of a furniture representative and had studied art history. The art collectors John and Dominique de Menil noticed him and took him under their wing as they soon recognized his abilities, especially his sharp eye for artistic quality. Hughes turned into a "patrician snob" and let people believe he was related to the business tycoon Howard Hughes.[45] On a journey to New York he met Warhol, who was fascinated by Hughes's elegant appearance. In *POPism* the artist later called him a "cute kid" and "dandy."[46] Benjamin Liu, Warhol's personal assistant in the 1980s, remarks about Fred Hughes: "Fred made the business, so to speak. Andy said that to me. ... He said, 'Oh, Fred is a brilliant decorator, not by profession, just by his eye, his taste.' ... There is a reason why Diana Vreeland loved Fred. It's because of his aesthetic, his intelligence, and his way of ... maybe his dandyism."[47] One of the first business deals that Hughes arranged was the sale of Warhol's artworks to the de Menils. Fred was also greatly beneficial in winning portrait assignments. He successfully convinced the de Menils to commission Warhol to do a portrait of Dominique de Menil and their private curator, Jermayne MacAgy. This led to further clients, who in turn recommended him to others.[48] Therefore it did not take long for Hughes to climb within the Factory hierarchy, outlasting Malanga, Name, and Morrissey. He started as a factotum, soon became vice president of Andy Warhol Films, Inc. and later the deputy director of the Warhol imperium.[49] Just after Hughes had started as a new manager at the Factory, Warhol liked to say, "I'm just a traveling portrait artist now. I just go where Fred tells me to go."[50] To a certain extent, Hughes therefore took on the role at Warhol's Factory that Gala assumed in Dalí's life. He, too, was sometimes the "bad guy" and could be unpleasant.[51] Furthermore, he liked to play the diva, as Brigid Berlin recalls, "Andy would come out and say 'Bridge, what do you think is happening to Fred?' 'Well, Fred is an American kid from Houston, Texas, who thinks he's Diana Vreeland now.' He talked in her accent."[52] Hughes continued to play an important role at the Factory even after Warhol's death. The will that the artist wrote on March 11, 1982 designated Hughes as an executor and bequeathed $250,000 to him. Warhol's brothers Paul and John Warhol were also each to receive

40
Quoted according to Watson 2003, p. 67.

41
Bourdon 1989, p. 208.

42
Ibid.

43
Ibid., p. 256.

44
Ibid., p. 294.

45
Ibid., p. 263, Bockris 1989, p. 281.

46
Warhol/Hackett 1980, p. 216.

47
Benjamin Liu in a conversation with the author on November 30, 2012 in New York.

48
Colacello in Heymer 2000, (n.p.).

49
Bourdon 1989, p. 264.

50
Quoted according to Colacello 1990, p. 90.

51
Hans Mayer in a conversation with the author on March 11, 2011 in Düsseldorf; Princess Ingeborg zu Schleswig-Holstein in a conversation with the author on June 30, 2011 in Hamburg.

52
Brigid Berlin in a conversation with the author on December 4, 2012 in New York.

"up to" \$250,000.[53] The main heir to the fortune, which was estimated at a total sum of between \$75 and \$100 million, was the Andy Warhol Foundation of Visual Arts. Fred Hughes went on to become president of the foundation, John Warhola its vice president, and Vincent Fremont its director.[54]

Vincent Fremont had become acquainted with the Factory through Paul Morrissey and at first had merely held the microphone for the movie *Trash* in 1969.[55] He had already been a great fan of Warhol in high school and started working for him from January 1971. Fremont reports:

Andy had a real American work ethic. He believed you start from the bottom and work your way up to being successful. When I first started working for him he gave me keys to his studio and I would open up the studio every morning at 9 a.m. I would clean up the place, sweep the floors, answer the phones and run errands. It was up to you to gain Andy's trust and let him know what you were capable of doing for him and with him. He made me vice president of Andy Warhol Enterprises, Inc. in 1974 when I was twenty-four years old. I collaborated on video projects with Andy and ended up producing all of his cable TV shows.

In my first few years of working at the Andy Warhol studio at 33 Union Square West in Manhattan, Fred Hughes and Paul Morrissey were both acting as Andy's managers. Paul was directing films that Andy produced and Fred was working on painting exhibitions and painting commissions for Andy. They were both vying for exclusive manager status. Paul left Andy's studio after making the films 3D Flesh for Frankenstein *and* Blood for Dracula *in Rome. Fred Hughes became Andy's exclusive business manager in 1975.*

In 1974 Andy opened a checking account for me called Andy Warhol Enterprises, Inc. SPL so I could write payroll checks and pay bills. Later when we changed the business structure, he had three checking accounts: AW #1 was personal, AW #2 was for business, and AW#3 was the account I used for payroll, paying bills, etc.[56]

Vincent Fremont, who succeeded in building up a good rapport with Warhol, was a reliable employee.[57] Brigid Berlin says that he was "the only person that Andy ever let go to the bank."[58] And furthermore:

He [Andy] freaked out when Fred and Vincent said that it was a good idea to get health insurance for everybody that worked there. ... He didn't understand this idea at all of everybody having health insurance and then telling him it would be cheaper for him and all that stuff. Then he's told one day, and this really freaked him out, there was gonna be a meeting and that Andy had to do a will. Well, he panicked. He almost wanted to walk in the door and say "Bridge, let's go shopping" (laughs). He couldn't deal with this. And then of course Fred had to have another little meeting with him because Fred got this bright idea that if Andy died there should be a foundation. Well, don't think for one minute that Andy knew what a foundation was. I mean, Andy was not thinking in those terms.[59]

One employee who contributed significantly to Warhol's recognition also as an author was Pat Hackett. She was studying at Barnard College and was looking for a job in the fall of 1968. She asked Warhol if he could use a copy typist and he said she could start work for him straight away. From

53 Bourdon 1989, p. 414; Bob Colacello reports that the Warhol brothers received about \$600,000 each. Cf. Colacello 1990, p. 498.

54 Ibid.

55 Fremont in McShine 1989, p. 441.

56 Vincent Fremont in a conversation with the author on June 28, 2012 in New York.

57 Bockris 1989, p. 324.

58 Brigid Berlin in a conversation with the author on December 4, 2012 in New York.

59 Ibid.

60
Hackett 1989,
p. ix.

61
Ibid., p. xi.

62
Ibid., p. x.

63
See the chapter
**Autobio-
graphies
Written
"With Four
Hands"**
in Part 4.

64
Ibid., p. xvi.

65
Colacello in
O'Connor/Liu
1996, p. 80.

66
Ibid., p. 82.

67
See the chapter
**Dali News
and Andy
Warhol's
Interview**
in Part 4.

68
Brigid Berlin in
a conversation
with the author
on December 4,
2012 in New York.

69
Vincent Fremont
recalls: "Andy
liked Brigid Berlin
transcribing and
typing his audio-
tapes, he liked
to see the white
stack of paper
grow higher and
+

then on Hackett went to the Factory several times a week after her seminars, to transcribe telephone calls.[60] When she was preparing for her exams she did not show up for a while. As Warhol no longer wanted to be without his new employee, he "sweetened the pot" by paying her travel expenses for the subway to and from the Factory.[61] Pat Hackett remembered Warhol later as a "polite and humble" employer:

He rarely told anyone to do things—he'd just ask in a hopeful tone, "Do you think you could …?" He treated everyone with respect, he never talked down to anyone. And he made everyone feel important, soliciting their opinions and probing with questions about their own lives. … And he was especially grateful for even the smallest extra thing you might do for him. I never heard anyone say "Thank you" more than Andy, and from his tone, you always felt he meant it. "Thank you" were the last words he ever said to me.[62]

In the years that followed, Pat Hackett became ever more important. The 1975 publication of *THE Philosophy of Andy Warhol (From A to B and Back Again)* was the first book that she contributed to significantly. At Warhol's request, she acted as co-author for *POPism*, which was published five years later.[63] In the years before 1976, Hackett had also started to keep a general and very sketchy Factory log for Warhol. In fall 1976 he began summarizing the daily events himself and communicating them to his employee on the telephone every morning. These telephone conversations form the basis for *The Andy Warhol Diaries*, which Hackett went on to publish two years after the artist's death.[64]

In 1970 Warhol found another important staff member in Bob Colacello. Colacello was born in Brooklyn in 1947 as Robert Colaciello. He studied stage direction at Columbia University and already as a student began writing movie reviews, which were published in the New York weekly *The Village Voice*. In 1970 he wrote a review of the Factory movie *Trash*, calling it "a great Roman Catholic masterpiece in the tradition of Maria Magdalena," which showed that everyone—even prostitutes, hustlers, and junkies—could be redeemed. Colacello then received a call from Paul Morrissey, was invited to the Factory, and it was suggested that he write for the magazine *Interview*.[65] He became chief editor after just six months and received a salary of fifty dollars a week.[66] Colacello worked for *Interview* until the beginning of 1983 and contributed significantly to its success. It evolved quickly from an unremarkable movie magazine to a glamorous magazine with reports about fashion, lifestyle, and the entire entertainment industry.[67]

As early as the 1960s, Warhol let wealthy young people, such as Edie Sedgwick, Jane Holzer, Ultra Violet, and Brigid Berlin, appear in his movies. Berlin remarks that Warhol upheld this preference into the 1970s: "What Andy liked to work there, were kids that came from good families. … Because, I guess, he thought we all had trust funds."[68] In 1976 Berlin took on the job of receptionist at the Factory. She answered telephone calls and transcribed tape recordings.[69] Fred Hughes, in particular, had a special talent for recruiting rich young people from good homes. Bob Colacello writes in *Holy Terror*: "… Fred found a ready pool in the growing number of 'English Muffins' landing in New York from London. They were the British equivalents of the rich young Italian immigrants who had landed the year before, and were soon to be followed by the 'French Fries.'"[70]

The first "English Muffin" to arrive at the factory was Lady Anne Lambton in 1973. Her father was the conservative politician Lord Anthony Lambton. Lady Lambton reports that at a charity ball Fred Hughes had invited her on a whim to come to the Factory:

I sat next to him and I said, "I don't know what to do and I don't know what I'm doing." I was seventeen ... and he said, "Well, you could come and work in the factory." That just got me depressed. I said, "You know, I've sat here and talked to you, to be polite and now you've offered me a job in a factory." ... I thought that it was a canned pea factory, not sure why. Didn't know it was The Factory he was offering me a job in. I felt that my life held more promise than watching peas pass on a conveyor belt. ... And then I left and bumped into [the art dealer] Robert Fraser on the way out and I said to Robert Fraser, "Who is that ghastly man? He's just asked me to go and work in a factory." And he said, "Not a factory—The Factory! That's Andy Warhol's Factory and he's Fred Hughes, who's as much Andy Warhol as Andy Warhol and you've just blown it." So, I said, "I don't think so," and went back: "Hello, let's start again." I said, "My name is Anne Lambton. I will come to New York and work in the Factory, if you may pay my ticket, accommodation, and give me a lot of money?!" And he said, "What can you do?" I said, "Nothing." He said, "Ok." ... So, wherever I was put, I couldn't do it. I couldn't understand accents, I thought everybody was a pervert, I didn't take the messages correctly. I was put on the door, so I was no good on the door, I didn't let the right people in, didn't keep the right people out. In the end I was put to sweeping up the Factory, which I did one morning. I used to sit and do my nails a lot. Oh, and they tried to put me on the Xerox machine and that made me cry, because I didn't know what a Xerox machine was. I thought it sounded like an episode of Doctor Who when they said, "Maybe you can work the Xerox" and Bob Colacello found me in the lift at the Westbury [Hotel] crying and he says, "What's wrong?" and I say, "You want me to use the Xerox machine and I don't know how to do it—what is it?"[71]

When Warhol went on tour with his book *THE Philosophy of Andy Warhol*, a suitable job was finally found for Lady Lambton. She became his bodyguard. She explains with humor what it meant to be Warhol's bodyguard: "... you sit by his side or walk with him and say, 'Don't you understand? Mr. Warhol doesn't want to speak to you at the moment.' And people were so surprised by this tiny little girl with a very gruff voice and an English accent being very polite, and they sort of backed off. They were usually all weirdos anyway ...."[72] Lady Lambton left the Factory after barely three years, after a car accident. Even so, she stayed in contact with Warhol up until his death. In the end he had suggested to her that they marry:

I was always really, really fond of him and he was always really, really fond of me ... It was so odd, he asked me to marry him in a club, he said "Gee, why don't we get married?" and I said, "Right. Are you asking me to marry you?" Then "So, ok. Give me nine portraits a year and half your money" and he said, "Well, gee, I'll give you six and a third." And I said, "No, I only want three months to look rough," and he said, "What would I have to do? Do I have to

70
Colacello 1990, p. 247.

+ higher as she typed away. Though a number of the tapes were interviews he had done to be included in *Interview* magazine, Andy just liked to see the volume of typed pages grow, knowing he would not read all of it or listen to the tapes again. It was almost like he thought of Brigid's typing as a conceptual art piece." Vincent Fremont in a conversation with the author on June 28, 2012 in New York.

71
Lady Anne Lambton in a telephone conversation with the author on August 11, 2012.

72
Ibid.

ask your father?" And I said, "Well, if you ask my father you had better do it by telegram, because if he sees you, there is no chance." So, then we were laughing and you'd think that was it—a joke. ... When he came over when I had a car crash and I was in a hospital and he announced to the press he was going to marry me, I didn't know whether it was real or not.[73]

After Lady Anne Lambton, Catherine Hesketh brought a British flair to the Factory. Hesketh, from the Guinness aristocratic dynasty of Irish origins, which became world-famous through the beer brewery founded in 1759, is the daughter of Jonathan Guinness, 3rd Baron Moyne. Hesketh reports how she came to be in the United States in 1975:

I went to America trying to get a job or trying to enter university. And I was having lunch with Robert Mapplethorpe and he had to take a picture for Interview *magazine and he took me with him .... Fred Hughes offered me a job. I got to know him first. ... So I came and stayed with Fred until I got an apartment of my own and started working in* Interview *magazine. ... I was called the European editor and I worked my way up from doing the subscriptions to organizing interviews and editing and thinking who should go in the magazine and choosing photographers. ... Bob Colacello was my boss. ... But there were lots of other editors, I was not the main editor. ... and I also became more and more friendly with Andy and so I went on a trip around America with him and Bob or him and Fred or whoever went along ... to deliver portraits or to go to openings. ... I went out with Andy on the road and went shopping with him, generally hung out with him.*[74]

Catherine Hesketh was also regularly in Warhol's company when he was out exploring New York nightlife. Marc Balet, who started at *Interview* the same year as she and became art director, still remembers his co-worker very well: "She was that kind of heiress who came to the Factory to work in the morning still in her gown from the night before. She'd been out all night. And she'd just come in a big dress or something and start fumbling through her desk. She couldn't find anything and she was madness. I just adored her. We all did."[75]

Marc Balet proved to be a lucky find for *Interview*. According to Bob Colacello, "... Marc had a natural feel for the clean, simple look that Andy, Fred, and I all favored."[76] Balet was born in 1948. After studying architecture at Rhode Island School of Design he went to Rome, where he won the Prix de Rome. Balet emphasizes that Warhol gave everyone a chance and relied on his instinct and intuition—degrees, schooling, and experience were not so important for him.[77] Balet worked for *Interview* until 1988 and, looking back, he remarks that he had learned everything about PR and marketing from Warhol. He says about his appointment at the Factory:

It was Upstairs, Downstairs at the Factory. We were Downstairs but there was lot of Upstairs going around. As Andy said in the Diaries, he liked me "cause I was a worker." And it was true ... as I told a friend of mine who I helped to get hired at the Factory, "You have to think of Andy as the ocean liner that we bring out to sea every day. We're just manning the little tug boats that get him out and back into port. There are lots of us on our little tug boats, and best to keep it that way. Remember: There is only one big ship coming into port, and that's Andy."

[73]
Ibid.

[74]
Catherine Hesketh in a telephone conversation with the author on August 27, 2012.

[75]
Marc Balet in a conversation with the author on December 3, 2012 in New York.

[76]
Colacello 1990, p. 249.

[77]
Balet in Johnson 2012, p. 103.

I said, "So, if you think of yourself as on the little tug boat, you're gonna do just fine. If you think you're gonna get on board that big Andy ship or something like that, you'd better watch out."[78]

In 1982 Benjamin Liu became Warhol's personal assistant.[79] Liu was born in Taipei, Taiwan, as the son of a diplomat. Due to his father's career, he lived in Turkey, the Philippines, and Greece as a child, before moving to San Francisco at the age of thirteen where he attended Sunnyvale High School. Liu met Victor Hugo, Halston's boyfriend, in 1979 in San Francisco. Hugo advised him to go to New York.[80] Warhol loved introducing Liu by saying, "That was Ming Vase the bodyguard. Drag queen by night, bodyguard by day."[81] Liu explained later that this was a good marketing ploy and he did in fact have a weakness for cross-dressing.[82] He described his tasks as Warhol's personal assistant as follows:

I was his personal assistant at the studio with Jay Shriver [who became Warhol's painting assistant in 1980]. My main job was to go and pick him up in the morning and take him home at night. I would pick him up at his home on 66th street and Madison and we would walk. We might go to the bookstore, the doctor, have lunch, or go to the Whitney Museum to see a show. In the evening I took him home. During the daytime I worked on the paintings and photographs. It was a full-time job, except at weekends. ...

The first week I worked there Brigid said to me: "Benjamin, you're going to be a 'lifer,'" which meant that I was going to work there all my life. And I said to myself: "I'll stay for three years." So after three years I stopped. Andy wasn't happy. Andy asked me to come every Friday. So I did. He told me if I came he would give me a box of chocolates every week. In fact people were always giving him boxes of chocolates and he didn't eat them anymore. I came back in 1985, left again for six months, then came back until the end.[83]

From 1977 until Warhol's death, Rupert Jasen Smith was his printer. Smith had heard that the artist was dissatisfied with his printer at the time, so he asked whether he could make some sample prints for him. This was the start of a fruitful cooperation.[84] Smith had high quality standards. His willingness to experiment led to Warhol's print works becoming more refined. Bernd Klüser, who published Warhol prints together with Jörg Schellmann, explains, "... Rupert Jasen Smith, the printer, was very important for all the projects. If he was motivated—and he had to try out many variations—then some projects were better because of his direct involvement in the work process. The role he played in the result cannot be underestimated."[85] Smith himself once remarked, "My main role with Andy is that I, along with my colorist and assistants, controlled the physical look of the paint and printing."[86] Over the years he determined the appearance of the paint and printing of more than 32,000 works on paper and more than 2,000 works on canvas.[87] This volume of assignments also made it necessary for Smith to take on assistants. At the end of 1978 he had five.[88]

Smith's only long-term assistant was the German-American artist Horst Weber von Beeren who was born in 1953 and had studied at the University of Fine Arts in Hamburg under the guest professor Joseph Beuys. Beuys had advised him to go to the United States. Weber von Beeren spent

---

78
Marc Balet in a conversation with the author on December 3, 2012 in New York.

79
Hackett 1989, p. 459, September 7, 1982.

80
Bullock 2011.

81
Warhol (1986) in Goldsmith 2004, p. 360.

82
In his diaries Warhol wrote about him: "... he really looked like a pretty girl." Cf. Hackett 1989, p. 216, April 1, 1979.

83
In Benhamou-Huet 2009, pp. 41f.

84
Smith in Feldman/Schellmann 1989, p. 23.

85
Bernd Klüser in a conversation with the author on April 30, 2010 in Munich (translated from the German).

86
In Feldman/Schellmann 1989, p. 27.

87
Horst Weber von Beeren in a telephone conversation with the author on June 22, 2011.

88
Smith in Smith 1986, p. 472.

his summers in New York beginning in 1971. In his first summer there he met Andy Warhol:

I simply introduced myself to Warhol in 1971 on Union Square, which then was a pretty shady place full of drug dealers. There was no special security at the Factory. I walked right in. Warhol looked like death and lingered in this little side room, still totally shaken from the shooting in 1968. He came out of his little box, asking me if he could take some photos of me. Also, whether I wanted money for being photographed, which would never have occurred to me. His camera was his connection and his defense mechanism—his little weapon. ... After some obligatory shallow compliments he crawled back into his hide-out and told me to look up Bob Colacello on the seventh floor, who had just started Interview *magazine.*[89]

In the period that followed Warhol photographed Horst Weber von Beeren repeatedly. In 1978, Weber von Beeren met Smith. "I met Rupert in the elevator at Warhol's, with a huge roll of canvasses under his arm. I asked him about it and he said they were the 'Warhols' he had just printed today. That I didn't understand—why an artist had his work done by someone else. Rupert invited me to his studio, which was a shambles. He printed all of Warhol's canvasses there."[90] When Warhol and Smith were working on the first print edition for the publisher Ronald Feldman and the volume of assignments was mounting, Horst Weber von Beeren made a "life-changing decision" and started to help with production.[91] He worked alongside Rupert Jasen Smith until 1985. "The working conditions were appalling," according to Weber von Beeren:

It was a true sweatshop and the toxic materials involved were frightening. It was unhealthy and hard work. ... My normal height helped to push the squeegee over the screen. It has to have a certain angle and weight to do this. Rupert in his high-heeled cowboy boots was too short to create the right amount of pressure. He spent less and less time at work pursuing the Warhol trappings, which was fine with us, because he was such a tyrant. The assistants made the real artistic decisions. For example, he ran into Warhol at a Sotheby's viewing of diamonds. Warhol hissed at him, "What are you doing here? Aren't you working?" The yellow diamond Rupert purchased turned out to be a zirconia. And I thought to myself, "Why isn't Warhol working?"[92]

Horst Weber von Beeren estimates that he must have printed around 20,000 papers and canvasses during his time at Smith's Studio.[93] However, he was not only Smith's and therefore Warhol's assistant, but also supported Dalí in 1979 in the realization of the stereoscopic painting *Athens is burning!* (*The School of Athens* and *The Fire in the Borgo*).[94] Weber von Beeren is therefore the only person who assisted both Salvador Dalí and Andy Warhol in their art production. It was Albert Field who originally brought him to Dalí. Field was a schoolteacher from New York, whose enthusiasm for the surrealist's art stemmed from a visit to his exhibition at the Museum of Modern Art in 1941. He decided to focus his interest in art entirely on Dalí and started cataloguing his works. Although he became a regular guest at Dalí's court, he was never able to realize his plan of compiling a complete catalogue of his oeuvre. Even so, in 1996 he published

---

89
Horst Weber von Beeren in a telephone conversation with the author on June 22, 2011.

90
Ibid.

91
The print edition is the portfolio "Ten Portraits of Jews of the Twentieth Century" from the year 1980. Cf. Feldman/Schellmann 2003, II.226-235.

92
Horst Weber von Beeren in a telephone conversation with the author on June 22, 2011.

93
Horst Weber von Beeren in an e-mail to the author on April 11, 2013.

94
Descharnes/Néret 1993, no. 1493, 1494.

The Official Catalog of the Graphic Works of Salvador Dalí.[95] Horst Weber von Beeren recalls assisting Dalí:

Albert Field had a disciple, Frank Hunter, whom I had known for years ... One day Frank Hunter said to me that Dalí was looking for an artist to do some painting for him. That is how I landed at Dalí's suite at the St. Regis Hotel, being served tea on faux-baroque silver dishes. Dalí needed color squares a la Mondrian for his double-panel series that nobody understood. So the second bedroom of the suite was turned into a studio, where he worked on two minuscule paintings on a huge easel. I remember Dalí as a very fickle painter, who rushed away all the time, because his wife screamed for him and he catered to all her whims. That he got so much work done despite the constant interruptions is commendable. The two paintings were rip-offs of Raphael's School of Athens. He painted little pestilence bubbles over the bodies to hide the anatomical inaccuracies. Dalí was Gala's poodle, she ran the show with her viciousness. Dalí was stuck in the European fascist time bubble of the 1930s. Warhol was present. You could feel he was at the cutting edge, while Dalí floated in a soap bubble of Surrealism, having long outlived his moment of importance. He was an anachronism.[96]

In the 1960s and 1970s many young artists were drawn to Dalí. In 1973, the German artist Heiner Meyer came to Cadaqués and stayed for a year. Meyer reports how he asked Dalí "quite naively" whether he could "become his student. And then of course he said that that was something he was not interested in at all, otherwise he would already have considered it. He was so involved with his genius that he could not take on anything else."[97] However, the ice was broken when Meyer spontaneously noticed the hidden portrait in the painting *Gala Contemplating the Mediterranean Sea which at Twenty Metres Becomes the Portrait of Abraham Lincoln – Homage to Rothko*, which Dalí was working on at the time. Dalí asked Meyer, who was looking for a job, whether he would be willing to make sure things were in order at the studio.[98] It was easy to meet Dalí personally in the small community of Cadaqués. However, also in New York, the artist was not difficult to contact. In 1973, the then still unknown Jeff Koons made a phone call to the St. Regis Hotel and was put through to the artist directly. Dalí suggested a meeting in the hotel lobby by saying, "I'm here—come and visit me." This was followed by an invitation to his exhibition at the Knoedler Gallery.[99] It was similar for Louis Markoya who acted as Dalí's assistant for five years in the early 1970s. Markoya reports:

I called him, and eventually spoke to him. He said I could come to meet him that evening (a Sunday) at 6 p.m. at the hotel.

I excitedly went to the St. Regis to be told I could find Dalí in the cocktail lounge. This was my first introduction to Dalí's "court," a large group of the rich, famous and bizarre. Dalí was seated at a table at the back of the room, with a long line of people who trailed off on seats to his right. As a richer, more famous, beautiful, or bizarre person arrived, they would sit next to Dalí and the others would move down. Watching this for a while I realized I did not really know what to say to him and left. What I left to do was to spend the next year teaching myself to paint, going to the library to find out about technique and mediums.

95
Gibson 1997, pp. 513f.

96
Horst Weber von Beeren in a telephone conversation with the author on June 22, 2011.

97
Heiner Meyer in a conversation with the author on February 16, 2011 in Bielefeld (translated from the German).

98
Ibid.

99
Koons 2014, pp. 56ff.

In that year I produced probably twenty paintings in the style of Dalí, which I photographed, and the next winter I called him again. This time, though, I would use the photos as a starting point for speaking to him.

I met Dalí again at the cocktail lounge in the winter of 1970/71, where he critiqued each and every picture … "this is nice"; "this he had done before," etc. At the end of which he stacked all of the photos carefully into a pile and completely surprised me saying, "We will do some collaboration." This was the start of an amazing five years of work.[100]

Louis Markoya completed drawings and ran various errands for Dalí, such as supplying books and taking care of purchases. He also researched in magazines and catalogues—for example in the *Edmund Scientific Catalog*—and gathered ideas that were welcomed by the Spaniard. Markoya did the preliminary work and Dalí then took over. He goes on to say:

I was assigned research projects (Cloning, Gerard Dou, etc.) and given authority to represent Dalí for certain research … like going to the NY Police and Detective bureau to get the methodology for fingerprinting. I was officially called protégé by Dalí upon my execution of the sign that said "DALI" for the Knoedler window for Dalí's show. He asked me to design it in the style of Warhol (which to me meant simple and boring) and that the signature had to be made from a typewriter, which I had enlarged and copied exactly. I was asked to play many roles and did absolutely everything I could for him, as I was happy to be helping a genius.[101]

Dalí's first assistant in Cadaqués was the Canadian Timothy Phillips. Dalí had been commissioned to portray his mother. Mrs. Phillips asked him to take on her son, who wanted to be a painter.[102] Dalí soon recognized that his protégé, who worked for him in the 1950s and 1960s, eased his workload considerably. In August 1953 he wrote about the "Dalínian fanatic" in his *Diary of a Genius*: "An angel sent him to me. I have set up a studio for him in a shed. Already he draws with great probity whatever I need, which allows me to dwell at length on the details I like best, with less of a feeling of guilt. Since six o'clock this morning, Philips [sic] has been under the house, drawing Gala's boat as I have asked him to do. … Philips [sic] paints my picture meticulously. I'll only have to undo everything to finish it."[103] Forty-six years later Timothy Phillips recalled his years at Dalí's side:

Emboldened by the example of the renowned master, I proceeded to act in ever stranger ways. In the beginning Dalí said (in "Dalínese"): "You is not enough crazy." When I parted company from him, he declared: "You is too much crazy!" …

I was working for Dalí before I was married, doing mathematical calculations. I also did very minor parts of lesser pictures and he complimented my sense of tone. It is very difficult to explain to anybody who doesn't paint what tone is. Generally, tone is what you see in a painting when you take a black and white photograph. If it's all pale you can't distinguish things, if it all depends on color it is not in tone. If it is in tone, it'll be 50 percent mid-tone, 25 percent light tone and 25 percent dark. And it will have a pattern of masses of tone. … So Dalí said to me that I had the total sense of a Velázquez, a big exaggeration, but I've tried to live up to it and in a lot of pictures I haven't.[104]

100
Louis Markoya in an e-mail to the author on May 17, 2010.

101
Ibid.

102
Descharnes/
Descharnes
2003, p. 66.

103
Dalí 1965, pp. 98f.

104
In Girst 1999.

In 1955 Dalí started to engage the services of the scene painter Isidor Bea. Bea was born in 1911 and came from Torres del Segre.[105] He had studied art and scenography in Barcelona. In particular, he had learned perspective and the technique of enlarging a small picture. Bea emphasized later that this procedure became a purely mechanical matter for him.[106] After the Civil War he initially began working for the scene painter Francesc Pou. Later he opened his own studio with two co-workers. Bea enjoyed a good reputation and received assignments from all the leading theaters in Barcelona.[107] In summer 1955 he was appointed to create a ceiling fresco in Palamós based on a small painting by Dalí. He managed to do so in just one day. When Dalí was invited to view the work he was so impressed by it that he wanted to meet Bea. This meeting marked the beginning of a cooperation that was to last forty years. The first painting that Bea assisted Dalí with was *The Last Supper*. He helped to set the proportions for the 65.63 × 105.12-inch work, so that it could be completed in the summer of 1955.[108] His new assistant enabled Dalí to increase the production of paintings and to tackle larger formats. Bea's task comprised devoting himself to less important parts of the works—such as the sky, clouds, and the sea.[109] As he was hardworking, reliable, and affable, the cooperation ran smoothly. Bea reported later: "When he was with me he was always perfectly normal, but the moment a journalist arrived he would begin to put on a show. … It had taken them [Dalí and Gala] a long time to achieve success, and having done so they weren't going to give anything away to anyone else. … They took me on as an assistant and by God I worked hard. I was a sort of robot imbued with the spirit of Dalí."[110] During the first summer of his new employment, Bea lived at the neighboring Hotel Port Lligat. Later he moved into a nearby cottage, as he was expected "to slave, like Dalí, from dawn to dusk." Apparently, the artist granted Sundays free, but only reluctantly after Bea pointed out that as a practicing Catholic he was obliged to attend mass and to rest.[111] After Dalí's death Bea confirmed that he also had helped him with his last oil paintings.[112]

At the end of 1959 Dalí began receiving an abundance of assignments and decided to take on a secretary. His choice was John Peter Moore, who was born in London in 1919 and became Dalí's "military adviser." Moore was given this title because of his career in the British army. He had enlisted willingly in 1936 and after two years he was admitted to the Royal Corps of Signals. At the start of the war, Moore was promoted to corporal and he soon went on to become lance sergeant in the British Expeditions Corps, and second lieutenant two years later. During the period that followed he served in the Department for Psychological Warfare. In his discharge notice of November 1, 1946 it said that he would be awarded the honorary rank of captain.[113] From then on Moore always referred to himself as "captain." He later said that he owed everything to the army as it had made him self-confident and tough.[114] During his military years Moore became friends with Randolph Churchill and fell in love with Churchill's sister Sarah. Their father, Sir Winston Churchill, recommended him to the movie producer and director Sir Alexander Korda. Korda appointed Moore for the next ten years as director of London Films International in Rome.[115] In 1955 Korda shot the

105
Tharrats 2007,
p. 182.

106
Gibson 1997,
p. 480.

107
Ibid.

108
Ibid.

109
Llongueras
2003, p. 218.

110
Quoted according to Gibson
1997, pp. 480f.

111
Ibid., p. 481.

112
Ibid., p. 598.
Unfortunately he
never revealed
details about
the extent of his
contribution.

113
Gibson 1997,
pp. 481f.

114
Ibid., p. 481.

115
Moore 2009,
pp. 13f., 57.

movie *Richard III* with Laurence Olivier in the lead role and commissioned a portrait of Olivier from Dalí for advertising purposes, for which the painter received a fee of $20,000 in Italian currency.[116] Owing to the strict foreign exchange control, Korda asked the painter to contact his man in Rome. Peter Moore had never heard of Dalí at this point.[117] In his memoirs, *Flagrant Dalí,* published posthumously in 2009, he reports that the painter also had another agenda. He had found out from Korda that Moore could arrange an unofficial audience with the Pope, as he was in charge of supervising the installation of a TV system at the Vatican at the time. Apparently, this meeting actually took place.[118] Moore maintained contact with Dalí in the years that followed. At the beginning of 1960, Dalí sent him a first-class TWA ticket and summoned him to New York.[119] He explained to him that he wanted a "military adviser," so as "to wage a psychological war in the art world."[120] Moore, who knew nothing about art, writes in his memoirs:

Dalí and I formed an efficient duo: he was a fantasist, I was strict. He was the bait, I was the shooter. He was the one who created, I was the one who elicited consent. We were a team, an implacable team who made the investors laugh while they were emptying their pockets. We had made the King Cole Bar at the St. Regis our business headquarters with a queue of potential clients, from eleven o'clock in the morning.

A producer wanted a portrait of his wife. An editor wanted a book cover. Another wanted illustrations for a theater flyer. Joe Kennedy wanted a bust of his son, John, who was to be elected as President the year after, in 1961. Everything ran smoothly.

In the space of two weeks I had gathered more than $500,000 for Dalí, which meant $50,000 for me.[121]

Moore, who spoke English, French, Italian, and soon also Spanish, did not receive a fixed salary, but a ten-percent commission on all contracts he negotiated. The sales of paintings and drawings remained under the monopoly of Gala, who in Moore's view was a "dead loss" as a saleswoman.[122] Moore was therefore only responsible for prints, sculptures, items of clothing, perfumes, and all else he came up with.[123] He was very creative when it came to marketing Dalí profitably, but he drew a clear boundary between professional and private realms.[124] There was no private contact, which is why he did not even invite Dalí to his wedding.[125] Moore, who did not sign a contract with the artist,[126] later claimed that during his first seven years he earned $230,000 a year tax-free and in the five following years as much as one million dollars.[127] He commented later on Dalí's fortune, that the artist had had $32 million in his bank account when he left him.[128]

In summer 1968 Dalí met the Catalan Enrique Sabater. Sabater was born in 1936 in Corçà in the Baix Empordá region. He was a journalist, but had many talents and had worked as a chauffeur for a radio station, employee at a travel agency, and public relations man for the urbanization of Empuriabrava.[129] As a journalist, the ambitious Sabater worked for the newspaper *Los Sitios* in Girona. This was how it came about that he visited Dalí in the summer of 1968 to interview him.[130] The two of them hit it off immediately and Sabater was soon visiting Port Lligat regularly. Dalí was

---

116
Ibid., p. 59.

117
Ibid., pp. 55, 58f. According to another version, Peter Moore met Dalí at the Palm Court at the New York Plaza Hotel. The painter appeared with Nanita Kalaschnikoff, complained about the music, and asked the violinists to play zarzuelas or a tango, attracting the attention of Moore, who appeared at his table and introduced himself. Cf. Etherington-Smith 1993, p. 337; Secrest 1986, p. 205.

118
Moore 2009, p. 62; Gibson 1997, pp. 482f.

119
Ibid., p. 494.

120
Moore 2009, p. 67.

121
Ibid., p. 72 (translated from the French).

122
Ibid., p. 82.

123
Gibson 1997, p. 494.

124
Moore 2009, pp. 75, 190.

125
Gibson 1997, p. 558.

126
Moore 2009, p. 71.

127
Gibson 1997, p. 496; see also Moore 2009, p. 190, who talks of around $200,000 per year.

128
Gibson 1997, p. 557.

129
Carol 1990, p. 110.

130
Gibson 1997, p. 536.

quick to recognize that the many talents of his fellow countryman, including his photographic talent, might be useful for him. Over the years he photographed Dalí during a variety of activities and events. One of Sabater's first duties was to find a suitable property for Gala, which he found in the Baix Empordà region in the village of Púbol. Because he had a pilot's license, he could search for suitable properties from the air and photograph them.[131] He soon began to play an increasingly important role in the Dalí household, and finally took over Moore's duties in 1974. It is said that Gala insisted on it and Dalí put up little resistance. Moore agreed to the decision, as he had a tumor that had to be treated urgently.[132] Gala apparently said to him: "He'll take a five percent commission instead of your ten percent, he's better looking than you are, he's younger than you are, he's more intelligent than you are *and* he speaks Catalan."[133] Sabater denied this later: "I was born here, I am a Catalan, I don't think a Catalan could accept less than an Englishman! I got more than ten percent because Mr. Moore was doing only the contracts for etchings, and contracts for TV shows, that sort of thing, but never for oil paintings, never."[134]

Sabater displayed great entrepreneurial qualities. On May 31, 1976 the company Dasa Edicions S.A. was registered in Girona—"Da" stood for Dalí and "sa" for Sabater.[135] Dasa Edicions S. A. produced postcards, posters, and also books, including the first Spanish and Catalan editions of *The Secret Life of Salvador Dalí*. In June 1976 the company Dalart Naamloze Vennootschap (Dalart N.V.) was founded in the Dutch Antilles, specialized in dealing with jewelry and objects, as well as reproduction rights. A third company was also founded there, under the name of Dasa Editions N.V. All of these companies were founded in the interests of tax benefits.[136] In the years that followed, Dalí created colorful gouaches with commercial potential. One of the companies in particular Dalart N. V., assigned the reproduction rights that made it possible to sell the original works as lithographs. Some of the lithographs were issued in print runs of up to 1,195 copies.[137] Dalí's collector A. Reynolds Morse noted in his unpublished diary that in 1979 the going rate for a reproduction print run was $100,000. Sabater apparently claimed the original and the rights for other editions of the same work as his own.[138] Ian Gibson writes that within a couple of years Sabater was "well into the multi-millionaire category." He was a "businessman and wheeler-dealer," who made Moore look like a "novice" in comparison.[139] Contrary to Moore, Sabater also had private contact with Dalí, as he later remarked: "The fact is that through no particular merit of my own I lived with them, lunched and dined with them and travelled with them almost every day for about twelve years."[140] At the beginning of the 1980s, voices spoke up around Dalí that were critical of Sabater's business practices. A. Reynolds Morse, in particular, expressed his concern. In May 1980 he wrote in his diary that Sabater had taken on the difficult task "of seeing the master through his critical transitional years from the peak of his greatness to the onset of senility and a nervous breakdown."[141] A few months before, "The Committee of Friends to Save Dalí" had been formed, to which Morse and his wife, Dalí's servant Arturo Caminada, Benjamin Castillo, a friend of the artist from Figueres,

131
Sabater in *Salvador Dalí Enrique Sabater*, p. 263.

132
Gibson 1997, p. 557.

133
Quoted according to ibid., p. 549.

134
In ibid., p. 558.

135
Catterall 1992, p. 49; Gibson 1997, p. 565.

136
Ibid.; Catterall 1992, pp. 48f.

137
Cf. Field 1996, pp. 182ff.

138
Gibson 1997, p. 568.

139
Ibid., p. 558.

140
In ibid.

141
Quoted according to Gibson 1997, p. 576.

Robert Descharnes, Nanita Kalaschnikoff, Antoni Pitxot, and Dalí's cousin Gonzalo Serraclara belonged. The committee saw itself as an "international, nonprofit organization chartered solely to preserve the physical well-being and artistic welfare of Salvador Dalí."[142] The Spanish and international press also mounted a campaign against Dalí's secretary and accused him of having accumulated a fortune at the artist's expense.[143] Sabater refuted this vehemently and made Gala and her "secret contracts" responsible for Dalí's demise. He had tried to prevent the muse from undertaking her "unfortunate commercial adventures." But since he did not succeed, he also informed the Morses and later even the Catalan prime-minister Jordi Pujol.[144] At the end of 1980 Sabater resigned from his post. According to a report, he delivered his resignation on March 12, 1981, whereupon Gala is said to have spat in his face.[145] Now she was forced to deal with the business herself. She soon sought help from the Frenchman Jean-Claude Du Barry, who had often brought the Dalís into contact with young and attractive people through his model agency in Barcelona.[146] In summer 1980 Gala had already approached Du Barry and asked him to come to Port Lligat to discuss business matters.[147] According to a press report, Du Barry declared himself willing at that point to negotiate some contracts that brought the Dalís $1.3 million.[148] Du Barry took over the Dalís' business for one month only (from December 1980 to January 1981). Prompted by Gala, he is said to have prepared "many irregular contracts for the exploitation of Dalí's work" and forged contacts with "shady dealers."[149] Du Barry explained: "I started to call Dalí's old clients, people Sabater had completely cut off and told them, 'If you want to do business with Dalí, call me.'"[150] Dalí's American lawyer Michael Ward Stout reported later that an "utterly chaotic situation" had emerged.[151]

Although Sabater was still in charge, Dalí called Robert Descharnes and asked him for help.[152] Descharnes, born in 1926 in Nevers in France, was a successful journalist and photographer.[153] He had met Dalí and Gala back in the winter of 1950/51 on the *S.S. America* crossing from Le Havre to New York.[154] During the following years a fruitful cooperation had ensued. Descharnes documented Dalí's activities in countless photographs and took over the organization of important exhibitions for the artist.[155] Between 1954 and 1962 he shot some scenes with Dalí for the movie *The Prodigious Story of the Lacemaker and the Rhinoceros*, which was never finished.[156] In the fall of 1962 Descharnes's book *Dalí de Gala* was published, the first luxuriously designed monograph about the artist. In the years that followed he wrote further books about Dalí's life and works. As his new secretary, Descharnes had taken up contact with the Paris-based Société de la Propriété Artistique et des Dessins et Modèles (SPADEM), which was to handle the artist's copyrights from January 1981.[157] Later on this task was taken over by Demart Pro Arte B.V., founded in 1985, with its head office in Amsterdam. Descharnes earned harsh criticism, as he himself acted as managing director of this company. Dalí had signed a contract on June 13, 1986 and thereby assigned his copyrights to Demart Pro Arte B.V until his one-hundredth birthday on May 11, 2004. Critics later felt that due to his poor state of health, Dalí was not aware of the significance of this contract, especially as it was signed without

142
Ibid., p. 573.

143
Ibid., p. 580.

144
Sabater in
*Salvador Dalí
Enrique Sabater*,
pp. 263f.

145
Carol 1990,
p. 131.

146
See the chapter
**Compan-
ions, Court-
iers, and
Superstars**
in this part.

147
Carol/Navarro
Arisa/Busquets
1985, p. 107.

148
Gibson 1997,
p. 584.

149
Ibid.

150
Quoted accord-
ing to ibid.

151
Ibid.

152
Carol/Navarro
Arisa/Busquets
1985, p. 61.

153
*Dalí per Robert
Descharnes*,
p. 173.

154
Descharnes
2002, pp. 95f.

155
*Dalí per Robert
Descharnes*,
p. 173.

156
See the chapter
**Filming with
a Camera
"Nailed
to the Floor
like Christ
on the
Cross"** in Part 4.

157
Romero 1989,
pp. 269f.

a notary. After Dalí's death, it was thus inevitable that Descharnes would become embroiled in a legal battle with the Spanish government and the Fundació Gala-Salvador Dalí founded on December 23, 1983, based in Figueres.[158] An agreement was first reached in 2004. The Fundació Gala-Salvador Dalí subsequently took over the rights management company and declared that peace had now returned to the art market.[159]

158
More details
in Gibson 1997,
pp. 612ff.

159
Otte 2006,
p. 138.

ENTOURAGE
4 WORK
5 ENCOUNTERS
6 VIEWS
OF
EACH
OTHER'S
WORK
AND
PERSONALITY

Salvador Dalí and Andy Warhol were involved in a wide variety of artistic fields. The following chapters discuss parallels between the two artists and the subject matter in their works. Examples are shown to illustrate their most important subjects and major individual works are presented. Subjects common to most artists, such as self-portraits, still lifes, and memento mori, are not presented.

Window Displays

On December 7, 1936, Salvador Dalí embarked on his second journey to the United States, together with Gala, which he later referred to as the "official beginning of my 'glory.'"[1] Dalí did indeed achieve considerable acclaim in America in late 1936. The group exhibition "Fantastic Art, Dada and Surrealism" opened at the New York Museum of Modern Art on December 9; thirteen works by Dali were shown—including his painting *The Persistence of Memory*.[2] "The biggest surrealist show on earth" drew crowds of visitors and was a great success among the public and critics.[3] The Bonwit Teller department store on Fifth Avenue commissioned several artists with window displays on the occasion of the exhibition. Of course Dalí was among them and his creations attracted the widest attention. As the *New York Weekly Telegraph* reported on December 26, 1936, under the title "Fifth Ave. Crowd Stops to View Dalí Window,"[4] crowds jostled in front of the store window to admire the surrealist works.[5] The artist later provided a description of his display for his autobiography *The Secret Life of Salvador Dalí*: "I used a manikin whose head was made of red roses and who had fingernails of ermine fur. On a table, a telephone transformed into a lobster; hanging on a chair, my famous 'aphrodisiac coat' consisting of a black dinner jacket to which were attached one beside another, so as entirely to cover it, eighty-eight liqueur glasses filled to the edge with green *crème de menthe*, with a dead fly and a cocktail straw in each glass."[6]

Dalí and Gala set out on a third journey to the United States in February 1939. When the couple arrived in New York, Bonwit Teller, remembering the great advertising success three years before, again ordered window displays; this time to present the new spring collection.[7] Dalí is said to have received a payment of $1,000.[8] As he writes in his *Secret Life*, he had only one condition: that he should be allowed to do what he wanted. Since he despised modern window dummies, he set off with Mr. Lee, who was responsible for the display design, and dug out from the attic of an old shop, "some frightful wax manikins of the 1900 period with long natural dead women's hair" covered with dust and cobwebs. Dalí decided to leave the manikins in this state, in order to achieve a striking contrast to the setting of upholstered satin and mirrors that he had devised. Dalí describes the displays as follows:

The theme of the display was intentionally banal. One of the displays symbolized Day, and the other, Night. In the "Day" display one of these manikins was stepping into a "hairy bathtub" lined with astrakhan. It was filled with water up to the edge, and a pair of beautiful wax arms holding up a mirror evoked the Narcissus myth; natural narcissi grew directly out of the floor of the bedroom

1
Dalí 1942, p. 344.

2
Aguer in Ades 2004, p. 493.

3
Jean 1961, pp. 271f.

4
Gibson 1997, p. 680, fn. 92.

5
Ibid., p. 368.

6
Dalí 1942, p. 344.

7
Gibson 1997, p. 387.

8
Goldman in Francis/King 1997, p. 113.

and out of the furniture. "Night" was symbolized by a bed whose canopy was composed of the black and sleepy head of a buffalo carrying a bloody pigeon in its mouth; the feet of the bed were made of the four feet of the buffalo. The bed sheets of black satin were visibly burnt, and through the holes could be seen artificial live coals. The pillow on which the manikin rested her dreamy head was composed entirely of live coals. Beside the bed was seated the phantom of sleep, conceived in the metaphysical style of Chirico. It was bedecked in all the sparkling jewels of desire of which the sleeping wax woman was dreaming. This manifesto of elementary surrealist poetry right out in the street would inevitably arrest the anguished attention of passers-by with stupor when the morrow, amid so much surrealist decorativism, lifted the curtain on an authentic Dalínian vision.[9]

The display opened on the morning of March 16, 1939, and attracted, as expected, crowds of viewers. Dalí also went along in the afternoon to see the effect of his display and was enraged: The old wax manikins had been replaced by ordinary mannequins, and the bed and the sleeper on it had been removed. The artist went to see the management of the department store and demanded the removal of his name and all parts of his display remaining in the window, as the falsification of his work could only damage his reputation. When this was refused, Dalí made his way straight to the display. His appearance in the store window caused a large crowd to gather immediately while he took the drastic measure that he tells of in his *Secret Life*:

I took hold of the bathtub with both hands, and tried to lift it so as to turn it over. I felt like the Biblical Samson between the pillars of the temple. The bathtub was much heavier than I had calculated, and before I could raise one side it slipped right up against the window so that at the moment when with a supreme effort I finally succeeded in turning it over it crashed into the plate glass, shattering it into a thousand pieces. The crowd immediately fell back in a wide semicircle with a movement of instinctive terror, dodging the glass splinters and the water from the bathtub which now was spilling onto the sidewalk. Then I coolly appraised the situation and judged it much more reasonable to leave by the hole in the window, bristling with the stalactites and the stalagmites of my anger, than to go back through the door in the rear of the shop window.[10]

Here, Dalí noticeably presents himself as an artist who "coolly appraised" the situation and made the most of it. In the edition of the *New York Post* released a day after the event, he remarked, "I took friends to see the window and there was this shocking modernistic figure substituted for my lovely old figure, in the center of the design. It ruined all meaning. So I dashed into the window to disarrange it, so that my name, signed in the window, should not be dishonored. I was never so surprised as when that bathtub just shot through the window when I pushed it and I was thereafter most confused."[11] This report is undoubtedly closer to the truth. The people standing in front of the display window scene were most surely entranced by the scene. The police came and led Dalí away. His gallery owner, Julien Levy, his patron Edward James, and Gala rushed to his aid. James's lawyer presented the artist with a choice; either be released on bail or wait in the prison cell until his case was tried. Dalí opted for the latter and after a short stay in the cell appeared before Judge Louis B. Brodsky.[12] In *The Secret Life*

9
Dalí 1942, p. 372.

10
Ibid., pp. 374f.

11
In "Surrealist Dalí Explains Fury for his Art; Never Meant to Smash 5th Ave. Window. Couldn't Bear Sight of Expurgated Version of his Work," in *New York Post*, March 17, 1939, quoted according to Gibson 1997, p. 388.

12
Dalí 1942, p. 375; Etherington-Smith 1993, p. 241.

he writes: "The judge who tried my case betrayed upon his severe features the amusement that my story afforded him. He ruled that my act was 'excessively violent' and that since I had broken a window I would have to pay for it, but he made a point of adding emphatically that every artist has a right to defend his 'work' to the limit. The following day the press reacted, giving me a warm and moving proof of its sympathy…."[13] All of the New York daily newspapers reported on the incident and it was stated that after the verdict, Judge Brodsky remarked, "These are some of the privileges that an artist with temperament seems to enjoy."[14] The incident launched an avalanche of press reports in the U.S. and Europe, with photos of the smashed display window and Dalí's arrest.[15] Dalí realized very early on how important spectacular public performances were for furthering his artistic career. Many years later he referred to the fiasco as "the most magical and possibly the most effective action" of his whole life.[16]

Dalí took every opportunity to refer to the incident repeatedly in his written works. Even in 1966, in his *Open Letter to Salvador Dalí*, he included a reminder of the "greatest of scandals 'to end all scandals,' in the very heart of the Court of Public Opinion, on Fifth Avenue, the palpitating and explosive heart of New York City."[17] In his autobiographical work *The Unspeakable Confessions of Salvador Dalí* published in 1973, he describes the event yet again, in this case going so far as to use the title "How Dalí Challenged America."[18] One year later Dalí illustrated the incident with the etching *A Shattering Entrance to the USA* for the portfolio "After 50 Years of Surrealism," which reviews the twelve most important stages in his life. It shows him at the moment he leaves the department store through the shattered window, taking a huge leap.[19]

Thanks to Dalí, New York department store window displays became tourist attractions in the 1940s. This was an early indication of the connection between the visual arts and the world of consumerism, which would reach its peak in Pop Art. Over the course of the 1950s, the extravagant and surrealist elements disappeared, however, and were replaced by simpler and clearer displays.[20]

During this transitional period, Andy Warhol gathered initial experience in the field of window displays in his hometown. In 1947, during his third year at the Carnegie Institute of Technology, he worked part time at Pittsburgh's largest department store, Joseph Horne's. He trimmed the store's windows and dressed the mannequins.[21] In the following year he was assigned with painting the backdrops for the display windows.[22] Viktor Bockris reports that Warhol ended up in the department store's display department, in a "group of colorful homosexuals" by whom he was particularly fascinated.[23] In order to fit in with his colleagues, he painted his fingernails a different color every day, let his tie hang into a paint pot, or dyed one shoe a different color from the other.[24] Warhol was delighted with his holiday job and got on very well with his boss Larry Vollmer, who recognized Warhol's talent immediately.[25]

Warhol later recounted, "I got something like fifty cents an hour and my job was to look for 'ideas.' I don't remember ever finding one or getting

13 Dalí 1942, pp. 375f.

14 Quoted according to Etherington-Smith 1993, p. 241.

15 The report in the *Daily News* from March 17, 1939 is printed in Abadie 1980, p. 74; the report in *Paris-Soir* from March 18, 1939 in Éluard 1989, p. 334, note 1 to letter 249. *TIME* magazine reported on March 27, 1939, see Gibson 1997, p. 682, fn. 155.

16 Dalí 1967, p. 42.

17 Ibid.

18 Dalí 1976, pp.185f. The original French edition *Comment on devient Dalí* was published in 1973.

19 Michler/Löpsinger 1994, no. 673; Field 1996, Original Intaglio, 74–8, H.

20 Goldman in Francis/King 1997, p. 114.

21 Bourdon 1989, p. 22.

22 Bockris 1989, p. 71.

23 Ibid., p. 72.

24 Ibid., p. 71.

25 Colacello 1990, p.19.

one. Mr. Vollmer was an idol to me because he came from New York and that seemed so exciting. I wasn't really thinking about ever going there myself, though."[26] What was exciting for Warhol were Larry Vollmer's stories about his time as a New York display decorator. Vollmer reported that he had installed, together with Salvador Dalí, a fur-lined bath in the Bonwit Teller display window. A dispute then sparked between him and Dalí, whereupon the painter attempted to remove his work, resulting in the famous mishap that launched an avalanche of press reports.[27] This story about Dalí was undoubtedly Warhol's first lesson in publicity, and it surely left a strong impression on him.[28] In this context it should be noted that Dalí never mentioned the name Larry Vollmer in his numerous personal accounts, but only Tommy Lee, the display director at Bonwit Teller, as well as a "gentleman" from the management with whom he entered into a discussion about his display.[29]

In 1945 Gene Moore began working at Bonwit Teller. He was display director from 1951 to 1961,[30] responsible for twenty-two display windows. At Bonwit Teller, Moore followed the tradition of Lee, who had worked with Dalí in 1939, and appointed young artists to design windows. Contrary to Lee, however, he commissioned unknown artists, in order to provide a platform for their talent, including James Rosenquist, Robert Rauschenberg, Jasper Johns, and Andy Warhol. Warhol presented an exception since he was already a successful commercial artist.[31] He had even already designed advertisements for Bonwit Teller. From 1955, he was appointed by Moore to design display windows.[32] Moore regarded Warhol as a professional and simply explained the theme of the display to him and then left the whole window display in his hands without making him present designs for approval.[33]

For one of his first displays, Warhol painted a stylized fireplace directly onto the window glass. He chose an unusual perspective, because the viewer of the display was behind the fireplace looking through it at a window dummy sitting on a bearskin.[34] For a display presented in October 1958, Warhol decorated the store window with a tailor's dummy and cotton reels. The floor of the display window was laid with panes of glass, with brown, marbled paper underneath them, while window dummies in front of a blue wall presented French and Italian fashion, illuminated by blue spotlights.[35]

In July 1955, Gene Moore had the idea of using wooden fences covered with graffiti and of setting them up close to the window glass.[36] Many years later he recalled in an interview, "I used to do once a year perfume windows, and I had an idea of doing, like, a fence—just a raw wood fence, and have Andy sketch all over, you know, like kids draw with crayon and stuff. Those were great fun. There were holes cut into it with perfume bottles [in the niches]. But with all of Andy's great sense of humor in his drawing, they really came off beautifully."[37]

For two fences created in 1955, with the mottos *Bonwit's Loves Replique* and *Bonwit's Loves Pot Pourri*, Warhol drew cupids, hearts, lips, flowers, butterflies and scribbles with the words "spring" and "kiss."[38] He also added pairs of initials, indicating couples that he knew, along with a couple of telephone numbers of friends whom he thought would not mind getting a call from a stranger.[39] Other interesting fences were created in 1957. One work

26 Warhol 1975, *Philosophy*, p. 22.

27 Bockris 1989, pp. 71f. Victor Bockris informed the author in an e-mail on October 15, 2012, that this information was based on an interview that Larry Vollmer had given him in 1983 in Pittsburgh.

28 Bockris 1989, p. 72.

29 Dalí 1942, pp. 372ff.

30 Smith 1988, p. 110.

31 Over the course of his career Moore employed more than 900 young artists. See Goldman in Francis/King 1997, 114.

32 Moore in Smith 1988, p. 111.

33 Goldman in Francis/King 1997, pp. 115f.

34 Moore in Smith 1988, p. 111. Ill. in Francis/King 1997, p. 104.

35 Smith 1986, pp. 29f.

36 Moore/Hyams 1990, p. 69.

37 In Smith 1988, p. 111.

38 Ill. in Francis/King 1997, pp. 103, 105. According to Bourdon the fence *Bonwit's Loves Replique* was created in July 1955. See Bourdon 1989, p. 50.

39 Ibid., p. 47.

had an India theme, with a veiled, six-armed female dancer, reminiscent of a Hindu god, between two elephants in front of the Taj Mahal.[40] Another creation with the title *Fleur de Rocaille* showed a female and male gardener with their tools, flanking a flower garden.[41] The holes in the fences mentioned by Moore, for presenting the perfume vials and other cosmetics in illuminated niches, blended harmoniously into the presentations. The Indian dancer balanced one vial on her left foot and two others in her hands, while a cupid presented a box with two vials. Warhol's works for Bonwit Teller's display windows in the 1950s were romantic and had a childish innocence, reminiscent of drawings by Jean Cocteau, but appearing more naïve. Contrary to Dalí, Warhol did not want to shock with his displays, but entice and seduce, making use of his idiosyncratic style that he had already applied successfully in his commercial assignments. At that time, Warhol not only decorated the Bonwit Teller display windows, but also received assignments from Tiffany & Co. and I. Miller.[42]

In the mid-1950s Warhol presented three framed drawings in a Bonwit Teller display window, hung one above the other next to a window dummy.[43] In April 1961, Moore decided to present five paintings by the artist from the previous year behind five female window dummies dressed in the latest spring fashions—one painting stood on an easel, while the four other works were hung up. The weeklong presentation was much less spectacular than Warhol's previous displays, thus it is hardly surprising that it attracted little interest from the art world.[44] The number of dummies was identical to that of the displayed works of art. When dressing and setting up the dummies, the color of the spring clothes was harmonized with the tones of the paintings. On display were the paintings *Advertisement, Little King, Superman, Before and After [1],* and *Saturday's Popeye.* As the titles indicate, the works were created based on comics and advertisements in newspapers. They were hand-painted, and the colors had run, which was characteristic of Warhol's works around 1960. The artist must have been pleased to be able to exhibit his paintings in the display windows of the Bonwit Teller department store. For him, the border between art and advertising was always fluid. In his photographic volume *America,* published in 1985, he alluded to this as follows: "When you think about it, department stores are kind of like museums."[45]

Infringing Artistic Freedom

In April 1939, Salvador Dalí received a lucrative contract to design a surrealist pavilion for the leisure area of the New York World's Fair, which was to open at the beginning of June. Initially, the plan was to call it *Bottom of the Sea,* but in the end Dalí decided on *Dream of Venus.*[1] In his *Secret Life* he emphasizes that his contract had granted him not only general supervision, but also "complete imaginative freedom."[2] Dalí had originally envisaged a palace made of artificial corals, with an L-shaped pond made of transparent plate glass for underwater performances expressing the workings of the subconscious. He had planned soft watches, "women pianos," a divan in the shape of Greta Garbo's lips, and "splendid female underwater swimmers,"

40
Ill. in Francis/ King 1997, p. 107.

41
Ill. in Kornbluth 1988, p. 124.

42
Smith 1986, p. 31; Bourdon 1989, p. 47. A decoration for Tiffany & Co. is depicted in Francis/King 1997, p. 102.

43
Ill. in Francis/ King 1997, p. 106.

44
Bockris 1989, p. 142.

45
Warhol 1985, p. 22.

1
Gibson 1997, p. 390.

2
Dalí 1942, p. 376.

whose choreographed underwater circles were to express the secrets found in dreams.[3] In his autobiography the artist writes, "They did 'approximately' what I ordered, but so badly and with such bad faith that the pavilion turned out to be a lamentable caricature of my ideas and of my projects."[4] The situation escalated when the organizers of the exhibition and one of the co-investors—a rubber producer from Andy Warhol's hometown of Pittsburgh—rejected Dalí's plan of setting up a reproduction of Botticelli's Venus with the head of a fish in front of the pavilion. The director of Gardner Display Works in Long Island City, who was the local rubber producer representative, sent an enraged telegram to William Morris, organizer of the World's Fair,[5] stating, "OUR SHOW IS SIXTY PERCENT AN UNDERWATER MERMAID AND FORTY PERCENT A SURREALIST SHOW SO WHY SHOULD FRONT BE ALL SURREALIST AND NOT PUBLICIZE THE MOST IMPORTANT PART OF OUR SHOW ... MEN'S PASSION TO SPEND A QUARTER WILL NOT BE AROUSED BY A GIRL WITH A FISH'S HEAD BUT A SUGGESTIVE MERMAID PRESENTATION ON THE FRONT OF THE BUILDING ... DALÍ'S FRONT MAY STOP THEM FOR A FEW SECONDS WHILE THEY SHAKE THEIR HEADS THEN WALK ON BUT WE WANT THEM TO STOP AND COME IN."[6] Dalí reacted quickly and boarded a ship to Europe even before the fair opened. Before his departure he composed a tract "to rid myself of the moral responsibility for such an adulterated work."[7] It bore the long title "Declaration of Independence of the Imagination and of the Rights of Man to His Own Madness" and in it Dalí stated that the erection of Botticelli's Venus with the head of a fish had been refused by the responsible committee with the words, "A woman with the tail of a fish is possible; a woman with a head of a fish is impossible." He also explained that the public had a greater intuitive understanding of art than "those 'middle-men of culture' who, with their lofty airs and superior quackings, come between the creator and the public."[8] Years later, Dalí referred to his tract as "my own personal declaration of war against stupidity. I had just given the powers of the irrational their standing in America. A Dalínian victory."[9] Dalí had it printed on leaflets, with a picture of Botticelli's Venus with the head of a fish, scattered down to the masses from a plane circling above New York.[10] This action contributed to the success of his pavilion at the World's Fair, along with the generous display of naked breasts in the show. *TIME* magazine wrote that the vast pleasure grounds at the fair contained "more public nudity than any place outside Bali."[11]

Two and a half decades later, Andy Warhol also experienced an affront to his artistic freedom at the New York World's Fair. In April 1964 he was among the ten artists who the architect Philip Johnson had appointed to create works of art for the New York pavilion's façade, which he had designed. Commissioned in addition to Warhol were Peter Agostini, John Chamberlain, Robert Indiana, Ellsworth Kelly, Roy Lichtenstein, Alexander Liberman, Robert Mallary, Robert Rauschenberg, and James Rosenquist.[12] Warhol had initially planned to contribute a Heinz pickle. According to a report by his then assistant Nathan Gluck, he had come up with this idea because the company Heinz, from Warhol's birth town Pittsburgh, was also represented with a pavilion at the World's Fair of 1939, where Dalí had caused a stir with

---

3
Gibson 1997, p. 390.

4
Dalí 1942, p. 377.

5
Etherington-Smith 1993, pp. 243f.; Schaffner 2002, p. 68.

6
Quoted according to Gibson 1997, p. 390.

7
Dalí 1942, p. 377.

8
In Finkelstein 1998, p. 333.

9
Dalí 1976, p. 187.

10
Depicted in Descharnes/Néret 1993, no. 717. In 1984, Warhol created the print portfolio "Details of Renaissance Paintings (Sandro Botticelli, *Birth of Venus*, 1482)." See Feldman/Schellmann 2003, II.316–319. Although he also produced paintings, he didn't like the subject. In his diaries he remarks, "The Details. I hate them. Like details of the Botticelli 'Venus.' But people are loving these best. It makes you wonder." Hackett 1989, p. 605, October 5, 1984. See also the chapter **Religious Art** in this part.

12
Frei/Printz/King-Nero 2004, *A*, p. 25.

his *Dream of Venus*; "... there was a Heinz Pickle Pavilion, and they gave everybody little pins that were Heinz pickles, and everybody wore them. And Andy had evidently seen these or heard about it or something and thought, 'Wouldn't that be great: for this year's World's Fair to do a Heinz pickle.'"[13] Why Warhol then abandoned this idea is unknown. He found a new theme by asking others for advice, such as his artist colleague Ray Johnson, who was a frequent guest at the Factory at that time and was referred to by Grace Glueck in the *New York Times* as "most famous unknown artist."[14] William S. Wilson, who got to know Johnson in 1956 and was a close friend of his, recalled:

Early 1964 I drive Ray uptown in my little car to a party ... Ray and I enter the foyer. Andy comes rushing out of the group of people in there, guides Ray into the bedroom. I'm standing in the foyer, I don't go in to these other people. ... I just stand there and wait. After quite a long time the door opens and Ray rushes without looking, no goodbyes, takes me by the elbow, 'We're getting out of here! We're ditching this joint!' And we are outside and back in my little car and Ray whose moods I knew in the finest gradations of grey and other colors ... Wow, he is furious! Andy has taken him into the bedroom and told him, he would pay him for an idea. He's been commissioned to make a work for the World's Fair, he does not have any ideas, if Ray provides him with an idea, he will pay him.[15]

After a lack of success with Johnson, Warhol was able to glean an idea for the pavilion design from the artist and moviemaker Wynn Chamberlain. Chamberlain, who had spent many years of his life in India, drew an interesting comparison as he reported:

When I got to India, it was very interesting because I realized that if you can make yourself totally empty, everything will come into you. ... if you make yourself an empty vessel and shut up and don't say anything and if you're at all bright, everything comes to you. That's a yogi's thing in India ... I was responsible for getting him those photographs because I knew this young policeman who was the son of the chief of detectives of New York City. And he could get anything he wanted. And I said Andy needed something to do for this World's Fair thing. So he went out and got me these highly secret pictures of the most wanted men in America. And then Andy did these big silk screens ... .[16]

Warhol used the photos from the list of "The Thirteen Most Wanted," which had been released on February 1, 1962, by the New York Police.[17] Nine of those wanted were pictured with a frontal and profile view, four just with a frontal or three-quarter view.[18] Warhol produced a total of twenty-two screen prints, which appeared very coarse-grained from close up, as pixels could already be seen even on the photos of just 1 ½ by 1 ⅕ inches that they were made from.[19] Furthermore, in some cases strips remained empty to the left and right, because the templates were too narrow for the four-square-foot screens. Warhol added three blank panels to the twenty-two screen prints, thus producing a total of twenty-five panels, which were arranged in five rows of five as a twenty-by twenty-foot mural, with an uneven distribution of individual panels. If two views of a face were available, then they did not always appear next to each other. The

13
In Smith 1986,
p. 323.

14
Glueck 1965.

15
William S. Wilson
in a conversation
with the author
on December 7,
2012, in New York.

16
Wynn Chamberlain in a telephone conversation with
the author on
August 26, 2011.
According to
John Giorno
this was on the
evening of
April 28, 1963,
when he was
also present.
See Giorno
1994, pp. 127f.
See also Giorno
in Harris/Farzin
2014, p. 23.

17
Frei/Printz/
King-Nero
2004, A, p. 25.

18
The complete
wanted list
is reproduced
in Harris/Farzin
2014, pp. 15ff.

19
Crone 1970,
p. 30;
Bourdon 1989,
p. 181.

20
Depicted in Frei/
Printz/King-Nero
2004, *A*, no. 547.

21
Bourdon 1989,
p. 181.

22
Quoted accord-
ing to Frei/
Printz/King-Nero
2004, *A*, p. 25.

23
Warhol/Hackett
1980, p. 72;
Bourdon 1989,
p. 181.

24
Quoted accord-
ing to Frei/
Printz/King-Nero
2004, *A*, p. 26.

25
Crone 1970,
p. 30.

26
Letter from
Warhol to the
New York State
Department
of Public Works
on April 17, 1964,
reproduced
in Harris/Farzin
2014, p. 58.
A photo of the
painted-over
mural is depicted
in Frei/Printz/
King-Nero 2004,
A, p. 49.

27
Quoted accord-
ing to Frei/
Printz/King-Nero
2004, *A*, p. 25.

28
Osterwold 1989,
p. 176.

29
See Dergan/
Monk 2009,
pp. 176ff.

1
Levy 1977, p. 71.

three blank panels were placed in the lower right-hand corner.[20] Perhaps this was meant to indicate that some criminals had already been seized, or that there was space available for others who were wanted.[21] After completing the mural, Warhol was cited in the *New York Journal-American* of April 15, 1964, "I was first contacted by Mr. Johnson about six months ago. The whole thing cost about 4000 [dollars]. That's all they gave me to do it. It took one day. I got the pictures from a book the police put out. It's called 'The 13 Most Wanted Men.' It just had something to do with New York, and I was paid to have it silkscreened. I didn't make any money on it."[22] Warhol was evidently not interested in why the men were wanted or whether they were still being pursued. On the other hand, he assumed jokingly at the time that his mural could lead to an arrest.[23] In the end, he used the wanted photos as readily as those of film stars. Problems were inevitable, because some of the pictured men had in the meantime been arrested, appeared before the court, and even been acquitted. The organizers were therefore afraid that the State of New York might be sued. In fact the *New York Times* reported on July 19, 1964, that Warhol had been threatened with legal measures, citing him as saying, "One of the men labeled 'Wanted' had been pardoned, you see. So the mural was not valid any more. I'm still waiting for another inspiration."[24] Warhol was ordered to take down his mural. He then suggested making a portrait of Robert Moses, the World's Fair boss, as a replacement.[25] Since Philip Johnson rejected this, after a brief dispute Warhol agreed to paint over the mural then and there "in a color suitable to the Architect," whereupon the color silver was chosen.[26] The reason for this could be read in the press the next day, namely, that the work of art had not achieved the desired effect, in Warhol's view, and Philip Johnson was cited as saying, "He thought we hung it wrong. He didn't like it the moment he saw it."[27] Warhol's painted-over mural hung on the New York Pavilion at the World's Fair for about four weeks. After that it was kept in a warehouse and later destroyed.[28]

As the screen prints for the *Thirteen Most Wanted Men* still existed, not long afterward the artist decided to make new prints of them, which he exhibited for the first time in April 1967 at Ileana Sonnabend's gallery in Paris.[29]

Culinary Delights

Salvador Dalí's most famous work is *The Persistence of Memory*, which is also known as *The Soft Watches*. The small-format painting was created in 1931 in Paris, where it was exhibited for the first time in the same year at the Galerie Pierre Colle. The young New York gallery owner Julien Levy, who was fascinated by Dalí's works, visited the exhibition and purchased *The Persistence of Memory* for $250. Levy recorded in his memoirs: "In those days $250 was a high price, more than I had ever spent for a painting, and this by a relative unknown at that. My father was also pleased when I told him that if he liked it 'so would America.' He urged in vain that I change the title, 'Persistence de la Mémoire' to 'The Limp Watches.'"[1] The plan worked out. Shortly thereafter, Levy presented the painting to the American public, who received it enthusiastically. In his *Secret Life* Dalí recounts the making of *The Soft Watches* and reports that he had been inspired by camembert cheese:

It was on an evening when I felt tired, and had a slight headache, which is extremely rare with me. We were to go to a moving picture with some friends, and at the last moment I decided not to go. Gala would go with them, and I would stay home and go to bed early. We had topped off our meal with a very strong Camembert, and after everyone had gone I remained for a long time seated at the table meditating on the philosophical problems of the "super soft" which the cheese presented to my mind. I got up and went into my studio ... .[2]

When Gala returned home from her visit to the movie theater and saw the painting, Dalí noticed upon her face an "unmistakable contradiction of wonder and astonishment." He asked her, "Do you think that in three years you will have forgotten this image?" She answered, "No one can forget it once he has seen it."[3]

Although Dalí liked to claim that painting was only an "infinitesimal part" of his genius and therefore the "least important aspect" of his personality,[4] he had a particular affinity to it. This he expressed in *50 Secrets of Magic Craftsmanship* published in 1948 in New York, a compendium he authored of anecdotes, viewpoints, and practical advice for painters. Dalí dedicated the work to "all the young, who have faith in true painting," whose task is "to save Modern Art from chaos and laziness."[5] He also defines painting within it in a very straightforward way: "Painting: representation upon a surface of 'visual reality' through colors. If intellectual elements intervene in this representation we have a second rate painting, called 'decorative painting.' If the elements that intervene are of the domain of ideas we also have a second rate painting called 'literary painting.' Conclusion: The only first rate painting is realistic painting."[6] Dalí adhered to this definition throughout his life. In light of this, he welcomed the emergence of Pop Art, which he referred to as an "affirmation of reality" and as "part of the healthy trend away from abstract expressionism."[7] In an interview in 1975 he reiterated his definition of painting and even highlighted Andy Warhol's leading role in Pop Art: "In the beginning of surrealism I said that painting is photography in color, made by hand, of images of the irrational or of reality. And after Andy Warhol allowed the period of the black despair of abstraction to pass, I said it again."[8]

In the early 1960s, when Andy Warhol ventured the transition from commercial artist to fine artist, he still worked conventionally at first and produced hand-painted pictures. The most significant works from this creative period include the thirty-two little *Campbell's Soup Cans* of 1962, which each measure 20 × 16 inches and appear identical at first glance, but have different flavors on the labels.[9] The playwright Robert Heide later reported that Warhol had once told him the story behind their creation: "Andy told me that, even though he had learned to draw the required bowl of fruit on the dining room table at art school, what he really wanted to paint was that can of Campbell's tomato soup (his favorite) from his mother's pantry. 'Many an afternoon at lunchtime Mom would open a can of Campbell's for me, because that's all we could afford,' he said. 'I love it to this day.'"[10] For Warhol it was not about the soup can as such, but about the idea of serial repetition. With

2
Dalí 1942, p. 317.

3
Ibid.

4
In Bosquet 1969, pp. 19f.; see also Pauwels/ Dalí 1985, p. 77.

5
Dalí 1948, p. 5.

6
Ibid., p. 18.

7
Quoted according to Descharnes 1984, p. 369; Dalí 1964, p. 46.

8
In Dalí 1975, "I Laugh Tremendously," p. 56.

9
Frei/Printz 2002, no. 051.

10
In Bockris 1989, p. 144.

regard to this, Marcel Duchamp stated: "If you take a Campbell's Soup Can and repeat it fifty times, you are not interested in the retinal image. What interests you is the concept that wants to put fifty Campbell's soup cans on a canvas."[11] The use of silkscreen printing soon opened up unimaginable possibilities for Warhol.[12] Wynn Chamberlain believed that there was an economic reason behind the idea of the serial:

He always, all his life, had his eye on the cost and so he realized that if he got small silk screen things ... if he did it small and just repeated it on the canvas it would be much less expensive than the screens he was using. So that's what he did. ... and people began to say, "Oh, he's invented the serial thing, bla bla bla bla bla." But it was all cost. It was cost-effective to do it that way. And he had very little imagination. So, his whole goal was to kill the imagination, which he almost succeeded in doing, you know, factory-made.[13]

David Bourdon correctly states that the concept and style of Warhol's soup can pictures led to the artist's name becoming so widely known.[14] Therefore, what was said of Dalí's *Soft Watches* applies also to Warhol's *Campbell's Soup Cans*—once seen, one does not forget them, and the name and even the face of the artist are automatically associated with them. In both cases, the work of art is based on a "culinary delight": Warhol's on tomato soup, and Dalí's on camembert.

Currier & Ives

In January 1965, Salvador Dalí signed a contract with the American publisher Sidney Z. Lucas granting the latter exclusive sales rights for his signed prints in North America. Until 1971, Lucas issued lithographs in print runs of 150 to 300 signed copies, most of which he declared to be originals.[1] The prints were sold through the Phyllis Lucas Gallery – Old Print Center in New York, which was run by his wife. The portfolio "Currier & Ives" from the year 1971, intended as homage to the company of the same name and consisting of six lithographs based on an original image in gouache with collage, is a remarkable edition.[2] Nathaniel Currier (1813–1888) and James Merritt Ives (1824–1895) were the first American lithographers who succeeded in establishing a market for their products. Their prints, featuring every imaginable theme—including politics, wars, misfortune, inventions, circus, hunting, and sports—were sold in the nineteenth century for prices ranging from twenty-five cents to three dollars apiece, depending on their size. It is assumed today that around 11,000 different pictorial motifs by Currier & Ives went into circulation.[3] Due to their popularity and the value given to them, the lithographs were able to achieve premiums of up to $25,000 in auctions in the U.S. in the twentieth century.[4] As Phyllis Lucas recalled, Dalí also valued the American company's prints: "Ever since Dalí walked into my gallery to buy Butterfly prints to incorporate into a collage, it was a dream of ours to put out a collection of works reflecting Dalí's interpretation of these famous prints by Currier and Ives. Dalí was a big fan of Currier and Ives."[5] The wide distribution and the considerable fame of the Currier & Ives prints were probably key reasons for Dalí, who always sought a mass impact, to take

---

Margin notes (left columns):

11
Quoted according to Bourdon 1989, p. 88.

12
In mid 1962, Warhol produced the silkscreened painting *Clocks*. The black and white image shows two Westclox clocks without hands. Frei/Printz 2002, no. 200.

13
Wynn Chamberlain in a telephone conversation with the author on August 26, 2011.

14
Bourdon 1989, p. 88.

→
14/15 [p. 372]

1
Dalí, 1971, pp. 5ff. However, not all prints are original lithographs. Cf. Michler/Löpsinger 1995, nos. 1143, 1147–1157; Field 1996, Cooperative Lithographs, 64-1, 65-1 to 65-6, 66-1, 66-3.

2
The publisher advertised the graphic prints as original lithographs. The print run was 250 copies on Rives and 50 copies on Japan. See *Dalí*, 1971, pp. 23ff.; in fact they are lithographs based on gouache works by the artist, see Michler/Löpsinger 1995, nos. 1345–1350; Field 1996, Cooperative Lithographs, 71-5.

3
Dalí, 1971, p. 22.

4
Salvador Dalí: Das goldene Zeitalter, p. 193.

5
Quoted according to Dalí: A Fifty Year Retrospective, p. 65.

on the project. The artist created six gouaches, each paraphrasing a graphic print by Currier & Ives. A still life with flowers and fruit in front of a landscape, a winter scene in Central Park, a yacht race, a scene from firemen's lives, and two horse races, served as templates. As was often the case with his gouaches, Dalí applied the paint in part directly from the tube onto the paper. He integrated the templates in the middle at the bottom edge of the gouaches. Almost all of the works include butterflies cut out of old prints, with which the artist refers charmingly to the fact that he visited the Phyllis Lucas Gallery for the first time when he was looking for butterfly prints.

The Currier & Ives prints distributed by the million were, of course, also known to Andy Warhol, who appreciated them just as much as Dalí did. Warhol was a frequent visitor to the New York Public Library, where he sought sources of inspiration for his illustrations. He found them there in the form of photos and prints from the graphic collection, which he liked to take home with him. It is reported that Warhol kept hold of the borrowed pictures long beyond their due date, or even claimed to have lost them, willingly paying the late charge or penalty fee, in order to be sure that nobody could discover his sources.[6] Around 1952/53 he put together the promotional book *Love Is a Pink Cake* with the author Ralph Thomas ("Corkie") Ward.[7] The simply designed book served as self-promotion for Warhol during his time as a commercial artist. It consists of a simple cover made of folded, white wax paper with a little sticker outlined in red with the words "love is a pink cake by corkie & andy" on it. The book contains twenty-five offset prints based on Warhol's drawings, on loose, light blue sheets of paper measuring 11 × 8 ½ inches. The prints are dedicated to famous personalities in myths and history who were unlucky in love. Almost all the prints are accompanied by Corkie Ward's humorous or ironic verses.[8] The lovers represented include Orpheus and Eurydice, Samson and Delilah, Antony and Cleopatra, and Napoleon and Josephine. Warhol used the 1846 hand-colored lithograph *The Lovers' Reconciliation* by Currier & Ives as the template for a print dedicated to Frederic Chopin and George Sand. However, from another lithograph published by Currier & Ives in the same year, *The Lovers' Quarrel*, he adopted only the male figure to create a dandy reminiscent of Oscar Wilde.[9] Sometimes the drawings look rather awkward, giving the impression that the line has been repeatedly restarted.[10] Warhol evidently drew all the figures for the portfolio freehand. But he did not slavishly adhere to the template and, for example, left out shadowing, background, or minor details.[11] For example, the fan that the lady is holding in her right hand on the lithograph *The Lovers' Reconciliation* becomes a cigar in Warhol's representation of George Sand. With this, he added his own personal touches, for example, by "eroticizing" his dandy and emphasizing his crotch with a very clear line.[12]

The subject of unhappy or unrequited love can also be viewed as an allegory for the relationship between Warhol and Corkie Ward. Warhol wrote several love letters to Ward, but Ward was not attracted to him so initially they simply remained friends.[13] However, Ward found even this friendship too tiring later on, as Warhol constantly demanded a great deal of attention

6
Bockris 1989, p. 105.

7
Schleif 2013, pp. 81, 84.

8
Feldman/Schellmann 2003, IV. 27-50. The total print run is not known. According to Rainer Crone it totalled around 200 copies. See Crone 1976, p. 106, and the pages that follow, which contain fourteen reproductions on light blue paper.

9
The Currier & Ives templates and Warhol's works are depicted in Smith 1986, pp. 51ff.

10
Schleif 2013, p. 82.

11
Bourdon 1989, p. 36.

12
Smith 1986, p. 50.

13
Bockris 1989, p. 94.

and was easily offended. He was also bothered by the young commercial artist's ambition to earn money, as he later remarked, "Andy did everything for money. His main goal was to learn how to do everything faster."[14]

Art for the Department Store and Disco Décor

Salvador Dalí dedicated himself only sporadically to printmaking until the early 1960s. He did, however, receive a commission from the Swiss-French publisher Albert Skira to illustrate a book edition of the work *Les Chants de Maldoror* by Isidore Ducasse, the self-proclaimed Comte de Lautréamont, which was published in 1934.[1] The photogravures it contains, based on drawings with Dalí's original reworking,[2] were widely appreciated and can be regarded as the highlight of the artist's early graphic work. The French publisher Joseph Forêt later convinced Dalí to create lithographs for Miguel de Cervantes's *Don Quixote*, which were published in the portfolio "Pages Choisies de Don Quichotte de la Manche" in 1957.[3] These were Dalí's first lithographs, as he had hitherto refused to create such works "for aesthetic, moral, and philosophical reasons."[4] He dramatized himself and the creative process to great effect when it came to events with a public appeal. For example, he filled two rhinoceros horns with bread dipped in lithographic ink, in order to "splatter" the sails of a windmill onto a lithographic stone, or he threw an egg filled with lithographic ink at a rotating lithographic stone.[5] Dalí also did watercolors, which were transferred to printing plates in a photomechanical process to add color to the lithographs.[6]

In 1960 Dalí began his more than ten-year cooperation with the French publisher Pierre Argillet, who commissioned him with various book illustrations.[7] The artist preferred to use the drypoint technique, whereby the image is etched directly onto the copper plate. Other publishers gave him similar commissions in the period that followed. Dalí recognized that there was a lot of money to be earned very quickly with prints. In his *Unspeakable Confessions* he writes: "The captain brings in two copperplates I am supposed to engrave for a Parisian publisher. Each morning after breakfast I like to start the day by earning twenty thousand dollars. I stick the plates down on my belly, raise my knees, and on that stand I set to work with the engraving point. I take real pleasure in cutting the metal as the steel tip moves along."[8] Since colorful prints, in particular, appealed to the public, Dalí was repeatedly asked by publishers to complete watercolors or gouaches. A printer then converted them lithographically or photomechanically.[9] Gouaches also served as templates for the portfolio "Memories of Surrealism," which the Hollywood actor and gallery owner Allan Rich edited in 1971.[10] In order to be able to claim the sheets as original artworks, Rich found a clever solution: "I said, 'Dalí, in order to make this an original, you have to put an etching on each one,' because Dalí never really did a lithograph. He didn't understand tusche. So people who say, Dalí has done an original lithograph—it's not right. He wanted to do photomechanical ones with me for 'Memories of Surrealism' and I said no. So I had Rigal [the printer] do the litho on stone and then I had Dalí do an etching."[11] Therefore, to be precise, the graphic

---

14
In ibid., p. 95.

1
Löpsinger/
Michler 1994,
no. 11–54;
Field 1996,
Original Intaglio, 34-2.

2
Details of technique see Mason 1992, pp. 24ff.

3
Löpsinger/
Michler 1995,
no. 1001–1012;
Field 1996,
Original Lithographs, 57-1.

4
Dalí 1965, p. 168.

5
Ibid., pp. 169f.;
Descharnes in
Löpsinger/
Michler 1995,
pp. 8f.; Maur
1989, pp. 442ff.

6
Löpsinger/
Michler 1995,
p. 14;
Maur 1989,
p. 442.

7
These include
the book illustrations *Poèmes
secrets d'Apollinaire* (1967),
*Poèmes de Mao
Tse-tung* (1967),
Goethe's *Faust*
(1968/69), and
Vénus aux fourrures by Leopold
von Sacher-Masoch (1969).

8
Dalí 1976, p. 267.

9
Michler/Löpsinger 1995, pp. 14ff.

10
Michler/Löpinger
1994, no. 494–
505; Field 1996,
Original Intaglio,
71–15.

11
Allan Rich in
a telephone conversation with
the author on
April 25, 2013.

art in the portfolio is mixed media. The principle of combining lithographic reproductions, based on a unique piece created by Dalí with an original etching, was applied repeatedly in the artist's graphic work.

Dalí was deeply addicted to fame and wanted to be so popular that his pictures would be for sale even in department stores. It was only prints that made this feasible. Large department stores and dispatch galleries did, in fact, order templates from him, from which lithographs or chromolithographs were produced in large quantities. Only in a few cases did the artist work on these himself. So as not to scare off potential buyers, the edition was done on various types of paper (Japan, Arches, Rives), so that the sheet numbering could be kept quite low. For profitability reasons, the traditional rule of printing ten percent of the edition as simply "artist's proofs" was also ignored. Today, the assumption is that there are as many as 500 copies of some of Dalí's prints.[12]

Impressive editions were also created during those same years, for example, the book objects *Moses and Monotheism* with texts from Sigmund Freud's eponymous late work, and *Alchimie des Philosophes* with Chinese, Indian, Greek, Hebrew, and Arabic writings by seminal alchemists from the second to the seventeenth centuries. For both works, Dalí etched the motifs with a diamond-tipped etching tool on plates of solid gold, which were then printed, together with lithographic or serigraphic secondary motifs, onto lamb's leather or lamb parchment.[13] Another unusual volume of prints is the book object *Dix recettes d'immortalité* from 1973, with texts by Dalí on the subjects of life and death, which he illustrated with eleven drypoint etchings with photogravures. This includes the first stereoscopic print in art history.[14]

With only few exceptions, Dalí signed all of his prints. When production reached its peak in the 1970s, the artist dedicated every free minute to accomplishing this task. Therefore, he was often signing prints while receiving visitors, giving interviews, or dictating texts for a new book. It is said that the artist's signature could vary spontaneously under the influence of a conversation or music.[15] His secretary Peter Moore reports in his memoirs that at the beginning of the 1970s, Dalí generally spent two to three hours a day signing prints, getting through an average of 1,000 sheets per hour.[16] According to his biographer Luis Romero, signing was what Dalí loved the most, calling out "more, more, more ..." and gesticulating excitedly.[17] In his memoirs *Vivencias con Salvador Dalí*, Emilio Puignau, the Dalís' architect in Port Lligat and Púbol, provides further insight into the artist's signing hours:

In his shack in the little street outside there were several boxes of these sheets, a table and Dalí sitting at it. I remember well those whole days that Dalí would spend signing in a totally automatic manner: a man placed a sheet on the table, Dalí would sign, and while he took it away someone else would put another in its place; and so on again and again as if it were a printing shop.

I couldn't fathom that Dalí would submit to such a tiresome, and, particularly, boring chore which had nothing whatsoever to do with his art. I told him, once only, that I couldn't understand what it was all about, and I dared to say to him: "If you sign so many blank sheets they'll be able to print any imitation they want on them, anything that looks like Dalí." His reply was: "I've already

12
Löpsinger in Maur 1989, p. 410, and Michler/ Löpsinger 1994, p. 28.

13
Salvador Dalí: Das goldene Zeitalter, pp. 246, 285.

14
Michler/Löpsinger 1994, no. 567–577; Field 1996, Original Intaglio, 73–20.

15
Michler/Löpsinger 1994, p. 24.

16
Moore 2009, p. 252.

17
Gibson 1997, p. 547.

been paid what they offered for the work. So what they do with them's no concern of mine."

In truth, Dalí was an Avida Dollars.[18]

Around 1965, Dalí started to sign blank sheets. Peter Moore later reported that a French publisher—according to A. Reynolds Morse, this was Pierre Argillet—had persuaded Dalí to sign a couple of blank sheets, so that he would not have to return to Paris to sign the prints. Argillet is said to have offered the artist ten dollars extra per signature and Dalí signed 10,000 sheets in this "first case."[19] The signing of blank sheets subsequently became a habitual practice. It is said that Dalí earned 100 dollars in cash for every signature.[20] It cannot be determined how many blanks Dalí signed during his lifetime. Ralf Michler and Lutz Löpsinger, the authors of the first catalogue raisonné of Dalí's graphic works, estimate that around 40,000 to 60,000 authentic pre-signed print sheets exist or are in "safe hands."[21] A look at the catalogue raisonné compiled by Albert Field reveals that around 10,000 blank sheets were used for authentic editions from the years 1978 to 1980.[22] Peter Moore, on the other hand, remarked that Dalí may have signed up to 350,000 blanks.[23] This signing practice did lasting damage to Dalí's reputation within collectors' circles and was also thoroughly milked by the media. Horst Weber von Beeren, who was assistant to Warhol's printer Rupert Jasen Smith at the time, caught wind of a flagrant detail:

Albert Field's disciple Frank Hunter told me the story, that French customs confiscated 40,000 empty sheets of graphic paper, which were all signed. Dalí had gotten $100 for each signature. Someone had alerted customs and it turned out to have been Gala, who was in a marital fit, though it was she who lived on that money. When I told Warhol this story, he loved it. He said, "That is so Andy Warhol. Oh, it is so me! I would like to do the same, just sign canvasses and papers and get paid for it."[24]

However, Warhol did not have the same endurance as Dalí when it came to signing prints. Brigid Berlin recalls that Warhol soon became bored.[25] Horst Weber von Beeren reports something similar:

At the end of an edition from Warhol, it just needed to be signed. For that, 100 plus prints were numbered and put on top of each other. One of us had to hold them up, and then let that page fall after Warhol signed it. Like an accordion. Andy rolled his eyes, made faces, like he had to carry cement bags, that it was all too much from the art dealers, to have him do it. It was so demeaning for a pop superstar. How dare they ...? It was hardest work for a diva (laughs).[26]

As of 1980, Dalí was no longer capable of signing because of his state of health. Despite this, countless signed prints continued to appear, as the art market was thoroughly flooded with forgeries. Furthermore, even before 1980 some excess (unauthorized) print runs were made. As Albert Field later explained, Dalí initially responded casually to this and reckoned that forgeries showed how famous he was.[27] Warhol had a similar view; his superstar Louis Waldon recalled, "He was reading the paper one day, and he says, 'Oh no, no, I don't understand it, Louis. Why are they buying these fake Dalís? My God, there's something like 20,000 of them out there. They're buying them up at these prices! I said, 'You don't like it.' ... 'Oh no, I like it! That's a compliment when somebody makes someone else's art.'"[28] It was not until an interview in 1984 for the magazine *Paris Match* that Dalí expressed his outrage about the flood of forgeries, saying, "We must denounce this extraordinary and unheard of phenomenon surrounding the work of Dalí, which is provoking plagiarism, forgeries and alterations, with which absolute fortunes are being made."[29] When this situation threatened to damage his reputation even further, the artist felt obliged to declare on June 1, 1985, by means of a notarial statement, that as of December 23, 1980, he had stopped signing sheets of paper meant for printing plates or any other use. On August 14, 1986, he gave a further statement, reaffirming that he had signed "no blank papers suitable for printing graphic works during 1980."[30] Even so, Dalí's reputation was already severely jeopardized. According to Löpsinger, almost ninety percent of all the Dalí prints on the market at the end of the 1980s were fakes.[31] The number of non-authorized prints is difficult to estimate—Ricard Mas Peinado estimates that there are somewhere between 100,000 and 300,000.[32]

Dalí's extensive print production of over 1,500 works and the ever larger print runs over the years—at the end of the 1970s there were editions of up to 1,195 copies[33]—are reminiscent of Andy Warhol's serial art production, which defines the entire oeuvre of the Pop Art artist. However, in Warhol's work, in contrast to Dalí's, prints and paintings are inextricably entwined. Warhol used the same technique in both media—silkscreen printing.[34] Many of the artist's motifs are present in both his painted and printed works. Popular pictures, such as *Marilyn*, *Campbell's Soup Can*, *Flowers*, or *Electric Chair*, appeared first as paintings and later as prints. From 1972, motifs were first formulated in print and subsequently influenced the painting. There are, however, distinct criteria for painting and prints in Warhol's work. First of all, there is the picture base—canvas was reserved for painting and paper for prints. Warhol also relativized the mechanical aspect of silkscreen printing in his painting work, accepting irregularities and tolerance margins. In other words, no two canvasses are identical and it is only with prints that seemingly identical pictures were produced. However, even here there were exceptions. Some prints have color variations and the individual prints are therefore unique.[35]

A turning point in Warhol's print creations came in 1977. He employed the experimental printer Rupert Jasen Smith, who—together with his most important assistant Horst Weber von Beeren—had a significant influence on Warhol's print work.[36] The works became more elaborate. This started with the choice of paper. Weber von Beeren explains, "Rupert said we needed Museum Board to get a good print. So he ordered it, but sometimes it didn't arrive, because the check bounced. The printed part was 39 × 39 inches, and then we cut one inch off on each side, so it looked like it was printed all the way to the edges."[37] Horst Weber von Beeren explains that the use of Lenox Museum Board demands a higher printing quality, because the smooth surface of the board makes every printing fault visible. On the other hand, on paper with a textured surface, such as Arches, mistakes are hardly noticeable.[38]

As from 1979, numerous works were created using "diamond dust." As Rupert Jasen Smith later reported, this was "a great trick because it solved

28 Louis Waldon in O'Sullivan Shorr 2014, *Book III*, p. 47. Louis Waldon added in a telephone conversation with the author on October 2, 2013 that the conversation took place in the 1960s.

29 In Saurat 1984, p. 94 (translated from the French).

30 The documents are reproduced in Michler/ Löpsinger 1994, pp. 6ff.

31 Löpsinger in Maur 1989, p. 410.

32 Mas Peinado 2004, p. 270.

33 Cf. Field 1996, Cooperative Lithographs, 79–1ff.

34 Geldzahler in Feldman/ Schellmann 1989, p. VII.

35 Warhol tried this method for the first time with the print *$1.57 Giant Size*, which was used as a record cover that was shown in 1963 on the occasion of the exhibition "The Popular Image" at the Washington Gallery of Modern Art. Cf. Feldman/ Schellmann 2003, II.2 and IIA.2; Maréchal 2008, no. 25.

36 See the chapter **Assistants, Employees, Secretaries, and Managers** in Part 3.

37 Horst Weber von Beeren in a conversation with the author on December 7, 2012 in New York.

38 Horst Weber von Beeren in an e-mail to the author on December 22, 2013.

a lot of problems, especially with images that did not look good by themselves."[39] "Diamond dust" provided a sparkling surface for Warhol's print and painting works, which led Warhol to refer to these works ironically one time as "disco décor."[40] The diamond dealer and designer John Reinhold, one of the artist's closest friends, reports:

The idea of diamond dust came from me. Andy always used to ask people: "What should I paint? What should I do? What should I do?" This was a constant thing not just with me, but with almost everybody. So one day when he came up to my office I decided to give him a jar filled with diamond dust and said, "Here. Do something with it." I didn't say what, I just said, "Here. Do something with it." So, that's how the diamond dust paintings began. But, in fact, diamond dust itself doesn't sparkle, so actually, these diamond dust paintings are not diamonds, they are crushed glass. Rupert would be crushing the glass for him. Then we had discussions about what to call the diamond dust paintings. Should we call them this, should we call them that, etc. But that's how the idea came to him, from that jar of diamond dust.[41]

Rupert Jasen Smith later clarified that he had used "diamond dust" for his own works since art school and had gathered some experience with it. That's why Warhol always said, "The diamond dust fell off Rupert's paintings and stuck to mine."[42] Horst Weber von Beeren still clearly remembers working with "diamond dust": "It was horrible work … The crushed glass, not diamond-dust, was rolled over the wet print and stuck to it. The glass was everywhere, in the eyes, the mouth, the clothes, even at home in the bed sheets. Andy kept saying it would fall off in ten years and collect at the bottom of the frame."[43]

Salvador Dalí had already experimented with similar effects in his graphic work from 1965. However, he used "gold dust" rather than "diamond dust," and first did so on the print *Gala mon seul désir* and on the prints of the portfolio "Le cirque" to create a glittering surface structure.[44] The publisher's catalogue says that it is an embellishment made of real gold.[45] Dalí's illustrations for the biblical texts *Songs of Solomon* (1971) and for Tristan Corbière's *Les amour jaunes* (1974) also feature golden highlights.[46] The Spaniard was evidently quite taken with Corbière's erotic fantasies, because he coated the drypoint etchings with pastose gold bronze of a permanently slightly sticky nature, which had been developed especially for this edition.[47] Perhaps Dalí wanted to allude with this to the exchange of bodily fluids during lovemaking.

Andy Warhol's print production, comprising a total of 413 sheets, also reached its peak during the 1980s, and ended abruptly with his early death in 1987. However, in contrast to Dalí, with few exceptions his print runs rarely exceeded 250 copies. Warhol's employees were also anxious to keep the market value of the print work stable. The artist reports in his diaries that in October 1981, Vincent Fremont bought back portfolios that had been auctioned at Sotheby's.[48] He recorded on May 17, 1986, "Fred was upset because I'm doing the Martha Grahams, that 300 more prints of mine will be in circulation."[49] Such considerations were quite alien to Dalí's secretaries or Gala.

39
In Feldman/
Schellmann
1989, p. 24.

40
In *Warhol
Shadows* (n.p.).

41
John Reinhold in
a telephone
conversation
with the author
on May 26, 2010.

42
In Feldman/
Schellmann
1989, p. 24.

43
Horst Weber
von Beeren in a
conversation
with the author
on December 7,
2012 in New York.

44
Michler/Löpsinger
1994, no. 134–140,
Field 1996,
Original Intaglio,
65-5, 65-6.

45
Sahli 1985,
no. 9–15.

46
Michler/Löpsinger
1994, no. 468–
479, 683–702;
Field 1996,
Original Intaglio,
71-17, 74-15.

47
*Salvador Dalí:
Das goldene
Zeitalter*, p. 242.

48
Hackett 1989,
p. 411, October 8,
1981.

49
Ibid., p. 733.

Salvador Dalí— The Father of Pop Art?

In the 1930s, Salvador Dalí created objects that were to become some of the most well-known works of the surrealist movement: *The Surrealist Shoe – Scatalogical Object Functioning Symbolically* (1932), *Retrospective Bust of a Woman* (1933), *Aphrodisiac Dinner Jacket* and *Lobster Telephone* (both 1936).[1] The objects are based on the principle of putting together everyday items, and they reflect the aesthetic of the poet Lautréamont. The poet, highly admired by the surrealists, described the beauty of a young man as the "fortuitous encounter upon a dissecting table of a sewing machine and an umbrella."[2] In view of the newly emerging Pop Art, in the 1960s Dalí described his surrealist objects as "Dalínian antecedents of Pop Art,"[3] highlighting his *Aphrodisiac Dinner Jacket*, in particular, as the "most glorious antecedent of Pop Art."[4] In an interview for *Playboy* magazine in 1964, he proposed:

... I have thought of a tremendous idea for you, for a most beautiful Pop-Art cover for Playboy: *photograph of Dalí's fantastic Aphrodisiac Jacket. It consists of one regular smoking jacket—but with plenty of little jigger glasses fastened onto the front. All of the glasses are filled with crème de menthe, and in every glass there is a dead fly in the bottom. Very luxurious, very brilliant object. Only two days ago Dalí discovers the real mathematical significance of this creation in the* Scientific American *magazine, about the smell of peppermint: it shows every kind of smell arranged mathematically, according to the constitutional geometry of its molecules, including the molecular arrangement of the smell of peppermint. So one of the greatest pop-art objects is now becoming completely scientific. Add to this creation plenty of straws, each in the middle of the green crème de menthe. Then put inside the jacket a nude model, showing the legs and the beginning of the bosom; her sex is not showing, but almost, almost. It is possible instead of a coat hanger to show the girl's face—but not the whole face, just up to the mouth. But you decide. Perhaps it is best to use a smoking jacket of moiré silk pattern. Some people tell me that in a shop for theatrical supplies you can get a "twist" jacket, which is more fancy and extraordinary than the usual ones—the kind twist boys like the Beatles would wear. Since the sexes of the Beatles is so ambiguous—nobody knows if it is boy or girl with the hair so long—the quintessence of ambiguity is this smoking jacket of Dalínian pop art. I propose that this is the most beautiful, the most fantastic cover for* Playboy.[5]

Two years later, Andy Warhol was asked in an interview: "Salvador Dalí has been quoted as saying that he is the father of Pop Art. Have you any comment on that?" Warhol answered: "I don't know. He's certainly been around a long time. But it's hard to understand what he is saying most of the time."[6] A kinship between surrealist objects and works of Pop Art is undeniable. The surrealists intended to make visible psychological content that they saw as being concealed behind the frequently banal surface of everyday reality. They often used an arsenal of everyday, ordinary items for this reason, as the Pop Art artists would later also do.

The *Aphrodisiac Dinner Jacket* was shown for the first time at the exhibition "Exposition surréaliste d'objets" in Paris, held by the Galerie Charles

1 Lobsters and telephones are signature features in Dalí's work. In 1938/39, he created a series of paintings, including *The Enigma of Hitler*, featuring a telephone receiver as main motif. In 1961/62, Warhol painted four versions of an antique candlestick telephone, all entitled *Telephone*. Twenty years later, he quite incidentally produced lobster paintings. See on this Cutrone in Bockris 1989, p. 453.

2 Lautréamont 1966, p. 263.

3 Dalí 1964, pp. 46, 48.

4 Ibid., p. 48; Dalí 1968, no. 85.

5 Dalí 1964, p. 48.

6 In Goldsmith 2004, p. 98.

Ratton in May 1936. It was displayed at the London "International Surrealist Exhibition" in June and the American public was able to admire the unusual object in late 1936. Simultaneous to the exhibition "Fantastic Art, Dada and Surrealism," from November 1936 to January 1937, Dalí presented the *Aphrodisiac Dinner Jacket* together with his *Lobster Telephone* in his window display for the Bonwit Teller department store.[7] The *Aphrodisiac Dinner Jacket* is currently considered destroyed. However, Dalí made two reconstructions during the heyday of Pop Art. The first was made in 1964 for his retrospective in Tokyo,[8] the second is signed by Dalí and dated 1967. The latter was shown in the two major Dalí retrospectives in the years 1979/1980 and 2012/2013 at the Centre Georges Pompidou in Paris.[9]

Silver Clouds

In her memoirs *Famous For 15 Minutes*, Ultra Violet writes that she got to know Salvador Dalí in 1960.[1] Three years later he introduced her to Andy Warhol who immediately invited her to make a movie together.[2] However, Ultra Violet first stood in front of Warhol's camera in March 1965.[3] Therefore, her statements are questionable.[4] Warhol's nephew, James Warhola, with reference to her book, remarked in an interview: "... Ultra Violet ... may have exaggerated some things possibly to make herself look a little more important, more at the center of things. ... It wasn't completely her fault, as her editors wanted her to make the book juicier, to sell more copies ... ."[5]

Ultra Violet reports in her memoirs:

On occasion Andy comes with me to tea at Dalí's, and one day in 1965 Dalí takes us upstairs to his studio in the St. Regis. The room is filled with his toys: stereopticons and boxes of cards to view in the machines, photographs of exotic places and beautiful people, including dozens and dozens of himself, stacks of back issues of Scientific American, *dried flowers, a white plaster Venus de Milo, yards of red velvet, a cardboard pyramid, live leeches in an aquarium, several gold-dipped lobsters, crabs, and sea urchins. Andy stares in fascination at this accumulation of odd objects. He plays with a foot-long, helium-filled silver blimp attached to a string. "Oh, how great!" he exclaims. "Where did you get this?"*

"At Schwarz's toy store," Dalí tells him.

A little later, on our way to F.A.O. Schwarz, Andy says to me, "Leave Dalí. He's too old, and he's not with it."

"He's still getting plenty of press attention."

Andy grimaces.

In the toy store we buy two blimps. I don't think much about the purchase until next year, when Andy's show at the Castelli Gallery features his Flying Pillows. Bigger than bed pillows, the helium-filled rectangles of silver Mylar are clearly derived from the toy blimps. They have the dreamy beauty of indoor clouds. One wafts gently out of the gallery window; several turn up as props the following season in one of Merce Cunningham's ballets; but four do not bring an estimated price of $20,000 at auction at Sotheby's in the spring of 1988.[6]

7
Dalí 1942, p. 344.
See the chapter
Window Displays
in this part.

8
Descharnes/
Descharnes
2003, p. 44.

9
Aguer in Martin/
Aguer/Bouhours/
Dufrêne 2012,
p. 188.

1
Ultra Violet 1988,
p. 68.

2
Ibid., pp. 78f.

3
Angell 2006,
p. 205.

4
See the chapter
The First Encounter
in Part 5.

5
In Prekop/Cihlář
2011, p. 105.

6
Ultra Violet 1988,
pp. 121f.
+

Ultra Violet later recalled that Dalí was quite outraged when Warhol exhibited his *Silver Clouds* at the Leo Castelli Gallery.[7] His friend, the painter Antoni Pitxot, confirmed this: "... Dalí told me once that he had advised Warhol to realize the famous, flying cushions filled with gas. Until he once said in an absurd manner: 'That's my idea, not Warhol's. I gave it to Warhol.'"[8] Dalí had already discovered the *Silver Clouds* for himself at the beginning of 1963. At the time, he met the actress Mia Farrow, who tells of her first encounter with the Spaniard at the St. Regis Hotel in New York in her memoirs *What Falls Away*: "In a single, unfurnished room of the hotel, Dalí kept a large, beautiful, silver helium balloon that he visited at various times during the day, noting and delighting in its autonomous, barely perceptible movements. 'I am penetrating more and more into the compressed magic of the universe,' Dalí said."[9] Even after Warhol presented his *Silver Clouds* to the New York public in April 1966 in his exhibition at the Leo Castelli Gallery, Dalí could not resist occasionally posing with the air sculptures he had "discovered"—for example, two years later in front of the camera of the British photographer Robert Whitaker, whom he had met the previous year.[10] Whitaker's photos show Dalí on the patio of his house in Port Lligat with a silver helium balloon the same size as Warhol's works.[11] Perhaps it did in fact come from Warhol's Factory. Dalí explained at the time that he was watching the reflections on the shiny helium balloon and that it was part of an experiment in photographing God. This experiment was to be carried out using a laser beam and a one-meter length of aluminum.[12] In addition, there is a film shot taken around the same time showing Dalí inside his house with a silver helium balloon. This recording is accompanied by a commentary by the artist, in which he explains why the balloons held such a special fascination for him:

I'm obsessed by helium cushions because I already belong to this society of Doctor Stinger who claims that he can prolong people's life and, in case of sudden death, instead of putting me in a box for dead people, like everyone, I mean the skeleton and ... not at all: I'll be preserved in helium at a very, very low temperature so my death would only be a temporary and curable illness, thus deceiving all divine Dalí's detractors of today.[13]

Warhol was presumably not deliberately seeking to recreate Dalí's silver helium balloon. The fact that he succeeded was more due to coincidence and collaboration with the Swedish electrical engineer Billy Klüver. At the time, Klüver was working at Bell Laboratories in Murray Hill, New Jersey, and had earned a reputation as "the artist's scientist."[14] Klüver later explained how the cooperation with Warhol came about:

In the summer of 1964, Andy asked me if I could make a floating light bulb for him. I went back to Bell Labs and discussed the problem with my colleagues. We looked into batteries, lights, a material to contain helium, etc. We did some calculations and tests and decided it could not be done without the bulb being very large, because of the weight of the batteries, lights, etc. Meanwhile, Harold Hodge found a material that was highly impermeable to helium and could be heat-sealed easily. Made by 3M, it was called Scotchpak and, we were told, was used by the army to wrap sandwiches. A friendly local salesman for 3M supplied

---

7
Ultra Violet in a conversation with Jeanine Barone for the author on October 18, 2009 in New York.

8
Antoni Pitxot in a conversation with the author on September 5, 2009 in Cadaqués (translated from the Spanish). Similarly, also in Pitxot 2014, p. 87. See also *Salvador Dalí:* Àlbum de família, p. 74.

+
Two photos by Philippe Halsman shot in 1965 show Dalí at his easel working on the painting *Le Voyage fantastique* with a "helium-filled silver blimp" to the top right of it. See *Dalí by Halsman*, pp. 61f.

9
Farrow 1997, pp. 70f.

→ **16** [p. 373]

10
Robert Whitaker's son Benjamin in an e-mail to the author on January 14, 2013.

11
Ill. in Ste. Croix 2006, pp. 82f.

12
Ibid., p. 82.

13
Dalí in a sound recording in the film *Le Divin Dalí*. Warhol had a quite different attitude to the end of his life: "The worst thing that could happen to you after the end of your time would be to be embalmed and laid up in a pyramid. ... I want my machinery to disappear." Warhol 1975, *Philosophy*, p. 113.

14
Bourdon 1989, p. 229.

us with several hundred feet of four-foot-wide metalized polyester film. This all took many months, not because it was complicated, but because both of us were doing a lot of other things.

We told Andy we couldn't make the light bulb, but showed him the material we had found. When Andy saw it he said, "Let's make clouds." Back to Bell Labs to figure out how to heat-seal irregular rounded surfaces. During this time we had left some of the Scotchpak with Andy; we built him a makeshift heat-sealing machine and brought him a bottle of helium. One day in the spring or summer of 1965 I came to the Factory. Andy had simply folded the material over and heat-sealed it on three sides and filled it with helium. Warhol's "pillows" were born. We added a valve so they could be refilled, and Andy found someone to make a lot of them. A roomful of the pillows were shown at the Leo Castelli Gallery in April 1966; they were called Silver Clouds.[15]

When Warhol presented the *Silver Clouds* to the public for the first time as part of his second exhibition at the Leo Castelli Gallery in April 1966, they were displayed in the size of 34 ½ × 49 ¾ inches in the front room of the gallery.[16] They floated and reacted to air currents, temperature fluctuations, static electricity, and also to the public, who felt an urge to give the clouds of aluminum-coated polyethylene a gentle prod. Warhol had had the rear room of the gallery decorated with his famous *Cow Wallpaper*. Apart from that, no other works of art were exhibited.[17] The display can be viewed as Warhol's attempt to denounce painting and sculpture as conventional forms of artistic expression.[18] The artist referred to the *Silver Clouds* once again shortly afterwards in order to explain that he had turned his back on painting: "Painting was just a phase I went through. But I'm doing some floating sculpture now: silver rectangles that I blow up and that float. Not like Alexander Calder mobiles, these don't touch anything, they just float free."[19] The *Silver Clouds* were offered for fifty dollars each. However, collectors refrained from making a purchase, because the cushions lost their helium. Klüver suggested offering the air sculptures together with a ten-year propellant supply contract. However, as this was not practically feasible, Castelli decided to sell Warhol's works together with little bottles of helium, so that the owners could refill the works themselves.[20] Warhol's statement that the floating sculptures were disposable art for those buyers whose excess of possessions had become a burden also did not exactly contribute to sales of the works. In a television interview at the time he suggested, "You open a window and let them float away and that's one less object."[21]

Filming with a Camera "Nailed to the Floor like Christ on the Cross"

Filming played an important role in Andy Warhol's work. He shot almost 650 movies in just five years. Even though most of the strips were not very successful from a financial point of view, they nevertheless made him one of the most significant underground filmmakers of the twentieth century. When Warhol started making independent movies in the summer of 1963, the trend was in full bloom in New York. Almost anyone who could afford a

15
In McShine 1989, pp. 430f.

→ **17** [p. 373]

16
Frei/Printz/ King-Nero 2004, *B*, no. 1868.

17
Bourdon 1989, pp. 228f.

18
Ibid., p. 232.

19
In Goldsmith 2004, p. 88. Similarly, also in Warhol 1975, *Philosophy*, p. 150.

20
Bourdon 1989, p. 230.

21
Quoted according to ibid.

16-mm camera started shooting amateurish, black-and-white, silent movies, which were artistic and pointedly non-commercial.[1] It was at this time that Warhol met the moviemaker and actor Jack Smith, whose steadfast disdain for conventional moviemaking techniques was to have a lasting influence on him.[2] Smith cultivated an amateurish use of technique: the hand camera shook, in some frames the heads of the protagonists were cut off, and parts of the movie were overexposed.[3] Warhol recognized the sign of the times and bought a Bolex 16-mm camera.[4]

As he was taking amphetamines at the time, which reduced his need for sleep, he soon found the theme for his first movie. In *POPism* he says, "I only slept two or three hours a night from '65 through '67, but I used to see people who hadn't slept for days at a time and they'd say things like 'I'm hitting my ninth day and it's glorious!' ... Seeing everybody so up all the time made me think that sleep was becoming pretty obsolete, so I decided I'd better quickly do a movie of a person sleeping."[5] Warhol was able to win over the poet and performance artist John Giorno as the sleeper for his movie. Giorno, with whom he had a relationship at that time, was working as a stockbroker on Wall Street and, by his own account, slept a lot.[6] It was filmed in Giorno's apartment. He undressed, went to bed, and was already asleep when Warhol started filming him. When the reel was filled, Warhol left the apartment without waking him up. The first reels turned out to be unusable because the camera had to be wound up manually approximately every twenty seconds, so the images had visible interruptions. For this reason, Warhol bought a motor for his camera and started again. As Gerard Malanga later recalled, Warhol wanted to simply press on a button. The movie was to run continuously and document life, recording reality in real time for the duration of the reel of film.[7] However, since the Bolex 16-mm camera could only record films of four minutes—Warhol commented later that they were in fact only three minutes in length—he had to produce numerous reels.[8] Initially he still experimented with an array of different filming styles with a variety of camera angles per film reel.[9] Then he decided on a minimalist style. He screwed the camera onto a tripod, switched it on and waited until the whole reel had run. During filming he avoided moving the camera. It was only when switching the reels that he occasionally changed its position, aiming it at the head or other body parts of the sleeping Giorno, whose lower body remained discreetly covered up. The movie *Sleep* has a length of five hours and twenty-one minutes and is a complex montage of various camera angles. The length of each varies greatly, but each one is repeated between five and twenty times.[10] Warhol recorded *Sleep* and his other early silent movies with twenty-four frames per second, but then projected them onto the screen as just sixteen frames per second.[11]

For much of 1964 Warhol produced black-and-white silent movies in a similar manner using a static camera. For these movies he chose everyday and trivial themes. *Kiss* is a collection of close-ups of couples who, for the most part, are kissing motionlessly, while *Eat* shows Warhol's artist colleague Robert Indiana eating a mushroom, and *Blow Job* records an oral sex act, whereby the camera is pointed exclusively at the face of the young actor DeVeren Bookwalter.[12]

1 Bourdon 1989, p. 164.

2 Warhol/Hackett 1980, pp. 31f.

3 Bourdon 1989, p. 164.

4 Warhol (1966) in Goldsmith 2004, p. 105; Warhol/Hackett 1980, p. 29.

5 Ibid. p. 33.

6 Bourdon 1989, p. 166.

7 Gerard Malanga in the documentary *Andy Warhol*.

8 Angell in *The Andy Warhol Museum*, p. 125; details about the length of individual reels, p. 143, fn. 16.

9 Angell in Ofner 2005, p. 93.

10 Ibid.; Schmidt in Meyer-Hermann, p. 01:40:00.

11 Schmidt in ibid. See also Warhol 1975, *Philosophy*, p. 95.

12 O'Sullivan Shorr 2014, *Book I*, p. 39.

Empire is a remarkable movie, lasting eight hours and five minutes and showing the tip of the Empire State Building recorded from 8 p.m. to about 2:30 a.m. Warhol shot it with a hired 16-mm Auricon camera, which could hold fifty-minute reels.[13] Jonas Mekas, who had also used an Auricon for his own movies, assisted him as a cameraman. Shortly afterwards Mekas propagated the movie in his commentary in *The Village Voice* with the words: "Last Saturday I was present at an historical occasion: the shooting of Andy Warhol's epic *Empire*. ... The camera never moved once. My guess is that *Empire* will become *The Birth of a Nation* of the New Bag cinema."[14]

Salvador Dalí's career as a filmmaker began in 1929. The movie *Un Chien andalou* was created that year, directed by Luis Buñuel, which became a milestone in movie history. Buñuel reports in his memoirs *My Last Breath* that he and Dalí wrote the script in Figueras within a week of "total identification."[15] Dalí, on the other hand, claimed to have written the script all by himself.[16] His school friend Jaume Miravitlles, who like Dalí made a brief appearance in the movie as a Marist Brother, declared later that Buñuel had confirmed to him in a letter that the original idea for the movie had come from Dalí.[17] *Un Chien andalou* broke with all viewing conventions and shows only few traces of commonplace dramaturgy. The scenes are connected according to the principles of coincidence.[18] Although critics were largely confused, the movie earned great praise in the press.[19] Robert Desnos wrote:

I do not know any film which works so directly on the spectator, any film which is made so specifically for him, which engages him in conversation, in intimate rapport. But whether it's the eye sliced by a razor, and whose crystalline liquid trickles viscously, or the assemblage of Spanish priests and grand pianos bearing its load of dead donkeys, there is nothing in it that does not partake of humor and poetry, intimately liked.[20]

The surrealists were so enthusiastic about the movie that they published the script in their magazine *La Révolution surréaliste* on December 15, 1929. The publication of this edition therefore marked Dalí's and Buñuel's admission into the surrealist movement. Charles and Marie-Laure de Noailles, leading patrons of art and literature in France at the time, were thoroughly electrified by *Un Chien andalou* and suggested to Buñuel that he shoot another movie.[21] This was how *L'Âge d'or* was born. In his memoirs, Buñuel plays down Dalí's involvement in the script for this movie.[22] However, in a letter to his fellow student Pepín Bello on May 11, 1930, he remarked that like the script for *Un Chien andalou*, he had also written this one together with Dalí.[23] Later, in his *Secret Life*, Dalí expressed his disappointment with regard to the movie and called it a "caricature of my ideas." He wrote, "The 'Catholic' side of it had become crudely anticlerical, and without the biological poetry that I had desired. Nevertheless the film produced a considerable impression, especially the scene of unfulfilled love in which one saw the hero, in a state of collapse from unsatisfied desire, erotically sucking the marble big toe of an Apollo."[24]

Over the following decades Dalí regularly developed new concepts for movies and wrote scripts. However, none of these projects could be realized. In 1937 he wrote the script *Giraffes on Horseback Salad* for a movie together with the Marx Brothers, whom he appreciated, especially Harpo Marx, whom he saw as the "most fascinating and surrealistic character in Hollywood."[25] The project was destined to fail, as most of Dalí's ideas were too extravagant and could not be realized with the filming techniques available at the time.[26] Even so, Dalí made it to Hollywood in 1945. Alfred Hitchcock had asked him to create a dream sequence for his movie *Spellbound* with Ingrid Bergman and Gregory Peck in the leading roles. However, once again it proved difficult to capture Dalí's ideas on celluloid. Therefore the dream sequence fell far short of Dalí's expectations and was shorter than originally planned.[27] Two years later, Dalí traveled to Hollywood once again to attempt a movie project together with Walt Disney, which was to bear the title *Destino*. Disney's idea was that *Destino* should be a six- to eight-minute animated short film included in a feature-length, musical anthology movie. Unfortunately, after three months of work on *Destino*, Disney changed his mind and abandoned the project.[28] In 1999, Walt Disney's nephew Roy decided to take the project up again and to complete the movie, which had its premiere on June 2, 2003 and was nominated for an Academy Award in the category of Best Animated Short Film.[29]

In 1954, Dalí and Robert Descharnes proceeded with the movie *The Prodigious Story of the Lacemaker and the Rhinoceros*. The concept of this movie was based on Dalí's curious discovery that Vermeer's *Lacemaker* was composed of rhinoceros horns.[30] In the scenes shot between 1954 and 1961, one can see Dalí working on a copy of the said painting by Vermeer in the Louvre and painting a rhinoceros horn according to nature at the zoo in Vincennes, where he also spurs the animal to attack a reproduction of the *Lacemaker*, albeit without success. Unfortunately the movie was never completed.[31] Robert Descharnes remarked in an interview that while shooting their movie together, Dalí was not concerned about montage like a director, but about the continuity of the images. Therefore he also dreamed of a camera that never moved and captured everything that passed by, rather like a spectator in a theater.[32] Dalí outlined this concept in his article "My Cinematographic Secrets," published in the French magazine *La Parisienne* in February 1954, as follows:

If I create my film, I want to be sure that it will be, from beginning to end, a succession of wonders, because there is no point in bothering to see shows that are not sensational. The more numerous my public, the greater the fortune my film will bring its author, who has so justly been baptized "Avida Dollars." But for a film to seem marvelous to its audience, the first indispensable requisite is that the audience can believe in the marvels that are revealed to them. One must therefore abandon, first of all, today's repulsive cinematographic rhythm, that conventional and boring rhetoric of camera movements. How can one believe, even for a second, in even the most banal melodrama when the camera follows the murderer everywhere, traveling even into the washroom where he goes to wash the blood off his hands? That is why Salvador Dalí, before he so much as begins his film, will take care to immobilize his camera, to nail it to the floor like Christ on the cross. Too bad if the action moves out of the visual field! The public will wait—distressed, exasperated, breathing heavily, stamping their

25
Cf. Dalí 1937, pp. 68, 132. At that time Dalí drew Harpo Marx. Ill. in Ades 2004, cat. 172; Soby 1941, cat. 58. In 1980, Warhol created the portfolio "Ten Portraits of Jews of the Twentieth Century," including portraits of the Marx Brothers and Sigmund Freud. See Feldman/ Schellmann II.226–235. In 1937/38, Dalí created four drawings of Freud. See Descharnes 1984, pp. 232f.

26
Details provided by Sánchez Vidal, Ades, Jeffett and Gale in Gale 2007, pp. 104ff.

27
Details provided by Cochran in Gale 2007, pp. 174ff.

28
Details provided by Bossert 2015, pp. 33ff.

29
Details provided by ibid., pp. 135ff.

30
Heiner Meyer tells of another discovery made by Dalí related to Vermeer's *Lacemaker*: "Dalí asked me, 'Why do you just put up with it all? Why don't you question it?' That's just the way society is. Something was tossed out there and people were fascinated by it and would never question it. Then he told a story. I think he gave a lecture on this at the university in Paris. When you cut open a cauliflower, the pattern of lines in it is always that of Vermeer's *Lacemaker*. But the very next moment he said that that was absolute nonsense, because you can, of course, always look for a line." Heiner Meyer in a conversation with the author on February 16, 2011 in Bielefeld (translated from the German). Dalí's lecture from December 17, 1955 is printed in Abadie 1980, pp. 144f.

31
Details in King 2007, pp. 117ff.; King in Taylor 2008, pp. 190ff.

32
In King 2007, p. 143.

feet, in ecstasy or, better still, bored to death—for the action to come back into the visual field. Unless some very beautiful and completely unrelated images distract the audience by parading before the immobile, bound, hyperstatic eye of the Dalínian camera, which will then finally be restored to its true purpose of being slave to my prodigious imagination.[33]

The painter Antoni Pitxot recalled that Dalí had claimed to him that he had given Warhol the advice to work with a static movie camera and that Warhol had then followed this advice. Dalí insisted repeatedly that the static movie camera had been his idea.[34] Whether this is actually the case is difficult to establish in retrospect. As described above, Warhol began filmmaking in the summer of 1963, when many amateurs were starting to shoot movies. There is reason to believe that Dalí and Warhol did not yet know each other well at this point. The intellectual exchanges between the two artists will be discussed in detail in Parts 5 and 6 of this publication.

Warhol's *Screen Tests* of Dalí

The production of movies went hand in hand with the birth of the Warhol superstars at the Factory. Jane Holzer became one of the Factory's first female superstars.[1] The attractive young woman with the blond mane of hair was married to a businessman and worked as a successful model in the early 1960s. David Bailey's photo of her, which appeared in November 1964 on the cover of *Show* magazine, designed by Nicholas Haslam, caused a stir. Haslam was also the one who had introduced Holzer to Andy Warhol.[2] The press gave Holzer the nickname "Baby Jane" in reference to the movie *Whatever Happened to Baby Jane?* with Joan Crawford and Bette Davis in the leading roles.[3] Her first role in a Warhol movie was in *Kiss*. Warhol produced more movie scenes with her in total than with any other female superstar.[4] Holzer also played one of the girls in the movie *Thirteen Most Beautiful Girls*, which is a series of filmed portraits each just a few minutes in length, for which the actresses posed close up and motionless in front of the camera. The whole movie is a composition of several so-called *Screen Tests*, which Warhol produced together with Gerard Malanga beginning in 1964.[5] Malanga later recalled,

First of all, the modus operandi was we would have the person seated in front of the camera, and the camera was at a distance of at least ten feet. We would vary the lighting from time to time. It was basically against a silver wooden panel which we would sometimes drape with a piece of black cloth or sometimes just leave it silver. The instructions were very simple: "Just look into the camera for three minutes." Most of the time, we'd walk away from the camera because we'd want the subject to look at the camera and not at us. We didn't want to become distractions, so we'd kind of meander off into the background and do something and come back in three minutes because the film would run out. So, basically the sitter was confronting his or her self, the camera became a mirror, metaphorically speaking, anything could happen during the three minutes. One interesting thing happened with a young girl named Anne Buchanan. She had long black hair, very petite looking, an angelic face, big eyes, and tears starting coming out of her eyes at one moment, but it was kind of a Daliesque jewel. It

33
Quoted according to Gale 2007, p. 158. Also published in Dalí 1965, p. 89.

34
Antoni Pitxot in a conversation with the author on September 5, 2009 in Cadaqués. See also Pitxot 2014, p. 87.

1
In *POPism* Warhol refers to the moviemaker Naomi Levine as his first female superstar. See Warhol/Hackett 1980, p. 32. See also Angell 2006, p. 97.

2
Haslam 2009, pp. 201f.; Holzer in O'Connor/Liu 1996, p. 47.

3
O'Connor/Liu 1996, p. 48.

4
Angell 2006, p. 97.

5
The term "screen test" was not introduced until the end of 1965, the movies were initially called "film portraits" or "stillies." See ibid., p. 15.

didn't drop, it came out of her eye, tears welled up in her eyes, it hung there like a Salvador Dalí jewel, and finally dropped. That was one instance of situation.[6]

Malanga determined the camera settings for many of the *Screen Tests.*[7] In several cases, it was due to his efforts that production of the *Screen Tests* was even possible. The actress Sally Kirkland, who was studying under Lee Strasberg at the Actors Studio, stood in front of the camera for two *Screen Tests* in 1964. This led to a unique symbiosis of Strasberg's method acting and Warhol's *Screen Test* production. Kirkland recalls,

Gerard Malanga persuaded me on Andy's behalf to do the Screen Test. *... When I did the* Screen Test *I remember Andy telling me: "I'm gonna leave the room for a while and I just want you to be completely and totally still." And I said to him "Why? I'm an Actors Studio trained actor. I wanna cry on cue. I wanna act." And he said "No, no. Just be completely still and look at the camera." So I was very frustrated—he was my first director, my very first director, but I was so hoping to be able to act, I didn't want to stay still. So what I did was what they call an emotional recall at the Actors Studio, where I remember something very sad in my life and the tears start coming out of my eyes and I thought: "Oh, good. I'll just keep looking at the camera and I'll think of this emotional recall and the tears will come." That made me feel better about doing nothing in front of the camera.*[8]

All *Screen Tests* were shot with Warhol's motorized 16-mm Bolex silent movie camera at twenty-four frames per second and projected at sixteen frames per second.[9] Consequently, every single blink and the tiniest facial movements of the subject could be seen. A total of 472 *Screen Tests* were recorded between 1964 and 1966.[10] Almost everyone who spent time at the Factory or paid a visit was asked to pose—in many cases more than once.

In 1965 Warhol produced two *Screen Tests* of Ultra Violet.[11] In both recordings she is wearing a suit with a standing collar. They were probably shot the first time she came to the Factory. In *POPism* it says that Ultra Violet was wearing a pink Chanel suit when she walked into the Factory.[12] During the night of February 6, 1966,[13] Warhol then produced a further *Screen Test* of her, wearing a black evening dress and a pearl necklace.[14] She was accompanied by Salvador Dalí. Ultra Violet said it was her idea to bring Dalí to the Factory for a *Screen Test,*[15] and she recounted, "Dalí liked to be everywhere. It's nice to be on screen. He didn't think much of the *Screen Test*. But I think it was great."[16] Dalí posed in front of the camera for two *Screen Tests*. In the first *Screen Test* he takes out a small, glittery handbag—probably belonging to Ultra Violet—shows it first from one side and then from the other, while looking in various directions. Then he holds the handbag against his cheek for a little while and drums on it rhythmically with his fingers, as if he were listening to music. In the second *Screen Test* Dalí is looking into the camera with his head held high. Roughly halfway through the recording, there is a sudden in-camera edit and he disappears from the screen. The rest of the recording shows the dappled wooden background that Dalí and Ultra Violet posed in front of for their *Screen Tests.*[17] The Warhol superstar Mary Woronov writes in her memoirs, "I saw Salvador Dalí strike too flamboyant a pose for his test, and when the arm holding his cane collapsed, the upper lip holding his mustache twitched and drooped, I liked him better that way."[18]

6
In *Andy Warhol Photography,* p. 118.

7
Jonas Mekas recalled in an e-mail to the author on July 31, 2011, that Malanga rather than Warhol operated the camera for his *Screen Test.*

8
Sally Kirkland in a telephone conversation with the author on December 16, 2012.

9
Angell 2006, p. 21.

10
Ibid., p. 12.

11
See ibid., ST346 and ST347.

12
Warhol/Hackett 1980, p. 210. In his diaries Warhol recorded: "… she did something great—she wore the exact same outfit as the day we met her in the sixties —a pink Chanel miniskirt suit with the same boots and her hair the same way." Hackett 1989, p. 119, March 19, 1978.

→ **18/19** [p. 374]

13
Gerard Malanga in an e-mail to the author on September 24, 2009.

14
Angell 2006, ST348.

15
Ultra Violet in a conversation with the author on October 18, 2008 in New York and in an e-mail to the author on April 17, 2009.

16
Ultra Violet in a conversation with Jeanine Barone for the author on October 18, 2009 in New York.

17
Angell 2006, ST67, ST68.

18
Woronov 2013, Pos. 1852. Similarly, also in O'Sullivan Shorr 2014, *Book I*, p. 101.

The first *Screen Test* of Dalí is unusual as he erroneously appears to be upside down. When viewing the recorded material for her catalogue raisonné of the *Screen Tests*, Callie Angell thought that perhaps it had been shot with the intention of projecting it under the second one. This would have led to a "playing card effect," in which the surrealist appeared the right way round above and upside down below. She pointed out, however, that she had no concrete proof to support this hypothesis and that it was therefore merely a supposition.[19] Gerard Malanga remembers that he shot the unusual *Screen Test* and remarks,

That was a mistake, the upside down Screen Test. *... I'm pretty sure I spliced that reel together ... I may have inadvertently turned it upside down without knowing it. Only because that was a print that was made from the original, that had one sprocket and one black side and the print may have had two ... a double-edged sprocket, so, it's hard to tell when it's upside down when you do that. 'Cause if it's one sprocket, I would have caught the mistake. But I may have inadvertently spliced the film backwards. Because, if you do it upside down, it also goes backwards. It was a mistake.*[20]

Greg Pierce, associate curator of film and video at the Andy Warhol Museum in Pittsburgh, discovered after recent research that the *Screen Test* was indeed a print made from the original that was read incorrectly. After changing its orientation—emulsion in, base out—Dalí's position in the frame is correct. The number "R. 1," which thought to be written on the tail leader is, in fact, handwritten but printed through on the head leader.[21]

The *Screen Tests* of Dalí were used shortly thereafter as part of Warhol's multimedia show *Exploding Plastic Inevitable*. Several "background reels" were found, which were projected onto the background during the performances of The Velvet Underground and Nico. Two of these reels contain a *Screen Test* of Dalí. The first reel runs for 22.5 minutes, with a projection of sixteen frames per second. It contains original material starting with the second *Screen Test* of Dalí followed by *Screen Test*s of Nico, Sterling Morrison, and Lou Reed. The reel ends with two rolls of a whip dance performed by Gerard Malanga and Mary Woronov.[22] The number "R. 2," which is written on the white head leader, indicates that the compilation is reel 2 of a double screen film. The second reel with the number "R. 1" was recently found. It also contains original material in the following order: the second *Screen Test* of Dalí, *Screen Test*s of Nico, Maureen Tucker, and John Cale, as well as two rolls of whip dances performed by Gerard Malanga and Mary Woronov.[23]

There is reason to believe that Dalí's *Screen Tests* were made for Warhol's multimedia show. As already mentioned, they were produced during the night of February 6, 1966. Just one day later, Warhol presented the Velvet Underground on the TV show *USA Artists* broadcast by WNET. From February 8 to 13, the band then performed together with Nico in the New York Film-Makers' Cinemathèque. At the time, however, the show was still called *Andy Warhol, Up-Tight*.[24] It is very likely that Dalí's *Screen Tests* were shown there. He is named as a protagonist in two advertisements placed on February 10, 1966, in the *Village Voice*, one of which announces: "Velvet Underground, rock 'n' roll; double screen films including: MORE MILK YVETTE starring Mario Montez

---

19
Callie Angell in an e-mail to the author on June 25, 2009.

20
Gerard Malanga in a conversation with the author on July 2, 2012 in Hudson, NY.

21
There is also a print made from the original second *Screen Test* of Dalí with the number "R. 2" handwritten but printed through on the head leader. Greg Pierce kindly provided the author with this information in e-mails on March 29, 2016 and April 21, 2016. See also Angell 2006, ST67.

22
Angell 2006, ST367.

23
Greg Pierce kindly provided the author with this information in e-mails on April 4, 2016 and April 21, 2016. This reel is the "lost reel" listed in Angell 2006, ST371. See also ibid., p. 265.

24
DeRogatis 2009, p. 102.

→
20 [p. 375]

and the Velvet Underground; UP-TIGHT series starring Barbara Rubin, Paul Morrisey [sic], Dan Williams (film makers); Mary Piffath & Gerard Malanga (whip dancing and leather); Nico, chanteuse; Nat Finkelstein, lobby photos; Bob Neuwirth, tapes & SALVADOR DALÍ."[25] Dalí did, in fact, make an appearance at a series of events to promote Warhol's show, but of course also for his own publicity purposes.[26] Victor Bockris, who co-authored the book *Up-Tight: The Velvet Underground Story* together with Gerard Malanga, remarks:

In April 1966 Dalí was part of the Exploding Plastic Inevitable's *month-long stand at the Dome in downtown Manhattan. His name was listed on some of the advertisements. All he had to do was walk through the crowd and be seen while the Dalí* Screen Tests *were shown on the wall behind the Velvet Underground. At that time Dalí's profile was popular in the counterculture among college students and rock'n'roll people, besides this was a sophisticated audience. All the ideas were Andy Warhol's.*[27]

So Dalí did not appear on stage during the events. It was nonetheless a clever move by Warhol to integrate the *Screen Tests* of him into the show, in order to be able to announce him as one of the participants. It paid off for Warhol. In an article on February 9, 1966 in the *New York Post*, Dalí's contribution was even worth a subheading for the author Archer Winsten:

Dalí Was There

A telephone conversation seems to be coming through a ruined loudspeaker. You can't hear what they are saying. Dalí appears on the screen behind. Then a dog shows up and barks. By this time the Velvet Underground, prodigiously amplified, prepares itself in a tuning session, then produces a rhythmic beat proving the session may not have been necessary.

Another Velvet Underground number, "Heroine," is accompanied by dancing figures on the stage and on the screen. Their movements are all the same and one can only note that they cannot be accurately described in a family journal.

What emerges most clearly is a sense of climatic noise, exhibitionistic movements, and the devil take the audience. The devil did get quite a number, for they left at regular intervals before the two-hour show had finished. Chanteuse Nico sang near the end of the proceedings.

Audience Can Take It

Andy Warhol, king of the put-on, bring-down, nothing movie, has here thrown together some meaningless stuff well calculated to reflect not only a meaningless world but an audience so mindless that it can sit still and take it and come back for more. It is even possible that the more Andy kicks his audience in its teeth, the more he shovels nonsense into its hanging-open mouth, the more they like it.

This is a strange taste, but we live in strange times. There is no disputing that a packed house, many of whom paid to get in, were there last night, and photographers for God knows what chi-chi magazines competed with the show in befuddling the audience.[28]

An ambitious movie project with Dalí was most likely being planned at the Factory in 1966. A telegram sent to Warhol by Philip ("Foo Foo") Smith on June 2, 1966 was discovered in Warhol's archive: "Making arrangements for

25 https:// warholfilmads. wordpress.com /1966-2/ (last accessed on April 16, 2016). See also Angell 2006, ST68.

26 Bockris/Malanga 2003, p. 36.

27 Victor Bockris in an e-mail to the author on July 16, 2010.

28 Winsten 1966.

up to 100,000 dollars to be available for our Warhol-Dalí flick. Call me today … without fail or the aforementioned can be written off, and you will find yourself on the receiving end of a 60,000 dollar lawsuit."[29] These lines reveal that the project had not gone beyond the planning stage. Smith sued Warhol later, as he assumed erroneously that he had rights to the artist's movies on account of his investments. He also referred to a spoken agreement with him. On April 1, 1968, Warhol was summoned to court, which he initially took to be an April Fools' Day hoax. As was to be expected, the charge was unsuccessful.[30] Robert Heide, who worked on various projects with Warhol at the time, had already sensed that Smith would cause trouble[31] and later recalled, "Foo Foo Smith was around the Factory a lot. He was a very idiotic man, a heavy amphetamine addict. He sued Andy because he felt he'd put money into some of his films."[32] It is questionable, however, whether the Warhol-Dalí movie project mentioned by Smith ever actually existed. In answer to the question of which project was being referred to, Gerard Malanga, who documented Dalí's visit to the Factory in his own movie, replied,

The only film that I'm aware of, other than the one I shot of Dalí's Factory visit, is a thirty-five-minute reel that Andy shot in Tiger Morse's studio back in 1967. … It's a color movie. … I think Dalí was there for the entire thirty-five minutes. It was a group shot just the way the photograph was. I'm pretty sure that's what the camera composition was. The camera was static, it was in one place. … I think we were all talking. The theme was like conversations between people. … Conversations like people talking next to each other, Tiger Morse like talking to somebody, whatever. … As I recall we were kind of all seated, sort of like in a group, actually in two tiers. I think Dalí was actually at the back. I even don't know if Dalí had said anything in the movie. … I remember Dalí donning an American Indian headdress and he looked quite grand. He was a trooper. He got into the spirit of things. That was one of his admirable qualities. … The reel was later included, I believe, in Andy's twenty-four-hour movie, ★★★★ *(Four Stars).*[33]

The designer Tiger Morse, who belonged to Warhol's entourage in the 1960s, opened her "tiny new boutique called Teeny Weeny" at the end of August 1966 on upper Madison Avenue in New York. Her "policy" was "man-made materials only—vinyl, Mylar, sequins."[34] *POPism* states, "…it was Tiger who made happenings pop, turning them from something artistic into big parties. She'd stand around in her silver jeans and huge sunglasses, having a ball herself."[35] The reel mentioned by Malanga, shot in Tiger Morse's studio, can unfortunately no longer be found and is considered lost. There are no references to Dalí in Callie Angell's notes regarding the five reels recorded in the late summer of 1966 either with Tiger Morse or in her studio. One strip was entitled *Tiger Morse* and integrated as Reel 14 in the twenty-four-hour epic ★★★★ *(Four Stars)*. Morse appears in this in front of a background of costumes and lights, holding a disco ball in her hand and talking about love.[36]

At the same time, Warhol posed with Tiger Morse and some Factory people for a photo by the French photographer Hervé Gloaguen, shot in the designer's studio.[37] Warhol is standing in the foreground with his movie camera and Malanga can be seen behind him, having donned the mentioned "American Indian headdress."

29
Quoted according to Angell 2006, p. 265.

30
Ibid., p. 265; Bockris 1989, pp. 313f.

31
Robert Heide in a conversation with the author on December 6, 2012 in New York.

32
In Bockris 1989, p. 313.

33
Gerard Malanga in a conversation with the author on July 2, 2012 in Hudson, NY, and in an e-mail to the author on September 24, 2009.

34
Warhol/Hackett 1980, p. 176.

35
Ibid., p. 177.

36
I thank Claire K. Henry, assistant curator, The Andy Warhol Film Project, for this information (e-mail on June 9, 2011). See also Patalas 1971, p. 100.

37
Gerard Malanga in an e-mail to the author on August 2, 2015. Ill. in *Andy Warhol: "Giant" Size*, p. 333.

Suicide—Andy Warhol's First Color Movie

Andy Warhol shot *Suicide*, his first color movie, in March 1965.[1] A month later the *New York World-Telegram and Sun* reported, "Pop artist Andy Warhol emerging as the Rossellini of the underground movies has a new one starring Roc [sic] Bradett, one of Salvador Dalí's favorite male models. In Andy's newest epic, Roc [sic] commits suicide seven times."[2] Finding information on the star of the movie, the young French-Canadian Rock Bradett,[3] is difficult. Ronald Tavel, who wrote several screenplays for Warhol and collaborated with him on his films, recalled, "Rock B. was a *Gentleman's Quarterly*-chic and trim, classically small-featured French film actor who jet-set his time in a kind of frenzy between expensive hotels on either side of the Atlantic. In that shuffle, he was symptomatic of a considerable block of the weekly Factory drop-ins, and contributed strongly to my overall impression then of the traffic through the artworld landmark."[4] Warhol spoke frequently about how exciting it would be to make a movie in which someone actually died. He instructed suicidal friends, of which there were plenty in his circles, to call him straight away if they got serious.[5] Eventually he met Rock Bradett. Ronald Tavel later said:

He [Andy] had met this guy who tried to kill himself by slashing his wrists twenty-three times. So he said, go and interview him and get the story, and I was to reproduce his life story and act out the roles of the people who provoked each suicide. So, on March 6, a Saturday, this kind of high-class faggot came to the Factory and he cooperated completely, as suicides will. That's part of why they attempt suicide. It was Andy's idea to just focus in on the wrists with all these slashes for each suicide and to have not blood but water spilled from a pitcher onto the wrists after each story. You never saw the guy's face and there was a bucket underneath to catch the water. Andy's last-minute inspiration was to get gorgeous flowers from a local florist, since the hands would get kind of dull just being there. So you saw this wringing of his hands tearing apart the flowers and in the middle of it he freaked out and took the bucket and threw it in my face. I was drenched.

Andy came up and said, "Oh, Ronnie, shall we stop? Oh, how awful."

I said, "No, go on, let's go on, I'm fine, the script is still legible. We'll discuss this afterwards."

So we continued and finished it. Then the guy took out lawsuits against us and the film was never shown.[6]

The situation was disconcerting as Rock Bradett told of his suicide attempts and his homosexual relations, not only in front of a running camera, but also in front of the crowd at the Factory, which included journalists who had gathered there.[7] According to Ronald Tavel, Bradett returned to the Factory when it was nearly empty and stole a painting. Warhol considered this act as ample remuneration.[8]

Dalí and Warhol as Actors

Andy Warhol was fascinated by Hollywood and the Hollywood star system. He became an "art celebrity" in the 1970s. It was thus an obvious

1
Warhol (1966) in Goldsmith 2004, p. 67; Tavel in Bockris 1989, p. 214.

2
Dever 1965.

3
Goldsmith 2004, p. 63.

4
Tavel 2015, p. 27.

5
Bourdon 1989, p. 200.

6
In Bockris 1989, pp. 214f. Similarly, also in Smith 1986, p. 486f.

7
Crimp 2012, p. 154, fn. 19.

8
Tavel 2015, p. 31.

move for him to also try his hand as an actor in foreign movie and television productions.

Warhol first took on a minor guest role in the Italian movie *Identikit* directed by Giuseppe Patroni Griffi, which premiered in May 1974 in Monaco and hit the screens in the U.S. in October 1975 with the English title *The Driver's Seat*. Even with Elizabeth Taylor in the starring role, the movie had only moderate success. Based on Muriel Spark's bestseller *The Driver's Seat*, it tells the story of Lise, played by Taylor, who takes time out and flies to Rome, where she experiences a series of adventures and becomes involved in a crime. Warhol plays the role of a British aristocrat and can be seen in two brief scenes representing altogether less than two minutes of the movie. The opening credits announce, "With the special participation of Andy Warhol." Also worthy of note is that his voice was dubbed in by a speaker with a British accent. In his *Philosophy of Andy Warhol* published shortly afterwards, the artist wrote, "When I played an airport person in a movie with Elizabeth Taylor, the lines they gave me were something like 'Let's go. I have an important date,' but it kept coming out of my mouth as 'Come on, girls.' But in Italy they dub everything in afterwards, so no matter what you don't say, you say it anyway."[1] In an interview in 1977, Warhol revealed about his movie debut, "Oh, I was just really rotten. I couldn't remember anything. I got too nervous. I shouldn't be nervous, and I can't think of why I get so nervous. It's just stupid. I can't remember anything."[2] Pat Hackett comments Warhol's stage fright, "He was a chatterbox. But the thing is, he would get nervous and have stage fright any time he had to say lines from a script. He'd watch himself on film or video afterwards and he'd say, 'There's something wrong with me, with the way I look. I just look too odd.'"[3]

Owing to the German actor and director Ulli Lommel, Warhol was able to put his acting abilities to the test again a couple of years later. Lommel became acquainted with the artist in August 1977 at a press conference in New York, on the occasion of the screening of his movie *Tenderness of the Wolves*, which is about a homosexual mass murderer. Warhol had read a critique by Vincent Canby in the *New York Times* saying that the movie broke taboos just as radically as his own movies.[4] Lommel writes in his memoirs that Warhol had asked him about his next movie project and wanted to know whether he could shoot it in Manhattan. Towards the end of 1977, they started to shoot the movie *Blank Generation* there.[5] The French movie star Carole Bouquet and the American musician Richard Hell played the leading roles. According to Lommel, Warhol wanted to be part of it.[6] In the movie, which is carried primarily by its music scenes, Warhol plays himself and appears for a few minutes towards the end. He is sitting in a fur coat in a TV studio and the camera circulates around him. Carole Bouquet interviews him and he takes a couple of Polaroid photos of her.

In the summer of 1978, Lommel shot his second movie in the U.S., in which Warhol was also involved: *Cocaine Cowboys*. Tom Sullivan had contributed to the script, which explains the film's autobiographical elements. At the time, Sullivan passed himself off in New York as a Texan oil heir and turned the heads of high society ladies. In reality, however, he was a drug

1
Warhol 1975,
Philosophy,
p. 83.

2
In Goldsmith
2004, p. 250.

3
Pat Hackett in a
conversation
with the author
on December 4,
2012 in New York.

4
Lommel 2012,
p. 14.

5
Ibid., pp. 16f.

6
Ibid., p. 18.

smuggler who earned millions by flying in marihuana from Colombia.[7] The Hollywood actor Jack Palance agreed to play the leading role. It was shot on Long Island. Most of the scenes were enacted in and around Warhol's house in Montauk. Warhol writes in his diaries, "Jack played a character named Rof, who used to be Jayne Mansfield's manager, and Tom plays one called Destin, who's a singer with a band. We went outside to do my scene where I'm taking pictures without knowing it of the people who run off with the coke. They decided to put me at the beginning of the movie and gave me some lines, which I'm terrible at. I just don't know how to be real."[8] Victor Bockris is also not very convinced of Warhol's acting prowess in this movie, in which the music scenes once again represent the highlights, and refers to the strip as the "nadir of his film career in more ways than one."[9] When he was shown the movie later, Warhol himself was not quite so disenchanted with his own acting performance. He recorded in his diaries, "And I decided I'm not so bad in it. They only let me do one take and I think if I'd been able to do more I would have gotten better. But I was better than in 'my first film,' *The Driver's Seat*. And *Cocaine Cowboys* has some good music in it. It's a dumb story, though. These dealers drop cocaine from a plane and a maid and a secretary find it and steal it. Tom said it cost him $950,000 to make it, but I don't see how, it was non-union."[10]

Although Warhol's performances as an actor were not very convincing, in the mid-1980s he was persuaded to take on a guest appearance in the then successful TV series *The Love Boat*. In the series, the passenger ship *Pacific Princess* sails around the world with Captain Merrill Stubing and his crew and anchors at various dream destinations. The passengers are all guest stars, for whom the script envisages a variety of adventures. Vincent Fremont recalls that the producer Douglas S. Cramer had contacted Fred Hughes to win over Warhol for a guest appearance.[11] Cramer reported later that it was also about a portrait assignment and that he had said to Warhol:

"I'll buy my portrait if you appear in The Love Boat *or in* Dynasty, *which was another of my series."*

Of course he thought it was an outrageous proposal. He wanted to be seen but he didn't want to say anything. … In The Love Boat *we would also work out ways to create moments for guest stars. The first idea was to bring Andy into the storyline as the cousin of one of the stars of the show and to have him on several episodes. But on discussing what he might do, we realized that Andy wasn't an actor. He wouldn't be capable of doing what we wanted. … One of the clauses of the contract was that he had to do me a double portrait for the price of 25,000 dollars, and one of the thousandth star to appear in* The Love Boat *for the same price. He was very nervous at the idea of playing his own role. We paid a maximum of 5,000 dollars for his appearance. It was he who was to have the final say in the choice of the thousandth star. He suggested people it was impossible to get hold of, like Catherine Deneuve, Brigitte Bardot, Doris Day … And finally Lana Turner, who had never had a Warhol portrait done, accepted. Otherwise, a fairly simple script had been written especially for him. Someone came especially from California to meet him twice in order to write it.[12]*

7
Ibid.; Hackett 1989, p. 362, March 13, 1981.

8
Ibid., p. 165, August 29, 1978.

9
Bockris 1989, p. 423.

10
Hackett 1989, p. 179, November 1, 1978.

11
Vincent Fremont in a conversation with the author on June 28, 2012 in New York.

12
In Benhamou-Huet 2009, p. 53.

Warhol refers to the incident in his diaries: "The story is that I go on *The Love Boat* and there's a girl on the boat named Mary with her husband, and she used to be a superstar of mine, and she doesn't want her husband to know that she used to be 'Marina Del Rey.' And I just have a few lines, things like 'Hello, Mary.' But one of the lines I have to say is something like 'Art is crass commercialism,' which I don't want to say."[13]

The movie shoots with Warhol started on March 26, 1985, in Los Angeles. His diaries state for this day: "Got picked up to go to *The Love Boat* set. Had to do my 'Hello, Mary' line, and the gay director is saying, 'Give it some pizzazz—Hel-*lo, Ma*-ry!' And I say, 'Hel-lo Ma-ry.'"[14]

During filming, Warhol developed the wish to shoot his own movie again. His last production had been *Andy Warhol's BAD*, for which Pat Hackett had written the script. Now he approached her again, as Hackett recalls, "I remember when Andy was on *The Love Boat* ... We were in L.A. at his bungalow at the Bel Air and he said to me: 'Just write another script for a movie and I'll give you the same deal I gave Paul [Morrissey].' Which was half. And I said okay, that I would think of a screenplay to write. So I was thinking of ideas. But then Andy died."[15] Vincent Fremont adds, "Roughly a year before Andy's death in February 1987, Andy asked me to option the film rights to Tama Janowitz's collection of stories, *Slaves of New York*. This would have been our first film production since *Andy Warhol's BAD* was made in 1977 but sadly Andy died in the midst of putting the project together. We would have been executive producers of the film."[16]

In the same year that *The Driver's Seat* came to movie theaters in Europe, with Andy Warhol in the cast, Salvador Dalí, who had been an "art celebrity" for decades, also received an offer to be part of a movie. The Chilean director Alejandro Jodorowsky, who had become a cult director on account of his movies *El Topo* (1970) and *The Holy Mountain* (1973), was planning a filming of Frank Herbert's novel *Dune*. Jodorowsky envisaged a ten-hour-long movie. The intention was also to commission Pink Floyd for the music and H.R. Giger for set and character design. As performers, the director hoped to be able to sign a contract with Orson Welles, Mick Jagger, and Salvador Dalí.[17] Jodorowsky provided a detailed report about this project later, which states:

Dalí accepts the idea of playing the emperor of the galaxy with great enthusiasm. He wants to film in Cadaqués and use a WC composed of two intertwined dolphins as a throne. The tails will form the feet, and of the two open mouths, one will serve to receive the "wee-wee," the other to receive the "poo-poo." Dalí thinks it is horribly bad taste to mix "wee-wee" and "poo-poo."

We tell him we'll need him for seven days ... Dalí replies that God made the world in seven days and that Dalí, being no less than a god, must cost a fortune: $100,000 an hour. Maybe when he gets onto the set he will decide to film more than an hour each day for the same price.

The condition, sina qua non, is to have the emperor on the scatological throne. He doesn't want to read the script: "My ideas are better than yours."[18]

Since Dalí adhered to his demand for $100,000 per hour, considerations were made later to hire him for just an hour and to use a replica of him

13
Hackett 1989,
p. 633, March 20,
1985.

14
Ibid., p. 635.

15
Pat Hackett in a
conversation
with the author
on December 4,
2012 in New York.

16
Vincent Fremont
in a conversation
with the author
on June 28, 2012.

17
Alejandro
Jodorowsky in
the documentary
*Jodorowsky's
Dune*.

18
Jodorowsky
1985, p. XII
(translated from
the French).

in the form of a polyethylene puppet for additional scenes. The artist also arranged for Amanda Lear to play Princess Irulan, the Emperor's daughter, in the movie.[19] Ultimately, however, Jodorowsky was never able to realize his movie *Dune*, as the investors withdrew. According to statements by the director, the project was rejected by Hollywood because decision-makers there considered it too French and not American enough.[20] There was also another problem. On September 27, 1975, General Franco had had five alleged terrorists executed, which triggered a wave of protest in the foreign press.[21] As part of the international coverage, Agence France-Presse asked Dalí for his opinion on the executions. The report stated that in his view there would be no more terrorism in Spain in a couple of months, because the perpetrators "are going to be liquidated like rats." It also proclaimed that in Dalí's opinion, three times the number of executions were needed, but for the time being these were enough.[22] The following day Dalí tried to relativize his statements and explained that he was against any form of terrorism and against capital punishment, in principle. However, as the latter existed in certain countries, he was not entitled as an individual to intervene in the application of the law in other countries.[23] Dalí's views unleashed a wave of outrage worldwide. According to press reports, abusive graffiti were scrawled onto his house and stones thrown through the windows. He also received death threats.[24] Alejandro Jodorowsky publicly declared, "I would be ashamed to use now in my work a man who in his masochistic exhibitionism demands the ignoble death of human beings."[25]

Watching TV Upside Down with Commercials Every Few Minutes

Andy Warhol repeatedly emphasized how important television was for him. In his *Philosophy* he reports that he started an "affair" with his TV set in the late 1950s and from then on close relationships with other people were no longer so important.[1] Warhol gave an exaggerated, but interesting insight into his TV habits in the article "TV," which was published in the December issue of *Esquire* in 1975. The article states: "Television is so important to my life I watch two color sets at the same time, doubling my pleasures, always in bed, usually while I'm talking on the phone to somebody who's watching the same thing. Sometimes I switch from color to black and white for a few seconds. That's very nice."[2] Warhol made many such revelations. When he was asked in an interview in 1969 whether he had a preference for any particular programs, he remarked, "I like it all. ... There's just so much to see. You can change all the stations. As soon as it gets a big picture, it'll be even more exciting. Everybody should have two television sets. So you can watch two at a time. Every time you see the President, he has three."[3] Warhol thereby cemented his image as an artist who was enthusiastic about or even addicted to television. Benjamin Liu, who was Warhol's assistant in the 1980s, emphasizes however:

Remember this is a man who actually, once he gets home, not only watches television. He reads books—mostly current books. It could be biographies. He

---

[19] Ibid., pp. XIIf.; Lear in the documentary *Jodorowsky's Dune*.

[20] Ibid., p. XIV.

[21] Gibson 1997, p. 560.

[22] Quoted according to ibid., p. 561.

[23] Ibid.

[24] Secrest 1986, p. 239; Gibson 1997, p. 562.

[25] Quoted according to ibid.

[1] Warhol 1975, *Philosophy*, p. 26.

[2] In Warhol 1975, "TV," p. 136. In his *Philosophy* Warhol states that he even played around with four TV sets at a time in his bedroom. See Warhol 1975, *Philosophy*, p. 26.

[3] In Goldsmith 2004, pp. 165f.

does like biographies. Of course he is hyper-intelligent. He reads more than one at the same time. And he does read the papers first thing in the morning, obviously The Post that he does like, not only for the column on page six. ... So, his knowledge is quite immense. To me, my analysis of Andy is ... it's the great film by Nicolas Roeg called The Man Who Fell to Earth, starring David Bowie. Remember that initial scene of him, he was an alien who fell to earth and it was a scene on multiple television screens and he is watching all of them. That to me is Andy. ... He knows a lot of stuff. Be it what we call more literary things or it could be just common gossip. Because, you know, as Truman Capote once said, common gossip actually is literature. What do you think Marcel Proust wrote? That was gossip.[4]

The photographer and antique dealer Roger Prigent, who was on friendly terms with Warhol, pointed out that the artist was also often critical towards television, despite all his glorifying comments about it: "Andy was crazy about television. He thought that it will be very important in the future because people here [in the U.S.] are TV oriented and TV dedicated. ... Andy Warhol was a genius because he had a point of view on everything. Andy was interested in everything. ... He had a vision, and he knew that TV was not so good but very important for the Americans."[5]

When asked what he thought of commercial breaks, Warhol answered in the aforementioned interview, "I like them cutting in every few minutes because it really makes everything more entertaining. I can't figure out what's happening in those shows anyway. They're so abstract. I can't understand how ordinary people like them. They don't have many plots. They don't do anything. It's just a lot of pictures, cowboys, cops, cigarettes, kids, war, all cutting in and out of each other without stopping. Like the pictures we make."[6]

According to Ultra Violet, Salvador Dalí was also not at all bothered by commercial breaks on television. At the symposium "The Dalí Renaissance" held at the Philadelphia Museum in 2005 she recalled:

One of my most surreal experiences with Dalí was watching an American movie on television, and Dalí never realized that every fifteen minutes there was a commercial. [laughter] He thought the commercial was part of the film. [laughter] No, really. Because Dalí would do such a film. So all of a sudden someone would be brushing his teeth—you would see the toothpaste being crushed—and Dalí would explain it and justify it. He would say, "Oh, this villain is brushing his teeth to clean up the vomit from before, to get a good flavor in his mouth." But then when the movie would come back, Dalí would say, "Is this another movie?" [laughter][7]

It is debatable whether Dalí really did not recognize commercial breaks as such, but there is no doubt that he—unlike Warhol—was anything other than a habitual television viewer. Amanda Lear remarked that he even considered television to be a "very vulgar medium":

It was something terrible. What we saw on French TV—people singing, dancing—he thought that was disgusting, really poor and pathetic. And when I became a television personality and a singer, he was very upset. We had a TV set in the Hôtel Meurice, and he asked that the TV set be turned upside down! And so I said, "But I'm on TV next," and he said, "That's why I'm putting it upside down. I'm sure it will be much better that way." So I had to watch myself

---

4
Benjamin Liu in a conversation with the author on November 30, 2012 in New York.

5
Roger Prigent in a conversation with the author on June 27, 2012 in New York. Nick Rhodes of Duran Duran adds: "... Andy was a very inquisitive person by nature. He wanted to know everything. Particularly, everything that was new, whether it was music, art, technology, design, fashion ... And one of the things that struck me the most when we first met him was that he was more attuned to modern life than most of my teenage friends at that time, or my friends in their early twenties. And Andy knew more about things and what was going on right across culture." Nick Rhodes in a conversation with the author on December 15, 2014 in London.

6
In Goldsmith 2004, p. 166.

7
In "Reminiscences of Dalí: A Conversation with Amanda Lear and Ultra Violet," moderated by Dawn Ades, in Taylor 2008, pp. 209f.

*completely upside down and without any sound as well, because he preferred
to imagine the dialogue and the sound rather than listen to all the rubbish we
were talking on TV.*[8]

Dalí also refers to his suggestion to turn the TV upside down in an
interview published in the 793rd issue of the U.S. *TV Guide* on June 8, 1968.
Interestingly, this also establishes a connection to Pop Art:

*"Mysalf," says Dalí, "never watch televeesion. Don't like TV. Only one very
leetle minute."*

"You never watch it at all?"

"Watch it upside down!" says Dalí triumphantly. "Through moiré *filter!"*

"Through taffeta?"

*"Taffeta filter. Changes completely. Is possible to see whatever my own
brain creates."*

...

*"Mmmmm," we say. "Referring back to your watching TV upside down—
how does that work, exactly?"*

*"Upside down! Everything in my brain. Project my brain on the screen.
Vary agreeable! My brain is superior of every other medium."*

...

"Mmmm," we say again. "What else would you like to see on TV?"

"Happenings. And things scientifiques*! Lots of things* scientifiques*! Sci-
entifique is fantastique! And lots of heepies, lame people, Op and Pop
artistes, who are most alive. Nevair filmed in advance. Everything filmed
in advance is dead."*

...

*"TV for masses. Don't like masses. Only like minority. Masses never cul-
tivé, never good taste. TV should be for to shock them. Force them theenk.
But nevair to please them. TV is for aristocrats to show them what they
don't understand."*

"What aristocrats?"

"Op and Pop artists," says Dalí. "Op and Pop artists superior to masses."

"Would the masses enjoy a TV run by Op and Pop artists?"

*"No, no. They would protest. The lame people, the wild ducks. They
wouldn't understand. They ..."*[9]

Dalí created a painting for the cover of the *TV Guide* with the title *Today, Tonight and Tomorrow*. It shows two thumbs in a desert landscape that
have transformed into televisions. Dalí explains in the interview:

*"Ees desert. Dalínian landscape. Desert of Spain. Also like desert of Cal-
ifornia. Put TV set in thumbs. In usual desert."*

"Does the desert symbolize TV?"

Dalí looks blank.

"My editor thought maybe you meant the 'vast wasteland.'"

Dalí looks blank. "No, ees usual Dalínian universe."

*"The cover just means ... thumbs in a desert? It doesn't actually have a
meaning?"*

*"No. Just thumbs." Dalí changes the subject. "Must uplift masses. Op and
Pop artists must uplift," he repeats.*[10]

8
In King 2007,
p. 183.

9
In Efron 1968,
pp. 8f.

10
In ibid., p. 10.

Andy Warhol had already designed a cover for the *TV Guide* two years before Dalí. During those years the *TV Guide* was the most widely read magazine in the U.S. As Roger Prigent once remarked with a laugh, it therefore had the biggest print run after the Bible.[11] Warhol was undoubtedly predestined to design the cover for the magazine. His design adorned the 675th issue of the *TV Guide* on March 5, 1966. The artist had asked Roger Prigent to take photographs of the actress Barbara Feldon from the TV series *Get Smart*. Warhol took a profile photo and made four portraits out of it with different coloring, composing them into a collage. He edited other photos of Barbara Feldon in different attire for the inner pages of the guide, which were presented under the title "Barbara Feldon + Andy Warhol = Pop Fashions."[12] In an interview that he gave in the summer of the same year, he remarked rather apologetically, "When I did the cover for the *TV Guide*, that was just to pay the rent at the Factory."[13]

Television as "Instant Fame"

In his book *THE Philosophy of Andy Warhol* published in 1975, Warhol refers to having his own regular TV show as "the great unfulfilled ambition of my life." He even already had a title in mind, *Nothing Special*.[1] Four years later, the artist did in fact start to broadcast a show of his own. Vincent Fremont reports:

In the 1970s Andy and I developed soap opera style video plays. They were never shown on cable TV at the time because he wanted me to keep learning the medium of TV. In 1979, Andy asked me to put together a video production team and I did. I hired Don Munroe to direct and Don brought in artist Sue Etkin to be our production manager. Andy invested in a professional video camera, lights, sound, and editing equipment. The first TV show was called Fashion *with Andy as the logo, then came* Andy Warhol's TV, *and finally on MTV we produced* Andy Warhol's Fifteen Minutes.[2]

Fremont also emphasizes that the artist was not concerned with producing art with his TV shows.[3] Warhol himself remarked about his thirty-minute show *Fashion*: "The whole idea is just to do a fashion magazine on TV ... We're trying to make the video magazine just like an *Interview* magazine ..."[4] *Andy Warhol's TV* and *Andy Warhol's Fifteen Minutes* were talk shows in which celebrities from the worlds of entertainment, fashion, and art chatted in front of the camera for half an hour. Debbie Harry, Liza Minnelli, Steven Spielberg, Giorgio Armani, Halston, Paloma Picasso, Georgia O'Keefe, David Hockney, and other famous personalities all had their say here.[5] The shows were also a platform for newcomers, as Suzan Etkin explains:

It was a mixture of people. Andy of course was the main collector of information. At the same time ... if someone saw a great band the night before, or ran into an interesting person at a club, then they were considering having them on the TV show, but primarily Andy had the last word on that ... He knew what was in, and what was going to be important and [what] really wasn't going to make it. He had a pulse for contemporary culture. I don't know who else really has that even now. ... Fashion, music, and artists—I think those were the top three categories. But there were a lot of people who hadn't made it yet … who were just unknown at the time … who were maybe going to become very famous later. He was a great talent scout. … I don't know if anybody ever thought of Dalí on the TV show, I remember that we had William Burroughs, who was kind of an older person on the show. But for the most part, the people who were on the TV show were kind of young.[6]

Etkin also discusses Warhol's appearances in the shows:

Andy had an understanding of the space and scale of television, that it was a flat rectangular plane, the machine was a box, but the screen had four edges. So his eyes would dart around the parameters of the screen. … like he was uncomfortable there … like he was trapped. He was always insecure to be on the other side of the camera, so this made a lot of sense to me. We were shocked when we realized how profound it was. … But I think as time wore on he became accustomed to it and then I think he liked it.[7]

Vincent Fremont reports that cooperating with his team made Warhol feel more secure and that he therefore got better and better.[8] Over time the artist developed a significant degree of routine, which led to him being in front of the camera for every episode of *Andy Warhol's Fifteen Minutes*.

Warhol could also occasionally be seen in foreign television productions. In 1981 he allowed himself to be persuaded to make a guest appearance on the TV show *Saturday Night Live*. His team recorded three one-minute scenes for this, which could then be seen on various shows.[9] The first scene was broadcast on October 3, 1981 and presented a cynical Andy Warhol who addressed the public saying: "In the first place, I never thought I'd ever be on *Saturday Night Live* because I hate the show. I never watched it. I didn't think it was that great and if you're home on a Saturday night, why ARE you home on a Saturday Night … ."[10] The day after the broadcast Warhol recorded in his diaries, "So many people must see *Saturday Night Live*, because instead of people on the street saying, 'There's Andy Warhol the artist,' I heard, 'There's Andy Warhol from *Saturday Night Live*.'"[11]

Salvador Dalí also recognized that television represents a kind of "instant fame," with which one can reach millions of viewers.[12] Yet Dalí had an advantage over his younger American colleague. He had no stage fright whatsoever and had no problem with presenting himself in front of a foreign camera. He thoroughly enjoyed it. The list of television programs produced with him is therefore long. Dalí not only gave numerous television interviews, but also appeared in newsreels and stood in front of the camera for television movies.[13] In December 1965 the British moviemaker Jack Bond shot the documentary *Dalí in New York* for the BBC. Bond accompanied Dalí with the camera for two weeks while the artist engaged in various activities. He invited Andy Warhol, whom he had met together with Dalí in New York before starting to shoot the movie, to a pre-screening.[14] Warhol was very much taken by *Dalí in New York* and called it "a truly terrific film." Jack Bond even recalls the following: "He said I had captured the essence of Dalí."[15]

A year later, the TV production *Autoportrait mou de Salvador Dalí* was made, directed by Jean-Christophe Averty. The title was an allusion to Dalí's 1941 painting *Soft Self-Portrait with Fried Bacon*. An English version with the

6
Suzan Etkin in a telephone conversation with the author on July 26, 2010.

7
Ibid.

8
Vincent Fremont in a conversation with the author on June 28, 2012 in New York.

9
Ibid.

10
Quoted according to *Saturday Night Live Scripts*. The second scene was used for the broadcast on October 10, 1981 and the third for the one on October 31, 1981.

11
Hackett 1989, p. 411, October 4, 1981. See also ibid., October 6, 1981.

12
Cowles 1959, p. 132; Lear in King 2007, p. 183.

13
Cf. Gale 2007, pp. 230f.; Montua 2015, pp. 483ff.

14
With regard to this encounter see the chapter **The 1960s** in Part 5.

15
Jack Bond in an e-mail to the author on June 19, 2012 and in a conversation with the author on July 27, 2012 in London.

title *Soft Self-Portrait of Salvador Dalí* was shot parallel to the French version, managing to win Orson Welles over as commentator. In this entertaining color production, Dalí provides insight into his life, thoughts, and work. It is noteworthy that he once again presents himself here as a pioneer of Pop Art. He claimed, referring to the book *The Trauma of Birth* by Otto Rank, to have a very clear picture of his life before his birth and to recall every detail of intrauterine images, which Op Art and Pop Art pictures are also associated with. He was, accordingly, already an Op Art and Pop Art artist before his birth.

In 1973, the British television director and producer Bruce Gowers shot *Hello Dalí* for the TV series *Aquarius* produced by London Weekend Television Ltd. The producer, Russell Harty, appears in the documentary as an interviewer. *Hello Dalí* provides interesting insight into Dalí's artistic activities during that year. Bruce Gowers remarks about the filming with Dalí:

It was a lot of fun. I mean, it wasn't really what you would call a "serious documentary." And, in fact, he didn't want to do that. He just wanted to have fun basically and he was wonderful to work with. He was basically only in front of the camera. He really had very little input into what we did. We just told him what we'd like to do and, if he loved it, we did it basically. We had no big budget and nobody controlling us and saying, you have got to do this or you have got to do that ... We had total freedom in what we did. ... On the last day of shooting he invited the whole crew to his place to dinner and we had the most outrageous meal, which was lobster with chocolate sauce on it, which I'd never had before. ... It was his way of saying thank you. ... We were all sitting around together, having a drink, presumably after dinner, and Salvador Dalí said, "I have no contract with you guys." Which we didn't, we'd signed nothing. And he said, "We'll have to write on something." So that's where the Marlboro packet of cigarettes came in. I broke a pack up and we wrote the contract on the back of a package of cigarettes. It was crazy. [16]

There is a highly amusing scene where Dalí uncovers a stuffed giraffe at his museum in Figueres; it is then turned into a burning giraffe using torches. Bruce Gowers recalls: "Underneath the little sequence with the burning giraffe, Dalí is telling a story about the word 'fire'. The word 'fire' in Catalan is 'foc.' And when he was in New York there was a fire in his hotel room. He was yelling out 'Foc! Foc! Foc!' And the man in the next room shouted back 'Go fuck yourself!'" [17] Owing to Dalí's strong accent, the scene slipped through censorship. [18] *Hello Dalí* was broadcast for the first time on November 11, 1973.

The documentary *Warhol* by David Bailey had been broadcast on British television eight months earlier, on March 27, 1973. In addition to Warhol, numerous members of his entourage also appeared before the camera. After its first broadcast, the movie was the subject of controversy. Two scenes that offended sensibilities at the time were the cause of this. In the first scene one can see Brigid Berlin producing one of her "tit paintings" by pressing her painted breasts onto paper. In the second scene David Bailey is lying in bed with Warhol in order to interview him. [19] As Bailey later recalled, Warhol

16
Bruce Gowers in a telephone conversation with the author on February 27, 2013.

17
Ibid. The anecdote is recounted similarly in Moore 2009, pp. 143f.

18
Bruce Gowers in a telephone conversation with the author on February 27, 2013.

19
Harrison 2003, pp. 61f.

prompted this scene: "He said, 'I'll only let you make a film if you'll go to bed with me.' And that's why we did the interviews in bed."[20]

Autobiographies Written "With Four Hands"

Salvador Dalí wrote prolifically during his lifetime including diaries, novels, essays, manifestos, movie scripts, poems, and theoretical treatises. His autobiography *The Secret Life of Salvador Dalí*, published by Dial Press in New York in October 1942, is without a doubt his most important and well-known literary work. Dalí completed his memoirs when he was thirty-seven years old. His comments on that were: "Customarily writers begin to write their memoirs 'after their life is over,' towards the end of their life, in their old age. But with my vice of doing everything differently from others, of doing the contrary of what others do, I thought that it was more intelligent to begin by writing my memoirs, and to live them afterwards."[1]

Dalí wrote his autobiography in French. Haakon M. Chevalier, known in the United States for his translations of French novels, was entrusted with the translation of the manuscript. Chevalier later remarked:

Mr. Dalí's manuscript, as to handwriting, spelling and syntax, is probably one of the most fantastically indecipherable documents ever to have come from the pen of a person having a real feeling for the value and the weight of words, for verbal images, for style. The manuscript is written on yellow foolscap in a well-nigh illegible hand-writing, almost without punctuation, without paragraphing, in a deliriously fanciful spelling that would bring beads of perspiration to a lexicographer's brow. Gala is the only one who does not get lost in the labyrinthian chaos of this manuscript.[2]

Recent research has shown that *The Secret Life of Salvador Dalí* has to be viewed as a work written "with four hands." As Chevalier indicated, Gala provided a fair copy of Dalí's manuscript. She made corrections, so that in many places the French original is dominated by her own style with lyrical accents, similar to that of her letters to Paul Éluard.[3] In Gala's diaries discovered just a few years ago, which also display this style, she writes about her "travaux d'arrangement du livre de D."[4] Gala had already helped with Dalí's book *The Visible Woman* published in Paris in 1930. In the *Secret Life* one reads: "Gala had in fact gathered together the mass of disorganized and unintelligible scribblings that I had made throughout the whole summer at Cadaqués, and with her unflinching scrupulousness she had succeeded in giving these a 'syntactic form' that was more or less communicable."[5]

Dalí's autobiography attracted great interest, which was reflected in both sales figures and reactions in the press. In the *Herald Tribune* it was referred to by Bertram D. Wolfe as "a fascinating and appealing book of self-revelation,"[6] who wrote, "it would then have had to take its place on the shelf with the *Droll Tales* of Balzac, the works of Rabelais, Boccaccio and Margret of Navarre, the *Ulysses* of James Joyce, and other variegated and semi-reputable companions, classics for the most part that could not get by the triple barriers of the customs, the post office and the Watch and Ward."[7] However, many people also recognized that Dalí was pursuing exclusively

20
In Bailey 2014, p. 69.

1
Dalí 1942, p. 393.

2
Ibid., p. 74.

3
Diego 2003, p. 123. It is only the 2006 critical edition of the *Secret Life* in the French original by Frédérique Joseph-Lowery that allows this to be verified in detail, see Dalí 2006, pp. 17ff.

4
Dalí 2012, p. 182.

5
Dalí 1942, p. 250.

6
Cowles 1959, p. 160.

7
Quoted according to ibid., p. 162.

one goal with his *Secret Life*. He formulated this to Luis Buñuel by saying: "I wrote it to make myself a star."[8] Dalí succeeded in this. His autobiography was to become a resounding success, with which he managed to spread his fame even further in the United States. However, there were also critical voices. Shortly after the book was published, a reader of the magazine *The Nation* referred to it as "perhaps the greatest feat of willed obscurantism of the times."[9] George Orwell wrote about the work in his 1944 essay, "Benefit of Clergy: Some Notes on Salvador Dalí," "Some of the incidents in it are flatly incredible, others have been rearranged and romanticized, and not merely the humiliation but the persistent *ordinariness* of everyday life has been cut out. Dalí is even by his own diagnosis narcissistic, and his autobiography is simply a striptease act conducted in pink limelight."[10]

Thanks to his diligent staff, Andy Warhol was also able to publish his first autobiographical text *THE Philosophy of Andy Warhol (From A to B and Back Again)* in 1975. The book, in which the artist comments on love, beauty, fame, work, time, death, economics, atmosphere, success, art, titles, the tingle, and underwear power, was received with jubilant praise. Barbara Goldsmith wrote in the *New York Times Book Review*, "Some people say California is the bellwether of America. I'd say Andy Warhol."[11] Warhol had initially entrusted Bob Colacello with the *Philosophy* project, but in the end it was Pat Hackett who compiled the majority of the book.[12] Colacello recalled that it was important for Warhol to have enough "nutty lines" in the book. It was also supposed to be humorous, but not so humorous that people would not know whether what was written was meant seriously or not.[13] When asked how he had written the book, the artist remarked in an interview in 1977, "I taped most of it talking to my secretary, Pat Hackett. I used to call her in the morning to tell her what I did the day before."[14] In saying so Warhol probably had his weekday morning routine in mind, which started in the fall of 1976 and provided the basis for *The Andy Warhol Diaries*.[15] As Hackett later reported, she carried out eight interviews with the artist and then wrote chapters one to eight and ten for the *Philosophy* book. The other chapters written by her were based on conversations that Warhol had had with Brigid Berlin and Bob Colacello.[16]

POPism: The Warhol '60s, published in 1980, was the artist's most significant autobiographical text. Warhol wrote this book, too, together with Pat Hackett. It says in the preface,

This is my personal view of the Pop phenomenon in New York in the 1960s. In writing it, Pat Hackett and I have reconstructed the decade, starting in '60 when I began to paint my first Pop canvases. It's a look back at what life was like then for my friends and me—at the paintings, movies, fashions, and music, at the superstars and the relationships that made up the scene at our Manhattan loft, the place known as the Factory.[17]

POPism is based on interviews that Hackett did with Henry Geldzahler, Emile de Antonio, and other personalities from the 1960s.[18] She says of Warhol's very headstrong instructions:

I remember when I started to do POPism *and I wanted to keep researching and talking to more and more people. Andy said, "You only need to talk to*

8
Quoted according to Buñuel 1984, p. 183.

9
Quoted according to Secrest 1986, p. 182.

10
Orwell 1946, p. 170.

11
Quoted according to Bockris 1989, p. 390.

12
Colacello 1990, pp. 207f.

13
Ibid., p. 210.

14
In Goldsmith 2004, p. 249.

15
Hackett 1989, p. xvi.

16
Ibid., p. xiii.

17
Warhol/Hackett 1980, Foreword.

18
Colacello 1990, p. 419.

one *person from each period. All you need is* one. *And then make* me *say what* they *said.*"

When we were writing POPism *together Andy gave me this instruction:* "*Never have me saying that I was 'the first person' to do anything. Always say that I was 'the first person I knew of' to do something, because you can never know for sure if somebody else has done something before you and maybe you just don't know about it.*"[19]

POPism was met predominantly with positive reviews. The *Boston Globe* referred to the book as "gossipy and alive, one of the best things you'll ever read about those crazy eight years—Warhol says the '60s ended in 1968. It's a Pop history in wraparound sunglasses and it reads like a dream."[20] Despite the "embroidered anecdotes, distortions, and incorrect dates," the book conveys an appropriate image of Warhol and the general atmosphere of the 1960s.[21] When Viva and Ultra Violet asked Warhol about the inaccuracies in the book, his standard phrase was, "Not my fault. I never wrote it, never read it."[22] However, a peek into Warhol's diaries reveals that this was one of the artist's typical evasive statements. It says under August 12, 1979: "I'd taken the *POPism* manuscript home with me to read and so I worked on that all afternoon and then called PH [Pat Hackett] and discussed it."[23] Hackett, who edited *The Andy Warhol Diaries* published two years after the artist's death, explains: "'Just make it up,' was a philosophy of Andy's. If a journalist called on the phone and wanted him to answer a question, he'd tell me, 'Oh just make it up.' *The Diaries* were not like that because they were diaries. But with other projects it would be like that. He thought making it up was better than the truth."[24]

Warhol Photographs Dalí

Photography clearly plays a central role in the work of Andy Warhol. Already as a commercial artist he often based his work on photographic source material. It was more convenient to copy contours than to create a new figure from scratch. He was also able to use the advantage of the photograph's recognition value for his own work of art. This criterion was also decisive when he began experimenting with the photo-silkscreen technique beginning in August 1962.[1]

Salvador Dalí, too, liked to use photographic source material from newspapers and magazines. His 1954 painting *Young Virgin Auto-Sodomized by her Own Chastity* is based on a photograph that appeared in an erotic magazine in the late 1930s.[2] For the painting *The Sistine Madonna* from the year 1958, Dalí was inspired by a photograph of Pope John XXIII that had been previously published in *LIFE* magazine.[3] He once said of his penchant for photographic templates: "I almost always use photographic documents, it's traditional. Praxiteles made direct casts of legs, arms, and anything that he was going to reproduce. For someone who draws as I do, a photograph is an extremely useful element."[4] On occasion, Dalí also painted over photographs that he found in newspapers or magazines. The gouache *Mae West's Face which May Be Used as a Surrealist Apartment* (1934/35), for which he used

19
Pat Hackett in a conversation with the author on December 4, 2012 in New York.

20
Quoted according to Rosenthal/ Prather/Alteveer/ Lowery 2012, p. 263.

21
Bourdon 1989, p. 386.

22
Quoted according to Ultra Violet 1988, p. 242. Similarly, also Viva in an e-mail to the author on April 17, 2012.

23
Hackett 1989, p. 235.

24
Pat Hackett in a conversation with the author on December 4, 2012 in New York.

1
In 1981, Warhol recalled in an interview: "The silkscreens were really an accident. ...Then someone told me you could use a photograph image, and that's how it all started." In Goldsmith 2004, p. 294.

2
Descharnes 2002, p. 72. Ill. in King/Brenneman 2010, p. 33.

3
See the chapter **Religious Art** in this part.

4
In Bosquet 1969, p. 72.

5
See the chapter
Mae West's and Marilyn Monroe's Lips in this part.

6
Ill. in Guldemond 2005, p. 261. In 1962, Warhol created two pencil drawings of Ginger Rogers, based on the cover of the magazine *Movie Play* issued in May 1946. Ill. in Crone 1976, cat. 269, 270.

7
Cf. Descharnes 1984, pp. 89, 91, 119; Descharnes/ Néret 1993, no. 391–395.

8
See the chapter **Mustache, Wig, and Other Signature Features** in Part 2.

9
Details about the history of the Photomaton in Pellicer 2010, pp. 29, 65ff.

10
Éluard 1989, p. 12.

11
Ill. in Martin/ Aguer/Bouhours/ Dufrêne 2012, p. 115.

12
Pellicer 2010, pp. 90ff.

13
La Révolution surréaliste, no. 12, p. 73.

14
Heinrich in *Andy Warhol Photography*, p. 10.

15
Cf. Golden 2015, pp. 38ff.

16
Bonanos 2012, p. 42.

17
Ibid., pp. 64, 68.

18
Ill. in ibid., p. 64. See also Guldemond, p. 50.

19
Frei/Printz 2002, p. 468.

20
Malanga in *Andy Warhol Photography*, p. 115.

21
Moore 2009, pp. 91f.

the cover of a magazine, is the most well-known example.[5] A similar work is *Ginger Rogers with butterflies and roses* from the 1940s, which Dalí created with collage, watercolor, and ink on printed paper. It shows the actress Ginger Rogers in a coat with a flower and butterfly pattern.[6]

Dalí rarely took photographs, and did so only in the early 1930s to produce templates for his paintings or to serve as a source of inspiration.[7] Warhol, on the other hand, became a passionate photographer over the years and the camera even became one of his signature features.[8] If there were no suitable photographic sources available, he simply produced his own. From 1963 to 1966 he worked a lot with photo booth pictures that only take minutes to develop. The photo booth is an invention by the Russian-American inventor Anatol Josepho, who registered the patent for his machine—the Photomaton—on March 27, 1925 in the United States. The first Photomaton was set up in New York in 1926 and two years later the first booths also appeared in Paris.[9] In March 1928 Paul Éluard wrote to his wife Gala: "I bumped into Fraenkel at the automatic photos. Five francs a roll. It's funny if you make a face."[10] Dalí and Gala, who became a couple a year later, also had their pictures taken in a photo booth. The shots show the painter with a strict demeanor, which softens slightly when he is photographed together with his good-humored muse.[11] Not long afterwards the surrealists also discovered the artistic potential of photo booth pictures and used them for their publications.[12] A photo collage of photo booth pictures of the surrealists, including Dalí, in which they all have their eyes closed was published in the magazine *La Révolution surréaliste* in December 1928. The photos are arranged around a reproduction of René Magritte's painting *La femme cach*ée, which bears the words: "je ne vois pas la [femme] cachée dans la forêt" ("I cannot see the [woman] hidden in the forest").[13]

Andy Warhol appreciated photo booth pictures because of their wealth of contrast, which produces a cosmetic touch-up. The flash directed right at the face smoothens facial features, hides skin blemishes, and erases wrinkles.[14]

Warhol began experimenting with a Polaroid instant camera in 1958.[15] The first model had been sold in Boston on November 26, 1948.[16] Bert Stern photographed the actor couple Jessica Tandy and Hume Cronyn in 1958, as well as Louis Armstrong and Salvador Dalí, using a Polaroid camera. The shots were used in a Polaroid advertising campaign in various print media.[17] The photo of Salvador Dalí, in which he is gazing at the viewer, was reproduced in a very large format in an advertisement to highlight the "exceptional quality in detail and tone."[18] Warhol purchased a Polaroid land camera in 1962, which he used to take pictures of friends and visitors to his studio.[19] Although Polaroid photos were entirely instantaneous, according to Gerard Malanga they did not satisfy Warhol's aesthetic drive.[20] Dalí was also experimenting with Polaroid instant camera technology at the time. His secretary Peter Moore later reported that the artist had, for example, photographed fishermen at work in Port Lligat.[21]

In March 1971, the Polaroid Company launched the Big Shot camera, which with a fixed focal point of three feet was conceived explicitly for portrait photography. The camera was fitted with a dual range finder. The photographer had to move back and forth until two images corresponded in the viewfinder. Warhol bought his first Big Shot shortly afterwards, which became an indispensable working tool for his portrait assignments.[22] He soon became quite skilled in handling the camera.[23] The artist appreciated the photos made with it and remarked in an interview in 1983, "The Polaroid gets rid of everybody's wrinkles, sort of simplifies the face."[24]

Even after the Polaroid Company stopped producing the Big Shot camera in 1973, Warhol continued to work with it. Since the model was rather prone to defects, he bought up all the cameras that he could find in New York shops. When Polaroid found out about Warhol's proclivity for the Big Shot, a special repair service was set up for him. The artist simply sent his faulty cameras to the company headquarters in Cambridge, Massachusetts, and got them back repaired and as good as new. Some of the managers at Polaroid even went one step further and on their travels around the world purchased any dusty leftover stock they found and sent it to Warhol.[25] When Warhol himself embarked on a journey he always had at least two Big Shots in his luggage. He kept a couple more at Fred Hughes's apartment in Paris, so he would always be well-prepared for his European portrait assignments.[26] During this period he met Dalí in the French capital, who had of course not failed to notice Warhol's passion for Polaroid photos. In Dalí's weekly report "Les six jours de Dalí" in the French magazine *Paris Match,* on June 16, 1973 he wrote about his younger colleague: "He lives with his mother and is passionate about Polaroid photography."[27]

Of course Dalí also let Warhol take several pictures of him with a Polaroid camera. The Pop Art artist took these color photos as snapshots with a Polaroid SX-70, and not as templates for a portrait. In October 1972 Polaroid introduced an integral film system, making it no longer necessary, like with the Big Shot, to separate the wet positive from the sticky negative, thereby producing less waste. The SX-70 also made it possible to focus on objects as close as 10 ½ inches away. The photographer could move freely, making action shots possible. This model was also not as bulky as the Big Shot. Therefore Warhol used the SX-70 on many occasions for shooting at social events.[28] Warhol's pictures of Dalí were shot in 1973 in New York. Warhol photographed Dalí together with Pandora at the cocktail lounge of the St. Regis Hotel.[29] Most of the shots of Dalí were taken during a lunch together with Alice Cooper, which took place on April 3, 1973 at the French restaurant La Goulue. What prompted this gathering was the presentation of Dalí's hologram *First Cylindric Chrono-Hologram. Portrait of Alice Cooper's Brain,* which was exhibited at the Knoedler Gallery.[30] Several of the Polaroids show Dalí with gesticulating hands. On two of them, Nanita Kalaschnikoff is to his right, while on two others, the rock musician Alice Cooper is to his left. Six of the Polaroids are signed by Dalí and one by Cooper.[31] These signatures were not a unique occurrence. Warhol frequently had the personalities who had just been photographed, including movie stars, musicians, fashion designers, and other celebrities, sign his Polaroids.[32] On two photos, taken on the same day, Warhol himself is in the picture, sitting at a table with Dalí. Therefore, somebody else must have released the shutter of his Polaroid

22
Printz/King-Nero 2010, p. 60.

23
Fremont in *Andy Warhol Polaroids 1971–1986*, p. 5.

24
In Ratcliff 1983, p. 114.

25
Fremont in *Andy Warhol Polaroids 1971–1986*, p. 5.

26
Ibid.

27
Dalí 1973, p. 4 (translated from the French).

28
Printz/King-Nero 2010, p. 60.

→ **49/46/47/ 48** [p. 395]

29
The Andy Warhol Foundation for the Visual Arts, Inc. cat. no. F311.00045. Another photo was taken during this encounter, showing Dalí with the actor Juan Fernández, who was part of the artist's entourage (The Andy Warhol Foundation for the Visual Arts, Inc. cat. no. F311.00046). Pandora kindly provided the author with this information in an e-mail on August 19, 2015.

30
See the chapter **The 1970s** in Part 5.

31
The Andy Warhol Foundation for the Visual Arts, Inc., cat. no. F313.00042, F313.00046, F313.00047, F313.00053, F313.00054, F313.00057, F313.00058, F313.00086.

32
Cf. Golden 2015, pp. 104ff.

33
Their friendship began when Malcolm Morley received a call from Dalí one Sunday morning saying he wanted to meet him. At the time, Morley was living at the Chelsea Hotel. At first he thought it was a prank. Andrew Lee kindly provided the author with this information in an e-mail on February 18, 2016.

34
The Andy Warhol Foundation for the Visual Arts, Inc., cat. no. F311.00035, F311.00036. On another Polaroid, Dalí is sitting next to an unidentified man (The Andy Warhol Foundation for the Visual Arts, Inc., cat. no. F311.00033).

35
Colacello in Steinorth/Buchsteiner 1992, p. 16.

36
Warhol/Colacello 1979, p. 19.

37
Colacello in Steinorth/Buchsteiner 1992, p. 16.

38
Ibid., p. 18.

39
Details of the encounters with Dalí in the chapter **The 1970s** in Part 5.

40
The Andy Warhol Foundation for the Visual Arts, Inc., cat. no. FL06.00327.

41
The Andy Warhol Foundation for the Visual Arts, Inc., cat. no. FL06.00458.

42
Warhol/Colacello 1979, pp. 124f.

43
Colacello 1990, p. 422.

44
Ibid., p. 420.

45
Bob Colacello in an e-mail to the author on September 11, 2013.

SX-70. Malcolm Morley, who was friends with Dalí,[33] is sitting between them, putting something on paper and thereby attracting the Spaniard's attention. Warhol, on the other hand, is concentrating totally on leaning in towards the two of them, in order to be in the pictures.[34]

Beginning in 1976, Warhol used a Minox 35EL for his snapshot photography. He had become acquainted with what was then the smallest camera available on the market during a stay in Zurich with the Swiss art dealer Thomas Ammann, who was working with Bruno Bischofberger at the time.[35] In *Andy Warhol's Exposures,* the artist states: "I love the new, small, automatic-focus 35-mm cameras like Minox and Konica. That's what I used for the photos in this book. I think anybody can take a good picture. My idea of a good picture is one that's in focus and of a famous person doing something unfamous. It's being in the right place at the wrong time. That's why my favorite photographer is Ron Galella."[36] Bob Colacello reported that Warhol shot at least one entire roll of black-and-white film a day—color being "too expensive" for him. He estimates that over 150,000 photos must have been taken between 1976 and 1987.[37] In time Warhol moved on from the Minox 35EL to newer models by Minolta and Olympus, which in the meantime had introduced autofocus and the automatic flash.[38]

Two shots of Dalí taken by Warhol with a compact camera exist.[39] The first was taken on March 17, 1976 and shows him at a table at the Metropolitan Club in New York together with the actress Candice Bergen, sitting between the two artists.[40] The second shot was taken on Palm Sunday in 1978.[41] It shows Dalí with a big pair of sunglasses, together with Ultra Violet, also sitting between the two artists. This photo was published in *Andy Warhol's Exposures.*[42] The photo was also used for the *Celebrity Collage* that Christopher Makos and Rupert Jasen Smith created under the supervision of Bob Colacello for the cover of *Exposures.* Apart from Dalí, the work shows Elizabeth Taylor, Margaret Trudeau, Steve Rubell, Bianca Jagger, Liza Minnelli, Jack Nicholson, Diana Vreeland, Halston, Truman Capote, Mick Jagger, Grace Jones, and prominently, to the right, Warhol himself. Colacello reports that his boss hated the collage, but made no effort whatsoever to edit it or have it edited.[43]

Andy Warhol's Exposures was published in 1979. Bob Colacello is stated as co-author, but in fact he acted as ghostwriter. Brigid Berlin assisted him in this. Colacello writes in his memoirs: "Almost every night that winter [of 1978/79], she came to my place, or I went to hers, and after I smoked two or three joints, I dictated to her, turning myself into Andy, imitating the way he talked and, as best I could, the way he thought. Every so often, Brigid would snap, 'That's you, not Andy. He'd never say that.'"[44] As already mentioned, an entire chapter of the book is devoted to Salvador Dalí. Bob Colacello reports that Warhol read through the whole text for the book prior to publication and modified it here and there. However, he cannot recall Warhol commenting on the chapter dedicated to Dalí.[45]

It would be an exaggeration to refer to Andy Warhol as a photo artist, as his shots conform entirely to the tradition of snapshot photography and he himself never pursued photography explicitly as an art. The photographer

Christopher Makos, who acted as Art Director for *Andy Warhol's Exposures* and produced all the lithographs for the book, remarked later about the photos it contains:

They were gimmick photos, very offhand and sloppy, but that was because Andy was often in extraordinary situations. ...

We never spoke of his photos as art. I mean, I would just ask him if he could try to focus better, use a little bit more care, and try actually to aim the thing once in a while. He definitely took more care after the publication of Exposures, because when the art dealer Bruno Bischofberger offered to turn his photos into portfolios, he began to take his pictures more seriously, as if to say, "These are my art photos."[46]

Due to his keen powers of observation, Warhol developed remarkable photographic proficiency over the years, and he also learned from professionals. Roxanne Lowit, who photographed Warhol as well as Dalí, comments:

One time Andy told me: "Roxanne, I learned something from you." I stood there in shock, I said "WHAT!?!" I was quite surprised that Andy Warhol would tell me he learned something from me. He actually learned from everybody, he was very good at watching and listening. He would reinvent the ordinary things he found around him and transfer them into art. I said, "What did you learn from me?" He reached into his pockets and pulled out two separate cameras: "Black-and-white and color!" I always had two small cameras with me. In one pocket I had a camera with black-and-white film. In another pocket I had a camera with color film. Two cameras ready at the same time and he did the same.

Like Dalí, Andy loved being in front of the camera and photographed by me. Andy was visually more reserved, Dalí was more theatrical.[47]

Dalí News and Andy Warhol's Interview

On the occasion of the opening of his exhibition "Recent Paintings by Salvador Dalí" at the Bignou Gallery in New York, Dalí published the first edition of a newspaper parody on November 20, 1945, which bore the title *Dalí News*. This was published under a crowning banner reading "GALA FIRST." The subtitle was *Monarch of the Dailies*. The choice of title was a play on words, referring to the *New York Daily News*. Printed in smaller type was also the ironic note, "Dalí Mirror incorporated," the meaning of which becomes clear only when one is aware that the *Daily Mirror* was the arch rival of the *Daily News*.[1] The artist's old school friend Jaume Miravitlles from Figueres helped him with the design of his four-page *Dalí News*. They had launched the school magazine *Studium* together with other classmates in 1919.[2] Miravitlles had gone on to make a name for himself in South America as a publisher and was living as a refugee in New York at the time.[3] The first page of *Dalí News* was titled "DALÍ TRIUMPHS IN APOTHEOSE OF HOMERUS," alluding to the painting by the same name, of which a section was reproduced on the second page and which was exhibited at the Bignou Gallery.[4] The first page depicted a section of the painting *Melancholy, Atomic Uranic Idyll*, which could also be seen at the exhibition, and

46
Makos 1988,
p. 104.

47
Roxanne Lowit
in a telephone
conversation
with the author
on July 24, 2012.

→ **23** [p. 377]

1
Gibson 1997,
pp. 435f.

2
Details provided
by Guillamet/
Ferrerós/Pascuet
2003, pp. 6ff.

3
Etherington-
Smith 1993,
p. 302.

4
Descharnes
1984, p. 286.

5
Gibson 1997,
p. 435.

6
Quoted accord-
ing to Ethering-
ton-Smith 1993,
p. 303.

7
The whole edition
is reproduced
in Abadie 1980,
pp. 116ff.

8
The whole edition
is reproduced
in ibid., pp. 124ff.

9
In Etherington-
Smith 1993,
pp. 302f.

10
Quoted accord-
ing to The Andy
Warhol Founda-
tion for the Visual
Arts 2007, pp. 40f.

11
Bob Colacello
in the docu-
mentary *Andy
Warhol: A
Life at the Edge*.

attracted widespread attention.[5] The exhibition was well-received and James Thrall Soby also made positive comments about it in a letter to A. Reynolds Morse on February 2, 1946, but he remarked about Dalí's newspaper, "Unfortunately, his *Dalí News* ... seems to have put people off a good deal, though personally I rather admire his refusal to appear repentant and his insistence on the megalomania to which he is and for so long has been committed."[6] Soby's sharp words can be explained by the fact that Dalí blew his own trumpet loudly in his newspaper and reported about his own artistic activities. He discussed the New York performance of his "first paranoiac" ballet *Mad Tristan* to music by Richard Wagner, his dream sequence created for Alfred Hitchcock's movie *Spellbound*, and he announced his forthcoming cooperation with Walt Disney.[7] The second and last edition of *Dalí News* was published on the occasion of the exhibition "New Paintings of Salvador Dalí" at the New York Bignou Gallery, which opened on November 25, 1947. The issue bore the header in capital letters "TRUMAN, MARSHALL, PICASSO, DALÍ, IN ARTISTIC CRISIS AND REBELLION SPREAD" and signaled that Dalí was still waging an editorial campaign against modern art. It also included the announcement of his forthcoming book *50 Secrets of Magic Craftsmanship,* of which he printed the first chapter and his "Fifty Secrets" as a preview. Furthermore, under "Tastes And Prophecies For The Next Ten Years," he listed his prophecies for the post-war world, stating consequently, "After the First World War, it was Romantics. After the Second World War, it shall be the Classicists."[8]

The two editions of the *Dalí News* also reflected the fact that Dalí and Gala were able to occupy themselves for hours with newspaper articles, which they pasted carefully into scrapbooks. A. Reynolds Morse later recalled, "The trouble was, they really did not understand English well enough to realize that many of the clippings were making fun of Dalí. All they cared about was how much space Dalí got."[9] Andy Warhol must have liked the Dalís' habit, because he once remarked, 'Don't pay any attention to what they write about you. Just measure it in inches.'"[10] Bob Colacello remarked later that the Pop Art artist was able to get himself very worked up if his name did not appear in the newspaper on a daily basis.[11]

In 1969 Warhol had the opportunity to launch his own magazine, *Interview*. He received support from his long-standing friend, the journalist John Wilcock. Wilcock later recalled:

The way Interview *began was with one of the occasional phone calls Andy made to me in which he—once again—was bitching about how Hollywood wouldn't give him a million dollars to go out there and make a movie. Off-handedly I said, "Well Andy, all my friends publish newspapers; why don't you produce a paper?" It was met with a noncommittal grunt, but ten minutes later Andy called again. "What kind of paper?" he asked in that querulous, uncertain voice.*

I remember telling him that a film paper would be an obvious choice ...

... I did suggest that he follow the example of Art D'Lugoff's Village Gate and call the paper Andy Warhol's inter/VIEW (he had come up with that title). No, he replied, he didn't want his name on it, nor did he want it printed in color. What style would the paper follow? I asked, figuring that anything Andy came

up with would be imaginatively innovative. "I want it to look like Rolling Stone,*"
he said determinedly, to my surprise.*

And thus Interview *was born and Andy began to carry a tape recorder
with him everywhere he went.*[12]

Gerard Malanga was named co-editor and given the responsibility of
managing all editorial aspects of the new magazine.[13] When he was asked
why he had started *Interview*, Warhol sometimes answered, "Umm, to give
Gerard something to do," or sometimes, "To give the kids something to do."[14]
Malanga left the Factory for good in November 1970, following an internal
dispute.[15] After his departure, Bob Colacello and Glenn O'Brien became involved with *Interview*. O'Brien, who became managing editor and art editor
in 1971, later remarked:

For the first year of its life, Interview *was an underground film magazine.
It got Andy Warhol and Paul Morrissey into film festivals and screenings. It
promoted Andy's own productions, like* Flesh *and* Trash. *And it quickly proved
to be an effective way to get the attention of the film stars, directors, and producers Andy and Paul wanted to meet. They discovered that the words, "Can
we interview you for our magazine,* Interview?*" worked surprisingly well. Later*
Interview *was a good foot in fashion-world doors, art-world doors, even White
House doors.*[16]

The early *Interview* magazine was referred to repeatedly as an "underground magazine." John Wilcock, who was listed on the imprint page during
the first year as the co-publisher, but was not yet involved in editorial work,
remarks, "It was never an 'underground' magazine. Andy always wanted it
to be interviews of people connected with film. ... We members of the underground press syndicate (worldwide) regarded underground papers as those
which were politically oriented and against the system. *Interview* was never,
to my knowledge, against the system."[17]

Thanks to Bob Colacello, who was appointed executive editor in 1975
and retained this position until 1983, *Interview* gained a new image almost
overnight and evolved from an "amateurish movie-fan magazine with tedious
dialogues and fussy-looking graphics into a sleek journal."[18] Colacello announced at the time, "We're trying to reach high-spending people. The trend
in our society is towards self-indulgence and we encourage that. We don't
want to give the whole picture. We leave out the things we don't like. We're
not interested in journalism so much as taste setting. We're the *Vogue* of
entertainment."[19] *Interview* addressed topics from the entertainment scene,
as well as the fashion world, which was playing an increasingly important
role in the United States in the 1970s.

Warhol's personal contributions undoubtedly contributed to the early
success of the magazine. For each edition he held an interview, in a casual
and chatty tone, focusing on trivialities as the main subject matter. Others
helped him with this, such as Catherine Hesketh, née Guinness, who started
as editor at *Interview* in 1975. She described the situation as follows: "Obviously, it is more interesting for people to hear Andy's questions than mine.
So, sometimes I had questions which were called his, or mainly his were left
in. But he was very good at interviewing himself and people wanted to open

[12] Wilcock 2009, p. 81.

[13] Bourdon 1989, p. 302.

[14] Quoted accord-
ing to O'Brien
in Francis/King
1997, p. 232.
See also Malan-
ga in Smith 1986,
p. 404.

[15] Bourdon 1989,
p. 307.

[16] In Francis/King
1997, p. 234.

[17] John Wilcock
in e-mails to
the author on
October 14 and
15, 2013.

[18] Bourdon 1989,
p. 302.

[19] Quoted accord-
ing to Bockris
1989, p. 370.

up to him. He just had that way about him. People wanted their things a little shocking or interesting. He was very good at eliciting information from people."[20] Three regularly published columns also received a resounding response. Fran Lebowitz compiled the column "I Cover the Waterfront," Glenn O'Brien the music column "BEAT," and Bob Colacello was responsible for "OUT," in which he reported with refreshing honesty and sometimes also in a blithe manner about nightlife in New York and other metropolises. It could scarcely be avoided that the name Salvador Dalí also popped up occasionally. Here are two examples:

Friday, Jan. 24 [1975]

Lunch at La Grenouille … <u>Dalí</u> was there with <u>Gala</u>, and a beauty named <u>Lorey Rodkin</u>. <u>Dalí</u> said he was looking for talented young artists in New York and Paris but couldn't find any. He said that was because it's impossible to have art in a democracy because if everybody is equal, who is the artist? … He also said he was opening a Hyper-Realist museum in Cadaqués, Spain where he would show his favorite artists, <u>Richard Estes</u>, <u>Malcolm Morley</u> and <u>John D'Andrea</u> [sic]. He said his really favorite artist is himself.[21]

Wednesday, Feb. 19 [1975]

The opening of Cecil's … <u>Guy Burgos'</u> answer to El Morocco. Everyone was there: … <u>Potassa de la Fayette</u> did a new dance called the Noblesse Oblige with Amanda Lear who came but did not leave with her rich uncle, <u>Salvador Dalí</u>.[22]

In the April 1973 edition, the "art in view" section said about Dalí:

SALVADOR DALÍ has just created a portrait of rock star ALICE COOPER in the form of a hologram, complete with a 3-D representation of Alice's brain as well as the diamond TIARA of WESTMINSTER, loaned to Alice by HARRY WINSTON, which adorns both Alice's body and brain. DALÍ himself wore a gold-trimmed translucent gown over his clothes to complete the image and ritual, as he shot lasers into Alice's brain. The result will be seen in early April when DALÍ shows us what makes a rock star tick, here in NEW YORK.[23]

This announcement was accompanied by a photo with the caption, "SALVADOR DALÍ caught in a melodic spell by the violin." It was shot by Ronnie Cutrone, who was *Interview*'s assistant editor at the time. The photo is one of a series of shots taken at the loft belonging to Dalí's close friend and confidante Pandora, and shows a relaxed Dalí, listening to the violin player. The surrealist was often Pandora's guest, and she later reported, "He became an innocent child—an embryo, an egg, at my loft. It was a sanctuary for him … where we could be two kids in a sandbox. He was relaxed there, as you can see in this photo. He's lying on the floor."[24] Ronnie Cutrone later described the exact circumstances that led to the photos:

I was doing two pages in Interview: *the art page and the music page, two very important pages. So, I was always busy. I used to run around to all of these events and parties. So, I was invited by Dalí to come in and if I want I could bring my camera and have any photos I like, bla bla bla, and they would be grateful if I did that, but I don't have to do that I could just come for the party. And I said "Ok, that's fair." So, I took my girlfriend at the time and went to the party. And it was a strange thing. He was sort of on a throne. … This was as close to a club party as you can make it, except it was really weird. What was*

20
Catherine Hesketh in a telephone conversation with the author on August 27, 2012.

21
Colacello 1975, March, p. 40.

22
Colacello 1975, May, p. 41.

23
"art in view," p. 17. See also the chapter **The 1970s** in Part 5.

24
In Michaud 1991, Summer, p. 5.

going on was Dalí would stand there with his gown and his stick that he carried and this throne or whatever it was. So, all the photographers were standing all knocked together, this bunch of people in the back. And Dalí takes his finger and he points it directly at me and he had like these long fingers and I was like "Oh my God, what's going to happen now?" So, he informs the people, the guards, that I should be picked out of the crowd and the only one permitted to come out into the middle of the floor and to take any photo I wanted, which really was a great opportunity … And he picked me out because he'd heard I was part of the Warhol studio. But then, it even gets crazier. So, I take all the photos and within about forty-five minutes this black man and this white girl come over to me and my girlfriend and they ask if they can rub our toes and we're like, "Well, I guess, if you want for a little bit" you know, because we were joking around, too, with it. … And then they ask if we want to go home with them and we said "No, you know what, we think we're going to pass on that." So, I mean, that's basically, what the scene was like.[25]

Dalí even appeared on the cover page of *Interview* in May 1973. An interview was printed inside, which Warhol's superstar Candy Darling had conducted with him. Since Dalí was fascinated by the drag queen, she was, as Glenn O'Brien remarks, the perfect person to interview him.[26] Dalí philosophized here about his "intrauterine memories" and reported about his plans to have beans printed with the images of Mao Zedong and Marilyn Monroe. It is also revealed that instead of "marijuana, dope and LSD," he consumed Vichy water, and that a version of his *Lip Sofas* with plenty of saliva would soon be marketed, which would always make the genitals a little wet when one sat on it.[27] The famous fashion photographer Francesco Scavullo photographed Dalí for the cover and inner pages of the volume.

In a certain way, the cover of the August 1976 edition of *Interview* was also a homage to Dalí. It features a black and white detail showing C.Z. Guest's head from the portrait Dalí painted of her in 1958. At the bottom right is the inscription "C.Z. by DALÍ." Richard Bernstein was responsible for the cover design at the time. Bernstein adopted the aesthetics of Warhol's portraits for the covers he designed, but mainly used pastel colors and soft contours. It was evidently Warhol's intention to present Dalí's portrait to a wide public. An interview he had held with C.Z. Guest was published within the volume:

CZ: … Andy, I want to tell you I was so impressed with that drawing you did of Mick Jagger, I can't tell you. I couldn't believe it. I had no idea what an artist you were. When Diana (Vreeland) showed it to me I said to Diana, "I think Andy has the talent of Dalí." I've never said that about another artist. I want you to see the painting he did of me. It's in the house in the country.

AW: I'm sure I've seen it before but could you describe it?

CZ: No. It's never been exhibited.

AW: Really? It's never been photographed?

CZ: No, no, no. Never, never, never.[28]

At the time the issue of *Interview* was published, C.Z. Guest was already fifty-six years old and there were certain rules for the cover design that Bob Colacello describes as follows:

25
Ronnie Cutrone in a telephone conversation with the author on July 8, 2012. Pandora remarked in an e-mail to the author on August 9, 2013 about the "throne" mentioned by Cutrone, "There was no Dalí throne in my loft. [Ronnie Cutrone] might have seen Dalí, [in my loft], reclining on a middle-eastern carpeted lounge that extended up a very high wall and under clouds on the ceiling."

26
Glenn O'Brien in an e-mail to the author on December 21, 2011.

27
Candy Darling 1973, pp. 12, 40. See also the chapters **Mao Marilyn** and **Mae West's and Marilyn Monroe's Lips** in this part.

28
Warhol 1976, p. 8. See also the chapter **Portraits of Socialites** in this part.

→ **21** [p. 376]

→ **22** [p. 376]

People magazine editor Richard Stolley has some famous rules about what covers sell best: Young is better than old, pretty is better than ugly, movies are better than music, music is better than TV, and anything is better than politics. The Interview *twist: Only young, only pretty, movies are best, but music, fashion, and society are also good, and anything, even politics, is better than TV. ... Our readers didn't watch TV, they went to discos. ... [W]hen we put older stars on the cover we did them the way they looked when they were younger: We used a thirties publicity shot for Ginger Rogers, and a forties [actually from 1958] Dalí portrait for C.Z. Guest.*[29]

Warhol made a great effort to find suitable personalities for the cover of *Interview*. This started already in the morning when he left the house. Brigid Berlin recalls:

Benjamin [Liu] would pick him up at the house and they'd walk down Madison Avenue and each would have a pile of Interview *magazines in their arms and Andy would hand them out especially if you were cute and he'd sign them. And then he'd say, "Oh, wow, we have a beautiful Factory. Why don't you come up for lunch?" (laughs) When I'd walk with him I'd have a bunch of* Interviews *and he would. And we would just have left the Factory and he'd see somebody cute, sign an* Interview *and say "Well, we have a Factory right up there. Why don't you come for lunch? Maybe we could put you on the cover of* Interview.*"*[30]

This game continued in the evening. Vincent Fremont recounts, "When Andy went out at night he would often promise the cover of his magazine, *Interview*, to people he would meet at a dinner. This might happen multiple times a week, which would drive Bob Colacello crazy. He did the same thing to me with the TV show, he would tell people they could be on the show."[31]

The format of *Interview* was unusual, up to eleven by seventeen inches and therefore significantly exceeding the standard format of a magazine. Up until August 1975 the cover photos were in landscape format, which made it possible to fold the magazine in the middle. At first the magazine was called *inter/VIEW* or *INTER/VIEW*. From May 1972 it was published as *Andy Warhol's Interview* and in March 1977 they went back to using just *Interview*. Marc Balet, who worked as art director for the magazine from 1975, recalls that it was Warhol's idea to remove his name from the title again: "I don't think you'd see Andy that much in *Interview* ... very rarely would Andy be in there nor were any of us 'cause he didn't want it to be self-promotion like that. ... He wanted it to become its own entity. ... Andy was so smart that he saw *Interview* should stand on its own."[32] However, the advertisements were important to Warhol. Paige Powell, who was responsible for advertisements at *Interview*, later felt that Warhol would have liked most of all for the magazine to consist entirely of advertisements. The artist asked her, even when an edition had already gone to print, "Oh, Paige, can't we get one more ad in?"[33] Vincent Fremont points out that the number of ads was an indication of a magazine's success. And success was important to Warhol, "He had to bring home the bacon as he always said."[34]

From 1980, *Interview* developed into a profitable business. In 1987 the printrun already amounted to 170,000 copies. The magazine had found its way into the center of society. Marc Balet recounts, "People have told me that

---

29
Colacello 1990,
pp. 251f.

30
Brigid Berlin in a
conversation
with the author
on December 4,
2012 in New York.

31
Vincent Fremont
in a conversation
with the author
on June 28, 2012
in New York.

32
Marc Balet in a
conversation
with the author
on December 3,
2012 in New York.

33
Quoted according to Bourdon
1989, p. 400.

34
Vincent Fremont
in a conversation
with the author
on June 28, 2012
in New York.

they came to New York because of *Interview*, because they saw *Interview* in a little store in Montana or Idaho and they went 'Oh, my God. There is this whole world out there that I must be a part of.' They would come to the city in search of that THERE that they saw in our magazine. It was kind of made up, anyway."[35]

Commercials for Braniff International Airways

Braniff International Airways was founded in 1928, with its head office in Dallas, and was largely unknown until the mid-1960s. This was set to change when Harding L. Lawrence took over as president in April 1965. Lawrence had his mind set on making Braniff International Airways known overnight. For this, he appointed Mary Wells from the Jack Tinker advertising agency, who attracted great attention to the airline through the "The end of the plain plane" campaign. Wells made use of color, bringing in the Italian fashion designer Emilio Pucci and the American designer Alexander Girard. Pucci created uniforms in bright colors for the stewardesses, who were called "hostesses" at Braniff, and Girard had the previously silver-gray airplanes painted in cheerful colors, while the cabins, ticket counters, and waiting lounges were given a colorful and extravagant design. Braniff International Airways opened the "Terminal of the Future" in 1968 at Dallas Love Field airport, with a mirrored ceiling and a wealth of color, where travelers could even admire Mexican art as well as paintings by Fernando Botero and Alexander Calder.[1]

In 1969, Braniff International Airways launched a major advertising campaign with TV commercials produced by the Lois Holland Callaway advertising agency, founded by George Lois, Ron Holland, and Jim Callaway. During the first phase, minute-long commercials were broadcast, in which a hostess welcomed a celebrity on board with the words "Thanks for flying Braniff, So-and-so." In addition to Gina Lollobrigida, Joe Namath, Sugar Ray Robinson, Emilio Pucci, Leonard Lyons, Tab Hunter, Mickey Rooney, and the rock band Vanilla Fudge, Salvador Dalí also made an appearance as "So-and-so."[2] After three weeks, the second phase broadcast thirty-second clips in which celebrities sat in a Braniff airplane and held bizarre conversations. These clips included appearances by Hermione Gingold and George Raft, Mickey Spillane and Marianne Moore, Bennett Cerf and Ethel Merman, Rex Reed and Mickey Rooney, Dean Martin Jr. and Satchel Paige, Salvador Dalí and Whitey Ford, as well as Andy Warhol and Sonny Liston. The conversation between Dalí and the baseball player Whitey Ford went as follows:

> *Whitey Ford: Now tell me the truth, don't you think a knuckleball is much harder to throw than a screwball?*
> *Salvador Dalí: Oh no, no, no, no, Whitey.*
> *Announcer voice over: Whitey Ford and his new friend Salvador Dalí always fly Braniff. They like our food. They like our style. And they like to be on time. Thanks for flying Braniff, fellas.*
> *Salvador Dalí: Ven you goddit—flaundit!*
> *Whitey Ford: Tell 'em, Dalí baby.*[3]

35
Marc Balet in a conversation with the author on December 3, 2012 in New York.

1
Danicke 2008, pp. 40f.

2
Stills in Guldemond 2005, p. 329.

3
Quoted according to Lois/Pitts 1977, p. 138.

Ford later reported in an interview that Dalí had written his text on a card based on how it sounded. Ron Holland took the card and had it signed by the artist, then went on to declare that he was now in possession of an original Dalí.[4] Peter Moore, who was Dalí's secretary at the time, states in his memoirs *Flagrant Dalí* that the artist proclaimed, shortly after the commercial broadcasts started, that he never traveled to the United States by airplane. Apparently Braniff International Airways immediately halted the broadcasting of commercials featuring Dalí and even demanded that Dalí return his fee.[5] Because of his fear of flying, Dalí first boarded an airplane in 1975. After the flight he said to his companion Amanda Lear, "I wish I had flown before, it is quite painless."[6]

In the commercial with Andy Warhol and the boxer Sonny Liston, the conversation was one-sided:

Andy Warhol: Of course, remember there is an inherent beauty in soup cans that Michelangelo could not have imagined existed.

Announcer voice over: Talkative Andy Warhol and gabby Sonny Liston always fly Braniff. They like our girls. They like our food. They like our style. And they like to be on time. Thanks for flying Braniff, fellows.

Andy Warhol: When you got it—flaunt it![7]

It is remarkable that the artist, notorious for his taciturn nature in public, was announced as "talkative Andy Warhol" and was the only one to talk in this commercial. However, Warhol's voice was later dubbed, which he evidently disliked, as he wrote in *Philosophy*: "I did an airline commercial once with Sonny Liston—'If you've got it, flaunt it!' I liked saying that, but then later they dubbed my voice, although they didn't dub his."[8]

After the broadcasting of the TV commercials, advertisements were placed in regional and national newspapers and magazines. One of the advertisements used a still photograph from the commercial with Warhol and Liston. The title read: "Andy Warhol and Sonny Liston fly on Braniff (When you got it—flaunt it.)"[9]

Braniff International Airways' success continued for another couple of years. In 1977 Emilio Pucci was replaced by Halston, who designed a rather more urban-looking uniform in soft brown tones for the hostesses. When the airline deregulation law was passed a year later, Lawrence further expanded the company. As of 1979, Braniff International Airways, in cooperation with Air France and British Airways, offered flights with Concorde. However, the enormous operational costs and the expansion policy led to ever increasing debt. On May 12, 1982, Braniff International Airways ceased operations due to insolvency.[10]

Advertisements for Nylons and Ladies' Shoes

Salvador Dalí created many advertisements for fashion, perfume, and cosmetics during the 1940s.[1] The most famous and perhaps most impressive designs include those for the company Bryans, a manufacturer of nylon stockings. The ads appeared in various magazines between 1944 and 1948, including *Harper's Bazaar*, *Town & Country*, and *Vogue*. Dalí came up

4
Berkow 1969.

5
Moore 2009,
p. 150.

6
Quoted according to Lear 1985,
p. 265.

7
Quoted according to Lois/Pitts
1977, p. 137.

8
Warhol 1975,
Philosophy,
p. 83.

9
Dougherty 1969;
Ill. in Lois/Pitts
1977, pp. 136f.

10
Danicke 2008,
p. 41.

1
Cf. the list in
*Salvador Dalí y
las revistas*,
pp. 336f. In 1969,
Dalí created
an advertising
poster for the
French mineral
water Perrier.
+

with light and humorous drawings in ink and watercolor, in most cases with collage whose main motif was an attractive female leg in stockings. Some of the advertisements feature pairs of legs or several of them. They were derived from "risqué" postcards of cabaret beauties that Dalí and Gala had collected.[2] The artist resorted in his designs to his tried and true repertoire of motifs that had brought him fame. The ladies' stockinged legs are staged within surrealist landscapes among soft clocks, elephants on spider's legs, butterflies, and ants. Sometimes they also become architectural elements, or the wings of Pegasus in an advertisement inspired by Greek mythology.[3] It is clear that Dalí wanted to seduce with his designs, rather than shock, which he undoubtedly succeeded in.

The advertising campaign left a lasting impression. *Saturday Review* of October 14, 1961 published caricatures by Al Hirschfeld, which present Pablo Picasso, Henri Matisse, Marc Chagall, and Salvador Dalí, taking up the respective style of each of the painters. For his Dalí caricature, Hirschfeld was inspired by a Bryans advertisement. He drew the face of the Spaniard in a surrealist manner, with tree branches as hair and two ladies' legs in stockings, of which one is growing out of Dalí's right eye, while the other is protruding from under his chin and has his grotesquely elongated left mustache tip woven around it.[4]

The advertising sector was "infected" by Dalí's numerous advertisements. In P.H. Erbes Jr.'s essay "Surrealism Invades Advertising," which was published in the magazine *Printers' Ink* in December 1943, the author explored the influence of Surrealism on the advertising industry. He concluded that the perspective of spatial depth and the dream-like distribution of various unconnected elements across the landscape were the most important stylistic elements that were adopted in advertising. Erbes Jr. remarked that it was actually curious that Surrealism, as a "radical, eccentric art form," was accepted more fundamentally and quickly by the most conservative element of American society, namely business, than by society per se.[5] The essay drew a resounding response. Dale Nichols countered in the *Printers' Ink* edition published at the beginning of March 1944, that the current wave of Surrealism was even dangerous. Surrealist advertising was based on the principle of drawing attention, which in his opinion was bad advertising. He emphasized that he was not against Dalí, but against poor advertising.[6]

One year after the end of the advertising campaign launched by the Bryans company, with the advertisements designed by Dalí, Andrew Warhola, as Andy Warhol still called himself at the time, visited advertising agencies and magazine editorial offices in an attempt to win assignments for illustrations and magazine editorials. He was awarded one of his first by Tina S. Fredericks, art director at the fashion magazine *Glamour*. Fredericks was taken by the young advertising designer's drawings and soon recognized his talent: "His ink lines were electrifying. Fragmented, broken, and intriguing, they grabbed at you with their spontaneous intensity."[7] The reason for the special impact of Warhol's work was his "blotted line" technique. Vito Giallo, Warhol's assistant in the 1950s, describes this technique:

+
See Michler/ Löpsinger 1995, no. 1231. Fourteen years later, Warhol was commissioned to create two posters for Perrier. Following this, he produced a series of paintings showing Perriers bottles. See Maréchal 2014, *Posters*, no. 30, 31.

2
Matthiesson in Gott 2009, p. 233.

3
Ill. in *Salvador Dalí y las revistas*, no. 185, 187, 192–194, 196, 198–199, 201– 202, 210–214, 216–218; *Dalí. Cultura de masas*, pp. 160f.

4
Ill. in *Salvador Dalí y las revistas*, no. 284.

5
Cf. Spies 1979, p. 106.

6
Cf. ibid.

7
In Kornbluth 1988, p. 11.

4

No one knew how he did that blotted line, which was so funny because it was extremely simple once you knew how to do it. But everybody had a different idea how he did it and nobody hit on the right, the correct way. … It was hard to make a mistake because he would do a pencil drawing, then fold the piece of paper in half. So the drawing would be on the left as a rule and I would trace it with a pen and ink and keep blotting it back and forth to get a perfect register. So, when I finished it was really a Warhol. It wasn't me at all.[8]

When Warhol declared to Tina S. Fredericks that he could draw anything, she suggested that he try shoes,

Perhaps put them on a background of ladders, so they can be followed by more ladders with girls climbing—to illustrate the next pages of articles on how to ascend the ladders of career success in various fields.

The shoe editor gave us six shoes, which Andy took home. "How soon do you need them?" Yesterday, of course—my standard answer. Indeed, he came back the following day. The brown paper bag, which would be the vehicle for most of his offerings, in hand. It contained a roll of beautiful drawings: shoes with the swells and cracks and wrinkles of true personality, full of character. Unfortunately they had none of what in those days we called "sell." I explained that our shoes had to look irresistibly sleek, chic—and new—so that Glamour readers would rush to buy them. "Oh," said Andy, and returned the next morning with flawless renderings.[9]

During the period that followed, Warhol received assignments for shoe illustrations from a series of fashion magazines.[10] These kinds of assignments were a lucrative source of income for him, as he recorded later in his *Philosophy*: "When I used to do shoe drawings for the magazines I would get a certain amount for each shoe, so then I would count up my shoes to figure out how much I was going to get. I lived by the number of shoe drawings—when I counted them I knew how much money I had."[11]

Beginning in 1955, advertisements for the shoe company I. Miller became Warhol's main source of income. Over a period of several years, he received an annual fee of $20,000, as well as a bonus if the agreed number of illustrations was exceeded.[12] Peter Palazzo, the art director at I. Miller, was pursuing the goal at the time of establishing an innovative graphic black and white style, to lend the shoe manufacturer a "strong, identifiable image." Palazzo was determined that the style of the new illustrations should be "gutsy."[13] He described his cooperation with Warhol as follows:

I was able to add an element in an area where Andy wasn't too strong—composition. Andy and I would discuss the ideas to make sure they were compatible. I would then make design and composition suggestions in rough form and Andy would go off and interpret them in his blotting technique. These were times when Andy would draw the raw elements and I would then compose them by photostatically resizing and rearranging them in the ad space to make a good decorative composition.[14]

Warhol liked this form of cooperation, as he stated later in an interview: "I was getting paid for it, and did everything they told me to do. If they told me to draw a shoe, I'd do it, and if they told me to correct it, I would—I'd do anything they told me to do, correct it and do it right."[15]

8
Vito Giallo in a telephone conversation with the author on May 25, 2010.

9
In Kornbluth 1988, p. 12.

10
Ill. in Maréchal 2014, *Magazine Work*, pp. 44ff.

11
Warhol 1975, *Philosophy*, p. 85.

12
Bourdon 1989, p. 42.

13
Ibid., p. 40.

14
Ibid.

15
In Goldsmith 2004, p. 18. Similarly, also in Warhol 1975, *Philosophy*, p. 96.

I. Miller advertisements, which were real eye-catchers and went against the conventions at the time, appeared in the *New York Times* almost weekly from 1955 to 1959. They were not a mere representation of a certain model, but a memorable stylization. In his designs, Warhol liked to present the footwear in front of a white background, making them appear almost caricature-like. Added to this was an unusual perspective with details. One advertisement merely showed the rear end of a stiletto, another just the tips of various models. There was a particularly memorable, L-shaped advertisement showing a woman's leg stretching across the entire length of the page, while the shoe at the bottom occupied the whole width.[16] Palazzo later recalled, "There was a lot *not* to like about these ads. The entire shoe industry, as well as the I. Miller sales people, initially hated them because they were used to literal renderings of shoes. But when the ads began to get recognition in the graphics, advertising, and fashion communities—and customers still came into the store—then management deemed the campaign a success."[17]

The novel advertisements attracted a great deal of attention and Warhol gained considerable fame as a result. The experts in the field were also impressed. In 1956 and 1957, Warhol received the "Award for Distinctive Merits" from the Art Directors Club. In 1957, he also received a medal as the highest award by the club. The magazine *Women's Wear Daily* is even said to have called the artist "the Leonardo da Vinci of the shoe trade."[18]

Shoe Fetishism

In his autobiography *The Secret Life of Salvador Dalí*, Dalí often mentions his passion for shoes and confesses to being a shoe fetishist. He states in a footnote:

All my life I have been preoccupied with shoes, which I have utilized in several surrealist objects and pictures, to the point of making a kind of divinity of them. In 1936 I went so far as to put shoes on heads; and Elsa Schiaparelli created a hat after my idea. Daisy Fellowes appeared in Venice with this shoe-hat on her head. The shoe, in fact, appears to me to be the object most charged with realistic virtues. ... One of my latest pictures represents a pair of shoes. I spent two long months copying them from a model, and I worked over them with the same love and the same objectivity as Raphael painting a Madonna.[1]

The painting Dalí is referring to is *Original Sin* created in 1941, showing a pair of tatty men's shoes, with Gala's naked leg next to them, adorned with a bracelet in the form of a snake designed by Fabergé. The jewelry was a gift from the patron Edward James, who was close to Dalí and Gala for some time.[2]

Ladies' shoes first appeared in Dalí's work after he met Gala. Initially, a few paintings showed a surrealist landscape with one or two ladies' shoes.[3] The 1931 oil painting *The Sense of Speed (Landscape with a Shoe)*, which was exhibited the same year at the "Newer Super-Realism" display at the Wadsworth Atheneum in Hartford, Connecticut,[4] is an interesting example. It shows a rock in the form of a ladies' shoe, on which there is a clock without hands. The function of the hands is taken over by a big and a small ladies'

16
Ill. in Bourdon 1989, p. 42. Further depictions of advertisements in Francis/King 1997, pp. 70ff.

17
In Bourdon 1989, pp. 40, 42.

18
Ibid., p. 42.

1
Dalí 1942, p. 122. Elsewhere Dalí reports of an alleged event while at school: one day he gave a student a "terrific kick on the buttocks" and trampled on his violin. When the teacher summoned him, he explained that it was not him, but *his* *shoes* that were the perpetrators. Cf. ibid., pp. 120ff.

2
Etherington-Smith 1993, p. 217. See also the chapter **Sterile Love and Voyeurism** in Part 2.

3
The Fish Woman (1930) and *Premature Ossification of a Railway Station* (1931).

4
Fundació Gala-Salvador Dalí, cat. 386.

shoe next to the clock face. This already heralds Dalí's famous *Soft Watches.* The association between Gala and women's shoes becomes especially clear in the drawing *Paranoic Metamorphosis of Gala's Face* created the following year. Dalí used his paranoiac-critical method in this meticulous portrait to transform the face of his muse into two compilations of various objects, with a ladies' shoe in each.[5]

Shortly before, Dalí had created the erotically charged object *Scatalogical Object Functioning Symbolically*, which is also known as *The Surrealist Shoe.* Here it is clear that Dalí was using it to process his first (unsuccessful) sexual experiences with Gala.[6] In the December 1931 edition of the magazine *Le Surréalisme au service de la revolution,* he describes it as follows:

A woman's shoe, inside of which a glass of warm milk has been placed, in the center of a soft paste in the color of excrement.

The mechanism consists of the dipping in the milk of a sugar lump, on which there is a drawing of a shoe, so that the dissolving of the sugar, and consequently of the image of the shoe, may be observed. Several accessoires (pubic hairs glued to a sugar lump, an erotic little photograph) complete the object, which is accompanied by a box of spare sugar lumps and a special spoon used for stirring lead pellets inside the shoe.[7]

In 1979 Dalí was asked in an interview for the Spanish *Playboy* whether the composition had any kind of meaning, whereupon he remarked, "The milk had to be lukewarm, because that's how I like to drink it, neither cold nor hot. I added the pubic hair and the photo automatically. They have no particular meaning."[8] The original *Surrealist Shoe* was unfortunately destroyed, so today the work of art is only known from a photograph that was published in the aforementioned edition of *Le Surréalisme au service de la révolution.*

The surrealist object was reconstructed in 1973 under Dalí's supervision, and twelve copies were produced.[9] The artist delivered an interesting interpretation of the work with his drypoint *The Curse Conquered,* which is part of the graphic series created one year later, "After 50 Years of Surrealism."[10] With this portfolio, Dalí took the opportunity to illustrate twelve important milestones in his life. The aforementioned print shows a red ladies' shoe that is clearly inspired by the *Surrealist Shoe.* As the liaison with Gala led to severe disputes and later to the breakdown of his relationship with his father, here, the shoe becomes a symbol of his oedipal liberation.

In the early 1930s Dalí posed for several photos with Gala's shoes. In a shot captured in 1932, he is balancing a shoe on his right shoulder and another on his head.[11] The following year, Dalí stood in front of the camera for Man Ray, who took a number of photos of the artist during his summer stay in Cadaqués.[12] Dalí once again posed for two of the photos with a shoe belonging to his muse. The first shows him wrapped in a white sheet, standing on a wall with a shoe balanced on his head. The second shows Dalí standing on his head, with his face behind a white sheet, presenting one of Gala's shoes on his chin.[13]

Man Ray's photos inspired the paintings that Dalí created shortly thereafter, *Seascape* and *Ambivalent Image.* The former features a variation

---

Margin notes:

5
Ill. in Descharnes/ Néret 1993, no. 430.

6
Regarding the artist's sexual experiences with Gala, see the chapter **Sterile Love and Voyeurism** in Part 2.

7
In Finkelstein 1998, p. 234.

8
In Calvo Serraller 2006, p. 1541 (translated from the Spanish).

9
Descharnes/ Descharnes 2003, p. 24.

10
Michler/ Löpsinger 1994, no. 666; Field 1996, Original Intaglio, 74-8, E.

11
Ill. in *Les Cahiers,* p. 4.

12
Man Ray 1988, p. 191.

13
Ill. in *Les Cahiers,* cover and p. 33.

of the *Surrealist Shoe* standing on a wall with a white sheet hanging between it and a tree, and the latter a ladies' shoe on a rock and a figure wrapped in a white sheet.

In two drawings from 1932 known as *Cannibalism of Objects,* Dalí represented a ladies' shoe particularly impressively. The works show a bearded, bald male figure, reverently devouring a ladies' shoe. He rips the lining out of the shoe with his teeth, while holding a spoon in his right hand.[14] A similar drawing was created five years later, this time showing a woman devouring a shoe.[15] In his essay "Concerning the Terrifying and Edible Beauty of Art Nouveau Architecture," published in the December 1933 edition of the magazine *Minotaure,* the artist explains, "Breton said: 'Beauty will be convulsive or will cease to be.' The new Surrealist age of 'cannibalism of objects' equally justifies the following conclusion: Beauty will be edible or will cease to be."[16]

On November 26, 1948, a stage production of the Shakespeare comedy *As You Like It* premiered at the Teatro Elisio in Rome, under the direction of Luchino Visconti. Visconti had asked Dalí to design the stage set and the costumes, in order to—as he later put it—"restore the Italian theater to an international level."[17] The performance was a success, which was due no least to Dalí's imaginative contributions. His designs were shown concurrently at the Dell'Obelisco Gallery and drew many viewers as "The First Exhibition of Salvador Dalí in Italy."[18] The art publisher Carlo Bestetti also published the book *As You Like It*, containing several of Dalí's stage sets and costume designs. In his accompanying text, "Bonjour!," Dalí says that his costumes were prophetic, that they were not clothes from the past, from the eighteenth century, but clothes of the future that would be worn over the forthcoming ten years.[19] As part of his stage and costume design project, Dalí also designed extravagant footwear for the individual characters in the theater piece. It is noticeable that four of the shoes were each decorated with a different animal, namely, a pheasant, a dove, a hare, and a bat.[20]

Salvador Dalí's surrealist shoe creations for Shakespeare's *As You Like It* bring to mind that a few years later Andy Warhol also drew attention with similarly fantastical footwear. As reported in the previous chapter, he had been awarded prizes for his designs for the advertising campaign launched by the shoe company I. Miller, and had worked his way up into the top echelons of New York commercial art. Also beyond the advertising and shoe world, there was enthusiasm for Warhol's work. Stephen Bruce, one of the founders and owners of the legendary Serendipity 3 on the East Side of Manhattan, persuaded the young commercial artist to offer the shoe drawings rejected by I. Miller for sale there. Bruce recalls,

He came in with the big portfolio he was working on for I. Miller Shoes on Fifth Avenue and they asked him to do some ads for the New York Times. *He came in with a lot of rejects and I said, "Why don't we frame them?" and he said, "What a good idea." So he gave me five or six of them and then he colored them right there and I took them right down to a framer and had them framed and put them out for—would you believe it—twenty-five dollars each. ... We sold them, they went very very quickly because at that particular time we had a sort of very eccentric fashion and Fifth Avenue clientele and they snapped at these*

14
Ill. in Martin/ Aguer/Bouhours/ Dufrêne 2012, pp. 161f. In 1969, Dalí created a drypoint entitled *The Bureaucrat,* showing a bearded man with a bald head devouring a ladies' shoe, cf. Michler/ Löpsinger 1994, no. 343; Field 1996, Original Intaglio 69-2.

15
Ill. in Descharnes/ Néret 1993, no. 655.

16
In Finkelstein 1998, p. 200.

17
Cf. *Dalí Shakespeare Visconti,* p. 11.

18
Gibson 1997, p. 453; Aguer in Ades 2004, p. 508.

19
Cf. *Dalí Shakespeare Visconti,* p. 9.

20
Ill. in *Dalí Shakespeare Visconti,* cat. 34.

pictures, you know, they felt something is happening in the art world. So they sold out very quickly and I said, "Let's do something different. I want you to do a shoe with the calf going all the way up the thigh." And then I cut the picture in half and framed it in two with the thigh one part and the ankle and the shoe the other part. And we sold those for seventy-five dollars. So it started the theme of shoes that were mostly returning in Andy Warhol's life. [21]

In 1955, when Warhol started his cooperation with I. Miller, he created a portfolio as a gift for business customers in which he presented extravagant drawings of shoes. Warhol called it *À la Recherche du Shoe Perdu*, as an allusion to Marcel Proust's series of novels *À la Recherche du Temps Perdu* [*In Search of Lost Time*]. Blotted line drawings were printed as offset lithographs for the portfolio, which were then hand colored with watercolors. For this purpose, Warhol held "coloring parties" at Serendipity 3, during which guests helped to paint the footwear in appealing colors. [22] A different model of shoe appears on each of the sixteen sheets, with a so-called "Shoe Poem" beneath it by the poet Ralph Pomeroy, a friend of Warhol. The "Shoe Poems" are witty plays on words, referring to well-known quotes, book and movie titles, sayings, and so on. For example, the recruitment slogan "Uncle Sam wants you!" became *Uncle Sam wants Shoe*, Gertrude Stein's *The Autobiography of Alice B. Toklas* became *The Autobiography of Alice B. Shoe*, Alfred Hitchcock's movie *Dial M for Murder* became *Dial M For Shoe* and Shakespeare's "to be or not to be" became *to shoe or not to shoe*. Warhol's mother Julia inscribed all of the "Shoe Poems" in her characteristic curlicue handwriting. [23] In addition to this portfolio, Warhol created a sheet that shows not only a ladies' shoe, but also the wearer's leg. Different color variants of this work are known. [24] Tony Curtis's collection included a sheet that was dedicated to him with Julia Warhola's calligraphy, signed and titled *The Some Like it Hot Shoe*. [25] Curtis famously played the main role, alongside Marilyn Monroe and Jack Lemmon, in the Billy Wilder classic *Some Like It Hot*. Leslie Curtis, who was married to the actor from 1968 to 1982, reports that Dalí knew by hearsay of the *Some Like it Hot Shoe*. Her husband mentioned the work during a dinner together at the French restaurant La Grenouille in New York: "I remember Tony talking about that piece—it was in our home in Bel Air—so Dalí never saw it. ... I don't know what they talked about. I was not privy to their conversation." [26]

Andy Warhol had therefore found his subject. From April 25 to August 5, 1956, the Museum of Modern Art exhibited a major overview entitled "Recent Drawings U.S.A.," which Warhol participated in with a shoe drawing. The shoe theme was also the focus of his solo exhibition "Andy Warhol: The Golden Slipper Show or Shoes Shoe in America," which opened on December 3, 1956, at the Bodley Gallery in New York, run by David Mann. It showed extravagant footwear for famous people. Once again it was Stephen Bruce who had suggested to Warhol to create shoe drawings and to name them after celebrities. [27] The artist made large blotted line drawings of shoes, which were then adorned with Dutch metal, imitation gold leaf, and appliqués made of gold foil and similar material. [28] Of course once again it was Julia Warhola who wrote the names of the respective personalities below the shoes and

---

21
Stephen Bruce in a telephone conversation with the author on July 6, 2011. Design for an invitation to the "Gee Cocktail Showing" at Serendipity 3 in 1957 in Gassen 1996, cat. 12.

22
Stephen Bruce in a telephone conversation with the author on July 6, 2011. See also the chapter **Assistants, Employees, Secretaries, and Managers** in Part 3.

23
Feldman/ Schellmann 2003, IV.69A–84A, IV.69B–84B. It is assumed that the print run was 100 copies, cf. Schleif 2013, p. 293.

24
Feldman/ Schellmann 2003, IV.85.

25
Ill. in Julien's Auctions 2011, lot. 206.

26
Leslie Curtis in a telephone conversation with the author on April 27, 2013. Details about the dinner in the chapter **The Extroverted Dalí and the Introverted Warhol** in Part 2.

27
Kornbluth 1988, p. 164.

28
Bourdon 1989, p. 51.

signed the works with her son's name. These included a boot with spur for Judy Garland, adorned with a feather and bourbon lilies, a spike-heeled, ankle-strapped shoe embellished with roses, hearts, and a bourbon lily for Zsa Zsa Gabor, a ladylike slipper for Julie Andrews, a western boot with spur for James Dean, a buccaneer's boot for Elvis Presley, and a shoe for Truman Capote with flowers sprouting out of it, alluding to his theater piece *House of Flowers*.[29] The works were offered at prices ranging from $50 to $225.[30] D. D. Ryan, a society lady, bought the shoe for Truman Capote and sent it to the author as a Christmas present. In her accompanying note she remarked that Warhol was in the process of becoming very famous. Capote was not quite of the same opinion, as he later recalled: "Even then I never had the idea he wanted to be a painter or an artist. I thought he was one of those people who are 'interested in the arts.' As far as I knew he was a window decorator. … Let's say, a window-decorator-type."[31] *LIFE* magazine had a similar view; reporting about the said exhibition on January 21, 1957, in a two-page article with the headline "Crazy Golden Slippers," referring to Warhol as a commercial artist who drew imaginary footwear "as a hobby." The subhead of the article was: "Famous people inspire fanciful footwear."[32] However, quite the opposite was the case, as Warhol's assistant Nathan Gluck later recalled: "He did a shoe, and then somebody said, 'Let's call this shoe *Judy Garland*, and let's call this *A Shoe for Zsa Zsa Gabor*.' I don't think Andy ever said, 'Let's make a shoe for Mae West.'"[33]

In 1980 Warhol took up shoes again as a subject. This was prompted by Ingeborg Princess zu Schleswig-Holstein, who worked at the Factory a short time later. "When Andy was in Germany he asked me 'Oh, what do you think I should paint?' … And I said to him 'Why don't you paint shoes again because your shoe drawings are so beautiful?' … Then I came to New York and he had indeed just started this shoe series."[34] However, in contrast to the 1950s, this time he painted a collection of various models rather than just individual shoes. Warhol arranged and photographed ladies' shoes and then had silkscreens made from selected photos for paintings and prints.[35] In order to convey the impression of disorder, he always showed only one example of each model in the compositions, of which some could be seen in profile and others as a top view.[36] Since the works were sprinkled with diamond dust, the series was entitled *Diamond Dust Shoes*. The use of diamond dust charmingly recalls the fact that Warhol also often gave his early shoe pictures from the 1950s a glittering surface.[37] Rupert Jasen Smith's studio was not only responsible for printing and applying the diamond dust, but also, by his own admission, he played an important role in the creation of the series. Smith reported:

When I lived on Duane Street, there was still part of the old wholesale shoe district there. One store went out of business and sold every old shoe from the 1940s through the 1960s, size 4AAA or size 14 drag queen shoes. I bought 2,000 pairs of shoes for Andy—the beginning of a new collection. The old designs were really great—wedges, cut-outs, spikes, etc. They look current even today. Andy began photographing the piles of shoes and then did drawings, large prints with diamond dust, and paintings, too. In terms of colors, I had suggested we do

29
Ill. in "Crazy Golden Slippers," p. 12f.; Crone 1976, p. 91; Kornbluth 1988, no. 37, 76.

30
"Crazy Golden Slippers," p. 13. According to Bourdon the prices were between $35 and $150, cf. Bourdon 1989, p. 51.

31
Quoted according to Bockris 1989, p. 125.

32
"Crazy Golden Slippers," p. 13.

33
In Smith 1986, p. 337.

34
Princess Ingeborg zu Schleswig-Holstein in a conversation with the author on June 30, 2011 in Hamburg (translated from the German).

35
Cf. regarding the prints: Feldman/Schellmann 2003, II.248–252, II.253–257.

36
Bourdon 1989, p. 380.

37
For the use of diamond dust see the chapter **Art for the Department Store and Disco Décor** in this part.

black, red, white, and multicolor versions. The black on black series was really nice, but everyone wanted the red shoes.[38]

Warhol commented ironically on his *Diamond Dust Shoes* series at the time of its creation: "I'm doing shoes because I'm going back to my roots. In fact, I think maybe I should do nothing but (laughs) shoes from now on."[39]

Mao Marilyn

Salvador Dalí often stressed that he was an apolitical person. In an interview in 1977 he expressed his "enormous admiration" for the poems by Mao Zedong and explained, "... I couldn't care less whether he is a communist or not. ... I am the only one who was able to commend and illustrate the poems by Mao Zedong with enthusiasm ...."[1] Dalí had expressed an interest in Mao Zedong's lyric poetry as early as 1965[2] and not long after that the French publisher Pierre Argillet presented him with the opportunity to illustrate the poems. He created eight watercolor and ink pen drawings that were transferred onto copper plates by engravers, reworked by Dalí as drypoints, and printed as a special edition, which was published in 1967 with poems by Mao Zedong translated into French, entitled *Poèmes de Mao Tse-tung*.[3] The most interesting illustrations include a portrait of the Chinese leader, with which Dalí set a counterpoint to the famous official Mao portraits of the 1960s. It shows a full body portrait, but without the head, which remains outside of the picture. When Argillet asked why he had portrayed Mao in this way, Dalí purportedly answered, "Well, the man is so tall that he didn't fit on the page!"[4]

In the same year Dalí approached the photographer Philippe Halsman and asked him to create a photomontage of the portraits of Marilyn Monroe and Mao Zedong. Halsman, who had been working with Dalí for years, accepted the challenge and created the double portrait *Mao Marilyn*.[5] To do so, he used a close-up of Mao and his famous photo of Marilyn that had appeared on the title page of *LIFE* magazine in April 1952.[6] Halsman also created a version of the double portrait that is known by the title *Marilyn Mao (Mao With Marilyn's Mouth as Eyes)*.[7] The subtitle describes the photographic composition. All the individual traits of the actress have disappeared and, in addition, the face of the Communist Party chairman is further distorted by the montaged irregular teeth. Dalí presented the two photomontages in November 1967 during a live performance on the French television program *Le petit dimanche illustré*.[8] One month later, *Mao Marilyn* was shown at the charity exhibition "Homage to Marilyn Monroe" at the Sidney Janis Gallery in New York. Andy Warhol was also represented in the exhibition with *Marilyn Diptych* and *Gold Marilyn Monroe*.[9] Sidney Janis remarked to the press at the time: "This is a selective exhibit focusing upon the avant-garde artists of the United States and Britain, France and Italy. Here, we are placing the photographer on the artistic level of the painter and sculptor. And so, with de Kooning, Claes Oldenburg, Andy Warhol, Peter Blake, Dalí, Marisol and George Segal, we also have photographers Richard Avedon, Cartier-Bresson, Philip [sic] Halsman and Bert Stern."[10]

38 In Feldman/ Schellmann 1989, p. 24.

39 Hackett 1989, p. 306, July 24, 1980.

1 In Calvo Serraller 2006, p. 1477 (translated from the Spanish).

2 Dalí in Bosquet 1969, pp. 13, 72.

3 Michler/ Löpsinger 1994, no. 209–216; Field 1996, Cooperative Intaglio, 67-1.

4 Quoted according to King in Taylor 2008, p. 100.

→ **29** [p. 381]

5 Halsman/ Halsman 1989, p. 66.

6 Halsman 1972, p. 35.

7 Ill. in King/ Brenneman 2010, cat. 86.

8 Cf. http://www.ina.fr/video/CPF88004673/salvador-dali-video.html (last accessed on April 11, 2016).

9 Cf. *Homage to Marilyn Monroe*, cat. no. 15, 47, 48.

10 Quoted according to Gavzer 1967.

It can be assumed that Warhol was already aware of Dalí's double portrait *Mao Marilyn* when the exhibition opened. A gray envelope sent during that year from the Sidney Janis Gallery, announcing the exhibition "Homage to Marilyn Monroe," was discovered in one of his *Time Capsules* in which he archived everyday items over the years.[11] *Mao Marilyn* was presented at the exhibition as part of an installation that was referred to in the press as *Mao Marilyn Monarchy* or *Mao Monroe Monarchy*.[12] The March 1975 edition of *Andy Warhol's Interview* provides information for understanding the title. Bob Colacello wrote in his column "Out": "He [Dalí] said, Mao was a modern monarchist because he knew that the cult of the personality was necessary to lead large numbers."[13] A press photo conveys an impression of Dalí's ten-foot-high installation, consisting of "2 non-starched, white, businessman-type shirts; 2 plaster fried eggs in a 'floating mirror'; 4 Con Ed flags; 2 big photomontages—MM [Marilyn Monroe] and Mao."[14] The exhibition met with mixed response. *TIME* magazine stated:

Of 50 works by 36 artists, by far the better half, from de Kooning, Rosenquist and Warhol, among others, predated her [Marilyn's] death in 1962. The recent works were second-rate or worse, with the booby prize going to Salvador Dalí for a ten-foot mobile, obviously whomped up for the occasion, that features a pair of Esso Tiger flags dangling beneath a photomontage of the faces of Marilyn Monroe and Mao Tse-tung. The idea seems to be that sex kittens and paper tigers are really siblings under the skin.[15]

Peter Schjeldahl wrote in the *New York Times*: "Not so much personal as eccentric is Salvador Dalí's 'Mao-Marilyn,' which combines all sorts of things with composite photos of the two luminaries whom it has pleased Dalí to see as one. It is simply ridiculous. ... The show did indicate to me that, of all artists who have tried to make major artistic statements about Marilyn Monroe, two may actually have succeeded. Willem de Kooning and Andy Warhol ... ."[16]

Mao Marilyn achieved wider acclaim when Dalí used the double portrait in his design for the cover of the December issue of the French *Vogue* published in 1971 on the occasion of the fifty-year anniversary of the fashion magazine. Worldwide public attention was focused on China at the time. The United States had refused to acknowledge the People's Republic of China founded in 1949 under the leadership of Mao and continued diplomatic relations with the Chiang Kai-shek regime that had fled to Taiwan. In answer to the question of what advice he would give the American president, Salvador Dalí remarked in the conversations with Alain Bosquet, "... I would advise him to recognize Communist China immediately. You simply cannot deny the existence of that enormous country."[17] From mid-1955 to the beginning of 1970, a total of 136 exchanges took place between the People's Republic of China and the U.S., with no progress achieved on the Taiwan issue. In December 1970 Mao Zedong declared that he wanted to invite President Richard Nixon to Beijing; in May 1971 he reiterated his willingness to enter into direct talks, and not long after that Nixon announced his visit to China. Since no U.S. president had ever traveled to the People's Republic, there were detailed reports of the events. The visit took place at the end of February 1972 and marked the start of the normalization of relations between the

11
Time Capsule 47, Andy Warhol Museum, Pittsburgh.

12
King in Taylor 2008, p. 107, fn. 14. The press photo is reproduced in ibid., p. 92.

13
Colacello 1975, March, p. 40. See also Colacello 1990, p. 175.

14
According to the discussion in the magazine *Mademoiselle*, quoted according to King in Taylor 2008, p. 92.

15
"People," 1967, p. 45.

16
Schjeldahl 1967.

17
In Bosquet 1969, p. 72.

two states. The constant presence of Mao in the media was one of the reasons for using the photomontage on the title page of *Vogue*. When asked about the motif, Dalí answered in the *Herald Tribune* of December 10, 1971, "The idea was to blend the two great matriarchal countries of the world, the United States and China. Those two civilizations are bound to have considerable impact on each other. For the next two years, people will talk about nothing else."[18] However, Dalí's assignment comprised not only the design of the cover, but also the interior of the magazine. The idea of appointing the Spaniard came from the French photographer Jean Jacques Bugat, who worked for the French *Vogue* at the time. Bugat recalls that Dalí remarked about the assignment, "I'm the greatest prostitute, the greatest whore: as long as they are paying I'm up for it!"[19] Dalí approached the task with enthusiasm and he was given absolute free rein with regard to the choice of themes, composition of texts, and design of the layout.[20] In the volume he remarks, "Salvador Dalí takes total responsibility for the Christmas 1971 issue of VOGUE which, to set it apart from all the others, will be called VOGUÉ just this once. Salvador Dalí has accomplished all this precious work gracefully, with the aim of glorifying the cult of his own personality and that of Gala."[21]

Dalí created a surrealist memorial to Mao Zedong not only on the cover, but also in the interior of the issue. *Vogue* had sent their star photographer Alex Chatelain, the editor Francine Crescent, and the top model Veruschka, whom Dalí had already met in the 1960s in New York, to Catalonia for photo shoots.[22] Dalí asked Veruschka to dress up as Mao and to pose for a shot that he would later describe in *Vogue* as: "Veruschka, an evocation of Mao on the banks of the Yang-Tse-Kiang."[23] Vera von Lehndorff, alias Veruschka, recalls this photo shoot: "We did not talk about it at all. After all, Dalí didn't call you. ... At that time we were often in contact through Peter Beard. *Vogue* had probably called me and told me that Dalí wanted to do the photo with me. Then we traveled to Cadaqués and took the photo."[24]

For another photo on the ensuing pages of the issue, young people were recruited in Cadaqués to gather around the swimming pool designed by Dalí on the patio at his house in Port Lligat.[25] These included the artist Howard R. Carr, who was part of Dalí's entourage at the time.[26] Carr explains:

I am the tiniest last person in the photograph on the horizon line. My legs are spread and I'm standing up on a piece of architecture, garden art architecture, a group of people off to my left and I had broken my arm before and my arm is in a sling. You can hardly tell that it's like a close-up of Dalí with Veruschka dressed as Mao. It was a real tight and crammed shot around the swimming pool. ... Those times in his garden were always really artistic and it was exploding with surrealist activity. ... They would have bullfighters and soccer players, a fascinating mix of people. And Dalí would always orchestrate some surrealist happening.[27]

Dalí wrote the following text for the group photo: "The Dalínians are in the habit of gathering at the end of the afternoon in this spiritual center (which now replaces those of yesterday: Le Bateau-Lavoir, La Ruche, the Café de Flore ...). With Pop architecture, a stretch of water under construction with, as a backdrop, the monumental enlargement of the polyester pack-

---

18
Quoted according to Taylor in Ades 2004, p. 463.

19
Jean Jacques Bugat in a conversation with the author.on December 29, 2013 in Paris (translated from the French).

20
Lear 1985, p. 208.

21
Dalí 1971, p. 159 (translated from the French).

22
Lear 1985, p. 210.

23
Dalí 1971, pp.178f. (translated from the French).

24
Vera von Lehndorff in a telephone conversation with the author on January 6, 2012 (translated from the German).

25
Lear 1985, p. 210.

26
See the chapter **Companions, Courtiers, and Superstars** in Part 3.

27
Howard R. Carr in a telephone conversation with the author on January 10, 2013.

aging for a radio."[28] As a brief explanation, with his "monumental enlargement of the polyester packaging for a radio" Dalí meant the big pavilion at the end of his patio, whose form was inspired by the polyester packaging for a radio.[29] The whole ensemble, decorated with advertising panels for Pirelli tires, Michelin men, and a plastic *Lip Sofa*, is "*la plus pop qui fût,*" as Amanda Lear put it.[30] Lear also reported that Dalí was jubilant that his *Vogue* edition would be a sensation that nobody would understand and everybody would be "cretinized."[31]

In 1972 Dalí used the photomontage *Mao Marilyn* again for a self-portrait in which he portrays himself as a renaissance artist with an extremely long neck.[32] It is noticeable that Halsman's creation covers the majority of Dalí's head, perhaps as an indication that Mao Zedong and Marilyn Monroe were often on his mind at the time.[33] Warhol must also have gained this impression when he attended a reception held by Dalí at the King Cole Bar at the St. Regis Hotel in 1973. Bob Colacello, who accompanied him, writes in his memoirs:

"Oh, are you doing any new art?" asked Andy.

Dalí said that he was putting "effigies of Mao Tse-tung and Marilyn Monroe," in vegetable emulsion, "on lee-tle white beans, and you swallow, and at thees momento is possible commun-i-on with Mao and Marilyn together in your stomach. Only—you take no whiskey."

Andy said, "Oh really" for the third time, and picked his tape recorder out of the ashtray, which was the signal to leave. Outside the hotel, he said to me, "I never know what Dalí is talking about. Do you think he was making fun of me? He was, wasn't he? But I don't care, he's just being entertaining, right? ... ."[34]

As Pandora reported, at the time Dalí really had hatched a plan to have beans made with the images of Mao and Marilyn: "He wanted to have imprinted on the beans Marilyn Monroe's portrait on one side and Chairman Mao on the other. We looked for a company that could stamp these images on beans, but we couldn't find one. ... For one of his openings in New York he wanted zillions of beans with these images on them ... like mountains of Marilyn and Mao beans all over the gallery. Spilling everywhere."[35] Dalí presented his idea of Mao-Marilyn beans to a wide public in the May 1973 edition of *Andy Warhol's Interview*. It included an interview that Candy Darling had held with him. When asked how the unusual pulses feel in the stomach, Dalí answered, "Uh feel very peaceafull. You in any ways look much better when you eat many Mao's and Marilyn's than before."[36] With the "peaceful feeling" in the stomach, Dalí was evidently alluding to the easing of tension in the relations between the People's Republic of China and the United States.

When the said edition of *Andy Warhol's Interview* was published, Warhol had already been producing portraits of Mao Zedong for over a year. There is a hypothesis that he had been inspired by Dalí's photomontage *Mao Marilyn*.[37] The French writer and photographer François-Marie Banier believes quite the opposite. In his essay "That little laugh Andy had," he writes, "Under Warhol's influence, I saw Salvador Dalí mix the face of Marilyn Monroe with the face of Mao, complaining all the while that Andy Warhol was copying him when it was he who had taken from the younger man the

---

28
Dalí 1971, p. 180 (translated from the French).

29
Descharnes/Descharnes 2003, p. 155. The packaging is now at the studio at the house in Port Lligat, cf. Pitxot/Aguer/Puig 2008, p. 67.

30
Lear 2004, p. 233.

31
Lear 1985, p. 210.

32
Ill. in Descharnes/Néret 1993, no. 1338. The work evokes Dalí's 1921 painting *Self-Portrait with Raphaelesque Neck*.

33
The unpublished typed manuscript "À cause de la sécheresse de Hans Hartung le Roi prend l'apparence génétique de Mao" of 1971 is at the archive belonging to Robert and Nicolas Descharnes, cf. King in Taylor 2008, p. 106, fn. 1. In 1971/72, Dalí wrote an exposé for the opera libretto *Être Dieu*, in which Mao Zedong and Marilyn Monroe also appear. The Spanish writer Manuel Vázquez Montalbán wrote the libretto, Igor Wakhévitch composed the music. The opera was recorded in 1974 with Dalí in the main role and published as a record. Details by La Salvia in Puyplat/La Salvia/Heinzelmann 2005, pp. 93ff. In 1975, Dalí published extracts from his book *El pequeño libro Lila-Dalí-Gala-Maorylin* in the catalogue *Picasso: Visage de la paix*. At the time he also created the collage *Symbiosis*, uniting the flags of the United States and the People's Republic of China, as well as the names Mae West, Marilin (sic) Monroe and Mao. The work served as a template for a lithograph. Cf. Michler/Löpsinger 1995, no. 1428; Field, Cooperative Lithograph, 71-4.

34
Colacello 1990, p. 173.

35
In Michaud 1992, vol 2, no 2.

36
Candy Darling 1973, p. 12. See also the chapter **Dalí News and Andy Warhol's Interview** in this part.

37
Cf. Taylor in Ades 2004, p. 463; Gorvy/Gold in Christie's 2006 (n.p.).

38
In *Andy Warhol: Red Books* (n.p.).

39
Printz/King-Nero 2010, p. 165; *LIFE* magazine is depicted on p. 192.

40
Colacello 1990, pp. 110f. Bruno Bischofberger confirmed to the author in an e-mail from Silvia Sokalski on September 2, 2009, that he had suggested to Warhol to portray Einstein.

41
Printz/King-Nero 2010, p. 166.

42
In Bourdon 1989, p. 317.

43
Ibid.

idea of appropriation and of fusing a specific individual with another person one idealizes."[38] As reported, however, Dalí's preoccupation with Mao had already begun in 1965 and he had asked Philippe Halsman two years later to create *Mao Marilyn*. Furthermore, in the paintings *Mae West's Face which May Be Used as a Surrealist Apartment* (1934/35) and *Shirley Temple, the Youngest Monster of the Cinema in her Time* (1939) the Spaniard had already paid tribute to movie stars. It is more likely that Dalí and Warhol reflected the phenomenon of Mao in their work independently.

Although Warhol was basically apolitical, even more so than Dalí, he could not remain impervious to Mao's media presence. The title page of *LIFE* magazine in March 1977 with the leader's photo and with the opening line "Nixon in the land of Mao" had left a lasting impression on him as well.[39] In addition to this, the Swiss gallery owner Bruno Bischofberger was putting him under pressure at the time to dedicate himself more to painting again. Bischofberger suggested that Warhol paint the most significant personality of the twentieth century. Bob Colacello reports in his memoirs:

Bruno and his staff researched the history books, brainstormed and pondered: Who? Finally, he came up with the perfect subject: the man responsible for both the technological richness and the technological terror of life in this century.

He flew to New York to present the idea in person. "I've got it," he told Andy. "Albert Einstein! The most important person of the twentieth century!"

"Oh," said Andy. "That's a good idea. But I was reading in LIFE magazine that the most famous person in the world today is Chairman Mao. Shouldn't it be the most famous person, Bruno?"

Bruno was horrified. "A portrait of a Communist leader did not seem like something easy to sell to Gunther [sic] Sachs or Stavros Niarchos, I told Andy," he says. "But Andy pointed out that Nixon had just been to see Mao, and if he was okay with Nixon, he would probably be okay with people like Gunther [sic] or Stavros, too."

Andy wasn't apolitical; he was ruthless. Mao was a brilliant choice, and Andy's timing was perfect.[40]

The book *Quotations from Chairman Mao Tse-Tung* had been distributed worldwide since the days of the Cultural Revolution and was already in its eleventh English edition at the time. Warhol was also in possession of the *Little Red Book* and it can be assumed that he used the official portrait of the leader of the Chinese Communist Party within it as a template for his silkscreens. However, this portrait is not a photo, but a reproduction of a painting by Zhang Zhenshi from 1952. It is doubtful whether Warhol was aware of this fact.[41] In September 1971 he remarked in a telephone conversation with David Bourdon, "I've been reading so much about China. They're so nutty. They don't believe in creativity. The only picture they ever have is of Mao Zedong. It's great. It looks like a silkscreen."[42] More than two months later he returned to this idea in another telephone conversation with Bourdon: "Since fashion is art now and Chinese is in fashion, I could make a lot of money. Mao would be really nutty ... not to believe in it, it'd just be fashion ... but the same portrait you can buy in the poster store. Don't do anything creative, just print it up on canvas."[43]

The *Mao* portraits represent a first dialogue in the artist's work between silkscreen printing and the painting process. Warhol decided to create them in the style of a painting, by painting a colored background with a paintbrush, with the image of Mao printed over it. He produced a total of 199 paintings that can be divided into five groups according to their size. Alongside this, thirty drawings, a portfolio of prints, a couple of individual prints, and wallpaper were created.[44]

The first *Mao* paintings, which are known by the name *Early Maos*, were produced by Warhol between March and June 1972. For the works, he selected a modest blue color scheme inspired by the template he had chosen. The *Early Maos* therefore allude to the "Blue Ants," meaning the workers who were obliged by the Cultural Revolution to wear identical blue working clothes, which Mao is also wearing himself in the portrait.[45] As Warhol had just started painting again at the time and did not employ an assistant, he created all eleven works himself. The *Early Maos* measure about 82 × 57 inches. As a rule, Warhol painted the canvas and then printed the motif over it. On some works, however, he added a few strokes of the brush even after printing.[46] The *Early Maos* were presented to the public at the Kunstmuseum Basel at the exhibition "Zehn Bildnisse von Mao Tse-Tung," which ran from October 21 to November 19, 1972. In early 1973 the works were then shown at Mario Tazzoli's Galleria Galatea in Turin.[47]

In November 1972, parallel to the exhibition in Basel, the *Mao* print portfolio was introduced at Leo Castelli's gallery in New York.[48] It was the first time that the American public had been confronted with Warhol's new "star." Warhol had selected a quirky color scheme for the portfolio consisting of ten silkscreens on paper, from which Castelli published 250 copies. Both the background and Mao's face and jacket appear in garish, unnatural-looking colors. The spectrum of flesh tones ranges from chocolate brown and blood red to vile green and deep blue.

Warhol had chosen a modest color scheme for the *Early Maos*. He started to experiment with loud colors in the paintings that followed from these. At the same time, the treatment of the canvas became more expressive. First he created four monumental works known under the title *Giant Maos*. These are the largest works in Warhol's oeuvre that are dedicated to a single subject.[49] In the case of one painting, Warhol's working method can be reconstructed in detail based on a black-and-white video recorded by Vincent Fremont and Michael Netter in December 1972, which is part of the so-called *Factory Diaries*. It shows that the artist painted the canvas from top to bottom.[50] Warhol also "embellished" the *Giant Mao* cosmetically. The work measuring 177 × 137 inches shows an androgynous Mao with eye shadow, rouge, and red lips. Warhol used his typical "makeup" that he had already tried out on his portraits of Marilyn Monroe, Elizabeth Taylor, and Jackie Kennedy. Mao's jacket also displays quirky color accents, creating the impression that he is wearing a colorful feather boa over his shoulder. In doing so, Warhol is undermining Mao's "imperious gravitas and masculine strength"[51] and is also playing with gender attributes, as Dalí did with his photomontage *Mao Marilyn*. The two works are examples of both artists'

44
Printz/King-Nero 2010, p. 167; Feldman/ Schellmann 2003, II.89, II.90–99, II.125A, III.A.6, III.A.7, III.A.8.

45
Warhol once said about Chinese culture: "I like this better than our culture. It's simpler. I love all the blue clothes. Everyone wearing blue. I like to wear the same thing every day. If I were a dress designer I'd design one dress over and over." Quoted according to Makos 2007, p. 43.

46
He also reversed the procedure for one work, first printing the picture and then painting over it, cf. Printz/King-Nero 2010, p. 184.

47
Ibid., p. 170.

48
Feldman/ Schellmann 2003, II.90–99; cf. also p. 358.

49
Printz/King-Nero 2010, p. 175.

→ **28** [p. 381]

50
Ibid., pp. 174f.; stills from the video p. 199.

51
Rajaratnam in Christie's 2006 (n.p.).

fascination with transvestites and transsexuals.[52] After the *Giant Maos*, Warhol embarked on the groups *50 × 42 Inch Maos* and *26 × 22 Inch Maos*. The *12 × 10 Inch Maos* from the *Mao* series, of which Warhol produced a total of 122 copies in 1973, are especially painterly. Owing to their format, he gave many of them away as gifts and some of the canvasses bear the abbreviated inscription "M.C." on the rear, for "Merry Christmas."[53]

On many of the canvasses, Mao's head stands out from the background due to a lighter patch of color, thereby giving the politician a kind of nimbus or the aura of a superstar. This was most fitting, as in 1968 Mao Zedong had become a cult figure of the student movement and was celebrated enthusiastically by young people in the U.S. and Europe. It was only after Mao's death in 1976 that the true face of his dictatorial rule became known. Warhol's *Mao* portraits were also a success because they had different effects on the viewer: they could be seen as "ominously and universally threatening, or a parody, or both."[54] When the German gallery owner and publisher Bernd Klüser commissioned Warhol in 1986 to create a series of portraits of Lenin, the artist harnessed the same effect. Klüser recalls, "There is no evidence that he wanted to knock communist icons off of their pedestals. He never allowed himself to become involved in discussions like that, he didn't like to get pinned down in talks about the content and intention of his works—also not in private conversations. He replied to such questions with the classical vacuous answers that are part of his myth."[55] In 1977, Warhol remarked in an interview, "We've been in Italy so much, and everybody's always asking me if I'm a Communist because I've done Mao. So now I'm doing hammers and sickles for Communism, and skulls for Fascism."[56]

Warhol's *Maos* were the reason for the subsequent great interest in the artist's portraits, which were to become his most important source of income from then on. His return to painting was much appreciated. The critic Douglas Crimp wrote that the artist had found an "unmachine-like painterliness": "... he has given us an image of Mao with such a brutal force that, however we formulated our mental picture of the Chinese leader a moment ago, he has supplanted it with his own."[57] Henry Geldzahler was enthusiastic about Warhol's choice of motif and remarked, "The irony that is obvious and front row centre in these images is the fact that they are produced cheaply to be sold dearly by an artist in the capitalistic capital of the world."[58]

An exhibition with *Mao* portraits was presented at the Musée Galliera in Paris in early 1974. According to a contemporary review, 136 works were shown, ten of which were drawings.[59] The exhibition was enabled by the involvement of Ileana Sonnabend, in whose gallery Warhol had already successfully exhibited. Sonnabend suggested that he design a *Mao Wallpaper* especially for the exhibition, as a leitmotif.[60] The artist took up the suggestion, as he had already designed his famous *Cow Wallpaper* for his second exhibition at the New York gallery belonging to her ex-husband Leo Castelli (they divorced in 1959) and had used it to decorate one of the back rooms.[61] Now Warhol created wallpaper consisting of a grid of identical Mao portraits, based on a drawing he had made the year before.[62] The reproduced

---

52
See the chapter
Companions, Courtiers, and Superstars
in Part 3.

53
Printz/King-Nero 2010,
pp. 176, 226.

54
McShine in
McShine 1989,
p. 19.

55
Bernd Klüser in a conversation with the author on April 30, 2010 in Munich (translated from the German). Dali on the other hand painted *Partial Hallucination. Six Apparitions of Lenin on a Grand Piano* in 1932, which can be regarded as a homage to Lenin. One year later he garnered the wrath of Breton when he painted *The Enigma of William Tell* showing Tell with Lenin's face as well as a grotesque elongated posterior.

56
In Goldsmith
2004, p. 239.

57
Quoted according to Printz/King-Nero 2010, p. 171.

58
Quoted according to Bockris 1989, p. 357.

59
Ibid., p. 182.

60
Ibid., p. 179.

61
See the chapter
Silver Clouds
in this part.

62
Feldman/
Schellmann
2003, II.125A.
+

drawing was given a color accent by printing a purple oval on Mao's face. This oval dominated the overall impression of the wallpaper that Warhol pasted onto the walls of the exhibition spaces.[63] The art critic Charles Stuckey wrote: "Installed edge to edge in uninterrupted horizontal rows, the paintings rivaled the decorative role of the wallpaper pattern. The wallpaper portraits dwarfed the smaller paintings and were themselves dwarfed by the larger ones. Altogether, 1,951 images of Mao loomed and receded as paintings and decoration in tandem orchestrated the gallery space."[64] The number of *Mao* portraits cannot be confirmed, as the French press mentioned as many as 1,900 or 2,000 heads.[65] Warhol himself, who was involved in putting his works up on the walls,[66] was delighted with the result, as Nicholas Haslam recalls: "I went to see the *Mao* show in Paris with John Richardson before it was hung—all these *Maos*. And Andy walked in and he said: 'Gee, these pictures are great. Who painted them?'"[67] When the French critics later asked Warhol why he had chosen Mao for his works, he answered that he had always been interested in fashion.[68]

Alongside the spectacular exhibition in Paris, in February 1974 ten *Mao* drawings were displayed at the Mayor Gallery in London. According to Warhol, he created drawings in "waiting periods," as "an exercise consisting of deliberate repetition and the gradual release of the hand."[69] It was the first exhibition since the 1950s to dedicate itself exclusively to Warhol's drawings.[70] The *London Times* attested: "it became clear that here was the most serious artist to have emerged anywhere since the war, and the most important American artist ... . Warhol is in some ways like Oscar Wilde. He hides a deep seriousness and commitment behind a front of frivolity. Compared with that of other American artists Warhol's view of America is bleak and uncomforting ... ."[71]

In a 1977 interview for the magazine *High Times*, Glenn O'Brien asked Warhol whether the Chinese party leader had ever seen one of the *Mao* portraits he had produced. Warhol replied,

I don't know. One of the big ones was shown in Washington at the Corcoran Gallery, and the director there told us that a delegation of Chinese was taking a tour of the place. They found out there was a big Mao *hanging there, so they went in through the back of the museum so they wouldn't see* Mao. *I guess they were worried about liking it or not liking it. It's all so different for them. We invited the Chinese ambassador to the Factory, but he never came.*[72]

Dalí reported in an interview for the Spanish newspaper *Tele/eXprès* at the beginning of August 1973 that he had given the Spanish ambassador gifts for Mao Zedong: "The ambassador Sanz Briz is taking my latest piece of jewelry with him to Beijing for Mao Zedong: a reproduction of the mummy of the Chinese princess who lived in the first century BC. He's also taking my illustrations of the *Little Red Book* and my combination of the faces of Mao and Marilyn Monroe with him. I am convinced that one can only cross the Great Wall of China through culture, and I can play an important role in this."[73] This is subject to correction, insofar as the "illustrations of the *Little Red Book*" must have been referring to the illustrated work *Poèmes de Mao Tse-tung* from the year 1967.[74] It is questionable whether the ambassador was

---

+ Ill. of drawing and wallpaper in Printz/King-Nero 2010, p. 223.

63 Excerpts from the exhibition at Musée Galliera, Paris, are depicted in ibid., pp. 180 and 254f.

64 Quoted according to Bockris 1989, p. 372.

65 Printz/King-Nero 2010, p. 521, fn. 44.

66 Ibid., p. 181.

67 Nicholas Haslam in a conversation with the author on July 20, 2012 in London. Victor Bockris reports that Warhol commented to Fred Hughes about the display: "Gee, these paintings are great." Hughes replied, "Now don't forget that you painted them." Cf. Bockris 1989, p. 372.

68 Printz/King-Nero 2010, p. 166.

69 Ibid., p. 172.

70 Ibid., pp. 171f., 182.

71 Quoted according to Bockris 1989, p. 372.

72 In Goldsmith 2004, p. 239.

73 In Calvo Serraller 2006, p. 1266 (translated from the Spanish).

74 Already at the end of February 1967, *Le Figaro* +

+
stated that the publisher Pierre Argillet would send Mao Zedong the five luxury editions of the work on traditional China paper. Cf. "Mao Tsé-toung illustré par Dalí."

75
King in Taylor 2008, p. 101.

76
Lear 1985, p. 248.

77
Calvo Serraller 2006, p. 1266.

78
In Bosquet 1969, p. 84. See also p. 76.

79
Warhol 1975, *Philosophy*, p. 116.

80
Marx in Bastian 1996, *I*, p. 9; cf. also Bastian 1996, *II*, pp. 20ff.

81
Dr. Erich Marx in a conversation with the author on April 13, 2011 in Berlin (translated from the German).

82
Hackett 1989, pp. 465ff.

83
Makos 2007, p. 6.

84
Hackett 1989, pp. 466f., November 1, 1982.

85
Ill. in Makos 2007, pp. 62ff.

86
Quoted according to ibid., p. 63.
+

really given the gifts mentioned by Dalí to take with him and whether these were in fact presented to Mao. According to another source, Dalí is supposed to have handed an advisor to U.S. president Nixon a copy of *Mao Marilyn* in 1972, in order to present it to Mao Zedong. When Nixon was admitted as a member of the Académie des Beaux-Arts in 1987, Robert Descharnes was given the opportunity to ask him about it and Nixon confirmed that *Mao Marilyn* was presented to Mao Zedong. Chairman Mao's reaction to the photomontage is not known.[75]

Amanda Lear reported that Dalí was invited to a palace in Beijing and was planning a journey to China with her. He had already envisaged the photomontage *Mao Marilyn* waving on the Great Wall of China.[76] In the accompanying text for the mentioned interview in *Tele/eXprés,* it also said that the surrealist had received an unexpected invitation to China.[77] However, Dalí never embarked on the journey. He hated traveling, as he emphasized in the mid-1960s: "Voyages are a bigger drag than anything else in the world. Thank God I don't have to go Yucatan or India. … I always stay in the same place: Venice, the Hôtel [Le] Meurice, Cadaqués, New York, and that's all! And from time to time I visit Lyon."[78] Interestingly, Warhol expressed a similarly negative opinion about travel. In his *Philosophy* he states, "I don't like to travel, because I really like slow time and for a plane you have to leave three or four hours ahead of time, so that's a day right there. If you really want your life to pass like a movie in front of you, just travel, you can forget your life."[79] In 1978 Warhol portrayed the German entrepreneur and art collector Erich Marx, who had purchased his first piece of art by Warhol shortly before that and in later years, according to his own statements, was able to purchase some of the best works by the artist from the 1960s, as well as a *Giant Mao*.[80] Marx reports on a stay of several days by the artist and his entourage in Berlin: "When they got into the car to drive to the airport, Warhol said: 'Always the same. We never know where we are flying to!'"[81]

Although Warhol was not keen on traveling, on October 27, 1982, he embarked on an eight-day journey to Hong Kong, accompanied by Fred Hughes and his girlfriend, the English aristocrat Natasha Grenfell, as well as the photographer Christopher Makos. It was a business trip. Warhol had been invited by Alfred Siu, a young industrialist from Hong Kong, to the opening of his nightclub "I" on the first floor of the Bank of America. Siu had commissioned portraits of Prince Charles and Princess Diana from Warhol. Further portraits Siu had envisaged were never realized.[82] Warhol was accompanied on the journey by a film crew appointed by the art dealer Jeffrey Deitch, which resulted in a twenty-nine-minute documentary about the journey.[83] From Hong Kong, they went on a three-day trip to Beijing, with excursions to the Great Wall of China and the Ming Tombs.[84] Mao Zedong had already died six years previously, but it was impossible to escape his presence. Warhol and Makos photographed each other on Tiananmen Square. In the background of the shots is Tiananmen Gate with a larger-than-life portrait of Mao hanging above it.[85] Warhol is said to have remarked before the photo shoot, "Gee it's big. Yeah, I painted Mao about four hundred times. I used to see how many I could do in a day."[86]

4

New York Salutes Dalí and Warhol

On the afternoon of November 14, 1934, the *Champlain*, with Salvador Dalí and Gala on board, docked in New York. Caresse Crosby accompanied the Dalís and provided valuable help when they stepped onto American soil for the first time. She explained to Dalí, "There are the gentlemen of the Press and they can take or leave you." Dalí understood straight away.[1] He did not leave his arrival in New York up to chance and together with the gallery owner Julien Levy, prepared the broadsheet "New York Salutes Me," which was distributed before he left the ship.[2] On the broadsheet, Dalí explained Surrealism, using André Breton's definition, and emphasized that he could now finally realize paintings that were "sufficiently lucid and appetizing" to be exhibited in New York. At the end of the text it said: "New York: why, did you erect my statue long ago, before I was born, higher than another, more desperate than another?"[3]

Dalí's arrival in New York sparked an avalanche of press reports. Newspapers covered the event and published interviews that he had given during an impromptu press conference in his hotel suite. The *New York Times* headline read: "SALVADOR DALÍ ARRIVES—Surrealist Painter Brings 25 of His Pictures for Show Here."[4] Not long after, *The American Weekly*, a Sunday newspaper supplement, presented three of his paintings and two of his illustrations for Lautréamont's *Les Chants de Maldoror* under the title "Written by a Madman—Illustrated by a 'Super-Realist.'"[5] Dalí went on to create numerous illustrations and design covers for the weekly.[6] These works are visions that take up aspects of American life. They were published in six full-page contributions, of which three were dedicated to the city of New York, under the titles: "New York as Seen by the 'Super-Realist' Artist, M. Dalí"; "How Super-Realist Dalí Saw Broadway"; and "Gangsterism and Goofy Visions of New York."[7] Cooperating with *The America Weekly* was a wise move as it gave Dalí the opportunity to reach a wide public that was not necessarily interested in art. The artist let his personal vision of America, which was still strongly influenced by American movies, flow into the contributions. He visualized his impressions of New York using his surrealist pictorial language. For example, a man finds a *Lobster Telephone*, or on Broadway a bald, bearded man greedily devours a lady's shoe, and of course, there is the obligatory soft watch. Also interesting in this regard is one drawing that was not used in *The American Weekly*. The work varies the motif of the nanny sitting on the beach at Port Lligat from the 1934 painting *The Weaning of Furniture-Nutrition*, with a bedside table cut out of her back. On the drawing it is no longer a bedside table, but the Statue of Liberty.[8]

In his *Secret Life*, Dalí reflects once again on the moment of his arrival in New York. He illustrated this passage with a little ink drawing. It bears the title *New-York?* and shows eight skyscrapers, offset in pairs, each taking on the silhouettes of the farmer couple in Millet's painting *The Angelus*. The skyscrapers are depicted with windows, which Dalí comments on in the text: "It looked like an immense Gothic Roquefort cheese. I love Roquefort, and I exclaimed, 'New York salutes me!'"[9] Elsewhere he says,

+
In this book Makos remarks in reply to the question of whether he had discussed Warhol's *Mao* paintings with him on Tiananmen Square (p. 83), "No. But we did feel special in Tiananmen Square standing in front of the big Mao painting."

1
Crosby 1953, p. 331.

2
Gibson 1997, p. 337.

3
Ill. in Abadie 1980, p. 41.

4
Gibson 1997, p. 337.

5
Ill. in *Salvador Dalí y las revistas*, no. 107.

6
Dalí designed the covers of the editions from November 7, 1937, January 9, 1938 and January 16, 1938. Ill. in Descharnes 1984, p. 156; *Salvador Dalí y las revistas*, no. 5, 6.

7
These contributions appeared in the editions of February 24, 1935; March 7, 1935; and May 19, 1935. Ill. in *Salvador Dalí y las revistas*, no. 108, 109, 112.

8
Ill. in Descharnes/ Néret 1993, no. 550.

9
Dalí 1942, p. 331.
+

4

The poetry of New York is old and violent as the world; it is the poetry that has always been. Its strength, like that of all other existing poetry, lies in the most gelatinous and paradoxical aspects of the delirious flesh of its own reality. Each evening the skyscrapers of New York assume the anthropomorphic shapes of multiple gigantic Millet's Angeluses of the tertiary period, motionless and ready to perform the sexual act and to devour one another, like swarms of praying mantes before copulation. It is the unspent sanguinary desire that illuminates them and makes all the central heating and the central poetry circulate within their ferruginous bone-structure of vegetable diplococcus.[10]

Dalí and Gala were permanent residents in the United States from 1940 to 1948, spending the summers in California and the winter months in New York, where they first resided at Hotel Saint Moritz and later at the St. Regis Hotel,[11] always reserving two suites, one of which Dalí used as his studio.[12] The St. Regis was also where he and Gala stayed in New York after 1948. Amanda Lear reports: "He spent a few months every winter there. It was usually after Christmas or just before Christmas and he would spend January, February, March until April. And in April, when it was St. Patrick's Day, then Dalí would say 'Now, I'm going back to Paris.'"[13] For the artist, New York was not only the ideal place to exhibit and take part in social life, but also to be inspired. The former model Nena Thurman, who met Dalí in 1963 in New York and became the artist's friend, recalls that the city held a great fascination for him: "Dalí was very vivacious and fun and he was very light. One thing he said to me for example: The reason he liked to come to New York and be in New York during the winters is because he loved the energy in New York. He said, 'The energy in New York is so thick with light and vibrancy you could cut it with a knife.'"[14]

In 1964 Dalí created several etchings of the New York cityscape.[15] The most interesting one is the work *Manhattan*, which shows the skyline of the metropolis from a bird's eye perspective, rising up from the mist and illuminated by rays of sunshine. A number of lines run parallel to each other with regular gaps between them. Peter Moore, Dalí's secretary at the time, reported later that in response to the question of what technique he had used here, Dalí had stated: "… Dalí has a special method which consists in using a fork!"[16]

When Andy Warhol came to New York for the first time in the summer of 1947 with Philip Pearlstein, nobody took any notice of him. Even when he moved to New York two years later he was not received like a star with a big press furor. Unlike Dalí, he had to work his way up the hard way as a completely unknown young commercial artist. In his *Philosophy* Warhol quite casually tells of this important event in his life.[17] Nonetheless, as his later works significantly reflect, the city of New York also held a great fascination for him.

In late 1962 Warhol created two large-format paintings of the Statue of Liberty.[18] The works are part of the *Optical Paintings* series in which he printed the motif in two colors slightly offset one on top of the other, mostly red and green, giving it structural depth when viewed through 3D glasses. The glasses, consisting of a cardboard frame with a red and a green lens, were in fashion at the time, especially for 3D movies. Several pairs of 3D glasses

+ Dalí had already transferred the farmer couple of the *The Angelus* to New York in the broadsheet *New York Salutes Me.* Cf. Abadie 1980, p. 41.

10 Ibid., p. 334.

11 See Mas Peinado 2004, p. 107.

12 A number of publications claim that the Dalís always reserved the same suite (e.g. Blume 2011, p. 18: suite 1610). The extensive correspondence addressed to Dalí at the St. Regis contradicts this. Sometimes Dalí stayed at the Presidential Suite. Cf. *Dalí et ses ateliers*, p. 53.

13 Amanda Lear in a telephone conversation with the author on March 13, 2010.

14 Nena Thurman in a telephone conversation with the author on July 11, 2012.

15 These are the works *Manhattan, Washington Gate, Plaza,* and *Statue of Liberty.* See Michler/Löpsinger 1994, nos. 112–115; Field 1996, original intaglio, 64–3.

16 Quoted according to Habarta 1988 (n.p.).

17 Warhol 1975, *Philosophy,* p. 22.

18 The formats are 77 5/8 × 80 3/4 inches and 80 × 61 inches. Cf. Frei/Printz 2002, no. 311, 312.

were found in Warhol's archive, but it is not known whether these had been intended for the *Optical Paintings*.[19] For the two *Statue of Liberty* paintings, Warhol used a souvenir postcard as a template.[20] The first painting shows the landmark twenty-four times, in four rows of six. The second painting presents the Statue of Liberty in four rows of four, with a third of the left edge of the painting recessed. The colors of the second work also differ from the first. Only the top row and the picture on the right in the second row are printed in both green and red. The other parts are in green.

The Statue of Liberty was restored from 1983 to 1986, on the occasion of its centenary. For the cover of his book *America*, which came onto the market in 1985, Warhol used a photo of the New York landmark with scaffolding. One year later he embarked on a new series of paintings of the Statue of Liberty. It was at just the right moment, because on July 5, 1986 the statue was re-opened with celebrations and fireworks, with U.S. president Ronald Reagan and French president François Mitterand in attendance. Parties were held all over New York during this "Liberty Weekend," which Warhol tells of in his diaries.[21] In his paintings he concentrates on the head of the Statue of Liberty, which is reminiscent of his portraits of celebrities, and indeed, Lady Liberty was the Star of the Year 1986. The works were presented from April 8 to May 30, 1986, thus even before the celebrations, at the Galerie Lavignes-Bastille in Paris, under the title "Andy Warhol—10 Statues of Liberty 1986." Paris was a suitable venue for the exhibition, because the Statue of Liberty had been a gift from France to the United States. As a reminder of these origins, Warhol added a signet of the French confectionery manufacturer Fabis to the bottom left of his paintings. It consisted of the inscription "Les bons biscuits FABIS," with a French and an American flag waving above it. Warhol used a camou-flage background for several paintings. As he had also started to concentrate on painting again at the time, there are both silkscreen and hand-painted versions.[22] The artist insisted on travelling to Paris to personally promote the exhibition. On April 12, 1986 he wrote in his diaries: "The dollar's gone down now in Paris so people are more interested in art. I had done the 10 Statues of Liberty thing ... ."[23]

Apart from the Statue of Liberty, other landmarks of the city also had star qualities for Warhol. In 1964 he shot the eight-hour movie *Empire*,[24] about which he remarked later in an interview: "In my other early movies there is just one scene with one star performing a very simple function—like the Empire State Building standing there all day."[25] Beginning in 1976, Warhol photographed further New York sights with his compact camera.[26] Some of these shots were included in his book *America*.[27] However, the majority of the photos pictured in the book show everyday life in the city, including demon-strators, a street parade, a couple in the park, policemen, a shoe cleaner, an older gentleman with a sign that says "Sotheby Cheats," a black worker, build-ing sites, street artists, a one-legged boy performing stunts with his crutches, and a break dancer. In the text, Warhol also expresses surprisingly critical words about life in New York:

The movies and TV like to separate everybody when they show New York, so you'll see a whole New York movie made up of rich people getting in and out

19
Frei/Printz 2002, p. 278. Patty (Oldenburg) Mucha, who was portrayed by Warhol with this technique, re-counted later that he had handed over his work with a pair of 3D glasses, but she found the paint-ing had a softer effect without the glasses. Cf. ibid.

20
Ibid. Ill. of the postcard p. 285.

21
Hackett 1989, p. 740, July 1 and 4, 1986.

22
Ill. of some versions of the painting in Blistène 1999, pp. 20ff. Warhol created further paintings of the Statue of Liberty in 1986, showing it as far as the waist. Ill. in The Andy Warhol Museum 2004, no. 350.

23
Hackett 1989, p. 724.

24
See the chapter **Filming with a Cam-era "Nailed to the Floor like Christ on the Cross"** in this part.

25
Warhol (1970) in Goldsmith 2004, p. 186.

26
See the chapter **Warhol Photographs Dalí** in this part.

27
Warhol 1985, pp. 130ff.

of limousines and spending their lives going to museums and eating lunches at stuffy restaurants. Or it's white and clean and middle-class, with these helpful upstairs neighbors who are always sweet and eccentric and cooking these "Old World" meals. Or it's a New York where criminals run the streets and every alley is filled with gangsters and everyone carries a gun or a switchblade and there's a murder every three minutes. Or maybe it's an "art" movie where the boys wear makeup and the girls have crew cuts and nobody has a personality like anyone you've ever met and everyone talks in this strange philosophic way and they're all sleeping with each other for no reason.

But the great thing is that all of this is true and in New York it's all happening at the same time.[28]

When *America* was published, Warhol himself had already become a New York institution and was just as famous as the star of his movie *Empire*. Nick Rhodes of Duran Duran, who met the artist for the first time in 1981, says of their first encounter:

A lady called Doreen D'Agostino [our press agent], who asked us, when we'd arrived in New York as excited teenagers from the U.K., "What would you like to do while you're in New York?" So, being slightly cheeky, I said, "Well, I'd like to go up the Empire State Building and meet Andy Warhol." These were the first things that came to my mind. They were two of the things that always looked appealing and exciting about New York. ... And so, to my great surprise, she said, "OK, then!" And I thought she was joking. ... The next morning she called us up. I was in my hotel, jet-lagged and sleeping and she said, "Well, will you be downstairs around mid-day?" And I said, "I thought it was your day off today?" And she said, "Well you asked to go up the Empire State Building and meet Andy Warhol so I've organized it. We're going to go to the Empire State Building first and then we're going to go over to the Factory to have lunch with Andy."[29]

Warhol had become famous not only through his art, but also through his constant presence at parties. The artist Suzan Etkin remarks, "Andy was involved, he was going to parties, he was meeting tons of people. He was definitely an insider: maybe *the* insider ... But also, I think he might have felt himself as an outsider, always looking in ... but he was inside and outside ... he could observe and participate."[30] Right before his death, together with Pat Hackett, Warhol completed *Andy Warhol's Party Book*, in which he talks about the best parties he went to and shares his experiences. The introduction states: "In the big cites like New York the party is essentially a mechanism for bringing together people who wouldn't otherwise be together, such as a wrestler and a sculptor."[31] Warhol never missed any important party in New York. Elsa Peretti, who arrived in New York in 1968 as a model, and became a successful jewelry designer, reports:

I first met Andy at a dinner, in Emily Staempfli's house. She always had a great mix of people. I noticed him sitting on a velvet sofa, a bordeaux color; he was very white and immobile, like a lizard.

Then, I met him often, because he was everywhere, a big part of New York, then of my group, and obviously part of my life. He was a voyeur, we always felt like performing for him and his camera. I remember he always used to say "OH GEE! ... This is greaaaaaaat!"

28
Ibid., pp. 132, 134.

29
Nick Rhodes in a conversation with the author on December 15, 2014 in London.

30
Suzan Etkin in a telephone conversation with the author on July 26, 2010. See also the chapter **The Extroverted Dalí and the Introverted Warhol** in Part 2.

31
Warhol/Hackett 1988, p. 8.

Some years later, I said to Andy, "Oh, I would like a portrait," and he said, "Of you?" And I said, "No, Andy, I really would like a portrait of you!" And he did it. It was his last self-portrait.[32]

In the 1970s Warhol was a regular guest at Studio 54, which opened in 1977 and became perhaps the most famous disco in the world. In *Andy Warhol's Exposures*, the artist states: "We've never had an earthquake in New York, but if we did, it would be at Studio 54. ... Studio 54 is the best thing that's happened to New York City."[33] Warhol's name soon became synonymous with New York nightlife. Nick Rhodes recalls:

I never imagined that Andy would become a friend. ... We used to go to dinners, go to the theater, hang out, go to parties, go to clubs, go to galleries together, go to artist's studios ... He was always wanting to do something and see something. He didn't see any point in staying in in the evening. ... [O]ne night when I was really tired, in New York, he said, "Oh, you've got to come to this, you've got to come to this, and you've got to come to that" and I said, "Andy, I can't. I've got too much tomorrow." I had a press day or something. And he said, "You are not going out?" And I said, "I don't think I can today." He said, "Well, if you don't go, you'll never know!" ... And the other thing he always said to me was: "If you don't like it you can always go home!" And I loved that enthusiasm. ... That was just the way he was. He had energy. He had an amazing energy.[34]

Coca-Cola is the Real Pop Art

Esquire magazine commissioned Salvador Dalí with an illustration for its Christmas edition in 1942. Dalí painted *Nativity of a New World*, which was reproduced in the volume on a fold-out color spread and referred to in the accompanying text as "a concept of the outcome of today's travail by the most discussed of all living painters."[1] The picture shows the arrival of the Three Kings at the manger in Bethlehem, but they come from American cultural circles, including a cowboy and a black man. Dalí made a sketch for the painting, which differs somewhat from the completed work. In the sketch, the Three Kings are represented in a rather classical manner and have laid down their gifts before the steps to the manger. Instead of gold, frankincense, and myrrh, the gifts include a telephone receiver and a Coca-Cola bottle.[2] This sketch was presumably the first work by Dalí to use the soft drink as a subject of his art.

One year later, in a room at the Del Monte Lodge Hotel in Pebble Beach, California, Dalí created the painting *Poetry of America – The Cosmic Athletes*. It shows the "obsessive images" that emerged for the artist during his years of American exile during World War II.[3] He wanted it to be understood as a "highly edifying" painting, in which he expresses his premonition of post–World War II racial unrest in America.[4] In the foreground are two male figures who symbolize American society. They are wearing football uniforms that are reminiscent of Italian renaissance costumes. The two players, a black man on the left and a white man on the right, face each other. The head of the white player is hollow, with a lit candle inside, and his arms are severed. The black player has a small male figure rising forth out of his back,

32
Elsa Peretti in a telephone conversation with the author on October 2, 2015.

33
Warhol/Colacello 1979, pp. 48, 53. See also the chapter **Addiction to fame** in Part 2.

34
Nick Rhodes in a conversation with the author on December 15, 2014 in London.

1
Swing 1942, p. 43.

2
Ill. in Descharnes/ Néret 1993, no. 803.

→ **24** [p. 378]

3
Descharnes 1976, p. 136.

4
Descharnes 1984, p. 257.

balancing an egg on his index finger, which represents the football. The black player, who stands for black America here, appears to be victorious. At the same time he refuses to acknowledge the white player, white America, who is showing him, according to Robert Descharnes, the "inevitable self-destruction of its white brother."[5] The scene is embedded in a landscape that bears references to Dalí's homeland, the Alt Empordà region, but also evokes the expanse of American desert regions. Dalí establishes a further link between his homeland and the New World: a clock is added to the mausoleum in the background, which resembles the "Molí de la Torre" on the property belonging to the Pichot family, friends of the Dalí's. From the clocks hangs the African continent, soft and melting, as if the artist wanted to warn of the decline of Africa. Robert Descharnes pointed out a detail that is attached to the nipple of the white rugby player by a thread: a Coca-Cola bottle. This is painted with photographic detail and dissolves from the bottom, transforming into a telephone receiver that melts into a black mass. For Dalí, the Coca-Cola bottle bore a premonitory aspect, as Descharnes wrote about the artist in 1973: "He pointed out to me recently that he had painted the bottle with photographic meticulousness nearly twenty years before Andy Warhol and the American Pop artists started to do the same thing. They were surprised to see this canvas by the Catalonian painter dated 1943 when they thought themselves to be the first ones to show an interest in this sort of anonymous and banal object."[6]

Dalí welcomed Pop Art in the 1960s because it turned away from the abstraction that he despised.[7] On the other hand, he also viewed Pop Art critically and only granted it "conséquences minimes" on its way to a new style of art:[8] "After Pop Art has passed, however, there *will* be coming a period of very objective painting in the style of Meissonier [a French academic painter of the late nineteenth century, popular for his photographic, highly detailed style]. This will not be sentimental, but classical painting. Of course, the Meissonier of tomorrow will not express the same reality as the Meissonier of yesterday. With the knowledge of our times he will create a new cosmology."[9] Dalí illustrated his hypothesis in the painting *Tuna Fishing* from 1966/67, which is the result of "forty years of passionate experiments in pictorial research." It brought together his various stylistic directions: Surrealism, "quintessential pompierism," pointillism, action painting, tachism, geometric abstraction, Pop Art, Op Art, and psychedelic art. Dalí referred to the large-format work bearing the subtitle *Homage to Meissonier* as the most ambitious picture he had ever painted.[10]

Despite his criticism of Pop Art, he liked to see himself as the "Father of Pop Art."[11] In his conversations with Charlton Lake, which led to the book *In Quest of Dalí* published in 1969, the artist recounts:

[P]eople are so tired of spots and splashes, they reach out for concrete images, but way out of context, and so we have the craze for Pop Art, in which an artist copies minutely a Coca Cola poster. But, as I said, in all those movements there is a little fragment of truth, however much it may be distorted. ...

... There are people like Arman and Roy Lichtenstein who seek to bring out the mystery of an object. Lichtenstein says, "I don't want anyone to feel the

5
Ibid.

6
Descharnes 1976, p. 136.

7
See the chapter **Culinary Delights** in this part.

8
Dalí 1967 (n.p.).

9
Dalí 1964, p. 46. See also Dalí in Lake 1969, pp. 26f.

10
Descharnes 1976, p. 162. The size is indicated here as 9'11" × 13'2".

11
See the chapter **Salvador Dalí— The Father of Pop Art?** in this part.

intervention of the artist in any way," and so he gets down on his knees before some anonymous machine-made object. That is the attitude of the absolute realist. Of course, when Vermeer painted his city of Delft, he didn't want to interfere in any way with things as they were. He wanted only to make a copy of what his eyes saw. He was in love with the city he was born in, and his act of love was to try to render exactly what he saw. The moral position of Roy Lichtenstein, although it's a caricature of that, is a true one and will have an elevating effect on others. The pure act of opening up his heart before reality, to fall in love with it—even if it is a Coca Cola poster—is something.[12]

Andy Warhol also associated Coca-Cola with Pop Art. Robert Heide reports that Warhol had once paid him and his partner John Gilman a visit. "There is a very heavy color litho on [a] metal outdoor advertising sign high on the wall in our apartment … it shows 'Betty the Coke Girl' and says 'Drink a Coca-Cola.' Andy commented on it one day saying 'That's the real Pop Art.'"[13]

Using advertisements as templates Warhol created two hand-painted Coca-Cola paintings in 1961. He did not copy them meticulously, but was deliberately casual in painting, letting the paint run.[14] In early 1962 he painted another version with an even coat of paint, which was therefore an almost faithful rendering of the advertisement. Warhol showed his works to the filmmaker Emile de Antonio. At the time, Warhol often invited him to his studio to pick his brain for ideas.[15] De Antonio later recalled: "He had painted two pictures of Coke bottles about six feet tall. One was just a pristine black and white Coke bottle. The other had a lot of abstract expressionist marks on it. I said, 'Come on, Andy, the abstract one is a piece of shit, the other one is remarkable—it's our society, it's who we are, it's absolutely beautiful and naked, and you ought to destroy the first one and show the other.'"[16] A couple of months later Warhol created a larger version of the painting favored by de Antonio, which differed only minimally from the smaller work.[17] Parallel to this, Warhol created the works *Close Cover Before Striking (Coca-Cola)* and *Close Cover Before Striking (Pepsi-Cola)*, which are based on matchboxes bearing Cola ads. He not only adopted the advertising graphics, but also the igniting strip, using sandpaper to imitate the surface structure. It should be noted that the representation of Pepsi-Cola advertisements was to remain an exception in Warhol's work.

A few weeks later Warhol started to make serial reproductions of Coca-Cola advertisements.[18] *Green Coca-Cola Bottles* shows 112 bottles of the drink, arranged in seven rows of up to sixteen bottles. Below these rows is a white strip with the famous red and undulating lettering "Coca-Cola." Since the bottles are arranged close together, they create a grid impression. However, on closer inspection one can see that this grid has irregularities. The reason for this is that Warhol initially painted the glass-green silhouettes and then printed the bottles on top. The bottles vary in terms of color application and tone. The technique used for printing the bottles is unknown. Warhol's assistant Nathan Gluck later remarked that the artist had used a balsa wood stamp,[19] but such a stamp was never found.[20] David Bourdon suggests that the irregular contours of the lettering on the bottles indicates the use of a

[12] In Lake 1969, pp. 45, 50.

[13] Robert Heide in a conversation with the author on December 6, 2012 in New York. In 1962, Warhol was asked in an interview what Coca-Cola meant for him, and he answered, "Pop." See Goldsmith 2004, p. 5.

[14] Frei/Printz 2002, no. 038, 039.
→ **25** [p. 379]

[15] De Antonio in Smith 1986, p. 293.

[16] In Bockris 1989, p. 136.

[17] Cf. Frei/Printz 2002, no. 082, 190.

[18] Frei/Printz 2002, no. 201ff.

[19] In Smith 1986, p. 321.

[20] Frei/Printz 2002, p. 182.

stencil, silkscreen, or a combination of the two.[21] While the painting *Green Coca-Cola Bottles* shows a frontal view of all the bottles, in the work *210 Coca-Cola Bottles* they are presented from a frontal view and also two different lateral views. There appears to be no system governing Warhol's choice of the three different views. The same applies to the intensity of the coloring. Apart from green, he also used brown to represent the bottles' contents. Some of the bottles create the impression of being full, while on others the coloring is so arbitrary that it evokes representations of shadows. Overall, the picture shows 210 Coca-Cola bottles presented in seven rows of thirty bottles. The canvas ends with a wide, white stripe at the bottom. It can be assumed that Warhol determined the number of Coca-Cola bottles based on the size of the canvas and thus did not attribute any particular significance to it.[22] In *POPism* the artist reports that he had intended to crop the canvas so that the bottles went as far as the edge of the frame. But then during a studio visit Robert Rauschenberg suggested that he leave a strip free at the edge if he wanted to show that he meant precisely this number of bottles and not an infinite number.[23]

As is well known, Billy Name was responsible for the design of the *Silver Factory*.[24] Nothing was safe from his silver foil and coatings, not even Coca-Cola bottles. Name recalls, "The Coca-Cola bottles were sitting in their yellow case in a corner of the Factory. I decided to spray the bottles silver … ."[25] The silver objects were displayed at the exhibition "The Museum of Merchandise," which the Fine Arts Committee of the Arts Council of Philadelphia YMHA organized in May 1967. The exhibition was based on a concept proposed by Marshall McLuhan: "Don't just put art in the environment—turn the environment into a work of art."[26] Warhol contributed three wooden crates with Coca-Cola bottles, which had been filled with the cheap perfume "Silver Lining" made by Cassell. This had also been Billy Name's idea: "… [I] suggested to Andy that we could fill them with a wholesale perfume and call it 'You're In' (urine) by Andy Warhol."[27] As it was specifically Coca-Cola bottles that Warhol had turned into perfume bottles, it caused trouble. The artist and the YMHA received letters from the Coca-Cola Company, advising them that the use of bottles for Coca-Cola was a flagrant infringement of trademark law.[28] As Warhol's perfume "You're In" came to an early end, very few bottles were sold. Furthermore, it cannot be determined precisely how many bottles were actually filled with the perfume.[29]

In *THE Philosophy of Andy Warhol*, Warhol writes that the notion of equality was intrinsic to American philosophy and explains this using the example of the consumption of Coca-Cola:

What's great about this country is that America started the tradition where the richest consumers buy essentially the same things as the poorest. You can be watching TV and see Coca-Cola, and you can know that the President drinks Coke, Liz Taylor drinks Coke, and just think, you can drink Coke, too. A Coke is a Coke and no amount of money can get you a better Coke than the one the bum on the corner is drinking. All the Cokes are the same and all the Cokes are good. Liz Taylor knows it, the President knows it, the bum knows it, and you know it.[30]

21
Bourdon 1989, p. 120.

22
Frei/Printz 2002, p. 188.

23
Warhol/Hackett 1980, p. 23.

24
See the chapter **Assistants, Employees, Secretaries, and Managers** in Part 3.

25
Billy Name in an e-mail to the author on August 9, 2010.

26
Frei/Printz/ King-Nero 2004, B, p. 280.

27
Billy Name in an e-mail to the author on August 9, 2010.

28
Scherman/Dalton 2009, p. 400; Frei/Printz/ King-Nero 2004, B, p. 408, Silver Objects, fn. 5. The letters to Warhol on May 18 and June 16, 1967 are in the archive of the Andy Warhol Museum, Pittsburgh, and were found in *Time Capsule 10*.

29
Frei/Printz/ King-Nero 2004, B, p. 280.

30
Warhol 1975 *Philosophy*, pp. 100f.
+

In March 1985 Warhol stood in front of the camera in Los Angeles for a commercial by the Coca-Cola Company. The artist was on the West Coast at the time, as he had allowed himself to be persuaded to appear in an episode of the TV series *The Love Boat*.[31] In *The Andy Warhol Diaries* it says:

Then they took me downtown to do the Diet Coke commercial. And there was a float and about eight ex-Miss Americas or Miss Universes and all the police were lusting after them, and I was wearing my Stephen Sprouse jacket. ... And I went and waited in my own private mobile trailer and I used the bathroom and that was fun, and then I guess the word the crew use for the actors is "talent" and so one girl opened the trailer door and said, "Where's the talent?" and she looked around and didn't see any I guess, so she left. I don't know, I guess she didn't recognize me. And we were on a big float with pansies. The girls sat on the pansies, and I had to say, "Diet Coke," and I drank it for the first time.[32]

Diarrhea of Dollars

Money played an important role for both Salvador Dalí and Andy Warhol— not just personally, but also in their art. Dalí loved pointing out at every opportunity that his business was flourishing. In the mid-1960s, talking about his regular stays in the United States, he said, "I live there now because I'm always in the middle of a cascade of checks that keep pouring in like diarrhea."[1] In his *Unspeakable Confessions* the artist dedicates an entire chapter to "How to Make Money."[2] The reader learns between the lines that the lack of money that Dalí and Gala suffered in the early 1930s influenced their later attitude to money. Dalí understood power, money, and gold as a "sovereign remedy" against fear.[3] Henry Geldzahler identified something similar with regard to Warhol: "He had been so traumatized by his impoverished youth that the speculative atmosphere in which he felt the New York art world was run inspired him with a fear that all could be lost 'in a minute,' as he liked to say, and that he could be left once again penniless and miserable."[4]

Dalí sometimes explained that he never knew whether he was rich or poor—he had no understanding of money as a means of payment. Luis Buñuel writes in his memoirs that already in his youth the painter forgot to take the change when paying.[5] Even later in life he had problems with this. Contemporary witnesses report that his inexperience led him to be extremely generous in taxis, often handing drivers hundreds of dollars.[6] Suzannah Fleming similarly explains:

Dalí loved money, but he didn't understand money. He really didn't understand. For example, whenever you'd take a taxi ride with him from the Plaza to the St. Regis—which is just around the corner—he wasn't confident with the fare. So it might be five dollars or ten dollars, but he didn't register what that was. So he would always give me a hundred dollar bill and I would pay the taxi driver. ... He would say to me "Dollars and le taxi arriving every day very mystery-ooooussssssly for Dalí." He explained that for him, the fare could be "one dollar or one-million dollares—is all the same for Dalí—is better for one beautiful Angel exactly one million."[7]

+
Similarly, also Warhol 1985, p. 22.

31
See the chapter **Dalí and Warhol as Actors** in this part.

32
Hackett 1989, p. 637, March 29, 1985.

1
In Bosquet 1969, p. 14.

2
Cf. Dalí 1976, pp. 160ff.

3
Ibid., pp. 168f.

4
In Geldzahler/ Rosenblum 1993, p. 18.

5
Buñuel 1984, p. 184.

6
Amanda Lear and Ultra Violet in "Reminiscences of Dalí: A Conversation with Amanda Lear and Ultra Violet," moderated by Dawn Ades, in Taylor 2008, p. 217; Moore 2009, p. 186.

7
Suzannah Fleming in a conversation with
+

4

Dalí's relationship with money also manifested itself in the decoration of his Teatre-Museu Dalí in Figueres, which he realized in the early 1970s. The ceiling fresco in the "Palace of Wind," the theater's former foyer, shows Dalí and Gala as giants supporting the celestial vault and bestowing spiritual and material showers of gold on the Alt Empordà region.[8] There is a representation of a naked woman with golden coins spilling down over her from the heavens. More golden coins are gushing out of her right leg and from a drawer appearing on her left thigh.[9] The 1973 documentary *Hello Dalí* by Bruce Gowers includes Dalí completing the ceiling fresco, and commenting:

Salvador Dalí, myself, is very rich, and Dalí love trrremendously money and gold, and Dalí sleep le *best after one day of work receive one tremendousss quantity of checksss, wis dollars and any kind of golden symbols, and sleep absolutely divine. Love gold. And* le *theme of this is one fluid, divine diarrhea of money, dollars and gold.*

Now every kind of money is le *more sa-tis-fac-torry for my brine (brain), and my brain every day becoming more cybernetic brain and plenty of golden printed cirqweets (circuits), electronic cirqweets. For dees* le *personality of Dalí is very clear is one cybernetic soft machine for create gold!*[10]

The Austrian painter Ernst Fuchs, with whom Dalí was on friendly terms, was of the opinion that gold was more important for Dalí than money: "Money was actually gold for him. He even represented it as such on the ceiling fresco at his Teatre-Museu Dalí. ... It's always shiny coins, never banknotes."[11]

Indeed, Dalí never painted banknotes, which were, however, present early on in Andy Warhol's work. In the 1950s Warhol created the drawing *One Million Dollar Bill*, showing a fantastical banknote with the portrait of a fantasy president wearing a monocle and the signature of the treasurer "Robert Paperbags." With the name "Paperbags," he was referring ironically to the fact that at the time he carried his works to art directors in paper bags rather than in a fine portfolio.[12] Around 1957 Warhol drew body studies of young men. He filled entire sketchbooks with drawings, many of them erotically charged.[13] A drawing from this time shows several one-dollar bills, some crumpled, strewn across the ground with a man's foot rising up above them.[14]

In the spring of 1962 Warhol created further drawings and his first paintings of dollar bills.[15] At the time he was experimenting with templates and seals, reproducing postage and trading stamps with them. Since it proved too difficult to make templates or stamps of banknotes and Warhol also did not feel like painting rows of money, he made drawings of the front and rear sides of a one-dollar bill and a two-dollar bill and had a printer make silkscreens of them. This was the moment that he discovered the silkscreen process for his work.[16] Many years later Warhol recalled in an interview, "The silkscreens were really an accident. The first one was the *Money* painting, but that was a silkscreen of a drawing."[17]

There are several anecdotes surrounding the creation of the *Dollar Bills* paintings. In *POPism* it says that one evening Warhol had asked several people for suggestions, until a female friend asked him, "Well, what do you love

---

+
the author on
July 20, 2012 in
London and
in an e-mail to
the author on
June 16, 2015.

8
Cf. Dalí 1971,
p. 176.

9
Ill. in
Descharnes/
Néret 1993,
no. 1382ff.

10
Quoted accord-
ing to Dalí 1975,
"Hello Dalí" (n.p.).

11
Prof. Ernst Fuchs
in a conversation
with the author
on May 14, 2010
in Klagenfurt
(translated from
the German).

12
Sometimes War-
hol also signed
drawings given
as gifts to friends
as "Andy Paper-
bag." Cf. Francis/
Koepplin 1999,
p. 39; Galster in
Smith 1986,
p. 304. Ill. of the
drawing in
Francis/Koepplin
1999, no. 138.

13
Bourdon 1989,
pp. 55f. Exam-
ples in Francis/
Koepplin 1999,
no. 142ff.
See also the
chapter **Large
Limousines**
in Part 2.

14
Ill. in Francis/
Koepplin 1999,
p. 39.

15
Ill. of some draw-
ings in Crone
1976, no. 251ff.

16
Gluck in Smith
1986, p. 315;
Bourdon 1989,
p. 106. The pre-
paratory draw-
ings are depict-
ed in Frei/Printz
2002, p. 146.

17
Warhol (1981) in
Goldsmith 2004,
p. 294.

most?" So he started painting money.[18] Elsewhere it states that Eleanor Ward, whose Stable Gallery is where the artist had his first exhibition in New York, whipped out her wallet during a visit to Warhol's studio, pulled out a two-dollar bill and said to him, "Andy, if you paint me this, I'll give you a show."[19] Ward, recalling this occasion explained: "I had given him my lucky two dollar bill to do a painting for the first show."[20] In view of the fact that Warhol was already doing drawings of banknotes in the 1950s, the truth of these anecdotes has to be relativized.[21]

The most impressive pictures from the *Dollar Bills* series include the large-format works *200 One Dollar Bills* and *192 One Dollar Bills*.[22] The banknotes are printed somewhat larger than the original templates and in the first work all the bills bear the round Treasury Department seal in blue on the right side, for which a second silkscreen was probably used.[23] While these pictures only present the front side of the bills, other pictures that Warhol produced at the time show both the front and the back. *Front and Back Dollar Bills* consists of two canvasses that form a diptych when hung up next to one another—the left canvas shows the front and the right one shows the back of forty one-dollar bills. The works *Two Dollar Bills (Front and Rear) [80 Two Dollar Bills (Front and Rear)]* and *Forty Two Dollar Bills (Fronts and Backs)*, on the other hand, present several rows of two-dollar bills. Each row has alternating depictions of just the front or the back. What all the depictions have in common is that a grid pattern determines the picture composition. The paintings *Many One Dollar Bills* and *One Dollar Bills* form an exception, whereby Warhol presents the bills in a wild jumble with a lot of overlapping, showing just the front of the banknotes.

Later, in his *Philosophy*, Warhol commented ironically on his *Dollar Bills* paintings: "I like money on the wall. Say you were going to buy a $200,000 painting. I think you should take that money, tie it up, and hang it on the wall. Then when someone visited you the first thing they would see is the money on the wall."[24] Just like Dalí in his *Unspeakable Confessions*, Warhol also devotes an entire chapter of his *Philosophy* entitled "Economics" to the subject of money. He writes, "I have a Fantasy about Money: I'm walking down the street and I hear somebody say—in a whisper—'There goes the richest person in the world.'"[25] Elsewhere he remarks, "I don't understand anything except GREEN BILLS. Not negotiable bonds, not personal checks, not Traveller's Checks."[26] Warhol's friend, the photographer Christopher Makos, later confirmed: "He never had credit cards; he carried cash. I think he liked it that way, because as a kid he'd never had any money. He didn't carry a wallet, but he always had crisp hundred-dollar notes somewhere on him in a neat brown envelope, and he'd whip them out when he wanted them."[27] Warhol also hoarded bundles of banknotes under the straw mattress of his bed. He explained to his life partner Jed Johnson, "You only feel as rich as the money you have in your pocket or under your mattress."[28]

In 1981 Warhol once again turned towards the subject of money. However, this time it was not about depicting banknotes, but the symbol for money—the dollar sign. He created paintings in different sizes, as well as some print editions on paper.[29] Although the paintings were produced using the

18 Warhol/Hackett 1980, p. 18. Warhol's assistant Ted Carey reported that it was the interior architect Muriel Latow who suggested during a visit to paint money: "The thing that means most to you and that you like more than anything else in the world is money. You should paint pictures of money." In Smith 1986, pp. 256f.

19 Warhol/Hackett 1980, p. 24. See also de Antonio, in Smith 1986, p. 295, as well as in Bockris 1989, p. 150.

20 In Smith 1986, p. 512.

21 Koepplin in Francis/Koepplin 1999, p. 40.

22 *200 One Dollar Bills* measures 80 1/4 × 92 1/4 inches and *192 One Dollar Bills* measures 95 1/4 × 74 1/4 inches, cf. Frei/Printz 2002, no. 125, 126.

23 Bourdon 1989, p. 108.

24 Warhol 1975, *Philosophy*, pp. 133f.

25 Ibid., p. 135.

26 Ibid., p. 129.

27 Makos 1988, p. 16.

28 Johnson also recalled: "One day, I asked him what he prayed for when he went to church. He said, 'Cash,' and I think he was serious …" In Aronson 1987, p. 194.

29 Prints in Feldman/ Schellmann 2003, II.274–286.

30
Bourdon 1989,
p. 384.

31
Ronnie Cutrone
in a telephone
conversation
with the author
on July 8, 2012;
Ingeborg Prin-
cess zu Schles-
wig-Holstein
in a conversation
with the author
on June 30, 2011
in Hamburg.

32
In O'Connor/Liu
1996, p. 70.

33
Ronnie Cutrone
in a telephone
conversation
with the author
on July 8, 2012.

34
In O'Connor/Liu
1996, p. 70.

35
Quoted accord-
ing to Ratcliff
1983, p. 94.

36
In McCabe/
Dalton 2003,
p. 38.

→
41/42
[pp. 390/391]

customary silkscreen process, they are based on hand drawings.[30] Warhol created various dollar signs: some are cursive, others are more curved, and others feature two vertical lines. The color scheme and composition of the paintings vary greatly. Dollar signs in a wide variety of colors and with shading appear individually or several times, in rows or layered, on a colored background. Warhol's assistants Ronnie Cutrone and Princess Ingeborg zu Schleswig-Holstein report that everyone hated these pictures at the time.[31] Cutrone later referred to them as "another variation of Warhol's love of money."[32] Cutrone was tasked with mounting the paintings for the exhibition at Leo Castelli, which opened at the beginning of 1982. At the time Warhol had also produced some paintings with knife and gun motifs. Cutrone recalled:

I called up Andy and I said, "Ok, all the paintings are down here at Castelli's. At what time do you think you'll come down?" So, he said, "Oh, Ronnie, I can't come down, could you do it?" And I said, "Well, you know, Andy, I'm great at installations but that's a big thing. Who approves them?" He said, "You know, I'll send Fred down there later." … So, I put together a show that I loved. It'd be two Guns, *three* Dollar Signs *and a* Knife. *Then it was* Dollar Sign, Dollar Sign, Dollar Sign, *then* Knife, Knife, Knife, Knife, Knife. *Then* Gun, Gun. *So it was all staggered around the room. And it was fairly big. So, Richard Serra comes into the room and he says, "Ronnie, this show is amazing. It looks like you walk in here and you get mugged." "Yes, Richard, that was the idea." … Leo Castelli comes in and goes, "Ronnie, this is beautiful. It's so beautiful the way you've done this." I say, "God, everybody is loving this. Thank you, thank you, thank you!" Fred walks in, dead drunk. And he comes in and he says, "You know what this show is? … Too European." And I said, "What the fuck does that mean too European?" And he said, "You know, it's serious and it's brooding." And I said, "Great, that's the way some art is supposed to be, don't you think?" "No, no, no, no, no." So, he puts up all the* Dollar Signs. *Now, I'm really angry so I go back and I say, "Andy, if you don't care enough about your work, I don't either. Fred's there, he's dead drunk, he's changed the whole show …" and he said, "Ronnie, please just let Fred do whatever he wants. He's been driving me crazy."*[33]

The exhibition, which displayed exclusively *Dollar Signs* paintings in the end, was a complete flop—not a single painting was sold. Ronnie Cutrone supposed that this would not have been the case if the *Knife* and *Gun* paintings had been displayed along with the *Dollar Signs*.[34] The critics also disapproved of the exhibition. In the April issue of the magazine *Artforum*, Thomas Lawson's review states: "Warhol's work has always been empty but now it seems empty-headed. Its great strength was to project nothing. … But that nothingness has now developed into something banal, unfortunately proving right all those critics who always hated Pop Art."[35]

Dollar signs also dominate the painting *The Apotheosis of the Dollar*, which Salvador Dalí completed in the year 1965. By coincidence, Warhol visited him in early 1965 at his studio in the St. Regis Hotel, where Dalí was working on the painting. The British photographer David McCabe, who captured the encounter between the two artists in numerous photos, reported that Dalí welcomed them with words such as, "Hello, welcome to my humble atelier for the fabrication of dollars."[36] *The Apotheosis of the Dollar* is a very complex and multilayered painting. The title Dalí chose provides a deciphering of the iconography: *Salvador Dalí Painting Gala, Taking Part in the Apotheosis of the Dollar in Which One Can Also See on the Left Marcel Duchamp Disguised as Louis XIV, Behind a Curtain in the Manner of Vermeer Which Happens Presently to Be the Disappearing but Monumental Face of Praxiteles' Hermes.*[37] José Nieto, the palace steward from *Las Meninas* by Velázquez is on the left side. Dalí stated as a reason for this: "Velázquez is a great precursor. And he is the precursor of my painting of the dollars. When you analyze the pattern of his brushstroke closely, you see that there are always two vertical lines and then a curved line. His vertical lines define the object, and the curved line rounds it off and creates the space around it. We might say that Velázquez was already painting the dollar sign at that time."[38] At the center of the painting are four pillars reaching up towards the sky, citing Bernini's winding bronze columns at the high altar of St. Peter's Basilica and displaying an S-shape or wave form, evoking the shape of the dollar sign. Two banners are wrapped around the pillars—the left one reading "Plus Ultra" and the right one "Non Plus Ultra." Behind the right pillar is a naked, androgynous Mercury with a caduceus. Dalí remarked:

First of all, I adore money. After Madame Dalí that is what I love the most, because I am mystic. In the Middle Ages the mystics were often alchemists, who tried to transform base metals into gold. Then, too, I am the incarnation of Mercury and also of Pollux, so I have the right, like them, to bear the caduceus. And that, when you analyze it, is the dollar sign: two parallel vertical columns with that sinuous inscription which is a reference to the serpent.

In Crete they represented the Dioscuri—Castor and Pollux—by two vertical bars bound together by a serpent, very much like the American dollar sign. And that is the true graphism of moiré: two vertical lines with a serpent between them—to put it in very simplified fashion.[39]

To the left behind the pillars are further Mercury personifications on Bernini columns, complemented by a naked female figure, somewhat closer to the viewer. Dollar signs proliferate between these columns, continuing towards the right. It is evident that Dalí's intention was to paint an altar devoted to the dollar. It is composed of a lined pattern that takes up the waved motif of the columns in various places. Works by the Op Art artist Bridget Riley may well have been the source of inspiration for this.[40]

The painting *The Apotheosis of the Dollar* is one of many examples of Dalí's provocative devotion to money. In his *Unspeakable Confessions* he states that his business flourished after this painting: "I was one of the kings of the world in terms of celebrity, rate of income, and the importance of my art and ideas. The rain of dollars was unabated. My chamberlain, Captain Moore, spent most of his time writing up contracts and laying out five-year plans of work for me."[41]

Car Crash

During their time in the United States between 1941 and 1948, Dalí and Gala spent the summers in California at the luxurious Del Monte Lodge

+
Details about this encounter in the chapter **The 1960s** in Part 5.

37
Dalí 1976, pp. 250f.

38
In Lake 1969, p. 49.

39
Ibid., p. 42.

40
Maur 1989, p. 370.

41
Dalí 1976, p. 251.

Hotel in Pebble Beach, which was also popular among celebrities from the movie business. Dalí had meanwhile achieved the same degree of fame as a movie star. Gala remarked at the time about their status at hotels: "Hotels are always happy to have us. Dalí makes publicity for a hotel. We do not ask for rates—they are given to us."[1] The couple resided at a special rate with an adjoining room converted into a studio that was free of charge. They met important personalities and were often invited to barbecues.[2] While among the rich and famous, Dalí got the idea of holding a benefit ball to raise funds for exiled European artists in the United States. He spoke to Alfred Barr, director of the Museum of Modern Art, who was enthusiastic about the idea. This was the start of the party "A Surrealist Night in an Enchanted Forest," which took place on September 2, 1941, in the Bali Room at the Del Monte Lodge Hotel. The invitation requested the following dress code from the guests: "you come in costume, preferably in a costume copied after your dream, or in a costume of a primitive animal or of the people of the forest."[3] More than 1,000 guests turned up,[4] including Hollywood stars such as Clark Gable, Bing Crosby, Edward G. Robinson, Bob Hope, Jackie Coogan, and Ginger Rogers. Gloria Vanderbilt, the Sanfords, the Winstons, and Alfred Hitchcock with his wife made the journey from the East Coast.[5] Dalí had transformed the ballroom into a surrealist setting with unusual props. The invited guests found themselves in a forest, for which countless pine trees had been set up. They sat at a long table together with store window mannequins wearing animal heads and dined on a menu with a first course served from a ladies' shoe. Gala sat enthroned on a giant bed that had been borrowed from the Warner Brothers Studios in Hollywood. She was dressed up as "Princess of the Forest," wearing a unicorn head with long blonde hair over her own. Dalí's costume consisted of an old anatomical medical chart with raised flaps, revealing the heart, the lungs, the liver, and other organs. He had sacks stuffed with newspaper hung from the ceiling, to create the impression of a grotto. In order to make the illusion perfect, he had even borrowed animals from the San Francisco Zoo, which were integrated into the scenery.[6] What was especially important for Dalí, however, was not the setting of a natural stage, but quite the contrary, a wrecked car, the significance of which he explained as follows:

In America people are always in automobile accidents, is it not so? We will have a wrecked automobile that is overturned. In it, we will have a nude model who lies there dead. From the automobile there will emerge two dancers—their bodies bandaged—and they will perform the dance of death.

When the guests walk in, it will be as if they had entered another world ... a dream world ... a world of fantasy.[7]

A wrecked Chevrolet was found in Monterey for a few dollars, which was set up opposite the bed.[8] As bookings for the party were being received continuously, the idea came up to remove the car wreck so that more tables could be set up for additional guests. However, Dalí categorically rejected this idea: "Nothing is to be moved. Nothing is to be touched."[9] Dalí had chosen a model a couple of days before.[10] A few hours before the party started, the naked young woman climbed into the wrecked car. In order to seem as

1
Quoted according to Cerwin 1966, p. 157.

2
Ibid., p. 159.

3
Briggs-Anderson 2012, pos. 128.

4
Ibid., pos. 290.

5
Ibid., pos. 444.

6
The number of props is indicated differently in different sources. Cf. ibid., pos. 140. According to Herbert Cerwin, Dalí's list included: "two thousand pine trees; four thousand gunny sacks; two tons of old newspapers; twenty-four animal heads; twenty-four store window mannequins; the largest bed available in Hollywood and two truckloads of squash, pumpkins, dried corn, melons, and other fruit." Cf. Cerwin 1966, p. 164.

7
Quoted according to ibid., p. 166. From the mid-1930s, Dali, who had no driver license, created paintings showing automobiles as geological fossils, overgrown by vegetation or in a state of metamorphosis. *Debris of an Automobile Giving Birth to a Blind Horse Biting a Telephone* +

8
Cerwin 1966, p. 167.

9
Quoted according to ibid., p. 174.

10
Ibid., pp. 172f.

genuinely dead as possible, she had taken a sedative, as suggested by the organizers. While she slept, parts of her body were covered with gigantic leaves, to shield her from curious onlookers.[11]

Furthermore, a dance duo had been hired for the *Dance of Death*. Shortly before the start of the event, a doctor arrived to work together with Dalí to prepare the dancers for the performance. They were bandaged and Dalí colored the gauze with red, to simulate the pair's injuries.[12] The guests were enthusiastic about the bloody *Dance of Death* and *Look* magazine later wrote: "Ballet about an auto wreck was the entertainment of the evening. ... Bloody and unbowed, the dance team of [Burt] Harger and [Charlotte] Maye emerges from the wrecked auto at one end of the room. Dalí, at least, had a wonderful time."[13] The extravagant event was a great success and once again brought Dalí nationwide publicity. A reporter remarked that the artist had "a flair for personal publicity that makes the late Barnum look like an amateur."[14]

When Alfred Barr asked in a letter about the financial support for the exiled artists, he was informed that due to the high expenditure, no money was left for the event's actual purpose. Herbert Cerwin, the Del Monte Lodge Hotel's public relations man at the time, writes in his memoirs: "We sent him a list of the props, including the evening slippers, and a breakdown of expenses. After that, we never again heard from Mr. Barr."[15]

Two decades later, Andy Warhol also created art around the *Car Crash* theme.[16] The works *Optical Car Crash* and *Green Car Crash* are part of the series *Optical Paintings* created at the end of 1962, in which Warhol experimented with a 3D effect and initially printed the motif in green or blue, then finally in red.[17] He used a photo as a template for both works and printed it a number of times closely together, creating a kind of visual grid on the canvasses.

One year later, Warhol's production of *Car Crash* works reached a peak. He was working at the time on the *Death and Disaster* series, dealing with catastrophes and accidents. In answer to the question of when he had started it, he remarked at the time in an interview, "I guess it was the big plane crash picture, the front page of a newspaper: 129 DIE. I was also painting the *Marilyns*. I realized that everything I was doing must have been Death. It was Christmas or Labour Day—a holiday—and every time you turned on the radio they said something like, '4 million are going to die.' That started it."[18] When questioned about the reason for the series he replied, "I believe in it. Did you see the *Esquirer* this week? It had 'The Wreck That Made Cops Cry'—a head cut in half, the arms and hands just lying there. It's sick, but I'm sure it happens all the time. I've met a lot of cops recently. They take pictures of everything, only it's almost impossible to get pictures from them."[19] Warhol found many of the templates for his images of misfortune in magazines such as *Newsweek*.[20] However, they were also provided by friends who had contacts at picture agencies and police photo archives.[21] He used three different templates for a series of fourteen paintings created at the beginning of 1963, known as *Early Serial Disasters*. The first is a newspaper photo showing a damaged car with a crumpled engine hood; the driver is hanging out of the

+
created in 1938 is an interesting example. In the same year, Dalí presented his *Rainy Taxi*, which actually had rainfall within it, at the "Exposition Internationale du Surréalisme" at the Galerie Beaux-Arts, Paris. See Aguer in Ades 2004, p. 495.

11
Ibid., p. 175; Briggs-Anderson 2012, pos. 337ff. with photos of the model in the car wreck.

12
Ibid., pos. 349ff.

13
Quoted according to ibid., pos. 353, 461.

14
Quoted according to Gibson 1997, p. 412.

15
Cerwin 1966, p. 177.

16
In 1962, *Harper's Bazaar* commissioned Warhol, who, like Dalí, had no driver license, to create a series of paintings of cars. Cf. Stavitsky 2011, pp. 15, 21ff. Twenty-four years later he created a series of paintings of (historic) Mercedes cars for Daimler-Benz AG. See Spies 1988, cat. 1ff.

17
See also the chapter **New York Salutes Dalí and Warhol** in this part, in which two *Statue of Liberty* paintings from the series are presented.

18
In Goldsmith 2004, p. 19.

19
In ibid., pp. 18f.

20
Bourdon in Smith 1986, p. 227.

21
Bourdon 1989, p. 142.

→
27 [p. 380]

opened passenger door. The second template is a UPI photo of an overturned Ford Customline.[22] The picture shows two dead bodies and three further victims lying injured under the car, hoping for help and rescue. The works based on this photo were later given the title *5 Deaths*, which is due to a misinterpretation of what happened.[23] Gerard Malanga, who assisted Warhol with making the paintings, later recalled, "When we were making the *5 Deaths* paintings, with the car upside down and the people underneath, Andy asked, 'Are they still alive?' as if the accident had actually occurred in front of us."[24] The source of the third template is also unknown. It shows a car whose left side has rammed against a tree and broken apart in the middle, causing the car door to fly open, revealing the driver's lifeless body to the viewer.[25] The templates were in black and white, but in Warhol's works they appear repeatedly on monochrome canvasses in the colors orange, red, turquoise, and silver. Some are conceived as a diptych, with the left canvas reflecting the photographic template, while the right is blank.[26] Gerard Malanga recalled that the works were perceived as "pretty shocking" at the time.[27] The use of light and joyful colors for the priming of the canvas was intended to take the "hard edge of death" and "darkness" out of the works, in order to make them less repulsive.[28] With the repetition of the images, Warhol also wanted to prove that viewers of an accidental death can be numbed and the grim details can dissolve into a "flamboyantly patterned abstraction"—"like a dress fabric," as he put it.[29]

In the mentioned interview, the artist explained the principle behind his series: "But when you see a gruesome picture over and over again, it doesn't really have any effect."[30] Three years later he relativized this in another interview and emphasized that the images were also suitable as a memorial to the unknown victims of the accident: "It's not that I feel sorry for them, it's just that people go by and it doesn't really matter to them that someone unknown was killed so I thought it would be nice for these unknown people to be remembered by those who, ordinarily, wouldn't think of them."[31]

A photo that Warhol discovered in *Newsweek* on June 3, 1963, served as a template for the *Burning Cars* series.[32] It shows a man who had been hurled out of an overturned and burning car and impaled on an iron bar protruding from a telegraph mast. Warhol primed one canvas in turquoise, as his only use of color. The image also recurs repeatedly in this series, but the canvasses have a blank space at the bottom. Gerard Malanga stated the reason for this as "bad mathematical calculations in terms of spacing" and added, "No canvas was ever stretched prior to our screening it. In some cases, it was already pre-cut. So, we had no idea that we were going to end up with that much space underneath. ... That's just an arbitrary thing. I mean, Andy didn't decide ahead of time that he was going to have that much space left over."[33]

Around the turn of the year 1963/64, Warhol produced a final series of images showing three car accidents. This time the artist only repeated the motifs two or four times per canvas, also avoiding the use of color, so that the viewer can concentrate better on the details of the dramatic scenes. For the work *Saturday Disaster* he used an unknown photo showing two accident

---

22
Stavitsky 2011, p. 44.

23
The caption reads: "Two Die in Collision. Los Angeles, Calif.: Three Survivors of a car-truck collision, pinned beneath their overturned automobile, wait to be freed by rescue squads here, June 17th. Two other passengers in the car, both sailors from the USS *Maddox* at San Diego, were killed." Cf. Frei/Printz 2002, p. 311.

24
Quoted according to *Andy Warhol: 5 Deaths*, p. 29.

25
Ill. of the known templates in Frei/Printz 2002, p. 329.

26
In summer 1963 Warhol created further variations on the *5 Deaths* series, which are small-format works that show the image of the dramatic accident just once.

27
In *Andy Warhol: 5 Deaths*, p. 24.

28
Gerard Malanga in a conversation with the author on July 2, 2012 in Hudson, NY.

29
Bourdon 1989, p. 143.

30
In Goldsmith 2004, p. 19.

31
Ibid., p. 94.

32
Frei/Printz 2002, p. 384.

33
In Smith 1986, pp. 398f.

victims who had been thrown out of a vehicle.[34] The work *Ambulance Disaster*, of which there are three versions, shows an accident victim whose upper body is hanging dramatically out of an ambulance. Warhol used a UPI photo as a template, whose caption reveals that in fact two ambulances on duty had collided and killed one of the injured who were on their way to hospital.[35] Finally, there is the shocking work with the title *Foot and Tire*, showing a shoe under the dual tires of an articulated truck. Upon closer inspection of the template, one can see that the severed foot is still in the shoe.

At the time that Warhol was working on his last *Disaster* series, Dalí also took up the subject again, this time in the form of a happening. Jonas Mekas later reported:

I actually met him in person in 1962 at my loft, which was also a Filmmakers' Co-operative office and a very busy place—a meeting ground for avant-garde experimental filmmakers, poets and musicians, where they projected their work and exchanged ideas.

One day Dalí came along with Ultra Violet and joined the crowd. He got interested in underground cinema (this was the term we used at the time) and in what we were doing, so I showed him some films. He was especially interested in Stan VanDerBeek. At the same time he decided he wanted to do some happenings/performances himself. He had met Peter Beard, who became a sort of manager of these semi-happenings, and I was asked to film a good number of them. ...

... Beard was always with the Vogue *magazine fashion crowd, so he provided willing models.*[36]

Vera von Lehndorff, known as Veruschka, was one of these models. Dalí realized a "shaving cream performance" with her, in which he covered her body with shaving cream, in order to create a living sculpture. The Warhol superstar Taylor Mead assisted him with this.[37] Von Lehndorff explains, "For Dalí, it was not so important that everything worked all the time. Others would say: I'm not happy with that yet, we have to do better. For him it was simply the action in itself that was interesting—squeezing shaving cream out onto a body lying there in a particular position. And that was it. Afterwards he was always pleased with everything."[38]

When Dalí held the *Major Accident* happening in December 1963 on 125th Street in snowy New York,[39] he was assisted by a different model: Nena Thurman, née von Schlebrügge. Thurman recalls,

It was a Sunday morning and I was luxuriating in bed, when the phone rang. It was Peter Beard, and he was most insistent that I get out of bed to meet him and Salvador Dalí for a special photo shoot. He explained that Veruschka, another top model at the time, had called in sick, and canceled the photo shoot. He had Salvador Dalí right there, and if I could please just do him this favor, they would come right over and pick me up in a car. I could not resist his plea and gave up my peaceful morning ...

When the car arrived I was ushered into the backseat next to Salvador Dalí and off we went. After an awkward silence, I leaned closer, pulled my dark glasses down, and said, as a way of explanation, "I'm very nearsighted"... (hence the dark prescription glasses). "Oh," he said, with a friendly smile "You are one

---

34
The back of the photo bears the note: "Mangled bodies of two victims in early morning crash. Body of 3rd is not yet seen in picture." Cf. Frei/Pintz 2002, p. 458; the photo is depicted on p. 464 as fig. 275.

35
The caption reads: "Chicago: Two ambulances, both returning from the same fatal accident, collided here early 1/9 injuring four of the ambulance men. Carol Czechowicz, 19, who was fatally injured in the accident in which two of her girl friends were seriously injured, was partly thrown from the ambulance carrying her to the hospital. She was pronounced dead on arrival." Cf. Frei/Printz 2002, p. 458; the photo is depicted on p. 464 as fig. 274.

36
Mekas 2007.

37
Taylor Mead reported in a telephone conversation with the author on June 2, 2010: "He sculpted the shaving cream a very Daliesque way. It was quite beautiful. But it got into the model's eyes and Veruschka began yelling, saying, 'My eyes are stinging.' So I removed the shaving cream from her eyes and Dalí said, 'You ruined my sculpture!'"

38
Vera von Lehndorff in a telephone conversation with the author on January 6, 2012 (translated from the German). See also Rohwer/Lehndorff 2011, pp. 130ff.

→
26 [p. 380]

39
Beard/Fahey 2008, *II*, p. 137.

of the blind people!" The ice was broken, and after that we became firm friends, for a number of years in NYC. ...

The photo shoot was about me looking like a car accident victim, draped on top of ... what looked like a banged up car wreck. Salvador was standing next to the car, his cane always in hand. To this day I can't say what the message of that was meant to be.[40]

Peter Beard documented the happening in photos and Jonas Mekas filmed it. Many years later Mekas commented:

We are talking about 1962–1963, when the golden age of the happening theater was already practically over. Nobody else took Dalí's happenings too seriously. There was nothing new in them. He was following others ... I was asking myself the question: why was he doing these performances? If you look at Claes Oldenburg, Allan Kaprow or Al Hansen's work, they have more spontaneity and freshness. Dalí's didn't have the same energy, but maybe by doing it he came closer to understanding what others were doing.[41]

However, with regard to Mekas's assessment, one should bear in mind that Dalí had already started much earlier, back in the 1930s, to stage spectacular actions—in other words, long before terms such as "happening" or "performance" had become commonplace. Therefore, one can refer to the speech at the opening of the London "International Surrealist Exhibition" in June 1936, which Dalí held in a diving suit as a metaphor for the subconscious that he wanted to immerse himself in, as a performance *avant la lettre*. The previously described *Dance of Death* during the "Surrealist Night in an Enchanted Forest" at the Del Monte Lodge Hotel in Pebble Beach is another example of this.[42]

In answer to the question of whether Warhol knew about Dalí's happenings/performances from the 1960s, Jonas Mekas remarks, "Andy was aware of them but he never was a part of them. I have never seen him with Dalí. I do not remember our talks about Dalí. But we must have talked about it."[43]

Mona Lisa in New York

The luxury liner SS *France* docked in New York harbor on December 19, 1962 with the world's most famous painting, Leonardo da Vinci's *Mona Lisa*, on board. The portrait, supposedly painted between 1503 and 1505 in Florence, portrays Lisa Gherardini, the wife of Florentine silk trader Francesco del Giocondo. The female form of his name led to the painting being known as *La Gioconda* (*La Joconde* in French). It is assumed that Leonardo never handed the portrait over to his client Francesco del Giocondo, but kept it for himself. Shortly before his death, he sold it to King Francis I, who collected Italian Renaissance works, thereby laying the foundations for the collection of paintings now exhibited at the Louvre in Paris. With the formal features of his half-length portrait, Leonardo referenced Florentine portraiture of the late fifteenth century. The Mona Lisa is sitting on a chair on a balcony that offers a view of an unfamiliar landscape. She turns partially towards the viewer, whom she looks at with a hint of a smile on her lips.

Margin notes:

[40] Nena Thurman in an e-mail to the author on September 21, 2011.

[41] In Mekas 2007.

[42] A list of further "ephemeralia, actions et performances" by Dalí in Martin/ Aguer/Bouhours/ Dufrêne 2012, pp. 47ff.

[43] Jonas Mekas in an e-mail to the author on July 31, 2011.

The *Mona Lisa* left Europe for the first time on December 14, 1962. Following U.S. President John F. Kennedy's and his wife Jacqueline's visit with French President Charles de Gaulle in 1961 to improve American-French relations, the French government felt obliged to send the painting overseas. The climate of rekindled friendship had prompted the idea of showing the *Mona Lisa* in the United States.[1] The media at the time provided detailed coverage of the painting's journey to the U.S.: from the press conference in which French journalists examined the watertight transport crate, through the painting's ride in a converted ambulance from New York to Washington, to its official reception on January 8, 1963, by the president, his wife, and vice-president Lyndon B. Johnson at the Washington National Gallery.[2] The painting was exhibited at the National Gallery from January 6 to February 3, 1963 and then from February 4 to March 4, 1963, at the Metropolitan Museum of Art in New York. More than 1.6 million people lined up at the museums to catch a glimpse of the *Mona Lisa*. The *New Yorker* magazine estimated that each visitor was granted a mere four seconds to do so.[3]

Before the first masses flocked to the painting in New York, Salvador Dalí staged an event involving several posters with a photomontage of the *Mona Lisa* by Philippe Halsman. Halsman had created this for the book *Dalí's Mustache* published in 1954. It shows a *Mona Lisa* counting coins, sporting Dalí's eyes and mustache.[4] On some of the posters, however, Dalí had had the face cut out. The event was captured on film by Jonas Mekas and in photographs by Peter Beard. Beard reports: "We got up at four in the morning and picketed the *Mona Lisa,* which had been brought to the Metropolitan, because Dalí just really wanted us to do it. And we had these *Mona Lisas* with the heads cut out and stuck our heads in. ... We were very obnoxious."[5] Dalí and his followers held up the posters with the *Mona Lisa*, let people put their faces in the holes, and picketed in front of the museum with further posters reading, for example, "Salvador DALÍ ON STRIKE against *MONA LISA*." It's obvious that the Spaniard tried to fight against the enormous attention the public paid Leonardo's famous painting.[6]

Dalí was given the opportunity to repeat the spectacle, alone, in an episode of the game show *I've Got a Secret* broadcast on February 25, 1963. He had been invited to present Leonardo's painting to the television public. The quizmaster Gary Moore opened a curtain, a poster of Halsman's *Mona Lisa* photomontage was behind it, again with the face cut out. Dalí stuck his face through the opening and proclaimed to the television public: "Only Salvador Dalí and Gala, Madame Dalí, know the significance and *le* tremendous tragical enigma of *Mona Lisa* de Leonardo da Vinci." Gary Moore added, "Maestro has just said 'I've got a secret.'" During the course of the show, Dalí was shown paintings that the panelists had made especially for this occasion. After a brief explanation by the respective creators, he evaluated the works consistently with "no comment." Dalí was then asked to paint a picture before a live camera. He used shaving cream, which he applied lavishly to the canvas, accentuated with a pressure spray gun after making the sign of the cross. When finished, the artist remarked, "Abstract!"[7] With this move he was once again making fun of the representatives of Abstract Expressionism.

---

1 Sassoon 2006, pp. 266f.

2 Ibid., pp. 267f., 294ff.

3 Ibid., p. 302.

4 On the subject of *Dalí's Mustache*, see the chapter **Mustache, Wig, and Other Signature Features** in Part 2.

5 Peter Beard in a Skype conversation with the author on September 24, 2010.

6 Scenes from Jonas Mekas' movie on http://jonasmekas.com/40/film.php?film=3 (last accessed on March 6, 2016).

7 *I've Got a Secret*, February 25, 1963.

4

The New York radio station WABC also took advantage of the *Mona Lisa* exhibition to launch a special program. Listeners were asked to send in their personal versions of Leonardo's masterpiece. Money prizes of $100 were offered for the largest, smallest, most artistic, and most humorous works.[8] Nat King Cole's version of the song "Mona Lisa" was played every hour to attract listeners to the competition. The promotion was a success—31,630 drawings arrived at the radio station.[9] Dalí had been persuaded to award the prizes, and did so on March 3, 1963. The event took place at the Polo Grounds Stadium in New York in order to accommodate the works, as some of those submitted were extremely large. A driving rain at the time, which soaked the exhibited artworks, did not stop Dalí from carrying out his job.[10]

Following the magazine *ARTnews'* coverage of the arrival of the *Mona Lisa* in the United States in its January 1963 edition, Dalí published "Why They Attack the Mona Lisa" in March of the same year. In his essay, he explains with reference to Sigmund Freud, why "a 'simple portrait' painted by the most complicated and ambiguous of all artists ... has had a power, unique in all art history, to provoke the most violent and different kinds of aggressions."[11] Freud had attempted to expose the endangered productivity and the repressed homosexuality of the Renaissance artist in his 1910 study *Leonardo da Vinci and a Memory of His Childhood*. The study focuses on Leonardo's oedipal relationship with his mother. The smile of the woman who sat as a model for *Mona Lisa* reminded him of his mother. In Dalí's essay he talks of "two main species of typical attacks upon *Mona Lisa's* archetypal presence." The first is "the ultra-intellectual aggressions, perpetrated by the Dada movement. Marcel Duchamp, in 1919, draws a mustache and goatee on a photograph of the *Mona Lisa*, and at the bottom he letters the famous inscription 'L.H.O.O.Q.' (*Elle a chaud au cul*)."[12] Dalí explains that this attack was

... a case of aggression by an artist against a masterpiece that embodies the maximum artistic idealization. It is explained by an insight of Freud whose sublime definition of the Hero is: "The man who revolts against the authority of the father and finally overcomes it." This definition is the antithesis of Dada which represented a culmination of the anti-heroic, anti-Nietzschean attitude to life. Dada seeks the anal, erogenous zone of the Mona Lisa, *and while accepting the "thermic agitation" of the Mother as a work-of-art, rebels against its idealization by masculinizing it. Dada paints the mustaches of the father on the* Mona Lisa *to enlist his aid in the denigration of the Art. In this gesture, the anti-artistic, anti-heroic, anti-glorification, and anti-sublime aspects of Dada are epitomized.*[13]

Thirty-five years after Duchamp, Dalí launched a similar attack on the *Mona Lisa*, together with Philippe Halsman. That is, the previously cited photomontage from the book *Dalí's Mustache*, showing her with the eyes and the mustache of Dalí. In the accompanying text, the painter explains that he sees "a paragon of beauty" when he looks at the *Mona Lisa*.[14] Philippe Halsman's daughter Irene says about the collaboration:

My father and Dalí were friends and collaborated for thirty-seven years. ... Sometimes they were like two schoolboys just having fun. They had a lot in common. They both had a good sense of humor. ... Both had a very good work

8
"It was 'smile time' at the Polo Grounds," p. 94; Fisher 2007, p. 72.

9
Martin/Bertran in Martin/Aguer/ Bouhours/ Dufrêne 2012, p. 54.

10
Fisher 2007, p. 72.

11
In Finkelstein 1998, p. 369.

12
Ibid.

13
Ibid., pp. 369f.; similarly, also in Dalí 1965, pp. 146f.

14
Dalí/Halsman 1954, p. 109.

→ **30** [p. 382]

ethic, they would start a project and finish it. My father was a perfectionist, as was Dalí, and both paid a lot of attention to details. I like the fact that there was never any competition. Philippe didn't want to be a painter, and Dalí didn't want to be a photographer. When Dalí had an idea for a picture he would tell Philippe, for instance: "Make me Mona Lisa." Then my father had to figure out how he would fulfill this challenge. He did everything pre-Photoshop, and people tell me—"before Photoshop there was Philippe Halsman." He did incredibly inventive things with … imagination and ingenuity—and especially liked doing them with Dalí … .[15]

Although it was Dalí's dream to equal the *Mona Lisa*, he also expressed certain reservations: "That is the trouble. Marcel Duchamp has already created a scandal by drawing a mustache on *Mona Lisa*. It would be plagiarism."[16] However, Halsman defended the project and promised to give *Mona Lisa* Dalí's striking eyes and big hands counting out money.[17] For the photo, he asked Dalí to assume the same pose as *Mona Lisa*. After that he cut the eyes and the mustache out of the photo and stuck them on a reproduction of the painting. Dalí and Halsman had planned from the beginning to replace the hands of *Mona Lisa* with Dalí's hairy hands, each holding a 10,000-dollar bill. The two 10,000-dollar bills were lent by the Bankers Trust Company and were brought by a courier with a revolver in a holster. Halsman photographed the banknotes in Dalí's hands. He sent the finished prints to the Secret Service Branch of the Treasury Department, in order to obtain reproduction permission. However, this was denied, on account of the fact that the photographic representation of bank notes was explicitly forbidden according to federal law, in order to prevent forgeries. Since Dalí had already left, the banknotes had to be replaced by coins and Dalí's hands by those of Halsman.[18] Only after American law allowed banknotes to be shown photographically was it possible to use the shot with him as *Mona Lisa* with the 10,000-dollar bills in his hands for a new edition of *Dalí's Mustache*.

Dalí describes the second "typical attack upon *Mona Lisa's* archetypal presence" in his essay "Why They Attack Mona Lisa" as "the primitive or naïve type of aggression, perpetrated by anonymous more-or-less Bolivians. It consists either of throwing a pebble at the picture or temporarily stealing it."[19] With regard to this, he refers to the case of the Bolivian painter Ugo Ungaza Villegas, who had hurled a stone at the *Mona Lisa* and had damaged the painting near her left elbow.[20] Dalí explains:

To explain the "naïve aggressions" against the Mona Lisa, *bearing in mind Freud's revelation of Leonardo's libido and subconscious erotic fantasies about his own mother, we need the genius of Michelangelo Antonioni (unique in the history of the cinema) to film the following sequence: a simple naïve son, subconsciously in love with his mother, ravaged by the Oedipus complex, visits a museum. For this naïve, more-or-less Bolivian son, the museum equals a public house, public rooms—in other words, a whorehouse, and the resemblance is reinforced by the profusion he finds there of erotic exhibits: nudes, shameless statues, Rubens. In the midst of all this carnal and libidinous promiscuity, the Oedipean son is stupefied to discover a portrait of his own mother, transfigured by the maximum female idealization. His own mother, here! And worse,*

15
Irene Halsman in a telephone conversation with the author on February 9, 2015.

16
Quoted according to Dalí/Halsman 1954, p. 121.

17
Ibid.

18
Ibid., p. 126.

19
In Finkelstein 1998, p. 369.

20
Sassoon 2006, p. 266.

his mother smiles ambiguously at him, which, in such surroundings, can only seem equivocal and outrageous. Attack is his one possible response to such a smile—or he can steal the painting to hide it piously from the scandal and shame of exposure in a public house.[21]

Dalí had already adopted Leonardo's *Mona Lisa* in a painting in 1934.[22] This same year he created *Imperial Monument to the Child-Woman*, which is considered the first major work in which the artist addresses his relationship with Gala. The "imperial monument" is a giant cliff formation, inspired by the Cap de Creus. This bizarre rocky landscape to the northeast of Cadaqués had fascinated him since his childhood. He was constantly discovering new figures and formations in it.[23] In the "imperial monument" one can also identify faces that express shame, as well as roaring lion's heads, hands, and naked female figures. Visible in a niche is Napoleon, Dalí's childhood hero, and right next to him in another niche, Leonardo's *Mona Lisa*.[24] Freud's Leonardo study had been published in Spanish for the first time earlier in the year that Dalí painted the picture, and it can be assumed that the painter had read it.[25] To the right of the monumental cliff structure, very close to the *Mona Lisa*, is the farming couple from the *The Angelus* by Jean-François Millet who appear regularly in Dalí's work beginning in 1932. In his book *The Tragic Myth of Millet's "Angelus"* written at that time, but first published in 1963, Dalí also establishes a connection between Leonardo's *Mona Lisa* and Millet's *The Angelus*. *The Angelus* painting had always held a fascination for him and in his book he explores this appeal in relation to Freud's study, according to which the painting contained hidden content: a representation of the Oedipus complex. The husband of the farming couple represented the male child's desire for his own mother and at the same time his fear of her. His hat concealed an erection, while the pitchfork stuck into the ground and the pushcart represent allusions to the sexual act. By choosing the attack on *The Angelus* by a "madman" at the Louvre in summer 1932 as a starting point, in his complex considerations Dalí also included Jean-Antoine Watteau's *The Embarkation for Cythera* in addition to Leonardo's *Mona Lisa*.[26] He elaborates:

Dr. Jacques Lacan, who was brought in to question the mentally sick man, obtained certain declarations from him that we consider "sensational." Indeed, the result of these declarations is that The Angelus, *in the mind of the author of the aggression in question is incontestably associated with* The Embarkation for Cythera. ... *The mentally ill man declared having had the intention of ruining the most famous painting in the museum. He had hesitated between the* Mona Lisa Gioconda, The Embarkation for Cythera *and* The Angelus *of Millet, and it was only after long doubts that he decided to attack the latter. The choice, among the works considered by him, of the* Mona Lisa *seems extremely comprehensible and coherent to us in view of the obsessive value of the picture: this value stemming from the well-known "mystery" of the* Mona Lisa *which, after all Freud has taught us about Leonardo, can only consist of the incestuous attraction that this work exercises over those with neurotic Oedipus complexes. For the latter it is quite clear that such a representation can only appear as the expression of the ideal type of desirable beauty which brings together all*

[21] In Finkelstein 1998, p. 370.

[22] The painting is often dated as 1929. Cf. Ades in Ades 2004, p. 222.

[23] Dalí 1976, p. 129.

[24] In *The Secret Life*, Dalí writes: "At the age of six I wanted to be a cook. At seven I wanted to be Napoleon. And my ambition has been growing steadily ever since." See Dalí 1942, p. 1.

[25] Dalí began reading Freud during his studies in Madrid, cf. Dalí 1942, p. 167. *Leonardo da Vinci and a Memory of His Childhood* was published together with *Totem and Taboo* in Spanish in *Obras Completas*, Biblioteca Nueva, Madrid, 1934.

[26] Dalí 1976, p. 156.

the most characteristic maternal attributes. The enigma which, through all the ages, is supposed to be hidden behind the smile of the Mona Lisa, *can only be identified with the enigma of the smile of the mother who becomes for all the sphinx questioned by every son about his own anguish.*[27]

Even in the run-up to the exhibition of the *Mona Lisa* in Washington and New York, the American public was swamped with reproductions of the painting. Television and other media reported extensively about the art event of the year. Around the turn of the year 1962/63 it was therefore impossible to avoid the *Mona Lisa.* Salvador Dalí was not alone in addressing the topic; Andy Warhol did so, too. The assumption is that Henry Geldzahler gave Warhol the idea to do a series of *Mona Lisa* silkscreens, and to use templates from a pamphlet published by the Metropolitan Museum of Art. At the time, Geldzahler was assistant curator of American twentieth-century art at the museum. As a thank you, Warhol gave him the painting *Four Mona Lisas*, which Geldzahler donated to the museum in 1965.[28] The artist used two reproductions from the aforementioned pamphlet for this work. In the upper half, the *Mona Lisa* appears twice in her entirety and in the lower half twice as an excerpt, concentrating on her face. Warhol had originally printed a third reproduction two times next to one another, showing only the hands of *Mona Lisa*, but this part of the canvas was later cut off and is now kept at the Andy Warhol Museum in Pittsburgh under the title *Mona Lisa's Hands.*[29] Warhol also created the silkscreen *Mona Lisa* showing Leonardo's work three times in a row, as well as two silkscreens that each bear the title *Double Mona Lisa.* One shows her face twice, side-by-side, while the other includes her face next to the complete image of her. Neither the composition nor the color scheme of Leonardo's painting was of interest to Warhol. What mattered to him were *Mona Lisa*'s fame and its media presence at the time.

The painting *Thirty Are Better Than One* shows five rows of six *Mona Lisas* printed next to one another with no gaps, forming a grid-like pattern, in a serial arrangement evoking a set of stamps. Looking more closely at the individual pictures, it is noticeable that the fine details of the original have disappeared—the light and dark contrast makes it difficult to see shades in between. Furthermore, many of the *Mona Lisas* are printed too dark or too light, or are blurred. As the working title reveals,[30] it is not about the quality of the original, but about unlimited repetition. At the time, Warhol had already begun experimenting with the silkscreen technique but had not yet achieved his later perfection.[31] Warhol's *Thirty Are Better Than One* went on to spark artistic and philosophical debate.[32] In this, Walter Benjamin's theory of the loss of aura, laid out in his 1935 essay *The Work of Art in the Age of Mechanical Reproduction,*[33] is exerted repeatedly. This theory will not be explained in any greater detail here, as Warhol did not take notice of philosophical approaches and they were certainly not the reason for his artistic confrontation with the *Mona Lisa.*

While for the aforementioned works Warhol used only black, in the painting *Colored Mona Lisa* he included yellow, red, and blue. Ivan C. Karp called it a quintessential pop painting: "cold, mechanical, tough, alien and bland."[34] In this work, the silkscreens appear randomly distributed across

27
Dalí 1986, p. 171.

28
In the museum documentation it says that the painting had been "made for Henry Geldzahler to commemorate the loan of the *Mona Lisa* to the Metropolitan Museum." Cf. Frei/Printz 2002, p. 293. The pamphlet is reproduced in Christie's 2015, pp. 77ff.

29
Frei/Printz 2002, p. 293

30
The title comes from a sticker by Ileana Sonnabend, who owned the painting, on the rear of the painting. Cf. ibid.

31
See also the chapter **The Ghost of Marilyn Monroe** in this part.

32
Bastian in Bastian 2002, pp. 30f.

33
Lüthy 1995, pp. 57ff.; Smith 1986, p. 174.

→
31 [p. 382]

34
Bockris 1989, p. 166.

the 126 × 82 ¼-inch canvas. In some cases they overlap or seem to be horizontal or upside down. Warhol used mainly the entire image shown in the painting; with only two detailed reproductions of the head and hands of the *Mona Lisa* in the lower quarter. He worked with the colors yellow, red, and blue only in the total views. It is questionable as to whether there was a purpose behind this "disorderly pattern."[35] Patrick S. Smith stipulates that the canvas was an "unadulterated accident," referring to Gerard Malanga, whom he interviewed in 1978.[36] At the time, Malanga called the work a "throw-away painting" and explained: "We had a piece of scarp painting on the floor—to get the excess paint off the screen. We put the screen on top of some piece of scarp and screened over it, and then we cleaned the screen. ... I guess it just happened to be sold, but I don't think that Andy intended that this was going to be something that he wanted to exhibit in this particular case."[37] Smith points out that Warhol and Malanga used, in addition to black, the colors yellow, red, and blue for the *Mona Lisa* series. Thus, it was necessary to clean the screen each time after completing a color variation.[38] At this point, it would be possible to object that there are no known color versions of the *Mona Lisa* from 1963.[39] David Bourdon thinks that Smith's theory is based on a misunderstanding and indicates that although some *Mona Lisas* are upside down or on their side, the figures are all arranged at right angles to each other. Evidently, care was given to avoiding any overlapping that would cover her face. Bourdon reaches the conclusion that *Colored Mona Lisa* is a "deliberately constructed painting."[40]

One and a half decades later, Warhol produced a second *Mona Lisa* series. The reason for this was rather commonplace, as his assistant Ronnie Cutrone recalled during the year of its creation. A customer wanted to purchase a *Mona Lisa* painting, which prompted Warhol to go into production.[41] The works from the year 1978 are slightly different to the works from the year 1963, as in the meantime Warhol had developed an expressive style for painting canvasses. The work *Four Mona Lisas* made in 1978 corresponds, in terms of its composition, almost exactly to the work of the same name from the year 1963, but the *Mona Lisas* now appear on an olive-colored background, painted cream white in the face and décolleté areas. On other paintings Warhol avoided this accentuation, with the *Mona Lisa* appearing to the viewer as though through a colorful veil of mist.

This "Warhol sfumato" is particularly evident on the works from the *Reversal* series created in 1979, in which the artist applied white *Mona Lisas* to a lightly painted canvas, with reversed color values. It is only upon closer inspection that one can recognize the silhouettes of the *Mona Lisa*. The most impressive work from this series is the 81½ × 425⅕-inch canvas *Sixty-three White Mona Lisas*. At first glance, only the expressively applied white paint of the representation dominates. Only upon second glance can one make out 36 *Mona Lisas* in three rows one below the other, of which not all are printed with reversed color values.

Warhol took up the *Mona Lisa* again in 1979 not only in the *Reversals* series, but also in the *Retrospective* series. Both series provide a "souvenir assortment of Warholian themes."[42] Many pictures in the *Retrospective*

Footnotes:

35 Osterwold in Felix 1993, p. 35.

36 Smith 1986, pp. 173f.

37 Ibid., p. 395.

38 Ibid., p. 173.

39 Cf. Frei/Printz 2002, no. 327–333.

40 Bourdon 1989, p. 162.

41 In Smith 1986, p. 287.

42 Bourdon 1989, p. 378.

series are based on overlapped blends of pictorial elements. Horst Weber von Beeren, who began assisting Warhol's printer Rupert Jasen Smith at the time, recalls that Warhol had given clear instructions regarding the arrangement of individual pictorial elements: "Overlap them! So they can't cut them apart and sell them separately!"[43] The work *Multicolored Retrospective* is an interesting example. A large-format, truncated *Flower* to the left corresponds with the *Mona Lisa, Marilyn,* and *Mao,* which all appear repeatedly. While *Marilyn* and *Mao* are interspersed across the canvas, the *Mona Lisa* appears a total of four times, arranged within a rectangle that delineates the borders of the picture at the top and bottom. The mentioned pictorial elements are printed as *Reversals* and are complemented by three *Campbell's Soup Cans,* which are also printed in blue, distributed across the canvas.

With the *Reversals* and *Retrospectives* series, Warhol provided a retrospective of his work from the 1960s and early 1970s.[44] It is noticeable that he included the *Mona Lisa* within his own treasure trove of motifs, independently of Leonardo, thereby appropriating it to a certain extent. As early as 1963 Warhol claimed in an interview with David Bourdon that he could not recall the name of the painter of the *Mona Lisa*: "You know, people have been comparing my soup cans to the *Mona Lisa* for so long now. 'How can you call this art?' they say. 'You can't paint as well as what's his name ... and your model isn't as pretty to begin with.'"[45]

Religious Art

In *The Secret Life of Salvador Dalí,* Dalí reports that his father was a self-confessed free thinker and, out of principle, did not raise him in the Christian tradition or send him to a Marist school, but instead, to a state school.[1] In his first year there, his teacher drilled into him that God did not exist and religion was "women's business." This concept became absolute truth for him at the time.[2] When Dalí went on to enter the circle of surrealists, he undertook—as he recorded in his *Diary of a Genius*—"the demonical and surrealist experiments of the first part of my life."[3] He was referring to the works he created from 1929 with an anticlerical pictorial language, in which he depicted his personal obsessive ideas. The paintings *The Lugubrious Game, The Font,* and *Profanation of the Host,* created between 1929 and 1930, form an early highlight, all showing a chalice and host. While in *The Lugubrious Game* the chalice and host appear next to an anus with a finger penetrating it, the painting *Profanation of the Host* shows a blood-imbued liquid, which could be sperm symbolized by saliva, running out of the mouth of the Great Masturbator into the chalice.[4] Dalí was emphatically neutral when, in *The Secret Life,* he later referred to the painting as "a painting of Catholic essence."[5] Noticeable is the extent to which the artist uses his autobiography to steer the public's perception of him with regard to religious matters. For example, he states: "For the unity of Europe will be made, and can only be made, under the sign of the triumph of Catholicism."[6] The Spaniard concludes his *Secret Life* by stating: "At this moment I do not yet have faith, and I fear I shall die without heaven."[7]

43
Quoted according to Horst Weber von Beeren in a conversation with the author on January 2, 2016 in Berlin.

44
Dalí's mural *The Dream of Venus* was created in 1939, and served as the background to the setting for his pavilion of the same name at the New York World's Fair. It was carried out by assistants, while Dalí added the main motifs, including soft watches, burning giraffes, and a drawer figure with a lobster. Cf. Maur, p. 274. See also the chapter **Infringing Artistic Freedom** in this part. Similarly to Warhol with his *Retrospectives* and *Reversals* series, Dalí resorted to his well-known repertoire of motifs.

45
In Goldsmith 2004, p. 11.

1
Dalí 1942, p. 36.

2
Dalí 1965, p. 6.

3
Ibid., p. 21.

4
For more detail with regard to this, see Gibson 1997, p. 282.

5
Dalí 1942, p. 308.

6
Ibid., p. 395.

7
Ibid., p. 400.

In *Diary of a Genius* published in the mid-1960s, Dalí proclaims that he found his faith again in 1949.[8] In the same year he painted *The Madonna of Port Lligat*, which he referred to in an interview at the time as his first religious painting.[9] He used Gala as his model for the Mother of God. The egg hanging by a thread from a shell over her head was inspired by Piero della Francesca's *Brera Madonna* (Montefeltro Altarpiece). In his 1948 book *50 Secrets of Magic Craftmanship,* Dalí examines the egg, which was "one of the greatest mysteries of the painting of Renaissance."[10] In 1984, Andy Warhol worked on the same subject as part of the print portfolio project "Details of Renaissance Paintings" initiated by Jörg Schellmann and Bernd Klüser. Warhol's prints show the egg hanging by a thread from the apsis shell.[11] Jörg Schellmann recalls, "We gave him the four pictures and the four excerpts. He asked, 'Have you not got any more famous pictures?' Whereupon we explained to him how famous they were in Europe and Andy was satisfied with that. ... Nobody found the fourth motif [Piero della Francesca] really suitable and none of us particularly liked Warhol's version. Therefore we did not make a print-run, but just trial proofs."[12]

In late November 1949 Dalí had the honor of being allowed to show his *Madonna of Port Lligat* to Pope Pius XII in a private audience, an encounter that lasted only a few minutes.[13] After this meeting, the painter apparently felt encouraged to take on a second, significantly larger version of the *Madonna of Port Lligat* the year after, as well as further religious paintings in the years that followed, some in monumental dimensions.

The question is whether Dalí had, in fact, reconciled with the Catholic Church in later years. In discussions with Alain Bosquet in the mid-1960s he remarked, "I rarely go to church, because I'm not a practicing Catholic. The only church I ever attend is the one in my little village of Cadaqués, and I do it only to set a good example for the people. ... I often cross myself on the forehead of others."[14] The journalist Manuel del Arco asked Dalí about his religious convictions in more detail back in 1951:

—*You say that you are a Catholic, yet I do not believe you to be entirely as God commands. Do you have any faith?*

—*Faith? No; but I hope to be able to reach it. I make an effort to achieve it; the practicing of it, the going to Mass, is like a way of obtaining it, a bother that I impose on myself. I lack the rational element of faith, which is the essential part for the Catholic believer.*

—*Do you think that to have or not to have faith is an involuntary matter?*

—*Exactly; if it would be voluntary I would have it, and in that case my faith would be overflowing. Cerebrally, intellectually, I am, but from the emotional point of view I am a skeptic; my intelligence brings me closer to God; my feelings continue full of skeptical residues.*[15]

Dalí's *Mystical Manifesto,* in which he attacks abstract art once again, was published a few months before this interview: "The two most subversive things that can happen to an ex-surrealist in 1951 are, first, to become a mystic; and second, to know how to draw. These two forms of vigor have just happened to me together and at the same time."[16] In the same year as the publication of this manifesto, Dalí met the Austrian artist Ernst Fuchs

---

8
Dalí 1965, p. 10.

9
In Calvo Serraller 2006, p. 160. In 1981, Warhol created a series of *Modern Madonna* drawings for which he photographed "actual" mother and child pairs. See Lüthy in Heymer 1999, pp. 5ff.

10
Dalí 1948, pp. 170ff.

11
Feldman/ Schellmann 2003, II.316A.

12
Jörg Schellmann in a conversation with the author on April 30, 2010 in Munich (translated from the German). The portfolios realized are "Sandro Botticelli, *Birth of Venus,* 1482," "Leonardo da Vinci, *The Annunciation,* 1472," and "Paolo Ucello, *St. George and the Dragon,* 1460." See Feldman/Schellmann 2003, II.316-327.

13
Arco 1984, p. 136.

14
In Bosquet 1969, p. 83.

15
In Arco 1984, p. 89.

16
In Finkelstein 1998, p. 363.

in Paris, who was then still unknown and spent nights in cafés because he had no money for decent accommodation.[17] Dalí soon recognized the young man's talent and praised his works enthusiastically: "You are the Dalí of the Germans, I am the Latin-Iberian Dürer."[18] He "ordered" the publisher of his *Mystical Manifesto* to help Fuchs.[19] A friendship developed between the two artists over the following years. Fuchs, for whom religion was an important source of inspiration, remembered Dalí "as a man who confessed to me over and over again with tears in his eyes, '*Je n'ai pas la fois. Je n'ai pas la fois. Je ne peux pas croire. Je suis damné.*'"[20] He also reported that he kept trying to strengthen Dalí's faith:

And I could even prove to him that he had faith by saying that a person who repeatedly calls himself a non-believer and is so serious about faith is re-deemed. He was so convinced that he was unworthy, that he had no faith, that he excused himself. ... Whenever Gala saw me she fled immediately. For her, I was the devil personified. Yes! Gala hated me because I gave Dalí this bee in his bonnet about religion. And she hated religion. ... She knew very well that I had brought him in contact with religion, like a virus. And she couldn't take it. She wanted to destroy this relationship through intrigue.[21]

Dalí's attitude to religion was influenced not only by colleagues, but also significantly by Gala. The jewelry designer Lee Brooks, whom Gala chose to accompany her one evening in 1974 in Paris, reports the following about one of their conversations: "I made the mistake of saying something about 'spirit.' And she looked at me and said, 'There is no such thing. There is only blood, bones, and gold.'"[22]

Religion consistently played an important role in the life of Andy Warhol and his family.[23] The Warholas were members of the Ruthene Church of the Byzantine-Slavic rite, which was united with the Roman-Catholic Church in the sixteenth century. Warhol's mother was a devout believer who attended Mass daily, sang in the choir, and often took her children with her to the St. John Chrysostom Church in Ruska Dolina (Rusyn Valley), Pittsburgh's Ruthene quarter. She made sure that Andy and his brothers said their prayers in the morning after getting up and in the evening before going to bed.[24] Even later, when Julia Warhola had moved in with her son Andy, she prayed with him before he left the house and looked favorably upon his regular church attendance.[25] In an interview published in 1966 in *Esquire*, she remarked: "Andy, he go to one o'clock mass at St. Paul's. He go every Sunday. He good religious boy."[26] Warhol's nephew Paul C. Warhola, who trained to become a priest, confirms his grandmother's and the family's religiousness:

I'm gonna say, my uncle had a high regard for the fact that I was going into the ministry, and of course, if you look at his early roots, my dad, my uncle, and my grandmother used to take him to the Eastern Byzantine Church. ... [I]t was probably maybe a two- or three-mile walk from their home. So, my uncle was brought up in the context of that religious setting and of course my grandmother had a very deep devotion and dedication to the Lord. She had her beautiful little corner at the house, in the basement, where it was like a little prayer corner and often we would see her there praying either in the morning or sometimes in the evening. ... I think certainly because of my grandmother's influence and growing

---

17
Habarta 2001, pp. 216f.

18
Fuchs 2001, p. 176 (translated from the German).

19
Habarta 2001, p. 217.

20
Prof. Ernst Fuchs in a conversation with the author on May 13, 2010 in Klagenfurt (translated from the German).

21
Ibid.

22
Lee Brooks in a conversation with the author on November 13, 2011 in San Francisco.

23
Paul Warhola in a conversation with the author on November 27, 2012 in Pittsburgh.

24
Bourdon 1989, p. 17.

25
James Warhola in a conversation with the author on December 2, 2012 in New York.

26
In Weinraub 1966, p. 101. See also the chapter **Muse and Mother** in Part 3.

up in that setting in Pittsburgh, my uncle really had a regard and a respect for spiritual things.[27]

Owing to his upbringing, Warhol was a devout Catholic throughout his life.[28] However, Warhol's "spiritual side" was known only to close friends, as Sir John Richardson remarked in his eulogy for the deceased artist at St. Patrick's Cathedral in New York on April 1, 1987.[29] The photographer Christopher Makos also emphasized that Warhol's faith was part of his private life: "In church he was Andrew Warhola and not the cool pop star Andy Warhol. I think it took a lot of pressure off him. It restored to him a perspective of the world that he had grown up with. In church he was the anonymous Catholic."[30] Warhol never commented in public about his religious views—not even in his autobiographical works. *The Andy Warhol Diaries* published posthumously are the only exception, and are valuable for gaining insight into the artist's "spiritual side." In these, he reports at times in detail about his church attendance. For example, on Easter Sunday of the year 1978: "Went to church. I took a peanut jar with me to get holy water and I spent a couple of hours doing that. You go in and you press a button and holy water comes out and you fill up your jar and take it home. It took another couple of hours to put it all over the house."[31]

For Warhol, church was a refuge where he could spend some time undisturbed. He sat in the pew right at the back when he attended mass.[32] In order to remain anonymous, he never went to confession or communion, as Dominican Father Matarazzo, prior of the St. Vincent Ferrer Church reported. He believed that Warhol "was bonding with a God and a Christ above and beyond the church."[33] Warhol evidently also found inner peace within the church. Catherine Hesketh, née Guinness, who started at *Interview* in 1975 and became friends with the artist, recalls that he was "a lot nicer and less cynical" after attending a church service.[34] "We'd always talk on the telephone, most evenings. But on Sunday evenings after he'd been to church he was very mellow, kind, and not so gossipy."[35]

Together with friends, Warhol also helped serve the homeless at the Church of Heavenly Rest on Fifth Avenue on major holidays, such as Christmas and Thanksgiving.[36] The parish priest later reported: "Andy poured coffee, served food, and helped clean up. He was a true friend to these friendless. He loved these nameless New Yorkers and they loved him back."[37] Perhaps Warhol was recalling the poverty of his childhood and youth. In his diaries he says, "And you see people with bad teeth and everything. And we're so used to all these beautiful perfect people. It's such a different world."[38]

In the early 1980s Warhol began capturing religious subjects in his work. With regard to this, Michael R. Taylor believes that his paraphrasing of Leonardo's *Last Supper* and Raphael's *Sistine Madonna* would have been inconceivable without Dalí's earlier variations on these works.[39] However, in contradiction to this, Warhol's group of works from the years 1985 and 1986 entitled *The Last Supper*, in the context of which the work *Raphael Madonna–$6.99* was created, was the result of a commission by the New York gallery owner Alexander Iolas.[40] In one of his last interviews, Warhol was asked why he had painted the *Last Supper*, to which he replied: "Because Iolas asked me

---

27
Paul C. Warhola in a telephone conversation with the author on June 28, 2013. He later decided to marry and leave the priesthood. "Once I began to mention to my uncle what I had in mind, I could see it, there was disappointment in his face and in the way he talked. He said 'Why do you want to do that?' ... And he tried to talk me out of it several times." Ibid.

28
Bourdon 1989, p. 403.

29
Richardson in Daggett Dillenberger 1998, p. 13.

30
Makos 1988, p. 53.

31
Hackett 1989, p. 120, March 26, 1978.

32
Bourdon 1989, p. 393.

33
In Daggett Dillenberger 1998, p. 33. In 1975, Warhol remarked in an interview with Lee Radziwill, "Well—I never feel that I do anything bad. But I do take communion sometimes." In Warhol 1975, "Lee," p. 5.

34
In Bockris 1989, p. 476.

35
Catherine Hesketh in a telephone conversation with the author on August 27, 2012.

36
Cf. Hackett 1989, p. 703, December 25, 1985, p. 777, November 27, 1986.

37
In Daggett Dillenberger 1998, p. 29.

38
Hackett 1989, p. 703, December 25, 1985.

39
Taylor in Ades 2004, p. 463. Taylor thinks that Warhol's *Raphael Madonna–$6.99* "... may have been inspired directly by Dalí's *Sistine Madonna*, since it takes as its point of departure a commercial reproduction of +

→ **33** [p. 383]

40
Thierolf in Schulz-Hoffmann 1998, pp. 23f.

to do the *Last Supper*. He got a gallery in front of the other *Last Supper*, and he asked three or four people to do *Last Suppers*."[41] The gallery mentioned was the Milan exhibition rooms at the Palazzo delle Stelline, right opposite the Dominican monastery Santa Maria delle Grazie, which has Leonardo's famous mural painting in its refectory. The Palazzo, formerly a monastery, then an alms house and orphanage, had been converted at the time into a bank, which still exists today. The decision was made to use the former refectory as an exhibition hall and Alexander Iolas was chosen to hold the first exhibition with Warhol's works based on Leonardo's *Last Supper*, which opened in January 1987 and was a success among the public.[42]

Dalí's version of the *Last Supper* was created in 1955. His painting was also the result of a commission. The American millionaire Chester Dale, a collector of French impressionism, had been so swept away by Dalí's work *Corpus Hypercubus,* completed the previous year, that he commissioned the work in question, which he went on to donate to the National Gallery of Art in Washington. The public was enthusiastic about the painting, but critics received it poorly.[43] The theologian Paul Tillich, who taught at Harvard University, called it "sentimental and trite" and found that Jesus looked like a "very good athlete on an American baseball team." Sherman Lee, director of the Cleveland Museum of Art, referred to Dalí's work as "the most overrated individual work" at an American museum. Originally in a room of its own, the museum directors felt obliged to hang the painting in a less prominent place because of this criticism.[44] A number of curators at the museum were disconcerted by the painting.[45] Dalí himself, however, viewed the many reproductions made of his *Last Supper* as a validation of his work. In discussions with Alain Bosquet, who also did not like the painting, the artist remarked:

According to the statistics, that painting you personally don't care for is the best seller of all modern paintings. There are more postcard reproductions of it than any da Vinci or Raphael. My strategy worked: At a certain point I decided to do paintings that would be more popular than anything in the world. My performance was marvelous. I would even go so far as to say that that painting is a thousand times better than all of Picasso's works put together. That one single painting![46]

The greatest challenge for Warhol when tackling Leonardo's *Last Supper* was to find suitable source material. Brigid Berlin recalls, "We'd go props shopping, because it could always be tax-deducted to gather ideas for doing *The Last Supper*. We'd buy the altars, any cards that I would see that looked like the *Last Supper*."[47] There were no pictures of Leonardo's work dating back to 1495–1497. Leonardo painted his *Last Supper* with tempera on plaster rather than using the fresco technique. This enabled him to work slower and devote himself intensively to representing the gestures and facial expressions of the individual figures, as well as to the light and shading. However, the decision to use the secco technique soon proved to be a mistake. Due to the prolonged humidity of the walls, the paint started to flake away from the plaster. Fine cracks were already appearing during Leonardo's lifetime and over time large areas of paint flaked off.

+ Raphael's altarpiece in Dresden, complete with its exceedingly low price-tag." Cf. Taylor in ibid., p. 389, fn. 4. This is incorrect, as Warhol did not use a commercial reproduction with a price tag as a template, as will be shown in the following.

41 In Goldsmith 2004, p. 385.

42 See Colacello 1990, pp. 486f.

43 See Cowles 1959, pp. 314f.; Secrest 1986, p. 216.

44 Ibid.

45 Gibson 1997, p. 488.

46 In Bosquet 1969, p. 15.

47 Brigid Berlin in a conversation with the author on December 4, 2012 in New York. See also Hackett 1989, p. 645, April 25, 1985, p. 662, July 10, 1985.

4

Based on a photograph of a nineteenth-century copy of Leonardo's *Last Supper*, Warhol created a series of silkscreens, some of which were of monumental size. The work *The Last Supper (Red)* measures 78 × 400 inches and *Sixty Last Suppers* measures 116 × 393 inches.[48] For many of the canvasses Warhol used only one color or none at all. In addition, there were works in which he decided to use a camouflage pattern. When asked about the reason for this he remarked ironically that he had had some camouflage material left over.[49] During the press conference for the opening of the exhibition, Warhol was also asked by a journalist: "What is your connection with Italian history and culture?" The artist answered provokingly with just one word, "Spaghetti."[50]

The Milan exhibition displayed only silkscreens. However, Warhol had also created an equally large number of handmade works as part of the *Last Supper* project. As a template for these he used an outline drawing of Leonardo's mural painting from the *Cyclopedia of Painters and Paintings* published in 1913 in New York.[51] These works focused entirely on the figures as subject, paying little attention to the spatial setting. Warhol set a counterpoint by integrating trademarks and advertisements, accentuated by a conspicuous color scheme.[52] As already mentioned, the painting *Raphael Madonna–$6.99* was created as part of this group of works; an outline drawing from the aforementioned encyclopedia served as source material here, too.[53] The most striking detail of the painting is the red price tag with a golden yellow "6⁹⁹," which was also used in some of the *Last Supper* paintings. It appears vertically in a prominent spot, right next to the Madonna with the child. The painting *Raphael Madonna–$6.99* also adorned the invitation containing the program for the memorial service at St. Patrick's Cathedral to mark Warhol's death.[54] The motif was once again a perfect choice. Vincent Fremont referred to Warhol's religious works over a decade later as "a kind of last will and testament," created during a period of intense activity, when the artist worked with fervor and was on a creative roll.[55]

Dalí's interpretation of the *Sistine Madonna* was also creative. In 1958, he completed the painting *Cosmic Madonna*, subtitled: *The cut end of Van Gogh's ear dematerializing itself from its frightful existentialism and pi-mesonically exploding in the dazzlement of Raphael's Sistine Madonna.*[56] Dalí reduced his depiction to the Madonna with the child. He dissected her into splintered particles, which dissolve her body and at the same time evoke the form of the cut end of Van Gogh's ear. The painting is an example of Dalí's "nuclear mysticism," the start of which he linked to the dropping of the nuclear bomb on Hiroshima on August 6, 1945, which shook him "seismically" and resulted in the nuclear becoming his "favorite food for thought."[57] After that the artist decided to tackle a pictorial solution to quantum theory and invented "quantified realism": "I plastically dematerialized matter, then spiritualized it in order to create energy. Each thing is a living being by virtue of the energy it contains and radiates, the density of the matter that makes it up."[58]

Another version, which Dalí also painted in 1958, bears the title of the original and is also known as *The Pope's Ear*. The starting point for this painting was the ear of Pope John XXIII in a photograph that had been published in the French magazine *Paris Match*. Dalí had the extract enlarged,

---

48
Cf. Daggett Dillenberger, pp. 107, 119.

49
In Goldsmith 2004, p. 383.

50
Morera in O'Connor/Liu 1996, p. 128.

51
Ill. in Schulz-Hoffmann 1998, p. 26.

52
In the painting *The Last Supper (Camel)* Warhol placed the trademark of the cigarette brand "Camel" between the apostles Philip and Matthew. However, he gave the animal a second hump and thereby turned the Arabian camel into a Bactrian camel. Ill. in ibid., cat. 12. Dalí had already taken up the cigarette brand "Camel" as a subject in the 1936 painting *Sun Table*.

→ **33** [p. 383]

53
Cf. Daggett Dillenberger 1998, p. 59.

54
Reproduced in ibid., p. 16.

55
Ibid., p. 38.

56
Fundació Gala-Salvador Dalí, cat. 746.

57
Dalí 1976, p. 216. In the case of Warhol, the involvement with the nuclear bomb explosion of August 6, 1945, is limited to the 1963 painting *Red Explosion (Atomic Bomb)*. It is part of the *Death and Disaster* series and shows the image of an atomic mushroom, printed repeatedly side-by-side in five rows.

58
Ibid., pp. 217f.

→ **32** [p. 383]

causing the pixels to become very prominent.[59] He transferred this enlargement onto the canvas and painted the Sistine Madonna with child as a bust portrait into the pixelated grid of the auricle. He then overlaid the composition with a gray moiré grid, using a stencil.[60] Dalí later described his work as follows: "Quasi-gray picture which, closely seen, is an abstract one; seen from six feet is the *Sistine Madonna* of Raphael; and from forty-five feet is the ear of an angel measuring five feet; which is painted with anti-matter; therefore with pure energy. Alchemist idea of the ear. Rabelaisian idea of birth through the ear."[61] It is no coincidence that Dalí chose an ear for his two versions of Raphael's *Sistine Madonna*. He was probably not only familiar with Rabelais's notion of being born out of an ear, but also with the traditional Christian teaching about the immaculate conception of Mary through her ear. Dalí painted the structure of the double helix of the DNA molecule onto the grid points of the papal earlobe, also a reference to the genetic principle of life. Two decades after creating his *Sistine Madonna*, Dalí commented on his work again: "With my moiréed canvases [sic], the microscopic texture of which contains three-dimensional images, I free the real from its terrifying vertigo by creating the gooseflesh of space-time which 'at all' can be or not be. In the same way, my *Sistine Madonna* is an ear made of antimatter or of the Virgin's face, depending on the stereoscopic effect."[62]

The painting was shown for the first time in April 1958 at the World's Fair in Brussels and at the end of the same year at the Carstairs Gallery in New York.[63] Dalí published his *Anti-Matter Manifesto* in the catalogue for the New York exhibition, explaining his motive as follows: "My ambition, still and always, is to integrate the experiments of modern art with the greater classical tradition. The latest microphysical structures of Klein, Mathieu and Tapié must be used anew to paint, because they are only what, in Velázquez's day, was the 'brush stroke,' about which the sublime poet Quevedo, already at that time, said that he painted with 'stains and distant spots.'"[64] However, Dalí's *Sistine Madonna* was scarcely noticed at first. This changed abruptly when the painting was displayed at the end of 1960 in an international Surrealism exhibition, "Surrealists' Intrusion in the Enchanters' Domain" at the D'Arcy Galleries in New York. André Breton, Marcel Duchamp, Édouard Jaguer, and José Pierre were the official organizers of the exhibition. Since Duchamp was the only one in New York, he was tasked with most of the preparations and decided also to present Dalí's *Sistine Madonna*.[65] Breton and his friends were furious about this, publishing a written protest in Paris entitled, "We Don't EAR It That Way," referring to Dalí as "Hitler's former apologist" and as "the fascist painter, the religious bigot, and the avowed racist, friend of Franco, who opened Spain as a drill-ground for the most abominable surge of barbarism the world has yet endured." It was illustrated with Gala's portrait from Dalí's painting *Assumpta Corpuscularia Lapislazulina*. As a reference to Duchamp's famous caricature of the *Mona Lisa*, Dalí's muse is wearing a mustache and under her hands folded in prayer it says, "*L.H.O.O.Q. (comme d'habitude),*" which can be read as follows: "*Elle a chaud au cul (comme d'habitude)*" ("She's feeling randy (as always)").[66] Dalí

59
Descharnes 1984, p. 355. Newspapers and magazines were often sources of inspiration for Dalí. On September 3, 1963, it says in his *Diary of a Genius*: "Today in the paper upside down, I see divine things moving at such a pace that I decide, in a sublime inspiration of Dalinian pop art, to have pieces of newspapers repainted containing esthetic treasures that are often worthy of Phidias." Dalí 1965, p. 219.

60
Maur 1989, p. 348.

61
In Descharnes 1972, p. 192.

62
Dalí 1976, p. 240.

63
Taylor in Ades 2004, p. 388.

64
In Finkelstein 1998, p. 367. Dalí is referring to a further painting that was shown at the exhibition, namely, *Velázquez Painting the Infanta Margarita with the Lights and Shadows of His Own Glory* (1958).

65
Polizzotti 1996, p. 880.

66
The protest is reproduced in Abadie 1980, p. 157.

took advantage of this written protest—he could not have wished for better publicity for his painting.

Dalí's *Sistine Madonna* is probably the "first halftone painting in art history."[67] In literature, the painting is repeatedly referred to as paving the way for Pop Art.[68] It is difficult to say to what extent it had a concrete influence on artists such as Roy Lichtenstein, Chuck Close, Richard Hamilton, Gerhard Richter, and Sigmar Polke. In 1966, when Pop Art became the leading form of artistic expression, Dalí provided a revealing explanation of why grid dots could conquer the art world: "... [I]t is because what they [the Americans] love most in the world are 'dots,' or bits of data, those information bits that symbolize the discontinuity of matter. It is for that reason that all today's Pop art is made up of information 'dots.'"[69] In the years that followed, Dalí used the grid technique frequently. One example is the *Portrait of My Dead Brother* created in 1963, which Jeff Koons called a "pre-Pop painting." Koons went on to remark: "It's like a Warhol silkscreen ahead of its time. I believe this style had a huge influence on many artists. For example, right now computer graphics seem to be based on his vision—with image gradation, geometric pixilation and morphing. The world today is viewed through Dalí's vision."[70] However, a year before the painting was made, Warhol had already started to produce silkscreen portraits of Marilyn Monroe, Elvis Presley, and other stars. Even so, one can agree with Koons that Dalí had an influence on other artists, after all, his first painting to use a grid technique, the *Sistine Madonna*, was created already in 1958.

A few years before creating his interpretations of the *Sistine Madonna*, Dalí had painted representations of crosses. In *Diary of a Genius* he refers to himself as "a specialist in crosses (the greatest who has ever existed)."[71] In 1951 he created the painting *Christ of St. John of the Cross*, inspired by a drawing of the crucifixion by Saint John. For his Christ, Dalí chose not to depict the crown of thorns, nails, and stigmata, in order to visualize his postulate of "beauty and joy" that he had set out in his *Mystical Manifesto*.[72] The source material for his painting was a photo on which the Hollywood stuntman Russ Saunders, who had been introduced to him by the movie producer Jack Warner, takes the place of the crucified.[73] Enlarged prints were made of this shot, ranging to the format of the planned painting, which Dalí also showed to his architect Emilio Puignau, whom he had appointed after his return to Spain to carry out a range of conversion works on his house in Port Lligat. Dalí asked him to make a true to scale drawing of the cross, which was then transferred onto the canvas.[74]

Puignau also assisted Dalí with the painting *Nuclear Cross*, which was completed in 1952.[75] It shows a cross shape composed of little golden cubes, floating over an altar stone. In the middle of the cross is a Eucharist bread in the form of a circle. In the painting *Arithmosophic Cross* created in the same year, Dalí presents a cross, which is also floating above an altar, composed of six wooden cubes, surrounded by a gloriole of elongated golden ashlars. Together with the painting *Corpus Hypercubus* created in 1954, the two paintings form a pair, for which Dalí found his inspiration in the *Treatise in Cubic Form* by Juan de Herrera.[76] As he explained, *Corpus Hypercubus*

67
Maur 1989,
p. 348.

68
Dehmer in
Henning 2012,
p. 108; King in
King/Brenneman
2010, p. 41.

69
In Descharnes
1976, p. 136.

70
Koons 2005.

71
Dalí 1965, p. 139.

72
Dalí writes here:
"I want my next
Christ to be a
painting contain-
ing more beauty
and joy than any-
thing that will
have been paint-
ed up to the
present. I want
to paint a Christ
that will be the
absolute con-
trary in every re-
spect to the
materialist and
savagely anti-
mystical Christ
of Grünewald!"
Finkelstein 1998,
pp. 365f.

73
Descharnes
1984, p. 318;
Gibson 1997;
p. 463.

74
Details in
Puignau 1995,
pp. 59ff.

75
Ibid., pp. 62f.

76
King in Ades
2004, p. 364.

... is based entirely on the Treatise in Cubic Form *by Juan de Herrera, Philip II's architect, builder of the Escorial Palace; it is a treatise inspired by* Ars Magna *of the Catalonian philosopher and alchemist, Raymond Lulle. The cross is formed by an octahedral hypercube. The number nine is identifiable and becomes especially consubstantial with the body of Christ. The extremely noble figure of Gala is the perfect union of the development of the hypercubic octahedron on the human level of the cube. She is depicted in front of the Bay of Port Lligat. The most noble beings were painted by Velázquez and Zurbarán; I only approach nobility while painting Gala, and nobility can only be inspired by the human being.*[77]

Although Dalí's *Corpus Hypercubus* was poorly received by art critics and cast off as "irrelevant kitsch," as already mentioned, the collector Chester Dale was enthusiastic when he saw the work for the first time in 1954. It is said that he purchased the painting at the time for $15,000. The very same year he donated it to the Metropolitan Museum of Art in New York, where it hung in the big entrance hall. The title was changed to *Crucifixion* in order to make the subject matter more accessible to the general public. In a press release, the painting was then referred to as an "outstanding modern religious painting, very serious, with few surrealist eccentricities."[78] Dalí was also allowed to express himself and said the following about his painting: "Juan Gris created beautiful cubism and Picasso continued it. Now myself has created one complete hypercubist painting."[79]

More than twenty years later, Dalí once again had the opportunity to dedicate himself to the hypercubus when, in 1975, he met the mathematics professor Thomas Banchoff who was teaching at Brown University in Providence, Rhode Island. In the years that followed a lively exchange of ideas ensued between the painter and the academic, who specialized in differential geometry of higher dimensions.[80] Banchoff recounts the circumstances of his first encounter with Dalí as follows:

I first met Salvador Dalí in New York City in the spring of 1975. In January I had given a mathematical lecture in Washington DC about computer graphics and the fourth dimension and I was interviewed by Tom Zito, a reporter for the Washington Post *newspaper. His story appeared the next morning on the first page of the Style section of the paper, together with a picture of me holding my flexible cardboard model of the unfolded hypercube, the central figure of Dalí's 1954 Corpus Hypercubicus. In the background was a copy of Dalí's painting. I recall telling my computer graphics colleague Charles Strauss back at Brown University that I was a bit concerned because I knew that the reporter had not had time to get permission for the reproduction of the picture.*

A few weeks later, when I returned from teaching a class, I found a note saying that I had received a call from a person in New York "representing Salvador Dalí." ... I called the number and a woman answered who said she was Dalí's appointments secretary while he was in New York City. His clipping service had sent him a copy of the Washington Post *article and he wanted to meet us in New York. I asked Charles and he said, "It's either a hoax or a lawsuit, but the worst we can get out of it is a good story." We did go down from Providence, Rhode Island, to New York, and we got not just one but a whole series of good stories.*

---

[77]
Quoted according to Descharnes 1976, p. 154. Raymond Lulle is also referred to later in this book as Ramon Llull.

[78]
Taylor in Ades 2004, p. 371.

[79]
Quoted according to ibid.

[80]
Banchoff 1990, pp. 105ff.

4

When we first met Dalí, he was more or less holding court in the cocktail lounge of the St. Regis Hotel, where I learned he would ... rent two suites, one for him and his wife Gala to live in and one that he would use as a studio for his current paintings. There were all sorts of people who would come to the lounge to meet him. Some were rather flamboyant artists or fashion designers or dancers, who greeted Dalí in various languages, English, French, or Catalan. He would direct them to seats in a large circle in front of him, and Charles and I were given seats of honor next to him, as something like "ambassadors from mathematics land." Dalí had just completed a series of works on process holograms on cylinders that would appear to move as you walked around them. Someone asked about a possible holomorphic film and I was impressed that Dalí's answer was very well informed. His next project, he explained, was stereoscopic oil paintings and he wanted to talk about mechanisms for presenting and viewing them. He was very interested in a set of stereo slides that he could observe using a small plastic viewer. He also seemed quite fascinated by the flexible polyhedral model that was featured in the Washington Post *article. He liked to manipulate it and at one point he said, "I may have this." It wasn't exactly a question. He explained that he wanted to create a special exhibit for the model in his new museum in Spain, in Figueres near Cadaqués, the place where he was born. I agreed and gave him the model.*

Since he was asking us for our technological opinions, I thought that this was an opportunity to ask him about the background to his famous painting. "Metaphysics!" he answered, and when I asked again, he mentioned a name that I did not catch the first time but which I then realized was "Ramon Llull." I was surprised to hear the name because I had just read a geometric work by that mystic and polymath. I had been sitting in on a history course in the Religious Studies Department at Brown University on "The History of the Church in the Twelfth and Thirteenth Centuries in Spain and Italy" and I became interested in his geometric speculations. Dalí was excited to learn that I knew about Llull. He said he was inspired by Llull's two-dimensional work on square arrays, and the follow-up three-dimensional interpretation by a disciple of Llull several centuries later, Juan de Herrera, the architect of El Escorial and author of a book on the cubic form. Now, several centuries later, Salvador Dalí, another Catalonian, had taken these ideas to the fourth dimension.

We continued to talk about stereoscopic images and he was particularly interested in our recent work in computer generated stereoscopic films of objects in a fourth spatial dimension. He asked us to come back in two weeks to show him some examples and to meet A. Reynolds and Eleanor Morse, owners of a large collection of Dalí's work. ... We looked at the films in Dalí's suite at the St. Regis and I met Gala for the first time. She said that she did not believe that the fourth dimension was real and she seemed skeptical when I claimed that the images were real projections of objects that could be built in a fourth dimension.

About once a year for the next ten years I would receive a call from Dalí inviting me to bring our latest images and to see what he was working on. We met at least six times in New York, once in Paris, and three times in Spain. I got the chance to see several of his paintings while they were in process, and I learned more about his techniques. Although in public his speech and actions seemed

264

showy and exaggerated, even outrageous, when he wanted to understand some-thing, he was very intent. The emphasis was on communication, and if one of us did not understand, things were repeated until they were clear. In one of our last meetings, in Púbol where Dalí retired after Gala died, once again he wanted to see some of the computer animations. He would exclaim that something was marvelous, especially when there was a sudden transformation of one object into another. The people around him were confused when he identified an ellip-tic catastrophe in the film on The Veronese Surface. He was right.

A number of times I have returned to study further the first painting that made a connection between us and I believe I finally have uncovered the reason Dalí became so impressed with the unfolded four-dimensional cross. In the Salvador Dalí Museum in Florida that houses the collection of the Morses, there are a number of books that appeared in Dalí's working art library, including Theory of Perspective for the Usage of Artists *by Emde-Sébastien Jeaurat written in 1750. One image from that volume shows two perpendicular views of a solid cross, superimposed on each other, almost the same shape as the unfolded four-dimensional hypercube. I can imagine that when Dalí again saw that shape in a popular article on geometry of higher dimensions, he recognized an image he had already seen in an art book. He saw its potential as an image of the tran-scendental unfolded into our reality for our benefit. The wooden model that was constructed for Dalí appears in the display case at the Salvador Dalí Museum in Figueres, along with a flexible moving copy of my original unfolded hypercube.*

I can honestly say that Salvador Dalí is the most interesting person I have ever met.[81]

For his exhibition at the Galería Fernando Vijande in Madrid, held at the turn of the year 1982/83 and bearing the title "Guns, Knives, and Cross-es," Andy Warhol also created representations of the cross. Bob Colacello reports in his memoirs:

"Guns, Knives, and Crosses" was Andy's big series for 1982. He had been collecting antique guns and daggers over the past year and photographing them so he could tax-deduct them as props. Then Fernando Vijande, a sleepy Spanish dealer we called "Fernando Hideaway," proposed a show in Spain. "What should I do, Bob?" Andy asked. "You went to school in Madrid." (I had taken my junior year abroad there.) The first things that came to mind were the Inquisition and the Civil War. "Oh, I can do the guns and knives for the war, right?" said Andy. "But what should I do for the Catholic thing." "Crosses," said Fred.[82]

The *Crosses* series is based on Polaroid photos. Warhol used un-adorned, industrially produced wooden crosses of two different types, which were photographed in various constellations. In some of the photos they appear to be arranged randomly. Other photos show a pattern of a dozen wooden crosses, grouped in fours in three rows.[83] For his paintings measur-ing 20 × 16 and 90 × 70 inches, Warhol decided to use this pattern of twelve and chose a black background, underlining the functionality of the cross-es. They are arranged irregularly with varying gaps between them. Most of the crosses veer slightly to the left or right, some crosses are touching and appear to transition from one to the other. On many of the canvasses the crosses appear in the same color. While the works with their somber color

81
Prof. Thomas Banchoff in a text based on a tele-phone conver-sation with the author on May 26, 2010.

82
Colacello 1990, p. 462. Else-where Colacello reports, that sometimes War-hol called taking holy water, genuflecting, kneeling, pray-ing, and making the sign of the Cross "all the Catholic things." Ibid., p. 119.

83
Ill. in *Andy Warhol CROSSES,* pp. 24f.

scheme evoke military cemeteries, the canvasses with garish and bold colors are associated with a wallpaper or fabric pattern.[84] This association is underlined further in the works with three rows of crosses in different colors. Warhol also created paintings showing a single cross in front of a black background. The symbol of Christianity appears monumental, poignantly sober, at a slightly sloped angle, with the shadow giving it the appearance of a corporeal object. All canvasses were initially painted with acrylics after which black oil paint was applied using a screenprinting process, masking out the crosses. This production process, which is a negative process, is still visible in the places where the colored background appears through the pitch black. Ultimately the viewer perceives the black as the top layer of color, owing to the reflecting gloss of the black oil paint.[85]

The Ghost of Marilyn Monroe

The portraits of Marilyn Monroe are among Andy Warhol's most well-known works. The famous 1966 interview "Andy Warhol: My True Story" contains the following statement by the artist:

I don't feel I'm representing the main sex symbols of our time in some of my pictures, such as Marilyn Monroe or Elizabeth Taylor, I just see Monroe as just another person. As for whether it's symbolical to paint Monroe in such violent colors: it's beauty, and she's beautiful and if something's beautiful, it's pretty colors, that's all. Or something. The Monroe picture was part of a death series I was doing, of people who had died in different ways. There was no profound reason for doing a death series, no "victims of their time"; there was no reason for doing it all, just a surface reason.[1]

It was due to the enormous attention that the media and the public paid to the early death of Marilyn Monroe that Warhol produced portraits of her.[2] The actress died on August 5, 1962, at a mere thirty-six years old. In the coroner's report, the cause of death was stated as "acute barbiturate poisoning—ingestion of overdose."[3] Warhol remarked in the said interview, "I wouldn't have stopped Monroe from killing herself, for instance: I think everybody should do whatever they want to do and if that made her happier, then that's what she should have done."[4] A few days after her death, Warhol got hold of a 1950s publicity shot of the actress.[5] He removed the lower half of the bust and had Monroe's head made into a silkscreen.[6] Warhol created a total of three series of *Marilyn* portraits: a series of different works made that same year, a group of five paintings two years later, and a print portfolio created in 1967.[7]

The first series starts with the painting *Gold Marilyn Monroe*, showing a color portrait of the actress on a monochrome gold canvas. The golden paint appears to have been applied by hand and also with a spray can.[8] David Bourdon sees the golden background as a "consistent and logical follow-up" to Warhol's *Golden Slippers* and the *Gold Book* of the 1950s and writes that the "tinselly treatment" of the painting was inspired by childhood memories of the many icons in the St. John Chrysostom Byzantine Catholic Church in Pittsburgh.[9] *Gold Marilyn Monroe* was among the works displayed at Warhol's exhibition at the Stable Gallery in New York, which opened in November

---

84
Plotzek in ibid., p. 17; Rosenblum in ibid., p. 9.

85
Plotzek in ibid., pp. 15f.

1
In Goldsmith 2004, p. 88.

2
It is reported that a couple of days after the death of the actress, during a visit to Serendipity 3, Warhol was asked by Stephen Bruce, one of the founders and owners of the restaurant, "Oh, Andy, will you do a book for us on Marilyn?" to which Warhol replied, "Well, okay." Cf. Sherman/Dalton 2009, p. 125. From 1952 to 1960 Warhol created several promotional books. Cf. Schleif 2013, pp. 79ff. However, he never realized a book about Marilyn Monroe.

3
Spoto 1993, p. 644.

4
In Goldsmith 2004, p. 94.

5
According to different sources the photo was shot by Frank Powolny or Gene Kornman. Cf. Frei/Printz 2002, p. 224.

6
Ill. in *Andy Warhol Photography*, p. 54.

7
Frei/Printz, 2002, p. 224.

8
Ibid., p. 226.

9
Bourdon 1989, p. 130. A photo of the interior of the church is reproduced in Daggett Dillenberger 1998, p. 18.

1962.[10] The architect Philip Johnson was enthusiastic about the portrait, bought it for $800 and donated it to the Museum of Modern Art.[11] When Warhol found out about it he wanted to give Charles Lisanby, his life partner at the time, a *Marilyn* portrait as a gift. Lisanby later remarked: "... he said, 'Oh, the Museum [of Modern Art] just bought *Marilyn Monroe*, and they're going to be famous. And I want to give you one of them.' To tell you the truth, I didn't particularly like them. I didn't want any. [Lisanby laughs] And he said, 'I want to give you one.' 'Well,' I said, 'I don't have any wall space here.' He said, 'Just store it. One day they're going to be worth a great deal of money.'"[12] Lisanby refused to accept the gift and added later: "I kept saying, 'I think it's wonderful what you're doing. Just tell me in your heart of hearts you know it isn't art.' He would never admit it, but I knew he knew it wasn't."[13] The curator William Seitz, on the other hand, was enthusiastic about Warhol's works and acquired a further *Marilyn* portrait for the Museum of Modern Art for $250. When a colleague called and asked, "Isn't it the most ghastly thing you've ever seen in your life?" he answered, "Yes, isn't it. I bought one."[14]

One reason for the vehement reactions was the coloring of the portrait, which a critic later referred to as "overworked Technicolor."[15] Warhol first painted various colored surfaces by hand, corresponding to the face, hair, eyes, eye shadow, lips, and neck, as well as the background of the photo.[16] He made the surfaces for the eyes, eye shadow, and lips significantly bigger than the outlines that were later printed over them. Printing could commence when the paint was dry. He did not proceed very carefully, which led his assistant Nathan Gluck to caution him:

"Now when you start silkscreening, you put little marks here, and you line up the screens with the marks, so, you know, when you screen, everything is exact." And Andy couldn't be bothered with this. So, when he got through, the lips ... were a little askew, the eyeshadow went a little high, or the hair went a little over to the left, and Andy would look at it, and you'd look at it, and it was all a little off-register. And you'd say to Andy, "Andy, it's a little off-register." And Andy would say, "I like it that way." And that's how it went.[17]

The artist Neke Carson, who was in regular contact with Warhol, views precisely this lack of precision as a brilliant achievement: "It wasn't the fact that he wanted to be a machine ... his brilliance was that he wanted to be a bad machine, a machine that didn't work very well. So, when he did these early silkscreens, they were done lackadaisically."[18] The varying outcomes of the printing were also due to the fact that occasionally the screen got clogged up, the squeegee was guided irregularly and with varying pressure, or the wrong quantity of color was used.[19] This resulted in each portrait having a different expression. The varying print quality is noticeable in the *Serial Marilyns* paintings, in which the face of Monroe appears serially on the canvas. As the faces are arranged in a grid and each individual portrait varies slightly from the one next to it, the pictures are reminiscent of a movie strip.[20] The most well-known images from this series are *Marilyn Dipytch* and *Marilyn X 100*. The latter is a monumental work measuring 81 × 223 ½ inches, on which Marilyn Monroe's face is depicted fifty times in color on an orange background on the left half of the canvas and fifty times in black

10
A photo of the exhibition opening, also showing the painting, is printed in Frei/Printz 2002, p. 226.

11
Bockris 1989, p. 156; Frei/Printz 2002, p. 226.

12
In Smith 1986, p. 372.

13
Quoted according to Bockris 1989, p. 157.

14
Quoted according to ibid., p. 156.

15
Ibid., p. 152.

16
Bourdon 1989, p. 124.

17
In Smith 1986, p. 316.

18
Neke Carson in conversation with the author on December 6, 2012 in New York.

19
Bockris 1989, p. 152; Bourdon 1989, p. 126.

20
Bourdon 1989, p. 124.

and white on the right half of the canvas, which is not primed. The *Marilyn Diptych* consists of a canvas with twenty-five colored faces of the actress appearing on an orange background, and a second canvas with twenty-five of her faces in black and white. Warhol had conceived the two canvasses as two independent works, but Emily Tremaine, who together with her husband purchased the works directly from the artist, convinced him to view them as a diptych.[21] The *Marilyn Diptych* as a concept evokes the work *Marilyn's Lips*, which likewise consists of two canvasses and achieves its effect through the contrast between color and black and white.[22] The art critic Peter Schjeldahl wrote: "Visually and physically the Marilyn diptych had majesty reminiscent of Pollock and Newman. The effect was like *Moby Dick* retold, to resounding success, in street slang, with a sexy actress standing in for the fearsome white whale. With his subject matter and technique in place, Warhol suddenly let loose a pent-up profound understanding of New York school painting aesthetics."[23] When the *Marilyn Diptych* and *Gold Marilyn Monroe* were displayed together with Dalí's installation *Mao Marilyn Monarchy* and works by several other artists, sculptors, and photographers in December 1967 at the exhibition "Homage to Marilyn Monroe" at the Sidney Janis Gallery in New York,[24] Warhol had the opportunity to deliver a commentary on his diptych. The press quoted the artist as follows: "She was absolutely beautiful and I had the feeling she was changing; that she was becoming more of herself than what a movie studio told her to be. I put this on canvas, as though it was a movie, so that you can see the change every second."[25]

In 1964, Warhol created five colored *Marilyn* portraits. As he chose a square format measuring 40 × 40 inches, which he was to adhere to from then on in most cases for his portraits, it was necessary to crop the top and bottom of the photographic template that had already been used two years before. The works became famous through the performance artist Dorothy Podber. She appeared at the Factory one day in September 1964 in motorbike attire, with her Great Dane, accompanied by two friends who were also wearing black leather. Podber asked Warhol if she could shoot his *Marilyn* paintings. When he replied that he did not mind, she took out a pistol and fired it at the said five portraits that were stacked against the wall, striking the forehead of the movie star.[26] "Andy was really disturbed by that," Billy Name later recalled, "She even stayed awhile afterwards, which agitated him even more. He asked me to tell her to leave and never come back, the only time he ever asked me to do that about someone."[27] William S. Wilson, a close friend of the artist Ray Johnson, who witnessed this event, remarked:

That story about the shooting has never been told correctly ever because people are careful for their friends. And so when Ray would tell the story he left out Billy Name, and when Billy tells the story he leaves out Ray. They don't want to get people into trouble. ... Dorothy never told that story right. ... Later Dorothy improved the story—that's not unusual—where she said, "I've come to shoot some pictures," meaning with a camera shooting pictures. Not true! ... What happened is that Ray took Dorothy Podber to Andy's Factory. He didn't know she had a gun. Ray did not repeat stories—this one he repeated three times, once to me but then other people involved, other events, and he acted

---

21
Frei/Printz 2002, p. 233.

22
See the chapter **Mae West's and Marilyn Monroe's Lips** in this part.

23
Quoted according to Bockris 1989, p. 152.

24
See the chapter **Mao Marilyn** in this part.

25
Gavzer 1967.

26
Bockris 1989, pp. 200f. According to another report, Warhol wanted to make a movie with Dorothy Podber and asked her at a party, "Can I shoot you," to which she purportedly answered, "Sure, if I can shoot you." Warhol then invited her to come to the Factory the next day. Cf. Sherman/Dalton 2009, p. 234. According to another source Warhol said to her at the Factory that he didn't have time for her at the moment, because he was currently shooting a picture, +

27
In Sherman/Dalton 2009, p. 234. See also Watson 2003, p. 174, who writes that Warhol said, "Ooooh, Billy, please don't let Dorothy come over here again like that." Bockris 1989, p. 201, reports that Warhol also complained to Ondine, "Your friend just blew a hole through ..." He then remarked, "But you just said she could."

it out, and I remember exactly where he was sitting—he played both parts. He and Dorothy were sitting in chairs. Billy Name is there and Andy is there, and the Marilyns are over there to the left. And according to Ray, Dorothy took the pistol out and shot.[28]

The shot penetrated all five paintings, but Warhol had the damaged canvasses repaired again.[29] He later told the art collector and entrepreneur Peter M. Brant that he had painted over the patches himself, ensuring that the restorations remained visible and appeared like makeup over a blemish.[30] The works were renamed *Shot Red Marilyn, Shot Orange Marilyn, Shot Light Blue Marilyn,* and *Shot Sage Blue Marilyn.*[31]

In 1967, Warhol published a portfolio of prints with ten *Marilyn* portraits.[32] The size of the sheets, each 36 × 36 inches, made it necessary to crop the photographic template even more than for the previously created portraits on canvas. For the works on paper, Warhol applied variations and a wide color palette. He used striking colors for both the background and Marilyn's face.[33] On each print, the color of the background corresponds to the color of the movie actress' eye shadow. Printed were 250 copies of the portfolio, offered for $500 each. In November 1987, a *Marilyn* portfolio with nine prints was auctioned at Sotheby's in New York for $125,000.[34] In November 2012 a complete set at the same auction house even achieved the sum of $1,650,000.[35]

In 1978, Warhol was asked in an interview whether he had ever met Marilyn Monroe. He replied, "Just a couple of times at a …"; changing the subject abruptly without finishing the sentence.[36] In 1955, Monroe moved to New York and began studying at the renowned Actors Studios, run by Lee Strasberg. Perhaps the artist met her at Serendipity 3, which they both liked to frequent. At the time Warhol was still completely unknown outside of the advertising sector and was not yet consorting with Hollywood stars. Therefore it is questionable that he really met Marilyn Monroe; more likely is that he saw her. Salvador Dalí, on the other hand, was already a celebrity in the 1940s and knew half of Hollywood. Dalí once said to Amanda Lear: "… I also met Marilyn Monroe! She had something childlike in her face which was very attractive. It contrasted with the well-rounded breasts she always displayed and which the Americans loved so much. I even arranged a secret rendezvous at the St. Regis for her to meet Dominguin, the bullfighter, but nothing came of it. She had to cancel in the last moment. A pity, because he looked very handsome dressed up as matador."[37] Many years later Lear added in an interview: "He [Dalí] met Marilyn Monroe—said she was nothing, just a little fat girl."[38] Women with a more gamine appearance corresponded to Dalí's ideal of beauty.[39] However, the British interior architect Nicholas Haslam, who knew both Monroe and Dalí, says quite rightly, "Dalí liked anybody famous. He adored Marilyn, I'm sure, because she was famous."[40] Dalí's fascination with Monroe was also ambivalent because her unbelievable presence and charismatic aura attracted the attention of her surroundings. The actress Sylvia Miles, who like Monroe had completed her training at the Actors Studio and also, by her own account, met her there for the first time, says fittingly, "To call her 'a little fat girl' … even on a bad day! … Marilyn

---

28
William S. Wilson in a conversation with the author on December 7, 2012 in New York.

+
whereupon Podber asked irritated: "Oh, can I shoot a picture?," "Sure" was Warhol's answer. Cf. Watson 2003, p. 174.

29
Bourdon 1989, p. 190.

30
Frei/Printz/ King-Nero, 2004, *A*, p. 278 of no. 1292.

31
However, traces of the damage can only be seen on the orange and light blue versions. Further details, ibid., pp. 272, 278.

32
Feldman/ Schellmann 2003, II. 22–31.

33
It is said that an out-of-focus color television set inspired him to this. Cf. Bockris 1989, p. 430.

34
Bourdon 1989, p. 263.

35
http://www. sothebys.com/ en/auctions/ ecatalogue/2012/ prints-n08896/ lot.346.html (last accessed: April 12, 2016).

36
Smith 1986, p. 522.

37
Lear 1985, p. 148.

38
In King 2007, p. 180.

39
See the chapter **Companions, Courtiers, and Superstars** in Part 3.

40
Nicholas Haslam in a conversation with the author on July 20, 2012 in London.

Monroe was probably in a crazy way in Salvador Dalí's mind more famous than him. ... Listen, you can't find something like Marilyn Monroe. She is bigger than us, bigger than all of us. ... She was better looking than him."[41]

It is a little known fact that Dalí followed Warhol's example in 1966 and also started to address the Marilyn Monroe phenomenon artistically. He created several watercolors on the subject of Homer's *Odyssey*, to which he later added individual sheets.[42] It was commissioned work for Giuseppe and Mara Albaretto, a doctor couple from Turin, who the artist had met in 1956.[43] One of the most interesting illustrations is the watercolor *Polyphemus*. Dalí's painting is reminiscent of Odilon Redon's painting *The Cyclops*, which shows a giant with a look that is both in love and naïve. Dalí's version presents the one-eyed giant with a powerful torso, a long white beard, and raised arms on the beach at Port Lligat. The masculine appearance contrasts with the face, which has female features. One can see an eye with long lashes, a button nose, and a radiantly smiling red mouth. Dalí was inspired by a Monroe photo for the face of his *Polyphemus*.[44] One year later, Dalí asked Philippe Halsman to create the mentioned photomontage out of the two faces of Marilyn Monroe and Mao Zedong.[45] In 1972, the Spaniard created the portrait *Marilyn Monroe* in oil on Plexiglas.[46] In this work, which seems like a caricature, the movie actress appears to be melting like a gelatinous yellow mass. He painted her red lips very prominently and particularly highlighted her eyes and breasts by means of transparent lenses, which are attached with nylon strings. The works show that Dalí was seeking to undermine Monroe's aura.

Similar to Warhol, Dalí also addressed the myth of the movie actress quite consciously. Among the illustrations that he created for his book *Dalí de Draeger* published in 1968, is a work showing Michelangelo's *Slave* with two car tires around his body. Dalí's *Slave* serves as an axis for the car tires and "is traveling at an accelerated speed on the downgrade," as stated in the accompanying text, with a Marilyn Monroe portrait projected onto his knee.[47] This portrait is the shot by Philippe Halsman that was on the cover of *LIFE* Magazine in April 1952 and had also been used for the mentioned photomontage *Mao Marilyn*.[48] A year after the publication of *Dalí de Draeger*, Dalí held a private event at the Draeger printing house.[49] He posed surrounded by models and shop window dummies in front of a giant light box, in which one can see a photo of him next to one of Marilyn Monroe.[50]

At the end of 1971, Dalí met the American actress Denise Sandell in New York.[51] Sandell reports that her agent pressured her to call the artist, so she did, and he spontaneously invited her to visit him at his suite at the St. Regis Hotel. She recalls their first encounter as follows:

The door flew open in front of me, I saw a white photographic backdrop rolling from the ceiling to floor and over the carpet. Dalí stepped from behind the door, ocelot at his side. His sweeping arm gesture told me to come in. I looked up into his eyes. Breathless in his gaze, transfixed in his widening stare, his eyes held me. Sighing smiling straight into his vision without blinking, I offered him my hand. "Je m'appelle Denise." His fingertips touched my palm raising my hand to his lips. Dalí: "Oui." He spun me on to the photo backdrop. Dalí: "Dans le centre." I twirled around a few times. Dalí was behind a movie

---

41
Sylvia Miles in a conversation with the author on July 1, 2012 in New York.

42
Heid in *Dalí: Mara e Beppe*, p. 17.

43
Cf. Gibson 1997, p. 486.

→ **29** [p. 381]

44
Maur 1989, cat. 275. See also Vescovo in *Salvador Dalí: Canvas & watercolours from the Albaretto Collection*, p. 60.

45
See the chapter **Mao Marilyn** in this part.

46
Ill. in Descharnes/ Néret, no. 1341.

47
Dalí had already created his version of *Slave* by Michelangelo in 1966. Cf. Descharnes/ Descharnes 2003, no. 282.

48
Dali 1968, no. 55. See also the chapter **Mao Marilyn** in this chapter.

49
I thank Jordi Casals for this information (Facebook message on January 4, 2015).

50
Photos in Casals 2005, pp. 104ff.

51
Denise Sandell in an e-mail to the author on December 5, 2015.

camera on a tripod ... I started laughing and dancing. He took the camera off the stand coming close and moving away. Dalí: "Baisez le camera!" Laughing, I blew him kisses. He moved around me. ... I made eye contact with the camera then put my lips to the lens as if it were him. He put the camera down and clapped "Bravo! You are the ghost of Marilyn Monroe." He returned the camera to the tripod, playing back what he'd recorded ... and announced "You will have a cover of Vogue magazine and I will put Mao's head on your face." I thought that was funny.[52]

The video recordings with which Dalí intended to recreate his *Vogue* cover with *Mao Marilyn* have not yet been found.[53] However, it is a given fact that like Warhol, he, too was experimenting with a video camera.[54] Pandora also reports that she was videotaped by Dalí on a number of occasions.[55] Her close friend, the moviemaker Steven Arnold, writes in his autobiography: "We [Pandora and I] posed for him nude, repeatedly had quiet evenings in his suite, being videotaped by a remote control camera that was ever present."[56]

In the years after their first encounter, Denise Sandell was often seen at Dalí's side.[57] When she reports on her time with him, it is evident that she was in love with him:

Dalí's desire for Marilyn was in her mouth—her lips were important to him. One time in public, he got angry with me, I forgot to wear red lipstick. He raised his voice "Where are your lips?" I smiled and bit my lips till they bled.

Any time he asked me to come to him or be with him, I did. In New York I would see him once or twice a week. ... he had parties often and invited me—I didn't particularly like to go to them, in Spain I did very much, and the opening of his museum ... In New York I was off catching plays at night and a theater student by day. His party guests, and people in that crowd were self-interested. When you're in love with somebody you may not want to be part of a circus. ... I liked to be only with him and he liked to be only with me. Dalí kept me away from his wife and Amanda. ... He treated me with love, dignity, and was gracious to me always.

On meeting Ultra Violet, she asked me, "Well, did you ever have sex with Dalí?" ... Dalí would whisper in my ear, "You can drink my cum from a silver spoon." He thought that would make me happy ... .[58]

Mae West's and Marilyn Monroe's Lips

At the time that Salvador Dalí first traveled to the United States, Mae West was a big movie star in Hollywood. She was considered a quintessential femme fatale and broke sexual taboos. West sparkled with frivolity and verbal wit in her movies—her most famous one-liner: "Is that a gun in your pocket, or are you just glad to see me?" In 1934/35, Dalí created the painting *Mae West's Face which May Be Used as a Surrealist Apartment*, for which he used the title page of a magazine.[1] He painted over the face of the actress with gouache and designed it as a view of an interior room with crimson walls. He transformed her eyes into two pictures with scenes of Paris, her nose into a fireplace with a golden clock on it, her sensual lips—which he refers to in his essay "The New Colors of Spectral Sex Appeal" as "rounded and salivary

52
Ibid., Denise Sandell in a telephone conversation with the author on November 27, 2011.

53
Regarding the *Vogue* cover see the chapter **Mao Marilyn** in this part.

54
In April 1960, as part of the 5th Annual Convention on Visual Communications at the Waldorf Astoria Hotel, New York, Dalí presented his video *Chaos and Creation*, which had been made on March 4, 1960, at Videotape Productions, Inc. in New York. Details provided by Sainsbury in Gale 2007, pp. 206ff. In the summer of 1965, Warhol first experimented with video recording equipment. See Warhol/Hackett 1980, pp. 119f. Starting in 1970, he documented his surroundings with a video camera as the so-called *Factory Diaries*. See Meyer-Hermann 2007, pp. 01:26:00ff. See also the chapter **Television as "Instant Fame"** in this part.

55
Pandora in a conversation with the author on November 20, 2011 in Mariposa, California.

56
Arnold, unpublished autobiography.

57
Photos of Dalí with Denise Sandell in *El ojo invisible*, pp. 103ff.

58
Denise Sandell in a conversation with the author on July 3, 2012 in New York.

1
Tusquets Blanca 2003, pp. 177f.

2
Dalí (1934) in
Finkelstein 1998,
p. 206.

3
Rose 1961,
p. 333.

4
Michi-Kusunoki
in Ades 2004,
p. 284. The sketch
is depicted
in Maur 1989,
cat. 140.

5
Cf. Michi-
Kusunoki in Ades
2004, p. 284.
According to
Descharnes/
Descharnes
2003, p. 40, the
first version
was created by
Jean-Michel
Frank in Paris and
two other ver-
sions were made
by Green &
Abbott. In *The
Secret Life* Dalí
comments on
the *Lips Sofa*:
"My idea as re-
alized by the
decorator, Jean-
Michel Frank,
one of my great
friends during the
Paris period …"
See Dalí 1942,
picture section
before p. 279.

6
Eight copies
were made plus
four EA copies.
See Descharnes/
Descharnes
2003, p. 41.

7
Pitxot/Aguer/
Puig 2005, p. 92;
Tusquets Blanca
2003, pp. 178ff.

8
Llongueras
2003, pp. XL
and LXIII.

9
Cf. *Salvador
Dalí Enrique Sa-
bater*, pp. 38f.

10
In Calvo Serraller
2006, p. 1349
(translated from
the Spanish).

muscles, horribly slimy with biological ulterior motives"[2]—into a sofa and her blonde hair into a curtain framing the entrance to the room. Mae West knew the portrait and it amused her. The English painter Sir Francis Rose reports in his memoirs about a lunch with the actress that took place at the end of the 1930s, to which also Harpo Marx was invited: "... they looked at some drawings Dalí had made. Mae West liked one, which I believe was only a magazine reproduction of a portrait of herself made out of furniture. Her hips were a scarlet sofa, her eyes were chandeliers, and her hair curtains. She said that she wondered if the idea could not be put to a practical use and converted into her new bathroom."[3] Unfortunately, the bathroom was never realized.

In 1936, Edward James had the idea of having Dalí do a surrealistic design for his drawing room in his house in London. Although the project was soon abandoned, the artist and his English friend and patron could not let go of the idea. James suggested recreating the *Lips Sofa* from Dalí's Mae West portrait. He commissioned two design firms to manufacture a total of five sofas, which were completed in 1938 in three different versions according to a special design sketch by Dalí.[4] It appears that Green & Abbott in London created the first version of the *Lips Sofa*, with a satin cover in the "shocking pink" of Elsa Schiaparelli's lipstick, as well as two sofas in red felt with black wool fringe lining the outer edge of the bottom lip. Two other sofas with a red felt and a pink felt base were presumably made by Edward Carrick, founder of Associated Artist Technicians, the first British school dedicated to film design and production.[5]

In 1974, a small number of the *Lips Sofas* were recreated in bright red with a beige base.[6] At that time a version was also made in a garish red, elastic, synthetic material, which had little lip wrinkles and therefore appeared more realistic than the preceding models. It ended up in the Mae West Room at the Teatre-Museu Dalí in Figueres. This room is a three-dimensional recreation of the painting *Mae West's Face which May Be Used as a Surrealist Apartment*. Dalí realized the installation together with the architect Oscar Tusquets Blanca and the master builder Pedro Aldámiz.[7] The curtain is a gigantic wig created by Lluís Llongueras and is included in the *Guinness Book of World Records*.[8] In order to be able to perceive the room as a whole, the visitor has to look through a reduction lens hanging from a camel sculpture—a gift from the cigarette manufacturer Camel.[9] When Dalí gave an interview for the Spanish newspaper *La Actualidad Española* a few days after the opening of his Teatre-Museu Dalí, he highlighted the Pop Art character of the Mae West Room:

Everything in it is a "Pop" take on the face of Mae West. This room contains an announcement of the next exhibition of the American hyperrealists, which I will soon show in the United States. I will mix a painting by W. A Bouguereau with those by the hyperrealists, in order to see the contrast between Pompier and avant-garde painting. In the room there is only one Bouguereau, a wonderful nude, but I have five others. The fragmentation of the face of Mae West will be his portrait that he will be able to use as a living room. I will add a TV under the camel's belly, and the person who sits on the lips of Mae West will see themselves through the TV screen that reflects West's entire face.[10]

However, the TV set announced by Dalí was never installed. Instead, an "inverted bathroom" was added in 1977 under the ceiling of the Mae West Room.[11]

Dalí had two further versions of the *Lips Sofa* installed in his home in Port Lligat. The first is in the entrance area of the house and is covered with a leaf-patterned fabric. The second is made of pink plastic and stands outside on the patio by the swimming pool belonging to the house. In an interview with Warhol's superstar Candy Darling, which was published in the May 1973 edition of *Andy Warhol's Interview*, Dalí described a further version of the *Lips Sofa*:

Candy: You and Mae West. You agree with Mae West a lot?

Dalí: Yes, because like it a sa-leev-a sofa.

Candy: Oh yes?

Dalí: Sa-lee-va sofa means one sofa with plenty of saliva. And for sit down is much better when something is humidity and not too much dry. And Mae West is very humid. And for this the best sofa is my best sa-lee-va sofa.

Candy: Sa-lee-va sofa. You mean it's moist your sofa?

Dalí: Yes.

Candy: It's moist and when you sit down you become wet?

Dalí: You become wet.

Candy: Marvelous.

Dalí: But it is only for la *summer time is not for winter.*

Candy: It is only used outdoors?

Dalí: Uh, no no no, inside the house but all time filled with liquid. All time your sex is a leetle wet. When you sit down on the saleeva sofa. But is not real saleeva. Is art-ee-fee-cial saleeva.

Candy: Then it must be covered with a porous material.

Dalí: EX-actly. And sharp realism because every leetle defect of the skin is reproduced in la *sofa. You know is like you sit down on lips. The lips completely real.*

Candy: Where is it?

Dalí: This is ready, for now is already in Paris in the market Saleeva sofa, my best saleeva sofa!

Candy: Will it be sold over here too?

Dalí: Yes ...[12]

The version of the *Lips Sofa* described by Dalí did not in fact make an appearance on the market in Paris or in the United States.

In *The Secret Life* Dalí establishes a link between the *Lips Sofa* and his Catalan homeland, by showing a photo of the "exact spot at Cadaqués" where "the jagged rocks made it uncomfortable to sit, which inspired the famous Divan in the Shape of a Mouth." Below it is a photo of the Casa Milà by Antoni Gaudí in Barcelona, about which the artist remarks, "The mouth, the sea, and its foam treated as aesthetic forms in wrought iron by the architect Gaudí of Barcelona."[13] It also becomes clear elsewhere in his autobiography that Dalí viewed the mouth as a special aesthetic form. The drawing *Project for an ultra-sophisticated oil lamp for the exclusive use of the aristocracy* shows an oil lamp consisting of a mouth with a nose, with a second, somewhat

11
Pitxot/Aguer/
Puig 2005, p. 92.

12
Candy Darling
1973, p. 40.

13
Dalí 1942, picture
segment before
p. 279.

smaller mouth with ears rising above it.[14] Elsewhere Dalí presents a design for a standing lamp, whose base is composed from the bottom to the top of a nose, an eye, and a mouth.[15]

In 1949 Dalí designed the impressive piece of jewelry *Ruby Lips* made of rubies with eighteen-carat gold and thirteen pearls.[16] Dalí commented on his creation: "Poets of the ages, of all lands, write of ruby lips and teeth like pearls. It remained for Dalí to translate this poetic cliché into a true surrealistic object."[17] Finally, one should also mention the vial for the perfume series *Le Parfum de Salvador Dalí*, which was presented to the public in October 1983 at the Musée Jacquemart-André in Paris in the presence of Princess Caroline of Monaco. What was presented was a perfume vial made by Lalique, according to Dalí's specifications, out of a kilo of pure crystal in the shape of curvaceous lips with a nose bottle top.[18] For health reasons, Dalí was unable to attend the presentation of the perfume.[19] The study for the vial was created with reference to the painting *Apparition of the Visage of Aphrodite of Cnidos in a Landscape* from the same year, showing a marble relief jutting far into a landscape bearing the facial features of the goddess of love. In the foreground one can see little miniatures that take up the motif of her lips.[20]

Andy Warhol also paid aesthetic homage to the charm of beautiful lips from early on. Remarkable drawings were created in the 1950s that already pre-empt the idea of serial art. The work *Lips* shows twenty-two female lips in different color nuances, ranging from deep red to pink and orange.[21] The drawing *Female Faces* dated 1960 also presents lips in different color nuances, all part of a stylized female face in profile, appearing eight times. With regard to the composition, Warhol let himself be inspired for this work by the renowned title page that Herbert Bayer had created in 1940 for the August issue of *Harper's Bazaar*.[22]

In summer 1962, Warhol once again took up the subject of lips. At the time he had just discovered the silkscreen technique and created his first portraits of Marilyn Monroe.[23] He used her smile as the motif for the painting *Marilyn's Lips*. The work consists of two large-format canvasses, with her lips arranged eighty-four times in twelve rows of seven on each.[24] While Warhol did not use color at all for the lips on the left canvas, the lips on the right canvas are presented in red against a pink background. In Lane Slate's documentary *Exhibition*, shot towards the end of 1962, the painting can be seen on both sides rolled up inwards. The size of the rolls indicates that it had previously been a single canvas that was divided between 1962 and 1965. At the beginning of 1965, Warhol's work was shown for the first time as a diptych at the Dwan Gallery as part of the exhibition "The Arena of Love."[25] Eric Shanes expresses the opinion that with his painting *Marilyn's Lips*, Warhol turned the facial feature into something repulsive through isolation and multiplication. At the same time Shanes emphasizes that certain physiognomic and anatomical details play an important "psycho-sexual" role in the perception of media figures. Warhol formulated it in his *Philosophy* as follows: "People look the most kissable when they're not wearing makeup. Marilyn's lips weren't kissable, but they were very photographable."[26] Shanes thinks that Warhol was inspired by Dalí's famous *Lips Sofa*, but in his opinion, the lips had been pushed "to the verge of total abstraction" through the repetition and therefore became something quite different.[27] Warhol was undoubtedly familiar with Dalí's design classic.

Apart from eyes, Warhol also liked to highlight lips in his portraits, and therefore made them his signature feature.[28] Horst Weber von Beeren, who was Warhol's printer Rupert Jasen Smith's assistant at the time, reports that a very special technique was used for the lips:

There are two kinds of portraits by Warhol. First, ones where the image was printed on a sloppy layer of acrylic paint—less desirable today. Second, there were the portraits where he taped out the shape of the face, which was then painted in with a flat flesh tone. He also put in the shape of eyes and eyebrows and the prominent shape of the lips in flat red. The background was in a different color. The lines were supposed to be elegant. The silkscreen portrait was printed in black on top of this acrylic paint. In this so-called "halftone," the lips were taped over, so that they wouldn't be black. Instead they were printed later in bright red silkscreen ink, as the focal point of the picture. With Liza Minnelli a new phase started [in 1978]. We painted a white rectangle on the flat acrylic lips, which with the red halftone on it looked like lip highlights. Male portraits did not get special lip treatment, they were just black halftone, printed on a flat acrylic shape of the face with a background color.[29]

Warhol was so fascinated by lips that he had them printed into blank books when making a female portrait. This marked the birth of the so-called *Lips Books*. Horst Weber von Beeren: "Andy had the idea to do a *Lip Book*. I remember two. Handmade paper was already bound into two books. They lay on the shelf. When a female portrait was printed, the lips were printed last and separately in red. Finally, an additional print was made on each page in each book."[30] Vincent Fremont later explained the function of the *Lip Books*: "Around 1980 Andy even had 'lips' books made; clothbound books containing many pages of silkscreened lips in various shapes and shades of red. If he thought a woman should have a certain look he would sometimes refer to these 'studies' of lips; they were his 'sketchbooks.'"[31] Warhol's friend, the photographer Christopher Makos, said of a portrait that a lady from Düsseldorf high society had commissioned, "I don't know whether Mrs. Düsseldorf knew she was getting Liza's lips, but they sure made her look better. The point was to make clients look glamorous. That was what they paid Goya for; that was what they paid Andy for."[32]

Portraits
of Socialites

By the early 1940s, Salvador Dalí had become a portrait painter of U.S. high society. Examples of his portrait art were exhibited in April 1943 at Knoedler in New York. In the preface to the catalogue, Dalí wrote: "As far as the portraits are concerned, my aim was to establish a rapport of fatality between each of the different personalities and their backgrounds, in a manner which, far from any direct symbolism, constitutes the sum of the mediumistic and iconographic volume that each person represented was

27
Shanes 1991, *Warhol*, p. 68. See also Shanes 1991, *Dalí*, p. 74, where he refers to Dalí's *Lips Sofa* as a direct precursor of Warhol's *Marilyn's Lips.*

28
Bourdon 1989, p. 338.

29
Horst Weber von Beeren in an e-mail to the author on May 13, 2013.

30
Horst Weber von Beeren in an e-mail to the author on November 25, 2015. Ill. of a *Lips Book* and some pages from it in Francis/King 1997, pp. 208f.

31
In Geldzahler/ Rosenblum 1993, p. 30.

32
Makos 1988, p. 103.

capable of releasing in my mind."[1] Word is that "café society" talked about the exhibition for a long time. The portraits of Mona von Bismarck (then Mrs. Harrison Williams) and Princess Gourielli, better known as Helena Rubinstein, attracted great attention.[2] The critics were less impressed, however, taking a dislike to the "lifeless technique," among other things.[3] The *New York Sun* stated:

There is no exhilaration in the portrayals. Nothing but plodding, plodding workmanship and an infinity of detail. So much for so much. Even the attempts to laugh off the money go for nothing. Our best-dressed lady, Mrs Harrison Williams, is shown in tatters and shoeless. All God's chillun's got shoes. All save Mrs Harrison Williams. It seems to be an extreme case. And it's not funny. The Princess Gourielli's face is carved upon a mountainside like the Gutzon Borglum monstrosities out west. It's not at all interesting.[4]

Contrary to the reviewer, Helena Rubinstein was delighted with her portrait. The cosmetics entrepreneur later said about the making of the painting:

Dalí suggested that he paint my portrait, and I readily agreed. He asked me to come to his hotel so that he might make a sketch of me. In three sittings he declared himself satisfied, although it was a month before the painting was ready. Dalí called me again and told me that he had selected a frame, and that he was ready to present the portrait to me. Dalí has great charm, and, although the portrait was wonderful, he made it seem more wonderful.

I find it difficult to describe. I am painted with my head jutting out of rocks, with strings of emeralds linked around my neck as though I were held in place by them. Dalí had many explanations for the symbolism in this portrait.[5]

The surrealist elements in Dalí's portraits became less prominent beginning in the late 1940s. An example of this is his *Portrait of Colonel Jack Warner* completed in 1951. The Hollywood producer had commissioned his portrait after Dalí had finished one of his wife Ann. Jack Warner later recalled: "After finishing a fabulous portrait of Ann, Dalí wanted to do one of me, too. I thought he would complete the portrait in no time at all—I was wrong, it took him five years! Of course he was not a house guest all the time. He would do several brilliant pen-and-ink sketches of my eyebrows, my mustache, and my little finger, then off he would go to his beloved Spain. This went on for all those years."[6] Warner also reported that he had requested some modifications to the portrait after seeing it for the first time. Dalí agreed with these, but went on to remark that Warner could gladly edit his own movies, but not Dalí's paintings.[7]

Sometimes Dalí mocked his clients in a subtle manner. For example, in 1952 the banker William Woodward Jr.'s wife Ann commissioned him to paint a portrait of her. Mrs. Woodward, who had embarked on her career as a model and actress under the name Ann Crowell, met the artist at a Park Avenue apartment belonging to her lawyer. Dalí purportedly remarked to her, "If I were a beautiful woman, I would be you."[8] When Ann Woodward turned up for her first sitting at the St. Regis Hotel she was wearing an evening dress. Dalí asked her about her favorite colors and her favorite place and she answered: pastel colors—blue, beige, green and gray—and a beach by

1
In *Dalí*, 1943 (n.p.).

2
In Cowles 1959, p. 226.

3
Ibid., p. 228.

4
Quoted according to Gibson 1997, p. 423.

5
In Cowles 1959, pp. 224f.

6
In ibid., p. 229.

7
Ibid.

8
Quoted according to Braudy 1992, p. 193.

the sea. Dalí promised her that he would paint a masterpiece. It was completed in April 1953. When he proudly unveiled the painting, she found it ugly and was horrified.[9] She had sat as a model repeatedly over the course of a year, but claimed never to have seen the painting.[10] The portrait shows Mrs. Woodward with an enlarged face that looks like a mask. Dalí shortened her neck and lengthened her already long upper lip.[11] Mr. and Mrs. Woodward refused to pay the arranged sum of $7,000. Dalí filed a suit and denied that Mrs. Woodward had not seen the portrait.[12] In order to avoid a drawn-out legal dispute, the defendants chose to pay the fee of their own accord. For the artist, the case had the pleasant side effect of plenty of headlines—for example, the *New York Post* ran a headline: "Horrified Lady Can't Brush Dalí."[13] In view of the torrent of press coverage, Dalí said of Ann Woodward, "This lady becomes more Dalíesque than I. She is trying to obtain publicity at my expense."[14] The portrait, which had gained notoriety, was initially offered for sale at the Carstairs Gallery, without success, and therefore remained in the ownership of the Woodward family.[15] Ann Woodward soon made new headlines—but this time not "at Dalí's expense." In October 1955 she heard noises in the house during the night, grabbed a weapon and fired two shots, killing her husband. She had mistaken him for an intruder. It was never determined whether it was an accident or murder.[16]

Portrait painting had become an important source of income for Dalí in order to support the exuberant lifestyle that he and Gala had become accustomed to during the years in the United States. In the mid-1950s Dalí's standard fee for a portrait was $7,000.[17] *Look* magazine reported in June 1947, on the other hand, that even back then he allegedly demanded up to $25,000.[18] When Dalí painted a portrait of the Briggs family in 1964, he charged $75,000, which is recorded as the highest price in his portrait career.[19] In the early 1970s, Dalí was asking $50,000, as *LIFE* magazine reported.[20] The article also stated that Aristoteles Onassis intended to have his wife Jackie Kennedy painted by Dalí at the time. He planned to collect Dalí in Cadaqués with his yacht and take him to Skorpiós. Dalí reportedly retorted, "If he can send his yacht from Skorpiós to Cadaqués, he has only to put his wife in the yacht and send her, too. It is easier to move a wife than all my paints and canvases."[21] Unlike Andy Warhol, Dalí did not portray Jackie Kennedy.[22] However, like his younger colleague, he stayed in contact with her—even after the death of her second husband. Amanda Lear writes in her memoirs, "Dalí said that Onassis's widow looked like a tadpole and that her eyes were set too far apart, but this didn't prevent him from kissing her warmly and agreeing to lunch."[23]

São Schlumberger was another client who was not happy with the portrait that Dalí painted of her. She was an attractive woman from Portugal, who had married the oil tycoon Pierre Schlumberger, from a respected French family, in Houston, Texas in 1961. Shortly after the wedding, Dalí was commissioned to paint her. He worked on the portrait from 1963 to 1965. The painting shows São Schlumberger in an elegant dress by Givenchy. In her hands she holds a necklace that Dalí had created for her.[24] A plain stretches in the background, with a stranded boat and an angel.

---

9 Ibid., pp. 193f.

10 Cowles 1959, p. 225.

11 Braudy 1992, p. 194.

12 Cowles 1959, p. 225.

13 Braudy 1992, p. 195.

14 "People," 1954, p. 32.

15 Braudy 1992, p. 195.

16 In detail ibid., pp. 287ff.

17 The 1954 portrait of Prince Artchil Gourielli is said to have cost this amount. Cf. Cowles 1959, p. 225.

18 "Dalí – Crazy," p. 95.

19 See Christie's 2016, lot. 365.

20 Wernick 1970, p. 51.

21 Quoted according to ibid., p. 48D.

22 In 1963, Dalí created a bust of John F. Kennedy decorated with paper clips. See Descharnes/Descharnes 2003, no. 220, 221. Dalí's etching *John F. Kennedy* from 1968 is part of the print series "Famous Men." See Löpsinger/Michler 1994, no. 226; Field 1996, Original Intaglio, 68-8 E. In the same year Warhol created the portfolio "Flash – November 22, 1963," which contains several portraits of Kennedy. See Feldman/Schellmann 2003, II.32-42.

23 Lear 1985, p. 270.

→ **35** [p. 385]

24 Sotheby's 2008, lot. 357.

Years later São Schlumberger revealed why she was not pleased with the portrait: "I was expecting a fantasy ... but he did a classic."[25] She confided to Warhol that Dalí had painted her as "too old-looking," which is why she initially declined the Pop artist's offer to also make a portrait of her.[26] Madame Schlumberger later changed her mind. In spring 1974 Warhol shot the obligatory series of Polaroid photos for the portrait of her at the New York Carlyle Hotel, from which he selected two shots.[27] Bob Colacello later remarked, "He had done something special for São: instead of four panels of the same pose in different colors, he had done two of one pose and two of another, full-face and three-quarter view."[28] At the time, Warhol preferred priming the canvas in a painterly way and applying the paint with expressive strokes of the paintbrush before the picture was printed onto it. Now and again he retouched these with further brush strokes, so that the portraits lost their impersonal character.[29] For his portrait of São Schlumberger, Warhol extended the photographic template on the sides, creating the impression that her arms continued beyond the canvas. Another portrait shows an expressive painting on the canvas in the upper area, which was no doubt intended as homage to the Matisse paintings in Madame Schlumberger's collection.[30] In his diaries, Warhol says admiringly, "She was wonderful. Her place is a palace [with] great Picassos, Rothkos, Matisses [and] a Chinese room."[31]

Warhol was also fascinated by C.Z. Guest. Bob Colacello writes in his memoirs:

Andy adored C.Z. because she talked faster than he could tape her, sent him orchids from her greenhouses in Old Westbury, and trusted him with her two children, teenage Alexander, and Cornelia, who was eight when Andy met her in 1975. C.Z. considered Andy a "good influence because he's a worker—and that's what it's all about these days: work, work, work." He was also impressed by the fact that C.Z. and Winston Guest, the legendary polo player and Phipps Steel heir, were "old money."[32]

Another reason for Warhol's admiration was undoubtedly the fact that C.Z. Guest was acquainted with many celebrities. In July 1962, she appeared on the cover of *TIME* magazine. Inside the magazine, one could read that she and her husband occasionally hosted elegant buffet lunches and small dinner parties, "seldom for more than 24—at which the guest list might include the Windsors, Henry Ford II, and Salvador Dalí, Italy's Donna Marella Agnelli, and Truman Capote."[33] Although her daughter Cornelia reported that her mother had asked Warhol repeatedly for a portrait, it was never realized.[34] On the other hand, Warhol created several portraits of Cornelia Guest in 1983, with a naked upper body. The works can be viewed as an allusion to Diego Rivera's portrait of Guest's mother, showing her as a naked odalisque.[35] However, this is mere speculation, as Warhol apparently never expressed such an intention to Cornelia.[36]

Dalí created a portrait of C.Z. Guest in 1958. In 1976 a black-and-white detail showing her head was published on the cover of the August issue of *Andy Warhol's Interview*.[37] The volume also printed a discussion that Warhol had had with her, over the course of which the portrait by Dalí came up:

CZ: ... the painting is exquisite. A lot of people didn't like it when it was first done. Bill Paley always liked it, though, and he has good taste in paintings, besides everything else.

AW: Are you in a strange setting or doing anything?

CZ: No, full face, and behind me he has sky, clouds and horses. It's beautiful.[38]

When Cornelia Guest had the portrait of her mother auctioned at Sotheby's in London in June 2011, however, she said that her mother had never liked it.[39]

C.Z. Guest also commissioned Dalí with a portrait of her son Alexander, who was eight years old at the time.[40] She did not like this portrait either, as she remarked later: "Dalí painted my son, too. But Salvador gave him what looked like a harelip and a huge head. He looked like one of those Velázquez dwarfs the king and the queen had around, and Winston would not accept the painting."[41] C.Z. Guest promptly returned the painting, which she viewed as too surrealistic, to the artist.[42] In the late 1960s the Guest family attempted once again to have one of their children painted by Dalí. Cornelia Guest recalls:

I met him years ago—when I was little—I was with my father. I went to see him in New York. My father wanted him to paint me. I must have been five or six years old. ... He was the most unbelievable man that I remember ... I remember the smell of the wax of his moustache. And I remember just listening to him and seeing this moustache and seeing that, I was just horrified—I remember sitting on my father's lap. And he wouldn't paint me because I was too young.[43]

Perhaps Dalí refused to paint Cornelia Guest because her mother had returned the portrait of Cornelia's brother, Alexander. Another reason might have been that Dalí was not at all child-oriented.[44] The actor and gallery owner Allan Rich, who edited Dalí's print portfolio "Memories of Surrealism" in 1971, mentions two incidents that document this:

I was often with Peter [Moore] and Dalí at the Ratskeller. I remember when I made the deal on "Memories of Surrealism" a little girl came over to the table and said—she was about ten years old—"Mr. Dalí, may I have your autograph?" He stuck his hand out and said, "Ten dollars, please." I gave him ten dollars and he wrote an autograph for the little girl.

When we had the opening of the Dalí exhibition for "Memories of Surrealism," we did it for the benefit of cerebral palsy at my gallery. ... Many many people came to the opening of the show. ... and a little girl was put on Dalí's lap while the press photographed it. While she was on his lap he made faces at her and went "Baaahlala." The little girl started to cry, and Dalí said, "Vedi good, vedi good." ... That's typical Dalí."[45]

While it was rare for Dalí to portray children, it was more common for Warhol to do so. He liked children, as his friend the photographer Christopher Makos recalled: "Andy needed to have contact with at least four or five kids a day. He loved smart ones as much as beautiful ones, but if they were dumb, he'd say, 'Oh God, not another one.'"[46] In 1983, Warhol even created the series *Toy Paintings* especially for children and it was exhibited from the end of the year at the Galerie Bruno Bischofberger in Zurich. He had also created child-friendly wallpaper for the exhibition.[47]

38
Warhol 1976, p. 8.

39
Morris 2012; Cornelia Guest in a telephone conversation with the author on January 3, 2013.

40
Salk 2013, p. 123. The portrait was dated by Dalí as 1959; see Fundació Gala-Salvador Dalí, cat. 664.

41
Quoted according to Hirschberg 2001.

42
Salk 2013, p. 123.

43
Cornelia Guest in a telephone conversation with the author on January 3, 2013.

44
Cf. Pauwels/Dalí 1985, p. 154. Regarding Dalí's relationship with animals, see the chapter **Mustache, Wig, and Other Signature Features** in Part 2.

45
Allan Rich in a telephone conversation with the author on April 25, 2013.

46
Makos 1988, p. 34.

47
Cf. *Ménage à trois*, pp. 164f.; +

4

Warhol accomplished his first commissioned portrait in summer 1963.[48] The taxi entrepreneur Robert C. Scull, an avid collector of Warhol's works, had ordered a portrait of his wife Ethel from him. The portrait consists of thirty-six panels showing Ethel Scull in different poses, seventeen in total. Some of the pictures are repeated, but inverted or in different colors.[49] For his silkscreens, Warhol used photo booth pictures, which he appreciated at the time because of their rich contrast. The initially highly skeptical Ethel Scull was so pleased with the shots that she later remarked, "I was so pleased, I think I'll go there for all my pictures from now on."[50] Until 1966, Warhol created further portraits based on photo booth pictures and from 1971 the Polaroid Big Shot camera became his main working tool.[51]

While Warhol's early portraits from the 1960s are characterized by monochrome priming and non-textured surfaces, as already mentioned the portraits from the early 1970s display a painterly style, forming a conspicuous counterbalance to the impersonal silkscreens. Bob Colacello is of the opinion that Warhol's European clients awakened the "latent abstract expressionist" in him. "'Should I do a little de Kooning,' he would say, as he slathered brightly colored swirls and zigzags of acryl around the subject's head. 'They'll like it, right? They're French. They'll think it's more intellectual.'"[52] In a 1974 interview Warhol remarked, "When I do the portraits, I sort of half paint them just to give it a style. It's more fun—and it's faster to do. It's faster to be sloppy than it is to be neat."[53] Sometimes the artist also added calligraphic flourishes by running through the still damp acrylic paint with his index and middle finger, drawing jagged and crisscross lines and contours, wiping the top layer of color away in the process and revealing the tone of the primer once again.[54]

Towards the end of the 1970s, Warhol returned to his bold and striking style with clearly delineated color segments. Furthermore, at the beginning of the 1980s, emerging in his portraits were sketched elements that outline and complete the photographic template. The magazine *Arts* interviewed the artist in 1981 and he explained in this conversation why he now also drew, providing an insight into his portrait painting:

> *AW: I really would still rather do just a silkscreen of the face without all the rest, but people expect just a little bit more. That's why I put in all the drawing.*
>
> *Barry Blinderman: As a portraitist, what do you feel is most important to express?*
>
> *AW: I always try to make the person look good. It's easier if you give somebody something back that looks like them. Otherwise, if I were more imaginative, it wouldn't look like the person.*
>
> *BB: How many shots do you take for each portrait? Do you take them all yourself?*
>
> *AW: Yes, I take them all. Usually about 10 rolls, about 100 shots.*
>
> *BB: Do you still use the SX-70?*
>
> *AW: No, I use the "Big Shot" now.*
>
> *BB: What's been the general response to the portraits from the people who commissioned them?*

---

*+ Feldman/ Schellmann 2003, IIIA.39.

48 Frei/Printz 2002, p. 410.

49 Bourdon 1989, p. 160.

50 In Antonio/ Tuchman 1984, p. 124.

51 See the chapter **Warhol Photographs Dalí** in this part.

52 In Heymer 2000 (n.p.).

53 Quoted according to Bourdon 1989, p. 330.

54 Fremont in Geldzahler/Rosenblum 1993, p. 30.

AW: The Polaroids are really great because the people can choose the photo they want. That makes it easier. And this camera also dissolves the wrinkles and imperfections.[55]

For Warhol, it was not about capturing the character of a person in his portraits, as he presented the faces of his clients embellished as "glossy masks."[56] He once explained, "I can make ordinary people look good, but I have trouble making beautiful people look good."[57] Later on he said about attractive women: "They're the ones that turn them down. I don't know why, because I work the hardest on them and don't fluff it off as easily."[58] Warhol was particularly keen to highlight the eyes and mouth, by adding an expressionist eye shadow and making the lips overly full and sensual.[59]

The list of personalities portrayed by Warhol is long. His circle of clients included people from around the world in the fields of the arts, film, music, fashion, industry, sport, and politics. As early as the fall of 1974, his portrait business was bringing in almost a million dollars per year.[60] Warhol never made a secret of the fact that his primary interest with regard to portrait assignments was the money, which was required to pay the "kids," meaning his employees.[61] Therefore, one of the "kids'" main tasks was to find clients for the portraitist Warhol. In order to sweeten this task for them, a commission was offered as an incentive.[62] Bob Colacello recounted:

… [I]n 1970, Andy Warhol was already telling reporters that he was "just a travelling society portrait painter." He was also doing his best to turn his entire staff into travelling society portrait salesmen. He did this by keeping salaries so low that the only way those of us who did not have rich parents could afford to live comfortably was to sell his art for a twenty percent commission. He was constantly urging us to seek out potential portrait clients, whom he jokingly called "victims." Rich kids who worked at the Factory—Brigid Berlin, Catherine Guinness, Averil Payson Meyer, Nenna Eberstadt—were urged to turn their parents into victims. "When's your mother going to have her portrait done?" he'd nag. "She can afford it, can't she?" Whenever one of us went to a dinner party at a rich person's house, Andy would ask, "Did you pop the question?"[63]

Brigid Berlin, one of these "rich kids," was able to witness the portrait production at the time:

It was all really funny because when the ladies would come, we would have lunch for the ladies. The same thing every day! If you were having your portrait done, you arrived. He had two pieces, they were blue and white of Pierre Deux fabric that we'd bought in the village. And they had to tie it around them so it looked strapless. Then Gigi, the makeup person, would come over and just garbed them in this white stuff.[64]

Gigi Williams:

… [T]he women would come in wearing gowns and jewels and all this makeup. And so Andy thought it would be better if I painted their faces white and did a harsh contour on the cheeks. And we would take off their jewelry and we would wrap them in canvas that was sitting around the Factory. And then he would take the portrait. And we'd sort of go laugh about it that here these people were coming in and we were like destroying them. … Andy was a bit wicked.[65]

55
In Goldsmith 2004, p. 294.

56
Bourdon 1989, p. 340.

57
Quoted according to, p. 327.

58
Ibid.

59
Ibid., p. 338. See also the chapter **Mae West's and Marilyn Monroe's Lips** in this part.

60
Bockris 1989, p. 378.

61
Geldzahler in Geldzahler/ Rosenblum 1993, p. 23.

62
Hackett 1989, p. xiv.

63
In Heymer 2000 (n.p.).

64
Brigid Berlin in a conversation with the author on December 4, 2012 in New York.

65
Gigi Williams in a telephone conversation with the author on May 5, 2014.

Brigid Berlin:

And they'd sit in a chair and they weren't allowed to look at themselves. And then we had this beautiful table that was from the Normandy with a green marble top and the base was really all art deco-like brass. And Andy took the Polaroids for the portrait with the twenty-five-dollar Polaroid, the Sharp-Shooter. ... Once these ladies were in the hot chair, I would just sit there and laugh to myself. He's gotten them in the chair. "Are you gonna take out the wrinkles? Are there gonna be any wrinkles?" There never was a wrinkle (laughs)—as flat as anything could be. And then the ladies would want to get up from the chair when the Polaroids were being pulled out, they had to wait one minute for them to dry. And Ronnie would be there, like grabbing up the Polaroids so that they couldn't get up and look at the ones on the table.

And then the next morning, this is right after a portrait has been done, he'd call me up, I mean, I can imitate exactly what he'd say to me, word for word,

"Hi, Bridge, what's new?"

"Andy, nothing's new. It's a quarter to nine in the morning."

"Well, are there any good invitations in the book?"

"Andy, the mail hasn't come yet."

"Well, did you do it last night? Was it big?"

"Oh, Andy, it was with a baseball player from Central Park."

"Oh, gee! How old was he? Do you think he could be Mr. Right? Is Vincent there?"

"He's in the back."

"You are not throwing out anything, are you, Brigid?"

"No, Andy."

"Is Vincent up in the front yet?"

"Yes."

"Bridge, is Vincent in a crabby mood?"

"No, Andy, he's fine."

"Well, would you ask him if the check came through? That's the check from yesterday's portrait."[66]

Portrait production often monopolized Warhol and his team, but there was of course also time for other projects. Ronnie Cutrone, Warhol's assistant, reported: "There were always a number of portraits to do. That was work. But then there were other times when Andy would say, 'OK, now what are we going to do for art?'"[67] For tactical reasons, Warhol and Fred Hughes explained to every client that their portrait was both a business and an artistic transaction. If a work proved to be particularly interesting, the artist reserved the right to produce some copies for his private collection.[68]

Warhol was of course criticized for his portrait production. Bob Colacello later stated: "Most of the New York art world, which during the 1970s was infatuated with Conceptual Art and left-wing causes, reacted to Andy's commissioned portrait work with outrage and jealousy, calling it embarrassing, reactionary, frivolous and commercial beyond critical redemption."[69] The exhibition "Andy Warhol: Portraits of the 70s," which opened in November 1979 at the Whitney Museum of American Art, was intended to do justice to the significance of Warhol's portrait painting. It showed two portraits each

66
Brigid Berlin in a conversation with the author on December 4, 2012 in New York.

67
In Bockris 1989, p. 400.

68
Guiles 1989, p. 365.

69
In Heymer 2000 (n.p.).

of altogether fifty-six personalities from the worlds of show business, art, fashion, politics, and business. The pictures were hung up in pairs in three rows in a checkerboard pattern and provided a colorful spectrum of celebrities including Dennis Hopper, Mick Jagger, Liza Minnelli, Sylvester Stallone, Truman Capote, Leo Castelli, Henry Geldzahler, David Hockney, Roy and Dorothy Lichtenstein, São Schlumberger, Diane von Fürstenberg, Halston, Yves Saint Laurent, and Golda Meir. Also shown were three *Giant Maos* and eight portraits of the artist's mother in a separate part of the exhibition.[70] Robert Rosenblum, a fine arts professor at the University of New York, concluded in his catalogue essay that Warhol had become a "celebrity among celebrities" and therefore an "ideal court painter to this 1970s international aristocracy that mixed, in wildly varying proportions, wealth, high fashion, and brains."[71] One month after the exhibition's opening, he expressed to Warhol his surprise about the negative critiques.[72] In *TIME* magazine, Robert Hughes stated that Warhol "was climbing from face to face in a silent delirium of snobbery," and Hilton Kramer from the *New York Times* referred to the faces as "ugly and a shade stoned if not actually repulsive and grotesque."[73]

Despite this criticism, Warhol continued to receive a constant flow of new portrait assignments. Most came from Germany, where his work was greatly admired by art historians and critics. Warhol wrote in his diaries in February 1980: "And all the Germans want portraits. Maybe because we have a good person selling there, Hans Mayer. How come we don't get many Americans portraits?"[74] Barely a year later he wrote: "At the cocktail party at Hans Mayer's house last night, there were a lot of people I'd done portraits of who I didn't recognize, so I thought they were potential new portraits. (laughs) Oh God, no wonder people think I'm out of it."[75] At that time Germany was already the largest market for Warhol, followed by France, Italy, and England.[76] Anyone could have the artist paint his or her portrait. The prices were staggered. Vincent Fremont provides details as follows: "Portrait commissions beginning around 1970 were $25,000 for the first 40 × 40-inch portrait and $15,000 for the second one, meaning two portraits for $40,000. If the client wanted more than two, the next portrait panels could be negotiated depending on how many more they wanted. By around 1986 the commission went up to $30,000 for the first portrait and $20,000 for the second portrait."[77] As a rule, four portraits were created. A clever business practice was developed in order to sell as many as possible. Bob Colacello commented on this: "Clients were encouraged to commission additional panels, at U.S. $15,000 each, of the same portrait in different colors, and those who didn't were considered 'cheap.' We were all trained to tell clients, 'Repetition is a very important element of Andy's aesthetic.' Of course, it really was, and the more serious collectors usually did order four or more panels."[78] Horst Weber von Beeren, who as Rupert Jasen Smith's assistant printed many portraits for Warhol, explains: "Andy liked clients like Diana Ross, who instantly signed a giant check, put all seven of the canvasses into her limousine and as a reward was on next month's *Interview* magazine. So much for editorial freedom."[79] The singer had commissioned four portraits of herself and one of each of her three daughters, for a total of $95,000.[80] Udo Kier, who played

---

70
Cf. Whitney 1979, pp. 24ff.; Bourdon 1989, p. 376.

71
In Whitney 1979, p. 15.

72
Hackett 1989, p. 249, December 20, 1979.

73
Bockris 1989, p. 432.

74
Hackett 1989, p. 263, February 19, 1980.

75
Hackett 1989, p. 361, March 8, 1981.

76
Vincent Fremont in a conversation with the author on June 28, 2012 in New York.

77
Vincent Fremont in an e-mail to the author on April 16, 2015.

78
In Heymer 2000 (n.p.).

79
Hort Weber von Beeren in an e-mail to the author on April 28, 2015.

80
Colacello 1990, p. 446.

the main role in Warhol's movie productions *Blood for Dracula* and *Flesh for Frankenstein* directed by Paul Morrissey, says of other well-heeled clients who had commissioned a portrait:

Andy always painted four. And I witnessed a purchase—without naming names—by one of these big families, in financial terms. The wife said, "That's really very nice. How many did Mrs. 'So-and-so' buy?" The reply was, "All four, of course." Then the woman went to the telephone, made a call, and bought all four. Then I asked Andy, "Tell me, what would you do—after all, a portrait of strangers is a very private matter—if she had only bought one?" To that, Mr. Warhol replied, "Then I would paint over it."[81]

Because of the flow of assignments, Warhol had his assistants prepare canvasses to have in stock in two colors: a flesh-colored tone for portraits of men and a somewhat more pink tone for portraits of women.[82] The canvasses were then painted with acrylic paint and in the end the portrait was printed as a silkscreen. Horst Weber von Beeren recalls that this last step often took place under great time pressure and explains:

Acrylic is water-based and silkscreen ink is oil-based. You can print oil-base on water-base, but not the other way around. For a natural, solid drying of the silkscreen ink it takes twelve to twenty hours. ... How many times did Warhol call Rupert's studio, where the art was being made, to hurry us: "Quick, quick the client is here. Put in more cobalt-dryer into the color and cook it up!" Cobalt-dryer is the most toxic substance but it speeds up the drying process. Then we hung the printed canvasses on a laundry line, like washed laundry across the street in Naples. Safety concerns were of no issue: we put the heater on full blast, even in the heat of the summer, and blow-dried them with hair-dryers until they were half dry, "tacky" as we called it. You still could imprint your fingerprint on it. We rolled them up and Rupert took them by subway or taxi through the backdoor of Interview *magazine to hand them to Andy, who presented them. The clients had waiting times of many months, but the actual product was done in a day.*[83]

Piss Pen versus Piss Painting

Urine provided Salvador Dalí inspiration for several artistic experiments. In the late 1950s, the American painter Constantin Alajalov, with whom Dalí was on friendly terms, reported :

... [A]rtists are immensely concerned with the techniques, mediums (painting), priming of canvasses, etc., etc. One day Dalí and I were talking about different painting mediums, and I asked him what he uses to mix his paints with, and, with a completely straight face, and in utmost seriousness, he said that he uses nothing but linseed oil, but, he added, he lets it stay in an open dish for a few days until flies land in it to die, and then, said he, "I wait till they decompose in it, adding their juices to the oil, and then I do a little pee-pee in it, and it gives me the best medium to paint with!"[1]

Dalí was heavily occupied by one of his urine experiments in the 1970s. Amanda Lear recorded that he was fascinated by the ballpoint pens in the hotel rooms at the St. Regis:

81
Udo Kier in a telephone conversation with the author on January 7, 2011 (translated from the German).

82
Hackett 1989, p. xv.

83
Horst Weber von Beeren in a conversation with the author on December 7, 2012, in New York and in an e-mail to the author on February 10, 2013.

1
In Cowles 1959, pp. 220f.

He had discovered that as the metal ring on the pen slowly rusted, it made minute spots in which he could make out a whole world. He had at least twenty of these pens and he accelerated the rusting process by peeing on them: the urine attacked the metal. Dalí kept these pens in a drawer where he gloated over them. He wanted to film these stains, and with them make his full-length psychedelic feature, "Journey to Outer Mongolia." He asked me to help him by peeing a couple of times on the pens, so that I would contribute to the rusting process.[2]

Robert Descharnes said that Dalí handed him an oxidized pen and suggested using it as a starting point for a movie. He was to turn the pen slowly, so that the Battle of Thermopylae would be played out before his eyes.[3] In 1974, the Spanish movie director José Montes-Baquer approached Dalí to talk to him about a documentary on audiovisual art in America, which he was shooting for the Westdeutsche Rundfunk. The painter seized the opportunity to show the director one of his oxidized pens and declared:

In this clean and aseptic country, I have been observing how the urinals in the luxury restrooms of this hotel have acquired an astounding range of rust colors through the interaction of the uric acid and the precious metals. For this reason, I have been regularly urinating on the brass band of this pen over the past weeks to obtain the magnificent structures that you will find with your cameras and lenses. By simply looking at the band with my own eyes, I can see Dalí on the moon, or Dalí sipping coffee on the Champs Elysées. Take then this magical object, work with it, and when you have an interesting result, come see me. If the result is good, we will make a film together.[4]

The German TV team did in fact spend a week filming the structures on the little metal ring and then presented Dalí with a thirty-minute video, which he found "infinitely better" than anything he had anticipated.[5] This marked the birth of the movie *Impressions de la Haute Mongolie – Hommage à Raymond Roussel*, which was awarded the Prix Italia in 1976.[6] Dalí retrospectively commented on it as follows:

It's a film which was made by some Germans who came to my hotel in New York, the St. Regis-Sheraton, to take some film of me. I'm always on the boil, and at the time I was having an extraordinary experience. ... I said to the Germans, you ought to film that, just focus on the pen, which I'll keep turning slowly, and record my voice, what I'm saying. They set to work. When this is shown on a screen, one sees fabulous lunar landscapes, strange, bearded, and magical, and you hear me describing them in exact detail: lakes, mountains, passes. You can see Outer Mongolia. It's better than my other films, including Le Chien andalou, *which I made with Buñuel almost half a century ago.*[7]

The oxidized ballpoint pen is the starting point for Dalí's movie, which purports to be a documentary and tells of a supposed expedition into Outer Mongolia to search for gigantic, white, hallucinogenic mushrooms. The effect of these mushrooms, which can reach a height of eighteen meters in six years, was many times stronger than that of LSD. A princess had guarded them during a famine and her subjects had become "cretins," as they were no longer able to distinguish between reality and fiction. Only towards the end of the film does it become clear that the images from what is supposedly

2
Lear 1985, p. 269.

3
Descharnes/ Descharnes 2003, p. 251. The battle described by Herodotus took place in 480 BC at the start of the second Persian War.

4
Quoted according to King in Gale 2007, pp. 222f.

5
Ibid., p. 223.

6
Bigwood in Abadie 1979, p. 353.

7
Dalí (1977) in Gómez de la Serna 1988, p. 223.

Mongolia are enlarged shots of the microscopically small traces of corrosion on the metal ring of the ballpoint pen.

Ultra Violet reported that Andy Warhol visited one of the "viewings of the Piss Pen." She also believed Warhol allowed himself to be inspired by the unusual exhibit for his own works:

The idea is bizarre enough to attract him. ...

Andy must find out now if his penis can produce art as marketable as his hand. Using his own urine (or an assistant's—who is ever to know?), he leaks it over a canvas previously covered with copper paint. What he gets resembles a large Polaroid picture in the making, a bad Polaroid that stops the Rorschach-like orange and green blobs resolve into a finished image. He calls the collection of murky images Oxidation Paintings *and exhibits them at galleries in Paris and Zurich and at Documenta Seven in Kassel ...*[8]

It is debatable whether Dalí's "Piss Pen" provided the inspiration for Warhol's *Oxidation Paintings*, which he started producing as early as 1977. In his diaries he tells of a lunch with Dalí on Palm Sunday in 1978: "He said that my idea of piss-painting was old-fashioned because it'd been in the movie *Teorema* which (laughs) is true, it was. I knew that."[9] In this 1968 work by Pier Paolo Pasolini, one of the movie characters decides to become an artist and experiments with painting techniques, including urinating on a canvas. Dalí liked this criticism of modern art, which is why *Teorema* was one of the few contemporary movies that he actually liked.[10]

Warhol was already working with urine in the early 1960s. The young commercial artist, who was just embarking on his career at the time, was concerned that his works needed artistic originality to be taken seriously. For that reason, he experimented with various techniques.[11] Warhol once placed a canvas in front of his door, in order to examine the artistic potential of the footprints left by visitors.[12] He liked the spontaneity of these works, as his later assistant Ronnie Cutrone described: "Like when he was much younger, he would take canvas late at night, when the cars couldn't park there and he would put a roll of canvas out, down on the street along the curb. Cars would pull in, cars would go out—he'd have all these tire tracks on a big piece of canvas and that was a painting."[13] On another occasion, Warhol peed on canvasses, but was not satisfied with the result.[14] When asked in 1976 in an interview if there were "any old non-representational paintings that no one knows about," he remarked, "The only ones I have are the piss paintings; I have a couple. That was a long time ago. Then there were the canvasses that I used to leave on the street and people used to walk on them; in the end I had a lot of dirty canvasses. Then I thought they were all diseased so I rolled them up and put them somewhere."[15] Ronnie Cutrone reported that Warhol brought these canvasses out again over a decade later: "... he unrolled one and looked at it and said 'Gee, I wonder if that would work now.'"[16]

For production of the *Oxidation Paintings,* the process unfolded as follows: The canvasses were spread out on the ground and primed with copper paint, then Warhol or one of his assistants, Ronnie Cutrone or Walter Steding, his friend Victor Hugo, or even one of the guests at the Factory did

---

8 Ultra Violet 1988, p. 261.

9 Hackett 1989, p. 119, March 19, 1978. Similarly, in Warhol/Colacello 1979, p. 129. Regarding this encounter see the chapter **The 1970s** in Part 5.

10 Lear 1985, p. 254.

11 See also the chapter **Coca-Cola is the Real Pop Art** in this part.

12 Bockris 1989, p. 136.

13 Ronnie Cutrone in a telephone conversation with the author on July 8, 2012.

14 Bockris 1989, p. 136.

15 Quoted according to Frei/Printz 2002, p. 469.

16 In Smith 1986, p. 287.

the urinating. In 1985 the artist remarked that a certain technique was required in order to produce an accomplished painting:

... [I]f I asked somebody to do an Oxidation Painting, they just wouldn't think about it and it would just be a mess. Then I did it myself. You know it's too much work ... when someone comes to try to figure out a good design or something like that. And sometimes it wouldn't turn green. I don't know. ...

... It was just copper paint and you would wonder why sometimes it did turn green and sometimes it didn't. It would just turn black, or something. I don't know what made it do that.[17]

Warhol's printer Rupert Jasen Smith reported that he had first shown the artist copper paint: "I introduced Andy to metallics. He uses them in a different way. And that we just paint the copper on; and, while it's still damp—slightly wet, Andy pisses all over them, and they turn green."[18] Vincent Fremont recalled that the Factory was filled with quite a distinct odor at the time: "Andy was taking a lot of B vitamins, and during the whole period the back room stank of piss."[19] Ronnie Cutrone was also taking a lot of vitamin B at the time. Warhol asked him not to pee after getting up in the morning, but to hold it in until he got to the Factory.[20] Cutrone explained, "I knew about vitamins and everything, so if you drink vitamin B, your pee comes out day-glow orange and day-glow yellow. I said 'Andy, we can get more color out of this.' So, then we started treating our bodies like paint brushes."[21]

A look at his diaries reveals that Warhol was working on increasing the production of the *Oxidation Paintings*. In October 1978 he wrote: "Doug Christmas wants to show the Piss paintings in Paris after we go to Denmark, so I'll have to drink more water and make more. I can do two a day now, and Fred told me to put two of them together, that they look more interesting that way."[22] One month later he noted: "I think I may try *brushing* the piss on the Piss paintings now."[23] Despite the fun factor during the production, Warhol took the *Oxidation Paintings* seriously. Walter Steding recalls that Warhol was committed to an idea and could get angry when it was deviated from:

One time Ronnie and I did a trick. There was a lot of down time at the Factory and we made some excrement out of foam rubber and painted them and put them on the canvas. ... And he was so upset when he saw that and he'd rarely go so far. He took it seriously. Ronnie came out of the other room, "Gee, Andy, you should see what Walter did on your pictures." He didn't think it would be funny. Not that, anyhow. He didn't like paint tricks.[24]

The oxidation process on the paintings took a few years before the coloring was stable.[25] In 1985, Warhol remarked that the *Oxidation Paintings* must not be exposed to great heat: "... when I showed them in Paris, the hot lights made them melt again ... it's very weird when they drip down. ... And then I realized why it dripped ... because there were just too many puddles, and it should have been less puddles ... and the puddles sort of dried ... But when the hot lights were on it, it just sort of ... the crystals melted."[26] Ronnie Cutrone additionally explained:

They were serious, because they looked like Japanese landscapes. Those were nice abstract paintings. ... We also had a joke name for the show, which was called "Piss Elegant." We loved them, because they did turn out to be very

17
In *Andy Warhol B&W Paintings*, pp. 38, 41.

18
In Smith 1986, p. 470.

19
In Bockris 1989, p. 419.

20
Hackett 1989, p. 55, June 28, 1977.

21
Ronnie Cutrone in a telephone conversation with the author on July 8, 2012.

22
Hackett 1989, p. 174, October 2, 1978.

23
Ibid., p. 182, November 13, 1978.

24
Walter Steding in a telephone conversation with the author on January 12, 2013.

25
Bourdon 1989, p. 371.

26
In *Andy Warhol B&W Paintings*, pp. 38, 41.

elegant. And they were also horribly mundane and sort of disgusting. They went to Paris and the lights were too hot for the show, so the piss started to melt a bit. Not a lot. So, it got all like sort of funky and it started to smell a bit. So, Andy's collectors are coming in for twenty-five and fifty-thousand-dollar paintings of piss and the room smells like a lavatory.[27]

Dalí and Warhol in Drag

Andy Warhol had a particular affinity to transvestism throughout his life, and played with his own appearance as well as gender perceptions and attributions. In answer to the question of why he dyed his hair, he once remarked in an interview, "… Edie's hair was dyed silver, and therefore I copied [that to] my hair because I wanted to look like Edie because I always wanted to look like a girl."[1] In 1979, Warhol posed in front of the camera for Paul Weiss in Washington. The photographer, who was only twenty-five years old at the time, was working on *American Beauties*, a series of photos for which he photographed men and women wearing ladies' hats from the 1940s and 1950s. Warhol liked the idea and let himself be photographed with hats, both alone and with his companions Bob Colacello and Chris Murray, at Weiss's studio. Paul Weiss recounts, "I had used natural light. … When Warhol saw the photos, he turned to Bob Colacello and said: 'My God, my skin looks so good!' He just loved the way that he was photographed and he asked me if I'd like to work for him in the Washington, DC area."[2]

When Warhol was working on his *Myths* series in early 1981, he posed as his own model in women's clothes and later recorded in his diaries: "I look pretty good in drag, and I thought it would be fun for me to pose for it myself, but Fred said to do myself in drag at a later date, not to use up the idea on this portfolio."[3] During the same year, the artist was given the opportunity to model in similar attire in front of his friend Christopher Makos's camera. For Makos it was about playing with identity, but to merely dress Warhol up as a woman would have been too simple.[4] Makos later recalled:

We both loved Duchamp, Dalí, and Man Ray, and the whole ambience of Surrealism. At the time I was thinking intensely about an important project that I wanted to be perfect for him. I knew that some people considered Andy to be a latter-day Dadaist and I saw quite clearly that I should take as my starting point some of the fabulous photographs of 1921 in which Man Ray portrayed Duchamp as Rrose Sélavy, wearing a woman's hat and dress. It was obvious that any endeavor would have to explore our own intuitions and not just express a shoddy copy of a work from 60 years before. …

We set to work. Halston suggested a sumptuous sequined evening dress that we didn't feel was right. We didn't want a drag act, so we worked exclusively on the face and hair, keeping the outfit Andy was wearing at the time—jeans, button-down white shirt, checkered tie, and cowboy boots. We were sure that the facial make-up and the wig would provide a wonderful contrast with the tie and jeans, which in turn would tone down the female caricature.

…

27
Ronnie Cutrone in a telephone conversation with the author on July 8, 2012.

→ **38** [p. 387]

1
Warhol (1966) in Goldsmith 2004, p. 113.

2
Paul Weiss in a telephone conversation with the author on March 30, 2015.

3
Hackett 1989, p. 358, February 16, 1981. See also the chapter **Working on Their Own Myths** in Part 2.

4
Christopher Makos in a conversation with the author on June 28, 2012 in New York.

4

The great day of the first session of poses arrived, and it was only then that we realized that a bit of make-up and a studied expression would not be enough to transform a man into a woman. So we decided to have two different sessions: in the first one Andy came made up in the same way as the women whose portraits he did for commissions. In those photos he has the same lost expression as the collectors portrayed by Cindy Sherman, who was always photographing them. I inserted these shots for their importance, knowing that they would become only richer with time.

There was the glamour session, and with the help of a professional theater make-up artist Andy became an extraordinary woman.

→ **36** [p. 386]

Eight wigs, two days of posing, sixteen contact prints, and 349 shots ... The result is that even now some people ask me if Faye Dunaway is actually concealed in one of the photos![5]

In the photos from the first session Warhol is wearing more discreet makeup than in the "glamour session" shots. In the latter he appears as a caricature of a woman, while in the first session Makos succeeded in convincingly capturing the artist's feminine alter ego. Warhol documented the whole photo session. On some shots one can spot a tape recorder on his lap, which appears to be running. Warhol also had photos of himself taken with his Polaroid camera and let Vincent Fremont film him with a video camera for almost an hour.[6] At the beginning of the video recording the artist says, "God. It must be hard to be a girl. Or a drag queen."[7]

If Salvador Dalí's account is to be believed, he already had problems with accepting his male identity as a child. In *The Secret Life* he reveals to readers that cross-dressing was one of his greatest passions at the time. An uncle from Barcelona had given him an ermine cape, a golden scepter, and a crown with a white wig attached to it as a gift. "That evening I looked at myself in the mirror, wearing my crown, the cape just draped over my shoulders, and the rest of my body completely naked. Then I pushed my sexual parts back out of my sight and squeezed them between my thighs so as to look as much as possible like a girl."[8] In his *Unspeakable Confessions*, Dalí adds, "I did not belong to any sex, I was neither boy nor girl, but perhaps angel or demon."[9] Dalí's 1950 painting *Myself at the Age of Six when I Thought I Was a Girl Lifting with Extreme Precaution the Skin of the Sea to Observe a Dog Sleeping in the Shade of the Water* testifies to his childhood wish to be a girl. It is evident that the child in the painting not only believes she is a girl, but in fact actually is.

Eric Schaal photographed Dalí and Gala at Hampton Manor, the country estate in Virginia belonging to their friend Caresse Crosby, in 1941 and 1942. Dalí worked frantically there, with Gala's support, on his autobiography *The Secret Life of Salvador Dalí*.[10] The book was announced in 1942 in the September issue of the magazine *Click*, for which Dalí created a collage, using photos by Schaal. Four of these photos show him dressed up as a maid.[11] The source of inspiration for the shots was a drawing that served as an illustration for his *Secret Life*. It shows a little girl who has put her doll aside and is fondly hugging a skeleton instead.[12] Schaal's photos show Dalí wearing a white blouse, a skirt with an apron and a blonde wig with long

→ **37** [p. 387]

5
In Makos 2002 (n.p.).

6
Ill. of the Polaroids in Francis/ King 1997, pp. 220, 222ff.

7
Quoted according to Meyer-Hermann 2008, p. 01:32:00.

8
Dalí 1942, p. 70.

9
Dalí 1976, p. 64.

10
See the chapter **Autobiographies Written "With Four Hands"** in this part.

11
Ill. in *Dalí versus Schaal*, pp. 118f.

12
In the *Click* announcement, Dalí referred to the little child
+

locks. In accordance with the book illustration, there is a doll lying at his feet and he is holding a skeleton in his arms, which appears to be returning his gesture and also has an arm draped around the artist's shoulder.[13] Dalí declined to wear makeup, which would not have appeared very convincing because of his prominent mustache. Contrary to Warhol, Dalí was not seeking to be a convincing woman, even though he also had a particular affinity to transvestism.[14] His intention was more to amuse and to illustrate that—as can be read in the text—"every man has as much right to be insane as he has to be sane." In the early 1940s anything else would have been scarcely conceivable anyway. The photos by Christopher Makos taken forty years later, on the other hand, give a sense of the seriousness with which Warhol approached the camera.

WORK

5 ENCOUNTERS

6 VIEWS OF EACH OTHER'S WORK AND PERSONALITY

– CONCLUSION

5

Salvador Dalí and Andy Warhol met frequently. Most of these encounters took place in New York. The following chapters attempt to reconstruct the encounters between Dalí and Warhol on the basis of sources, documents, and statements by contemporary witnesses. They seek to illuminate, in particular, the development of the two artists' relationship over time. First of all, however, it is necessary to determine when and where Dalí and Warhol met for the first time.

The First Encounter

Amanda Lear writes in her memoirs *My Life with Dalí* that Salvador Dalí and Andy Warhol first met in the mid-1950s: "Dalí had met Warhol when he was just a window dresser; he had come to show him his drawings of shoes. Dalí admitted that he was quite talented ... ."[1] Lear adds:

During the few winter months in New York Dalí liked to entertain. He was like a king holding court. So he would hold it downstairs in the King Cole Bar at the St. Regis, which was a beautiful lounge. And there he had his table every afternoon; he used it to call the five o'clock tea. And he would invite anybody to tea who would want to talk with him. So there were a lot of artists, ... a lot of musicians, ... a lot of actors, models, pretty boys, pretty girls, everyone. And Andy Warhol came one day and he said to Dalí, "I am the window dresser in a big department store." He was doing the windows at Bonwit Teller's. His specialty was making drawings of shoes and they were very, very good drawings, I must say. And Dalí encouraged him and said, "Well, instead of making shoes, you can also make other things." In fact, Dalí always claimed that he was the first one to encourage Warhol toward this Pop period.[2]

It is by all means conceivable that Dalí and Warhol met as early as the mid-1950s. After all, as described by Lear, anyone could show up at Dalí's tea-time at the St. Regis Hotel.[3] However, at the time, as a commercial artist, Warhol was still completely unknown outside of the advertising industry. Dalí had also been designing advertisements for years and had influenced the advertising style in the United States,[4] but for him, advertising was just one field of creative activity among many and not the focus of his artistic work. It is therefore questionable whether the commercial artist Andy Warhol was of any interest at all to the fine artist Salvador Dalí, who at the time, in the 1950s, had attained worldwide fame. Perhaps they found a topic of conversation in their window displays for Bonwit Teller—as Dalí had also designed window displays for the department store in 1936 and 1939.[5] However, it is unlikely that Warhol, who was always monosyllabic when faced with people he did not know, would have even been capable of such a spontaneous exchange with Dalí, because the Spaniard was always surrounded by people during tea-time at the St. Regis. It is also doubtful whether Warhol would have even had the opportunity to do so. It is quite probable that the comment Lear attributes to Dalí about encouraging Warhol is simply fictitious. Amanda Lear states in her autobiography *Je ne suis pas du tout celle que vous croyez ...*, published in 2009: "The maestro always thought that nothing happened without him."[6] The Austrian artist Ernst Fuchs, who was on friendly terms with Dalí, had a similar view:

1
Lear 1985, p. 113.

2
Amanda Lear in a telephone conversation with the author on March 13, 2010.

3
See also the chapter **Companions, Courtiers, and Superstars** in Part 3.

4
See the chapter **Advertisements for Nylons and Ladies' Shoes** in Part 4.

5
See the chapter **Window Displays** in Part 4.

6
Lear 2009, p. 65 (translated from the French).

5

As he always had a tendency to refer all signs of the time to himself, of course he also undoubtedly related the Warhol phenomenon to himself. Once, I recall, he said: "Today everyone wants psychedelic art, and everything has to be psychedelic. But I myself am the drug. I myself am psychedelic, as it were." He always made everything revolve around himself in this way. And the station of Perpignan was of course the center of the world, because he was there. Therefore he actually saw the whole world as something he had, in fact, invented.[7]

The painter Harald Stevenson, born in 1929 in Oklahoma, came to New York in 1949, like Warhol, and the two soon met at Serendipity 3. They became friends and Stevenson also appeared in a few of Warhol's movies.[8] Stevenson reports that he last saw Warhol two days before the Pop artist's death. They met for a drink at the King Cole Bar at the St. Regis, where Dalí met people on a regular basis until the end of the 1970s, and found themselves immersed in a discussion about Warhol's magazine, *Interview*.[9] Stevenson had met Dalí through the Greek art dealer Alexander Iolas, who had specialized in surrealist art and had enabled Warhol's first exhibition in New York in 1952. Iolas also presented the last exhibition during the artist's lifetime, held in Milan, showing a series of works inspired by Leonardo da Vinci's *Last Supper*.[10] Harold Stevenson says about a first potential encounter between Dalí and Warhol in the 1950s:

To my recollection, Dalí and Andy would have met at the place called the Serendipity, which was a little coffee shop. I don't know the exact moment but probably 1950 or 1951 ... in the public eye it was the first place to go. And so Salvador Dalí knew it and Andy knew it. And I'm sure they met there. They weren't the greatest friends. I mean they barely knew one another. So Dalí didn't have time for Andy. Nobody on earth knew who Andy Warhol was at that moment. And Dalí was a snob, you know. Do you think he would spend time with an unknown? ... at that moment Salvador Dalí was at the very peak of his fame. Dalí was probably the most famous artist in the world. So, how would an obscure unknown person like Andy try to get the attention of Salvador Dalí?[11]

Unfortunately, Stephen Bruce, who opened Serendipity 3 with two friends in 1954, cannot confirm that the first encounter between Dalí and Warhol took place there. He thinks, however, that it is by all means possible, particularly since celebrities such as Marilyn Monroe, Cary Grant, Bette Davis, Truman Capote, and Tennessee Williams frequented the restaurant in its early days. With regard to Warhol and Dalí, he explains, "both were seeking celebrity status and attention all the time."[12] John Giorno, who was Warhol's life partner in 1963 and 1964, is also inclined to believe that Dalí's and Warhol's paths crossed as early as the 1950s. At the time, according to Giorno, it was indeed not unusual to bump into Dalí in New York. He had also seen Dalí and Gala once from a distance. However, it could not be called a true encounter. The first "formal meeting" did not happen until later.[13]

In *Andy Warhol's Exposures* there is a passage in the chapter dedicated to Dalí that might provide a clue as to when the two artists first met: "Actually, I met Dalí in the sixties when one of my superstars, Ultra Violet, brought him to the Factory."[14] However, the book, which was published in 1979, was actually written by Bob Colacello, and furthermore, Warhol was an advocate

293

7
Prof. Ernst Fuchs in a conversation with the author on May 13, 2010 in Klagenfurt (translated from the German).

8
Cf. Angell 2006, pp. 193f.

9
Clark 2009.

10
Harold Stevenson in a telephone conversation with the author on February 8, 2011. More details about Warhol's *Last Supper* series in the chapter **Religious Art** in Part 4.

11
Harold Stevenson in a telephone conversation with the author on February 8, 2011.

12
Stephen Bruce in a telephone conversation with the author on July 6, 2011.

13
John Giorno in a conversation with the author on March 13, 2011 in Besançon.

14
Warhol/Colacello 1979, p. 129.

of the "just-make-it-up philosophy."[15] Colacello therefore also writes in his memoirs *Holy Terror*: "Andy and Dalí had been introduced by Ultra Violet in the sixties ..."[16] Ultra Violet also reported that she had brought Dalí to the Factory, so that Warhol could do a *Screen Test* with him.[17] This took place on the evening of February 6, 1966.[18] However, Dalí's visit to the Factory could not have been the very first encounter of the two artists, because Warhol had already visited Dalí at his studio at the St. Regis in early 1965, together with the photographer David McCabe, who captured this encounter in numerous photographs.[19]

Ultra Violet, on the other hand, writes in her memoirs *Famous For 15 Minutes* that Dalí had introduced her to Warhol "one day in 1963," when they had tea at the St. Regis.[20] This would mean that the two artists already knew each other at that point. In relation to this, Jean-Michel Bouhours states, "The date on which Dalí and Warhol met remains uncertain. Ultra Violet situates it around 1963; which firmly contradicts the poet and photographer Gerard Malanga ... who places it later on December 18, 1965 at the Gallery of Modern Art."[21] Malanga reports that he met Dalí for the first time in the context of the opening of his retrospective in New York at Huntington Hartford's Gallery of Modern Art.[22] This took place on the evening of March 17, 1965.[23] He emphasizes, however, that he cannot recall seeing Warhol there.[24] In an attempt to clarify this, John Giorno confirms that it was Ultra Violet who brought Dalí and Warhol together, but that the first encounter between the artists proceeded differently. He reports that the first "formal meeting" took place on January 10, 1964:[25]

It was a very cold winter, and it had snowed a really deep snow. But then half of it melted and froze again. Ultra Violet was an old friend of mine at that point, and she was arranging this formal meeting with Dalí and Andy for the first time. ... We were all in awe of Dalí. ... I knew the St. Regis really well for a number of reasons and Andy did too, but when we arrived there for drinks we were like little urchins. The arrival was around seven o' clock and we went up to the bar and sat in one of the banquettes. But instead of ordering something, we did not order anything. ... I had a hangover and we were acting like urchins. The place was completely empty and we waited and waited. And then, after about ten or fifteen minutes, Ultra came down to say that Dalí and Gala were coming down, which they did about five or ten minutes later. And so we were sitting there, but it was really awkward. ... Andy and I were really good friends, it was like a lover relationship where you just talk, but there it had become this really awkward situation. What happened was that we ordered drinks. ... Apart from that almost nothing happened. Gala was very charming and the one who generated the conversation. She would just talk in that relaxed way and Ultra was like that too, so Andy did not say much. Dalí was relaxed and cheerful and just the way he was. The conversation was mostly about nothing, and once or twice Andy actually got to say, "Oh yes," (laughs) or maybe even three words, because it was an answer to a question. But that was it.[26]

John Giorno also recalls that at this first "official meeting" with Dalí, Warhol was "on speed," in other words, he had taken amphetamines. He says that the artist wasn't nervous, but one could feel that it was an important moment for him. Giorno believes that Warhol evidently thought the time had come for him to be officially introduced to Dalí. After all, Warhol had achieved a degree of fame through his participation in the exhibition "New Realists" at Sidney Janis in New York, which ran at the end of 1962.[27] He was also able to look back on two solo exhibitions at this point: at the Ferus Gallery in Los Angeles and his first solo exhibition at the Stable Gallery in New York.[28] As Dalí attentively followed new art movements, he would have also been aware of Warhol and have had an interest, on his part, in getting to know his younger colleague.

Neither Dalí nor Warhol ever made any great effort to recall the exact circumstances of their first encounter. Dalí was keen to declare that he had encouraged Warhol to become a fine artist. It is similar for Warhol. He would probably have wished for "more glamorous" circumstances for his first encounter with Dalí. This was no doubt also a reason why, in his book *Andy Warhol's Exposures*, he relocated the first encounter to the Factory and liked to claim that Ultra Violet had brought Dalí to him. The two artists were thus both eager to claim that they had the upper hand during their first encounter.

The 1960s

The exhibition "NOT SEEN and/or LESS SEEN by/of MARCEL DUCHAMP/RROSE SÉLAVY 1904–1964" was held at the Cordier & Ekstrom Gallery in New York from mid-January to mid-February 1965. It showed early drawings and paintings by Duchamp. The playing-card size invitation he designed featured a reproduction of the *Mona Lisa*—without a mustache—with "*L.H.O.O.Q.*" and "*rasée*" inscribed below it.[1] Not only Marcel Duchamp, but also many famous names from the art world—including Salvador Dalí and Andy Warhol—attended the opening on January 13, 1965.[2] Dalí was undoubtedly the most famous contemporary artist at the time next to Picasso. Warhol's participation was an indication that he, too, had become one of his generation's most famous artists.

Several weeks later Dalí and Warhol met at the Fischbach Gallery in New York, where Wynn Chamberlain had a major exhibition of nude portraits in early February.[3] Chamberlain's wife Sally recalls,

I will never forget the evening in February 1965 when Wynn's Naked Nudes were revealed at the Fischbach Gallery on Madison Avenue. A huge crowd had come, drawn by Allen Ginsberg's short piece for the invitation entitled, "Why I like to see myself naked." The U.S. Postal Service had unsuccessfully tried to suppress this flyer and that night police patrolled the streets outside the gallery to keep innocent eyes from seeing the degree of nakedness being displayed. The center of all eyes was Poets Dressed and Undressed, a double portrait of poet Frank O'Hara and his friends.

...

Barnett Newman, Larry Rivers, and Salvador Dalí congratulated Wynn, saying he had opened up a new direction in painting the human body. Frank O'Hara stood in front of Poets exclaiming, "Aren't they great? Aren't they eye openers?" Andy Warhol sidled through the crowd, saying "wow," while Gala

27
Ibid.

28
Warhol's first exhibition at the Ferus Gallery took place from July 9 to August 4, 1962, the second from September 30 to October 1963. His exhibition at the New York Stable Gallery lasted from November 6 to 24, 1962. Cf. Frankel Nathanson in McShine 1989, pp. 407f.

1
The exhibition ran from January 14–February 13. Cf. D'Harnoncourt/McShine 1973, p. 28. The invitation card is reproduced on p. 315.

2
Tomkins 1999, p. 506.

→
40 [p. 389]

3
The exhibition was held from February 2–19, 1965. Cf. Morgan 1995, p. 320.

Dalí, her cash-register eyes scanning the guests, held on firmly to her protégé William Rothlein, whom she and Dalí had named Adil, because he looked so much like the young Dalí.

... I remember Gala hissing in my ear that she and Dalí were ensorcelled by Adil and they were going to make him an international star. ... But there was such a huge crowd there that I don't remember any interaction between Dalí and Andy.

I think the next morning when Andy called Wynn (at that time he called him daily, always asking Wynn what he should do next, along with asking who he had seen at what gathering or where we were going that night), he put down the nudes, saying something like he preferred Wynn's former Magic Realist style, which would probably sell better than these nudes.[4]

As already mentioned, William Rothlein met Dalí and Gala for the first time in May 1964.[5] He reports that Warhol occasionally appeared at Dalí's tea-time gatherings. Rothlein dates the encounters between the two artists as February 1965.[6]

There were so many different people around Dalí at that time who would come to see him in the afternoon at the St. Regis Hotel. ... Dalí and Warhol were just very respectful of each other. ... Dalí was very animated and always in control of the whole situation and very, very high strung, very nervous, moving around quite a bit ... always the center of attention. And Warhol would sit there very quietly and never move, listen and just be very soft. He spoke very softly. ... Warhol was very cool and just reserved, extremely reserved, and almost shy-like. He was the opposite of Dalí. ... Warhol was just very diminutive. He was small next to Dalí but very agreeable also. He was much more approachable and more down-to-earth in a sense. You could talk to him. ... I liked Andy. Andy was always a gentle guy. ... He knew my relationship with Dalí and Gala. He never tried to probe and find things out. He never even asked me about Dalí. ... He was very himself. He was very self-contained. ... He was just very self-confident, quiet and assured of who he was. Andy had self-respect.[7]

Ultra Violet reports that at the time, Warhol sometimes accompanied her to tea with Dalí at the St. Regis. One day the Spaniard even took them up to his studio, which is where Warhol saw a "foot-long, helium-filled silver blimp attached to a string," which may have provided the inspiration for his *Silver Clouds*.[8]

Around that time, Dalí and Warhol also met at a party held by Henry Geldzahler. Warhol's assistant Billy Name took the opportunity to document the artists' encounter in photos. One photo shows them together with Ultra Violet and Leo Castelli who is turning toward Dalí, in conversation with him, while Warhol is listening in on the conversation and smiling. Rather than standing next to each other, the artists are keeping their distance. Billy Name recalls this moment as follows: "I was very young at the time of Henry Geldzahler's party. It seemed as if all the stars of the art world were in attendance. I thought the party was for Dalí and Gala, but could have been mistaken. It might have been for everyone. The music was provided by La Monte Young. The party included people such as Warhol, Johns, Chamberlain, Cage, Newman, Castelli."[9] Name also observed that Dalí and Warhol

4
Sally Chamberlain
in two e-mails
to the author on
October 24, 2015.

5
See the chapter
**Muse
and Mother**
in Part 3.

6
William Rothlein
in an e-mail
to the author on
September 1, 2015.

7
William Rothlein
in a telephone
conversation with
the author on
October 23, 2011.

8
Ultra Violet 1988,
pp. 121f. See
also the chapter
Silver Clouds
in Part 4.

→
39 [p. 388]

9
Billy Name in
an e-mail to the
author on
August 9, 2010.
+

did not talk to one another that evening and thinks that the reason for this was that Dalí was already a real star in the art world, while Warhol's fame had only just begun.[10]

In order to create his image, in 1964 Warhol asked the photographer David McCabe from Great Britain to accompany him with a camera for a year. McCabe took more than 2,500 photos, showing the artist at the Factory, at exhibition openings, at parties, and other activities.[11] One special experience was the visit to Dalí's studio at the St. Regis in March 1965, where the Spaniard was working on the paintings *The Apotheosis of the Dollar* and *Le voyage fantastique*.[12] McCabe reports that it was Warhol's idea to record the encounter in photos:

Whenever he might call and say Nureyev is coming to the studio or Judy Garland or whoever, he would ask, "Could you come over?" It was just a few minutes for me to go from my studio on West Thirty-Seventh Street to his Factory. So, it wasn't unusual for me to get a telephone call like this. And Andy called me and said, "I'm going to go see Dalí, can you come with me?" To me it was a thrill because my heroes were people like Dalí and Picasso. I wasn't quite sure at this point what Pop Art was ...[13]

The encounter between the two artists was an experience for McCabe also because Dalí pulled out all the stops to receive his guests in due fashion:

He opened the door to the suite and he was wearing this black crazy wig. And nothing was really said, because there was opera music playing at such a loud volume that it was like theater, like welcome to my lair. And he just grabbed Andy and pulled him in and sat Andy down. He was working on a painting for which he had this beautiful Inca headdress. And he just grabbed the headdress, pushed Andy into a chair and placed this Inca headdress on Andy's head and pointed at me and was basically saying, "Shoot!" You know, he was like a director. ... I think we were both swept up in it. And Dalí was pouring glasses of wine. I never saw Andy drink wine, normally, but Andy was ... so in shock at not being in control that he just started to knock back glasses of wine. ... There was no dialogue. Andy and Dalí did not talk to each other nor did Dalí actually address me verbally because the music was playing at such a decibel that conversation wasn't possible. So, Dalí would point at me with his cane ... I don't think I had an opportunity to shoot more than ... one or two rolls of film, which is only thirty-six or seventy-two frames. ... While I was trying to photograph him the cat jumped on him and started to claw him. I had no idea that he had this wild animal in his suite. The ocelot seemed to be just as crazy as he was. ... At one point Gala came in and wanted to be photographed with Andy. And Dalí took his cane and chased her out of the room. He didn't want her to be photographed with them. And everything happened so quickly. It was a whirlwind. ... It was just a crazy moment and all I could think was: Just keep shooting! Just keep shooting! ... Andy looked at me ... I could tell that he just wanted to get out of there. Like he didn't really expect any of this drama. So, while Dalí was chasing her [Gala] around, Andy and I, we just slipped out of the place and we left. ... We went down to the street, took a taxi back to his Factory and just looked at each other like, "Oh my God, how insane was that?!" ... Andy and I were stunned at Dalí's energy and his perception. It was an incredible performance (laughs).

→
41/42
[pp. 390/391]

10
Billy Name in an e-mail to the author on July 2, 2009.

+
More photos of the party in O'Sullivan Shorr 2014, *Book I*, pp. 56, 58.

11
McCabe/Dalton 2003, pp. 4ff.

12
Dalí had received the assignment for the painting *Le voyage fantastique* in February 1965. Cf. Aguer in Ades 2004, p. 528. The photos by David McCabe show that the painting is almost complete. See McCabe/Dalton 2003, pp. 39ff.

13
David McCabe in a telephone conversation with the author on June 14, 2010.

5

... The meeting that we had at the St. Regis only lasted for maybe less than one hour. ... It was the only time in all of that period that I photographed Andy, when Andy was not in control. He was a total control freak. ... Usually, wherever we went, Andy was always the boss and I had never seen him quite so overwhelmed as when he was in the presence of Dalí.[14]

David McCabe's photos clearly show Dalí dominating the event. Warhol looks frozen and is clutching his wine glass tensely. Dalí evidently wanted to force his younger colleague into a walk-on role. The art dealer Ivan C. Karp said that Warhol usually knew how to turn situations to his advantage, but it did not work with Dalí.[15] Karp later recalled, "I met Dalí on several occasions and I dimly recall participating in a panel discussion with him and Andy. ... The discussion concerned Andy's art and the prevailing climate of art in New York."[16] Ivan C. Karp could adopt a very direct approach when judging artists and their works.[17] He said about Dalí: "Dalí was blessed with virtuoso skills, but sorely deprived of a 'vision.' He may simply remain a curiosity."[18]

Warhol traveled to Paris on the occasion of his exhibition of the *Flowers* paintings, which was held in May 1965 at Ileana Sonnabend's gallery. On April 30, he arrived in the French capital by plane, accompanied by Gerard Malanga, Edie Sedgwick, and Chuck Wein.[19] Dalí was also staying in Paris at the time, as he regularly traveled from New York to Paris after St. Patrick's Day, when, as he said, "everything becomes green."[20] The opening broke all visitor records and the French press reported gushingly about Warhol.[21] John Ashbery wrote in the European edition of the *International Herald Tribune*: "'Le Pop Art' became a respectable *franglais* term in record time. Reporters are always asking Brigitte Bardot and Jeanne Moreau what they think of it; it is the theme of a striptease at the Crazy Horse Saloon, and there is even a Pop Art dress shop in the Rue du Bac called 'Poppard' decorated with photo-murals of Blondie strips."[22] The Pop Art striptease mentioned here took place as part of an event organized by Dalí. The *New York Post* of May 9, 1965, announced: "Salvador Dalí will be host at a reception for Andy Warhol, the Pop Artist, at the Crazy Horse Saloon in Paris. The saloon will be turned into an art gallery for the Dalí-Warhol event."[23] The reception took place in the evening after the opening. Warhol went to the Crazy Horse together with Edie Sedgwick and her university friend Edmund Hennessy who was living in Paris, and sat at a table with Dalí. Suddenly a spotlight was cast on them and a loudspeaker announced the presence of the "father of Surrealism" and the "father of Pop." Dalí took a bow and enjoyed the attention, while Warhol squirmed.[24] Later on in *POPism* Warhol talked about his forays into Paris nightlife and also mentioned in passing his encounter with Dalí:

We had fun in Paris, staying up all night, going to nightclubs like Castel's and New Jimmy's, which was Régine's club. At Castel's there was this crazy thing where the music would suddenly stop and everyone would just dive onto the dance floor and feel each other up—a free-for-all grope—skirts pulled up, pants pulled down—this happened three or four times a night. They'd just filmed part of What's New, Pussycat? *at Castel's, and it seemed like the whole town was popping with stars like Terence Stamp, Ursula Andress, Peter Sellers, Woody*

14
Ibid.

15
In McCabe/
Dalton 2003,
p. 41.

16
Ivan C. Karp in
e-mails to the
author on February 25, 2010, and
March 2, 2010.

17
Bourdon 1989,
p. 82.

18
Ivan C. Karp in
an e-mail to the
author on February 25, 2010.

19
Bockris 1989,
p. 223.

20
Amanda Lear in
a telephone conversation with
the author on
March 13, 2010;
Farrow 1997,
p. 70. See
also the chapter
**New York
Salutes Dalí
and Warhol**
in Part 4.

21
Bockris 1989,
p. 223,
Bourdon 1989,
p. 205.

22
Quoted according to
Dergan/Monk
2009, p. 164.

23
Lyons 1965.

24
Edie Sedgwick
is said to have
asked Dalí how it
felt to be a famous author, and
he apparently
reacted with
amusement at
the unintended
joke. Cf. Watson
2003, p. 207.

Allen, Romy Schneider, Capucine, Shirley MacLaine, Peter O'Toole, Dalí, Zou Zou [sic], Donald Camel [sic], Vadim, Jane Fonda, Catherine Deneuve, Françoise Dorléac, Françoise Sagan, Jean Shrimpton.[25]

Dalí and Warhol met not only at the Crazy Horse, but also at the discotheque La Locomotive on Montmartre. Charlton Lake reports in *In Quest of Dalí* that Dalí had invited him to the day club, as there was a party there with "teenagers. All very Dalínian. They adore me."[26] Lake went to the club and saw Dalí make an entrance with Gala and his entourage. When the artist stepped into the overcrowded disco, the music stopped, a spotlight was directed at him and his arrival was announced: "the Master Salvador Dalí." The Spaniard bowed in two directions, and the young people became ecstatic. The enthusiasm soon culminated on the dance floor and Dalí's entourage also joined in.[27] Lake writes: "I heard one of them ask for Andy Warhol. 'I called his hotel. He's not there. He must be on his way,' said a long-legged girl wearing tight trousers and a suede jacket, and smoking a curved-stem clay pipe."[28]

By this point Warhol and Edie Sedgwick had achieved great popularity and were among the most frequently photographed couples in New York. They were celebrated as cult figures wherever they appeared. *TIME* magazine wrote in August 1965 that their names were "magic names" and remarked that the artist and his superstar frequented "more parties than a caterer."[29] They reached the pinnacle of their popularity when they appeared at the opening of Warhol's first American retrospective at the Institute of Contemporary Art in Philadelphia on October 8, 1965. The crowd was beside itself and reacted to Warhol and Sedgwick as if they were pop stars. Walter Hopps, then director of the Pasadena Art Museum, reported in retrospect: "That Philadelphia exhibition of Andy's was one of the most bizarre mob scenes I've ever witnessed. ... It was the first time I saw a young avant-garde artist have a show mobbed as if it were a movie premiere ... all kinds of people clamoring to get at Andy as if he were a star. The kind of adulation, curiously, that would be associated with a Salvador Dalí daydream. Dalí would have loved to have pulled off such a thing and, as far as I know, never quite has."[30] Their wide popularity also brought Warhol and Sedgwick an invitation to *The Merv Griffin Show*, which was broadcast on television on October 6, 1965. Warhol chose to reply monosyllabically with "yes" and "no" and to whisper answers into Edie's ear.[31] Dalí did not appear on the show until two months later, on December 30, 1965.[32] The Spaniard was aware of the competition that Warhol represented for him. This was another reason why he tried to create a stir at public events. For example, *Newsweek* reported in mid-January 1966: "It was opening night at New York's Roosevelt Raceway, but for a while it looked more like the camp town races. Mustachioed Salvador Dalí was there with a pet ocelot. Pop nymph Edie Sedgwick made the scene in hip-hugging, silver lamé bell-bottomed trousers and a T-shirt; her companion, Andy Warhol, wore dirty dungarees and a leather jacket."[33]

Serendipity 3 was a famous, trendy meeting place for celebrities, the two artists thus inevitably also met there in the 1960s. The owner Stephen Bruce recalls one encounter:

25
Warhol/Hackett 1980, p. 112.

26
Lake 1969, p. 257.

27
Ibid., p. 258.

28
Ibid., p. 259.

29
Bourdon 1989, p. 210.

30
In Stein/Plimpton 1982, p. 252.

31
In 1977, Warhol remarked in an interview: "I was on *Merv Griffin* a couple of times, and I was so nervous I couldn't even get a word in." In Goldsmith 2004, p. 250.

32
See the chapter **Dalí's View of Warhol and his Work** in Part 6.

33
"Trotting to the Bank."

5

They came at different times, and they were surrounded by their entourages ... It was in the late afternoon around 3:30 or 4. And it was just a coincidence that they just so happened to come in and they all joined together. I'd said to Andy, "Salvador is here" and he said, "Well, let me go and say hello to him right away." Then they wound up sitting together at one large table. ... At that time everything happened very quickly. You didn't think of having a memory or snapping a picture. It was all [happening] live.[34]

Dalí and Warhol also met quite often in the winter of 1965/66. In December 1965 Dalí stood in front of the camera for Jack Bond's documentary *Dalí in New York*.[35] Even before shooting started, he invited the moviemaker to accompany him to the opening of the René Magritte retrospective at the Museum of Modern Art. This took place on the evening of December 13, 1965. Bond writes in his unpublished autobiography *Mad Jack*:

At seven sharp, I was downstairs [in the foyer of the St. Regis]. Four of us were going in a taxi to Magritte's exhibition. Dalí, myself and two of his friends, the painter Larry Rivers and a delightfully enigmatic man, Andy Warhol. The doorman hailed us a cab and on the way Dalí told me he had telephoned Magritte that afternoon to ask if we could arrive with pineapples on our heads. Magritte's response was negative. "If you arrive looking utterly ridiculous then you will not be allowed in." Said one true surrealist to another.[36]

It was a special privilege for Jack Bond to be able to witness the encounter of three such significant twentieth-century artists. He comments on the experience:

You have to remember that Dalí and Warhol, when together, did not talk about art at all, either theirs or anybody else's. They were mainly interested in fun and being funny, Dalí in particular was a great comedian. Above all they loved mocking and running down any pretentiousness on the part of others. Magritte they saw as ridiculous, on account of the way he dressed and comported himself. They saw him as a provincial bank manager and indeed when I was with them at the Magritte retrospective, we did propose the idea of borrowing money from him.[37]

Bond adds that it was he who turned to Magritte to ask him jokingly for money.[38]

Dalí and Warhol met again during a different visit to the Museum of Modern Art. Their artist colleague Harold Stevenson, who was visiting the René Magritte retrospective together with Edie Sedgwick, later recalled: "We [Edie and I] were very good friends. I took her to an exhibition once of artist René Magritte. And we were photographed by everyone and with the artist Salvador Dalí. He came up to me and said, 'I want to be photographed with you and Edie.' And I said, 'Well, get in here.'"[39] Stevenson also later reported that Warhol was present at the photo shoot and filmed him together with Edie and Dalí.[40] Dalí and Warhol did not speak to one another during the encounter, but instead, ignored each other.[41] Unfortunately, there is no trace of the film recordings mentioned by Harold Stevenson.[42]

Just a couple of days later, on December 17, 1965, a major Dalí retrospective opened at the Huntington Hartford Gallery of Modern Art in New York. New York was totally under the spell of Surrealism that December.

34
Stephen Bruce in a telephone conversation with the author on July 6, 2011.

35
See the chapter **Television as "Instant Fame"** in Part 4.

36
Bond, unpublished autobiography.

37
Jack Bond in an e-mail to the author on June 19, 2012.

38
Jack Bond in a conversation with the author on July 27, 2012 in London.

39
In Brinkley Davenport 2006.

40
Letter from Harold Stevenson, in Hohenberg/Scheips 2006 (n.p.).

41
Harold Stevenson in telephone conversations with the author on February 8, 2011 and July 3, 2015.

42
Claire K. Henry, assistant curator, The Andy Warhol Film Project, kindly informed +

Many reviews emphasized the relationship between Magritte, Dalí, and Pop Art. Emily Genauer called the two surrealists "Pop's papas" in the *New York World-Telegram and Sun*:

The question, then, is why so many usages of the original surrealists, surviving in the decades since only as components of individual artists' idioms (Dalí's and Magritte's particularly), have suddenly become a common currency of a whole style again. The answer is, of course, that pop is also a non-esthetic, sociological expression. It, too, is a catch-all movement for many diverse talents united principally by their opposition to current cultural values, and by their need to make themselves heard ... Well, other times, other protests.[43]

Almost all of the reviews referred to Magritte's work as an "integral antecedent of Pop Art."[44] Dalí must have been irritated by the talk, as he considered himself the sole "father of Pop Art."[45]

The opening of Dalí's retrospective was a significant social event that drew almost 1,000 visitors. The *New York Times* stated: "Although the invitations read 9 p.m. until midnight, guests were slow in arriving, delayed by the inevitable cocktail and dinner parties. New arrivals were still in line in the check room after 11."[46] Of course Warhol did not want to miss out on such an important social occasion. He appeared with an entourage, including the playwright Robert Heide, who was working on various projects with him at the time. Heide recalls that Warhol kept his distance to Dalí that evening, recounting,

... I was at the Huntington Hartford Museum on the top floor. Dalí was there and he had this ocelot. Andy was keeping very distant from him. Andy would have a fear of saying the wrong thing so he often wouldn't talk. There were high emotions and I think the two artists were kind of like looking at one another in an alienated way. I remember Salvador Dalí was giving him a weird kind of look. There was something dark between them from both sides. I think Andy was whispering to somebody who was with him ... I don't know exactly who it was. But that was it, that was the scene.[47]

The guests at the gallery also included Warhol's assistant Gerard Malanga, who met Dalí for the first time that evening:

... I attended the opening and queued up in the receiving line. My mentor and friend, the filmmaker Marie Menken, fitted me in an old black tie for the occasion. This would be my public introduction to Dalí. When I reached Dalí to shake his hand, I introduced myself as "Count Gerardo Malanga," and as a spontaneous gesture of wit, he replied "I knew your father very well." The con conned the con. We were friends forever.[48]

As already reported, Dalí also met the model Bettina Cirone that evening.[49] She went on to become a successful photojournalist and photographed not only Dalí, but also Warhol, with whom she was also on friendly terms. Cirone recalls that she often saw the two of them together in the 1960s:

I often saw Andy at the King Cole room where Dalí would hold court in the St. Regis Hotel, but never at Dalí's private parties. Maybe he invited Andy to other events and gatherings. Andy often brought a small entourage of people with him as well. Warhol and I didn't become friendly until years later, during

---

+
the author in an e-mail on September 11, 2015 that there is no record of such a film.

43
Quoted according to Zalman 2012, pp. 24f.

44
Ibid., p. 31, with source index.

45
See the chapter **Salvador Dalí—The Father of Pop Art?** and **Coca-Cola is the Real Pop Art** in Part 4.

46
Robinson 1965.

47
Robert Heide in a conversation with the author on December 6, 2012 in New York.

48
Gerard Malanga in an e-mail to the author on September 27, 2009. See also the chapter **The First Encounter** in this part.

49
See the chapter **Companions, Courtiers, and Superstars** in Part 3.

the 1970s and 1980s, when I started to photograph him at events and parties and he saw my credits on those photos in newspapers and magazines. That is when he asked me to do my own regular column with photographs in Interview magazine. I liked the idea, but I was so busy in those prolific decades selling my work to the leading newspapers and magazines nationally and internationally that I never got around to it before Andy's untimely death. ...

During the Dalí years, Andy and I had never even spoken to each other. Back then, Andy would hang around Dalí like a groupie but not so much a peer. At least that's the way it looked to me, even though it may not have been the case. Usually Andy was standing and Dalí was sitting like an important authority figure with Andy in the background like he was Dalí's disciple. They would have brief conversations. I don't know what they talked about because I wasn't listening. ... Dalí was a stronger more imposing presence, whereas Andy was mild-mannered and appeared humble. He was soft-spoken. Andy always appeared shy and soft spoken as long as I knew him. He was always at ease. Just like a regular guy. Dalí was le grand maître. I thought back then that Dalí was a little dismissive regarding Andy. He talked with him, he communicated with him, but he didn't seem to be as impressed by Warhol as Warhol was by Dalí. To me, it looked like Warhol was a Dalí groupie.[50]

That winter Dalí invited Warhol and Ivy Nicholson to a party. Nicholson knew both artists, had posed as a model for Dalí, and appeared in some of Warhol's movies. However, her connection to Warhol was stronger than her connection to Dalí.[51] Nicholson remarks that she was Warhol's official girlfriend at the time; they went out together and he flirted with her in public.[52] She made an interesting observation at Dalí's party:

He had me sit next to him at his table—Salvador Dalí. He had Andy Warhol sit rather far away with a group of young, attractive, mostly male actors. ... The talk of the town was that Andy and Dalí were on the same level of genius, that Andy was definitely as big a genius as Salvador Dalí. So having him seated him far away was kind of an insult, which a few other people seemed to have been shocked by, but were too discrete, I'm presuming, to say anything. I mean, it kind of made people wonder: "What? You are not having Andy at your table?" But no one discussed it.[53]

Nicholson recalls that Warhol did not say anything. However, one could see that he was not happy with the situation.[54]

After Warhol had visited Dalí a few times at his studio at the St. Regis, it was now high time for a return visit. This took place on the night of February 6, 1966. It was the first time that Dalí set foot inside the Factory, which by now was a trendy meeting place known as the Silver Factory. The Warhol superstar Taylor Mead later remarked: "In Andy's Factory we met everybody. I really don't know who I met, The Rolling Stones, everybody."[55] Therefore, Dalí must have seen it as his social duty to pay Warhol a visit. Gerard Malanga supposes that it was Paul Morrissey who called to invite Dalí. Warhol was too shy to utter an invitation. Malanga is also sure that Dalí only came to the Silver Factory this once. He was not the type of artist to visit the studio of a colleague without an invitation.[56] Nat Finkelstein documented Dalí's visit to Warhol in photographs.[57] Finkelstein later recalled:

50
Bettina Cirone
in a telephone
conversation with
the author on
August 11, 2014.

51
See the chapter
**Compan-
ions, Court-
iers and
Superstars**
in Part 3.

52
Ivy Nicholson
in a telephone
conversation
with the author
on December 10,
2013.

53
Ivy Nicholson
in a telephone
conversation
with the author
on November 20,
2009.

54
Ivy Nicholson
in a telephone
conversation
with the author
on December 10,
2013.

55
Taylor Mead
in a telephone
conversation
with the author
on June 2, 2010.

56
Gerard Malanga
in a conversation
with the author
on July 2, 2012 in
Hudson, NY.

57
The photo is
printed in
Finkelstein 1989
(n.p.).

He came in, unnoticed, and like a three-card-monte dealer moved to the periphery, where with pickpocket's fingers he toyed with small objects so as to draw attention away from the more crowded couch area to where the spotlight belonged ... DALÍ. He then started to prowl up and down the sideline seemingly engrossed with his finger dancing and oblivious to all else. I stepped in front of him and grabbed two quick impromptus. He looked directly into my camera before I even had it to my eye. He was a pro.[58]

These shots brought Nat Finkelstein an invitation to a dinner. He recalled the evening as follows:

We met at the bar of the St. Regis Hotel: Dalí, Gala, Andy, and myself. Dalí, after a brief nod in my direction, whispered in Andy's ear. Andy then turned to me and explained that Dalí wanted me to parachute over an enormous chess board and to photograph Dalí as he arranged human pieces into a tableau. I replied that I would be happy to accept the commission but that fees and guarantees would have to be arranged with my agency. Dalí and Gala immediately buzzed into Andy's ear. Andy relayed the message to me that it should be a great honor to do this for Dalí. I responded directly to Dalí and Gala, "I'm a professional photographer. This is what I do for a living. I have a wife and child, so if I became disabled doing this job, their livelihood is gone, too. You do not give your paintings away; I do not photograph for free." Gala whispered, "But this is Dalí!" I replied, "But I am Finkelstein!" Again, the three heads were put together. Without an adieu, the three left the table. The waiter presented me with their bar bill.[59]

When Dalí came to the Factory on February 6, 1966, Warhol took the opportunity to produce two *Screen Tests* of him.[60] Gerard Malanga, who shot them, can still remember it well: "Dalí arrived at the Factory with an entourage of people, including Isabel Dufresne, who later took on the name Ultra Violet. I don't remember seeing Gala there, though she very well may have been. ... I also shot some black-and-white footage of the visit which many years later I incorporated into my movie, *Gerard Malanga's Film Notebooks*."[61] This twenty-seven-minute movie premiered in 2005 at the Vienna International Film Festival. The movie provides insight into the atmosphere of the Factory. For example, there is an encounter between Bob Dylan and Gerard Malanga, Edie Sedgwick putting on makeup, and The Velvet Underground without sound, as well as Salvador Dalí strutting through the Factory. Malanga also recalls that movies were shown that night during Dalí's visit.[62] Warhol evidently wanted to give his guest a taste of his movie production. Nat Finkelstein also took photos showing Dalí together with Gerard Malanga and the Warhol superstar Mary Woronov during the movie screenings. The shots show a relaxed Dalí, who for once does not appear to notice that he is being photographed.[63]

A day later Warhol produced three *Screen Tests* of Marcel Duchamp. These were made during the opening of the exhibition "Hommage à Caissa," for the benefit of the Marcel Duchamp Fund of the American Chess Foundation, which took place at the Cordier & Ekstrom Gallery in New York.[64] For the exhibition organized by Duchamp, more than forty artists contributed works on the topic of chess, including Arman, Victor Brauner, Alexander

---

58
In ibid.

59
In Finkelstein 2003, p. 78.

60
See the chapter **Warhol's Screen Tests of Dalí** in Part 4.

61
Gerard Malanga in an e-mail to the author on September 24, 2009.

62
Gerard Malanga in a conversation with the author on July 2, 2012 in Hudson, NY.

63
Photo depiction on http://planet groupentertain ment.square space.com/the-louis-walden-interview/ (last accessed on January 25, 2016). In an e-mail on March 9, 2016, Gerard Malanga kindly informed the author that the photographer was Nat Finkelstein.

64
Angell 2006, ST 79–81.

Calder, Max Ernst, Jasper Johns, Roy Lichtenstein, Richard Lindner, René Magritte, Joan Miró, Robert Motherwell, Claes Oldenburg, Robert Rauschenberg, Man Ray, James Rosenquist, George Segal, Daniel Spoerri, Jean Tinguely, and Salvador Dalí.[65] Dalí designed an unusual chess game. He formed the figures according to the fingers of his hand, the king and queen according to his and Gala's thumbs, each with a molar as a crown, while the St. Regis Hotel's salt shakers served as model for the rooks.[66] In 1971, the jeweler F.J. Cooper, Inc. of Philadelphia manufactured chess sets of thirty-two pieces, sixteen in sterling silver and sixteen in silver gilt.[67] Duchamp and Dalí played chess against each other at the exhibition opening.[68] Duchamp recalled the following in an interview, which was published in the July 1966 issue of the magazine *Art and Artists*:

Recently I met Andy Warhol, at Cordier & Ekstrom, during the American Chess Foundation sale. It was at the end of the exhibition: Dalí had just finished his piece, and they had laid on a little ceremony. Warhol had brought his camera and he asked to pose, on the single condition that I keep my mouth shut for twenty minutes.

...

It's very odd: in my case I had a girl on my knees, at least, nearly: a very cuddly little actress came and sat by me, practically lying on top off me, rubbing herself up against me. I like Warhol's spirit. He's not just some painter or movie-maker. He's a filmeur, and I like that very much.[69]

The "very cuddly little actress" was the model Benedetta Barzini. That evening she stood in front of Warhol's camera with Duchamp for one of the three *Screen Tests*.[70] Barzini reports: "I know that I was there because Nicki Ekstrom (who was courting me) wanted me there—got the dress from Genrich and didn't bother to wash my hair—I have no specific recollection of the event ... I was sort of distant from considering the situation 'important'—as usual I was waiting for the moment to 'escape.'"[71] Barzini cannot recall having seen Dalí that evening, but thinks it was possible that he did not stay until the end.[72] Nat Finkelstein, who accompanied Warhol to the opening and took numerous photographs, later said:

Andy's coming to this art show was like a guerrilla attack. That's what made him, as a matter of fact that's what made all of us ... [feel] like "Fuck you man, we'll kick our way in here." Duchamp was surrounded by his phalanx of defenders. Andy was attacking—we were his point men. These people who were surrounding Duchamp and his newly emerging pop artists were the same breed of people who might commission a handler to import and show a poodle. ... When we came in to the Duchamp show, they expected us to be ... different. They expected us to be outrageous, this was our job. We were supposed to chew slippers and bury bones in the sofa. Their main concern was that we didn't piss on the Aubusson.[73]

Dalí and Warhol probably did not cross paths on this occasion, but in the mid-1960s they met quite often at social events. James Warhola reports that he visited his uncle regularly at the time in New York and lived at his house.[74] He was still a child and was in the habit of sitting in front of his uncle's bedroom door in the morning with his siblings waiting for his stories.

65
Hahn 2001, p. 121, fn. 9;
Marcadé 2007, p. 487.

66
Pitxot/Aguer/Puig 2011 pp. 75f.

67
Ibid., p. 75;
Descharnes/Descharnes 2003, no. 276.

68
Hahn 2001, p. 121, fn. 9.

69
In Hahn 1966, p. 7.

70
Angell 2006, ST81.

71
Benedetta Barzini in an e-mail to the author on July 29, 2012.

72
Benedetta Barzini in an e-mail to the author on September 14, 2012.

73
In Finkelstein 1989 (n.p.).

74
James Warhola in Prekop/Cihlář 2011, p. 105.

"When his door would open, then we would go in. This was in the mid-1960s. We'd ask him, 'Who have you met who's famous?' And I remember specifically he would say 'Salvador Dalí.' We really wanted to know if he met the Beatles because the Beatles were the most famous. ... He would always rattle off a lot of names that we never knew. But I knew Salvador Dalí."[75] James's father Paul also later recalled that the name Dalí cropped up in conversations with his brother.[76] His other son Paul C. Warhola even had the opportunity to meet Salvador Dalí personally. Paul was studying theology at the time at The Catholic University of America in Washington D.C. He visited his uncle in New York during the semester holidays, together with a couple of fellow students in early 1966.

It was very unusual because my uncle was very private, he never allowed any visitors and for him to allow me the opportunity to bring several of my classmates up ... we were probably there for maybe four or five days. ... This was either the first or second day of our visit and my uncle asked us, "What are you doing tonight or maybe tomorrow night?" And we said, "Well, really not too much of anything." He said, "Well, I got some tickets to an art opening. Would you be interested?" And I looked at them and we said, "Sure." So, he gave us the tickets, but he didn't even mention that it was Salvador Dalí, because, I know, if he had mentioned it, I probably would have started asking a lot of questions ... "Gee, do you know him?" and so forth.[77]

The exhibition opening left a lasting impression on Paul C. Warhola.

There were maybe three, four, five floors with a lot of Dalí's paintings interspersed there and so it really was a very nice evening. ... We kind of mingled among the crowd and went to the different rooms. ... Salvador came out probably at about ten or ten-thirty, in a rather dramatic style to say the least. He came out, of course dressed superbly, with this beautiful blonde on his right arm and she happened to be carrying an ocelot in her arms. ... He started greeting people and talking with the people that I'm sure ... knew him. ... Had I known ahead of time I would have definitely introduced myself, which I didn't, because I didn't realize the regard that Salvador had for my uncle and my uncle towards him.[78]

In December 1966, Warhol met the nineteen-year-old, lanky Texan Rodney La Rod, who became his new boyfriend. The artist wrote about him later in *POPism*: "He was over six feet tall. He greased his hair and wore bell-bottoms that were too short, and he'd stomp around the Factory, grab me, and rough me up—and it was so outrageous that I loved it, I thought it was really exciting to have him around, lots of action."[79] Ondine, an early regular guest at the Factory, confirmed that he had never experienced Warhol before as "so completely in love, so sensitive and so mature" with a boyfriend.[80] Although it was common knowledge on the scene that nobody was allowed to touch Warhol,[81] this evidently did not apply to Rodney La Rod. Gerard Malanga later remarked: "It appeared to be a physically violent relationship but Rodney was always very corny about his physical overtures towards Andy. It wasn't like he slugged him, they were always love taps, or Andy pushing him away or trying to block the punches."[82] In May 1967, the bizarre relationship suffered a crisis and Warhol allowed himself to be persuaded by his entourage to split up with Rodney La Rod. "Andy would cry,"

75
James Warhola in a conversation with the author on December 2, 2012 in New York.

76
Paul Warhola in a conversation with the author on November 27, 2012 in Pittsburgh.

77
Paul C. Warhola in a telephone conversation with the author on June 28, 2013.

78
Ibid.

79
Warhol/Hackett 1980, p. 210. In his diaries, Warhol calls Rodney La Rod "my old crush from the sixties." Cf. Hackett 1989, p. 76, September 29, 1977. La Rod gave Warhol the nickname "the Great White Father." Cf. Bockris 1989, p. 267.

80
Ibid., p. 268.

81
See the chapter **Sterile Love and Voyeurism** in Part 2.

82
Bockris 1989, pp. 267f.

Ondine recalled, "Finally, he actually approached us and said, 'Do you think I should?' And we said, 'Yeah, plain dump him because he's a monster.' Andy was the only person I've ever met who took his friends' advice about love, and he dumped him."[83] Owing to this relationship with Rodney it is possible to reconstruct another encounter between Dalí and Warhol, which must have taken place around the turn of the year 1966/67. Gerard Malanga says about it:

We went to dinner with Dalí on another night. … It wasn't anything special. We were just all getting together for a dinner in a restaurant near the St. Regis. It was in the neighborhood. … Andy, Paul Morrissey … I'm not sure if Edie was there. … Andy was with this boy, some nutcase … a sort of a sadist, named Rod la Rod. … Rod would punch Andy like hitting around but like heavy stuff. … And Paul would try to stop him and say "Enough is enough." He did it that night with Dalí at the dinner table. It was all small talk and enjoy the meal … If anybody was talking it was Dalí. … It was Andy's shy period. … Dalí and Andy were sitting next to each oher. I was sitting across the way.[84]

Warhol spoke very little in Dalí's presence and observed instead. Gerard Malanga suspects that Dalí felt attracted by the "mysterious behavior" of his younger colleague.[85] Malanga, who left the Factory for good in 1970, also remembers that he sometimes went to Dalí's receptions at the St. Regis together with Warhol. He had the impression that the two artists enjoyed each other's company.[86]

On September 19, 1968, on the occasion of the publication of the album *The Marble Index* by his former superstar Nico, Warhol gave a party to which about 200 people were invited. It was the first party at the Factory since the attempt on his life.[87] Warhol was starting to take part in New York social life again and it is known that his path and Dalí's crossed repeatedly in the years that followed. For example, on November 20, 1968, when Roy Lichtenstein invited him to his Bowery Studio, where his works were exhibited that he had created for Twentieth Century Fox to promote the movie *Joanne* by Michael Sarne.[88] The event at Lichtenstein's studio also served the purpose of introducing the main actress in the movie, Geneviève Waïte, to New York society. The invited guests included senator Jacob K. Javits, Leonard Bernstein, Lauren Bacall, Charlotte Ford, as well as Dalí and Warhol.[89]

Leslie Curtis, who married the actor Tony Curtis in April 1968, remembers another coincidental meeting of the two artists around this time:

The only time I saw them together was one time when we were meeting with Dalí again for dinner … I think we were on Fifth Avenue … Andy was walking and Tony hailed him. We saw him—he was very distinct-looking, you know from the back you could recognize him if you knew him—and he turned around and he skipped a little bit almost towards us and everyone was effusive and said hello and what not, and he and Dalí embraced. … I think because it was spontaneous that it was very cordial and brief, you know. I didn't feel any stiffening.[90]

In the years that followed, Dalí and Warhol met more frequently for dinners together at elegant New York restaurants. Several other guests were regulars at these meals. The Indian singer and actress Asha Puthli remembers a weekend brunch at Trader Vic's, which took place in 1970, a few days

83
Ibid., p. 270.

84
Gerard Malanga in a conversation with the author on July 2, 2012 in Hudson, NY.

85
Gerard Malanga in an e-mail to the author on September 24, 2009.

86
Gerard Malanga in a conversation with the author on July 2, 2012 in Hudson, NY, as well as in an e-mail to the author on September 24, 2009.

87
Bourdon 1989, p. 297.

88
Roy Lichtenstein created three designs for a movie poster. There are two preliminary sketches with the titles *Girl in Water* and *Policeman*. Dr. Jack Cowart, Executive Director of the Roy Lichtenstein Foundation, kindly provided the author with this information in an e-mail on April 30, 2013. A design with the title *Joanna* was used in newspaper advertisements and was printed as an offset lithograph. See Corlett/Fine 2002, Ill. 24. However, Lichtenstein's designs were not used for the movie poster.

89
Archerd 1968.

90
Leslie Curtis in a telephone conversation with the author on April 27, 2013.

after her first encounter with Dalí.[91] However, she did not observe any interaction between the artists.[92] There were no noteworthy conversations between Dalí and Warhol, as Dalí always dominated the event. This is also reported by Warhol's superstar Viva, who was present at some of these encounters at the King Cole Bar at the St. Regis: "Both Andy and Dalí were surrounded by their entourages—that may be where Andy got the entourage idea—and I don't think they exchanged more than a couple of words with each other. The table was always huge with at least twenty people. ... Andy didn't talk. Dalí talked about himself."[93]

The encounters between Dalí and Warhol in the 1960s were sporadic and should not be overrated in retrospect. Many artists had contact with each other during this time. Dorothy Lichtenstein remarks about the relationship of her husband Roy to Andy Warhol: "They were friends in this small scene with a common dealer, but everyone hung around with everyone at this time, at the Factory, in the Hamptons, when Andy was occasionally out in Montauk, or exhibition openings. ... It was basically a 'casual' relationship."[94] Amanda Lear says with regard to this: "In these old days you could meet so many different artists, great artists, downstairs at the St. Regis, and they would say hello to each other. Not anymore. Nowadays it's more full of jealousy."[95]

The 1970s

In the 1970s, Salvador Dalí and Andy Warhol met more often than they had previously. Bob Colacello remarks that Warhol kept company with few colleagues during this decade, but quite often with Dalí. He explains this on account of the similarity of the two artists,

I would say Andy was more like Dalí than he was like Jasper Johns or Rauschenberg or Lichtenstein or Frank Stella or Robert Motherwell. These guys were all intellectuals. Andy was not an intellectual. Dalí was a kind of camp intellectual. I mean, he made fun of his intellectualism. ... Dalí had a Dadaist inside of him, and so did Andy. Duchamp was really Andy's idol. But Andy was very comfortable with Dalí, he was very comfortable with Larry Rivers ... Larry was more like Andy, too, or more like Dalí. He had a motorcycle and young girlfriends. He had an affair with Frank O'Hara. These were Andy's kinds of artists.[1]

Bob Colacello and Amanda Lear report that Dalí and Warhol met regularly in New York in the 1970s.[2] Warhol's biographer Victor Bockris says about the frequency of their encounters: "If it had not been for Gala they might have spent more time together. She was scornful of everyone, including Dalí. That was her role. But Andy did not tolerate the kind of brutality that Gala exercised."[3] Bob Colacello adds, "Andy had a problem with Gala, but he also liked Gala. He thought it was funny that she was so mean."[4] An interesting detail is that Warhol, as sign of his "sympathy," dedicated a *Campbell's Soup Can* drawing to Gala.[5] But he clearly felt more sympathy for Dalí, whom he gave several paintings as gifts.[6] Bob Colacello:

Andy did enjoy seeing Dalí. I don't think we ever said no to an invitation from Dalí, except when maybe there was something more important for business. Dalí would usually call himself, which was very charming. He didn't have a

91
See also the chapter **Companions, Courtiers, and Superstars** in Part 3.

92
Asha Puthli in an e-mail to the author on January 2, 2012.

93
Viva in an e-mail to the author on April 18, 2012.

94
Dorothy Lichtenstein in an e-mail from Dr. Jack Cowart to the author on May 12, 2010.

95
Amanda Lear in a telephone conversation with the author on March 13, 2010.

1
Bob Colacello in a telephone conversation with the author on September 22, 2010.

2
Ibid.; Amanda Lear in a telephone conversation with the author on March 13, 2010.

3
Victor Bockris in an e-mail to the author on July 16, 2010.

4
Bob Colacello in a telephone conversation with the author on September 22, 2010. See also the chapter **Muse and Mother** in Part 3.

5
Víctor Fernández kindly provided the author with this information in an e-mail from Enrique Esteban Zepeda on November 11, 2015.

6
Details are provided in the chapter **Exchange of Gifts** in Part 6.

secretary call. He would actually call me, and he would call Andy, and say "Count Valpolicella. Here is Dalí. Come for tea este *Sunday." And that was so nice. Dalí, for all his airs, could be quite simple and down to earth in a funny way.*[7]

In the fall of 1971, Dalí met the artist and moviemaker Steven Arnold. Arnold was born in Berkeley near San Francisco in 1943. After graduating from high school in 1961, he traveled to Paris, where he enrolled at the École des Beaux-Arts.[8] Disappointed by the course, he traveled back to San Francisco via Spain and Morocco and began studying at the San Francisco Art Institute in the mid-1960s.[9] He shot his first movies in 1971. Dalí was among the artists who influenced him most, intellectually.[10] He met him personally that same year, when the designer Kaisik Wong, who was also from San Francisco, introduced them at the St. Regis Hotel. During their first encounter, Arnold showed Dalí stills from his movie *Luminous Procuress*, whereupon Dalí said, "Dalí must see this film made by my little prince, tomorrow. Dalí will arrange a screening at the Rizzoli screening room, tomorrow at eight o'clock."[11] *Luminous Procuress* was the first feature-length art movie to be admitted to the collection at the Whitney Museum of Art in New York. Pandora, Steven Arnold's lifelong friend, muse, and collaborator, who plays the main role, comments, "*Luminous Procuress* is a journey of two young gentlemen of self-discovery through a series of magical moving tableaux. The film was compared to (a West-Coast) Fellini's *Satyricon*, and Steven was compared to Cocteau. The film has also been referred to as a 'motion painting,' which is a divine compliment."[12] The Cockettes, a psychedelic theater troupe that had formed in San Francisco in 1969, had their movie debut in *Luminous Procuress*. As the group also caused a stir in New York in 1971, they were presented in *Interview* the same year, also discussing their role in Steven Arnold's movie.[13] Dalí loved the movie and called it a masterpiece. He invited the crème de la crème of New York society to the screening he had arranged, including Warhol. In his autobiography Steven Arnold reports: "The next night, film under my arm, I went to the Rizzoli screening room one hour before Dalí had requested because I thought I had been dreaming—but sure enough, the projectionist told me Dalí had booked the screening room to show my film at seven forty-five that evening. Dalí arrived with Ultra Violet, Andy Warhol, and many other people he had called to come to see my film. Even Gala, Dalí's wife, came."[14] However, as the projector failed, the event had to be postponed and finally took place in the Grand Ballroom at the St. Regis Hotel. Around 300 guests appeared, including Warhol, who came with a big entourage.[15] The two large bars were decorated with ice sculptures and spectacular flower arrangements. An East Indian dancer performed in native costume and Denise Sandell played Marilyn Monroe as entertainment for the guests.[16] It was on this evening that Dalí met Pandora.[17]

Since Pandora frequently accompanied Dalí in New York in the years that followed, she was witness to a further encounter between him and Warhol:

We were dining in a beautiful restaurant. Andy Warhol was there with Truman Capote. Dalí recognized him and made a conscious effort to be pleasing and

7
Bob Colacello in a telephone conversation with the author on September 22, 2010.

8
Arnold, unpublished autobiography.

9
Weiermair 1996, p. 11; Pandora in a conversation with the author on November 20, 2011 in Mariposa, California.

10
Weiermair 1996, pp. 10f.; Arnold, unpublished autobiography.

11
Quoted according to ibid.

12
Pandora in an e-mail to the author on May 31, 2011.

13
Loney 1971, p. 7.

14
Arnold, unpublished autobiography.

15
Pandora in an e-mail to the author on January 27, 2016; Arnold, unpublished autobiography.

16
Michaud 1991, Fall, p. 6.

17
See also the chapter **Companions, Courtiers, and Superstars** in Part 3.

kind. Dalí greeted him and said, "Oh, you must put Pandora in a film." Warhol lit up, but I think he knew that his films were not the correct place for me. I was only in Steven's films; I wasn't interested in being in anyone else's films. I think Warhol would not have known what to do with me ... He knew Steven's films, and they operate on a completely different level than the Warhol films. I would say the Warhol films are very earthbound and Steven's films are very heaven-bound ... I told Dalí that it would not be a proper fit. He said, "Oh." I think Dalí understood.[18]

Perhaps the encounter described by Pandora is the same as the one reported on in 1973 in the April issue of the *Rolling Stone* magazine. Printed there is a conversation between Warhol and Capote, also witnessed by Bob MacBride, with whom the author was working on a television production at the time. The conversation starts at Capote's apartment and continues in the Oak Room at the Algonquin Hotel, at the bar of the Carlyle Hotel and at the restaurant Trader Vic's. As Warhol, Capote, and MacBride are having a drink at the bar of the Carlyle Hotel, they meet Dalí.

Andy: ... Oh, is that Dalí? Oh, look at Dalí.

Truman: Oh, we see him everywhere.

Andy: Oh, look at all the transsexuals.

Bob: Are those transsexuals?

Andy: Who knows ...

Truman: Well, Dalí's got on a real costume tonight. ... It's really a tragedy. He was a fantastic technician.

Andy: No, he really is great. Really.

Truman: But he's so unbelievably corny.

Andy: No, he really is a great artist. He's really one of the best artists. ... Oh, he's coming over to see us.

(Dalí comes over, greets Andy and Truman, and returns to his party.)

Andy: He's really a great artist.

Truman: Well, you're really sweet. I don't think Dalí's painted a good painting ... mmm ... since 1930. At the most. Never in my life have I seen a more disgusting picture than The Last Supper *in the National Gallery.*

Andy: Well, that was his Drunk Period. He's stopped now. He paints very well again. The ones five or six years ago were really painted badly, but now. ...

Truman: What would a really good Dalí painting get at auction now?

Andy: I don't know, because the really good Dalís never come up. And that's good. He gets a lot. He just did a Datsun commercial.[19]

David Bailey shot the documentary *Warhol* in February 1972.[20] The filming took place in and around New York and allowed Bailey to take numerous photos of Warhol, members of the Factory, and personalities from the art scene.[21] After the filming, Bailey and Warhol saw each other again in Paris. Dalí was also staying in the French capital at the time and invited the photographer to an event.[22] Bailey could not resist photographing himself with Dalí in front of a mirror.[23] He said later about the Spaniard, whom he had already met in 1962: "I never really liked Dalí's paintings ... in fact I thought they were rather silly but I liked him.—HE was the artwork really."[24]

18
Pandora in a conversation with the author on November 20, 2011 in Mariposa, California.

19
Warhol/Capote 1973, p. 46.

20
See the chapter **Television as "Instant Fame"** in Part 4.

21
Bailey 2014, p. 69.

22
Bailey later recalled: "There was some big ball going on and he said, 'Come around,' and Andy Warhol happened to be in Paris, too." In ibid.

23
Ill. in: ibid., pp. 78f.

24
Ibid., p. 14.

5

→
44 [p. 393]

Among the many photos that Bailey took that spring in Paris are also some shots showing Dalí and Warhol together. On one photo they are posing next to each other, Warhol is wearing a leather jacket and has his tape recorder in his hand, while Dalí is wrapped in a fur coat and has his chin resting on the handle of his cane.[25] Other photos were taken in Dalí's suite at Hôtel Le Meurice. In some of the photos, Warhol is sitting on the armrest of the armchair Dalí is seated on. There is no visible interaction between the artists. Dalí is clutching his cane, Warhol has his jacket over his right arm and is holding a glass of wine in his left hand.[26] One shot shows the two of them together with the model Penelope Tree, David Bailey's life partner at the time. In this photo Warhol is also sitting on the armrest and Tree is sitting on a chair, while Dalí is standing behind her, balancing his cane on her head.[27] Penelope Tree recalls this moment as follows: "Andy just went, 'Oh Wow' and Dalí didn't say anything, just looked theatrical and pointed his cane. I was feeling uncomfortable, maybe because unconsciously I knew that someday someone would ask me what it felt like to be hanging out with two major geniuses of the twentieth century and my reply would be … a little tense and not very connected!"[28]

Dalí had his first solo exhibition in spring 1943 at the Knoedler Gallery in New York.[29] He exhibited his works there regularly until into the 1970s. At the beginning of the 1970s, Sir John Richardson was vice president at Knoedler and witnessed an encounter between Dalí and Warhol at an exhibition opening:

Andy was totally passive. I mean, it's not how Andy treated people. Andy was a presence. Things happened to Andy. Andy was, to my mind, like a holy idiot, you know, like out of a Russian novel. He didn't impinge on people, people impinged on him. You wouldn't see him chatting in a corner. They [Dalí and Andy] were like Garbo meeting Myrna Loy. They were two presences. They were both so fixed in their personas: Dalí was busy being Dalí and Andy was busy being Andy. It was like a huge Hollywood opening: the stars are there, but they don't impinge. … There was obviously an enormous amount of culture of some kind, which Andy had managed to absorb, and wisdom, but on the surface all you got was, "gosh" and "wow." Overtly, there was nothing to be seen in the sense that words were exchanged. Andy wouldn't have engaged in any intellectual conversation, nor would Dalí for that matter. Dalí was too busy taking a crack at peoples' view of life. He was always trying to do something shocking or outrageous.[30]

The "Holograms conceived by Dalí" exhibition was shown at Knoedler from early April to mid-May 1972. The holograms are an expression of the Spaniard's enthusiasm for three-dimensional painting. The works were created with the help of the Hungarian engineer Dennis Gábor, who was awarded the Nobel Prize in Physics in 1971 for his invention and development of holography. Dalí explains in the exhibition catalogue *The 3rd Dimension: The 1st World Exposition of Holograms conceived by Dalí*: "All artists have been concerned with three-dimensional reality since the time of Velázquez, and in modern times, the analytic cubism of Picasso tried again to capture the three dimensions of Velázquez. Now with the genius of Gábor, the possibility

25
Ill. in Harrison 2003, p. 65.

26
In one photo, Fred Hughes is in the foreground. Ill. in *Andy Warhol: Transcript* (n.p.).

27
Ill. in Bailey 2014, p. 70.

28
Penelope Tree in an e-mail to the author on June 9, 2010.

29
See the chapter **Portraits of Socialites** in Part 4.

30
Sir John Richardson in a conversation with the author on July 3, 2012 in New York.

→
43 [p. 392]

of a new Renaissance in art has been realized with the use of holography. The doors have been opened for me into a new house of creation."[31] Art critics perceived Dalí's holographic compositions as anything other than innovative at the time. Robert Hughes wrote maliciously in *TIME* magazine: "Dalí has simply used a new medium to transmit his old mannerisms."[32] The artist himself declared through his gallery that the significance of his holograms would later be recognized in art history.[33] Dalí was indeed the first artist to make use of the holographic technique.

In April 1973 he showed his work *First Cylindric Chrono-Hologram. Portrait of Alice Cooper's Brain*, also at Knoedler. Alice Cooper remarked in an interview at the time about the unusual portrait: "He told me the reason he wanted to do the hologram with us was because we were the most confusing people he'd ever met. That's the only thing that we really have in common—confusion."[34] The rock musician provides an insight into the background to the work of art in his memoirs: "It was a major production, filming in this big, white video production room. He [Dalí] had cameras arranged in a circle. I wore $2 million worth of Harry Winston diamonds, a necklace and a tiara. No shirt. I held a Venus de Milo microphone and bit its head off as I was shot in the round. Before the shoot, security men guarding the jewelry checked all the exits."[35] Elsewhere Cooper draws an interesting comparison between Dalí and Warhol:

My influences weren't just rock stars, but artists and cultural icons. Salvador Dalí, an early and lasting influence, was a big fan. ... Andy Warhol was in love with our celebrity (or, for that matter, anybody's celebrity).

Andy Warhol was a permanent fixture at Max's Kansas City and Studio 54. He was the darling of the New York underground. We became acquaintances at this time, mostly because of my notorious infamy and out of pure curiosity. Andy was a media gourmet and I was on the cover of every single magazine, which meant he had to have Polaroids of us together. That was his addiction. ...

Andy was hard to get to know. He wasn't like the personable John Lennon, the surreal Salvador Dalí, or the chummy Peter Sellers who you could really be friends with. Andy was at the center of his own universe, with lots of strange little satellites revolving around him. He would only really recognize you if you were glamorous or hugely famous, and he didn't play golf.[36]

In *Andy Warhol's Exposures*, Warhol writes in turn about Alice Cooper: "I meet most rock stars through their girlfriends. Cindy Lang introduced me to Alice Cooper, who reminds me of Salvador Dalí, except Dalí doesn't drink beer and play golf."[37] Warhol evidently sensed that there was a kind of spiritual kinship between Dalí and the rock musician with his ghoulish stage shows.

Warhol also reports in *Exposures* that he paid Dalí a visit at the time. However, the surrealist's holograms did not make too much of an impression on him.[38] "One night we all met in Dalí's suite instead of downstairs in the King Cole Bar as usual. The suites at the St. Regis are very Italian Baroque, lots of marble, gilt, and candelabra, but Dalí makes his even more Baroque. He rearranges the furniture to look like art, and adds a

31
In *The 3rd Dimension*, p. 1.

32
Quoted according to Etherington-Smith 1993, p. 373.

33
Gibson 1997, p. 551.

34
In Swift 1973, p. 38.

35
Cooper/Zimmerman/Zimmerman 2007, p. 146.

36
Ibid., p. 139.

37
Warhol/Colacello 1979, p. 196.

38
Bob Colacello in a conversation with the author on June 26, 2012 in New York.

few bloody crucifixes from Spain plus a hologram or two. Dalí loves everything old-fashioned and everything avant-garde, like holograms—3D photo-sculptures."[39]

As is well known, Bob Colacello wrote *Andy Warhol's Exposures*. Colacello reports in his own memoirs about the encounters with Dalí and writes that Warhol took him to tea with Dalí for the first time in April 1973: "Dalí's teas were regular Sunday-afternoon events and had nothing to do with Darjeeling and crumpets, everything to do with champagne and strumpets. They were always held in the King Cole Bar of the St. Regis, beneath the 1906 murals by one of Andy's favorite painters, Maxfield Parrish, and were followed by dinner at Dalí's favorite restaurant, Trader Vic's in the Plaza Hotel."[40] This particular encounter between Dalí, Warhol, and Colacello took place on April 1, 1973. A. Reynolds Morse, who also attended, recorded an amazing detail in his diaries: "Andy Warhol had come in with a color Polaroid camera and was flashing photos of Gala and Jesus. He took a few of Dalí."[41] Unfortunately, photos of Gala and Jeff Fenholt have never been found. As reported in *Andy Warhol's Exposures*, Gala absolutely refused to let Warhol take her picture.[42] Bob Colacello continues in his memoirs:

Dalí himself, in a gold brocade dinner jacket, was attended by an elegant middle-aged Spanish lady, whom he introduced as "King Louis the Fourteenth," and our young disco-dancing friend Juan de Jesús, whom he introduced as "the Crown Prince." Neither was wearing a crown. Dalí carried a gold-topped scepter, waving it in the air whenever he wanted to make a point, which was often. He rose to greet Andy and waved for us to sit at the table. ...

... he offered Andy "a magnif-ico i-dea." "Oh, what is it?" asked Andy ... Dalí said that Andy should paint a triptych of Clara Petacci, Eva Braun, and Eva Perón, with "La Petacci" in the middle, hanging upside down, "naked and muerta like they find her with Muss-o-lini." "Oh, really," said Andy again, this time meaning, "Is he for real?" Dalí pounded his scepter and declared "Sí, sí, sí!!! Dalí even give you the título: 'The Three Great Whores of the XX Century'"— that's how he pronounced it, "ex-ex."[43]

As Colacello goes on to report, Dalí called the Factory the next day to pronounce an invitation: "Dalí invite Warhol and Valpolicella to the lunch *para el* brain *de* Alice Cooper *en* La Goulue, *mañana* at one o'clock sharp!"[44]

For the May issue of *Andy Warhol's Interview* with Dalí on the cover,[45] Colacello wrote a short report about the lunch, which appeared in the "Small Talk" section:

... Dalí threw a lunch at La Goulou in honor of ALICE COOPER, his snake and his brain. Alice came later, left early and didn't bring his snake, preferring to have full attention focused on his brain—that is, the hologram-portrait of his brain made by Dalí on display across Madison Avenue at Knoedler's Gallery, where Dalí and Cooper later gave a press conference. Lunch, nonetheless, went on and on without the guest of honor. Seated at the opposite ends of the long L-shaped table: CANDY DARLING, in a turban; POUTASSA [sic], in a big black hat; Queens of the North and South, respectively. In the middle, again: King Louis Quatorze, Crown Prince Juan de Jesus, and El Maestro who insisted on ordering "Lamb chops for everybody," at the height of the meat boycott.

39
Warhol/Colacello 1979, p. 128. The further text describes how the French author and photographer François-Marie Banier asked to be allowed to use the bathroom at the Dalís' suite, which Gala vehemently denied out of fear of venereal diseases. More details are provided in the chapter **Illness Phobia** in Part 2.

40
Colacello 1990, p. 172.

41
Morse 1973, vol. XVII: 1972–1973. The mentioned Polaroids of Dalí are probably those showing the artist together with Pandora and Juan Fernández. See the chapter **Warhol Photographs Dalí** in Part 4.

42
Warhol/Colacello 1979, p. 127.

43
Colacello 1990, pp. 172f. Warhol also asked Dalí "if he was doing any new art." See the chapter **Mao Marilyn** in Part 4.

44
Ibid., p. 173. According to Colacello, Warhol did not take part in the lunch. Cf. ibid., p. 174.

45
See the chapter **Dalí News and Andy Warhol's Interview** in Part 4.

A few tables away, PRINCE and PRINCESS RAINER of MONACO (read GRACE KELLY!) looked amused, or was it confused.[46]

Pandora recalls that Warhol took part in the meal with a couple of people from the Factory and they all walked along to the Knoedler Gallery afterwards.[47] As already mentioned, Warhol took several photos with his Polaroid camera of Dalí during their lunch together. In two of the photos, Nanita Kalaschnikoff is sitting to Dalí's right, while in two others, Alice Cooper is sitting to his left. Two other Polaroids show Warhol sitting at the table with Malcolm Morley and Dalí. They were probably taken later that day.[48] Morley was invited by Dalí to participate in the Knoedler exhibition. He recalls, "The show at Knoedler in 1973 had other artists in it as well. I had a piece called *The Toys* in it. Dalí would walk around with a stamp that said 'Dalí.' If he approved of something he would stamp it. As he stamped my painting he looked at me and said 'Velázquez.' I thought it was an enormous compliment."[49]

At the lunch at La Goulou, Warhol was photographed by Dalí's later secretary Robert Descharnes. In the two shots Warhol is holding his Polaroid camera in his hand and is sitting next to the collector Eleanor Morse. His tape recorder is on the table. According to Descharnes, the photos were taken on April 3, 1973.[50] Unfortunately, not all of Warhol's tape recordings have been transcribed. In the archive of the Andy Warhol Museum in Pittsburgh there is a recording with Dalí, which according to a note on the case, was recorded at La Goulue on March 31, 1973, therefore on a different day.[51] There are other sources that provide clues about the lunch at La Goulue. The Spanish press reported on the event in passing on April 27, 1973. There, it was stated that apart from the rock singer Cooper, the "inevitable" Warhol and some transvestites had attended.[52] A letter written by A. Reynolds Morse to Warhol on April 17, 1973, is evidence that not only Morse's wife Eleanor, but also he himself had lunch with them. The letter says:

Dear Mr. Warhol:

It was a pleasure to have seen you at Dalí's soirée and luncheon.

I sincerely hope that if you ever come to Cleveland that you will visit us and take a look at the museum. We would enjoy having your reaction to it. A copy of my book on Picasso and Dalí, which is a comparison of their lives and works, will be sent to you later on. However, before you get that you will receive a copy of "Dalí ... A Collection" in which I analyze and illustrate the 93 oils in Eleanor's and my collection.

Very truly yours,

SALVADOR DALÍ MUSEUM

A. Reynolds Morse

President.[53]

Morse kept his word and sent Warhol the promised books. The artist later put the two illustrated works in one of his many *Time Capsules*, in which he famously kept practically everything, and the letter in another. [54]

Pandora reports that Warhol was also present at the opening event at the Knoedler Gallery. There was a technical hitch during the press conference.

46
"Small Talk,"
p. 46. Similarly,
in Colacello
1990, p. 174.

→
46/47
[p. 395]

→
48 [p. 395]

47
Pandora in a
conversation
with the author
on November 20,
2011 in Mariposa,
California.

48
See the chapter
**Warhol
Photographs
Dalí** in Part 4.
There is also a
single shot of
Malcolm Morley
with Dalí in the
background.
The Polaroid is
signed by Morley
(The Andy Warhol
Foundation for
the Visual Arts,
Inc., cat. no.
F313.00059).

49
Malcolm Morley
in an e-mail
from Andrew
Lee to the author
on February 23,
2016.

→
45 [p. 395]

50
Descharnes
2002, photo ex-
cerpt, photo
no. 14. Nicolas
Descharnes
kindly informed
the author in
an e-mail on
March 17, 2016
that there are
two photos.

51
These are tape
recordings no.
1870 and 1872,
kept at the Andy
Warhol Museum,
Pittsburgh.
The Andy Warhol
Foundation for
the Visual Arts,
Inc. decided
that Warhol's
tape recordings
should only be
made accessible
to the public fifty
years after his
death.

52
"U.S.A.
GENTES,"
p. 26.

53
Letter from A.
Reynolds Morse
to Andy Warhol
on April 17, 1973
in the archive
of the Andy
Warhol Museum,
Pittsburgh.

54
*Time Capsules
89, 90* at the ar-
chive of the Andy
Warhol Museum,
Pittsburgh. On
the subject of the
Time Capsules
see the chapter
**A Passion
for Collect-
ing** in Part 2.

5

Dalí was seated at a very large table. There were perhaps eight or ten of us standing behind the table. There were so many television cameras in the room that they did not have enough electrical outlets for all the equipment. The television technicians were disconnecting other equipment in order to connect their own. ... The television media were all asking questions at the same time. One of the networks asked Alice Cooper how he felt about Dalí's political views and Alice responded that he personally had nothing to do with politics. ... There was so much confusion with all the press vying for Dalí's time and attention. Dalí was very polite in answering the media until they wanted him to repeat everything due to some failure of their equipment. This is when Dalí slammed his cane down on a table (which made an extremely loud sound) and proceeded to instruct them to ask Candy Darling and me about his exhibition. I have no remembrance of what Candy said. I spoke of Dalí's wish in communicating the fourth dimension; manifesting creation beyond holograms. ... Dalí was very happy that we did that, and then the next morning he called me and said, "Did you see yourself on television?" I said, "No, I never watch television." He replied, "Oh, I don't watch television either." I knew that he watched the interview because he wanted to know if I did.[55]

Dalí and Warhol met again in 1973 in Paris, as they had already the previous year. In the issue of the magazine *Paris Match* on June 16 of that year, Dalí recounts his weekly schedule: "Monday ... I had a visit by Andy Warhol, the official prophet of all the avant-gardes."[56] The encounter took place at Hôtel Le Meurice, where Dalí always resided during his stays in Paris. Warhol visited Europe often that year—especially Rome—where his movies *Flesh for Frankenstein* and *Blood for Dracula* were shot, directed by Paul Morrissey. He went on trips to other European cities from Rome to clinch portrait assignments.[57] The Paris encounter between Dalí and Warhol took place during the period between Easter and mid-May.[58] It can be verified that Warhol was in Paris on April 27 and May 10, to photograph Ileana Sonnabend and Denise von Thyssen for a portrait.[59]

Susi Wyss confirms that Dalí and Warhol occasionally met at Hôtel Le Meurice. She reports that the two artists also met at social events in Paris:

I was there once at Hôtel [Le] Meurice when Dalí and Warhol had a dinner together. ... They barely spoke to each other. They said "Hello" and were introduced: "This is that one and that is that one." ... They did not sit together at the table, as many people do when they are friends. Each had his fans around him and they had many—ten, twelve, fifteen people ... On the same evening the two of them were also at Madame Rochas. ... I also saw the two of them at the big parties that Yves Saint-Laurent threw.[60]

Warhol's superstar Jane Holzer recalls that the two artists were also at the surrealist ball held by Guy and Marie-Hélène de Rothschild in December 1972 at Ferrières Castle, at the gateway to Paris. Holzer reports that she had been to Dalí's suite at Hôtel Le Meurice beforehand with Fred Hughes, where Warhol was already. He and Hughes wore tuxedos that evening.[61] The Rothschild's had proclaimed a "Dîner de Têtes Surréalistes" on their invitation.[62] Numerous celebrities attended the tryst and came with imaginative and ostentatious head coverings, and some wore masks. While Warhol was

55
Pandora in an e-mail to the author on November 19, 2009, and in a conversation with the author on November 20, 2011 in Mariposa, California.

56
In Dalí 1973, p. 4 (translated from the French).

57
Printz/King-Nero 2010, p. 265.

58
On May 14 Warhol was back in New York. Cf. Printz/King-Nero 2010, pp. 269, 272.

59
Ibid., pp. 269, 271. As neither April 27 nor May 10 were a Monday, Dalí can only have received Warhol on April 23, April 30, or May 7.

60
Susi Wyss in a conversation with the author on October 25, 2013 in Paris (translated from the German).

61
Jane Holzer in e-mails to the author on September 9 and 13, 2015.

62
"A Surrealist Parisian Dinner Party chez Madame Rothschild, 1972."

accompanied by Jane Holzer and Fred Hughes, Dalí came with Amanda Lear. She writes in her memoirs:

Dalí had a sumptuous headdress made for me to go to the surrealist ball; it was a shark's head, crowned with artificial roses. He was planning to make his own entrance in a paraplegic's wheelchair, with an umbrella opening and closing above his head. ... All Parisian society was there: Leonor Fini, Yves Saint Laurent, Marie-Hélène de Rothschild and many others, including famous actresses, artists, and bankers.

We were sitting at the same table as Audrey Hepburn, whose head was encased in a birdcage. Our table was entitled "The Table of Metaphysical Perspectives" and each dish also bore a surrealist name.[63]

Dalí and Warhol had probably already seen each other at the "Proust Ball" that the Rothschilds had held in December of the previous year. An invitation was found in one of Warhol's *Time Capsules* addressed to "Andy Warhol at Hôtel Le Meurice."[64] Warhol was evidently staying in Paris at the time, at the same hotel as Dalí.

Bob Colacello reports in his memoirs that Dalí and Warhol met for dinner again in New York in the fall of 1973:

The following fall, like clockwork, Dalí returned to the St. Regis, and Andy returned to tea, still pining for Gala's portrait. Once again Dalí, in brocade, and Gala, in black, were accompanied by Louis XIV and Jesus Christ. And Crown Prince Juan and the starving young beauties, and Pandora, who was rumored not to be a drag queen after all, and Holly Woodlawn, in a reverse-drag tux of her own. Halston floated in with his coat over his shoulder, Iolas-style. "Gee, Bob," said Andy, "why can't we get a setup like this." It seemed to me we had. Dalí's British business manager, whom he introduced as El Capitán del Dinero (the Captain of Money), told Andy he could be making seven million a year by doing plates, coins, prints, and books like Dalí. Gala wasn't as forthcoming. "I'm not interested in your doing my portrait," she said, "because you're not a technical enough painter."[65]

Enrique Sabater reports that the relationship between Dalí and Warhol intensified markedly from 1974, the year he took over from Peter Moore.[66] This is the reason why an entire chapter of *Andy Warhol's Exposures* is dedicated to Dalí. Details about the Sunday invitations by Dalí and Gala are revealed to the reader: "Every Sunday afternoon they have people in for tea—champagne tea. Then Dalí takes everyone to dinner at Trader Vic's. He's very generous. There are never less than twenty people—all the starving young beauties and transvestites in town."[67] One can glean details of Dalí's first tea party in winter 1973/74 from the "New York Small Talk" section of the February issue of *Andy Warhol's Interview*, where it says:

DALÍ IS BACK: And up to his fabulous old tricks. His first Sunday tea at the King Cole Bar of the Hotel St. Regis brought out all the young beauties about town including models JANE FORTH, GRACE JONES, RAMONA SAUNDERS and others too divine too mention. On hand to greet them was the entire Court of Dalí including Queen GALA, in a black tuxedo, Crown Prince JUAN DE JESUS in white, and that mysterious blonde lady who is known as KING LOUIS QUATORZE. After a brief question-and-answer period for the media

63
Lear 1985, p. 219.

64
Time Capsule 81 at the archive at the Andy Warhol Museum, Pittsburgh.

65
Colacello 1990, p. 174.

66
Sabater in Mas in *El ojo invisible* 2004, p. 145.

67
Warhol/Colacello 1979, p. 127.

drove that always swarms around El Maestro (asking his opinion on everything from holography to anal sex for women), the champagne began to flow. Among the sippers: HALSTON with VICTOR HUGO and STEPHAN [sic] SPROUSE; the gilded PANDORA of "Luminous Procuress" fame; fashion stylist BETSEY JONES [sic]; and several Spanish titles. HOLLY WOODLAWN looking fresh as a daisy, didn't have a drop. "I restrict my drinking to my nightclub act," said Holly, who is off on a national tour after she closes at Trude Heller's.[68]

Louis Markoya, who was Dalí's assistant at that time, provides detailed information about the location of Dalí's tea parties at the St. Regis:

Dalí held regular meetings of all sorts during the week in the King Cole Bar. But court, at least from 1970 to 1976 was always Sunday night in the cocktail lounge, which was closed for Dalí's exclusive use during those evening hours—every Sunday he was there. Started at 6 p.m. ended around 8 or 9 p.m. or whenever Dalí wanted to go out for dinner.

It's very difficult to find anyone that even remembers the cocktail lounge as it was removed years ago, and of course because of the Parrish painting, the King Cole Bar is always mentioned. ... the cocktail lounge had its walls decorated with many harlequins, which Dalí actually liked ... Dalí would hold court every Sunday while he was in New York, usually three months of the year, in that time Warhol would come to the court perhaps two or three times, and see Dalí another few during the week in my experience. ... At one Sunday party, Dalí had me fill condoms with helium to float in the room, but to make them float at head level, Dalí made me buy every stamp the St. Regis front desk had to paste on the condoms, not only to form windows in the blimp like structures, but to weigh them down so they would not be caught on the ceiling ... crazy stuff. But perhaps a nod to Warhol as the Factory had the silver helium balloons floating around everywhere. ... There was talk of anti-gravitational protection from Dalí, and because the condoms were covered with postage stamps Warhol made some comment about them being delivered, unfortunately I did not hear the entire comment.[69]

Maybe it was Dalí's intention to mock Warhol's *Silver Clouds* with his special decoration for the cocktail lounge. In this context, it should be recalled that Dalí always claimed that it was he who had inspired Warhol to create the flying sculptures.[70] On another day, Warhol took a Polaroid of Louis Markoya and tried to win him over, as already mentioned.[71] Markoya recalls,

On one of these Sunday gatherings, during a break where Dalí was called away, I was left with Warhol and a few of his entourage, and some models from Dalí's entourage. ... Warhol was asking me to come to the Factory, and went on to request that I come and work for him, as he said Dalí was old and his fame dwindling. He felt that I would be a better protégé and assistant for him than Dalí. ... I felt Dalí was the premiere genius of modern art, and while Warhol was famous and loved, in my mind nothing in comparison to Dalí. Soon after this occurred I took the Polaroid portrait that Warhol took of me and signed and threw it in the trash, something my wife likes to bring up as me being too quick to act ... to be honest I felt it was the right action, even though I've lamented it. I never felt Warhol running around the room with his Polaroid snapping pictures like crazy was art, and my tossing his portrait of me was the ultimate showing of my feelings and commitment.[72]

68
"New York Small Talk," p. 29.

69
Louis Markoya in e-mails to the author on March 11 and 12, 2016.

70
See the chapter **Silver Clouds** in Part 4.

71
See the chapter **Companions, Courtiers, and Superstars** in Part 3.

72
Louis Markoya in e-mails to the author on March 10 and 11, 2016.

The former model Chris Royer reports that Warhol was also a regular guest at Dalí's dinners at Trader Vic's that followed the "champagne tea" at the St. Regis:

... Trader Vic's ... was famous at that time and considered a really hot place to go to in New York. It was downstairs in the Plaza Hotel and done in Kontiki style with palm trees, exotic plants, coconuts, and more. They had amazing drinks like the Zombie, a wonderful Hawaiian menu, brilliant blue and purple orchid flower garlands, which were given out to the guests. ... A regular was Andy Warhol, who would also bring his guests or Interview staff. Personalities like Amanda Lear, Holly Woodlawn, and Potassa fascinated both Dalí's and Andy's strong visionary senses. A lot of the creative thought processes would instantly happen in that element; Andy and Salvador Dalí thrived on this environment. Andy went one step further and carried a tape recorder and camera, while Dalí got inspired by watching the interaction of people at the table. This was part of setting up the stage for his art creations.[73]

Enrique Sabater also recalled later that Warhol was a frequent guest at Dalí's Sunday dinners at Trader Vic's or at Laurent, which opened exclusively for the surrealist's gatherings on Sundays.

Warhol didn't miss even one. He was usually accompanied by two or three young people, who were sometimes obliged to leave on Dalí's instructions, as they were smoking illegal substances under the table. Dalí was very strict in these situations.

...

He [Warhol] understood, and said nothing. He was an open, friendly person. He was always the last to arrive, and I always kept him a seat at the head of the table. He carried a tiny camera, and took thousands of photos at the meals. I suspected at times that there was no film in the camera, and that he was simply staging a show.[74]

Sabater elaborated in answer to the question of what the two artists talked about: "American politics and art. They talked of Klimt and Kandinsky, of hyperrealists like Estes. They described experiences of their visits to the New York exhibitions. It was all very funny and interesting. At the end of the seventies they often spoke about religion. Warhol was a practicing Catholic, Dalí non-practicing."[75] Louis Markoya confirms that the two artists talked about art: "They talked mostly about art, the area museums and the current shows in the area, and a little about their own current ideas."[76] Amanda Lear also recalls such conversations:

... the new tendency, "What do you think of hyperrealistic?" This was a big period. They were launching this new kind of painting that was very ... photographic. And so Andy and Dalí were talking about this, they were talking about musicals. They were talking about anything, boys, girls, whatever. They were chatting away. Warhol wasn't talking much in front of Dalí, because Warhol was always the type of man who said, "Oh, really? Oh, oh! Oh, really? Oh, that's interesting! Oh, really?" ... Dalí was doing all the talking because Dalí always had his opinion about everything ... .[77]

Baron Roger de Cabrol, who was often at Dalí's side at the time, reports on the other hand: "Dalí was always polite, and Andy Warhol, too. ... they

73
Chris Royer in a telephone conversation with the author on October 7, 2013.

74
In Mas in *El ojo invisible*, p. 145.

75
In ibid, pp. 145f.

76
Louis Markoya in an e-mail to the author on May 17, 2010.

77
Amanda Lear in a telephone conversation with the author on March 13, 2010.

would talk about what was happening in music and things like that. But there was no deep discussion about art."[78] However, the favorite conversation topic of both of the artists was sex. In *Andy Warhol's Exposures,* it says,

Dalí likes to talk about sex a lot. And so do I. I never know what he's talking about, but every so often I recognize the word "masturbation" because it sounds the same in every language. I think he thinks that masturbation has something to do with art. It could be art, couldn't it? When Dalí talks about sex he uses big words like synthesis, dialectic, energy, whereas I stick to four-letter words. If only Gala would let me tape record our sex talks it would make a great Broadway play. I'd like to produce it, with Woody Allen as Dalí and Warren Beatty as me.[79]

Bob Colacello adds: "Andy would be holding his tape recorder and laughing at what Dalí said. He didn't understand most of it because Dalí would switch from English to Spanish to French. Andy only spoke English. But Andy would laugh, and I think they would talk about sex a lot. Andy would try to ask him about sex."[80] Glenn O'Brien remarks about Warhol: "I think he was puzzled by Dalí being so hung up on Gala. Andy was always trying to figure out people's sexual orientation, particularly if it was unclear. ... I was with them once or twice. I would say their communication was semi-verbal, but they were very cordial, deferential and complimentary of one another. But everyone had trouble understanding Dalí's fanciful and heavily accented English."[81] Ultra Violet said later: "Warhol never had anything to say. He had nothing to say to anyone. Dalí had a lot to say. ... Dalí was so prolific and an extrovert. Warhol was an introvert. Dalí had a lot to do. He said 'I am not a painter. I am a writer.' He had much to say and he had an audience to listen—Warhol."[82] This may have been true of the relationship between Dalí and Warhol, but it was not applicable to all situations. Of course Warhol was also talkative and anything other than monosyllabic in the presence of friends and people close to him.[83] The actress Sylvia Miles, who took on the female lead role in Warhol's movie *Heat* directed by Paul Morrissey, reports:

Andy really adored me. He loved me. I have more pictures of Andy kissing me than I have of boyfriends. ... Andy, who I always think of as being very talkative, because when I was with him he was always talking. And when he was with Dalí—nothing. ... In a situation like that Andy was not as overtly in charge. ... He listened to him more than he talked to him. He took a back seat in front of him.[84]

The French flacon designer Pierre Dinand describes why Warhol had no choice but to take a back seat: "Dalí was a permanent showpiece, a one-man show, inventing crazy words. His speech was like his painting, baroque and surrealistic. He always put superlatives over the words: for Dalí, Warhol was 'extraordinaturalistic' and the shy Warhol would not answer. I do not recall any word from Warhol in front of the Master Charisma-Cosmo-Chronologic."[85] Dalí, on the other hand, dominated the conversation not just with Warhol, but basically with everyone. The jewelry designer Lee Brooks comments: "From what I understood, he never asked a question, because he didn't wait for the answer. And, if you asked a question, he would answer

---

78
Baron Roger
de Cabrol in a
conversation
with the author
on December 5,
2012 in New York.

79
Warhol/Colacello
1979, p. 129.

80
Bob Colacello
in a telephone
conversation
with the author
on September
22, 2010.

81
Glenn O'Brien in
an e-mail to the
author on December 21, 2011.

82
Ultra Violet in a
conversation
with Jeanine
Barone for the
author on October 18, 2009
in New York.

83
See the chapter
**The Extroverted Dalí
and the
Introverted
Warhol**
in Part 2.

84
Sylvia Miles in a
conversation
with the author
on July 1, 2012 in
New York.

85
Pierre Dinand
in an e-mail
to the author on
April 20, 2012.

half of it and then go off on something else. So, there wasn't any ... in-depth communication ... ."[86]

At that time Dalí and Warhol met not only at the St. Regis, but also at special events. Louis Markoya reports that Warhol took Dalí and him as his guests to the David Bowie concert from the Ziggy Stardust tour at the Radio City Music Hall on Valentine's Day 1973. Other people from Warhol's entourage attended. Shortly thereafter, Warhol invited Dalí and his assistant to a preview of his 3D movie *Flesh for Frankenstein*, directed by Paul Morrissey. Louis Markoya recalls, "It was a small group and private, more or less Warhol showing off his 3D versus Dalí and his 3D. ... I distinctly remember a 3D scene in *Frankenstein* where entrails fall through a grate towards the audience with a quick camera change of view, which Dalí liked and Warhol was proud of."[87]

Suzannah Fleming remembers another encounter between Dalí and Warhol, which can be dated to early 1974.[88] Fleming, who regularly posed as a model for Dalí at the time,[89] had said to him that she would like to get to know Warhol personally sometime, also because his superstar Candy Darling was her idol.[90] Dalí had never spoken about Warhol with Fleming before, but now he took the opportunity to prepare his muse duly for the encounter.

The only thing Dalí ever said to me about Warhol was that he believed he was someone who was fascinated with the idea of sex, but that he was in fact completely asexual himself. He said he was certain that Andy's penis was perpetually flacid, and this was what had turned his hair white. ... essentially he was saying Warhol had a morbid fascination with sex and perversion, but was a virgin or asexual – detached from his own sexuality—I guess. How Dalí knew this—or whether or not he was correct—I don't know. I never spoke to him about it afterwards. I do think I got a sense that Dalí was trying to steer me clear from any fascination with Warhol, because it might detract from my fascination with Dalí![91]

Then came the big moment of the encounter at Trader Vic's, which Suzannah Fleming remembers as follows:

It was always the same huge table reserved for Dalí. He always sat me next to him and Gala would be seated directly opposite us with her own entourage. ... I'm fairly sure Amanda Lear was at the same event, too, and sat on the other side of Dalí from me. Somehow I remember the idea being discussed of the "flanking blondes" and/or of Dalí's "lionesses" or "sphinxes." Who observed this I don't remember, but I definitely recall it struck Dalí as amusing when he heard it. I don't think I knew who Warhol came with, but it seemed as though he was surrounded by a couple of people he knew well. I can remember thinking to myself, as I went over to Warhol, that I might just end up being "The Next Candy Darling" (someone I greatly admired). ... I can remember saying to Warhol something to the effect that I was one of Dalí's "lesser-known muses" (which was very true!). ... I don't really remember what Warhol said at all. Whatever it was it wasn't very much, and the man next to him—whom he obviously knew—was far more responsive and in a way seemed to be responding for him as a kind of proxy. Warhol just sat there and kept looking in the direction of Dalí and back to his talkative friend. ... he struck me in his behavior as being uneasy as if he

86
Lee Brooks in a conversation with the author on November 13, 2011 in San Francisco. Michael Ward Stout reports similarly: "Warhol was always the person who asked questions and Dalí liked to talk. ... Dalí's intellectual conversations were more reserved for mathematicians and physicists and scientists ..." Michael Ward Stout in a telephone conversation with the author on June 9, 2010.

87
Louis Markoya in e-mails to the author on March 12 and 23, 2016.

88
Fleming recalls that the encounter took place "sometime after *Andy Warhol's Interview* did an article about Amanda Lear." Suzannah Fleming in an e-mail to the author on December 29, 2011. The article appeared in the January 1974 issue. Cf. Lester 1974, pp. 26f.

89
See the chapter **Companions, Courtiers, and Superstars** in Part 3.

90
Suzannah Fleming in a conversation with the author on July 20, 2012 in London.

91
Suzannah Fleming in e-mails to the author on December 23 and 25, 2011.

was bracing himself for Dalí to do something truly unpleasant to him. ... It was incredibly awkward and the exchange could not have lasted for more than a minute or so. Everyone within earshot was listening intensely to what I had to say, and more especially to Warhol's response, but basically it was entirely a misfire and rather dry and Waspish! I somehow got the impression he was very nervous about Dalí—which struck me as very odd. I could hear Dalí's voice rising—making yet another extraordinary Dalían pronouncement—and he was definitely looking right at Warhol! ... I got the impression he [Dalí] felt quite possessive of me. ... I looked back at Dalí across the table and it seemed he was a small, jealous child glaring directly at Warhol—as if to say, "Mine, not yours!"[92]

Suzannah Fleming also recalls another interesting detail: Warhol sat at the outer edge of the table at the party. This may be explained by the fact that he was always the last guest to arrive, as Enrique Sabater reports.[93] However, perhaps it was not a coincidence. Victor Bockris says: "They were both world people. They had a worldwide following and were both known by a single name. They were equals. In the international world of major celebrities the most famous people rarely mix with their equals. They prefer to spend time surrounded by their own court. Otherwise they cannot maintain the control that is the basis of their power, as Andy illustrates in the *Exposures* chapter."[94]

In fall 1974, Victor Bockris had the opportunity to interview Dalí at a reception at the St. Regis, together with Andrew Wylie. Bockris explains:

We were at the height of our interviewing period. In fact we had tried to interview Salvador the previous Sunday, but had to abort the mission when he refused to be tape-recorded. When we returned on this night a week later, Wylie had a cassette recorder in the inside pocket of his jacket. We got there early and thus were able to sit directly in front of Dalí, who sat on a sort of throne with various beautiful people to his left and right. We got off to a good start talking about sex and were able to hold his attention long enough to record over an hour of conversation with him. Andy Warhol and his entourage came in about twenty minutes into the interview and took a seat directly behind us. ... The cassette tapes we used were forty-five minutes long. When they ended they made a clicking noise. So forty minutes into the interview Wylie was going to go outside the room and turn the tape over so nobody would hear the click that would have come at forty-five minutes and we could record on its other side. Andy realized what we were doing ... "Going to change your tape?" Andy asked coyly. ... Andy made us feel really good because we ended up leaving the hotel at the same time as he did. As he floated by he smiled at us and said, "Goodnight girls!" And we thought, we're in, he likes us! He likes us![95]

As was to be expected, Warhol had also had his tape recorder running.[96] The interview of Bockris and Wylie with Dalí was not published until 1975 as the cover story in *The Coldspring Journal* and in December 1976 under the title "Sex, Money & Murder" in the erotic magazine *National Screw*.[97] The interview primarily revolves around sex. Dalí willingly provides the information that he preferred the anus to the vagina, speaks about the dolphin as "the most beautiful fucking animal in the earth" and reports that Lorca had tried to seduce him. Just as Dalí was remarking that he was afraid of sex and needed masturbation to prove to himself that "that little object is

92
Suzannah Fleming in e-mails to the author on December 12, 23 and 29, 2011.

93
Suzannah Fleming in a conversation with the author on July 20, 2012 in London.

94
Victor Bockris in an e-mail to the author on July 16, 2010.

95
Victor Bockris in e-mails to the author on September 9 and 12, 2015.

96
Tape recording no. 37 at the archive of the Andy Warhol Museum, Pittsburgh.

97
This information is thanks to Victor Bockris, from an e-mail on September 10, 2015.

something," Warhol entered the room with his entourage. His appearance was worthy of mention by Bockris and Wylie:

At this very moment, the glass doors at the back of the room open slowly, revealing Andy Warhol, carrying his dachshund, followed by two male members of his entourage. Warhol stands carefully in the doorway for a few moments surveying the scene and chatting in undertones with one or two men who approach him, then, preceded by one of his escorts, he heads across the room and takes a seat behind the two young men. He is wearing his costume of the moment which is a green velvet jacket, a white Brooks Brothers shirt, and blue and white striped tie, levis and brown boots similar to Dalí's but with higher heals. [98]

Bockris also remembers, "Dalí immediately ordered an aide to see if Mr. Warhol wanted a drink." [99] In the further course of the interview, on the subject of God, money, and art, Dalí saw it as his duty to highlight the significance of his younger artist colleague. The concrete context was the relationship between classicism and originality in art: "Classicism has more possibility of originality because is tradition. For instance, Andy Warhol create Pop Art, and his Pop Art is very good for the possibility of hyperrealism because is one tradition. In the people blocking tradition, as abstract expressionism, the tradition is blocked, and most everyone commit suicide. You know, Rothko commit suicide. But in the classicism is the contrary. Originality is one product of tradition." [100]

When Dalí spent time in New York he liked to visit French restaurants, including La Côte Basque opposite the St. Regis Hotel, as well as Le Cygne, La Goulue, La Caravelle and La Grenouille. [101] Around 1973/74, Dalí celebrated "the return of the flies" at La Grenouille. Pierre Dinand, who took part in the celebration, recalls,

Dalí was reigning on a throne at the King Cole Bar of the St. Regis Hotel with his dirty velvet jacket and his tall cane. There was his name written on the throne and nobody was allowed to sit there. ... His secretary was present, cashing the money from the lithographs (cost fifty cents) that Dalí was selling for $1,000 each to rich businessmen, with a squashed fly that he would take from a little box and squash himself on the litho for an extra $1,000. ... If the client wanted two flies squashed on the litho, it would be $2,000, three flies $3,000 and so on. ... You couldn't find flies in New York at the time. So he had worm flies coming from Mexico, keeping them in a plastic box in his rooms on the second floor, until one day a cleaning lady put the box down, and the flies flew all over and outside the room into the hotel. Dalí was first very upset, but quickly found this happening very creative. ... Dalí was thrilled. "Another surrealist happening," he said ... . He sent someone to buy butterfly nets and asked all the hotel grooms and attendants to catch the flies—the one-thousand-dollar flies. ... In the evening we went for dinner at La Grenouille to celebrate the return of the flies with Gala, Warhol, and Carlo Bilotti.

Another night at La Grenouille, I remember that Dalí was asked to test the wine. He brought a glass to his lips, looking up, then after a long minute of silence, he declared with his incrrrrredible accent, "The wine is fine, but the ceiling needs a new paint job." ... Dalí and Warhol spoke of the ceiling color, and Warhol left the decision to Dalí. ... "Paint it red please, come to my room I will give you the right

98
Bockris/Wylie 1976, pp. 16f.

99
Victor Bockris in an e-mail to the author on July 16, 2010.

100
In Bockris/Wylie 1976, p. 17.

101
Pierre Dinand in an e-mail to the author on September 8, 2012.

*color." The owner came to the hotel, got the color touch and had the ceiling paint-
ed again the following morning. Gala was sitting between Warhol and me, with
Dalí and Carlo Bilotti on the other side. Gala was touching me under the table,
with the obvious approval of Dalí, who was trying to find lovers for his wife … .
She even gave me her room number, "Come to see me, young man." I declined.*[102]

Another French restaurant in New York that Dalí liked to visit was
Lutèce. He also met Warhol there. *Andy Warhol's Exposures* includes a report about a lunch together, organized by Bob Colacello, that took place on
February 10, 1975.[103] Gala and the actress Paulette Goddard took part in this
meal. Goddard, who was famous for her jewelry collection, was born in New
York in 1910 and had regular contact with Dalí and Warhol. From 1936 to
1942 she was married to Charlie Chaplin, her second marriage, and played
a role at his side in the movies *Modern Times* (1936) and *The Great Dictator*
(1942). She was later married to the actor Burgess Meredith from 1944 to
1950.[104] In 1948 Dalí planned to include Goddard and Meredith in his movie
The Wheelbarrow of Flesh, which had never been realized.[105] On account of
the shared movie project, Dalí and Gala were invited by the acting couple to a
traditional Thanksgiving dinner. *Andy Warhol's Exposures* explains the meal:

*… Paulette was in a very good mood and telling funny stories. She told
about the Thanksgiving that Dalí and Gala spent with Paulette and Burgess Meredith at their house in Nyack, New York. Paulette said that she was so thrilled by
the idea of the great maestro Dalí coming to her house for Thanksgiving dinner
that she decided to do something really special. Instead of turkey she served a
whole stuffed pig with an apple in its mouth. When the butler appeared carrying the pig on a silver plate, Dalí clapped and Burgess got hysterical. "Merle,
Merle," he cried, "What have you done to my Merle?"*

*Paulette said, "How was I to know that was his favorite pig? I mean re-
ally, calling a pig Merle. It wasn't long after that Thanksgiving that we were
divorced."*[106]

Warhol recorded this conversation on tape on February 18, 1974 at
Trader Vic's.[107] Thus, two different encounters were merged as one in *Exposures*.

Warhol had met Paulette Goddard in spring 1973 at the opening of a
gold exhibition at the Metropolitan Museum of Art. They shared a passion for
gold and diamonds.[108] They became friends and often appeared together in
public. At the time Goddard exclusively wore Arctic fox fur in all imaginable
variations. Tellingly, she called Warhol "the white fox" on account of his al-
abaster skin and startling white hair and eulogized: "He is the best audience
I have ever found. I like to talk and he likes to listen."[109] An entire chapter of
Andy Warhol's Exposures is dedicated to the actress.[110] Furthermore, Warhol planned a book about her, which was to bear the title *HER*.[111] Although
he gathered a wealth of taped material for this, the project never got under
way,[112] because Goddard was not prepared to grant a genuine insight into her
life. She explained later: "Warhol taped me for eighty hours and I wouldn't
tell him anything."[113] Bob Colacello adds in his memoirs, "Andy hadn't helped
matters, admittedly, by starting off lunch with 'Well, now that we're really
working, tell us what we really want to know: How big was Charlie's cock?'"[114]

102
Pierre Dinand in
e-mails to the
author on April
18, 2012, Sep-
tember 7 and 8,
2012; and in a
conversation
with the author
on March 1,
2013 in Paris.
See also the
chapter **Muse
and Mother**
in Part 3.

103
The dating is
possible, as
Warhol made a
tape recording
of the encounter
and Bob Cola-
cello reported
about it in the
issue of *Andy
Warhol's Inter-
view* published
one month later
in the section
"OUT." Cf. tape
recording no.
1378 at the ar-
chive of the Andy
Warhol Museum,
Pittsburgh;
Colacello 1975,
March, p. 41.

104
In 1958 Goddard
wedded the
author Erich Ma-
ria Remarque,
with whom she
lived in the Ticino
region until
his death in 1970.

105
Dalí in Calvo
Serraller 2006,
p. 84. Details
about the movie
project in
Sánchez Vidal
in Gale 2007,
pp. 196ff.

106
Warhol/Colacello
1979, pp. 128f.

107
Tape recording
no. 63 at the ar-
chive of the Andy
Warhol Museum,
Pittsburgh.

108
Colacello 1990,
p. 194.

109
Quoted accord-
ing to Morella/
Epstein 1985,
p. 214.

110
Warhol/Colacello
1979, pp. 156ff.

111
Colacello 1990,
pp. 207ff.

112
Warhol/Colacello
1979, p. 159.

113
Quoted accord-
ing to Morella/
Epstein 1985,
p. 215.

114
Quoted accord-
ing to Colacello
1990, p. 209.

5

The guests at the lunch at Lutèce on February 10, 1975 included not only Dalí, Gala, and Paulette Goddard, but also the Iranian politician Fereydoun Hoveyda, who was a United Nations ambassador at the time, and his German wife Gisela. In *Andy Warhol's Exposures*, Warhol elaborates on the luncheon:

Things got off to a bad start when Gala grabbed my tape recorder and threw it in a vase of flowers. I didn't dare say a word. Then Gala ordered poached eggs on dry toast after the maître d' had spent fifteen minutes reeling off every incredible gourmet dish you can imagine. But what really got Gala going, I think, was the fact that Paulette was the center of attention. Poached eggs just can't compete with rubies.

Paulette was wearing her ruby earrings, her ruby necklace, her ruby bracelet, and her ruby pin in the shape of lips with diamond [sic] teeth by Dalí. Ever since Dalí made jewelry like that, I've wanted to make jewelry too. The closest I've come is filling a Heinz pickle jar with a bunch of semiprecious stones for H. Stern jewelers. It's not something Paulette would wear.

...

Then Bob crossed his leg and accidentally barely brushed Gala's shoe. Suddenly Gala punched Bob real hard in the arm and said, "How dare you kick Gala!"

Bob hesitated for a moment and punched her back. I couldn't believe it.

Gala punched Bob back. Paulette muttered, "Go to it, Bob!"

Bob hit Gala again. Gala hit Bob again. Bob hit Gala again.

Dalí laughed, but all I could think was, now she'll never let me take her picture and Dalí will always be the only artist who painted her.

Finally Bob hit her so hard that she broke down and kissed him on the cheeks. I guess he finally proved himself to her. It was the first time she was ever nice to him. ...

Gala decided to leave before dessert because she hates anything sweet. Dalí escorted her to their limo. The moment they were out of sight everyone started talking about Gala's shocking behavior, except me—I was too busy fishing my tape recorder out of the flowers.

...

... [Dalí came back], sat down at the table, and said, "Gala go! Fantastique!"

After lunch, Dalí asked Ambassador Hoveyeda to take him around the corner to the Pleasure Chest, the biggest sex shop in town.[115]

Dalí and Warhol met again in the evening on the same day. Bob Colacello's column "OUT" in the March issue of *Interview* states: "Back at the Factory, Mick Jagger dropped by for tea and champagne. He was on his way from Nicaragua to Haiti. He gave us a lift in his limo to Warren Beatty's screening of *Shampoo*. Dalí was there with Amanda Lear. Sylvia Miles was there with Rudolf Martinus. ... *Shampoo* is the best movie to come out of New Hollywood yet."[116] *Shampoo* is a U.S. American movie satire by Hal Ashby. It recounts twenty-four hours in the life of the love-crazed hairdresser George Roundy, played by Warren Beatty, who delighted his female customers not only with his professional skills as a hairdresser. The figure is inspired by Gene Shacove, the hair stylist of Beverly Hills stars, whom Dalí was extremely amiable towards at a dinner with Tony and Leslie Curtis.[117] Julie Christie and Goldie

323

115
Warhol/Colacello 1979, pp. 128f. Similarly, also in Colacello 1990, pp. 286f. Dalí was not the only artist who painted Gala. She had already been portrayed by Max Ernst and Giorgio de Chirico in the 1920s. For example, simply recall the 1922 painting *At the Rendezvous of Friends* by Ernst. De Chirico painted Gala in December 1923. Cf. Gateau 1994, p. 106. The "ruby pin in the shape +

116
Colacello 1975, March, p. 41.

117
See the chapter **The Extroverted Dalí and the Introverted Warhol** in Part 2.

+
of lips with diamond teeth" is the piece of jewelry *Ruby Lips* made of rubies with eighteen-carat gold and thirteen pearls as teeth. See the chapter **Mae West's and Marilyn Monroe's Lips** in Part 4.

118
Lear 1985, pp. 268f. Lear eternalized herself, like many other prominent visitors to the Factory, in a guest book that was used there between 1977 and 1984. Cf. Dedichen 2013, p. 131.

119
Lear 1985, p. 254.

120
Hackett 1989, p. 423, December 27, 1981.

121
Pat Hackett in a conversation with the author on December 4, 2012 in New York.

122
Lynn Karlin in an e-mail to the author on May 2, 2013.

→
50/51/52
[pp. 396/397]

Hawn play the leading female roles in *Shampoo*. In her memoirs, Amanda Lear explains how she and Dalí ended up at the screening of the movie:

Sometimes I had lunch at Warhol's "Factory" in Union Square. His magazine, Interview, *was enjoying enormous success, and it had recently featured Dalí and Gala on the cover. Warhol was always very pleasant to me, always asking for news of Dalí and his work. … He took me for a Chinese meal with Warren Beatty and his current girlfriend Michelle Phillips, ex-singer of The Mamas and the Papas. The conversation came round to the subject of LSD, and Warren asked me about its effects and the sensations it produced. The next day I met him again in the lift of the St. Regis and he invited Dalí and me to a special preview of his film* Shampoo. *I managed to persuade Dalí to join me, Shirley MacLaine, Warren and his producers.*[118]

There is no evidence as to whether Dalí liked the movie *Shampoo*, but it is doubtful. As Amanda Lear reports, there were hardly any contemporary movies that he liked.[119] Warhol probably liked it more, at least well enough for him to watch it again on television years later.[120] Pat Hackett captured the meeting of the artists at the screening in a photo. She reports:

I took a photograph of Andy and Dalí once at a screening of Warren Beatty's movie Shampoo *at the Columbia Pictures screening room on Fifth Avenue. Jed, Andy, Fred and I went to the screening, and it was at the time when we were trying to raise financing to make our movie* Bad. *And we loved* Shampoo *so much and thought it was so great that we wondered who would ever give us money to make* Bad! *Warren's sister Shirley MacLaine was at the screening, and some other Hollywood types. Getting invited to movie screenings like this was one of the reasons Andy had created* Interview—*if you had a magazine, you'd always get invited because you'd either review it or give it publicity. And Dalí was there, too. Andy always seemed amused when he was with Dalí, he thought it was great that Dalí was so expressive and outgoing—not like, say, Jasper Johns and Robert Rauschenberg, who always seemed uptight around Andy, as if they were afraid that being seen with him was bad for their "serious artist" images.*[121]

The occasion was a social event that drew reporters and photographers. These also included the photographer Lynne Karlin, who remembers the evening as follows: "There I was shooting for *Women's Wear Daily* at the screening for the film *Shampoo* in NYC and was delighted to come across these two iconic figures, whose work couldn't be more contrasting, Dalí and Warhol, absorbed in intimate conversation. I wished I could have heard what Dalí was saying at that moment I took the pictures."[122] Karlin succeeded in capturing Dalí and Warhol together on three photos. The first photo shows how Dalí has laid his right hand on Warhol's left shoulder and is about to greet him with a friendly kiss on his right cheek. In the second photo, Dalí and Warhol are shown together again, posing for photographers. Dalí manages to attract attention with his raised cane. The third photo shows the two artists together with Bob Colacello. Owing to Dalí's hand gesture, it is clear that he is the one who is talking, while Warhol and Colacello are listening to his performance, evidently amused. In all three photos, Warhol is holding his tape recorder in front of himself protectively with both hands and appears typically shy and reserved. The fact that he was once again forced into a walk-on role by Dalí is also confirmed by Sylvia Miles, who was also invited to the screening:

When Andy was with Dalí and you wanted to photograph them together you had to get Andy, come and do it. It wasn't like he was that looking to get photographed. He was reticent. He was in awe. ... Also it could very well be that he did not want to. In other words he wanted to retain his own sense of fame and power and not also be included in a group. But I think that all those people got a kick out of each other basically. ... Salvador Dalí was a very interesting man because he was a little weird, a little sadistic. He liked to make people feel uncomfortable. ... Actually what happened is that he wanted me, too, but I didn't give him the opportunity. ... I think Andy was kind of more interested in taking in what was going on and what he was doing so that he could remember it—store it in his brain.[123]

It was 1975 when Dalí's American solicitor Arnold Grant retired. Grant had represented many celebrities from the worlds of politics, film, and sport and became well-known as the husband of Bess Myerson, who was crowned Miss America in 1945. To Dalí's delight, Arnold Grant always accepted artworks as remuneration.[124] He was replaced by Michael Ward Stout, a young and ambitious lawyer from Wisconsin, who had met Dalí at a reception at the St. Regis. Dalí took a liking to Stout, who reminded him of his father. Stout was an admirer of Motherwell and Rauschenberg. He was not interested in Dalí's art or his public performances. Even so, he and Dalí found their way to each other and Stout went on to represent the artist's interests, but did not accept artworks as payment.[125] His duties soon went beyond legal responsibilities. He became an important helper in the preparations for Dalí's "$3,000 Sunday dinners at Trader Vic's."[126] Stout, who often participated in these events, recalls that the Spaniard regularly invited Warhol:

Andy Warhol would bring many friends, and Dalí would invite his crowd. He was always interested in colorful, amusing people. So he would have a list, including Warhol, and then some elegant, wealthy people from Europe or from New York, and perhaps a scientist and a mathematician—a very amusing mix always. I was a very young lawyer just trying to organize the dinner and help the secretary get the limousines and make sure that people sat at the right places. The dinners were often, but not always, at Trader Vic's, because, unlike many of the elegant restaurants around at the time, it was open on Sunday. This was in the days of Studio 54, and Sunday night was an interesting night to go there, so people would come to Dalí's dinner parties before going to Studio 54, and Dalí would usually go home.[127]

Baron Roger de Cabrol also remembers that Warhol always appeared at Dalí's dinner parties with a large entourage:

He would come in a group of twenty, twenty-five and then they would leave and Dalí would have to pay for everybody. ... Dalí used to be upset when they would all come and have dinner at his expense at Trader's Vic. That he didn't like. ... I saw his reaction. The secretary Enrique Sabater would pay everything, so I don't think Dalí knew exactly what was going on. ... Gala didn't like that whole crowd ... It would start with like ten people being invited and then it happened that fifty, sixty people came to dinner. ... It was like a big party.[128]

123
Sylvia Miles in a conversation with the author on July 1, 2012 in New York.

124
Moore 2009, p. 151.

125
Gibson 1997, p. 564.

126
Ibid., p. 572.

127
Michael Ward Stout in a telephone conversation with the author on June 9, 2010.

128
Baron Roger de Cabrol in a conversation with the author on December 5, 2012 in New York.

5

Warhol evidently enjoyed attending Dalí's dinners with a number of people. He liked to say: "The best dates are when you take the office with you."[129] A Warhol tape recording testifies to the fact that he appeared at one of Dalí's dinners in 1975 accompanied by Fred Hughes and Bob Colacello.[130] Michael Ward Stout recalls that Dalí also often invited Warhol for lunch:

Dalí was a big presence in New York throughout the 1950s, 1960s, and 1970s. So, many people wanted to have lunch or dinner with him because those lunches and dinners were always very amusing and fun, in a way that I don't think happens much anymore. Warhol wanted to be around celebrities and Dalí always had a lot of celebrities around him: kings, queens, and countesses; rock and roll stars; nightclub performers; movie stars; ballet dancers; and opera singers. It was interesting for Warhol because they both were interested in celebrity.[131]

On March 17, 1976, St. Patrick's Day, George Mason organized a dinner at the Metropolitan Club in New York.[132] Mason liked bringing people together and often chose the Metropolitan Club for this purpose.[133] He was friends with Dalí and Warhol, as well as with Candice Bergen, and wanted to acquaint the two artists with the actress. Gala also appeared that evening.[134] George Mason reports: "The room is grand and the tables are far enough apart to allow a good meal without being disturbed. The room and club, which are located on the corner of Sixtieth Street and Fifth Avenue, are of the grand style and a perfect setting for such a good and elegant dinner. Dalí loved the room … ."[135] The fact that Dalí felt at ease at the Metropolitan Club is documented by photos with him posing quite proudly within the club's rooms. Mason had asked the young photographer Jade Albert to document the evening photographically. Albert, who also photographed for *Interview*, recalls, "It was my job to freeze the moment. I remember being overwhelmed with my own curiosity. I don't recall the conversation, but I thought the body language was beyond magical. It was 'a night to remember.'"[136] Warhol also acted as photographer that evening. He took a snapshot of Candice Bergen and Dalí, who is wearing glasses, with his compact camera, with neither of them noticing that they were being photographed.[137] Jade Albert succeeded in capturing the special atmosphere of the dinner in her shots. One photo shows Warhol sitting at a table together with Candice Bergen, with a female hand in the foreground holding a cigarette. The smoker that evening was the art historian Frances Beatty, who can still remember Mason's invitation well:

… he used to give dinner parties all the time and was going out with my friend Shelley Wanger, who after that became the editor of Interview *magazine. … I said to him, "George, I'm not going to go any more to your parties because there all these ridiculous hangers-on who are just coming because it's a free meal etc. They don't have anything to say and they are of no interest whatsoever." I was getting my PhD in Art History and I didn't want to waste my time with a lot of superficial people. George called me up and he said "I'm having this party and you're really going to want to come. I've got Candy [Candice Bergen] and Andy, and Salvador Dalí is coming." George used to see Salvador Dalí at the St. Regis.*[138]

Frances Beatty has special memories of the encounter with Dalí:

I remember sitting next to Dalí … he turned to me and one of the things he said to me was, "Mademoiselle, I am making a movie about pissing on a

130
Tape recording no. 793 at the archive of the Andy Warhol Museum, Pittsburgh.

129
Quoted according to Bockris 1989, p. 381.

131
Michael Ward Stout in a telephone conversation with the author on June 9, 2010.

132
Dating is possible due to tape recordings at the archive of the Andy Warhol Museum, Pittsburgh (no. 124 and 128). George Mason also told the author in an e-mail on August 23, 2012, that Candice Bergen, Dalí, and Warhol only dined together this once at the Metropolitan Club.

133
Shelley Wanger in a telephone conversation with the author on July 23, 2012.

134
George Mason in e-mails to the author on June 8, 2011, and February 4, 2016.

135
George Mason in an e-mail to the author on June 22, 2011.

136
Jade Albert in an e-mail to the author on June 30, 2011.

137
The Andy Warhol Foundation for the Visual Arts, Inc. cat. no. FL06.00327.

138
Dr. Frances F.L. Beatty in a conversation with the author on June 27, 2012 in New York.

→
54 [p. 398]

carrot." And I said, "Oh, well that's very interesting," even though I didn't think it was interesting at all and I thought, how am I going to get through the next three hours talking to him? Not that that couldn't be an interesting idea, but he was just saying it, really, to shock me, and it didn't shock me in the least. I was a bit prejudiced against him. I appreciated his genius, his early genius, but he seemed to me to be a poseur and I was a young intellectual. So I was more critical than star-struck about him. I knew that he liked the nineteenth-century salon painter Ernest Meissonier, who is not an artist that most people then liked at all—he is and was very out of fashion—but Dalí liked him, perversely. I knew a fair amount about Meissonier and about Pompier paintings, which Dalí loved. So I started to talk to him about that and he brightened up and he actually had a conversation with me about them, because obviously there were not many people that he hung around with at Studio 54 who even knew who Meissonier was, much less about Pompier paintings.[139]

Shelley Wanger was also sitting next to Dalí that evening, but she did not engage in any serious conversation with him: "I sat there and just let him talk. And a lot of the conversation on his part was a bit on the surreal side ... Dalí was like a performance. You could laugh or smile. He didn't really want you to talk to him. I mean, he just wanted to have an effect. He used to say very strange things to try and get a reaction. He told me I looked like a seahorse, probably because I have a rather prominent nose. That was fine—I am very fond of seahorses."[140] Jade Albert released the shutter at the moment when Shelley Wanger touched Dalí's famous cane and the two of them looked at each other. Wanger cannot recall a conversation with Warhol and reports: "He would watch, and listen, he was, as you know, a voyeur and a catalyst. Things would happen around him. We did not really talk that night, though one night when I ran into him he mentioned one of my great aunts, who was a painter with a very whimsical style whom he admired."[141]

However, over the course of the evening Warhol loosened up and initiated a conversation with Candice Bergen, which the actress responded enthusiastically, as shown by Jade Albert's photos. Mason remembers that the atmosphere was good that evening and that all those present had a good time.[142] Shelley Wanger remarks in retrospect: "It was great fun on the level of who was there, but I felt quite shy and in that group rather wished I could have been invisible. It was interesting to be with them, of course, but I don't remember really finding a lot of the conversation that fascinating. ... on my side of the table there was a certain level of nonsense. It would have been different if Isaiah Berlin had been there."[143] Candice Bergen reports that Warhol had his tape recorder on his lap throughout the entire evening.[144] He recorded, for example, himself saying that you actually can get pregnant from sitting on the john.[145] The host of the evening, George Mason, describes how Dalí and Warhol interacted during the dinner: "They did talk together but I remember it was sort of awkward and stiff. ... [T]hey circled each other, taking measure ... like two lions, cats ... . Both had egos and, at first, they were cautious, but then enjoyed the irrational chats about trips and parties. Andy's voice was quite soft, so it was difficult for Dalí to understand him. The

139
Ibid.

→
53 [p. 398]

140
Shelley Wanger
in a telephone
conversation
with the author
on July 23, 2012.

141
Ibid.

→
55 [p. 399]

142
George Mason
in an e-mail to
the author on
July 26, 2012.

143
Shelley Wanger
in a telephone
conversation
with the author
on July 23, 2012
and in a conver-
sation with the
author on De-
cember 3, 2012
in New York.

144
Candice Bergen
in an e-mail to
her assistant
Alex McCann on
July 6, 2012, of
which extracts
were forwarded
to the author.

145
Tape recordings
no. 124 and
128 at the archive
of the Andy
Warhol Museum,
Pittsburgh.

146
George Mason in e-mails to the author on June 22, 2011 and February 4, 2016. Mason adds, "Dalí enjoyed the attention of the ladies and called each a funny and meaningful name. He called Shelley Wanger a seahorse, which is a reference to the clitoris. He called the French girl [who attended the dinner]—I have forgotten her name—"his staff" meaning his erection. Dalí loved to focus on what would surprise people and make them think." George Mason in e-mails to the author on June 22, 2011 and March 23, 2016.

147
Warhol reports for example in his diaries that he was invited to dinner by George Mason on June 9 and 30, 1977. Cf. Hackett 1989, pp. 50, 56.

148
George Mason in an e-mail to the author on June 22, 2011.

149
Ibid.

150
Bob Colacello in a telephone conversation with the author on September 22, 2010.

151
This painting may have been the second version from 1976. The first had already been made in 1974/75. Dalí created it for his Teatre-Museu Dalí in Figueres. The first version measures 445×350 cm, the second 252.2×191.9 cm. Cf. Descharnes/Néret 1993, no. 1446, 1447.

152
Pierre Dinand in a conversation with the author on March 1, 2013 in Paris.

153
See the chapter **Warhol photographs Dalí** in Part 4.

154
See the chapter **Portraits of Socialites** in Part 4.

→ **29** [p. 381]

table chat kept the interest alive and the evening was filled with laughter. ... Gala did not talk with anyone."[146]

Mason saw the two artists regularly at the time.[147] From his encounters with them he was able to establish that both Dalí and Warhol were interested in finding out more about each other: "Andy was curious about the dinners and parties Dalí gave and asked about how Gala handled Dalí's money. ... Andy liked the stories about Dalí's habit to shock and cause controversy. Dalí liked to give decadent parties/dinners with naked models lying in front of the guest as either objects or as serving plates for the food. Andy liked Dalí's knowledge of how to show people possibilities by shocking them and opening their minds to the new."[148] Mason remarks about Dalí's interest in his younger colleague: "Dalí asked about Andy's portrait price points because, at the time, Andy was doing quite a few portraits. ... Dalí was curious about Andy's lifestyle, gayness, and all about the NYC hotspots and parties. Andy was in the news quite a bit for the parties he attended with the rich and famous."[149]

Not only was Warhol often in the media, he tried repeatedly to persuade Dalí and Gala to let themselves be portrayed by him. As Bob Colacello reports, in the back of his mind, he was thinking of an exchange: "Andy liked to trade art with other artists; for example the portraits he did of Rauschenberg and Lichtenstein, they were trades. Either they did a portrait of Andy or I think they gave Andy one of their paintings and then Andy did their portrait. ... So he wanted to do a trade with Dalí, but I think he would have preferred doing Gala's portrait, not Dalí's. But he might have wanted to do Dalí's, too. I don't remember now."[150] Pierre Dinand remembers portraits that Warhol produced of Dalí and remarks that at the time, the Spaniard was working on the painting *Gala Contemplating the Mediterranean Sea which at Twenty Meters Becomes the Portrait of Abraham Lincoln – Homage to Rothko*.[151] Dinand, who was often in Dalí's company at the time in New York, recalls,

I remember that Warhol was working on a Dalí portrait. He showed Dalí four figures of Dalí in green, red, pink and blue. I saw them. That was at the King Cole Bar. What I remember is that Dalí didn't like them. Warhol had taken a picture of Dalí with a Polaroid and then probably changed the Polaroid so there was one completely blue. I remember there was one pink, one green .... They were rolled, so he took them out and showed them to Dalí. Dalí looked at them. Maybe he thought it was great, but he was jealous. I don't know. His reaction was very bizarre. I think his reaction was shock. ... So, why didn't he like them? I don't know. But he looked at them and never spoke about them anymore. Maybe Warhol destroyed them.[152]

Perhaps Warhol used one of the Polaroid photos he had taken of Dalí as a template for his portraits of him.[153] Unfortunately, the works have never turned up again. Perhaps they were indeed destroyed when they were painted over.[154]

There is another anecdote surrounding a Warhol artwork, which emerged around 1973/74. Louis Markoya reports:

Dalí knew very well of Warhol's silkscreen methods ... and of course is a long time supporter and practitioner of classical methods and technique. Dalí had been pumped and primed about his Mao Marilyn piece; it was on the cover

of Vogue and he was assured by many it was a work of epic genius. Being presented with the Warhol work gave Dalí the perfect opportunity to make an art happening out of the event and place the piece in its true historical context, according to Dalí. There were perhaps a half dozen people in the room. Warhol had arrived with one other person to carry the work till the last second (don't know who). We had moved from the King Cole Bar (Dalí, Peter Moore, and myself) to a private room at the St. Regis. When handed the Marilyn print, Dalí immediately lays it down and unzips. When the pissing starts, Warhol's surprised look turns to all smiles, he said nothing. Dalí made some comment about the genius of his Marilyn was not matched by this work and the chemistry of his piss would transform it.[155]

According to Markoya's report, there were few people present at the "art happening." In wider society, Dalí always treated his younger colleague with great respect. Louis Markoya explains, "Dalí respected Warhol for the attention he was getting, not because he felt he was the genius the art world was adoring."[156] If the two artists met by chance in a restaurant, their respectful attitude toward each other was clear to all. Pandora, for example, reports, "If I was accompanying Dalí to dinner and Andy was dining at the same establishment, Dalí would make a point of going over to his table and greeting him, often with humor, and Andy would rise to greet the 'Divine One.' It was easy to see that Andy appreciated this acknowledgment, even though he was a celebrity himself."[157] The Spanish architect, painter, and designer Oscar Tusquets Blanca, who was on friendly terms with Dalí for a number of years, also describes an occasion from the 1970s in his memoirs, documenting that Dalí always conducted himself very appropriately towards Warhol in public. He reports on a dinner where "a pretentious and impertinent Frenchman dared to claim that Warhol wasn't more than a clown, Dalí expelled him from the table. At first, the silly Gallic man thought it was another joke from the Master, but when he saw his rage (rare but terrifying when it occurs), he had no choice but to leave the table, in the middle of dinner, with his tail between his legs."[158]

Two further Dalí–Warhol encounters, which took place on March 13 and 19 of the year 1978, can be reconstructed on the basis of tape recordings by Warhol.[159] The second encounter is also recorded in his diaries:

Palm Sunday. ... Walked down to Laurent on 56th Street for lunch. Chris Makos was just in a leather jacket and his boyfriend [Peter Wise] didn't have a tie, and it looked like a good restaurant, but they were prepared for Dalí's crowd so they didn't care.

Ultra Violet was sitting next to Dalí ... I'd brought two copies of the Dalí book so Dalí could sign them and it turned out that one of them had already been signed "To Fred" so Dalí re-signed it to me. ... And Dalí was really sweet, he'd brought a plastic bag full of his used-up palettes as a (laughs) present to me.[160]

Christopher Makos adds in his memoirs that Warhol also handed Dalí a gift during the lunch:

At one point ... the two exchanged gifts. Andy pulled out one of his recent paintings ... and Dalí seemed pleased. Then Dalí reached round and pulled up to the table a large clear plastic bag full of rubbish. Andy said, "Oh, that's great.

155
Louis Markoya in an e-mail to the author on May 17, 2010. Markoya added in an e-mail to the author on August 15, 2012 that the *Marilyn* portrait was a canvas in muted colors, with an estimated size of between 20 × 20 and 30 × 30 inches. Another anecdote circulating on the internet, the truth of which cannot be verified, is that Dalí tied Warhol to a spinning board at his suite at the St. Regis and poured paint over him in front of the eyes of the other guests. Cf. Blume 2011, pp. 20f. Lesley M. Blume told the author in an e-mail on November 29, 2011, that her account is based on information from the in-house historian from the St. Regis, Richard Blodgett, who in turn cites the following internet sources: "When Warhol met Dalí"; http://daliplanet.blogsome.com/2008/06/28/the-st-regis-hotel/ (last accessed on November 29, 2011). Louis Markoya is named as an eye-witness. However, as Markoya informed the author in an e-mail on May 17, 2010, although he had never heard about the anecdote, he can imagine that it was the case.

156
Ibid.

157
Pandora in a letter to the author in August 2009. Similarly, Roxanne Lowit in a telephone conversation with the author on July 24, 2012.

158
Tusquets Blanca 2003, p. 162 (translated from the Spanish).

159
Tape recordings no. 1010, 1032 at the archive of the Andy Warhol Museum, Pittsburgh.

160
Hackett 1989, pp. 118f.

What is it?" Dalí said, "This is trash from my studio." Andy just nodded vaguely and smiled, because he thought that his own gift to Dalí was so much more valuable, while all he got was a bag of rubbish. It was original, but it didn't seem to be worth very much."[161]

The clear plastic bag full of rubbish has been kept in the archive at the Andy Warhol Museum in Pittsburgh. It measures around 19 × 13 inches and contains a used cardboard palette, which is curled under slightly with sheets of waxed paper in various sizes stuck together by paint residue. On the surface are crumpled and torn bits of waxed paper and scraps of paint are scattered throughout. The plastic bag also contains paint residue. One piece of waxed paper was signed by Dalí in purple felt tip ink.[162] He did so retrospectively, after handing Warhol the gift, because the bag also contains a black plastic pen with the imprint "Andy Warhol Enterprises Inc." Warhol was quite practical in such matters. When Joseph Beuys handed him a work of art in March 1981, consisting of "two bottles of effervescent water" that exploded in his suitcase, he recorded in his diaries: "... I can't open the box now, because I don't know if it's a work of art anymore or just broken bottles. So if he [Beuys] comes to New York I've got to get him to come sign the box because it's just a real muck."[163] In order to give Dalí's gift a certain value, Warhol asked him to sign it—Dalí did so by signing a piece of waxed paper from the plastic bag, for which Warhol himself gave him one of his pens. As already mentioned, there is a tape recording that Warhol made that day, as well as a transcript of it.[164] The transcript begins after Dalí, Gala, and Ultra Violet have already left the room and the lunch is finished. Warhol remains at the table with Christopher Makos, Peter Wise, and Catherine Guinness. As the four of them look for a pen, there is a remark that there one is in the plastic bag.[165] The bag from Dalí found its way into the archive at the Andy Warhol Museum because Warhol had deposited it in one of his many *Time Capsules*. When these were opened after his death, a red Latex glove was also found there with traces of oil paints and remnants of masking tape on the fingertips.[166] The quoted diary entry about the lunch with Dalí shows that Warhol accepted the gift of his older colleague with humor later on. But Peter Wise recalls, "Dalí thought this was hysterical and everything, and afterwards Andy expressed to us that he was very upset and hurt. And then he said he didn't think it was funny at all, and Dalí thought it was. It wasn't like he felt he was disrespected. His feelings were hurt. ... It's one of the few times I heard him say, 'Oh, my feelings are hurt.' And lots of people say Andy didn't have any feelings, of course he did."[167] In the photography book *Warhol/Makos in Context* by Christopher Makos, it is also revealed that Gala was not very amenable with the photographer at the lunch:

... I [sat] in a place of demi-honor next to Dalí's wife Gala. After about five minutes and three or four of my tries at conversation, she turned to me, looked me right in the eye and said very evenly, "nothing you could say would interest me." I was presented with Mrs. Dalí's back for the remaining 2 hours and 55 minutes or so. (I did notice that with all this good French food, she ordered a plain hamburger, well done, with mashed potatoes, chopped and mixed it all up together on her plate with a little ketchup and ate about two bites.)[168]

161
Makos 1988,
p. 74.

→
57 [p. 400]

162
Object no.
TC 190.71.1 –
TC 190.71.3.
Visual inspection on November 28, 2012 at the archive of the Andy Warhol Museum, Pittsburgh.

163
Hackett 1989,
p. 361, March 8,
1981.

164
As Matt Wrbican kindly told the author in an e-mail on August 15, 2012, some tape recordings had been transcribed about twenty years earlier on behalf of The Andy Warhol Foundation for the Visual Arts, Inc. by Brigid Berlin, who listened to around 300 tape recordings.

165
Insight into the transcript on November 26, 2012 at the archive of the Andy Warhol Museum, Pittsburgh.

166
The glove was most likely in the plastic bag and fell out, as it was found next to it. Cf. Object no. TC 190.72. Viewed on November 28, 2012 at the archive of the Andy Warhol Museum, Pittsburgh.

167
Peter Wise in a conversation with the author on June 28, 2012 in New York.

168
Makos 2006,
March 1978.

Christopher Makos and Enrique Sabater captured the encounter between Dalí and Warhol at the Laurent in a series of photos.[169] In one of the shots taken with Sabater's camera, he is seen helping Dalí hand the plastic bag to Warhol.[170] Warhol also took a photo with his compact camera during the lunch, showing Dalí and Ultra Violet, who was sitting between him and Dalí.[171] However, the most well-known photo of this encounter was taken by Christopher Makos. It bears the title *Dalí Kissing Andy* and shows the two artists leaning towards each other, blocking Ultra Violet out, poised for a kiss on the lips. It was Makos's idea to photograph Dalí and Warhol in this pose: "I was doing an article of people kissing each other for *Interview* magazine. ... And in February ... we have Valentine's Day. ... The theme was because of Valentine's Day; it's about love and romance and people kissing. I have more pictures of people kissing each other."[172] In the photograph *Dalí Kissing Andy*, Warhol is smiling and appears to be enjoying the situation. Dalí's face, on the other hand, displays no evident emotion, also because he wears sunglasses, which he didn't remove during the meal. Christopher Makos thinks that Dalí did not attribute much significance to the "kiss" and Peter Wise adds that it all happened very quickly.[173]

Owing to the tape recording of the lunch on Palm Sunday in 1978 it is possible to reconstruct another encounter between the two artists that occurred a week later. The transcription of the recording starts with Warhol calling to the departing Dalí, "Thanks a lot, see you next week." Not long afterwards it is reported that Dalí would like to see sometime how "fist fucking" was practiced. Warhol informs those present that Victor Hugo had declared himself willing to demonstrate this sexual practice for Dalí. Hugo was Halston's life partner and one of Warhol's friends. Christopher Makos asks straight away whether it would be possible to witness the spectacle, to which Warhol and Catherine Guinness reply in unison "Yeah."[174] That Dalí was indeed able to enjoy the live experience of "fist fucking" through Warhol can be gleaned from an interview that the surrealist gave a year later for the Spanish weekly magazine *Cambio 16*, in which he elaborated: "In the United States, they censored a television show because I said the words masturbation and ejaculation. But then, they have sexual practices such as *fist fucking*, which is to shove a clenched fist into someone else's anus. Andy Warhol took me to a place in New York where they even shoved the head in. To me that's an aberration."[175]

Dalí and Warhol also met each other at an array of social events during the 1970s. Chris Royer, who at the time was one of Halston's elite known as the Halstonettes, recalls that she also saw the two artists at fashion shows:

If Dalí was coming to an event or to a fashion show, he usually sat back with people that were from his staff and Gala. But with Andy it was different, he would come in and immediately start taking pictures of people and also use his tape recorder. If it was a fashion show where you had to sit, Andy waited until the last minute to sit down. When Andy met Salvador Dalí, let's say at a fashion show, he greeted him in a cordial manner. Just normal conversation "Hello, how are you?" bla bla bla and that would be pretty much it.[176]

Royer also reports about an observation she made when she witnessed Dalí and Warhol together at a party at Halston's house:

---

169 Cf. ibid. and also *El ojo invisible* 2004, p. 130.

→ **56** [p. 400]

170 Víctor Fernández kindly provided the author with this information in a Facebook message from Enrique Esteban Zepeda on September 9, 2015.

→ **Cover**

171 Andy Warhol Foundation for the Visual Arts, Inc. cat. no. FL06. 00458. The photo was published in *Andy Warhol's Exposures*. Cf. Warhol/Colacello 1979, pp. 124f.

172 Christopher Makos in a conversation with the author on June 28, 2012 in New York. Other celebrities Warhol kissed in front of Christopher Makos's camera include Liza Minnelli, John Lennon, and the architect Phillip Johnson. Ill. in Makos 2006, February 1978, March 6, 1979.

173 Christopher Makos and Peter Wise in a conversation with the author on June 28, 2012 in New York.

174 Transcript, viewed on November 26, 2012 at the archive of the Andy Warhol Museum, Pittsburgh.

175 In Rubio 1979, p. 93 (translated from the Spanish).

176 Chris Royer in a telephone conversation with the author on October 7, 2013.

5

There seemed to be a rivalry between Dalí and Halston and it was funny to watch, because they were so very territorial with their friends. There were definitely boundary lines and I recall when Dalí came to a party at Halston's chic eastside townhouse, he sat with his entourage and just watched the party going on. Andy on the other hand was always going around taking pictures and talking to everybody. I noticed he stayed far away from both Halston and Dalí.[177]

Another Dalí and Warhol encounter occurred on April 3, 1978, at Studio 54 when a big party was given on occasion of the Academy Awards ceremony at the Dorothy Chandler Pavilion in Los Angeles. The British actress Vanessa Redgrave was causing a furor, winning an award that evening for her role as a Jewish resistance fighter in the movie *Julia*. The politically active Redgrave had caused a stir previously through her role in the documentary *The Palestinians* and because of her support of Palestinians. She even received death threats later from radical followers of the Jewish Defense League, when in her speech she thanked all those who "have refused to be intimidated by the threats of a small bunch of Zionist hoodlums whose behavior is an insult to the stature of Jews all over the world and to their great and heroic record of struggle against fascism and oppression."[178] The speech was met with both catcalls and applause and prompted a scandal. Warhol followed the event with interest, as he and Truman Capote were the hosts for the evening at Studio 54. In his diaries, however, he expressed a certain lack of interest in the issue:

I'm never going to let my name be put on a party again because all it does is get you in trouble with the people you forget to invite or who don't get in for some reason. The invitations got all screwed up. I mean, a hand-delivered invitation from me to myself arrived at the office in the afternoon.

…

I hated the Awards, I hated the whole thing. I hated every nominee and I hated everything that won. I must be really out of it. … And there was Vanessa Redgrave doing her same stupid Communist routine up on stage that she did for us at 860 once.[179]

Dalí was also among the guests invited to the party, as recalled by Horst Weber von Beeren,[180] who was also present: "It was the Academy Award night, a.k.a. Oscar night, which made history … Warhol sat mesmerized in front of the giant TV screen. I have never seen him more focused. You actually could observe him, which normally was instantly noticed by him. At this moment, Dalí walked in and I saw both of them together in the same room. Dalí walked instantly out again, because he was not the center of attention."[181] It was not uncommon for Dalí to make only a brief appearance at Studio 54. Baron Roger de Cabrol recalls,

Dalí and I went there many times. He didn't like it that much because it was so noisy and everything and he was already of a certain age. I mean, Studio 54 was wild. … people would bump into you. When he would come in, it was like Moses and the Red Sea. Everybody would see him, everybody knew him. He would stay fifteen to twenty minutes. He liked to go to bed early, he liked to paint, he liked his comfort, and he liked restaurants. That's what he enjoyed.[182]

332

177
Ibid. It is noteworthy that Dalí called Halston "The Shepherd." Cf. Lear 1985, p. 269.

178
Quoted according to http://aa-speechesdb.oscars.org/link/050-4 (last accessed on April 12, 2016).

179
Hackett 1989, pp. 120f., April 3, 1978.

180
At the time, Horst Weber von Beeren occasionally assisted Warhol's printer, Rupert Jasen Smith, and soon thereafter worked for him full time.

181
Horst Weber von Beeren in a telephone conversation with the author on June 22, 2011.

182
Baron Roger de Cabrol in a conversation with the author on December 5, 2012 in New York.

5

In 1978 Warhol met the diamond dealer and designer John Reinhold.[183] They soon forged a friendship and Reinhold became one of the artist's closest confidants.[184] Reinhold reports,

I had a cousin whose name was Henry Geldzahler. Henry was my first cousin. ... Henry had introduced me to almost every artist he knew while I was growing up, so I found it really odd that suddenly he would say, "Now it's time for you to meet Andy." I said "Yeah. That would be great." One day soon after Andy came up to my office and spent quite some time there. Later on that evening he called and said, "Would you like to have dinner tonight?" I was very excited and I said, "I'd love to." But then he rattled off many, many names of people who were coming to the dinner and I hadn't realized that so I said, "Andy, I thought you meant having dinner with you. I'm really not interested in having dinner with ten or twelve other people." So he canceled the crowd and we had dinner together that night alone. And that's basically how it began.[185]

As Warhol and Reinhold saw each other frequently in the years that followed, it was inevitable that one day they were invited together to one of Dalí's dinners. Reinhold remembers:

The particular dinner I was at was at the Plaza Hotel. Dalí and his wife were there with about twelve or fourteen people they had invited to join them. At a certain moment he and his wife got up, said good night to everybody and left all the people they had invited sitting there. He did take care of the dinner but he would get up early and leave. He did that the two or three times I had dinner with him. We were always many, many people. I am not totally sure, but I would suspect that Andy was at that dinner at the Plaza, because otherwise I don't know how I would have been invited. I remember the table was very large because we were so many people. My conversation with Dalí was always minimal because every time I saw him we were so many people that it was impossible to have a conversation.[186]

The reason for Dalí's sudden departure from the table was not exceptional—he always went to bed early. For his entourage, this meant they could go out and do something with Warhol. Amanda Lear explains,

In the evening I used to go out with Warhol and those people, because Dalí went to bed very early. I was with Dalí all day and then in the evening after dinner Dalí went to bed and I was going to Max's Kansas City. And at Max's Kansas City we used to meet everybody. There was a German singer called Nico. She was a great friend of mine. I love Nico. She was very sweet. And she used to say: "Amanda, you can stay with me if you want." She was always offering me to stay with her at her place because I was in a hotel. And there were all those Warhol people there. And that's how I got to meet them a little more and I was invited to the Factory and I did some photographs also for Andy Warhol's Interview.[187]

It can be discerned from Warhol's diaries that the artists also saw each other again in winter 1978/79. The entry for December 16, 1978, states: "At Studio 54 later, I asked Potassa if she'd ever had sex with Dalí, and she said, 'No, he just picked my cock up once and kissed it.' She said Dalí was coming back to town and that we had to resume our friendship. And Potassa only drinks champagne. '*Schom-pon-ye.*' She said when Dalí kissed her cock he said, '*Magnifico!*'"[188] Dalí did not miss any opportunity to show himself with Potassa de la Fayette in New York, but Warhol also had steady contact with

---

183 He is mentioned in Warhol's diaries for the first time on April 19, 1978. Cf. Hackett 1989, pp. 127f.

184 Colacello 1990, pp. 487f.

185 John Reinhold in a telephone conversation with the author on May 26, 2010.

186 Ibid.

187 Amanda Lear in a telephone conversation with the author on March 13, 2010.

188 Hackett 1989, p. 188.

189
See the chapter
**Compan-
ions, Court-
iers, and
Superstars**
in Part 3.

her.[189] Potassa provided ample fodder for conversation for the two artists. Warhol's close confidante and friend Brigid Berlin still has vague recollections in this context of two further encounters between Dalí and Warhol:

It's funny but I don't remember that much. I remember Dalí in cabs talking about Potassa, but I really wasn't listening. ... Dalí was in the front with the cab driver. And I was sitting with Andy in the back. ... I think we had dinner at Quo Vadis. ... Dalí bored me because I thought it was just too much. And then it was difficult to understand him. And in the cab with him ... He was like just his eyes were going at everybody on the street. Andy would be in the back saying, "Oh, how exciting!" ... I think one night we even went out to dinner with Dalí and [Alexander] Iolas.[190]

190
Brigid Berlin in a
conversation
with the author
on December 4,
2012 in New York.

Catherine Hesketh, née Guinness, remembers another Dalí and Warhol encounter that took place around 1978. Hesketh, who had started three years previously as editor of *Interview*, reports that for Warhol it was always something special to visit Dalí at the St. Regis: "Andy always looked forward to going to the St. Regis to see Dalí. ... We met at the St. Regis and I know that Andy wanted Dalí to hold up an *Interview* magazine, so Andy could take a photograph of him with it, which he did. ... I'm sure Andy would have wanted to use it for *Interview* magazine, but I don't know whether he did or not."[191] Dalí may have even gone to the Factory later to talk about the publication of the shot and perhaps other things. Walter Steding, who became Warhol's assistant at that time, remembers seeing the surrealist there once. "*Interview*'s office was right next to the Warhol Factory and there were two different groups of people, a mix of people, two different types of Andy—the magazine advertising Andy on one side, the artist, the free and all that on the other side."[192] Unfortunately, the photo of Dalí with an *Interview* magazine in his hand has not showed up as yet.

191
Catherine
Hesketh in a tele-
phone conver-
sation with the
author on August
27, 2012.

192
Walter Steding in
a telephone
conversation with
the author on
January 12, 2013.

The entry in Warhol's diaries on March 4, 1979, indicates that Dalí invited him to dinner again that day. "We were going over to Laurent, where Dalí had invited us for dinner, he had about forty people there. He's really generous with these kids."[193] After spending the summer in his Spanish homeland, Dalí made his final trip to New York in December 1979.[194] One month later he and Gala contracted viral flu. Dalí had never had a long illness, but he was afraid that he would not recover this time and fell into a depression. Gala gave her husband valium and other sedatives to calm him down, which also made him lethargic. To combat the fatigue, she also gave him "unknown quantities of one or more types of amphetamine." The uncontrolled dose, without medical supervision, caused Dalí nervous damage, according to Albert Field, making his hands shake uncontrollably.[195] Owing to his poor state of health, Dalí could no longer take part in the social life of New York in the same way as before. It is unlikely that he met Warhol (often) that winter. The actress Mia Farrow, who was friends with Dalí, reports in her memoirs that she saw him for the last time in 1980, at the St. Regis: "... he lowered himself to his knees and kissed my hand, and then had trouble rising to his feet."[196] On March 20, 1980, Dalí and Gala flew back to Spain, accompanied by Enrique Sabater. Owing to his condition, the painter lay in a separate compartment.[197] He never returned to New York and never saw Warhol again.

193
Hackett 1989,
p. 209.

194
Gibson 1997,
p. 572.

195
Field 1996,
p. 227.

196
Farrow 1997,
p. 248.

197
Gibson 1997,
p. 574.

ENCOUNTERS

6
VIEWS
OF
EACH
OTHER'S
WORK
AND
PERSONALITY

—

CONCLUSION

—

IMAGES

Part 5 presented encounters between Salvador Dalí and Andy Warhol over a period of more than fifteen years. During this time, the artists became even better acquainted. The chapters that follow pursue the question of the views each developed of the work and personality of the other, also focusing on the issue of the extent to which jealousy determined their relationship and whether there was a true friendship between the artists.

Exchange of Gifts

From April 8 to May 31, 1970, an exhibition with works of Andy Warhol was shown at the newly opened gallery belonging to Folker Skulima in Berlin. It was the young art dealer's first exhibition in his spaces on Fasanenstraße. Shown were a large-format *Car Crash* painting, a *Silver Liz*, the complete *Marilyn* print portfolio, the prints *Cooking Pot, The Kiss (Bela Lugosi)*, and *Suicide*, six *8-Inch Flowers*, a golden and a blue *Jackie* portrait, and the work *Campbell's Elvis*.[1] What the exhibition visitors did not know was that Salvador Dalí had once owned some of these works. Fortunate circumstances had allowed Folker Skulima to purchase the six *Flowers* paintings, the two *Jackie* portraits showing the president's wife in grief, and the *Campbell's Elvis*— a total of nine works—from Dalí in Cadaqués one month before the exhibition opened.

Skulima knew the Spanish artist Manuel Díez Rollán from Berlin, who regularly assisted Dalí in Port Lligat at the time.[2] Rollán knew that Skulima was interested in Pop Art and had also found out by coincidence that Dalí owned some of Warhol's works. He suggested to the gallery owner that they visit the surrealist together and broach the subject of the works as part of the conversation.[3] Folker Skulima recalls: "And that is how I did it. Of course I also had money with me—plenty of money. Because it was common knowledge that Dalí always liked to see and also count out banknotes."[4] It went according to plan and the transaction was indeed agreed upon straight away. Dalí greeted the guests, they chatted and drank pink champagne. Gala was present, but appeared uninterested and did not say a word. A bit later, the governor of Girona joined them with a land surveyor, because Dalí had requested that the southern border of his plot of land be measured. "Dalí asked if I wanted to go with them," explains Skulima,

... and one could hardly say no. ... So I clambered up the whole mountain with them. ... Dalí was very nice, but also very self-confident. The five meters that it was all about were a must. ... When we were back down at the bottom, more pink champagne was drunk and I gradually worked my way round to my crucial question. I had heard, and Manolo had said, and it was not so important for him to really have them. But I would so like to do a Warhol exhibition at my gallery. ... Dalí said straight away: "If you want. We'll manage to sort it out. What were you thinking of financially?" Then I proposed the sum and he said: "Yes, that seems fine to me. Captain Moore administers a lot of my affairs and takes care of such money transactions. It would be best to see to it tomorrow with him." He also remarked that I must not misunderstand him and think that he did not find the works good and explained: "I have Warhol's work and that of other artists in my head. Therefore I do not need the works anymore." And I had them the next day

1
Folker Skulima in a telephone conversation with the author on June 29, 2011.

2
Rollán was working at the time, e.g., on the giant sculpture *Debris Christ*, which is in the olive grove in Dalí's garden. His son, Manuel Donato Díez, told the author this in a conversation on March 20, 2013, in Nordstemmen and confirmed it with photos. See also Descharnes/Descharnes 2003, pp. 104f.

3
Folker Skulima in a telephone conversation with the author on September 17, 2009, and in a conversation with the author on February 26, 2011 in Berlin.

4
Folker Skulima in a telephone conversation with the author on September 17, 2009 (translated from the German).

after just an hour. We may have telephoned beforehand, but then I had the works straight away. The very same day I got into the car and drove back to Berlin.[5]

Folker Skulima recalls that Dalí concluded the transaction rather soberly. He did not get to see the works by Warhol. Skulima thinks that the Spaniard would probably have hated showing them all to him. He remarks discreetly about the sales price: "A person as clever as Dalí would never have given the works as a gift. The question is, of course, what he thought of them and how successful and expensive Warhol was. I can only say: Warhol was not so expensive at the time, but somehow I found it great to purchase these authentic Warhols of this provenance. ... In any case it was a good price."[6]

Warhol was unable to attend the exhibition opening in Berlin. A few years later, however, Skulima had the opportunity to discuss the show with him at a reception in New York:

[H]e had this great memory and knew exactly when this show had been and asked, "What did you display?" That's what every artist wants to know. ... And I told him in detail. And of course, I also said, "The Flowers *and the two* Jackies *and the* Campbell's Elvis *were from Salvador." ... It is, of course, not really befitting to sell gifts, but such things are to be expected of Dalí. Warhol was very, very monosyllabic and really only said one single word: "Typical." ... During this conversation I also said to Warhol, "I know of course how often you go out with Dalí when he is in New York." He replied, "You know that? Everybody probably knows that. Whenever Dalí comes to New York we do something together."*[7]

The nine Warhol paintings that Skulima purchased from Dalí in March 1970 had been gifts from Warhol to Dalí. Although this was not openly declared, it was known to those involved. Skulima recalls that the works that he bought from Dalí were signed on the back.[8] The *Campbell's Elvis* from 1962 is signed "Andy Warhol 1964" on the back.[9] It can be assumed that this work was the earliest present given by Warhol to Dalí, as according to John Giorno, the two artists were introduced to each other officially in early January 1964.[10] The work measures 16⅛ × 20 inches and shows the head of Elvis Presley six times, four of which are incomplete. The heads are overlaid with a vertically printed section of a Campbell's soup can label.[11] The six *8-Inch Flowers* and the two *Jackie* portraits were all created in 1964.[12] Since Warhol produced numerous variations of the motifs, it is not possible today to establish exactly which paintings Dalí had owned. However, based on the exhibition poster that Skulima had printed at the time for the exhibition, it is possible to identify at least one *Flowers* painting, on account of the coloring and the small drops of paint next to the blossom on the top right. The painting in question is a canvas measuring 8 × 8 inches, showing four red flowers against a black and white background.[13]

Whether Dalí reciprocated and thanked Warhol with return gifts as early as the 1960s, as was the case during the following decade, is unknown. The Andy Warhol Museum's archive contains not only a plastic bag with rubbish from Dalí's studio, which Warhol received as a gift on Palm Sunday in 1978,[14] but also a plate from the French restaurant La Goulue in New York, which Dalí had signed with black felt tip pen over the entire glossy surface.[15] This plate could also have been a (spontaneous) gift from

---

5
Ibid.

6
Ibid.

7
Ibid.

8
Ibid.

9
Cf. Frei/Printz 2002, no. 289.

10
See the chapter **The First Encounter** in Part 5.

11
It is difficult to determine which motif was printed first, leading to various reproductions of the work in the literature in both portrait and landscape formats. In Crone 1970, p. 137, Felix 1993, p. 35, and Lumpkin 1998, p. 234, the work is reproduced in portrait format and in Frei/Printz 2002, no. 289, in landscape format.

12
Cf. Frei/Printz/King-Nero 2004, A, no. 1116-1140, 1192-1233 (*Jackie*); Frei/Printz/King-Nero 2004, B, no. 1573–1719 (*8-Inch Flowers*).

13
Frei/Printz/King-Nero 2004, B, no. 1647. There is no mention of the painting being signed. Visual inspection of the exhibition poster on February 26, 2011 in Berlin.

14
See the chapter **The 1970s** in Part 5.

15
Visual inspection on November 28, 2012 at the
+

+
archive of the
Andy Warhol
Museum, Pittsburgh.

16
See the chapter
The 1970s
in Part 5.

17
Further details
in the chapter
**Dalí's View
of Warhol
and his Work**
in this part.

18
See the chapter
**A Passion
for Collecting** in Part 2.

19
Sotheby's 1988,
vol. V, lot
2880–2884.

20
Ibid., lot
2885–2887.

21
Ibid., lot 2965.

22
See the chapter
**Art for the
Department
Store
and Disco
Décor** in Part 4.

23
Sotheby's
1988, vol. II,
lot 910, 1012.

24
See the chapter
**The First
Encounter**
in Part 5.

25
Sotheby's 1988,
vol. II, lot 910.

26
Sotheby's 1988,
vol. III, lot 2117.

27
Matt Wrbican
kindly provided
the author with
this information
in an e-mail on
August 15, 2012.

28
In Livingston
1952, p. 22.

the Spaniard to his younger colleague, as the two artists met often at La Goulue.[16]

Dalí's gifts to Warhol and the described transaction with the Berlin gallery owner Folker Skulima say something about the value that the surrealist attributed to the works of the Pop Art artist.[17] If Dalí had really appreciated Warhol's works he would no doubt have made more of an effort when selecting his return gifts and would not have sold the younger artist's works.

Warhol was evidently graced far more rarely with works of art from Dalí than vice versa. However, some of Dalí's works were found in his art collection, including drawings, prints, and jewelry items. This was revealed when Warhol's estate was auctioned at Sotheby's in New York from April 23 through May 3, 1988.[18]

Five ink drawings were auctioned that served as illustrations for the book *Wine, Women and Words* by Billy Rose, published by Simon and Schuster in New York in 1946. According to the auction catalogue, the provenience of the corresponding lots was Billy Rose, New York, which means that they were not gifts from Dalí.[19] References are missing for the drawings *Rocking Chair, Tailpiece for Major Mahatma,* and *Chanel: Grand Central Powder Room.*[20] However, it is improbable that they were gifts from Dalí. Drawings by the Spaniard were very much in demand already then.

Twelve signed etchings were called up at Sotheby's, which were offered as a mixed lot. As the prints were neither depicted nor detailed in the auction catalogue, it is not known what sheets these were. One can only glean from the text that the etchings were made around 1970, some in color and two printed on vellum.[21] The works were presumably individual prints and it is possible that they were gifts from Dalí. It is well known that his print production had reached its climax at the time.[22] Dalí ensured a continuous supply in those years, so a single gift was of no consequence.

Sotheby's also auctioned an exhibition poster signed by Dalí in 1960 and an autograph sheet with several signatures in India ink and red gouache.[23] As these lot numbers were not as valuable in comparison to the other works, they could have been gifts from Dalí. With regard to the exhibition poster, however, it must be noted that Dalí signed it as early as 1960, at a time when—according to John Giorno—Warhol had not yet been officially introduced to him.[24] It is also noticeable that the poster does not bear any personal dedication to Warhol. It belongs to a batch of posters that have personal dedications from artists such as Roy Lichtenstein, Claes Oldenburg, Andrew Wyeth, or Christo.[25]

Finally, there are the three jewelry items created by Dalí, which were part of Warhol's collection and were also auctioned at Sotheby's. A silver medallion from the year 1966 was called up, showing a trumpeter riding on a unicorn on one side, and two surrealist figures on the other. The framing and hanger loop are made of fourteen-carat gold.[26] The second item is the medallion *Tristan and Isolde* from the year 1953, on which Dalí commented in the catalogue *DALÍ: A Study of his Art-in-Jewels,* of which Warhol owned a copy:[27] "Filtre d'amour."[28] It shows the faces of Tristan and Isolde in eighteen-carat gold. They are positioned towards each other so that the shape of a wine chalice appears between them. Constructed of platinum, the piece is set with thirty-nine diamonds and a cabochon garnet representing red wine in the chalice.[29] The third piece of jewelry designed by Dalí is a pair of ear clips from 1949 bearing the title *The Honeycomb Heart*. Speaking about his melting heart formed of honeycombs, Dalí commented: "There's a little bit of sweetness in the heart of every woman."[30] The earrings are made of eighteen-carat gold and are set with diamonds and rubies.[31] It can be inferred from the auction catalogue that the latter two items of jewelry were not gifts from Dalí. Warhol had bought them at Alemany and Ertman in New York. It can also be ruled out that the third piece of jewelry was a gift, as Dalí would never have handed such a valuable piece of jewelry to his younger colleague.

Seventeen years after the big Warhol estate auction at Sotheby's, a variety of Pop memorabilia was auctioned at Christie's in London in the fall of 2005. The lots included an advertising poster from 1978 for Warhol's portraits of Muhammad Ali, with a dedication and signature: "to Dalí Andy Warhol."[32] The auction catalogue unfortunately does not provide any further information about the 30 × 24-inch poster. It can be assumed, however, that it was a gift given to Dalí by Warhol towards the end of the 1970s.

Dalí's View of Warhol and his Work

Despite his egocentrism, Salvador Dalí was always very interested in the work of younger colleagues. James Rosenquist, who met him for the first time in 1959,[1] reports: "Salvador Dalí was curious about young artists. He invited me to lunch at the St. Regis and to his birthday party. He put some George Segal sculptures in the back of a taxi and drove around New York, and apparently visited Andy Warhol. I think this attitude of Salvador Dalí was generous compared to other older artists."[2] Michael Ward Stout, Dalí's American lawyer, points out that Dalí did not find all young artists equally interesting:

There were many artists who came to see Dalí in those days but Dalí was not particularly interested in most of them. I think he found other artists boring, but he found Warhol very interesting. They both were artists who liked to be around many people and liked to be around celebrities. My law firm represents artists—many artists, perhaps sixty or more. Many artists are very reclusive, or they are not interested in a very visible, high social life, which existed so much in the 1960s and 1970s. Dalí and Warhol liked to go to the most elegant restaurants and nightclubs, and be with the richest people, titled people, the most pretentious people. I think that most artists were not like that, but more bohemian. Warhol was very sophisticated. He was at ease in Paris, London, New York, and Los Angeles. Many American artists in those days were not very international. Although Warhol did not speak French, everyone else spoke French in international society in those days.[3]

It is therefore hardly surprising that Dalí followed Warhol's artistic career with interest. His comprehensive library included, for example, the important catalogue for Warhol's exhibition held in 1968 at the Moderna Museet in Stockholm.[4] Amanda Lear reports that Ultra Violet acted as Dalí's "mole" and kept him informed about what was going on with Warhol.[5]

29
Sotheby's 1988, vol. III, lot 2118. See also *Dalí: Jewels – Joyas* (n.p.), where a similar medallion is presented.

30
In Livingston 1952, p. 18.

31
Sotheby's 1988, vol. III, lot 2119. See also *Dalí: Jewels – Joyas* (n.p.), where a similar brooch is presented.

32
Christie's 2005, lot 134.

1
Cf. Rosenquist/ Dalton 2009, pp. 91ff.

2
James Rosenquist in an e-mail to the author on March 30, 2010.

3
Michael Ward Stout in a telephone conversation with the author on June 9, 2010.

4
Lucia Moni from the Centre for Dalinian Studies at the Fundació Gala-Salvador Dalí, Figueres, +

5
Lear 2009, p. 67.

+
kindly provided
the author with
this information
in an e-mail
on July 7, 2014.
Dalí's library
comprised
4,333 books.
Cf. Altaió 2004,
pp. 340, 342.

6
See the chapter
**Shoe
Fetishism**
in Part 4.

7
Leslie Curtis in
a telephone
conversation
with the author
on April 27, 2013.

8
Baron Roger
de Cabrol in a
conversation
with the author
on December 5,
2012 in New York.

9
Dalí 1948, p. 22.

10
Pandora in a
conversation with
the author on
November 20,
2011 in Mariposa,
California.

11
Dalí 1964, p. 46.

13
Warhol/Hackett
1980, p. 13. In
his *Philosophy*
Warhol stated:
"I can't under-
stand why I was
never an abstract
expressionist,
because with my
shaking hand
I would have
been a natural."
Warhol 1975,
Philosophy,
p. 150.

12
Dalí 1975,
"I Laugh Tremen-
dously," p. 56;
Dalí in Bockris/
Wylie 1976,
p. 17. See also
the chapters
**Culinary
Delights**
in Part 4 and
The 1970s
in Part 5.

14
Leonard Kessler
in a letter to the
author in August
2011. See also
Bockris 1989,
p. 135.

Warhol's work was occasionally a topic of conversation for Dalí, for example, at a dinner with the actor Tony Curtis, who loved the visual arts.[6] Curtis also painted, created assemblages and pursued contact with artists such as Dalí, Warhol, Balthus, and Joseph Cornell. Leslie Curtis, with whom he was married from 1968 to 1982, recalls:

I don't know if Dalí took Andy Warhol seriously as an artist. ... I never heard him express that, but sometimes he would talk, when we had our dinners and everything under the sun was talked about, but I had the feeling that he reserved judgment. I think too he was conscious of how his art had impressed people of being sometimes sensational and provocative. Though he had this part of him that thought that Andy was doing something similar and he was not going to judge him the way he had been judged.[7]

Baron Roger de Cabrol, who could often be found in Dalí's company in the 1970s, cannot remember the Spaniard ever making a negative comment about Warhol.[8]

Dalí only appreciated artists who were masters of their trade. In his book *50 Secrets of Magic Craftsmanship* published in 1948, he passed on a rule of life to young painters: they had to first of all learn drawing and painting in the style of the Old Masters, after that they could do what they wanted and everyone would respect them.[9] Another decisive criterion for Dalí was that a work of art had to appeal to him emotionally. "Just like everyone else," reports Pandora, "if he did not have a direct experience from the paintings, if he could not feel the paintings, if he could not feel the emotion in some sort of consciousness within the paintings, they were not important to him. He had to have an impact from the paintings that resonated within him from some point, either from the heart, or the mind, or the soul."[10]

This therefore raises the question of whether Warhol's artistic language corresponded to Dalí's views. The surrealist liked to call Pop Art "part of the healthy trend away from abstract expressionism."[11] He repeatedly singled out Warhol as a special example of this.[12] Warhol could also not identify with the "world of the abstract expressionist" and referred to it as "very macho."[13] His former fellow student Leonard Kessler recalls a coincidental meeting during which Warhol expressed his views very clearly:

The episode took place at Arthur Browns Art Supply in midtown New York ...

It was in the 1960s.

There was my old buddy Andy purchasing art supplies ... "Andy, so what's new? Are you still doing the I. Miller Shoe ads for the New York Times?"

"No, I am doing POP ART."

"What's Pop Art?"

"Campbell's Soup Cans. I want to kill abstract expressionism. I hate it ... It's mushy ... gooey ... It doesn't say anything ... You could be a pop artist using some of the characters in your Kid's books."

I don't think so, I thought. Soup cans ... It will never sell.[14]

Despite the (in his opinion) positive influence of Pop Art on art, Dalí was critical of its artists and therefore also of Warhol. He explained to Charlton Lake,

... these Pop Artists are very little ones. But the important thing is that they aren't attempting to stylize something out of existence or make an interpretation of something or show how much the artist is suffering. What interests them is to show things as they are. ...

... These Pop people are very mediocre, even bad: there isn't an artist among them. But they paint things as they are and in that sense they are in the classical tradition.[15]

Dalí's criticism of the Pop artists also stemmed from the fact that he could not tolerate the idea of any other artist of the same stature beside himself. Baron Roger de Cabrol remarks, "Dalí considered himself above all the others. For example, he always told me, Cézanne couldn't draw circles, and Matisse couldn't draw hands."[16] Dalí also took a clear stance in numerous public appearances, for example, on *The Merv Griffin Show* on December 30, 1965, where his answer to the question of who the greatest painter in the world was: "Today Dalí. But, you know, modesty is not my specialty. Believe *que* today *le* best painter is Dalí but *si* Dalí compare my painting, *le* painting of Dalí, or *le* big masterpiece of Renaissance period the same *que* Velázquez and Raphael or Vermeer, in this moment Dalí is absolutely nothing. Dalí is only good because *les autres* painters is so bad."[17] Another remark that Dalí let slip five years later to a reporter is interesting in this context: "My time is valuable, $10,000 a minute. President Nixon has time to give interviews, Andy Warhol has time to give interviews, the Beatles have time for interviews. I don't have time for interviews. Don't you see, there are people waiting who want to give me money!"[18] This attitude was significantly influenced by Gala. Timothy Phillips, Dalí's assistant in the 1950s and 1960s, once remarked: "... she didn't like Dalí giving too much credit to anyone. Her idea was that Dalí should be some kind of a demigod, a Renaissance man who simply absorbed everything osmotically and gave it back in his own way. ... The idea that anyone could influence Dalí was alien to her."[19] Horst Weber von Beeren, who assisted Dalí in 1979,[20] reports that Gala demonstrated this view to him personally in a drastic manner:

Gala thought Dalí as the greatest of artists, on par with Michelangelo and da Vinci. ... One day, I was asked how much money I wanted for my help and I simply asked for a recommendation for my immigration process. Gala was furious. I showed her some transparencies of my work and she tried to rip them apart with the remark, "Dalí is the Greatest, there is no one else besides him!" The transparencies were stable and her physical weakness so advanced, that she did not manage to rip them ... .[21]

This probably also explains why Jeff Fenholt, Gala's last big love, states that Dalí liked neither Warhol nor his art. Fenholt adds that Dalí called his younger colleague "Soup Cans."[22] Dalí's assistant, Louis Markoya, reports that he once heard the surrealist calling the Pop Art artist "Warhola"— but he cannot say for sure whether Dalí knew that this was Warhol's birth name or whether it was just a coincidence.[23]

Despite this, a certain high regard remained. The French flacon designer Pierre Dinand recalls that Dalí may have discounted Warhol's art as mere decoration, but also admired it in a certain way. "Dalí spoke about Warhol

15
In Lake 1969, pp. 286f.

16
Baron Roger de Cabrol in a conversation with the author on December 5, 2012 in New York.

17
The Merv Griffin Show, December, 30, 1965.

18
In Steiner 1970, *Salvador Dalí,* as well as Steiner 1970, *Magical Meeting.*

19
Girst 1999.

20
See the chapter **Assistants, Employees, Secretaries, and Managers** in Part 3.

21
Horst Weber von Beeren in a telephone conversation with the author on June 22, 2011.

22
Jeff Fenholt in an e-mail to the author on May 31, 2010.

23
Louis Markoya in an e-mail to the author on May 17, 2010.

one day and said: 'He is interesting, but he is not really painting. He is designing on the walls of New York. He is using serigraphy with colors. That's not a real way to paint.' But in a way he was admiring Warhol's work. He did not quite understand what he was up to."[24] Ultra Violet was of the opinion that Dalí had not been able to find a connection with Warhol's works, but by all means recognized their revolutionary aesthetics:

Dalí thought Warhol's work was nothing. It was nothing, except the Campbell's Soup Can ... *The soup can represents an industrial still life—before that still lifes were of carrots, onions, fruit. Now you had all that in the can of soup. Dalí did not take him seriously because Dalí was a surrealist spirit. ... Dalí thought of Warhol's work—the* Campbell's Soup Can—*as a coup de poing of art because no one thought of doing that before. ... But Dalí still thought it was a joke. He didn't think it had the power it has today.*[25]

Amanda Lear reports that Dalí also liked the aspect of serial art production in Warhol's work:

He obviously liked the basic idea that the more often a piece of art is reproduced, the more it becomes valuable. That's what happened with the Mona Lisa. Mona Lisa *is not really a very good painting according to Dalí. It's just a mystery why it became the most famous painting in the world. Well, it's simply because when it came to the Louvre they printed the post card, you know, they printed the reproduction. And the printer made a mistake. Instead of printing 500 or 1,000 he printed 10,000 of the postcard. And suddenly everybody received the postcard of the* Mona Lisa. *And so it is luck that it became the most famous painting in the world ... You see this painting appear in papers, in magazines, on postcards so many times that at the end you like it. So starting from this, Dalí explained it to Andy Warhol and said: "You don't do just one painting, but you reproduce it many times. So you do your* Marilyn *15 million times and suddenly it's not a film actress anymore. It's something else. It becomes a complete different entity, an idol, an icon." He wasn't crazy about the result, the final result, with all the lipstick and the red and green splash all over the face. But he liked the basic idea of the Warhol philosophy, I must say.*[26]

There is also an interesting report from Edgar Froese, the pioneer of electronic music and founder of the band Tangerine Dream, who met Dalí in Cadaqués in the summer of 1967. Froese studied painting, sculpting, and graphic design at the Berlin Academy of Arts and had traveled to Spain with his band at the time, The Ones,

... to perform in a small club for two hours a day. As a student of sculpture, I had modeled a Dalí head and had it cast in a synthetic resin mixture. ... My gift as a guest was honored with a protracted photo shoot and an invitation to play a concert at his house. He wanted to hear some of the peculiar music, to establish how he might use it for an open-air vernissage in his olive garden. We stayed at Dalí's house the whole afternoon and were impressed by his hospitality and unbounded openness.[27]

Froese later recalled that he had also asked Dalí his opinion about Warhol at the time:

On this morning of a hot summer day in the year 1967 he replied to the question of whether he could accept Warhol in the new era of a changed visual

24
Pierre Dinand in a conversation with the author on March 1, 2013 in Paris.

25
Ultra Violet in a conversation with Jeanine Barone for the author on October 18, 2009 in New York. See also Ultra Violet in "Reminiscences of Dalí: A Conversation with Amanda Lear and Ultra Violet," moderated by Dawn Ades, in Taylor 2008, p. 215.

26
Amanda Lear in a telephone conversation with the author on March 13, 2010.

27
Edgar Froese in an e-mail to the author on November 30, 2011 (translated from the German).

consciousness: "Every true work of art is completely emancipated when it enters the world, it does not need applause because it is alive and exudes a consciousness. The works of Warhol bear the date of their time and will for a long time fill it with inspiration for others." What do a Campbell's can and the Perpignan station [which Dalí viewed as the 'center of the universe'][28] *have in common?" I asked. "They exist within the same universe of creative possibility and emanate from the sources of higher worlds of thought, to which a mediocre plagiarizer has no access—in art it is only ever about the original." ... As far as I can tell from the conversations, Dalí was very fascinated by the commercial psychology approach of Warhol's work.*[29]

However, Dalí not only admired the "commercial psychology approach" of Warhol's work, which went hand in hand with a "coup de poing," but also another aspect. Peter Beard says,

... Dalí loved everything that was boring. He loved Roy Lichtenstein for the incredible boredom of the human. And I think he loved Andy Warhol because he just saw the existential man and he saw a living sculpture and somebody who was doing very boring things like copying food, and Brillo boxes. He really loved that, as I said, the boredom and the satire and he loved Pop Art. ... He loved exclaiming how boring Roy Lichtenstein was. But he really loved it. He absolutely loved the idea of stretching boredom. It's kind of like a different subject.[30]

Ernst Fuchs confirmed that Dalí liked the idea of boredom and welcomed it when this became a subject of art, as for example in Warhol's movie *Sleep*:

He was interested in all contemporary movements and, for example, he once made a comment when he saw that movie where a sleeping man is watched the whole night and day. He said quite spontaneously after the movie had finished, "A pity it's already over. I would have liked to have watched it for much, much longer." It was too short for him. ... For sure that was not meant ironically, but in his notion of the eternal image that was, as it were, just a short recording. He always looked for the eternally valid in his paintings, the unalterable and everlastingly unique, so to speak.[31]

Dalí's view of Warhol was therefore ambivalent. Louis Markoya explains,

... Dalí was very critical of Warhol's art. There was no technique, no subject, and nothing to be attracted to. Dalí felt there was nothing in Warhol's art, and that Warhol's genius was in duping the critics into thinking what he was doing was genius. Dalí could not understand the public's or critic's embrace of Warhol. ... They shared a very strange relationship. ... Dalí admired Andy's popularity and fame ... and likely felt he was more deserving.[32]

Horst Weber von Beeren reaches the same conclusion: "Dalí had respect for Warhol, because they were both hopelessly corrupt and famous. Their idea of art was how to make the most money out of it, the easiest way. Frank Hunter [Albert Field's assistant], Gala and I had tea and sandwiches at the St. Regis, when Dalí walked in and picked up the word: 'Warhol'. The way he responded, 'Warhol is a good artist!' conveyed the respect."[33] This explains why Dalí liked to heap praise on Warhol's person as an artist, but not on his works. The moviemaker Jack Bond remembers that Dalí said to him in December 1965 that Warhol was a "profound figure of the future. He's gonna be very important, Jack."[34] These words were uttered when Bond met Dalí, Warhol, and

---

28
Dalí 1976, pp. 156ff.

29
Edgar Froese in an e-mail to the author on November 30, 2011 (translated from the German).

30
Peter Beard in a Skype conversation with the author on September 24, 2010.

31
Ernst Fuchs in a conversation with the author on May 13, 2010 in Klagenfurt (translated from the German).

32
Louis Markoya in e-mails to the author on May 17, 2010 and November 30, 2011.

33
Horst Weber von Beeren in a telephone conversation with the author on June 22, 2011.

34
Jack Bond in an e-mail to the author on June 19, 2012 and
+

+
in a conversation with the author on July 27, 2012 in London.

35
See the chapter **The 1960s** in Part 5.

36
Jack Bond in an e-mail to the author on February 9, 2016.

37
Lluís Llongueras in e-mails to the author on February 2, 2010, and September 19, 2012 (translated from the Spanish).

38
Antoni Pitxot in a conversation with the author on September 5, 2009 in Cadaqués (translated from the Spanish).

39
Dalí 1973, p. 4 (translated from the French).

40
Goll 1976, p. 246 (translated from the French).

1
James Warhola in an e-mail to the author on September 13, 2011.

2
See the chapter **The 1960s** in Part 5.

3
Paul C. Warhola in a telephone conversation with the author on June 28, 2013.

Larry Rivers in the foyer of the St. Regis in order to drive together to the opening of the René Magritte retrospective at the Museum of Modern Art.[35] Jack Bond adds: "Andy's reaction to the praise from Dalí was a beatific smile. Andy was always gracious when praised."[36] Lluís Llongueras recalls that about ten years later Dalí made a remark referring to Warhol as "very promising."

… At the end of the 1970s, (around 1977, approximately), at his request, I went with my team to comb his hair in a suite at Barcelona's Hotel Ritz. That was the day that we put curlers on his head to give volume to his hair, which he wanted, and also as a "game." (The picture was spread widely by the press and in books about Dalí).

On that day, too, an unknown American painter visited him expressly to show him his work (which didn't satisfy him, nor was it remarkable), and I remember that … he drew a parallel, saying … "All those young men want to be like Andy Warhol" (more or less) … During a visit to Port Lligat, when a critic (an unknown as well) asked him for his opinion regarding Andy and his Factory, I heard him say that "he was very promising." Dalí explained that Andy visited him at the St. Regis and that before that he had started as a "window dresser" with lots of art and promise. He believed in him as an original artist with personality.[37]

As his friend and confidant Antoni Pitxot recounted, Dalí's praise can be explained by the fact that he—just like Warhol—had been a "lover of the new idea." "They were the type of persons that didn't like to talk about things of the past. They loved to talk about what had a future projection."[38] Therefore, it followed that Dalí referred to Warhol in the magazine *Paris Match* on June 16, 1973, as the "official prophet of all the avant-gardes."[39] However, one must approach such comments by Dalí with caution. The author and lyricist Claire Goll writes in her memoirs, "Dalí always proceeded with affirmations even when he wanted to flay his competitors: 'I have a lot of respect for American painters because they have clean feet,' he said."[40]

Warhol's View of Dalí and his Work

The brothers James and Paul C. Warhola report that for their uncle, Andy Warhol, meeting Salvador Dalí was always something special. For example, James Warhola says,

My uncle brought up Salvador Dalí's name to me on several occasions, so I always got the impression that Andy had a great respect for him. Actually I think I may have initiated the conversations a few times, since I did some school reports on Dalí. To me there were only two art world greats—Picasso and Dalí, but Andy never had anything to say about Picasso, as far as I can remember. He definitely liked Dalí, he seemed to be excited to tell me that he had met him and visited him when he came to NYC.[1]

Paul C. Warhola, who went to the opening of a Dalí exhibition for his uncle in 1966,[2] adds, "… just even in some brief comments, I could see that he had a high regard for Salvador. … The indication to me was that it was almost like an accepted thing that he's a great artist."[3]

Warhol always spoke publically of Dalí with admiration. In *Andy Warhol's Exposures* he declares, "Dalí's one of my favorite artists because he's so big."[4] Ivan C. Karp felt that this quote documented Warhol's "reverence for FAME and the Famous no matter how it was achieved or by whom. Andy was in awe of *all* the artworld luminaries. And whether or not he enjoyed their work, I never heard him criticize it. Dalí was charming and appealing in the small social events we both attended."[5] As *Exposures* was written by Bob Colacello, it is also worth taking a look at his own memoirs *Holy Terror* with regard to this, where one can find similar accounts:

There was one artist who genuinely fascinated Andy, in the same way that movie stars and models did: Dalí. It wasn't that Andy liked Dalí, or his work, that much. He was taken with Dalí's scene, which was not unlike his own in the sixties, and with Dalí's wife, Gala, who had no equivalent in Andy's world, or any other. ...

... More than any other artist, Dalí lived the life of an international grand seigneur. *Though Andy was catching up fast.*[6]

Dalí and Warhol were two artists of different generations. At the time that Warhol began achieving fame, Dalí had already reached his pinnacle. In 1978, Patrick S. Smith interviewed the art director Jack Wilson and asked him whether Warhol had ever mentioned the surrealists during their time studying together at the Carnegie Institute of Technology. Wilson said he hadn't and remarked, "I don't remember him commenting upon the Surrealists. No. Now, he was very much aware of Dalí. I wouldn't understand Andy liking Dalí, because Dalí had too much academic structure. We were certainly exposed to Surrealism in terms of history—de Chirico and the Dadaists. There was a lot of discussion on it."[7] The photographer Christopher Makos, Warhol's friend in later years, reports that Warhol loved "Duchamp, Dalí, and Man Ray, and the whole ambience of Surrealism."[8] Another important aspect for him was that Dalí was European: "Andy was an American artist and I think he had this kind of unreasonable respect for European artists. American artists always thought that Europeans were bigger."[9]

When Warhol and Dalí met personally, Dalí had already been a celebrity firmly anchored in collective awareness for quite some time. Victor Bockris says,

The counterculture in the U.S. adopted a number of icons, including Freud, Dalí, and Chaplin, among others. Of these figures only Dalí actually materialized! And he had a magic presence, because he was so affiliated with the surrealists that to see him actually walking by in his cape with his cane almost defied the imagination. There was an aura around his head like a halo.

...

Andy Warhol was a great appreciator of art and other artists. He had a more European than American perspective. He also loved de Chirico and Man Ray. I know he thought Dalí was really great. He loved artists who made their art in their own way. And he loved great talkers and eccentric geniuses.[10]

John Giorno recounts with regard to the first encounter between Dalí and Warhol, which he remembers to have taken place on January 10, 1964:[11] "The day when we were sitting on that banquette with Dalí, Andy was in awe of Dalí and enormously impressed. ... The battle—the era of Surrealism—which was the reason Dalí had become such a great artist, was over. But Andy saw that star that he wanted to become and that he would become. But

---

4
Warhol/Colacello 1979, p. 129.

5
Ivan C. Karp in an e-mail to the author on February 25, 2010.

6
Colacello 1990, p. 172.

7
In Smith 1988, p. 21. Wilson remarked in addition that many movies were shown at the Carnegie Institute of Technology because of their artistic value, including *Un Chien andalou.* Ibid, p. 18.

8
Makos 2002 (n.p.).

9
Christopher Makos in a conversation with the author on June 28, 2012 in New York.

10
Victor Bockris in an e-mail to the author on July 16, 2010.

11
See the chapter **The First Encounter** in Part 5.

it was all non-verbal, because you don't know these things when you're at the beginning."[12] The photographer David McCabe made a similar observation when he photographed Warhol together with Dalí at his studio at the St. Regis the following year:[13] "Andy kept his thoughts pretty much to himself. I think he was very, very impressed by Dalí and, obviously, by Picasso. But I think in a way that Dalí's ability to promote himself in an almost outrageous way interested Andy. I don't think that Picasso ever really went to the extent of Dalí as far as self-promotion [is concerned]. And, possibly, Andy learnt a lot from 'Salvador Dollars' or whatever he called him."[14] Nick Rhodes, who was friends with Warhol, also sees this connection.

We talked about art a lot. ... We talked about Cocteau, Man Ray ... Dalí ... We spoke about how he was excited to meet him [Dalí] because he was a great admirer of his actual skills. ... I think Andy appreciated Dalí's outlandish character ... Andy said to me that he was fascinated by Dalí's ability to work the media and manipulate them. And I think, certainly, he borrowed some of that himself. ... I think that Dalí was very important to Andy because of his iconic status. Because what Andy wanted more than anything, really, was to become like the icons that he was portraying. I don't think he would have probably publically said that to anyone because he wasn't particularly egoistical. He could be very subtle with people and was never forcing himself into a position deliberately where he would try to stand in the limelight.[15]

Glenn O'Brien has a similar view: "I think in a way Andy learned more from Dalí than anyone, because Dalí was the first artist to master using the press. He wanted to be as famous as possible and went so far as to appear on the TV show *What's my line*."[16] Dalí especially understood using the power of photography. Ron Galella recalls that the Spaniard would always stop for him to strike an animated pose.[17] Warhol was clearly fascinated and inspired by that, went one step further and became friends with the infamous paparazzo, which was at that time "politically incorrect" in the art world.[18] Ron Galella remarks,

Andy wrote ... that I was his favorite photographer. I think that was because he admired my persistence, guts, and love of photographing celebrities such as Jackie, Liz Taylor, Elvis, etc. We both had the same "social disease"— we both wanted to meet and photograph celebrities, but he was too shy to be like me.

Other photographers largely ignored Andy. I shot him, not only because he was a famous artist, but because his physical look, with his silvery wigs and fair skin, had unique features. Many times Andy would simultaneously photograph me as I was photographing him. Then as friends we would exchange information as to who was at the other events of the evening. Unfortunately, he died too soon. I miss him.[19]

Gerard Malanga is also of the view that Warhol saw a kind of role model and paragon in Dalí:

Dalí was the first artist who had this ability to make contact with the commercial art world. The idea that he is so popular as a fine artist, I think, was part of Andy's attraction to Dalí. It's a very strong connection. ... Andy liked being around artists. He found artists fascinating to be around ... partly for

12
John Giorno in a conversation with the author on March 13, 2011 in Besançon.

→ **41/42** [pp. 390/391]

13
See the chapter **The 1960s** in Part 5.

14
David McCabe in a telephone conversation with the author on June 14, 2010.

15
Nick Rhodes in a conversation with the author on December 15, 2014 in London.

16
Glenn O'Brien in an e-mail to the author on December 21, 2011.

→ **9** [p. 368]

17
Ron Galella recalls about shooting Dalí: "My favorite take of Dalí is from the opening of his exhibit, March 7, 1974, at one of the Madison Avenue galleries. He was holding a paintbrush, painting two young nude girls. It's my favorite because he did not pose for me, he only painted. I got him in his natural element." Ron Galella in an e-mail from Anthony Miller to the author on March 11, 2016.

18
O'Brien in Galella 2008 (n.p.).

19
Ron Galella in an e-mail from Anthony Miller to the author on March 11, 2016.

inspiration, but just to feel that chemistry, because Andy wanted to be looked upon as an artist in a way. He wanted to be taken seriously. ... I think it was a kind of simpatico *relationship. I mean, Andy was not on Dalí's level as far as knowledge of, let's say, art history, Surrealism, or just talking ... Dalí could do that, but Andy couldn't do that. ... There is one component that people seem to avoid or not be aware of, which is that Andy and Dalí represented for each other a mutual admiration society. And I say that in the sincerest way because they truly liked each other.*[20]

Malanga assumes that Warhol's admiration for Dalí also had a positive influence on Dalí's view of Warhol: "Dalí was also fascinated with Andy, but I think this had much to do with the attention Andy showered on him. ... Andy, to Dalí's mind, may have represented a new breed of artist where the spotlight not only centered on the artwork per se, but on the artist's personality as well. Dalí was very psychoanalytical, in that regard. He may have seen a little bit of himself in this young, new artist."[21] Ultra Violet held a similar view. She also remarked that not only was Warhol fascinated by Dalí, but the same was true vice versa: "They treated each other with great curiosity, investigations, and mutual investigations."[22] Her colleague Viva describes the relationship between the two artists in a similar way as it was "based on their mutual celebrityhood and genius with publicity."[23] Bob Colacello is of the opinion that the special relationship between the two artists also had a positive influence in turn on Warhol: "Andy liked Dalí and I think Dalí liked Andy because in many ways they were similar. They had the same sense of humor. Dalí also said a lot of things for effect, in fact, almost everything he said was for effect. He was also quite warm. I think Dalí really liked Andy and Andy then would bond with him, because Andy felt very secure. And when people liked him then he liked them."[24]

Warhol's admiration for Dalí was also still evident in later years, when the younger artist was on the way to increasing fame. His superstar Holly Woodlawn once remarked about Dalí in an interview: "He was the star and Andy was like a fan. Andy worshipped stars. One 'was,' and the other looked up to."[25] Ultra Violet made the same observations: "Dalí looked down on Warhol and Warhol looked up to Dalí because he wanted that fame."[26] The notion that Dalí looked down on Warhol should not be overrated. "Warhol had a higher respect for Dalí than Dalí had for Warhol," according to Christopher Makos, "It's not that Dalí was a bigger known artist, it's just that Dalí had an enormous personality that was hard to beat. Also Dalí commanded much higher prices for his paintings, so they were really not equals. ... I think that Dalí was looking a little bit down on everybody ... not just on Andy, everybody. I mean, Dalí felt that he was above everybody."[27] Dalí himself did not mince his words,[28] while Warhol was quite different in this respect. Gigi Williams, makeup artist at the Factory, emphasizes: "Andy always treated everyone with respect and awe."[29] Her ex-husband Ronnie Cutrone, who was Warhol's assistant in the 1970s, added: "Andy was not a mean person. Like he would never say bad things about an artist's work. I mean, privately, very privately ... he would go 'ugh, eew' ... He would never purposely hurt somebody in public."[30] Compared to Dalí, Warhol was therefore significantly

20
Gerard Malanga in a conversation with the author on July 2, 2012 in Hudson, New York.

21
Gerard Malanga in an e-mail to the author on September 24, 2009.

22
Ultra Violet in a conversation with the author on October 18, 2008 in New York and in an e-mail to the author on April 17, 2009.

23
Viva in an e-mail to the author on April 18, 2012.

24
Bob Colacello in a conversation with the author on June 26, 2012 in New York.

25
Quoted according to Michaud 1992, vol. 2, no. 1, p. 8.

26
Ultra Violet in a conversation with Jeanine Barone for the author on October 18, 2009 in New York.

27
Christopher Makos in a conversation with the author on June 28, 2012 in New York and in an e-mail to the author on July 25, 2009.

28
See the chapter **Dalí's View of Warhol and his Work** in this part.

29
Gigi Williams in a telephone conversation with the author on May 5, 2014.

30
Ronnie Cutrone in a telephone conversation
+

+
with the author on July 8, 2012. It was an exception for Warhol to make a negative remark about a colleague. Marc Balet recalls, "The only artist I remember Andy talking bad about was Botero, that he hated Botero … . He didn't like fat people. … So, he would say bad things about Botero. I remember thinking: Oh, I get it totally." Marc Balet in a conversation with the author in December 3, 2012 in New York.

31
In Goldsmith 2004, p. 238.

32
Sir John Richardson in a conversation with the author on July 3, 2012 in New York.

33
Warhol/Colacello 1979, p. 128.

34
See the chapter **Companions, Courtiers, and Superstars** in Part 3.

35
In Michaud 1992, vol 2, no. 1, p. 8.

36
Glenn O'Brien in an e-mail to the author on December 21, 2011.

37
Victor Bockris in an e-mail to the author on July 16, 2010.

more diplomatic when asked about other artists. In an interview with Glenn O'Brien, which was published in 1977 in the magazine *High Times*, it says:

O'Brien: Who is the richest artist in the world?

Warhol: I'll bet there are a lot of artists that nobody hears about who just make more money than anybody. The people that do all the sculptures and paintings for big building construction. We never hear about them, but they make more money than anybody.

O'Brien: What about Dalí?

Warhol: I don't think getting your name around means that you make a lot of money.

O'Brien: Do you think you or Dalí is more famous?

Warhol: There's Calder, too. Miró is still alive.[31]

Warhol preferred not to get anyone's back up by making noncommittal statements. Sir John Richardson recalls, "Dalí's name would come up in a group of people, and Andy never said anything very revealing about people. Andy was very positive about Dalí. Dalí's reputation in the world is what Andy wanted for himself."[32]

Dalí's pompous behavior, his non-stop stream of talk, and his colorful entourage were a large part of the fascination that Warhol had for him. In *Andy Warhol's Exposures* he states: "It's like being with royalty or circus people. That's why I like being with Dalí—because it's not like being with an artist. He wouldn't be caught dead in a loft."[33] As already reported, it was not only Warhol who felt drawn towards Dalí, but also many members of his entourage.[34] Holly Woodlawn, who occasionally mixed with the surrealist's "circus people," once remarked: "Dalí was the party! He was the life of the party. Andy sucked the life out of the party."[35] Dalí undoubtedly relished the attention that the Factory people paid him. As Glenn O'Brien says, "I think Dalí liked Andy's surrealist taste in people. I think they both loved glamor and the spotlight."[36] Victor Bockris also sees this parallel: "I think that Dalí and Warhol were both great people users. They both knew how to create a circus around themselves, how to associate with other celebrities in a manner that drew attention to themselves."[37]

The former Halston model Chris Royer, who often witnessed the said "circus" at the time, recalls that Warhol liked Dalí's vibrant and eccentric behavior. She also thinks that, in return, Dalí appreciated Warhol's quiet personality:

They were very, very respectful of each other, but also very careful. Andy never really went into elaborate discussions with Dalí about his art. He was pretty much "Boy, that was really great!," "Wow, I really liked that!," "Oh, look at those pea pods and mushrooms!" (laughs) And then he would talk about Holly Woodlawn in the next sentence, like "Look at Holly's dress! Do you like that? I don't know, maybe she's wearing a Halston?" Andy closely watched Dalí, and Dalí in turn watched him. They were watching one another to see how each would interpret the movements of everything that was happening …

Andy would say to me, "I really like Salvador Dalí, the way he's so animated," because Andy was much more reserved and shy. He said "I couldn't do that." He was mesmerized by the passion of Salvador Dalí, with his signature mustache and dramatic gestures using his cane. Andy loved that drama, and although it was not his style, he was always amused to see it through Dalí. It was fascinating because I think, in a strange way, Dalí loved the quietness of Andy. It was interesting to see how they appeared to interact without a single word. They almost communicated through their eyes instead of words.[38]

Pat Hackett adds that Warhol especially liked Dalí's ready wit. She wrote a note at the time that documents this: "Andy really enjoyed Dalí, they'd have dinner sometimes with their respective entourages. One time someone quoted to Dalí something one of his critics had said and Dalí responded, 'I agree. I am anti-Dalían.' Andy loved that, he said to me, 'Wasn't that a great thing to say? To be against everything you're *for*?! Why didn't *I* think of that?'"[39] Warhol was convinced that he could not keep up with Dalí in certain respects.

The moviemaker Jack Bond recalls that Warhol was "clearly entranced" both by Dalí as a figure and by his work and therefore felt flattered to be in his company.[40] Edgar Froese also noted that Warhol admired his Spanish colleague's "professional eccentricity" and "highly skilled expressive impulse." During the first U.S. tour of his band Tangerine Dream, Froese—who had already met Dalí in 1967—[41] was introduced to Warhol after a sound check at the Avery Fisher Hall (now the David Geffen Hall) in New York. The encounter took place in 1977 and that same evening led to an invitation to a party, presenting the musician with the opportunity to exchange a few words with Warhol:

"When did you meet Dalí the last time?" I asked, just to get any kind of conversation going, which was difficult with Warhol. "He was in town with some German model who he wanted to cast in plaster, called Veruschka or something like that, why is he doing that, as he can paint." I wanted to know whether he liked Dalí's works. "Oh yes" he said and gazed somewhat absent-mindedly after a guy who was disappearing into the half-dark. It was difficult to reach him with words. He said suddenly more to himself: "Dalí is standing with one leg in the coat pocket of Velázquez and with the other leg in a mental institute—but I love him, he is one of the few originals and he is so fantastic, a genius as a one-man show." ...

... However, Warhol knew very well that the era of uniqueness, which Dalí had still worked on for years, was over.[42]

Ronnie Cutrone also confirmed that Warhol appreciated Dalí's combination of

genius and madness ... Dalí was like a freak. He would put on so many airs. It wasn't like he was bad or did evil things or said evil things, it was just that because of his act he was hard to approach, I mean that was the thing, like he is a crazy person on the outskirts of life. So, Andy and I thought he was a bit of a joke in a way, but we appreciated what he did and thought his art was great. ... Andy really thought a lot of his persona that he had made up. ... He [Dalí] was such a performer. ... Andy and I, in our ten-year work marriage, we said things about Dalí, but not much. He was in another world. We just respected him as an artist who did the amount of work that he did and in such a grand style. That's what we liked. But see, Dalí was not Andy's type of artist really—except for the publicity.[43]

Due to their pronounced addiction to publicity, Dalí and Warhol were rejected by many of their colleagues. Philip Pearlstein, who started his career

38
Chris Royer in a telephone conversation with the author on October 7, 2013.

39
Pat Hackett in an e-mail to the author on August 12, 2013.

40
Jack Bond in an e-mail to the author on June 19, 2012 and in a conversation with the author on July 27, 2012 in London.

41
See the chapter **Dalí's View of Warhol and his Work** in this part.

42
Edgar Froese in an e-mail to the author on November 30, 2011.

43
Ronnie Cutrone in a telephone conversation with the author on July 8, 2012.

in the field of abstract expressionism and returned to figurative painting in the 1960s, remarks,

… in 1950 I started to study art history at the N.Y.U. Institute of Fine Arts and a Spanish art historian gave a course in Modern Art and talked about Salvador Dalí … And I began being interested in Dalí myself. … I think at that point he was regarded almost as a joke, very eccentric, the same way that Duchamp was sort of dismissed as just the chess player, that became so much of a sensationalist, and everybody thought of him as somebody out to grab attention. He wasn't thought of very highly among the artists that I was associating with that time … neither was Warhol, they thought he was a joke, too. No one took them seriously.[44]

In the 1970s Dalí and Warhol also played the role of outsiders in academic art discourse. Bob Colacello says,

At that point Dalí was very out of favor in the art world. Don't forget, in the 1970s, Conceptual Art and Minimalism were the dominant movements in the New York art world, certainly on the more intellectual side, let's say, and among critics and curators and many collectors of contemporary art. And Dalí was seen as very old fashioned, even reactionary. His politics went totally against the grain of the art world. He was a monarchist. He got along with Franco. This was all horrifying to the liberal left-wing intellectuals of the art world. I think Andy was afraid to be too associated with Dalí. I mean, he admired like everyone did, Dalí's technique. But Andy himself believed in making art fast and cheap and modern. His silkscreens could be done very quickly. So I mean this painstaking Renaissance style painting was very démodé and very much against what Andy's image was. … He loved Dalí's portraits because he had seen Dalí's portrait of C.Z. Guest and he loved that portrait. We even put it on the cover of Interview *magazine. Andy would say things he meant and also say things that fit his image, because he was ninety percent image and ten percent human being. …*

Andy wasn't very beloved by the New York art world in the 1970s. He, too, was seen like Dalí as being too campy … especially when he started doing society portraits. … This horrified the New York art world. In Europe they understood Andy more … In Europe they weren't exposed to his social life on a day to day basis in the gossip columns.[45]

Whereas Warhol's society portraits, despite the criticism, were a breath of fresh air in the art world in the 1970s due to their unmistakable modernity, Dalí's late work was considered outdated, often referred to as "kitsch." Dalí himself responded to the accusation by launching into the offensive. For example, when he created the painting *The Battle of Tetuán* in 1962, he explained to the press that the painting was the "product of indigestion" and that he had decided to paint "the most kitsch work imaginable."[46] Ultra Violet later recalled that Warhol also referred to Dalí's art as "kitsch."[47] The Pop artist in fact considered some of the surrealist's late works as "painted really badly" and products of his "drunk period."[48] Warhol also expressed gentle criticism at the end of 1982 during a press conference in Madrid, on the occasion of the opening of his exhibition "Guns, Knives and Crosses" at the Galería Fernando Vijande. The daily newspaper *Cinco Días* wrote about the artist from America: "He also admires Dalí. However, he says about him 'He's wrong.' He [Warhol] doesn't believe in kitsch, nor that anyone is old."[49]

44
Philip Pearlstein in a telephone conversation with the author on April 13, 2010.

→ **22** [p. 376]

45
Bob Colacello in a telephone conversation with the author on September 22, 2010.

46
Gibson 1997, p. 503.

47
Ultra Violet in a conversation with Jeanine Barone for the author on October 18, 2009 in New York.

48
Warhol/Capote 1973, p. 46. See the chapter **The 1970s** in Part 5.

49
In Candela 1983 (translated from the Spanish).

In the Bilbao daily newspaper *Hierro*, it said that Warhol did not agree with Dalí's contempt for his generation.[50] Although it was difficult, as usual, to draw longer statements out of Warhol during the press conference, he defined his art as "that what you want to do."[51] It was precisely this aspect that also fascinated him about his Spanish colleague. "Andy loved that Dalí could get away with anything," according to Christopher Makos, "He'd say 'The sky is blue and I'm amazing right now' and people would listen to him and I don't think people would listen to Andy in that way."[52] The painter Peter Wise has a similar view: "I think what he was impressed with was that anything Salvador Dalí would do, anything he touched, became art, because he said it was art. And Andy was a little bit like that, too. Andy just looked at him as being a big mad magician in a way that Andy wanted to be a magician ... put something on a table because you did it, it's art. Because when Dalí did it, it's a Dalí."[53] The fact that Dalí applied his artistic creativity to all conceivable fields also exerted a particular fascination on Warhol. Dalí's American lawyer in the U.S., Michael Ward Stout, says,

Andy Warhol was very enamoured with Salvador Dalí, very admiring, because I think they shared a philosophy. Part of their philosophy about art is that it could be made rapidly and mass-produced for many people. In the 1930s, Dalí licensed his name and his designs to Elsa Schiaparelli, making him, I believe, the first artist to ever do so. Warhol thought that was very interesting. ... Clearly, they found each other amusing. I think their relationship was one of mutual admiration.[54]

Brigid Berlin finds Warhol's admiration for Dalí hard to understand:

It'd be the only time that I have ever said this in an interview because five million people say, "What was Andy like?" And they'd say, "Oh, he was really great." Well, that would be a question that I could ask Andy about Dalí and it would be "Gee, isn't he great?" But I have no idea why he thinks he's great. ... the thing that turned me off was the me Dalí. Just like walking in a room, sitting down on a chair, the me Dalí, is like the "King of the World" has just arrived here. And you'd just think: "Fuck! What is this about?" You wanna get away from it and not sit and chat. ... Andy was just as excited and thrilled to know the day that Joan Collins and Liberace were coming to the Factory ... he called me and said "Is he here yet?" And when Liberace walked in the door and he was all in white, you remember with all that [sic] jewels, and went up the elevator, I think Andy would have really died and gone to heaven meeting Liberace. But I don't feel that he had that feeling with Dalí. ... I did hear Andy say—quote—when Picasso did the plates and Andy saw the plates, he said, "Gee, this is so great. I want to do as much work as Picasso did."[55]

In *POPism* Warhol writes, "Picasso was the artist I admired most in all of history, because he was so prolific."[56] Bob Colacello adds: "Andy had in his mind that he was competing with Picasso in terms of fame and productivity. That's what Andy wanted to be—as important as Picasso. And now it's almost a cliché to say that the two most important artists of the twentieth century are Picasso for the first half and Warhol for the second half."[57]

Warhol's interest in other artists was also an expression of the fact that he was constantly looking for new ideas. The playwright Robert Heide

50 "ANDY WARHOL, un fenómeno cultural y sociológico."

51 "En su muestra madrileña" (translated from the Spanish).

52 Christopher Makos in an e-mail to the author on July 25, 2009 and in a conversation with the author on June 28, 2012 in New York.

53 Peter Wise in a conversation with the author on June 28, 2012 in New York.

54 Michael Ward Stout in a telephone conversation with the author on June 9, 2010.

55 Brigid Berlin in a conversation with the author on December 4, 2012 in New York.

56 Warhol/Hackett 1980, p. 114. In his *Philosophy* Warhol recounts, "When Picasso died I read in a magazine that he made four thousand masterpieces in his lifetime and I thought, 'Gee, I could do that in a day.' So I started.+

57 Bob Colacello in a conversation with the author on June 26, 2012 in New York.

emphasizes this point: "I knew that he admired surrealists. I think he really was in awe of Dalí. He was very interested in other artists and what they were doing. Ray Johnson was one he was very interested in. Even … later in life you saw him with other artists, finding out what they were doing. They all knew one another. There was a competitiveness, but it was a healthy competitiveness."[58] Dalí was an artist who willingly provided information about his ideas and projects. Elsa Peretti remarks, "Dalí gave a lot of himself, and constantly shared his ideas and his very strange thoughts, speaking in Catalan, French, and English with a fascinating, deep voice."[59] Dalí also had no issue with telling Warhol about it. Louis Markoya comments on this: "Warhol was known as an art idea thief, but Dalí felt he could talk to Warhol because he felt that Andy could never come close to executing the ideas of Dalí."[60] Amanda Lear reports that when she went to the Factory Warhol always asked her "for news of Dalí and his work."[61] "Warhol was always very friendly with me," says Lear,

Every time he came to Europe I saw him in London, I saw him in Paris. He wrote about me in his book very kindly. He was not bitchy with me. But with many other people we suddenly discovered that he was not such a nice person. … He was not always nice. But anyway, my friend was very obviously Salvador Dalí. So I was always with Dalí and not so much with Warhol. … They were very curious about each other because they couldn't go and spy in each other's atelier. Warhol would say "And what is Dalí painting at the moment?" I would explain to him, "Well, at the moment he started a crazy discovery about stereoscopic, 3D painting." … And so I would explain that to Andy Warhol. He would ask, "Oh really? But how is he doing it? What is he using?"[62]

For Warhol, therefore, it was always something special to meet Dalí, part for entertainment, part for inspiration. On March 19, 1978 he recorded in his diaries: "Dalí is so full of ideas, and he's ahead in some things, but then he's behind in others. It's odd. He was telling me about a book that's just been written in Paris about a brother and sister who were so in love that the brother (laughs) ate her shit. … And then he said something great—he said that the punks are the 'Shit Children,' because they're descendents of the beatniks and the hippies, and he's right. Isn't that great? The Shit Children. He *is* smart."[63]

Jealousy or Friendship?

Despite the great admiration that they had for each other, Salvador Dalí and Andy Warhol were both always mindful of defending their own position with regard to the other. The musician Edgar Froese, who became acquainted with the two artists, describes their distanced closeness:

An acquainted journalist … met both of them several times in New York and got to know what he called "the friendly cosmos of creative fire and water." Elements that could by all means merge in the case of Dalí and Warhol, but did not necessarily have to do so, as each had his own enormous international playground. However, as is always the case with two professional narcissists, each watered the other's roots, while fastidiously ensuring that the brother's artistic leaves did not grow larger in spirit than one's own.[1]

+
And then I found out, 'Gee, it takes more than a day to do four thousand pictures.'"
Warhol 1975, *Philosophy*, p. 148.

58
Robert Heide in a conversation with the author on December 6, 2012 in New York.

59
Elsa Peretti in a telephone conversation with the author on October 2, 2015.

60
Louis Markoya in an e-mail to the author on May 17, 2010.

61
Lear 1985, p. 268.

62
Amanda Lear in a telephone conversation with the author on March 13, 2010.

63
Hackett 1989, p. 119.

1
Edgar Froese in an e-mail to the author on November 30, 2011 (translated from the German).

Carter Ratcliff was even clearer when he wrote in 1983: "Andy Warhol may well be America's best-known artist. Only such figures as Norman Rockwell and Andrew Wyeth provide him any competition, while on the international scene, his aura rivals that of Salvador Dalí."[2] When Ultra Violet was asked more than twenty years later at the Philadelphia Museum of Art symposium, "The Dalí Renaissance," about the relationship between Dalí and Warhol, she answered: "... Dalí was *the* most famous artist, the most *publicized* artist in the forties, fifties, and early sixties, and I think Warhol was extremely jealous, or he wanted to have that position."[3] In a later conversation, she added, "All Warhol wanted was Dalí's fame. ... Warhol was jealous but he didn't say that."[4]

Brigid Berlin, however, one of Warhol's closest confidantes, denies vehemently that there was any jealousy involved: "I never heard Andy ever once say, 'Oh, he's so fantastic. Why can't I be like Dalí?'"[5] Sylvia Miles confirms, "I think Andy was a little ... not jealous ... but a little in awe of Salvador Dalí. ... Andy was very aware. ... He thought that Dalí was the real point—the real thing."[6] Christopher Makos also believes that Warhol was not jealous of Dalí, but simply knew that he himself did not possess some of the Spaniard's abilities.[7] Ronnie Cutrone was of the opinion that Warhol's jealousy was only evident in one area, if at all: "Andy was not so jealous about fame, Andy was jealous about money. ... The only thing I ever heard him say in jealousy about another artist ... he said 'How come Jasper Johns gets three-hundred-and-fifty-thousand dollars for a painting and I get twenty-five?' ... At that time Andy had ten times more publicity ... ."[8] In the 1960s, despite the hype surrounding his person, Warhol was not yet as commercially successful as he would be later on. Gerard Malanga explains, "Andy was as famous as you could get in the 1960s. ... Andy started getting a lot of PR, a lot of press. ... Whether he was financially successful as an artist is another thing. But as far as the press media is concerned, as they say in the press, Andy made good copy."[9] So perhaps Warhol was in fact envious of Dalí's immense commercial success. From this point of view he was undoubtedly a role model for him.[10]

When the two artists met in the 1960s, Warhol was still at the beginning of his artistic career. Therefore there was no reason for Dalí to be jealous of his younger colleague. According to Amanda Lear,

And so Andy Warhol started his brilliant career, of course, and when he was already quite famous he never forgot Salvador Dalí and he came regularly to have a drink with Dalí. He came from the Factory ... he was surrounded by a court. Dalí liked that because he liked colorful people and every time Warhol would arrive with all those transvestites and all those crazy people around, Dalí thought it was very funny and very entertaining. ... Dalí was usually quite jealous of other artists having success. He wanted to be the only one, the king, the god ...

Later on when Warhol became very very famous and everyone was talking only about Warhol—"Warhol is the Pope of painting"—at this stage, yes, Dalí was probably a little bit jealous: "It's too much, it's ridiculous." But this is normal between artists. Even in the 1930s, in the days of Surrealism, they were all jealous of each other, Max Ernst, Paul Éluard, and Breton. They were fighting and criticizing each other. I think it's quite normal and anyway it's good, it's stimulating.[11]

2 Ratcliff 1983, p. 8.

3 In "Reminiscences of Dalí: A Conversation with Amanda Lear and Ultra Violet," moderated by Dawn Ades, in Taylor 2008, p. 211. Similarly, also in Prekop/Cihlář 2011, p. 250.

4 Ultra Violet in a conversation with Jeanine Barone for the author on October 18, 2009 in New York.

5 Brigid Berlin in a conversation with the author on December 4, 2012 in New York.

6 Sylvia Miles in a conversation with the author on July 1, 2012 in New York.

7 Christopher Makos in a conversation with the author on June 28, 2012 in New York.

8 Ronnie Cutrone in a telephone conversation with the author on July 8, 2012.

9 Gerard Malanga in a conversation with the author on July 2, 2012 in Hudson, New York.

10 See the chapter **Warhol's View of Dalí and his Work** in this part.

11 Amanda Lear in a telephone conversation with the author on March 13, 2010.

By the late 1960s Warhol had already started overtaking Dalí in terms of fame. Gerard Malanga says, "In the 1970s when Andy became more and more famous, Dalí became older and older. So Dalí could not keep the pace."[12] The former model and Warhol superstar Ivy Nicholson, who went with the artist to one of Dalí's parties in winter 1965/66, made an interesting observation:[13]

And I noticed during the many years I knew Salvador Dalí—three or four years—some days he was compassionate but some days he was insanely jealous and especially of people with talent ... And I think most of the time he acted like he had a lot of love for other beautiful people, that includes the beauty of being a famous artist like Andy. But then he was almost like a grown-up, but a childish person in his envy. ... The greater the art the more insanely jealous he seemed to be. ... And that is why I am presuming that it was not exactly a nice gesture towards Andy when he invited him to that particular dinner; to have him seated so far away was definitely, without a question of a doubt, a big insult. And Dalí was like that all the time I knew him. It took me a while to figure it out.[14]

Ultra Violet reported later that at a certain point Dalí had to admit to himself that his heyday was over. She concluded this at a party that *LIFE* magazine held on January 10, 1969, in honor of the three astronauts Walter M. Schirra Jr., Donn F. Eisele, and R. Walter Cunningham, who had embarked on October 11, 1968, in the Apollo VII on a space flight to circle the Earth 163 times in over 260 hours. Many celebrities and people from show business were invited to the party.[15] "Warhol was invited, and I was, too, but Dalí was *not* invited. And that's when I think he realized maybe his time was up, as far as fame was concerned. He was very crushed."[16] Ultra Violet added that Dalí was upset that Warhol was coming into his own.[17] The French author and photographer François-Marie Banier, who met both artists frequently, even thinks that the elder suffered as a result of the success of the younger.[18] Louis Markoya, Dalí's assistant in the 1970s, remarks,

Dalí and Warhol were very competitive ... it was not really about their courts, it was about fame, or perceived fame. If Warhol was in the papers and magazines Dalí was upset, if Dalí was getting more press, Warhol would step it up. While I cannot speak specifically about Warhol, Dalí did not see why Warhol got the attention he did, and what attention Warhol did get, Dalí wanted. It seemed to be similar for Warhol, as he would refer to Dalí as old and washed up behind his back, but pal with him in public.[19]

Warhol's later commercial success, in particular, was a thorn in Dalí's side. When Horst Weber von Beeren assisted Dalí in 1979 and Warhol's name came up, he felt the "artistic respect" of the Spaniard, which he subtly associated with the question of "who made more money."[20] Warhol was already overtaking Dalí at this point. "Dalí only thought badly of Andy Warhol," according to Susi Wyss, "because he was making more money than him. Dalí was very jealous. ... It was talked about at the time. It was simply common knowledge. ... Prince Ruspoli and all these people talked at the dinners if they were not there. ... I occasionally heard Dalí saying quite nasty things— but not only about Warhol. How he put others down, as if he was trampling on them with his boot."[21] Louis Markoya adds, "Dalí would often throw out little quips about Warhol. One time I had Dalí sign an issue of *Interview*

13
See the chapter
The 1960s
in Part 5.

12
Gerard Malanga
in a conversation
with the author
on July 2, 2012
in Hudson, New
York.

14
Ivy Nicholson in
a telephone
conversation
with the author
on November 20,
2009.

15
Ultra Violet 1988,
pp. 198ff.

16
In "Reminis-
cences of Dalí:
A Conversation
with Amanda
Lear and Ultra
Violet," moder-
ated by Dawn
Ades, in Taylor
2008, p. 215.
Similarly in a
telephone con-
versation with
the author on
August 11, 2008,
and in a con-
versation with
Jeanine Barone
for the author
on October 18,
2009 in New York.

17
Ibid.

18
François-Marie
Banier in an
e-mail to the
author on Octo-
ber 24, 2011.

19
Louis Markoya in
an e-mail to the
author on May 17,
2010.

20
Horst Weber von
Beeren in a tele-
phone conver-
sation with the
author on June 22,
2011.

21
Susi Wyss in a
conversation
with the author
on October 25,
2013 in Paris
(translated from
the German).

where Dalí appeared on the cover. I had previously had the issue signed by Warhol, and when Dalí saw the signature he first asked what it was. When I told him it was Andy Warhol he told me he would sign it, but I had ruined all its value by the Warhol signature."[22] For this reason, Markoya describes the relationship of Dalí and Warhol as "cordial and full of venom."[23]

Warhol's diaries convey some of the cordiality between the two artists. The entry on December 16, 1978, for example, documents a conversation with Potassa de la Fayette, in which she tells Warhol that Dalí is coming back to New York and that the two artists will have to resume their friendship.[24] The passage shows that the interaction between the artists in public conveyed the impression of friendship. The mentioned photo by Lynn Karlin, where Dalí is greeting Warhol with a kiss on the cheek, and the shot *Dalí Kissing Andy* by Christopher Makos can also be regarded as documenting such a personal and artistic closeness.[25] Ultra Violet, however, observed, "Their relationship was not intimate. It was an artist to artist relationship. But with one looking up and the other looking down."[26] Amanda Lear, who shared her own fifteen-year friendship with Dalí, underlines this view:

No, it wasn't a friendship, absolutely no. Dalí denied many friends or real friends. … He knew everybody because he was incredibly famous. … But friends— he had only very few friends who were allowed to come to his house in Spain or to a dinner with him. And usually they were not painters because there was always this rivalry or jealousy with all the painters. … Dalí appreciated Andy Warhol. He liked him the same way he liked Richard Estes or William de Kooning. Dalí admired them. Dalí admired also Francis Bacon, but he wasn't friends with him.[27]

Dalí was indeed very selective when it came to choosing friends. His assistant Timothy Phillips hit the nail on the head: "No one could be friends with Dalí without having either talent or intelligence or both."[28] Dalí especially appreciated Warhol's intelligence. As already reported, he once remarked to Antonio Pitxot that Warhol was the most intelligent person from New York.[29] Pitxot later recalled, "Each time I heard Dalí speak about Warhol, he was using terms of sympathy and admiration for his intelligence, which is what Dalí admired the most—the intelligence of a person. The pictorial abilities or techniques were an issue that didn't surprise him, because he had already passed through it. However, he was always amazed by intelligence."[30] In this respect, Dalí viewed Warhol as his equal. When asked about his relationship with Warhol in a 1979 interview for the Spanish weekly magazine *Cambio 16* on the occasion of his retrospective at the Centre Georges Pompidou in Paris, he expressed his admiration for his American colleague very pointedly:

Warhol and I are very good friends. He has diamond-like intelligence. And also, his historical value is incontestable, because thanks to him and to Pop Art, it's back into figurative art. He painted those Campbell's soup cans exactly the same, and people started to realize that a taxi, for example, has wonderful reflexes, that one can spend a whole life painting a telephone booth. Without Warhol, hyperrealism would not exist, or it would have come at a later time. Anyway, I had already painted a Coca-Cola bottle in 1946, long time before Warhol.[31]

22
Louis Markoya in an e-mail to the author on May 17, 2010.

23
Ibid.

24
Hackett 1989, p. 188. See also the chapter **The 1970s** in Part 5.
→ **50** [p. 396]
→ **Cover**

25
See the chapter **The 1970s** in Part 5.

26
Ultra Violet in a conversation with Jeanine Barone for the author on October 18, 2009 in New York.

27
Amanda Lear in a telephone conversation with the author on March 13, 2010.

28
In Girst 1999.

29
Antoni Pitxot in a telephone conversation with the author on August 5, 2009.

30
Antoni Pitxot in a conversation with the author on September 5, 2009 in Cadaqués (translated from the Spanish).

31
In Rubio 1979, pp. 90f. (translated from the Spanish). It is remarkable that Dalí painted a Coca-Cola bottle even before he remembers here— in 1943. See the chapter **Coca-Cola is the Real Pop Art** in part 4.

CONCLUSION – IMAGES

Until into the 1990s, Salvador Dalí and Andy Warhol had bad reputations among art critics and art historians. The critic Robert Hughes wrote in *TIME* magazine on the occasion of the exhibition "Salvador Dalí: The Early Years," held at the Metropolitan Museum of Art in New York in 1994: "Was any painter a worse embarrassment than Salvador Dalí? Not even Andy Warhol."[1] The strong public presence and popularity of Dalí and Warhol were much more significant at the time than their status in the art world. Their enormous economic success had long been more a cause for attacks against both, and led to repeated criticism of the seriousness of their work. However, this changed over the course of time. When Warhol displayed his *Flowers* at the Leo Castelli Gallery at the end of 1964 and the works sold straight away,[2] Thomas B. Hess wrote rather admiringly in the magazine *ARTnews*: "He follows close to the trail of the divine Salvador Dalí—of whom Arshile Gorky once said (addressing a group of integrity-soaked cold-water-loft abstractionists): 'I profoundly admire Dalí, for his immense financial success.' In other words, Warhol makes empty metaphysical vessels that are continually being filled with real money, which is an undeniable triumph, sociologically."[3] After Hess penned these lines, a new viewpoint gradually emerged. As Robert Hughes attested at the beginning of the 1980s: "To be one's own PR outfit was, in the eyes of the New York artists of the forties and fifties, nearly unthinkable—hence the contempt they felt for Salvador Dalí. But in the 1960s all that began to change, as the art world shed its idealist prejudices and its sense of outsidership and began to turn into the American Art Industry."[4] Dalí, who had been dubbed "Avida Dollars" by André Breton with blatant disparagement, had paved the way for this and the first public uproar about it had already blown over when Andy Warhol stated in his 1975 book *THE Philosophy of Andy Warhol*:

Business art is the step that comes after Art. I started as a commercial artist, and I want to finish as a business artist. After I did the thing called "art" or whatever it's called, I went into business art. I wanted to be an Art Businessman or a Business Artist. Being good in business is the most fascinating kind of art. During the hippie era people put down the idea of business–they'd say, "Money is bad," and "Working is bad," but making money is art and working is art and good business is the best art.[5]

One might assume that this standpoint professed by Warhol met with Dalí's approval, but this was not the case. Although he and Gala conducted themselves according to this way of thinking, he justified his views in a quite traditional manner. The astrologer Michaël Delmar asked him about this concretely in an interview for the French underground magazine *Façade* in 1978:

M.D.: With regard to this, Andy Warhol said: "Supreme art is business." Do you share his opinion?

S.D.: Not at all. But me, I love money more than he does: because it is a form of spiritualization of vile material. I love money because I am MYS-TICAL and MYS-TIFYING and all matter has to be like in the era of the Middle Ages, that's to say spiritualized. Ramon Llull, Nicolas Flamel, the mystics have always wanted to transform matter into gold, INTO GOLD!! (he shouts) MATTER TRANSFORMED INTO GOLD!![6]

1
Hughes 1994,
p. 68.

2
Bourdon 1989,
p. 193.

3
In Madoff 1997,
p. 281.

4
Hughes 1992,
p. 247.

5
Warhol 1975,
Philosophy,
p. 92.

6
Delmar 1978, p. 7
(translated from
the French).

With commentaries like this, Dalí held on to the myth of the eccentric divine artist and he used it to emphasize that the only difference between himself and a madman was that he was not mad. In the 1970s Dalí's appearances started to take on an involuntarily comical effect. Warhol's confidante Brigid Berlin, who met the Spaniard at the time, remarks, "I never found Dalí to be a person that I would have fun with. He's too extreme. ... Even if Dalí was trying to be funny and amusing he didn't come off that way because of this and the whole contraption. It was the whole look or walking in with the cape flying. And you think to yourself, this is so absurd. ... I thought Gala was interesting. She was tough on Dalí because if she showed up he kind of came down a bit."[7] Dalí, who had been given the name "Wizard of Was" at the time,[8] had become anachr onistic. What had been new in the 1930s, 1940s, and even in the 1950s and had therefore had great entertainment value for the public, only had a limited effect in the 1960s. Robert Hughes wrote on the then current cultural change:

Television was producing an affectless culture. Warhol set out to become one of its affectless heroes. It was no longer necessary for an artist to act crazy, like Salvador Dalí. Other people could act crazy for you: that was what Warhol's Factory was all about. By the end of the sixties craziness was becoming normal, and half of America seemed to be immersed in some tedious and noisy form of self-expression. Craziness was no longer suggested uniqueness. Warhol's bland translucency, as of frosted glass, was much more intriguing.[9]

Warhol had recognized the signs of the times earlier and more radically than Dalí and hit the nail on the head with his famous declaration: "In the future everybody will be world-famous for fifteen minutes."[10] This so frequently cited statement is of lasting relevance in view of the development of media, especially the internet.[11] Dalí, who always had a very self-centered view, evidently struggled with this vision that Warhol expressed so aptly and assertively. Dalí still clung to the notion of the godlike artist whose geniality was superior to the everyday and commonplace.

From the point of view of today's selfie era, however, Dalí's massive self-staging, which also inspired Warhol, is more current than ever. So while Dalí was still bound up with the image of the artist as a genius, as in past centuries, Warhol created the slogan for a new artist personality and thereby took a decisive step ahead of Dalí, making a lasting contribution to art history, as stated by Henry Geldzahler: "Through his 'dumb blonde' persona, he quickly became associated in the public's mind with the new Pop movement. It is rare in our country and in our century for an artist to gain the recognition of the man on the street: Picasso, Dalí, Jackson Pollock—the list is short. ... Warhol captured the imagination of the media and public as had no other artist of his generation. Andy was Pop, and Pop was Andy."[12] However, Dalí had previously achieved something similar with regard to Surrealism, emphasizing: "Surrealism is myself."[13]

It is quite evident today that Warhol found his—probably most important—role model in Dalí, with regard to the development and promotion of his own artist personality as a "brand." He was also inspired by him on occasion in terms of approaches to art. In 1980 Warhol remarked in an interview:

7
Brigid Berlin in a conversation with the author on December 4, 2012 in New York.

8
Richardson 2001, p. 291.

9
In Madoff 1997, pp. 378f.

10
In Warhol/König/Hultén/Granath 1968 (n.p.).

11
In 1980, Warhol said in an interview: "There's so much TV around that you could be famous for five minutes on TV. If you're on TV the night before they will recognize you for five minutes too. It works both ways. The second day they forget about you." Quoted according to *Andy Warhol: Guns, Knives, Crosses* (n.p.).

12
In Feldman/Schellmann 1989, pp. VIIf.

13
Dalí/Halsman 1954, p. 65.

"Today the kids are painting the same way we did twenty years ago, like it's
new to them or something. When Salvador Dalí used to come around in the
'60s, he thought he had done everything we were doing. We thought it was
new, but we were doing things he had already done."[14] Warhol also appreciated Dalí's business acumen. He even liked his practice of signing large
quantities of blank sheets, even though he was never tempted to take such a
step himself. Vincent Fremont remarks, "Andy understood how important
your name was once you attained a certain level of fame. He branded his look
and his name before there was a term or phrase called 'branding.' Andy liked
to make money, [he] painted and made drawings of money, but never sold
out, never sold his name. Andy was always in control."[15]

Warhol was also cleverer than Dalí when it came to public appearances. He presented himself as an artist without an opinion, who did not
want to commit himself and instead let others talk for him. In 1977, in an
interview with Glenn O'Brien for the magazine *High Times,* he answered the
question of whether he stood to the left of Dalí by saying: "On the bias."[16]
Dalí, on the other hand, had something to say about everything and made
quite a few enemies with his clearly stated standpoints. He supported the
monarchy as a form of government, in a rather eccentric manner, and was
against democracy. His snobbish justification for this was that artistic genius
could not flourish in a democracy. It never occurred to Warhol, on the other
hand, to refer to himself as a genius. Francesco Clemente, who created the
Collaborations with him and Jean-Michel Basquiat in the 1980s, writes in
his essay "King for a Day": "Warhol knows that democracy loves to fantasize
about genius but hates to meet one. Democracy celebrates the face from the
crowd, chosen to be king for a day."[17]

Warhol recognized that the self-description of the artist as a genius
cult had run its course in the second half of the twentieth century and it had
become necessary to redefine oneself for a new era. Even so, he was repeatedly referred to as a genius. Ultra Violet was of the opinion that Dalí and
Warhol were both geniuses in their own way.[18] In Dalí's case it was technical
mastery and the imagination that Picasso had once humorously compared
to an "outboard motor continually running."[19] Warhol's creativity could best
be compared with a sponge that absorbed everything. Nick Rhodes says, "He
did it all with vibe by choosing and knowing what was cool. ... He's got such
remarkable taste, which is what a lot of it is about: it's putting things in the
right place. And he could do that better than anyone else."[20] Peter Beard, who
emphasizes that Dalí and Warhol were both "so different and so similar,"
says of the two artists' genius: "... they had enormous overlaps and enormous
respect for each other. And they were in the same ballpark. I don't like the
word genius, but of course we do have Picasso. I would say they were both
geniuses. ... And they became geniuses even more. One of their genius elements was to exponentially exaggerate the originality that they each had."[21]

Through their originality, their accomplished self-staging, and no least
their systematic self-marketing, Salvador Dalí and Andy Warhol made an
important contribution to the development of art, which places them among
the most seminal artists of the twentieth-century.

359

14
In Ratcliff 1983,
p. 108.

15
Vincent Fremont
in a conversation
with the author
on June 28, 2012
in New York.

16
In Goldsmith
2004, p. 263.

17
In Cypryański
2000 (n.p.).

18
Ultra Violet in a
conversation
with the author
on October 18,
2008 in New York.

19
Cf. *Salvador Dalí,*
1939 (n.p.).

20
Nick Rhodes in a
conversation
with the author
on December 15,
2014 in London.

21
Peter Beard in a
Skype conversa-
tion with the
author on Sep-
tember 24, 2010.

IMAGES

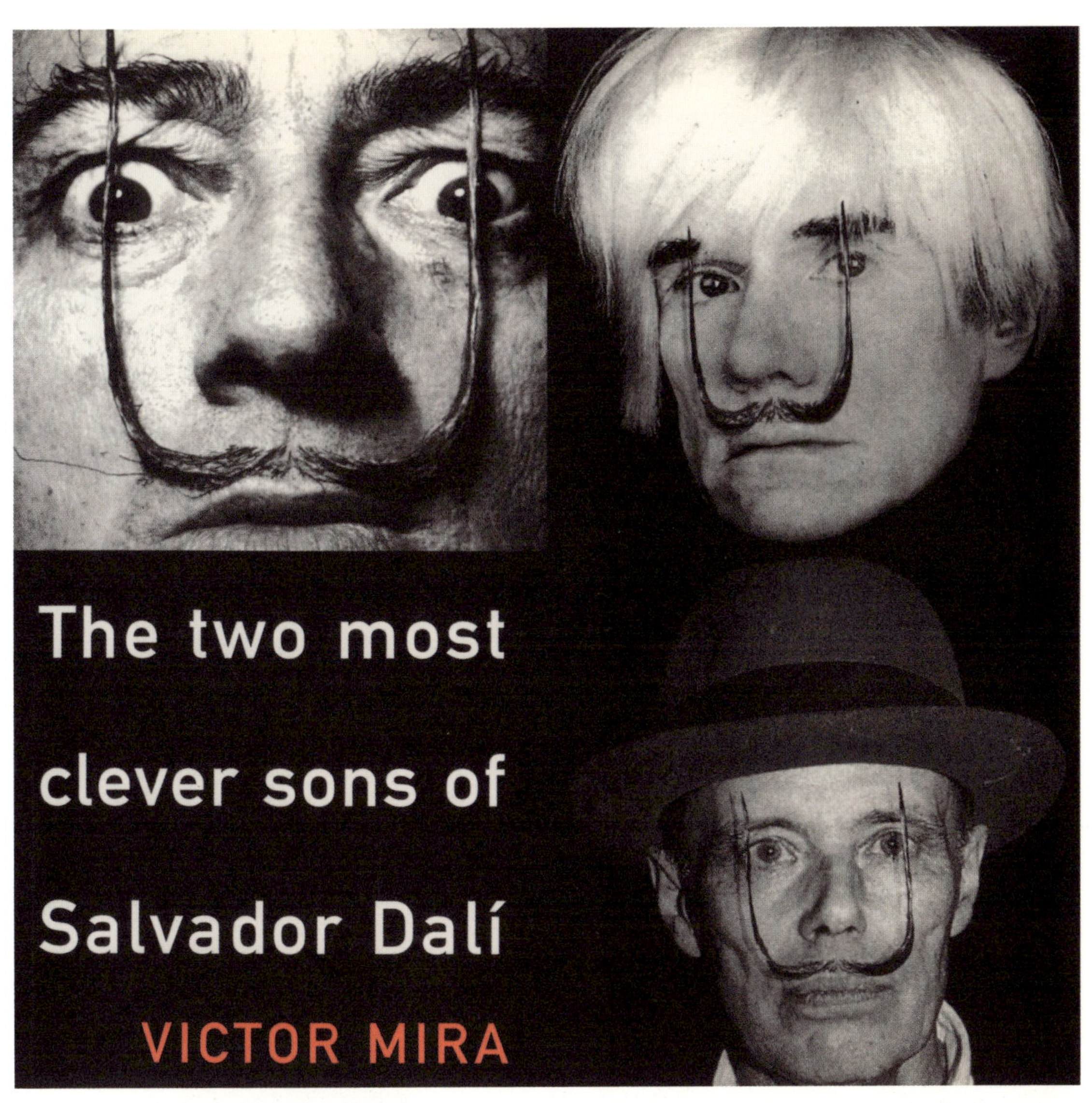

1
Cover of Víctor
Mira's *The two most
clever sons of
Salvador Dalí*, 1998.

2
Salvador Dalí,
1967. Photograph by
Philippe Halsman.

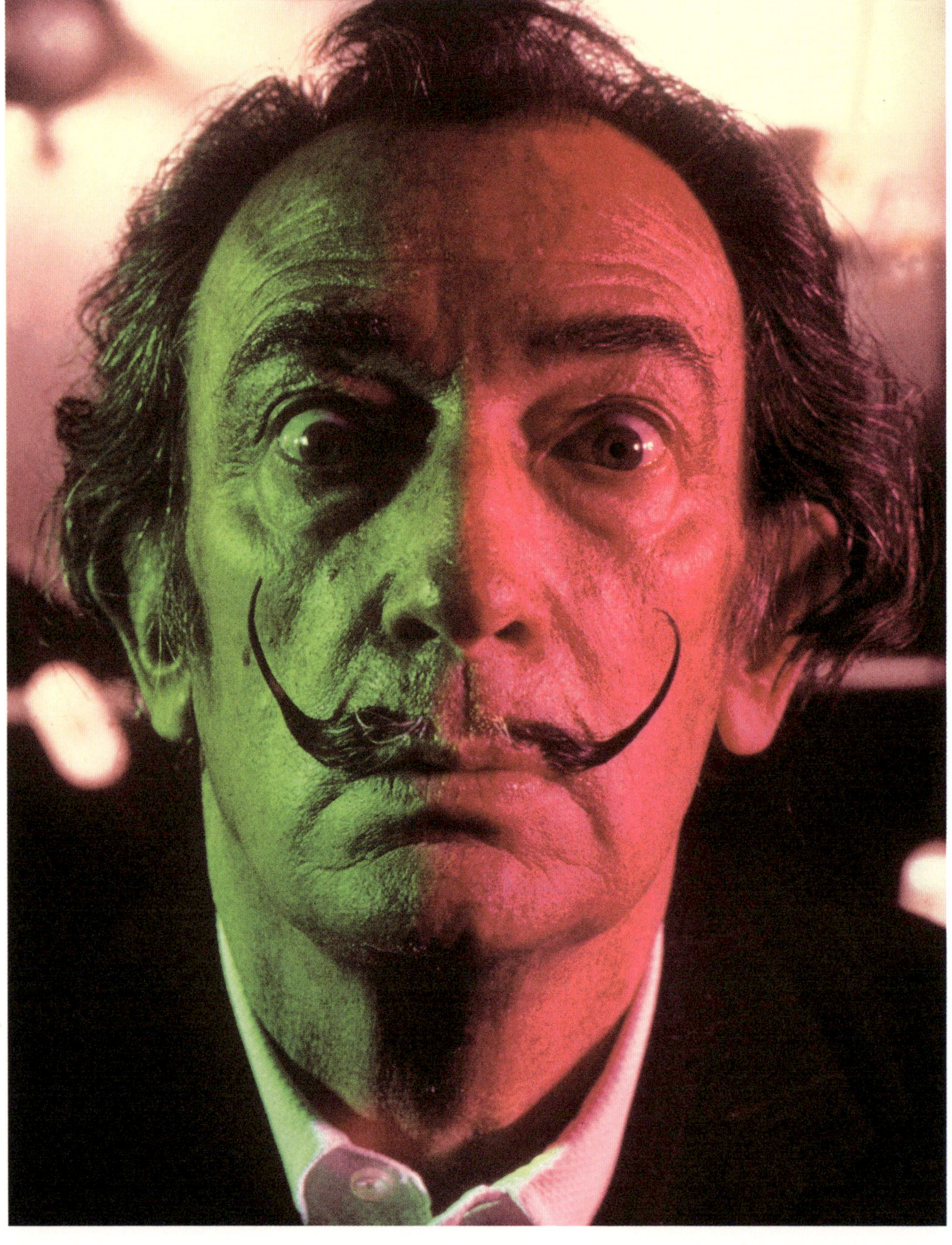

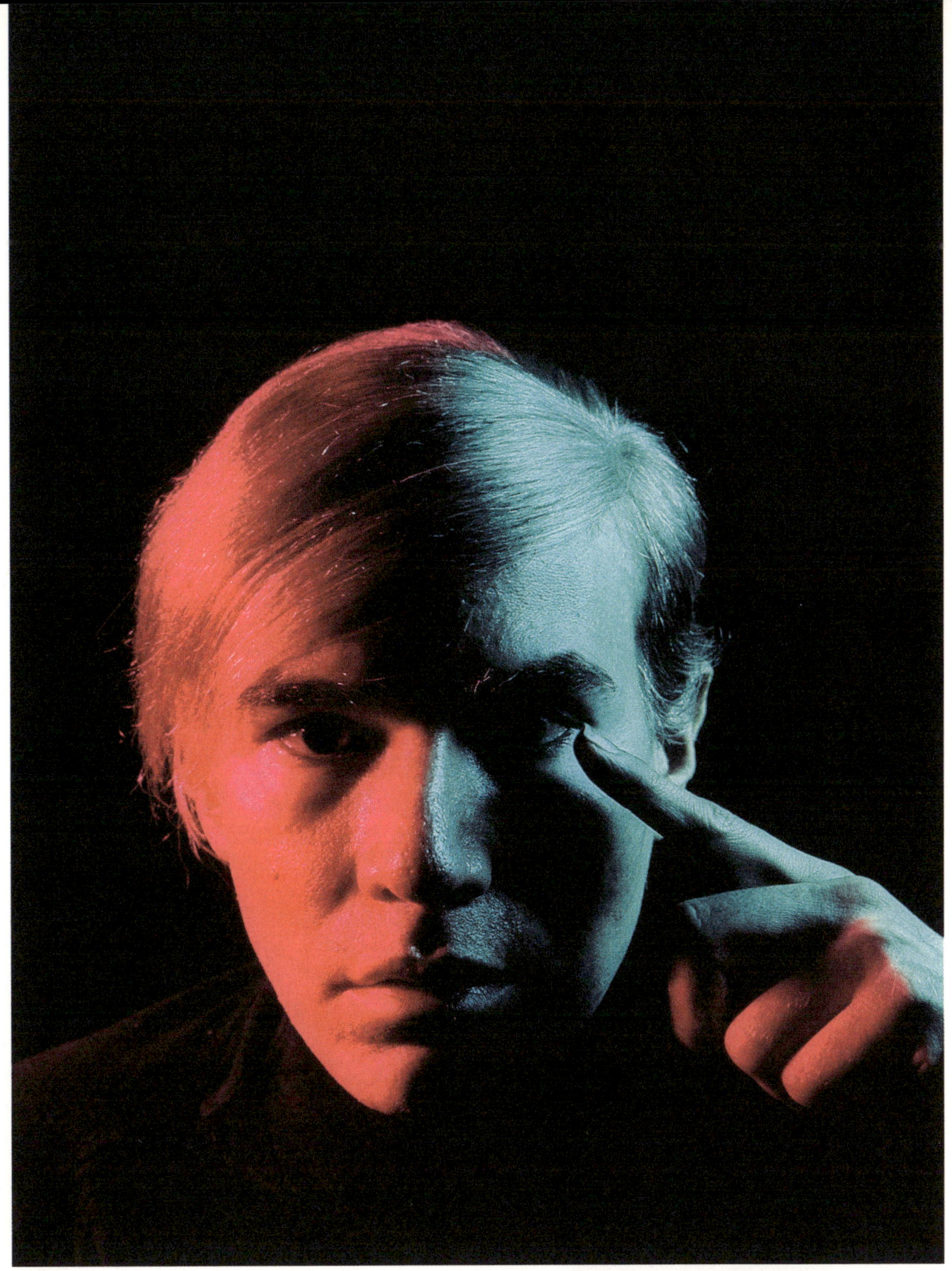

3
Andy Warhol,
1968. Photograph by
Philippe Halsman.

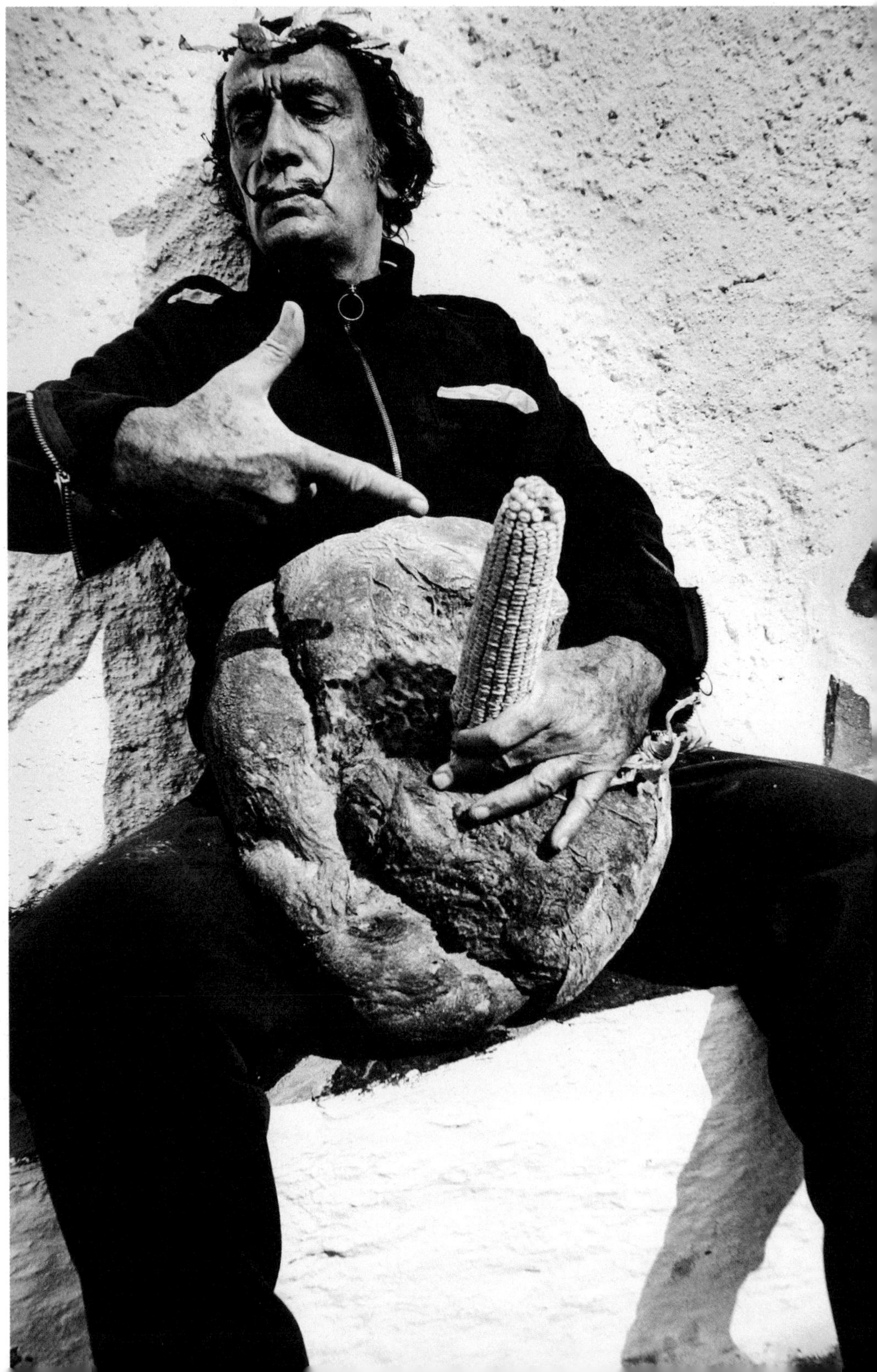

4
Salvador Dalí at
his home in Port Lligat,
1968. Photograph
by Robert Whitaker.

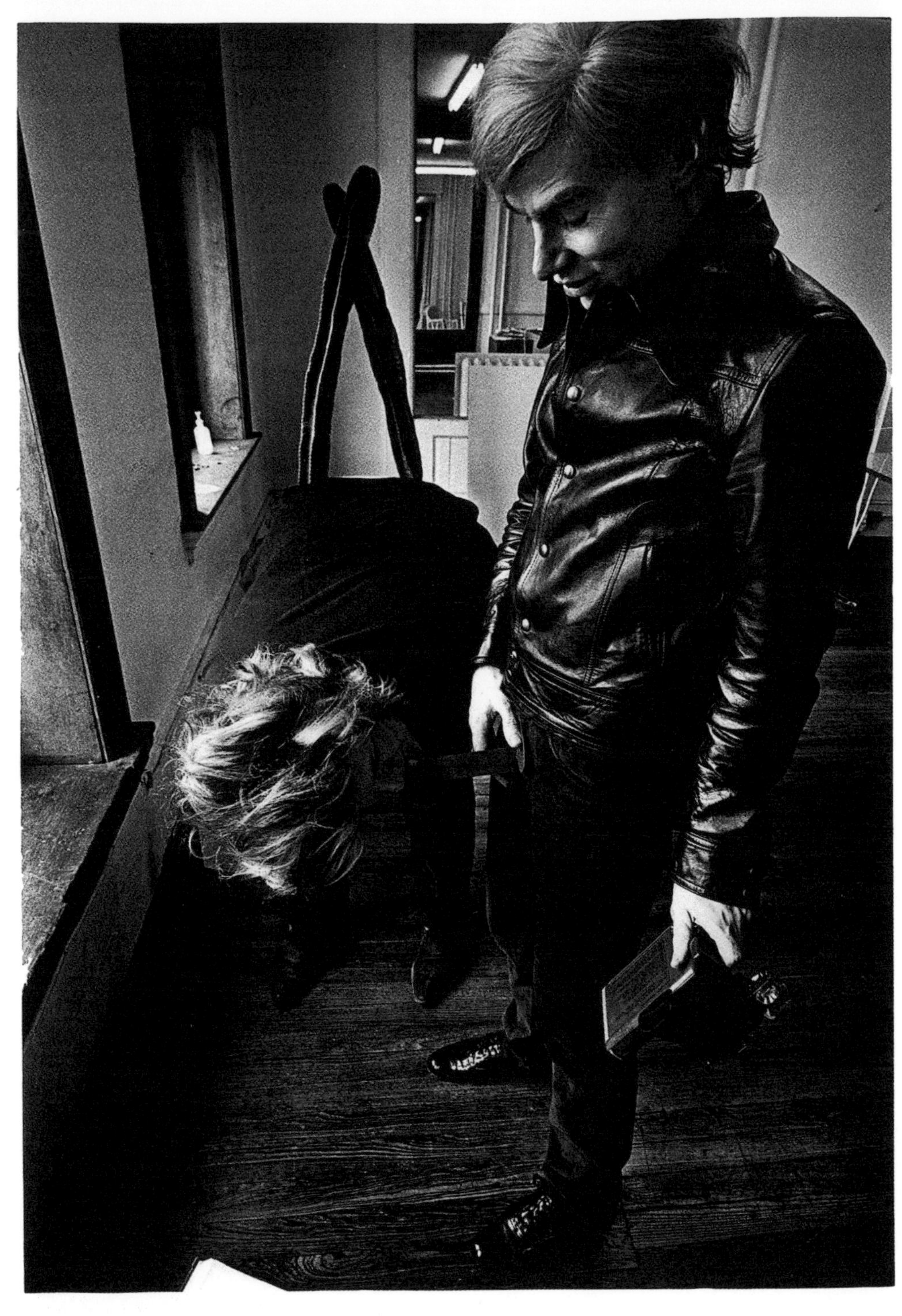

5
Brigid Berlin and Andy
Warhol at the Factory
in New York City, 1969.
Photograph by Harry
Shunk & János Kender.

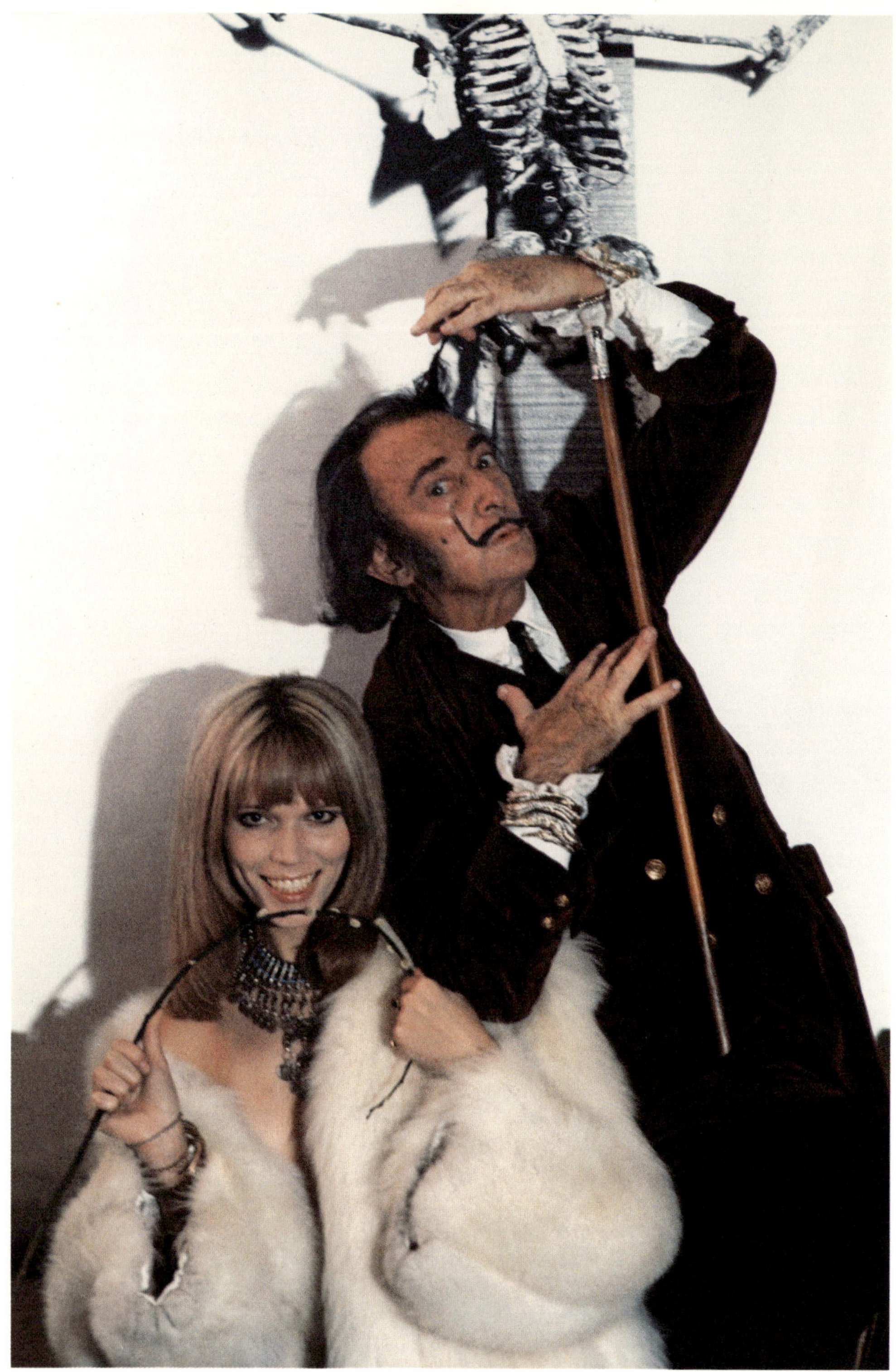

6
Salvador Dalí and
Amanda Lear in Paris,
1969. Photograph by
Giancarlo Botti.

7
Andy Warhol with Edie
Sedgwick and Chuck Wein
in New York City, 1965.
Photograph by Burt Glinn.

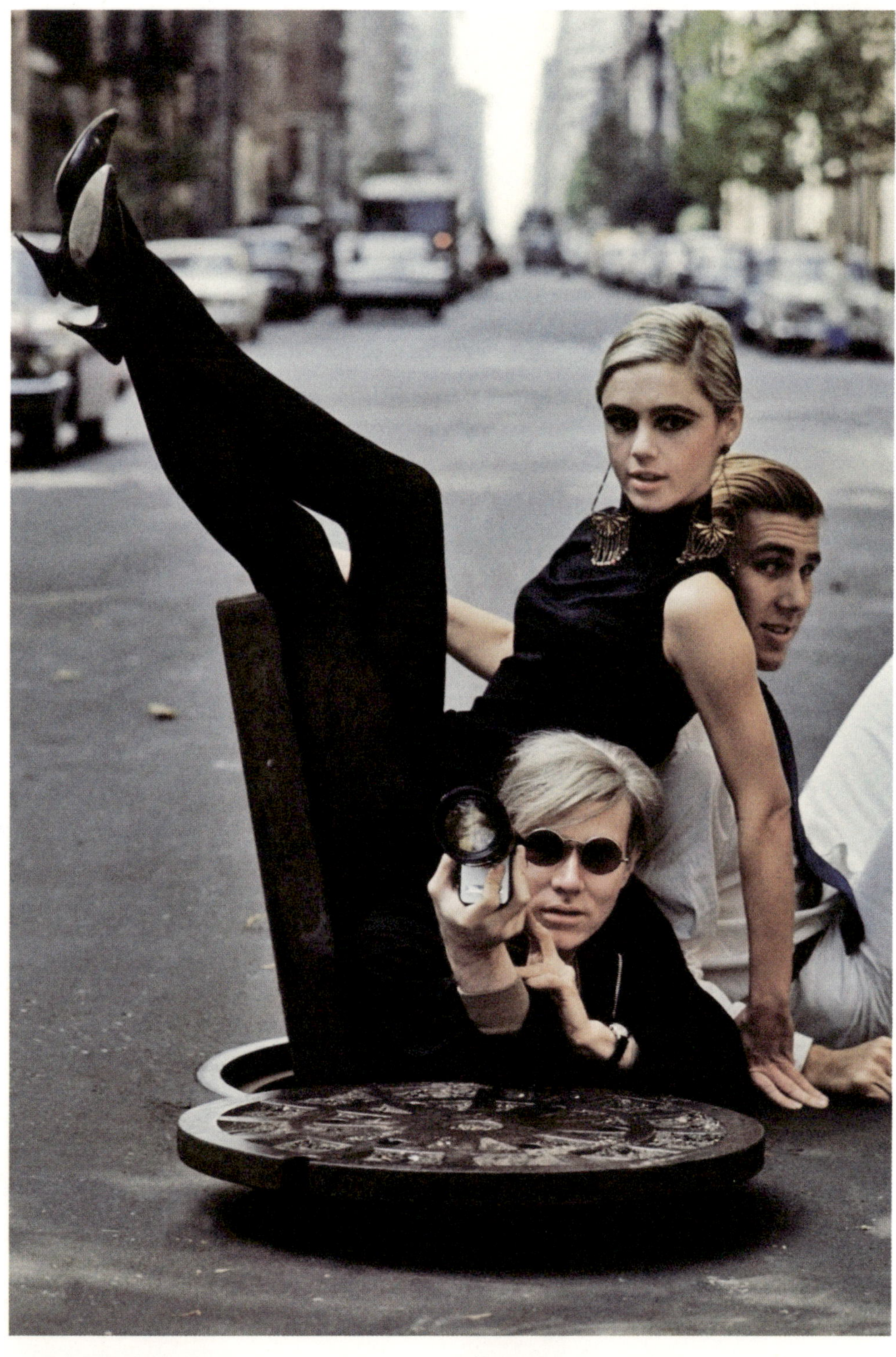

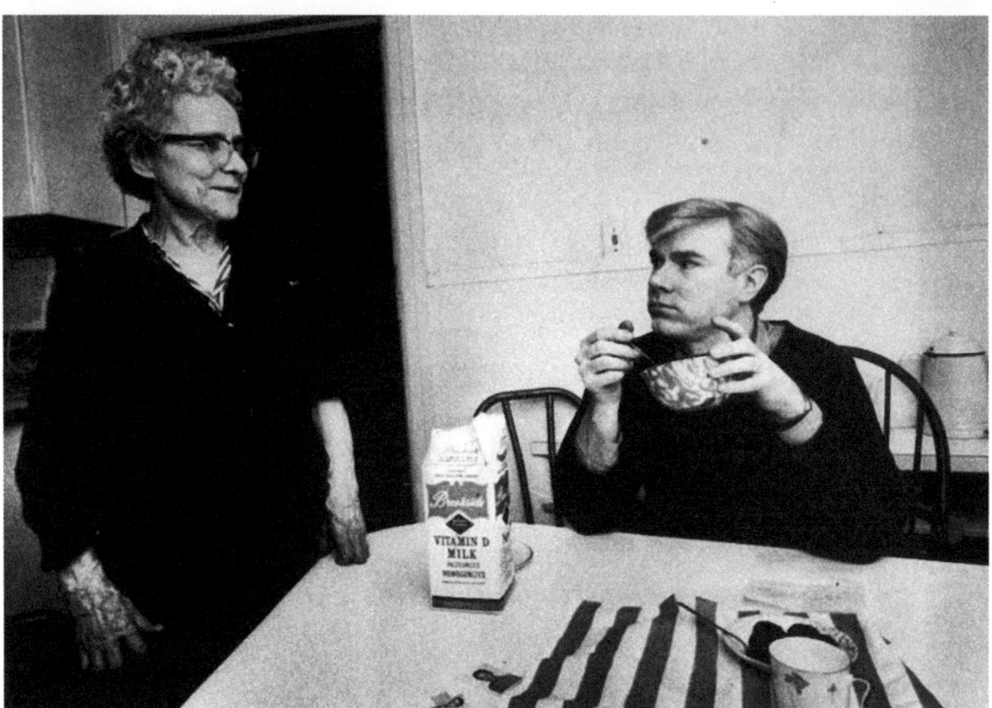

8
Andy Warhol with
his mother Julia
at home in New York
City, 1964. Photograph
by Ken Heyman.

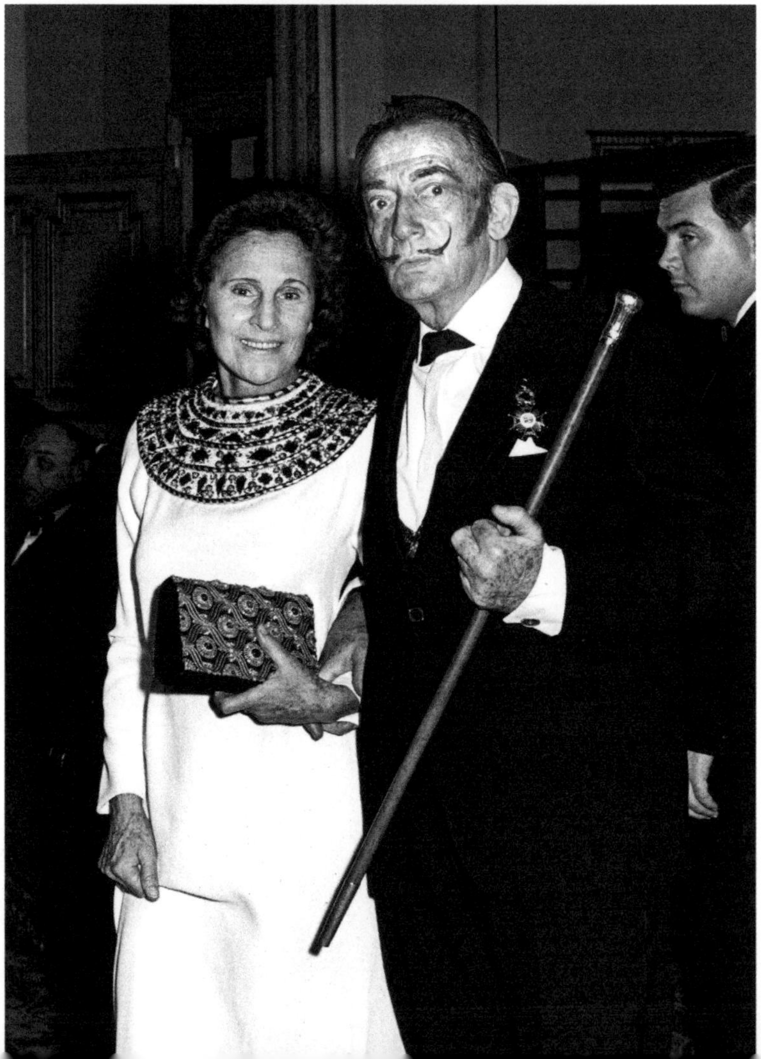

9
Gala and Salvador Dalí
at the St. Regis Hotel
in New York City, Feb-
ruary 6, 1968. Photo-
graph by Ron Galella.

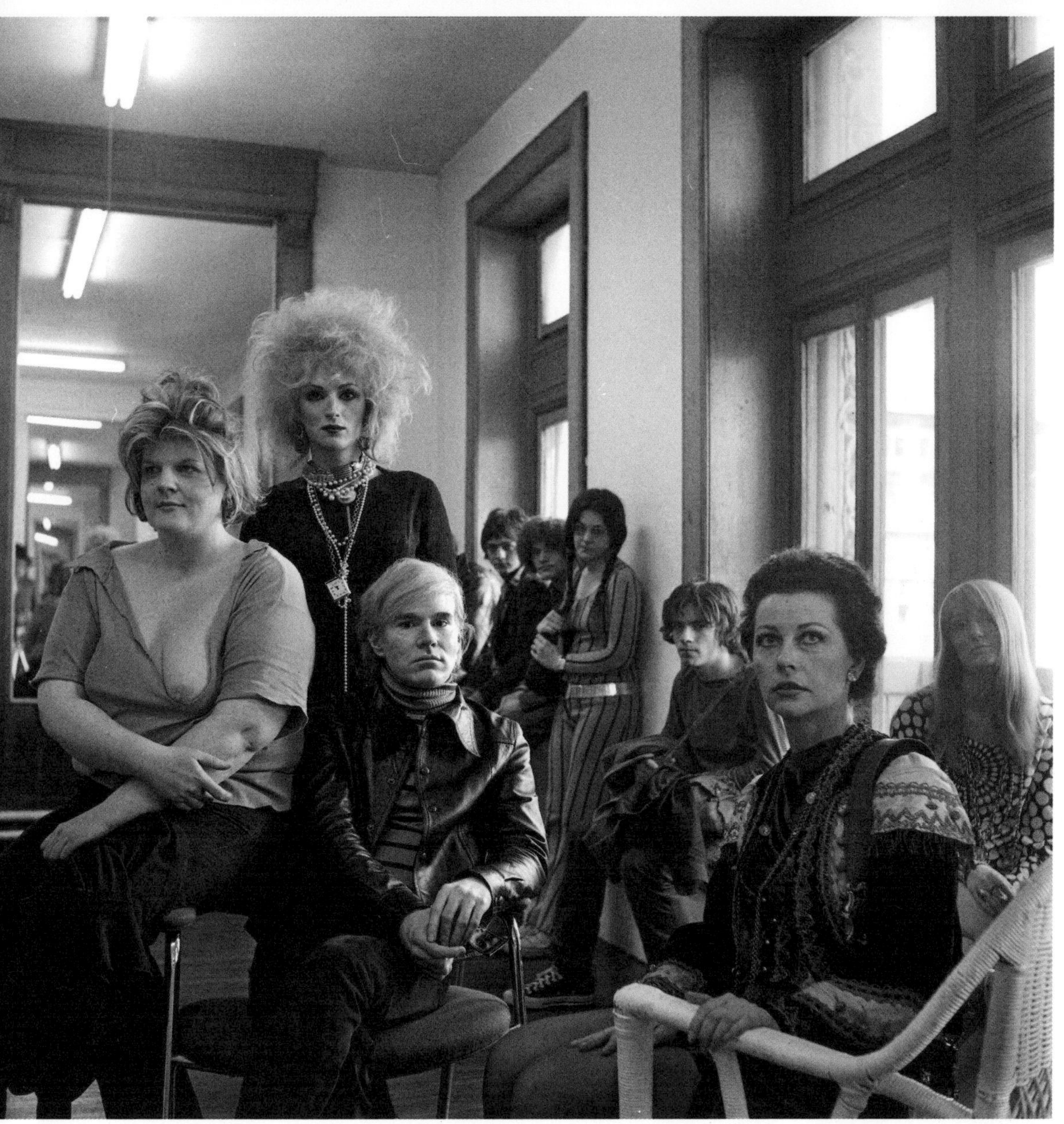

10
Andy Warhol with Brigid
Berlin, Candy Darling,
and Ultra Violet at the
Factory in New York City,
April 24, 1969. Photo-
graph by Cecil Beaton.

"**Whenever I photographed the surrealist artist Salvador Dalí, he would stop—sometimes along with his wife, Gala—and strike an animated pose, full of life. When in New York City, he was usually at the St. Regis Hotel, where I photographed him many times.**"

Ron Galella in an e-mail from
Anthony Miller
to the author on
March 11, 2016.

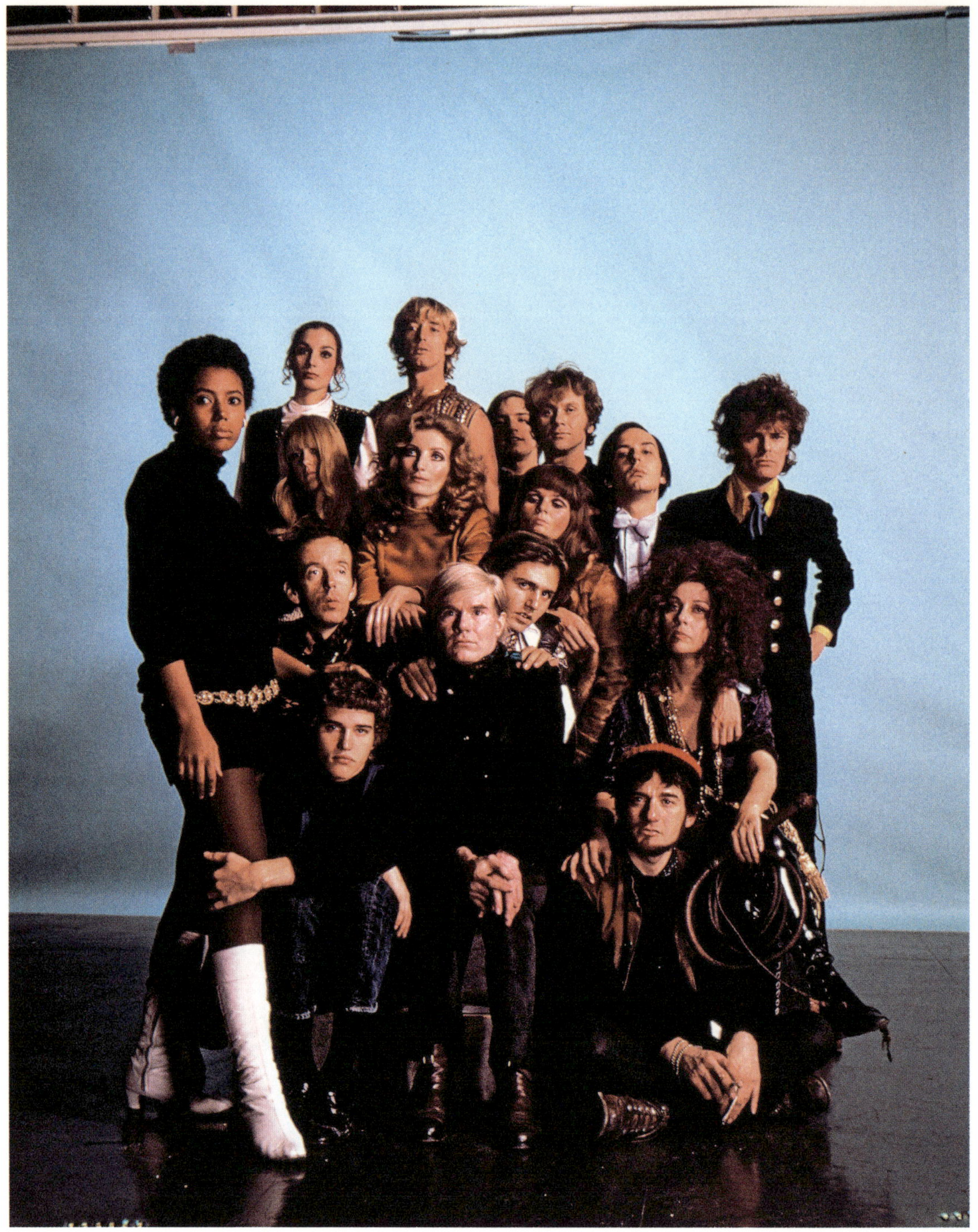

11
Andy Warhol and his
entourage from the Factory
posing at the *LIFE* studio in
New York City, 1968. Photograph by Philippe Halsman.

"Top row: Geraldine Smith, Eric Emerson, Joe Dallesandro (partly ob-
scured), Louis Waldon, Fred Hughes, Paul Morrissey. 2nd row: unidentified black girl, Ingrid Superstar, Viva, unidentified girl. 3rd row: Taylor
Mead, Gerard Malanga (with hands on Andy's shoulders), Ultra Violet.
Bottom: Jay Johnson, Andy Warhol, Ondine." **Gerard Malanga** in an e-mail to
the author on
April 10, 2016.

12
Salvador Dalí with
Elsa Peretti in Port
Lligat, 1966.
Photograph by Oriol
Maspons i Casades.

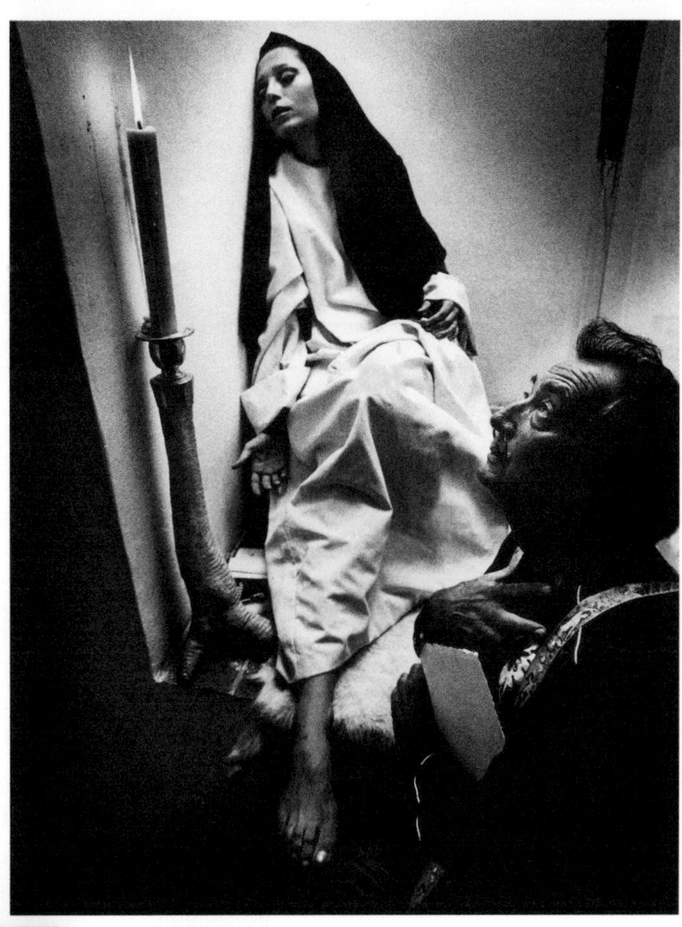

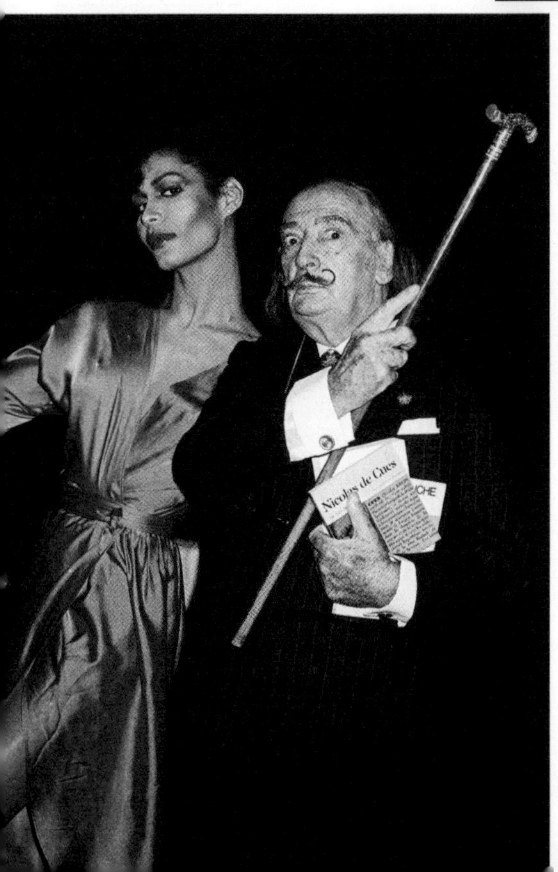

13
Salvador Dalí with
Potassa de la Fayette in
New York City, 1979.
Photograph
by Roxanne Lowit.

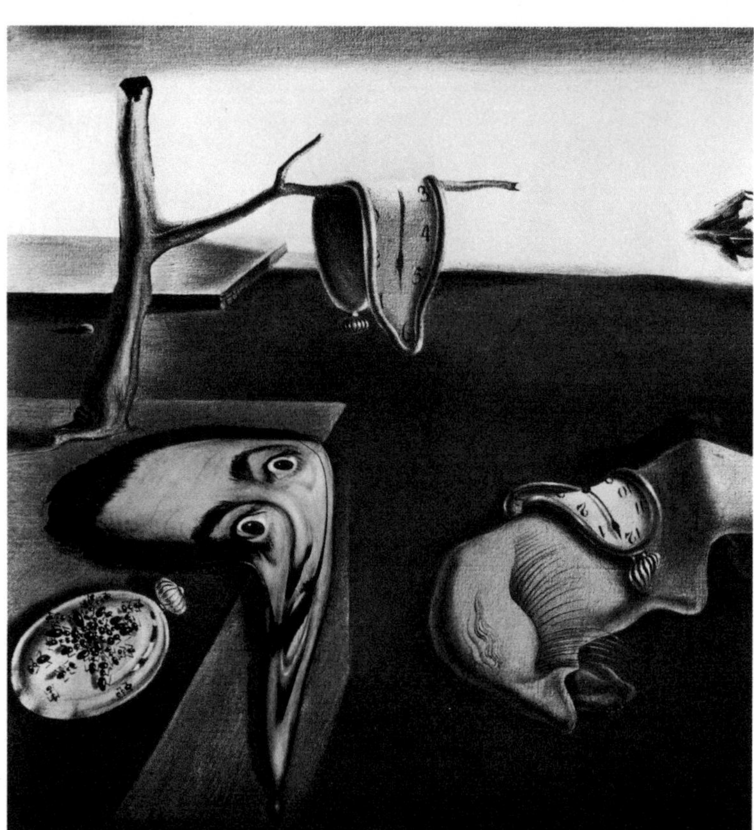

14
Philippe Halsman.
*Surrealism is Myself,
Dali's Mustache*,
1953–54.

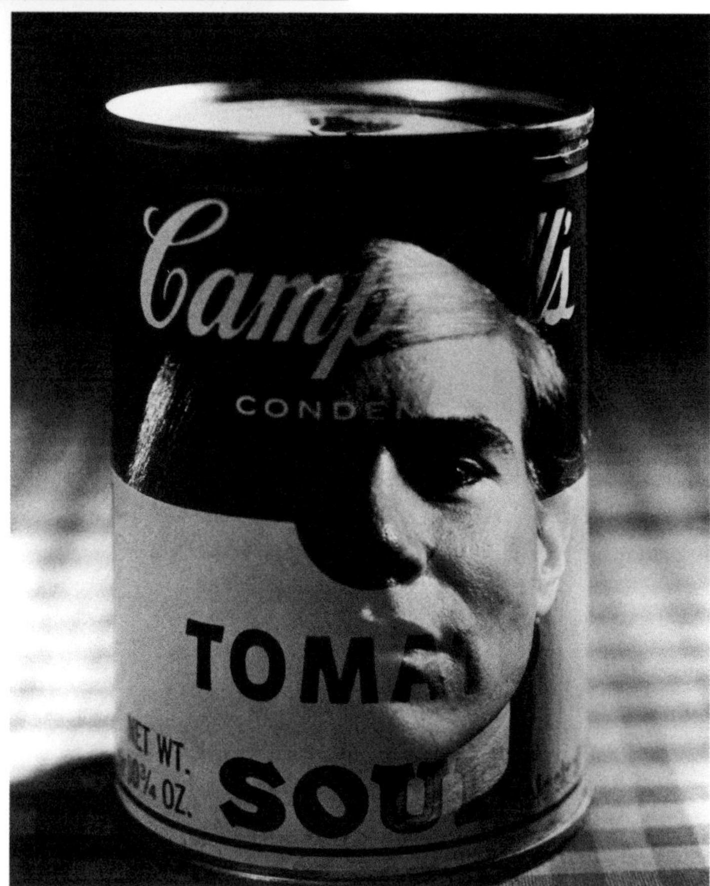

15
Philippe Halsman.
*Concentrated
Andy Warhol*, 1968.

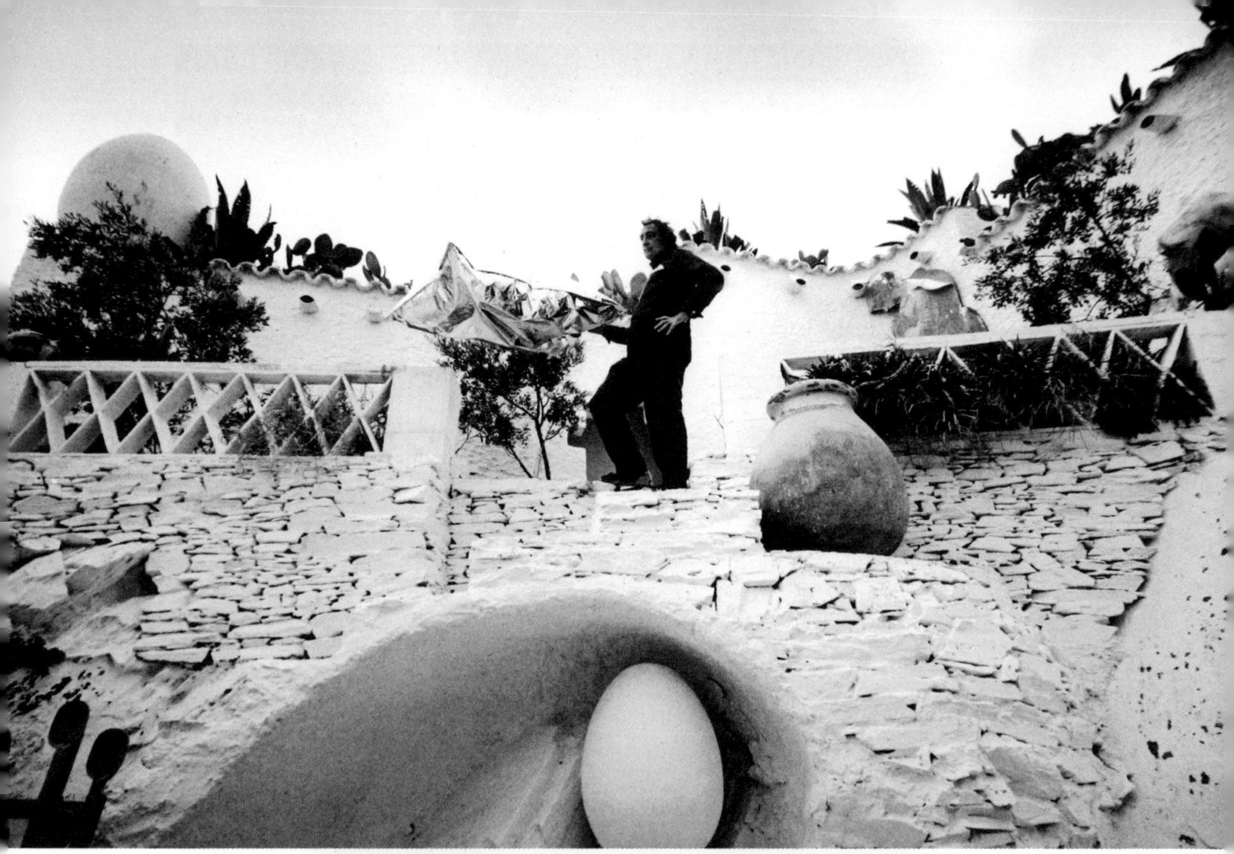

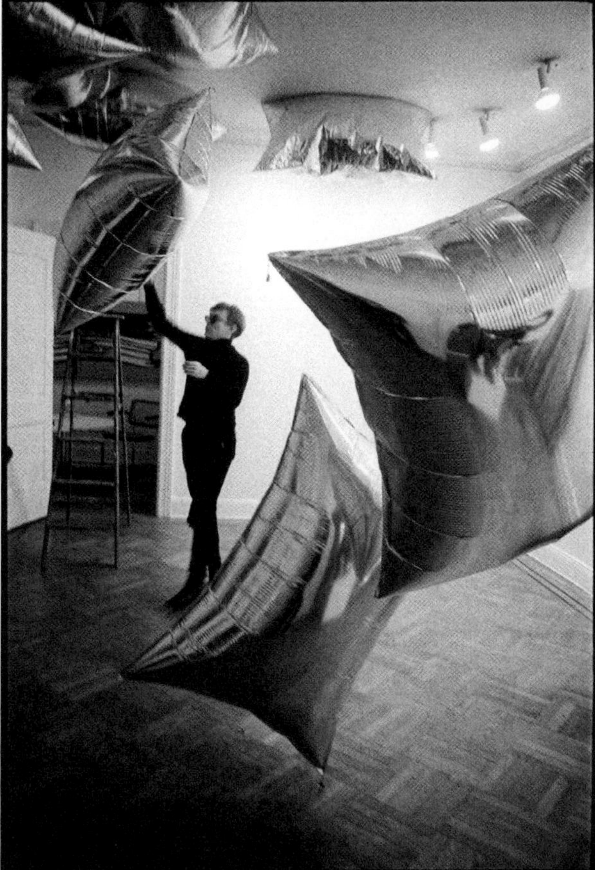

16
Salvador Dalí with a
silver helium balloon at
his home in Port Lligat,
1968. Photograph
by Robert Whitaker.

17
Andy Warhol with his
Silver Clouds at the
Leo Castelli Gallery in
New York City, April
1966. Photograph by
Nat Finkelstein.

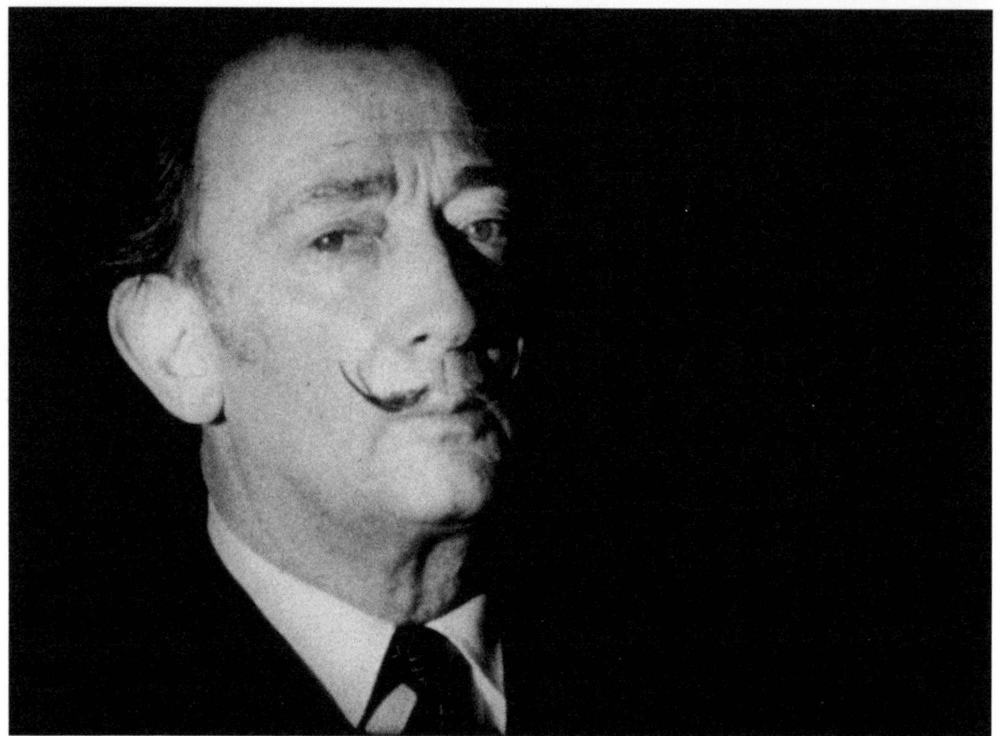

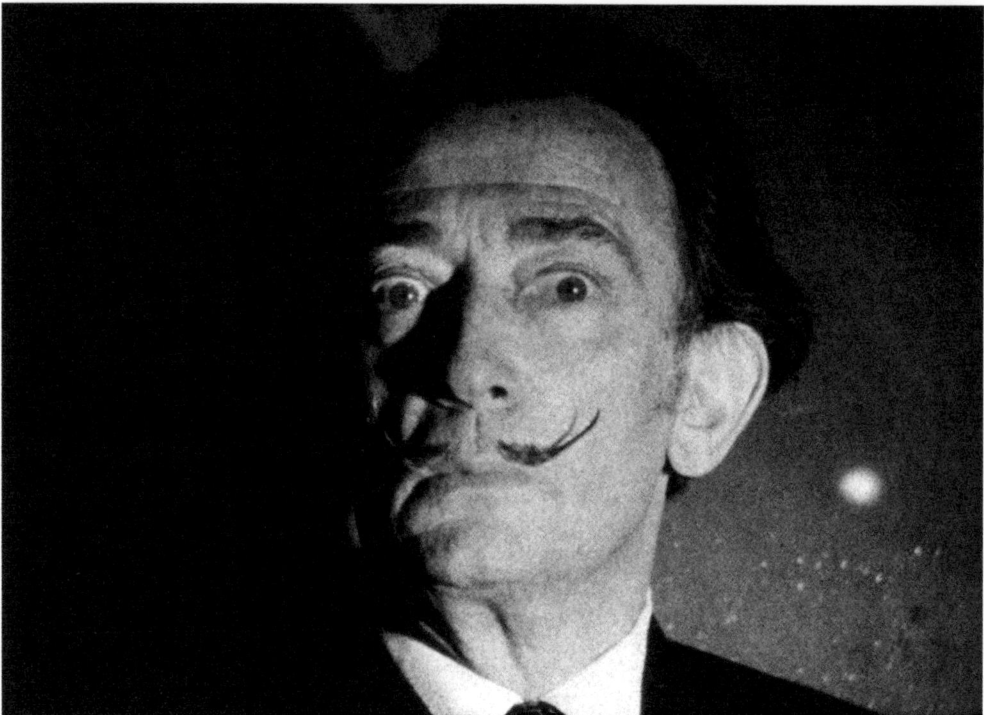

18
Andy Warhol. Still from
*Screen Test: Salvador
Dalí #1*, February 6, 1966.
16-mm film, black-and-
white, silent, 3.7 minutes
at 16 frames per second.
The Andy Warhol
Museum, Pittsburgh.

19
Andy Warhol. Still from
*Screen Test: Salvador
Dalí #2*, February 6, 1966.
16-mm film, black-and-
white, silent, 3.7 minutes
at 16 frames per second.
The Andy Warhol
Museum, Pittsburgh.

Film-Makers' Cinematheque

41st St. THEATER

125 West 41st St.   564-3818

ANDY WARHOL, UP-TIGHT

presents live

THE VELVET UNDERGROUND, ROCK' N' ROLL MUSIC

John Cale (vocal, viola, piano, bass, guitar, crystal glass), Lou Reed (guitar, autoharp, piano, harmonica, car horn, vocal) Maureen Tucker (drums, maraccas, tambourine); Sterling Morrison (guitar, bass, kazoo, vocal)

THE UP-TIGHT SERIES

Up-tight Rock 'n' Roll, Whip Dancers, Film-maker- Freaks, Tapers, Anchovie Filming live episodes of the "Up-tight" series featuring:

EDIE SEDGWICK
GERALD MALANGA
MARY PIFFATH
DONALD LYONS
BARBARA RUBIN
BOB NEUWIRTH
PAUL MORRISSEY
NICO
DANIEL WILLIAMS
NAT FINKLESTEIN
BILLY LINICH
AND
SALVADOR DALI

ANDY WARHOL'S new movie, "MORE MILK YVETTE" starring Mario Montez and The Velvet Underground

Tues. thru Mon., Feb. 8 to Feb. 13th
Weekdays 8 pm, 10:00 pm
Sat. and Sun., 2:30 pm, 8 pm, 10:30 pm

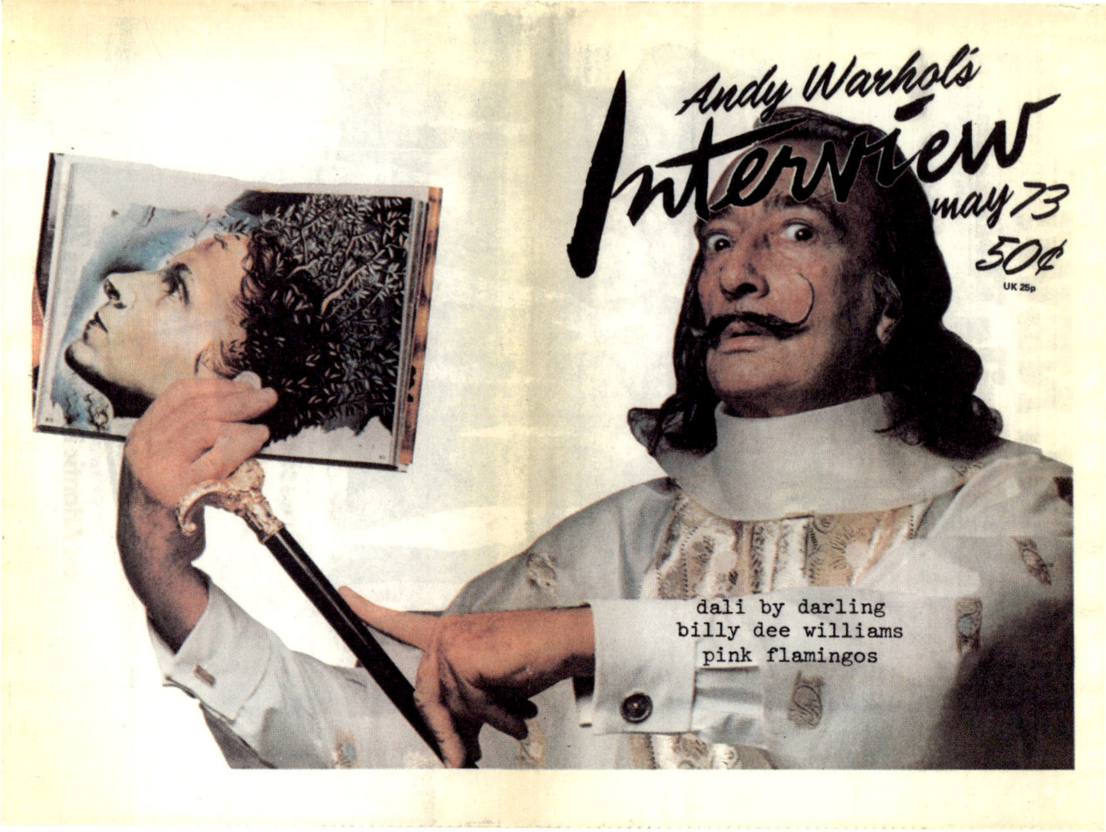

21
Cover of *Andy Warhol's Interview*, May 1973.

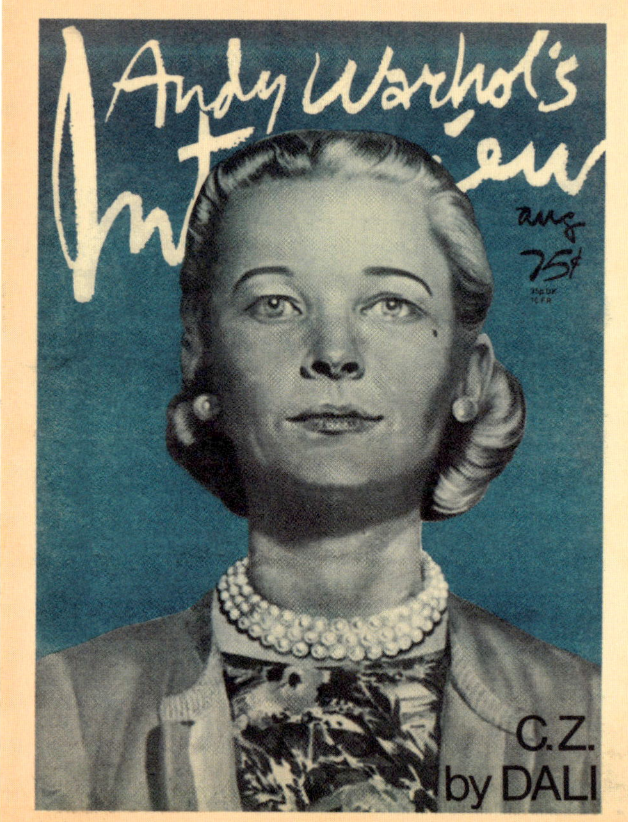

22
Cover of *Andy Warhol's Interview*, August 1976.

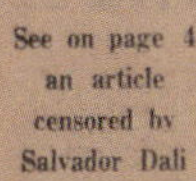
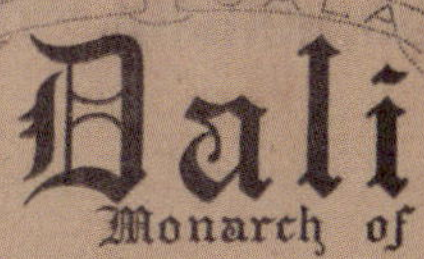
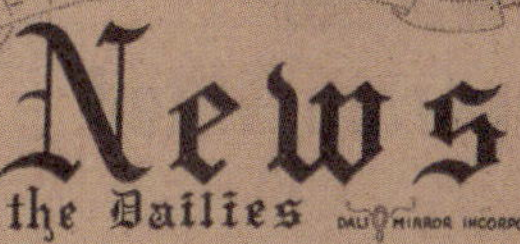

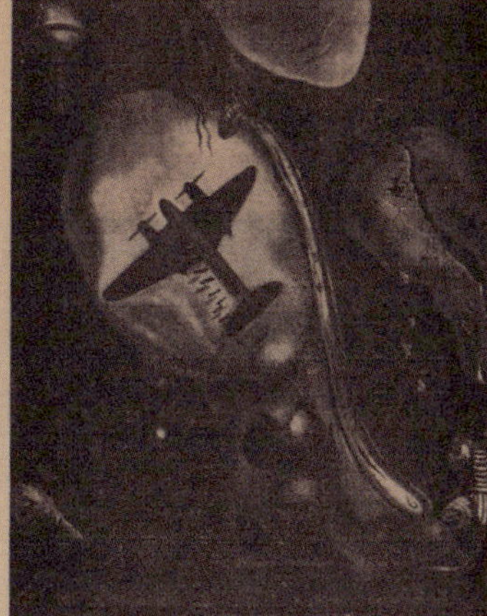
ATOMICA MELANCHOLICA
Recent painting by Salvador Dali.

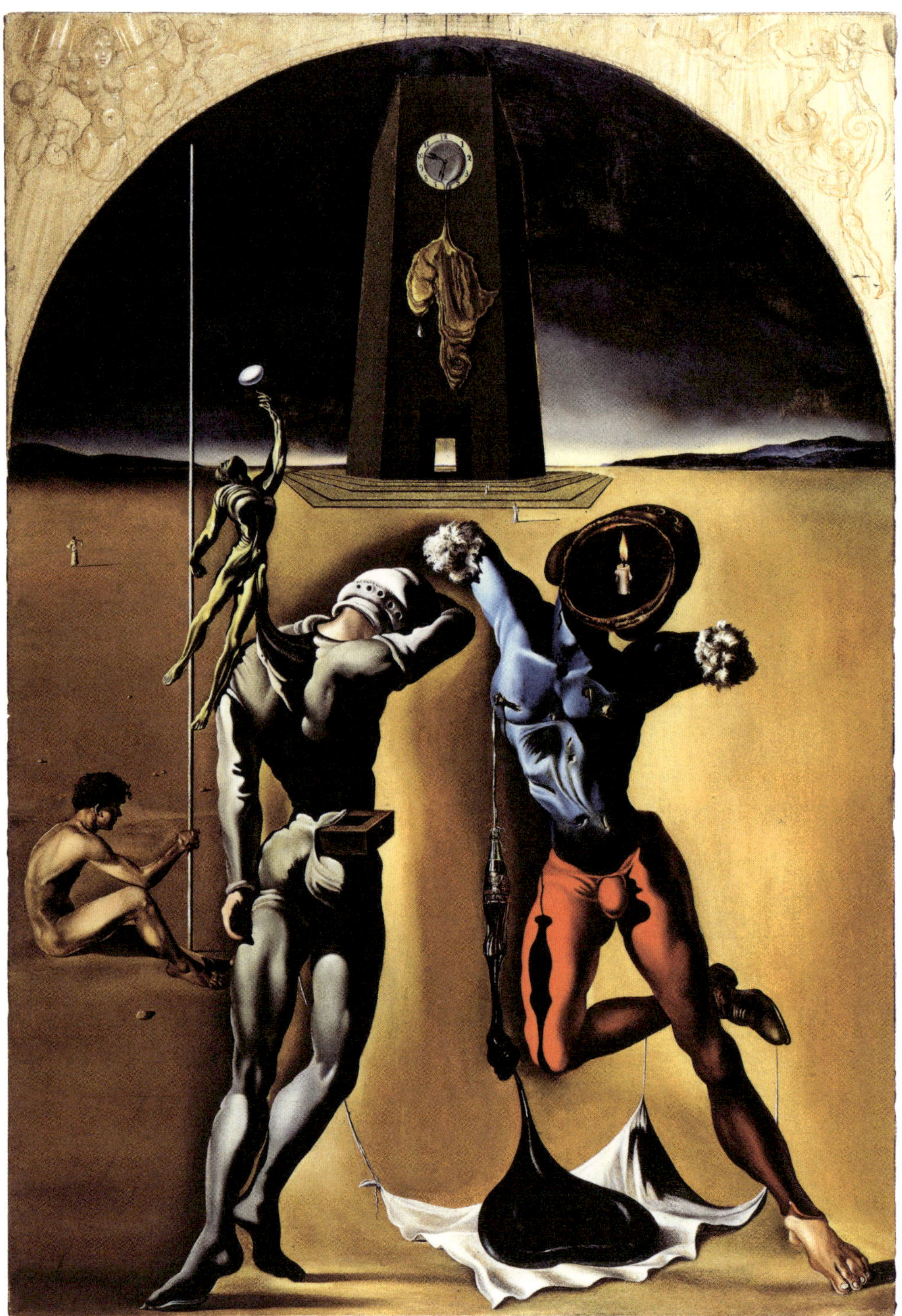

24
Salvador Dalí. *Poetry
of America (The Cosmic
Athletes)*, 1943. Oil on
canvas, 45²/₃ × 31¹/₁₀ in.
Town Hall of Figueres,
on permanent deposit
at the Fundació Gala-
Salvador Dalí, Figueres.

25
Andy Warhol. *Coca-Cola [3]*, 1962. Casein on cotton, 69 3/8 × 54 in. Private collection.

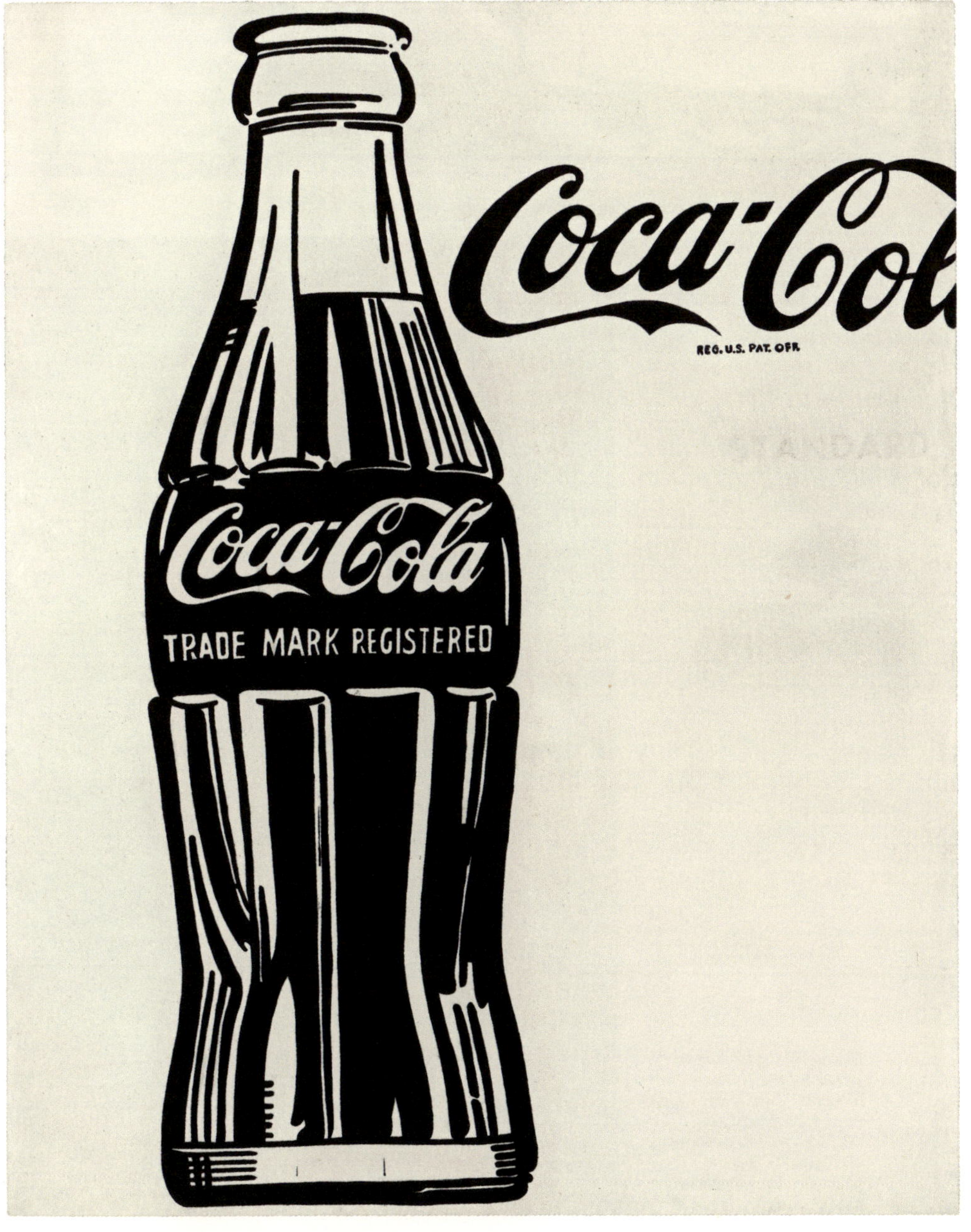

Coca-Cola
REG. U.S. PAT. OFR.
Coca-Cola
TRADE MARK REGISTERED

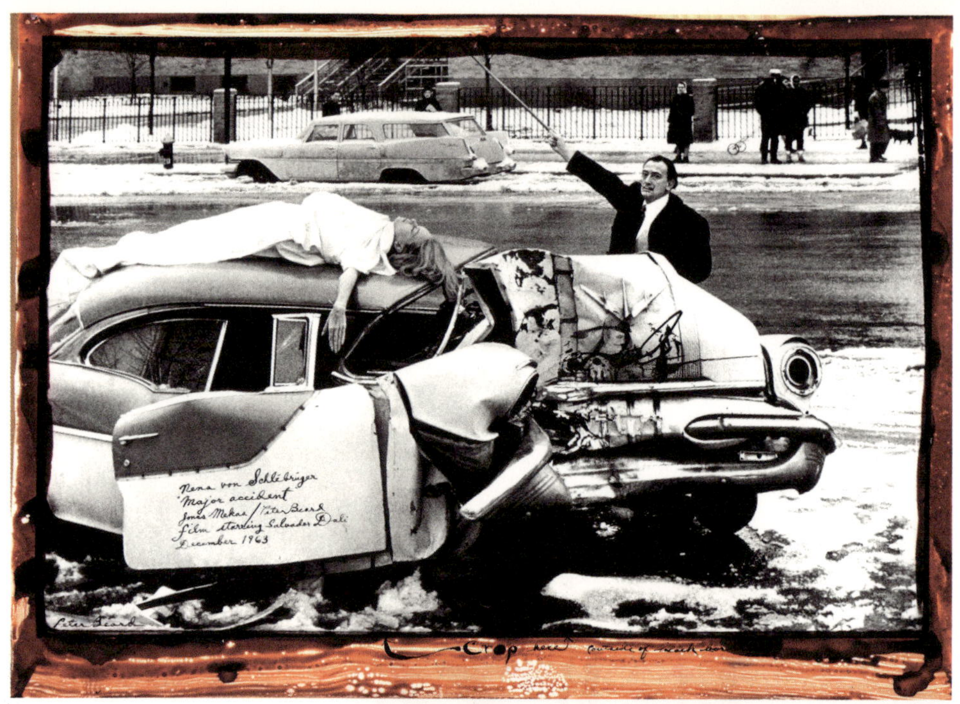

26
Peter Beard. *"Major Accident" with Dalí and Uma Thurman's Mother on 125th Street, December 1963.* Gelatin silver print with blood and ink.

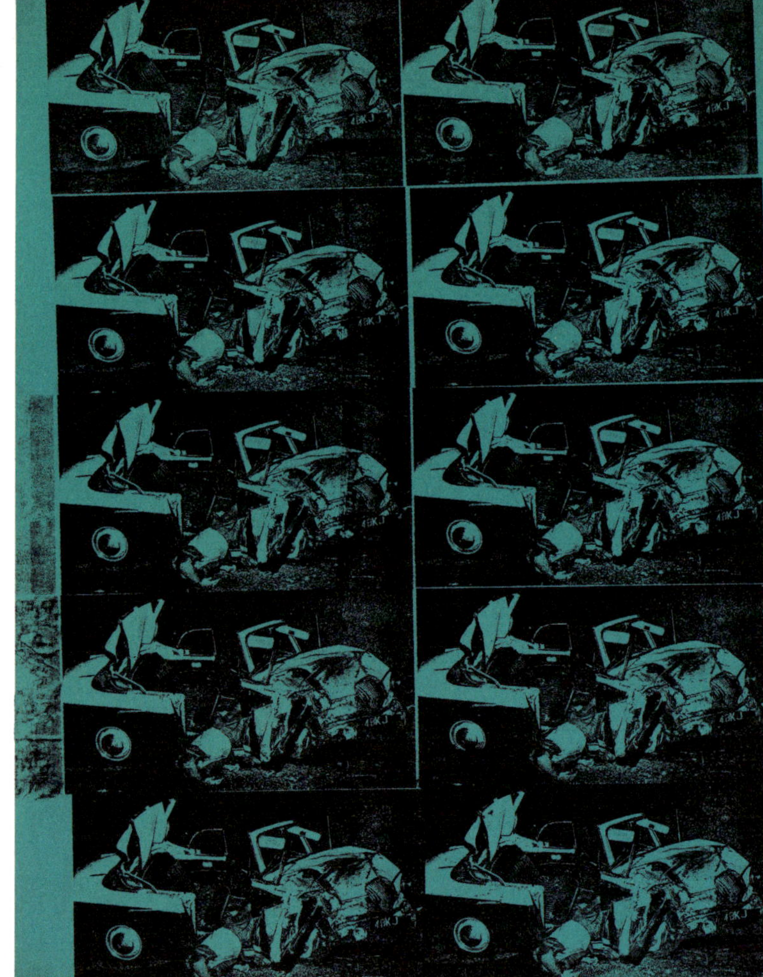

27
Andy Warhol. *Green Disaster #2 (Green Disaster Ten Times)*, 1963. Acrylic, silkscreen ink, and pencil on linen, 107 1/3 × 79 1/8 in. Museum für Moderne Kunst, Frankfurt am Main.

28
Andy Warhol. *Mao*,
1972. Acrylic, silkscreen
ink, and pencil on linen,
176 ½ × 136 ½ in. The
Art Institute of Chicago,
Mr. und Mrs. Frank G.
Logan Purchase Prize
and Wilson L. Mead funds.

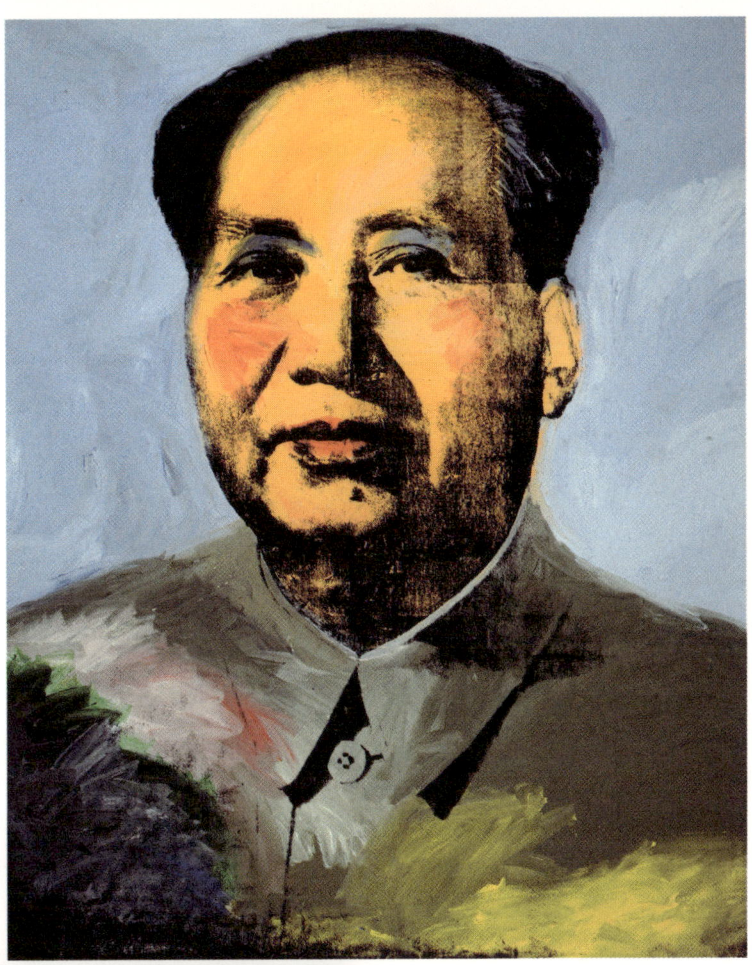

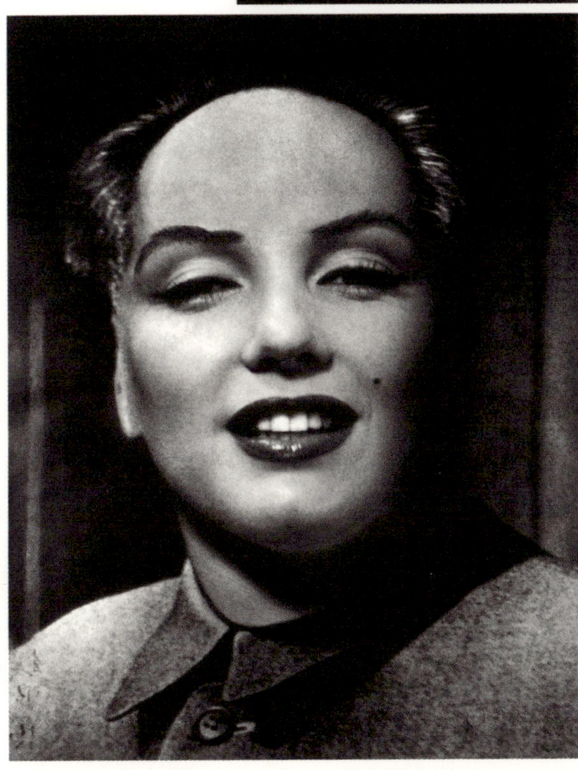

29
Philippe Halsman.
Mao Marilyn, 1967.

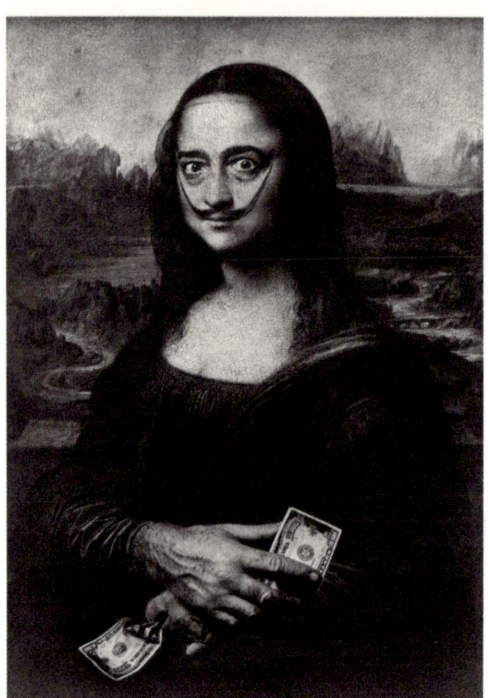

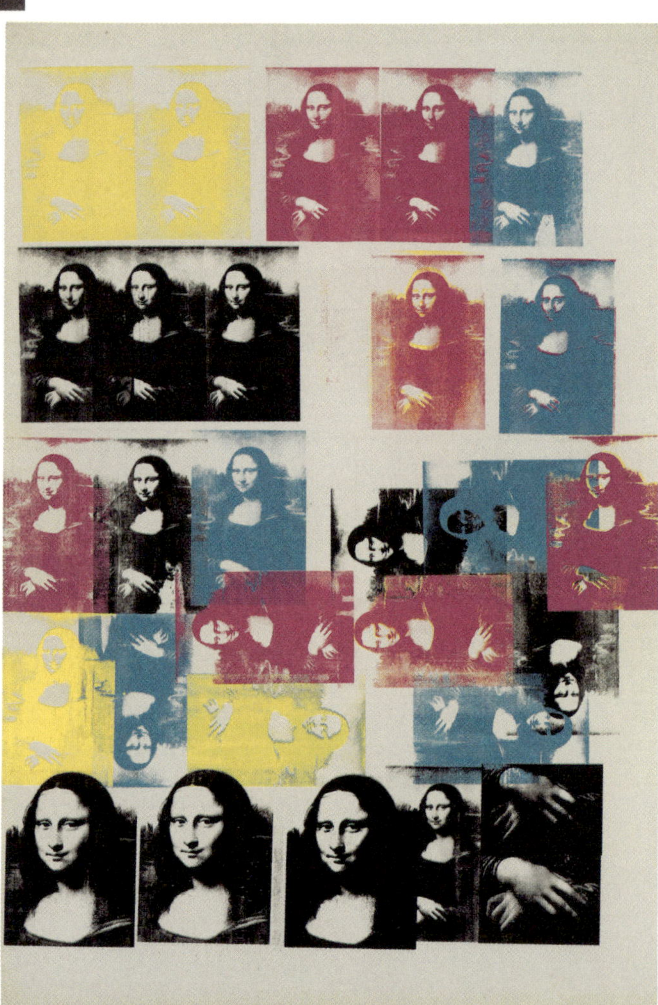

31
Andy Warhol. *Colored
Mona Lisa*, 1963. Silk-
screen ink and pencil
on linen, 126 × 82 1/4 in.
Private collection.

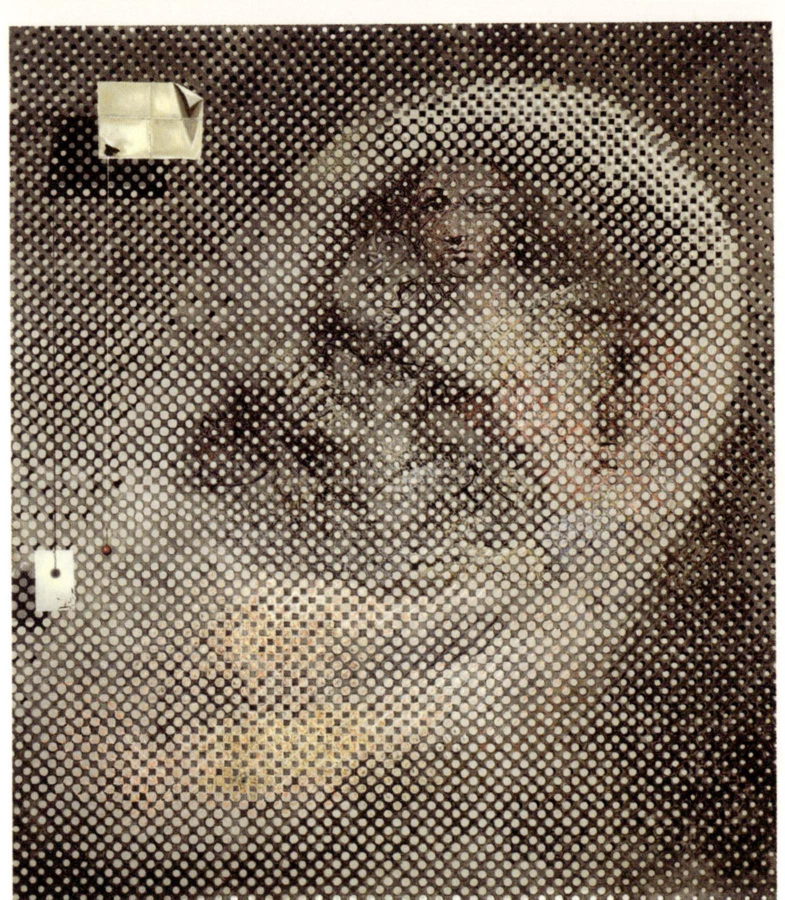

32
Salvador Dalí. *The Sistine Madonna (Quasi-grey picture which, closely seen, is an abstract one; seen from two meters is the Sistine Madonna of Raphael; and from fifteen meters is the ear of an angel measuring one meter and a half; which is painted with anti-matter; therefore with pure energy)*, 1958. Oil on canvas, 88⅞ × 75¼ in. The Metropolitan Museum of Art, New York, gift of Drue Heinz, in memory of Henry J. Heinz II, 1987.

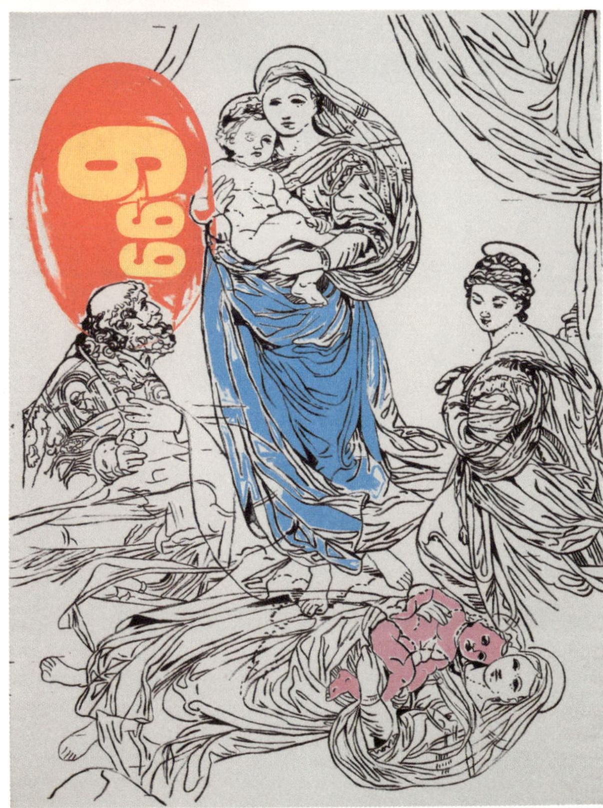

33
Andy Warhol. *Raphael Madonna—$6.99*, 1985. Acrylic and silkscreen ink on linen, 156¼ × 116 in. The Andy Warhol Museum, Pittsburgh.

34
Andy Warhol. *São
Schlumberger*, 1974.
Acrylic and silkscreen ink
on canvas, four panels,
40¼ × 40¼ in. each.
Private collection.

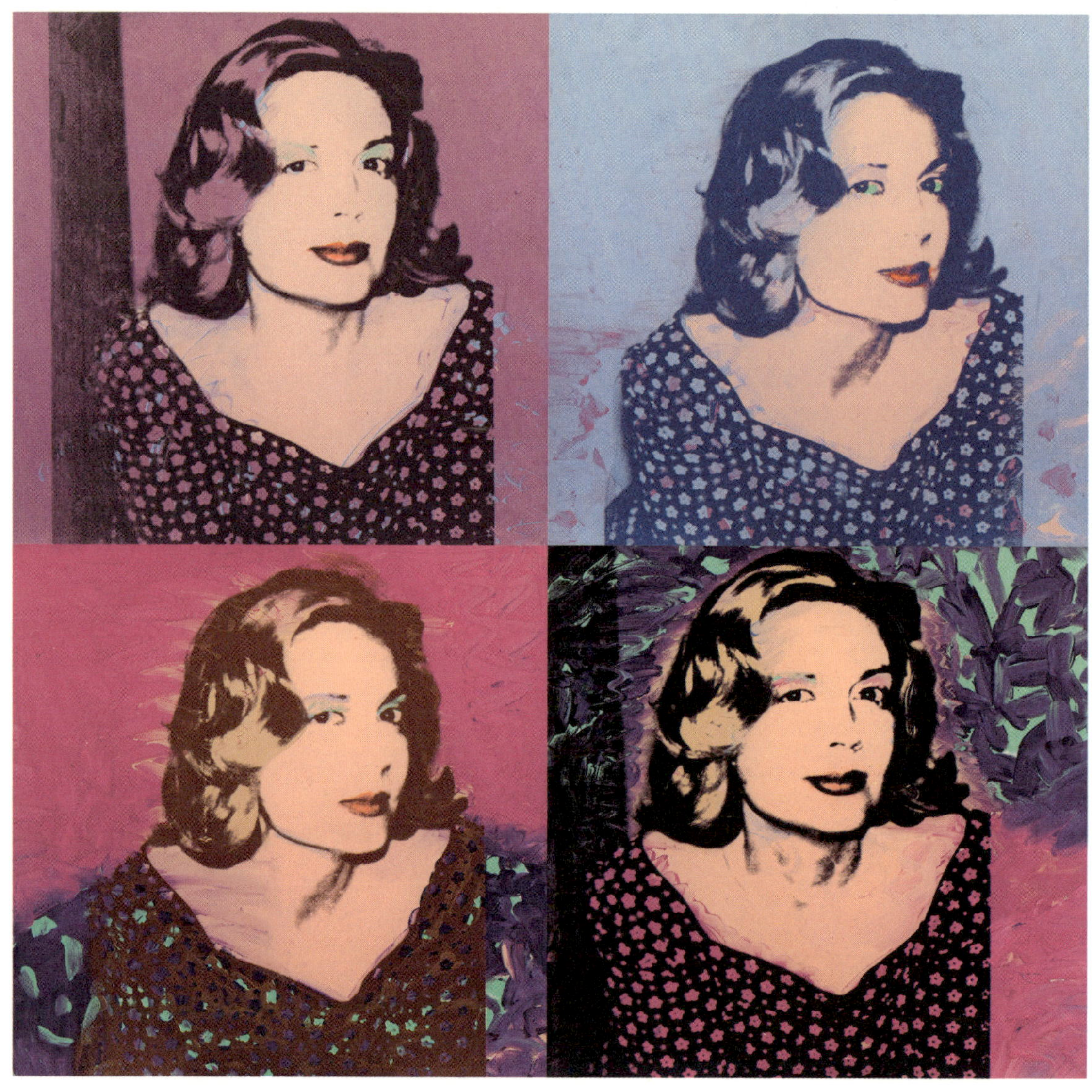

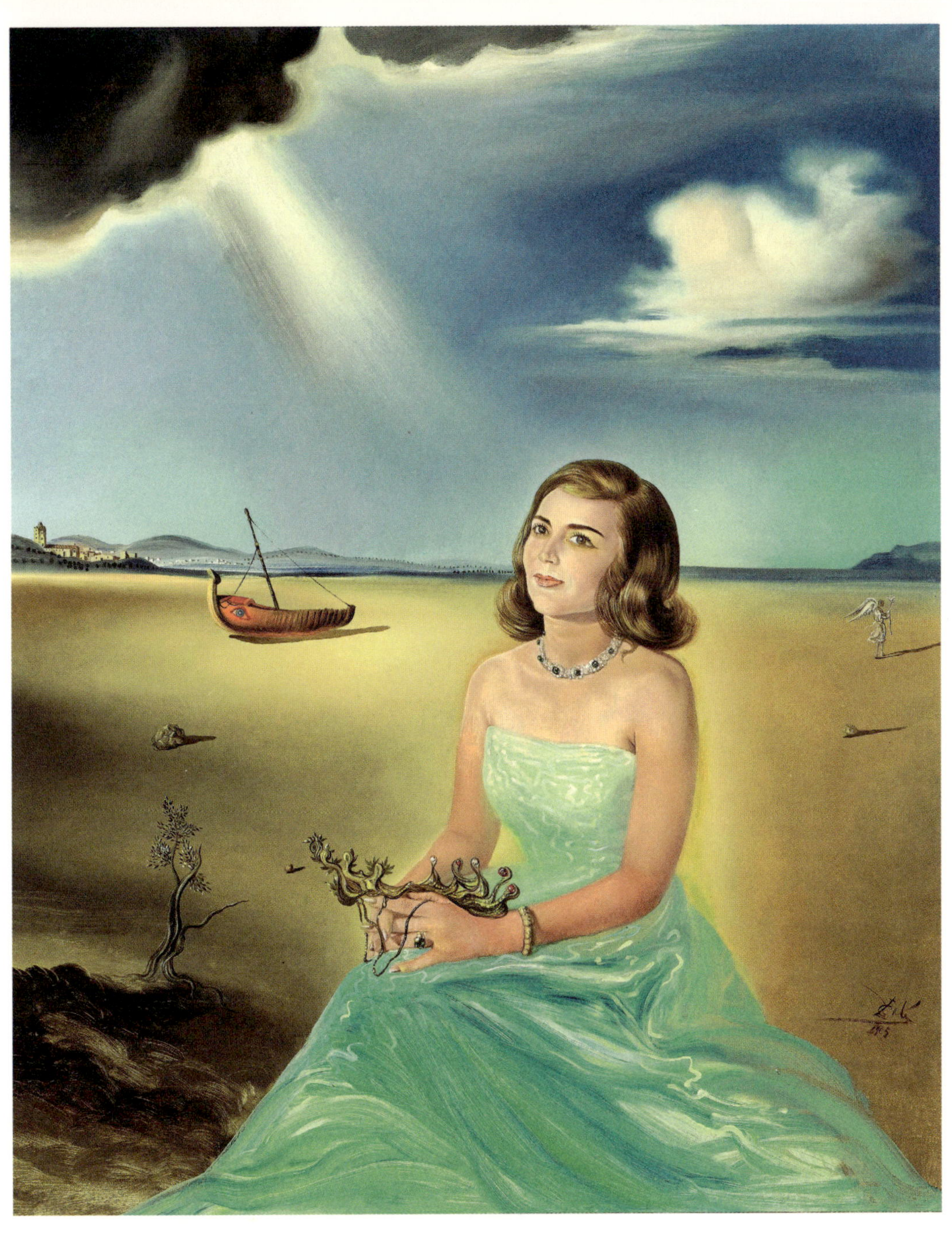

35
Salvador Dalí. *Portrait
de Madame Schlumberger*,
1963–65. Oil on canvas,
45 3/8 × 35 1/4 in.
Private collection.

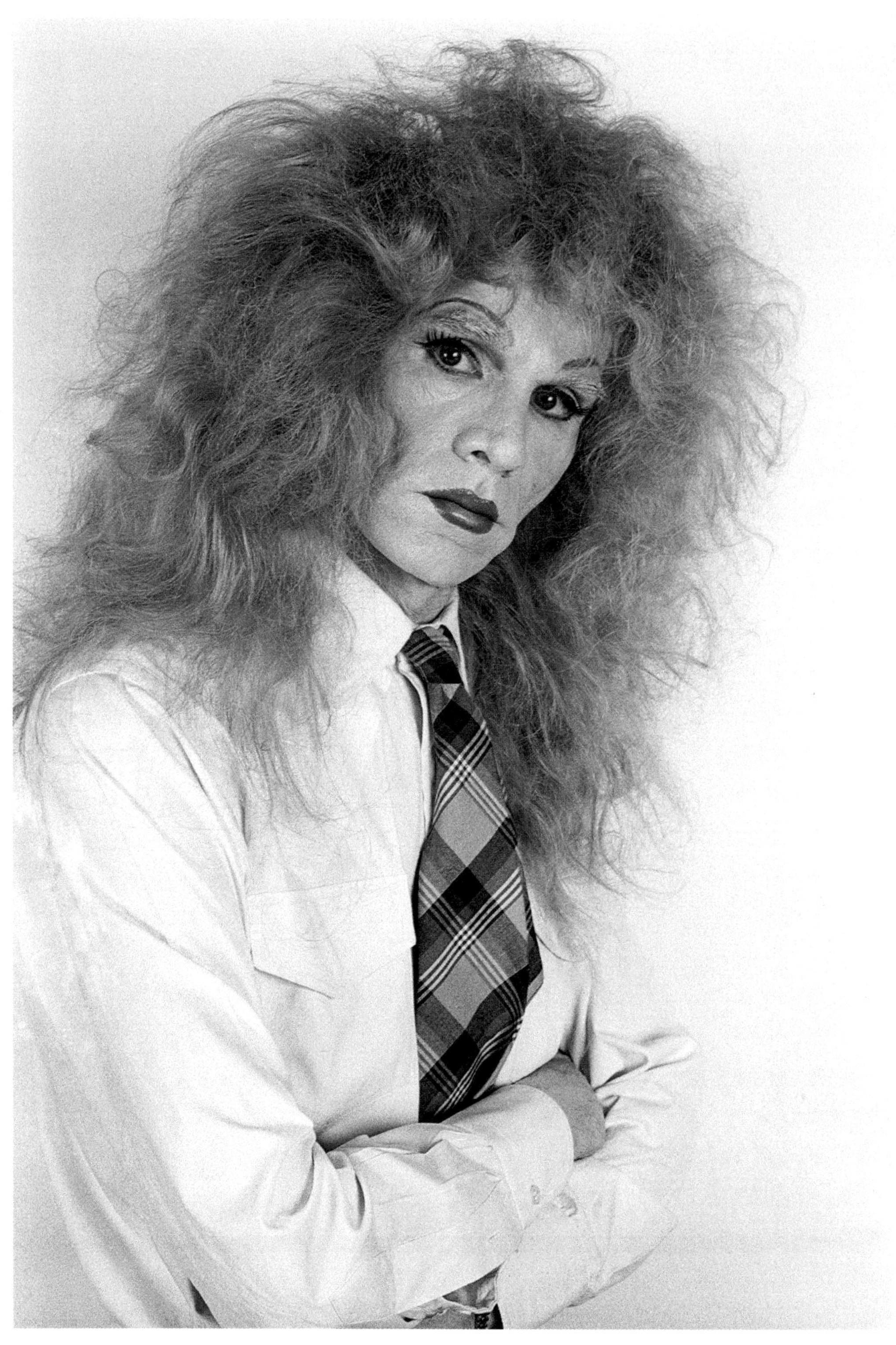

36
Christopher Makos.
Altered Image, 1981.

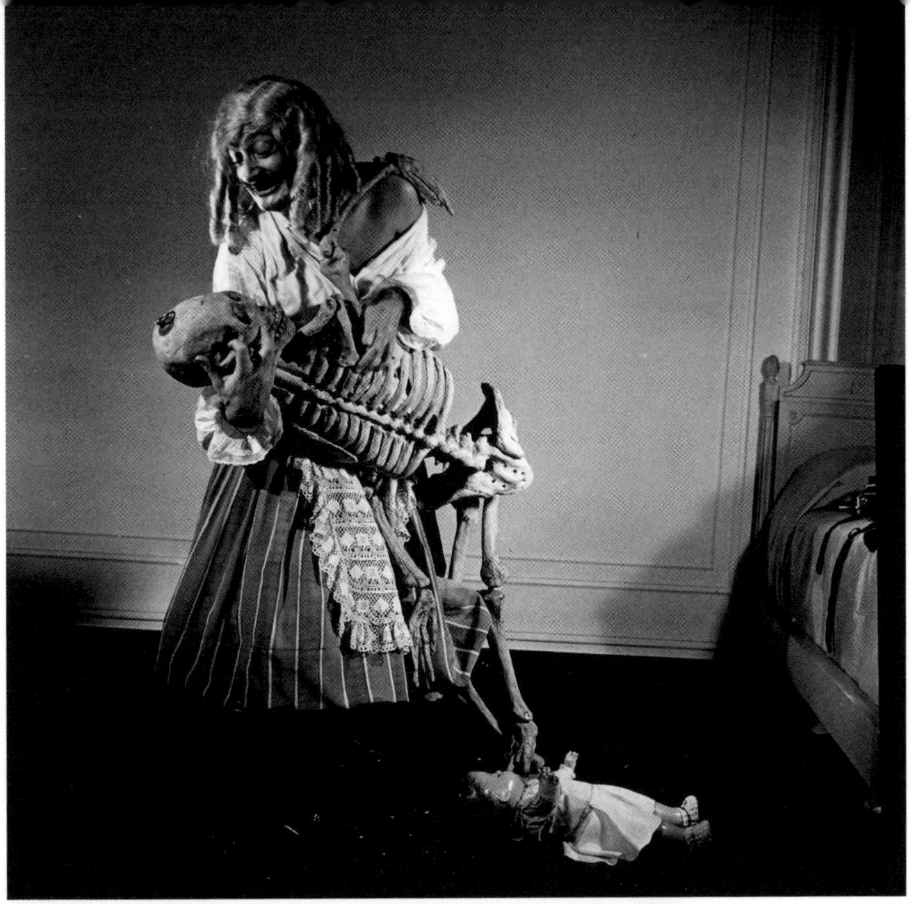

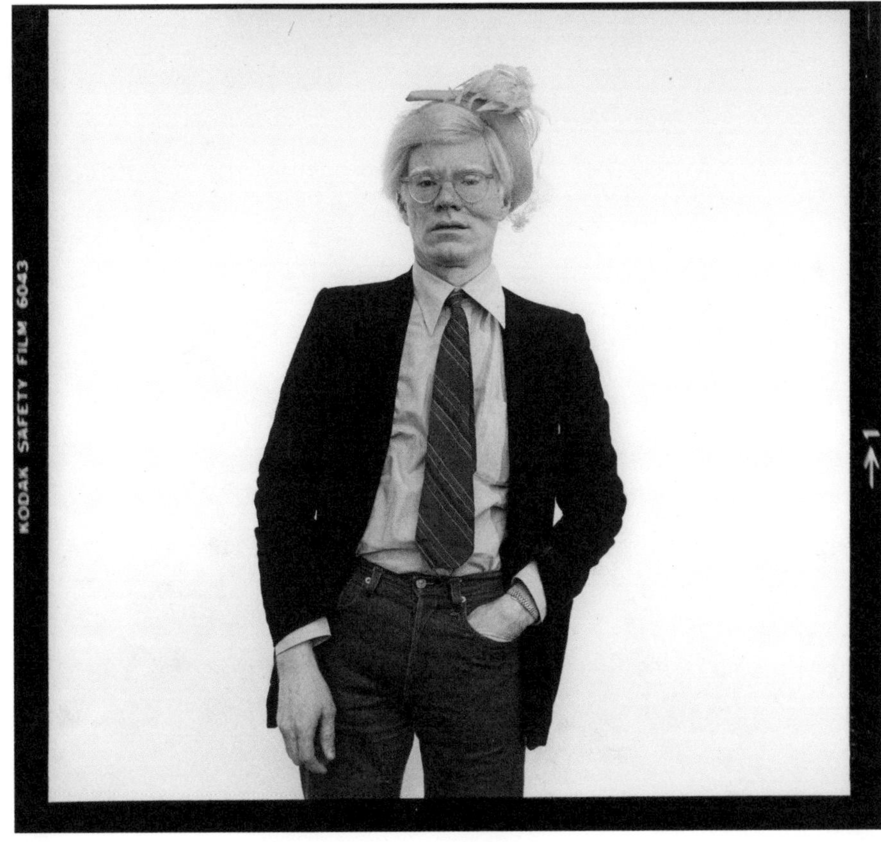

37
Salvador Dalí
dressed as
a maid, 1942.
Photograph by
Eric Schaal.

38
Paul Weiss. *American Beauties*, 1979.

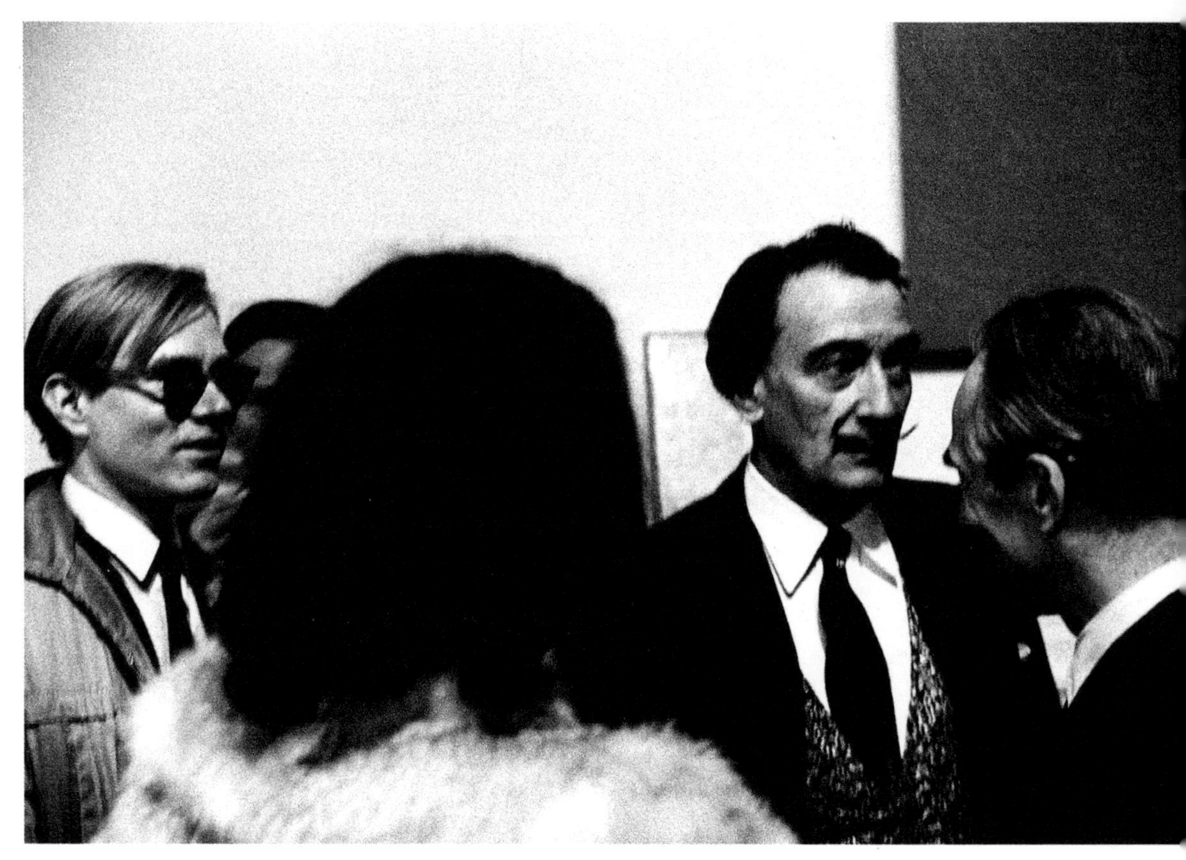

39
Andy Warhol, Ultra
Violet, Salvador Dalí,
and Leo Castelli at
a party held by Henry
Geldzahler, 1964.
Photograph by Billy Name.

"Wynn and Marilyn Fischbach, owner of the gallery, were so frightened the police would close the show for obscenity that before the opening Marilyn, Wynn, Donald Droll who ran the gallery, and I smoked a few joints and drank quite a lot of champagne to get through the evening."

Sally Chamberlain in an e-mail to the author on October 24, 2015.

"... that night I introduced Wynn to Gala. He was very excited to meet her."

William Rothlein in an e-mail on March 16, 2016.

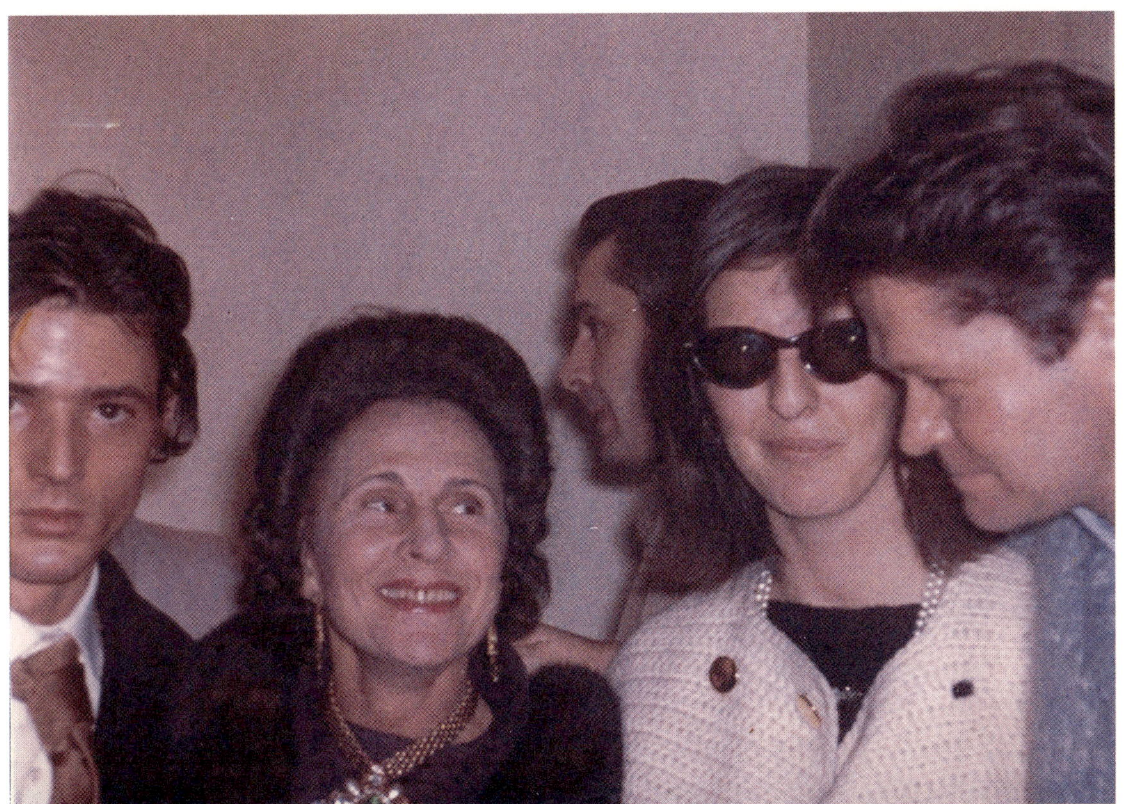

40
William Rothlein (Adil), Gala Dalí, Sally and Wynn Chamberlain at Wynn Chamberlain's opening at the Fischbach Gallery, February 1965.

41
Andy Warhol with
Salvador Dalí at the
St. Regis Hotel,
New York City, 1965.
Photograph by
David McCabe.

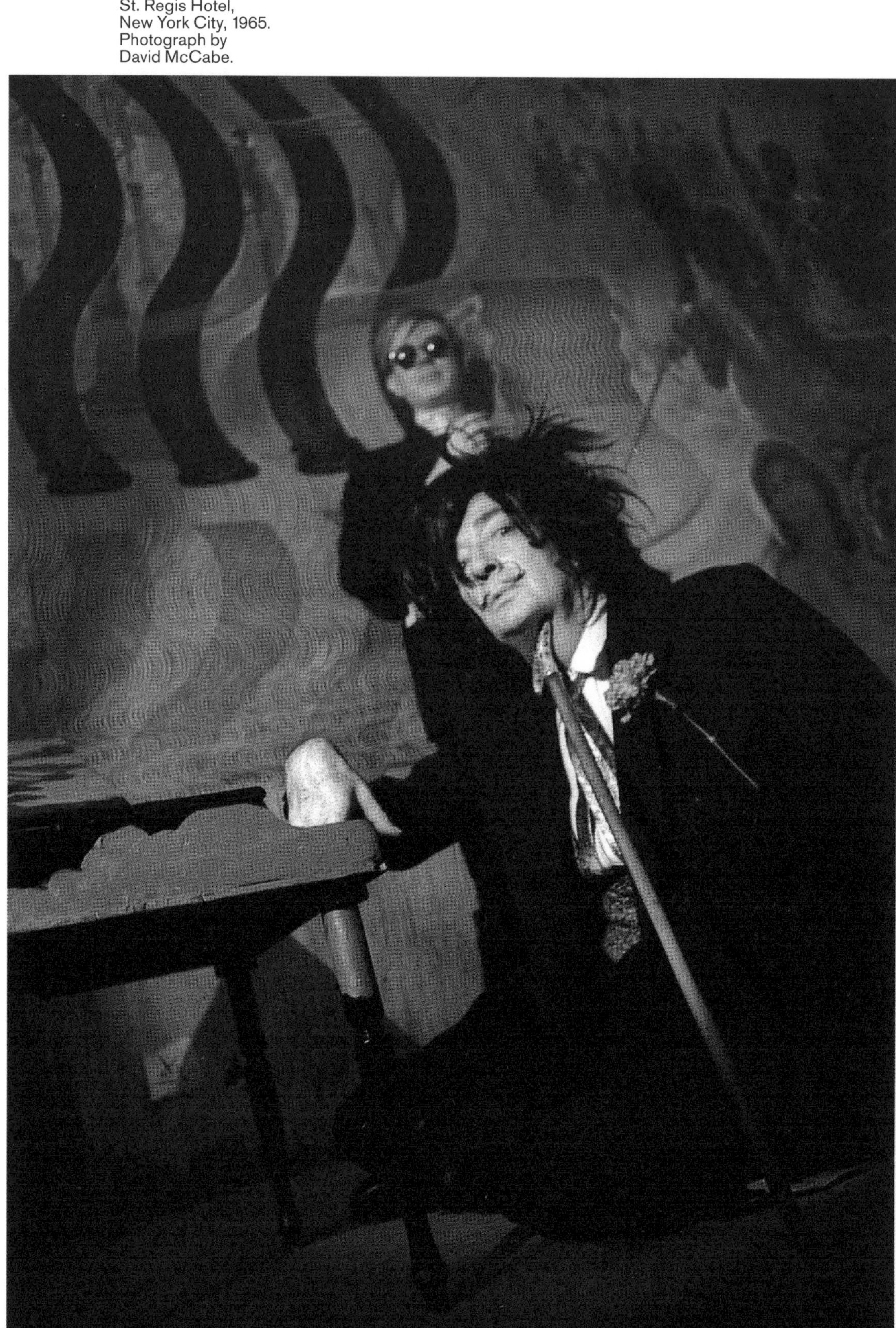

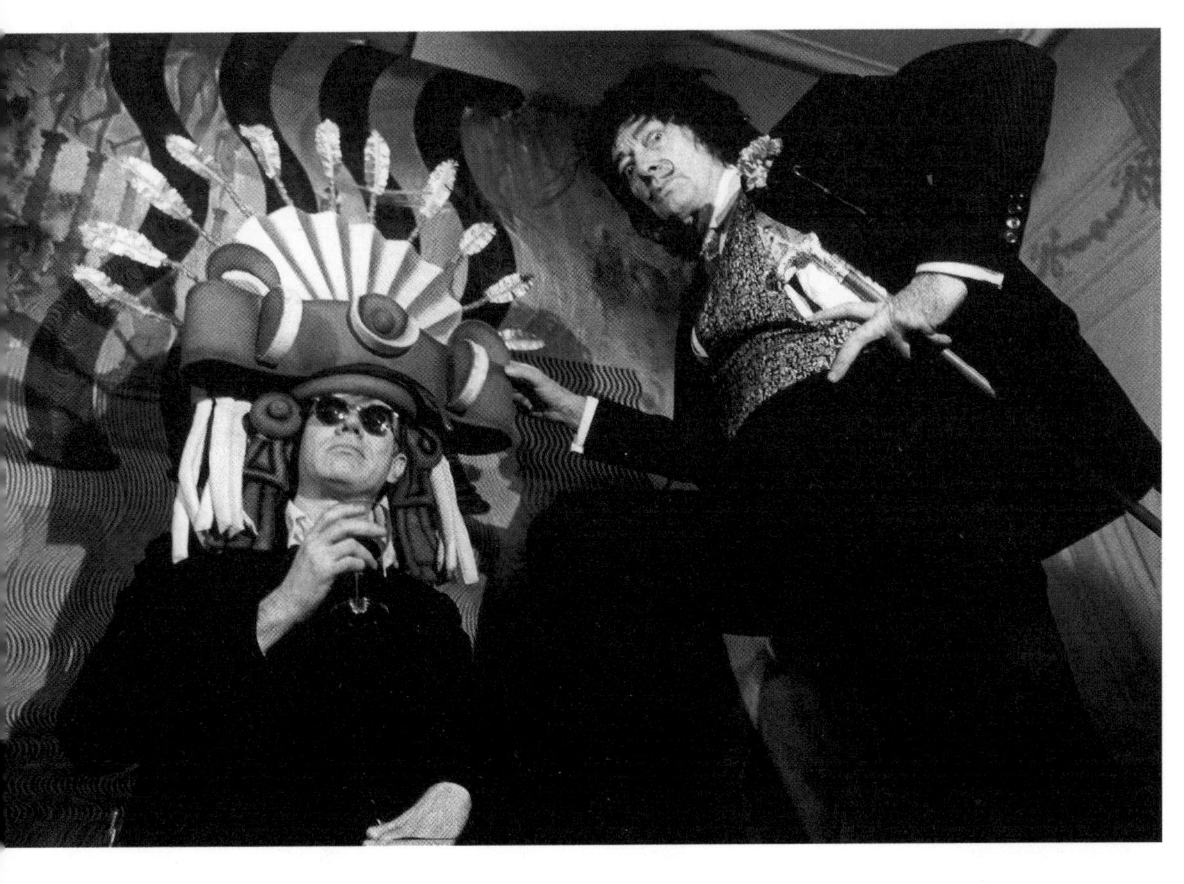

42
Andy Warhol wearing
an Inca Headdress
with Salvador Dalí at
the St. Regis Hotel,
New York City, 1965.
Photograph
by David McCabe.

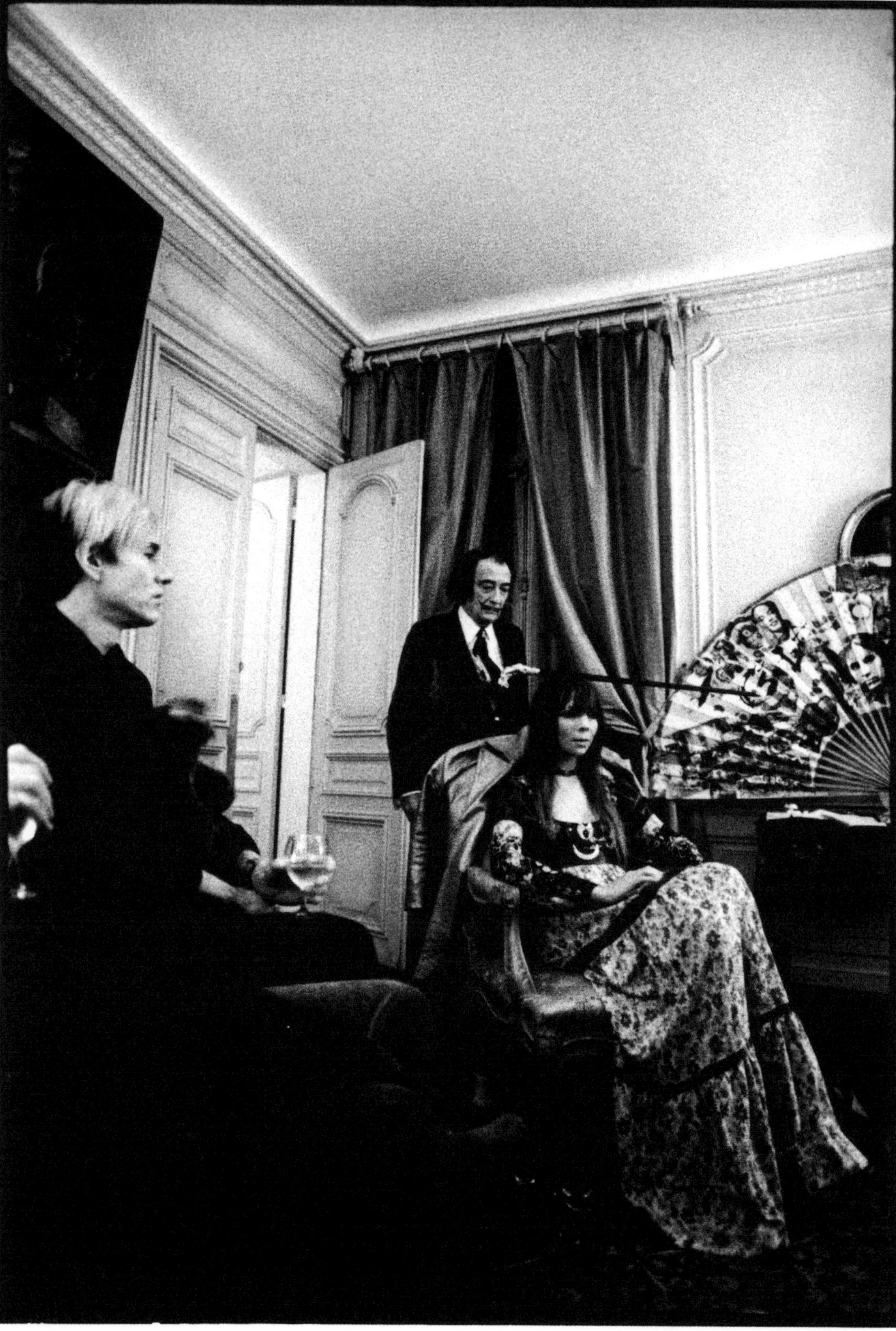

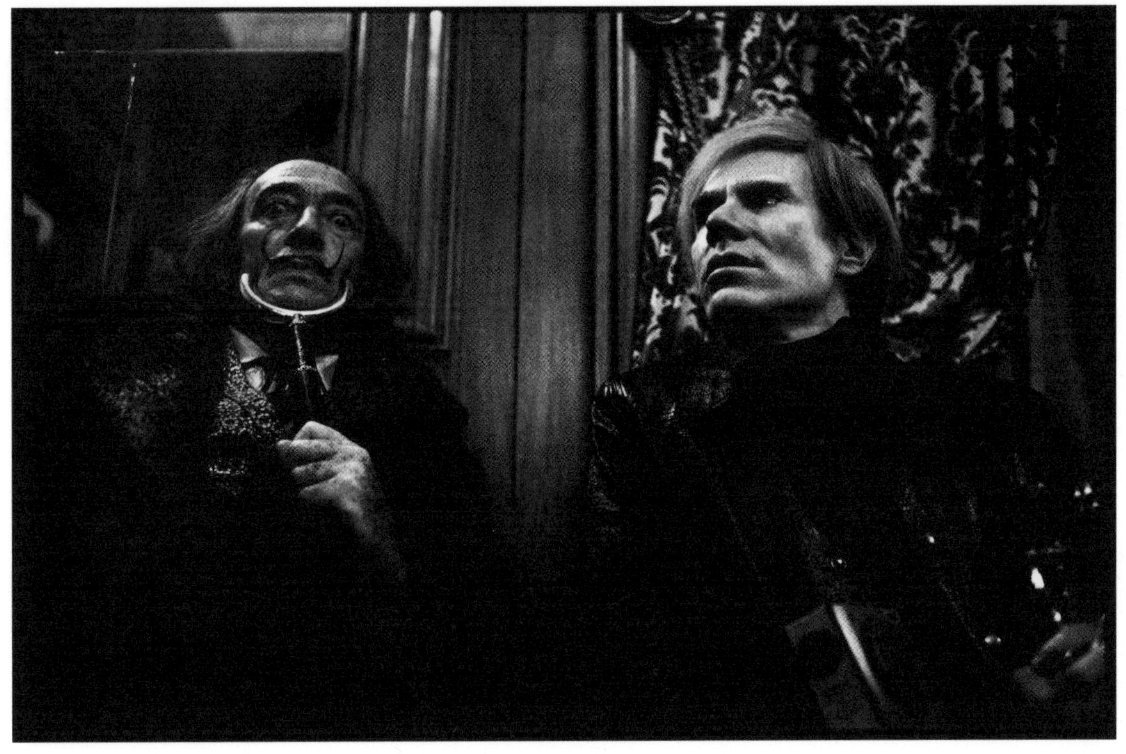

43
Andy Warhol,
Salvador Dalí, and
Penelope Tree,
1972. Photograph
by David Bailey.

44
Salvador Dalí and
Andy Warhol, 1972.
Photograph
by David Bailey.

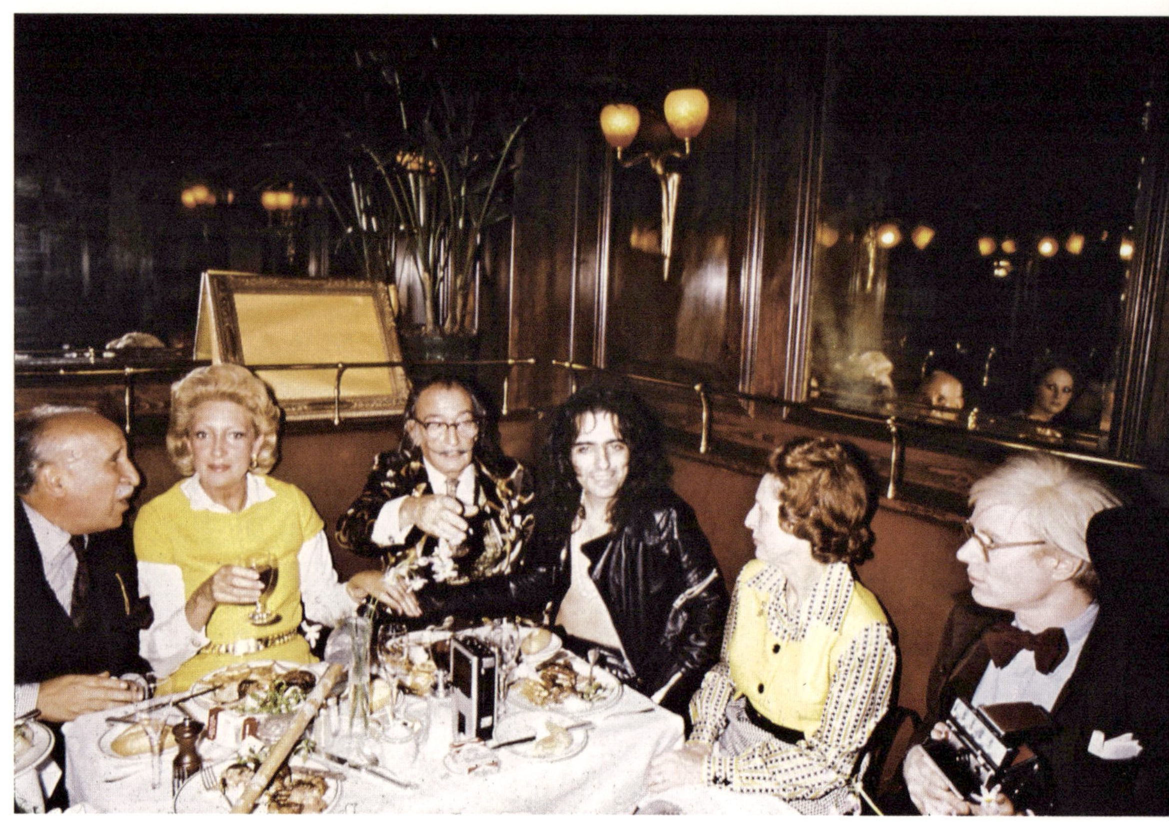

45
Lunch at La Goulue
in New York City, April 3,
1973. From left to right: unidentified
man, Nanita Kalaschnikoff
(Louis XIV), Salvador
Dalí, Alice Cooper,
Eleanor Morse, and Andy
Warhol. Photograph
by Robert Descharnes.

**"Dalí didn't always enjoy being photographed,
however, Warhol with his Polaroid camera interested him."**

Pandora in an e-mail to
the author on
March 19, 2016.

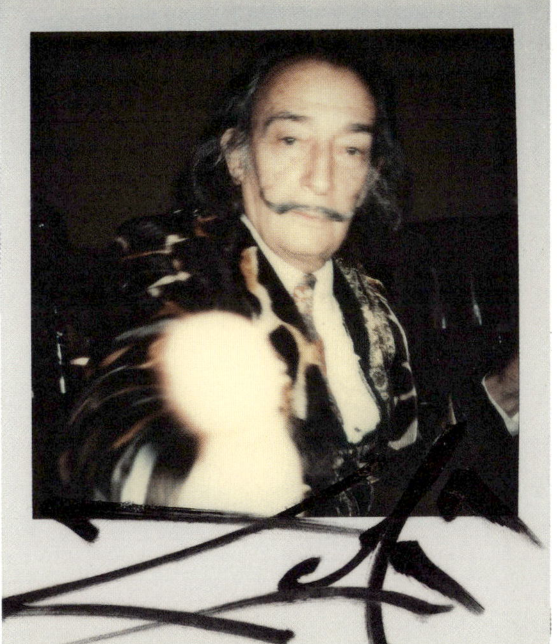

46
Andy Warhol. *Salvador Dalí*, 1973. Polaroid Type SX-70, 4¼ × 3½ in. The Museum of Fine Arts, Houston.

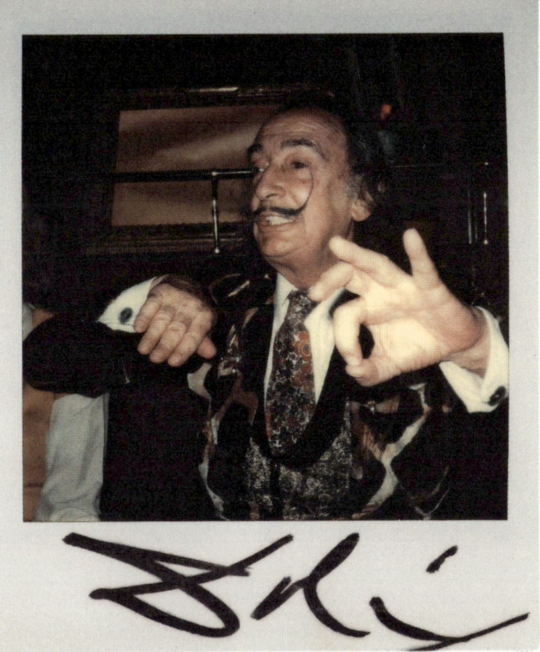

47
Andy Warhol. *Salvador Dalí*, 1973. Polaroid Type SX-70, 4¼ × 3½ in. The Museum of Fine Arts, Houston.

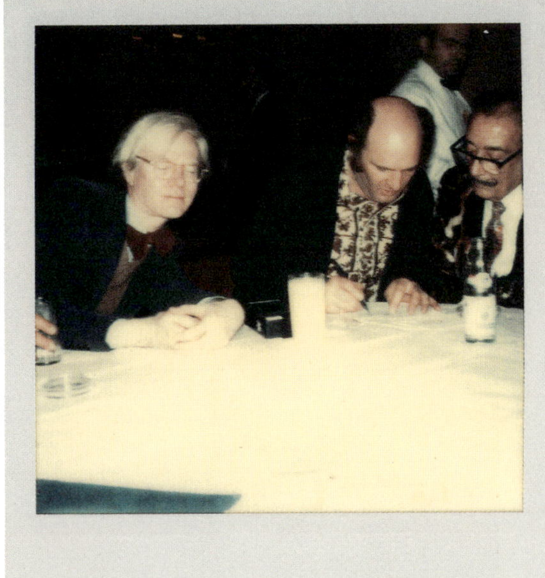

48
Andy Warhol. *Andy Warhol, Malcolm Morley, and Salvador Dalí*, 1973. Polaroid Type SX-70, 4¼ × 3½ in.

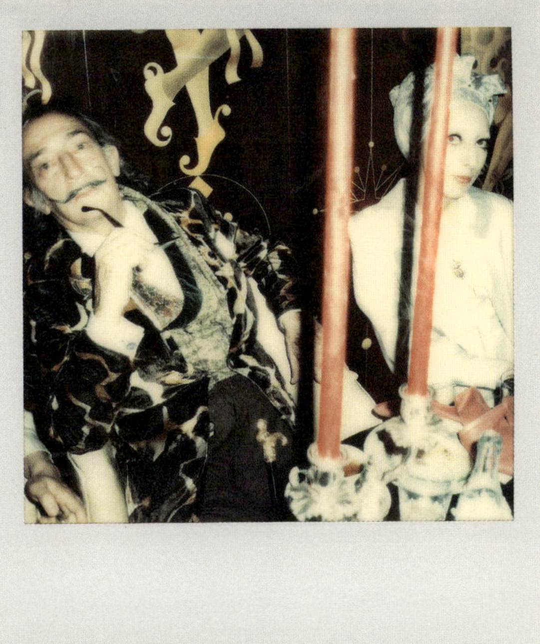

49
Andy Warhol. *Salvador Dalí and Pandora*, 1973. Polaroid Type SX-70, 4¼ × 3½ in.

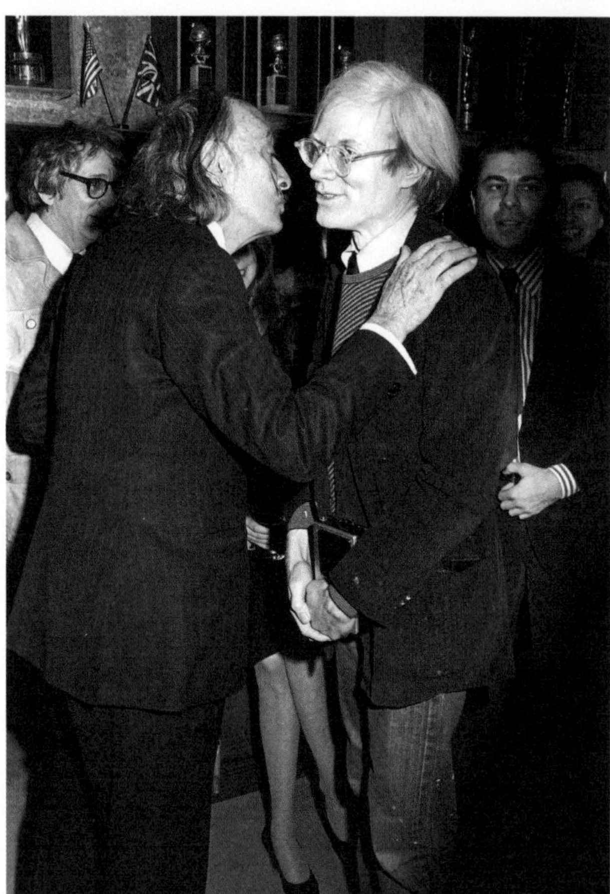

50
Salvador Dalí and Andy
Warhol at the *Shampoo*
Screening Party at
the Columbia Pictures
screening room on
Fifth Avenue in New York
City, February 10,
1975. Photograph by
Lynn Karlin.

51
Salvador Dalí and Andy
Warhol at the *Shampoo*
Screening Party at
the Columbia Pictures
screening room on
Fifth Avenue in New
York City, February 10,
1975. Photograph by
Lynn Karlin.

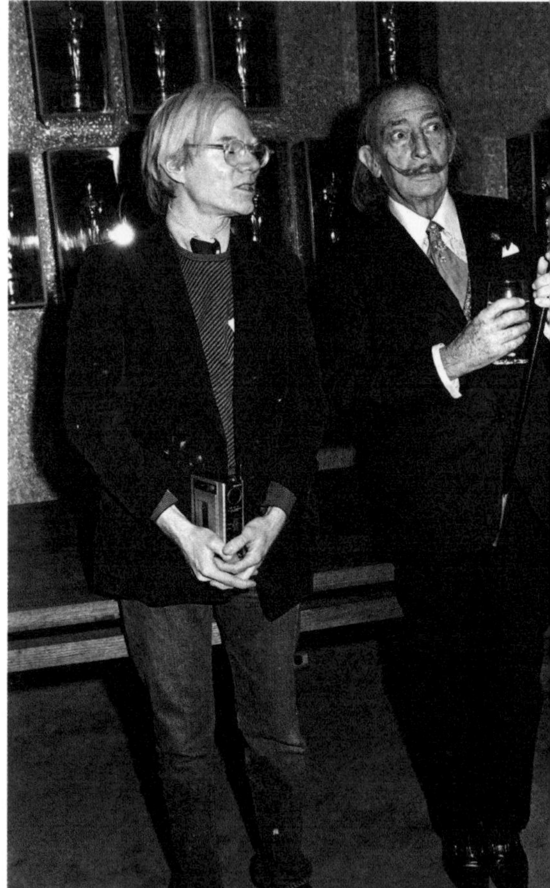

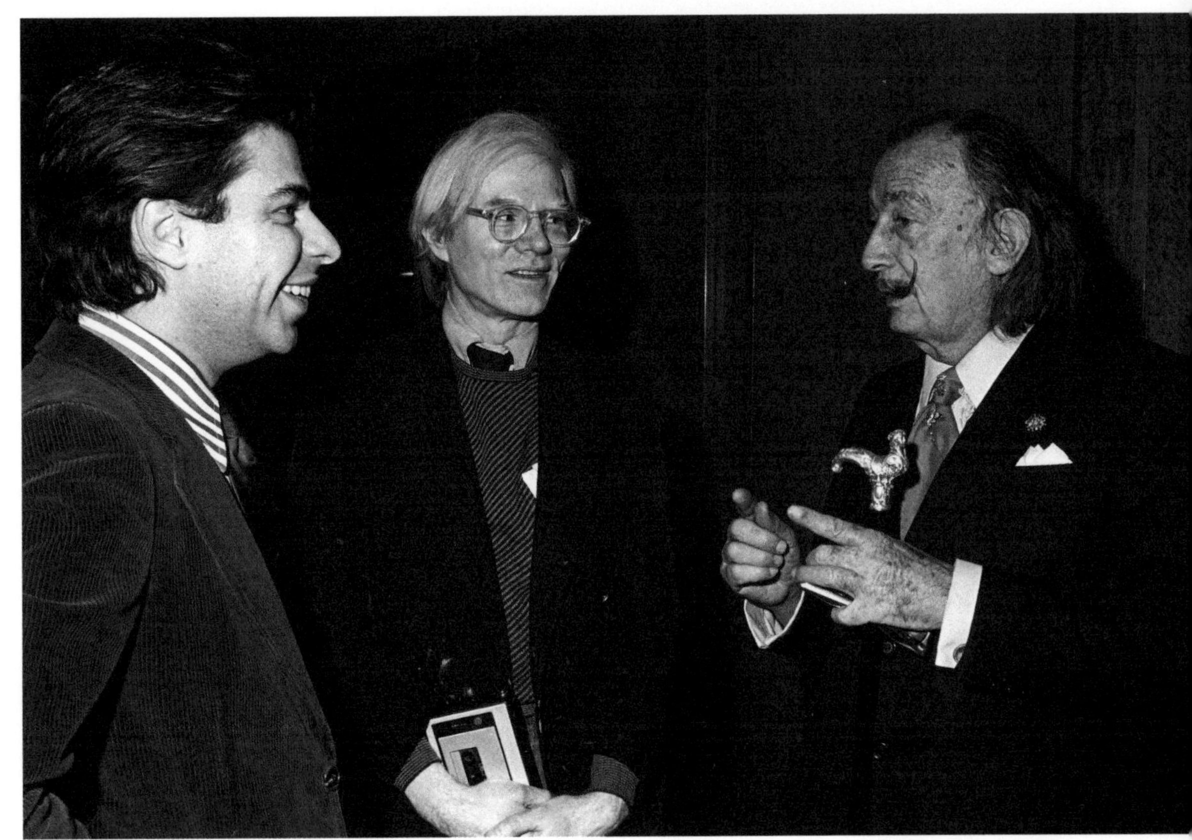

52
Bob Colacello, Andy
Warhol, and Salvador
Dalí at the *Shampoo*
Screening Party at the
Columbia Pictures
screening room on Fifth
Avenue in New York
City, February 10, 1975.
Photograph by Lynn Karlin.

"Conversations between Dalí and Andy were always entertaining." **Bob Colacello** in an e-mail to the author on April 26, 2016.

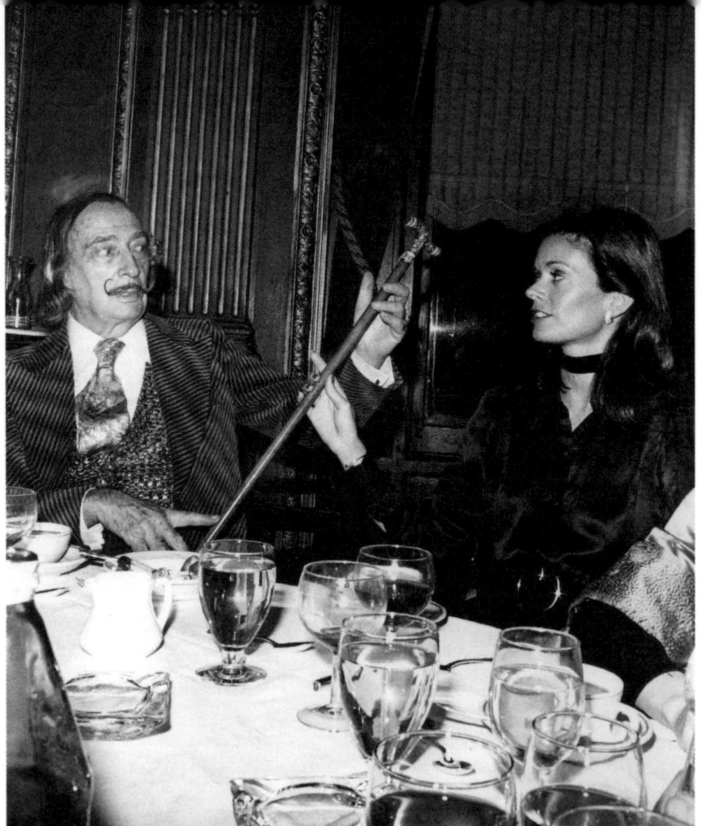

53
Salvador Dalí and
Shelley Wanger at the
Metropolitan Club in
New York City, March
17, 1976. Photograph by
Jade Albert.

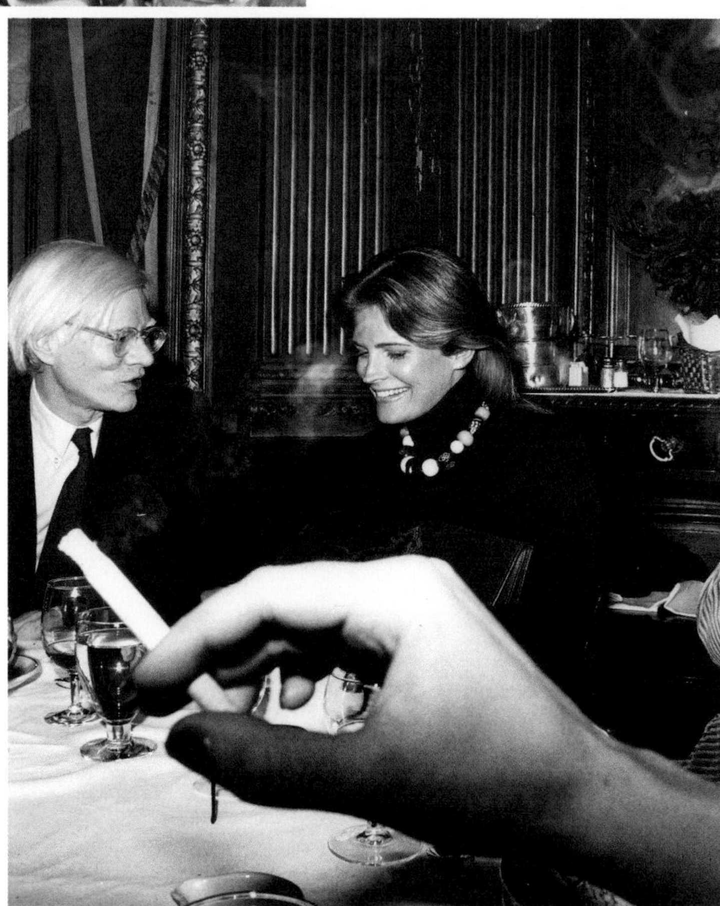

54
Andy Warhol and
Candice Bergen at
the Metropolitan
Club in New York City,
March 17, 1976.
Photograph by Jade
Albert.

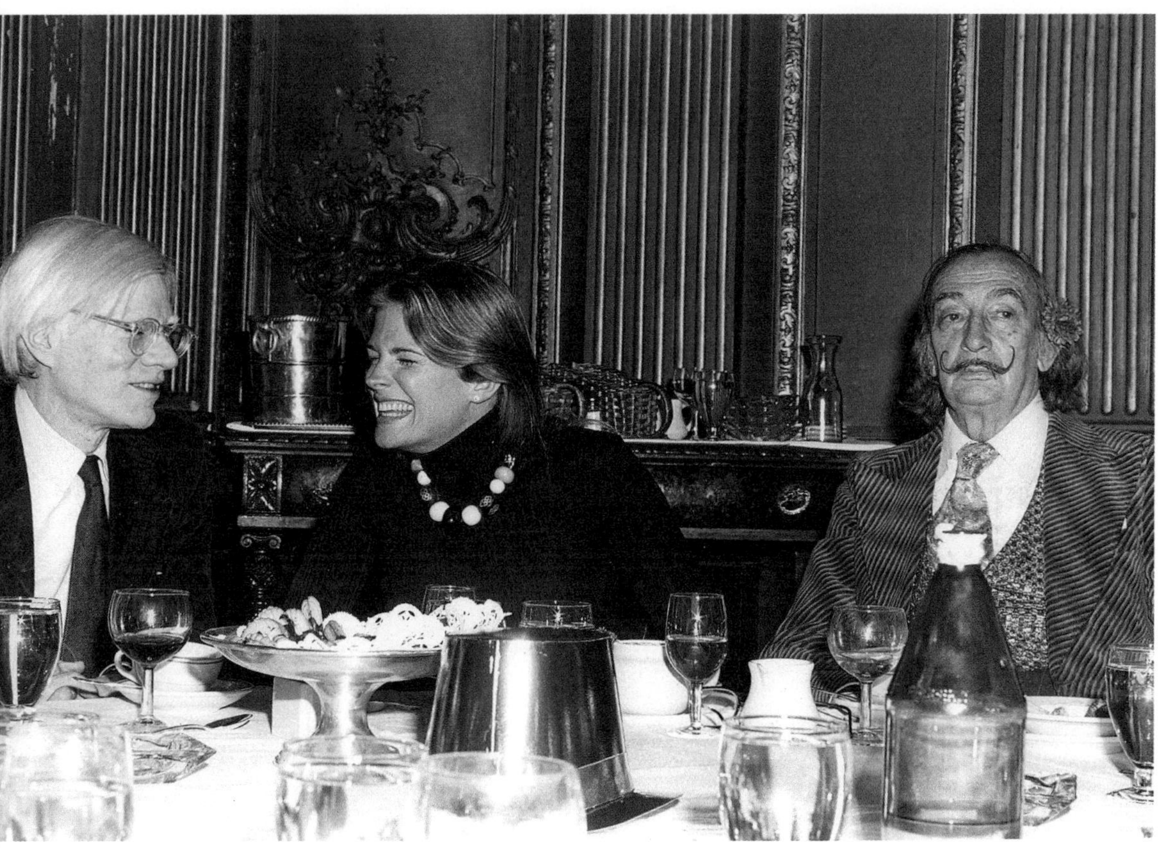

55
Andy Warhol, Candice Bergen, and Salvador Dalí at the Metropolitan Club in New York City, March 17, 1976. Photograph by Jade Albert.

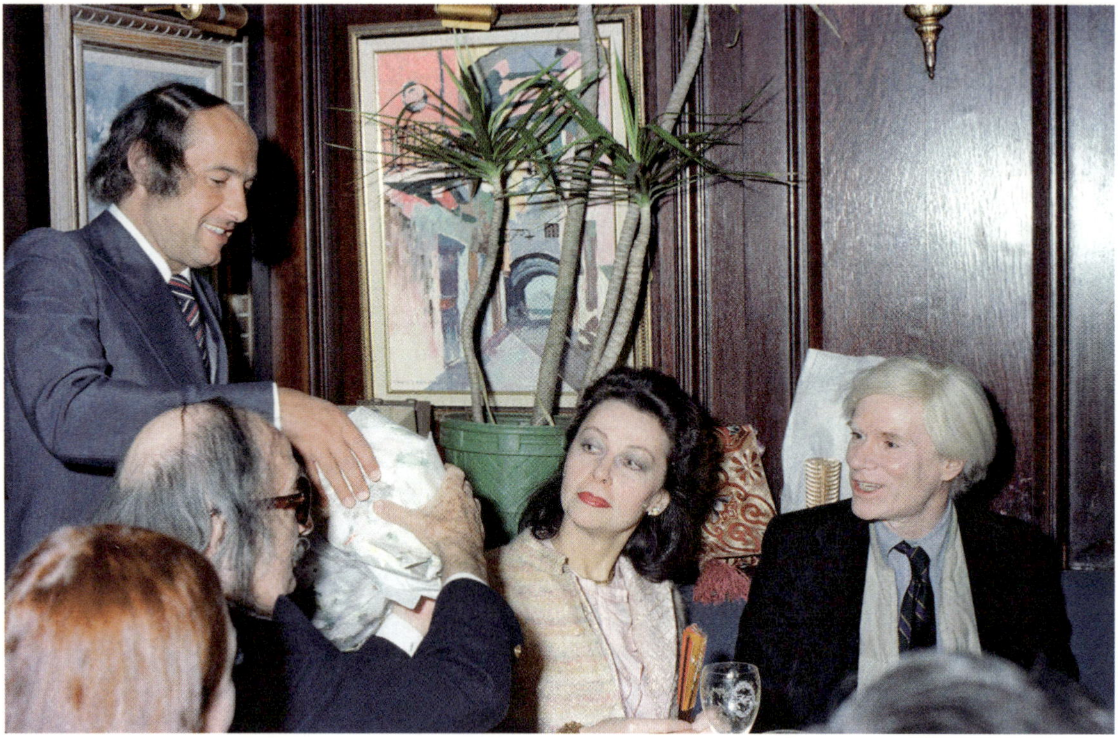

56
Lunch at Laurent in
New York City: Enrique
Sabater (standing),
Salvador Dalí, Ultra
Violet, and Andy Warhol,
March 19, 1978.
Photograph by Enrique
Sabater.

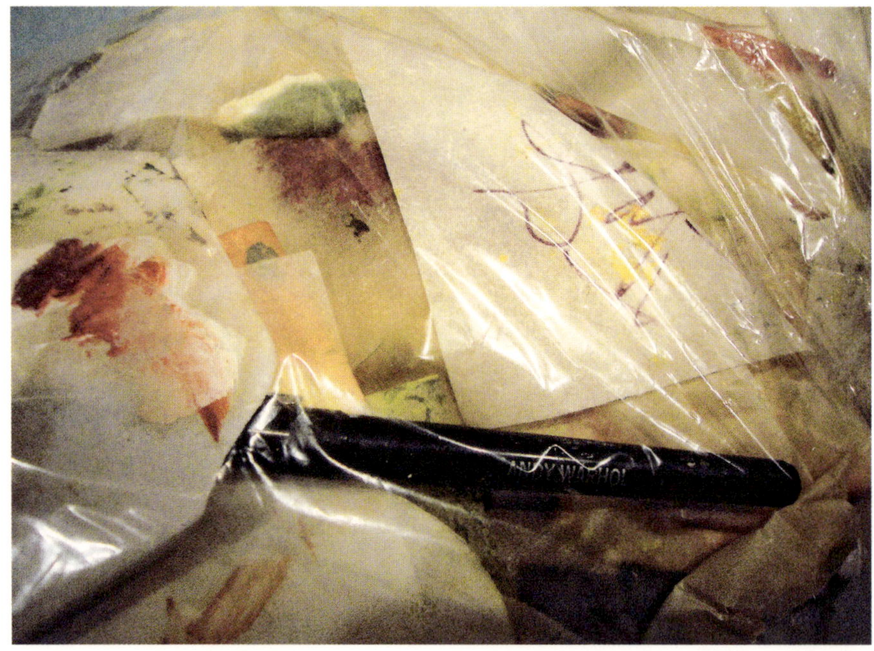

57
Salvador Dalí's gift
to Andy Warhol
on March 19, 1978.
Photograph
by Torsten Otte.

Afterword and Acknowledgements

The idea for this study was born after reading the highly amusing chapter dedicated to Salvador Dalí in *Andy Warhol's Exposures*. According to this 1979 volume, Andy Warhol met Salvador Dalí in the 1960s, when Ultra Violet brought him to the Factory. As a logical consequence, I contacted the late Ultra Violet and asked for an interview. This was my first interview for this study; it took place by telephone, on August 11, 2008. Two months later I met Ultra Violet at her studio in New York. One of the interesting things she said was that Dalí and Warhol were intrigued by each other. This truly inspired me, and led to the comprehensive interviewing of other contemporaries over the years. These interviews took place either face-to-face or by telephone. All interviews were recorded and transcribed, and in many cases, edited by those interviewed. In addition, several interviews took place by e-mail and a few by post. The final interview took place on March 11, 2016. I am profoundly grateful to all the wonderful people who took the time to share their memories for this study:

Jade Albert, April Ashley MBE, Marc Balet, Prof. Dr. Thomas Banchoff, François-Marie Banier, Benedetta Barzini, Peter Beard, Dr. Frances F. L. Beatty, Candice Bergen, Brigid Berlin, Bruno Bischofberger, Victor Bockris, Jack Bond, Lee Brooks, Stephen Bruce, Jean Jacques Bugat, Baron Roger de Cabrol, Howard R. Carr, Neke Carson, Sally Chamberlain, Wynn Chamberlain, Bettina Cirone, Bob Colacello, Prof. Dr. Rainer Crone, Leslie Curtis, Ronnie Cutrone, David Dalton, Robert Descharnes, Pierre Dinand, Manuel Donato Díez, Suzan Etkin, Ronald Feldman, Jeff Fenholt, Suzannah Fleming, Vincent Fremont, Edgar Froese, Prof. Ernst Fuchs, Ron Galella, Vito Giallo, John Giorno, Bruce Gowers, Cornelia Guest, Jonathan Guinness (3rd Baron Moyne), Pat Hackett, Irene Halsman, Bibbe Hansen, Nicholas Haslam, Robert Heide, Catherine Hesketh, Susan "Viva" Hoffmann, Jane Holzer, Gisela Hoveyda, Jasper Johns, Lynn Karlin, Ivan C. Karp, Leonard Kessler, Udo Kier, Sally Kirkland, Bernd Klüser, Lady Anne Lambton, Amanda Lear, Vera "Veruschka" Gottliebe Anna Countess von Lehndorff-Steinort, Dorothy Lichtenstein, Benjamin Liu, Lluís Llongueras, Roxanne Lowit, Christopher Makos, Gerard Malanga, Louis Markoya, Dr. Erich Marx, George Mason, Hans Mayer, Albert Maysles, David McCabe, Taylor Mead, Jonas Mekas, Heiner Meyer, Sylvia Miles, Mario Montez, Malcolm Morley, Chris Murray, Billy Name, Jeremiah Newton, Ivy Nicholson, Glenn O'Brien, Claes Oldenburg, Yoko Ono, Pandora, Philip Pearlstein, Elsa Peretti, Antoni Pitxot, Roger Prigent, Asha Puthli, John Reinhold, Gerhard F. Reinz, Nick Rhodes, Allan Rich, Sir John Richardson, James Rosenquist, William Rothlein, Chris Royer, Jörg Schellmann, Nena Thurman, Ingeborg Princess zu Schleswig-Holstein-Sonderburg-Glücksburg, Stephen Shore, Folker Skulima, Daniel Spoerri, Walter Steding, Jon Stevens, Harold Stevenson, Michael Ward Stout, Penelope Tree, Monique van Vooren, Joan Vehí, Ultra Violet, Santi Visalli, Geneviève Waïte, Louis Waldon, Shelley Wanger, James Warhola, Paul Warhola, Paul C. Warhola, Horst Weber von Beeren, Paul Weiss, Susan Whitaker, John Wilcock, Gigi Williams, William S. Wilson, Peter Wise, Holly Woodlawn, Mary Woronov, Jamie Wyeth, and Susi Wyss.

I would like to express my gratitude for the generous support provided by the Centre for Dalinian Studies at the Fundació Gala-Salvador Dalí in Figueres under the direction of Montse Aguer. My sincere thanks go to Bea Crespo and Lucia Moni.

It has been a privilege to do research at the archives of The Andy Warhol Museum in Pittsburgh with Warhol's *Time Capsules* as its keystone. I am grateful for the assistance of Matt Wrbican, chief archivist at the museum. I would also like to thank three other members of the museum staff for providing me with helpful information: Greg Pierce, associate curator of film and video; Greg Burchard, senior manager, rights, reproductions and photographic services; and Erin Byrne, lead cataloguer at the museum archives.

I also owe a great deal to Michael Dayton Hermann, director of licensing at The Andy Warhol Foundation for the Visual Arts, Inc., in New York.

I would like to thank the late Callie Angell, adjunct curator, as well as Claire K. Henry, senior curatorial assistant, of The Andy Warhol Film Project at the Whitney Museum of American Art in New York for their support.

It has been a pleasure to work with Scheidegger & Spiess, and I thank them for enthusiastically embracing the publication of this book. I am grateful to the publisher, Thomas Kramer, and the chief editor and project manager, Cornelia Mechler, as well as the creative Dalí & Warhol project team, including Karoline Mueller-Stahl, Lynne Kolar-Thompson, Lisa Rosenblatt, Charlotte Eckler, and Lisa Schons. My recognition also extends to 2×Goldstein+Fronczek for the creative design of this book.

My thanks to all who assisted me in the project in different ways, including anyone inadvertently missing from this list:

Susan K. Anderson, Christina Apostolaki, Carey Ascenzo, Jeanine Barone, Nejma Beard, Steve Bello, Jean-Paul Biondi, Lesley M. M. Blume, Reiner Boller, Jimmy Camicia, Ruth Carreras, Sean Carrillo, Sam Chamberlain, Sharon Cho, Susan Cipolla McCabe, Ron Clark, Beverly Coe, Gary Comenas, Dr. Jack Cowart, James Dagon, Vishnu Dass, Lowina Debowski, Nicolas Descharnes, Mike Dibb, Shelly Dunn Fremont, Richard L. Feigen, Víctor Fernández, Ellen Fisher Turk, Greg Frank, Muriel Fritz, Bianca Froese-Acquaye, Angelika Fuchs, Anni Fuchs, Samo Gale, Anne Gans, Ingeborg Gayda, Ian Gibson, John Gilman, Hervé Gloaguen, Gianfranco Gorgoni, Rachel Graham, Sebastian Guinness, Sara Gunasekara, Craig Highberger, Marlies Jackson, Jessica Kitz, Selina Lamberti, Andrew Lee, Joanna Ling, Silvia Lüdi-Sokalski, Peter Marino, Ricard Mas Peinado, Ann Marshall, Alex McCann, Anthony Miller, Carlos Miragaya, Elizabeth Murray Finkelstein, Lithgow Osborne, Stefano Palumbo, Linda Peitz, Dr. Meike Pfaff, Silvia Reissner, Marcia Resnick, Laura Rubin, Amanda Season Keeley, David Rickett, Katherine Robinson, Yann Saunders, Manuela Scheidler, Thomas Schröder, Mario Siegel, Stephen Snyder, Eric Sundermann, Michael Tighe, Michael Van Horne, Benjamin Whitaker, Susan Yung, and Enrique Esteban Zepeda.

Special thanks to my partner, Mike Deppe, for his support in many fields and his creative ideas.

Finally, I want to express my gratitude to my parents, Ingrid and Hubert Otte, who have provided encouragement and support. My father, Hubert Otte, died during the work on this book; it is dedicated to his memory.

Torsten Otte
Berlin,
April 2016

Torsten Otte is an attorney as well as an art historian, and the author of a biography of Salvador Dalí. He lives in Berlin.

Bibliography

1
Catalogues Raisonnés

Salvador Dalí

Descharnes, Robert, and Nicolas Descharnes. *Dalí: Le dur et le mou – Sculptures & objets.* Azay le Rideau: ECCART, 2003. Print.

Field, Albert. *The Official Catalog of The Graphic Works of Salvador Dalí.* Astoria, New York: The Salvador Dalí Archives, 1996. Print.

Fundació Gala-Salvador Dalí. *Salvador Dalí Catalogue Raisonné of Paintings (1910–1964).* Figueres: 2004. Web. http://www.salvador-dali.org/cataleg_raonat/index.php?lang=en (last accessed on April 11, 2016).

Michler, Ralf, and Lutz W. Löpsinger. *Salvador Dalí: Das druckgraphische Werk 1924–1980 – Œuvrekatalog der Radierungen und Mixed-Media-Graphiken.* Munich: Prestel, 1994. Print.

———. *Salvador Dalí: Das druckgraphische Werk II 1956–1980 – Œuvrekatalog der Lithographien und Holzstiche.* Munich, New York: Prestel, 1995. Print.

Sahli, Charles. *Salvador Dalí: 257 Editions originales 1964–1985.* New York: Art Inter; Paris: Michèle Broutta; Cologne: Orangerie-Reinz; Bern: Senans, 1985. Print.

Andy Warhol

Angell, Callie. *Andy Warhol Screen Tests: The Films of Andy Warhol Catalogue Raisonné Volume 1.* New York: Abrams in association with Whitney Museum of American Art, 2006. Print.

Feldman, Frayda, and Jörg Schellmann, eds. *Andy Warhol Prints: A Catalogue Raisonné.* Munich, New York: Editions Schellmann; Munich: Schirmer/Mosel Verlag; New York: Ronald Feldman Fine Arts, Inc., 1989. Print.

———. *Andy Warhol Prints: A Catalogue Raisonné 1962–1987.* Fourth edition. New York: D.A.P. / Distributed Art Publishers, Inc. in association with Ronald Feldman Fine Arts, Inc. / Edition Schellmann, The Andy Warhol Foundation for the Visual Arts, Inc., 2003. Print.

Frei, Georg, and Neil Printz, eds. *The Andy Warhol Catalogue Raisonné Volume 01: Paintings and Sculptures 1961–1963.* London, New York: Phaidon Press, 2002. Print.

Frei, Georg, Neil Printz, and Sally King-Nero, eds. *The Andy Warhol Catalogue Raisonné Volume 02A+02B: Paintings and Sculptures 1964–1969.* London, New York: Phaidon Press, 2004. Print.

Maréchal, Paul. *Andy Warhol: The Complete Commissioned Magazine Work 1948–1987: Catalogue Raisonné.* Munich, London, New York: Prestel, 2014. Print.

———. *Andy Warhol: The Complete Commissioned Posters 1964–1987: Catalogue Raisonné.* Munich, London, New York: Prestel, 2014. Print.

———. *Andy Warhol: The Record Covers 1949–1987: Catalogue Raisonné.* Montreal: The Montreal Museum of Fine Arts, Montreal; Munich, London, New York: Prestel 2008. Print.

Printz, Neil, and Sally King-Nero, eds. *The Andy Warhol Catalogue Raisonné Volume 03: Paintings and Sculptures 1970–1974.* London, New York: Phaidon Press, 2010. Print.

Others

Corlett, Mary L., and Ruth E. Fine. *The Prints of Roy Lichtenstein: A Catalogue Raisonné 1948–1997.* Easthampton, MA: Hudson Hill Press, 2002. Print.

López-Rey, José, and Odile Delenda. *Velázquez: Das vollständige Werk.* Trans. Egbert Baqué, Ursula Schmidt-Steinbach, and Brigitte Wölk. Cologne: TASCHEN GmbH, 2014. Print.

2
Exhibition Catalogues

Salvador Dalí

Abadie, Daniel, ed. *Salvador Dalí: retrospective 1920–1980.* Paris: Centre Georges Pompidou, 1979. Print.

———, ed. *La vie publique de Salvador Dalí.* Paris: Centre Georges Pompidou, 1980. Print.

Ades, Dawn, ed. *Dalí.* New York: Rizzoli, 2004. Print.

Aguer, Montse, and Lea Mattarella. *Dalí: un artista un genio.* Milan: Skira, 2012. Print.

Altaió, Vicenç. *Dalí: una vida de llibre – a life in books.* Barcelona: Destino, 2004. Print.

Dalí. New York: Knoedler Gallery, 1943. Print.

Dalí. New York: Phyllis Lucas Gallery – Old Print Center, 1971. Print.

Dalí: A Fifty Year Retrospective. Las Vegas: Silverstate Fine Art Collection, 2001. Print.

Dalí by Halsman. Figueres: Fundació Gala-Salvador Dalí, 2011. Print.

Dalí. Cultura de masas. Barcelona: Fundación "la Caixa"; Figueres: Fundación Gala-Salvador Dalí; Madrid: Museo Nacional Centro de Arte Reina Sofía, 2004. Print.

Dalí et ses ateliers. Figueres: Fundació Gala-Salvador Dalí, 2013. Print.

Dalí: Jewels – Joyas. London, Venice: Umberto Allemandi & C., Turin, 2001. Print.

Dalí Lacroix Gala: El privilegio de la intimidad. Santiago de Compostella: Fundación Eugenio Granell, 2000. Print.

Dalí: Mara e Beppe – Bilder einer Freundschaft. Augsburg: Römisches Museum, 2000. Print.

Dalí per Robert Descharnes. Cadaqués: Museu de Cadaqués, 2007. Print.

Dalí Shakespeare Visconti. Figueres: Fundació Gala-Salvador Dalí, 2016. Print.

Dalí versus Schaal. Figueres: Fundació Gala-Salvador Dalí, 2006. Print.

El ojo invisible: Enrique Sabater fotografía a Salvador Dalí. Barcelona: Lunwerg Editores, 2004. Print.

Gale, Matthew, ed. *Dalí & Film.* London: Tate Publishing, 2007. Print.

Gott, Ted, ed. *Salvador Dalí: Liquid Desire.* Melbourne, Victoria: Council of Trustees of the National Gallery of Victoria, Melbourne, 2009. Print.

Guldemond, Jaap, ed. *It's All Dalí: Film, fashion, photography, design, advertising, painting.* Rotterdam: Museum Boijmans Van Beuningen, 2005. Print.

Habarta, Gerhard, ed. *Salvador Dalí: The Graphic Art.* Cadaqués: Museu Perrot-Moore; Vienna: Habarta Verlag, 1988. Print.

King, Elliott H., and David A. Brenneman. *Salvador Dalí: The Late Work.* Atlanta: High Museum of Art; New Haven and London: Yale University Press. 2010. Print.

Livingston, Lida, ed. *Dalí: A Study of his Art-in-Jewels.* Greenwich, Connecticut: The New York Graphic Society, 1952. Print.

Martin, Jean-Hubert, Montse Aguer, Jean-Michel Bouhours, and Thierry Dufrêne, eds. *Dalí.* Paris: Centre Pompidou, 2012. Print.

Mason, Rainer Michael. *vrai Dalí – fausse gravre – l'œuvre imprimé 1930–1934.* Geneva: Cabinet des estampes du Musée d'art et d'histoire, 1992. Print.

Matt, Gerald A. *Le Surréalisme c'est moi! Hommage an Salvador Dalí.* Vienna: Kunsthalle Wien, Verlag für Moderne Kunst, 2011. Print.

Maur, Karin von. *Salvador Dalí 1904–1989.* Stuttgart: Verlag Gerd Hatje, 1989. Print.

Nilsson, John Peter, and Matilda Olof-Ors. *Dalí Dalí featuring Francesco Vezzoli.* Stockholm: Moderna Musset; Göttingen: Steidl, 2009. Print.

Pollock to Pop: America's Brush with Dalí. St. Petersburg, Florida: The Salvador Dalí Museum, 2005. Print.

Salvador Dalí. New York: Julien Levy Gallery, 1939. Print.

Salvador Dalí: Àlbum de família. Figueres: Fundació Gala-Salvador Dalí; Barcelona: Fundació "la Caixa," 1998. Print.

Salvador Dalí: Canvas & water-colours from the Albaretto Collection. Milan: Electa, 1997. Print.

Salvador Dalí: Das goldene Zeitalter – Illustrationen 1920–1980 aus der Sammlung Richard H. Mayer. Bamberg: Kunstgalerien Böttingerhaus 2003. Print.

Salvador Dalí Enrique Sabater: Reciprocitats 1968–1980. Cadaqués: Museu de Cadaqués, 2008. Print.

Salvador Dalí y las revistas – Volumen I Número I. Figueres: Fundació Gala-Salvador Dalí, 2008. Print.

Soby, James Thrall. *Salvador Dalí.* New York: The Museum of Modern Art, 1941. Print.

The 3rd Dimension: The 1st World Exposition of Holograms conceived by Dalí. New York: Knoedler Gallery, 1972. Print.

Andy Warhol

Andy Warhol at the Dalí. St. Petersburg: The Salvador Dalí Museum, 1998. Print.

Andy Warhol B&W Paintings: Ads and Illustrations 1985–1986. New York, London: Gagosian Gallery, 2002. Print.

Andy Warhol CROSSES. Cologne: Erzbischöfliches Diözesanmuseum, 1999.

Andy Warhol: Guns, Knives, Crosses. Madrid: Galería Fernando Vijande, 1982. Print.

Andy Warhol Photography. Thalwil / Zurich, New York: Edition Stemmle, 1999. Print.

Andy Warhol Polaroids 1971–1986. New York: Pace/MacGill Gallery; London: Anthony d'Offay Gallery; Paris: Galerie Liliane & Michel Durrand-Dessert, 1992. Print.

Andy Warhol: Red Books. Göttingen: Steidl; New York: Pace/MacGill Gallery, 2004. Print.

Andy Warhol's Time Capsule 21. Pittsburgh: The Andy Warhol Museum; Frankfurt am Main. Museum für Moderne Kunst; Cologne: DuMont, 2003. Print.

Andy Warhol: 5 Deaths. New York: Stellan Holm Gallery, 2002. Print.

Baldwin, Gordon, and Judith Keller. *Nadar Warhol: Paris New York Photography and Fame*. Los Angeles: The J. Paul Getty Museum, 1999. Print.

Bastian, Heiner. *Andy Warhol Retrospective*. London: Tate Publishing; Los Angeles: The Museum of Contemporary Art, 2002. Print.

Benhamou-Huet, Judith. *Warhol TV*. Paris: La maison rouge et Angelo Cirimele – ACP, 2009. Print.

Blistène, Bernard. *Andy Warhol: The Statue of Liberty*. Paris: Galerie Thaddaeus Ropac, Paris. Print.

Cheim, John, ed. *Andy Warhol Nudes*. Woodstock, New York: The Overlook Press, 1995. Print.

Christie's. *Andy Warhol: Colored Mona Lisa*. Wednesday, May 13, 2015. New York: 2015. Print.

Christie's. *Andy Warhol's Mao*. Wednesday, November 15, 2006. New York: 2006. Print.

Coblentz, Patricia, ed. *Andy Warhol's "Folk and Funk."* New York: Museum of American Folk Art, 1977. Print.

Crone, Rainer. *Andy Warhol: Das zeichnerische Werk 1942–1975*. Stuttgart: Württembergischer Kunstverein, 1976. Print.

Cueff, Alain, ed. *Le grand monde d'Andy Warhol*. Paris: Éditions de la Réunion des musées nationaux, 2009. Print.

Cypryański, Piotr, ed. *Andy Warhol Polaroids: Celebrities and Self-Portraits*. Cologne: Jablonka Galerie; Krakow: Starmach Gallery, 2000. Print.

Dedichen, Henriette, ed. *Warhol's Queens*. Ostfildern: Hatje Cantz, 2013. Print.

Dergan, Rose, and Bob Monk. *Warhol from the Sonnabend Collection*. New York: Gagosian Gallery, Rizzoli, 2009. Print.

Factory Work: Warhol Wyeth Basquiat. Hanover, London: University Press of New England, 2006. Print.

Francis, Mark, and Margery King. *The Warhol Look: Glamour Style Fashion*. Pittsburgh: The Andy Warhol Museum; Munich, Paris, London: Schirmer/Mosel, 1997. Print.

Francis, Mark, and Koepplin, Dieter. *Andy Warhol: Drawings 1942 – 1987*. Boston, New York, London: Bulfinch Press, 1999. Print.

Gassen, Richard W., ed. *Andy Warhol: Sammlung José Mugrabi*. Milan: Mazzotta, 1996. Print.

Harris, Larissa, and Media Farzin. *13 Most Wanted Men: Andy Warhol and the 1964 World's Fair*. Queens, NY: Queens Museum, 2014. Print.

Heymer, Kay, ed. *Andy Warhol Headshots*. Cologne: Jablonka Galerie, 2000. Print.

———, ed. *Andy Warhol: Modern Madonna*. Cologne: Jablonka Galerie, 1999. Print.

Heymer, Kay, and Julia Garnatz, eds. *Andy Warhol Polaroids: Ladies & Gentlemen Sex Parts and Torsos*. Cologne: Jablonka Galerie, 2003. Print.

Husslein, Uwe, ed. *Nico: Stationen einer Popikone*. Cologne: Popkultur Köln e.V., 2008.

McShine, Kynaston, ed. *Andy Warhol: A Retrospective*. New York: The Museum of Modern Art, 1989. Print.

Menage à trois: Warhol, Basquiat, Clemente. Bonn: Kunst- und Ausstellungshalle der Bundesrepublik Deutschland, 2012. Print.

Meyer-Hermann, Eva, ed. *Andy Warhol: A Guide To 706 Items In 2 Hours 56 Minutes*. Rotterdam: NAi Publishers, 2008. Print.

Ofner, Astrid Johanna, ed. *Andy Warhol Filmmaker: Eine Retrospektive der Viennale und des österreichischen Filmmuseums*. Vienna: Viennale, 2005. Print.

Rosenthal, Mark, Marla Prather, Ian Alteveer, and Rebecca Lowery. *Regarding Warhol: Sixty Artists, Fifty Years*. New York: The Metropolitan Museum of Art, 2012. Print.

Schleif, Nina, ed. *Reading Andy Warhol*. Ostfildern: Hatje Cantz, 2013.

Schulz-Hoffmann, Carla, ed.; *Andy Warhol: The Last Supper*. Munich: Staatsgalerie Moderner Kunst München, 1998. Print.

Smith, John W., ed. *Posession Obsession: Andy Warhol and Collecting*. Pittsburgh: The Andy Warhol Museum, 2002. Print.

Solomon, Alan R. *Andy Warhol*. Boston: Institute of Contemporary Art, 1966. Print.

Sotheby's. *The Andy Warhol Collection*. April 23–May 3, 1988, Vol. I–V; New York: Sotheby's, Harry N. Abrams, Inc., 1988. Print.

Spiess, Werner. *Andy Warhol: Cars*. New York: Solomon Guggenheim Museum, 1988. Print.

Stavitsky, Gail. *Warhol and Cars: American Icons*; Montclair Art Museum, Montclair, New Jersey, 2011. Print.

Steinorth, Karl, and Thomas Buchsteiner, eds. *Andy Warhol Social Disease: photographs '76-'79*. Tübingen: Institut für Kulturaustausch, 1992. Print.

The Andy Warhol Foundation for the Visual Arts. *20-Year-Report 1987-2007*. New York: The Andy Warhol Foundation for the Visual Arts, Inc., 2007. Print.

The Andy Warhol Museum. Pittsburgh: The Andy Warhol Museum, Pittsburgh; New York: Distributed Art Publishers; Stuttgart: Cantz Publishers, 1994. Print.

Warhol, Andy, Kasper König, Pontus Hultén, and Olle Granath, eds. *Andy Warhol*. Stockholm: Moderna Museet, 1968. Print.

Warhol: Art. Fame. Mortality. St. Petersburg, Florida: The Salvador Dalí Museum, 2014. Print.

Warhol Myths. Düsseldorf: NRW-Forum Kultur und Wirtschaft, 2007. Print.

Warhol Shadows. Houston, TX: The Menil Collection, 1987. Print.

Whitney, David, ed. *Andy Warhol: Portraits of the 70s*. New York: Random House in association with the Whitney Museum of American Art, 1979. Print.

Zdenek, Felix, ed. *Andy Warhol: Retrospektiv*. Ostfildern: Hatje, 1993. Print.

Others Bailey, David. *Bailey's Stardust*. London: National Portrait Gallery, 2014. Print.

Bastian, Heiner, ed. *Sammlung Marx – Band I*. Berlin: Hamburger Bahnhof Museum für Gegenwart, 1996. Print.

———, ed. *Sammlung Marx – Band II*. Berlin: Hamburger Bahnhof Museum für Gegenwart, 1996. Print.

Chéroux, Clément, ed. *Man Ray Portraits: Paris – Hollywood – Paris*. Paris: Centre Pompidou, 2010. Print.

Christie's. *Impressionist & Modern Art Day Sale*. February 3, 2016, London, King Street. London: 2016. Print.

Christie's. *Pop Memorabilia*. Wednesday, September 28, 2005, South Kensington. London: 2005. Print.

D'Harnoncourt, Anne, and Kynaston McShine, eds. *Marcel Duchamp*. New York: The Museum of Modern Art; Philadelphia: Philadelphia Museum of Art, 1973. Print.

documenta III, Handzeichnungen. Kassel: Hessische Druck- und Verlagsanstalt, 1964. Print.

dOCUMENTA (13): Das Begleitbuch / The Guidebook. Ostfildern: Hatje Cantz Verlag, 2012. Print.

Henning, Andreas, ed. *Die Sixtinische Madonna: Raffaels Kultbild wird 500*; Munich, London, New York: Prestel, 2012. Print.

Homage to Marilyn Monroe. New York: Sidney Janis, 1967. Print.

Julien's Auctions. *Property from the Estate of Tony Curtis*, Beverly Hills, CA, September 17, 2011. Beverly Hills, CA: 2011. Print.

Lumpkin, Libby, ed. *The Bellagio Gallery of Fine Art: Impressionist and Modern Masters*. Las Vegas, Nevada: The Bellagio Gallery of Fine Art, Mirage Resorts, Incorporated, 1998. Print.

Ray Johnson…Dalí/Warhol and others…"Main Ray, Ducham, Openheim, Pikabia." New York: Richard L. Feigen & Co., 2009. Print.

Sassoon, Donald. *Da Vinci und das Geheimnis der Mona Lisa*. Bergisch Gladbach: Gustav Lübbe Verlag, 2006. Print.

Picasso: Visage de la paix. Figueras: Galeria de la cupula, 1975. Print.

Sotheby's. *Impressionist & Modern Art Day Sale Afternoon*, New York, May 8, 2008. New York: 2008. Print.

Sotheby's. http://www.sothebys.com/en/auctions/ecatalogue/2012/prints-n08896/lot.346.html (last accessed on April 12, 2016).

3
Works by Salvador Dalí
and Andy Warhol

Salvador Arco, Manuel del. *Dalí in the Nude (Dalí al
Dalí Desnudo)*. Trans. Antonio Cruz, and Jon Berle. St. Petersburg, Florida: The Salvador Dalí Museum, 1984. Print.

Bockris, Victor, and Andrew Wylie. "A Conversation with Dalí." *National Screw*. New York: December 1976. 14–18. Print.

Bosquet, Alain. *Conversations with Dalí*. Trans. Joachim Neugroschel. New York: E. P. Dutton & Co., Inc., 1969. Print.

Calvo Serraller, Francisco, ed. Dalí, Salvador; *Salvador Dalí Obra Completa – Volumen VII: Entrevistas*. Trans. Inés Serra, Agustín Martínez, Enrique Gaínza, José Destéfano, Marisa Abdala, Felip Tobar, Javier Ruiz Portella, Carles Andreu, and Kirsti Baggethun. Barcelona: Ediciones Destino; Figueres: Fundacío Gala-Salvador Dalí; Socieded Estatal de Conmemoraciones Culturales, 2006. Print.

Candy Darling. "Dalí by Darling." *Andy Warhol's Interview*. New York: May 1973. 12–13, 40. Print.

Dalí, Salvador. *Aufzeichnungen eines werdenen Genies: Tagebücher 1919–1920*. Trans. Theres Moser. Munich: Schirmer/Mosel, 2004. Print.

———. *Dalí by Dalí*. Trans. Eleanor R. Morse. New York: Harry N. Abrahms, Inc. Publishers, 1970. Print.

———. *Dalí de Draeger*. Trans. Eleanor R. Morse. New York: Abdrale Press, Harry N. Abrams, 1968. Print.

———. *Diary of a Genius*. Trans. Richard Howard. Garden City, New York: Doubleday & Company, Inc., 1965. Print.

———. *"Hello Dalí."* Cleveland, Ohio: The Salvador Dalí Museum; Figueras: Teatro Museo Dalí, 1975. Print.

———. *Hidden Faces*. Trans. Haakon M. Chevalier. New York: Dial Press, 1944. Print.

———. *Hommage à Meissonier*. Paris: Hôtel Meurice, 1967. Print.

———. "I Laugh Tremendously." *Newsweek*. New York: October 27, 1975. 56. Print.

———. *La Vie Secrète de Salvador Dalí: Suis-je un genie?*. Édition critique des manuscrits originaux de *La Vie Secrète de Salvador Dalí*, de Gala et Salvador Dalí, établie par Frédérique Joseph-Lowery. Lausanne: L'AGE D'HOMME, 2006. Print.

———. "Les six jours de Dalí." *Paris Match*. no. 1258. Paris: June 16, 1973. 3–4. Print.

———. "Playboy Interview: Salvador Dalí." *Playboy*. Chicago: July 1964. 41-48. Print.

———. *The Secret Life of Salvador Dalí*. Trans. Haakon M. Chevalier. New York: Dial Press, 1942. Print.

———. "Surrealism in Hollywood." *Harper's Bazaar*. New York: June 1937. 68-69, 132. Print.

———. *The Tragic Myth of Millet's Angelus*. Trans. Eleanor R. Morse. St. Petersburg, Florida: The Salvador Dalí Museum, 1986. Print.

———. *The Unspeakable Confessions of Salvador Dalí*. As told to André Parinaud. Trans. Harold J. Salemson. New York: William Morrow and Company, Inc., 1976. Print.

———. *Vogué – Numéro du cinquantenaire 1921/1971 realisé par Salvador Dalí*. Paris: December 1971. Print.

———. *50 Secrets of Magic Craftsmanship*. Trans. Haakon M. Chevalier. New York: Dial Press, 1948. Print.

Dalí, Salvador, and Philippe Halsman; *Dalí's Mustache: A Photographic Interview*. New York: Simon and Schuster, 1954. Print.

Delmar, Michäel. "Salvador Dalí: Astroview." *Façade*, No. 6. Paris: 1978. 6-8. Print.

Efron, Edith; "He Prefers to Watch TV Upside Down." *TV Guide*, Vol. 16, No. 23. Randor, PA: June 8, 1968. 6-10. Print.

Finkelstein, Haim, ed. and trans. *The Collected Writings of Salvador Dalí*. Cambridge: Cambridge University Press, 1998. Print.

Guillamet, Jaume, Joan Ferrerós, and Rafael Pascuet, eds. *Studium, la revista del jove Dalí*. Figueres: Brau Edicions, 2003. Print.

Mercouri, Melina, and Salvador Dalí. "A Redbook Dialogue." *Redbook*. Dayton, Ohio: February 1965. 52, 90–95. Print.

Pauwels, Louis, and Salvador Dalí. *The Passions According to Dalí*. Trans. Eleanor R. Morse. St. Petersburg, Florida: The Salvador Dalí Museum, 1985. Print.

Andy Warhol Cohen, Scott, and Andy Warhol. "Andy Warhol Talks About Sex, Art, Fame and Money." FORUM. New York: January 1981. 18–23. Print.

Hackett, Pat, ed. *The Andy Warhol Diaries*. New York: Warner Books, 1989. Print. © 1989 by the Estate of Andy Warhol. Used by permission of Grand Central Publishing. All rights reserved.

Warhol, Andy. *America*. New York: Harper & Row, Publishers, Inc., 1985. Print.

———. "C.Z. by Andy." *Andy Warhol's Interview*. New York: August 1976. 8-11. Print.

———. "Lee." *Andy Warhol's Interview*. New York: March 1975. 4–6. Print.

———. *THE Philosophy of Andy Warhol (From A to B and Back Again)*. New York: Harcourt Brace Jovanovich, 1975. Print.

———. "TV." *Esquire*, Volume 84, No. 6. Chicago: December 1975. 136–137. Print.

Warhol, Andy, and Truman Capote. "Sunday with Mr. C.: An Audio-Documentary by Andy Warhol." *Rolling Stone*, No. 132. San Francisco: April 12, 1973. 28-48. Print.

Warhol, Andy, and Bob Colacello. *Andy Warhol's Exposures*. New York: Andy Warhol Books/Grosset & Dunlap, Inc., 1979. Print.

Warhol, Andy, and Pat Hackett. *Andy Warhol's Partybook*. New York: Crown Publishers Inc., 1988. Print.

———. *POPism: The Warhol '60s*. New York: Harcourt Brace Jovanovich, 1980. Print.

**4
Books and
Articles**

Salvador Dalí Argillet, Jean-Christophe. *Le siècle de Dalí*. Boulogne: Timée-Editions, 2004. Print.

Baudoin, Edmond. *Dalí par Baudoin*. Paris: Centre Pompidou/Aire Libre, 2012. Print.

Bona, Dominique. *Gala*. Paris: Flammarion, 1995. Print.

Bossert, David A. *Dalí and Disney: Destino*. Los Angeles, New York: Disney Editions, 2015. Print.

Bouhours, Jean-Michel. *Dalí*. Paris: Centre Pompidou, 2012. Print.

Briggs-Anderson, Barbara. *A Surrealistic Night in an Enchanted Forest*. BookBaby, 2012. E-book.

Carol, Márius. *Dalí: El final oculto de un exhibicionista*. Barcelona: Plaza & Janes Editores, S.A., 1990. Print.

Carol, Márius, Juan José Navarro Arisa, and Jordi Busquets. *El último Dalí*. Madrid: Ediciones El país, 1985. Print.

Casals, Jordi. *Salvador Dalí à Monte-Carlo*. Paris: Draeger, 2005. Print.

Catterall, Lee. *The Great Dalí Art Fraud and other Deceptions*. Fort Lee, New Jersey: Barricade Books, 1992. Print.

Cowles, Fleur. *The Case of Salvador Dalí*. Boston, Toronto: Little, Brown and Company, 1959. Print.

Dalí, Ana María. *Salvador Dalí visto por su hermana*. Barcelona: Editorial Juventud, S.A., 1949. Print.

Dalí, Gala. *Carnets intimes*. Neuilly-sur-Seine Cedex: Éditions Michel Lafon, 2012. Print.

"Dalí – Crazy Like a Fox." *Look*. Iowa: June 10, 1947. 95–99. Print.

Descharnes, Robert. *Dalí: The Work, The Man*. Trans. Eleanor R. Morse. New York: Harry N. Abrams, Inc., 1984. Print.

———. *Dalí: L'héritage infernal*. Paris: Éditons Ramsay-La Marge, 2002. Print.

———. *Salvador Dalí*. Trans. Eleanor R. Morse. New York: Harry N. Abrams, Inc., 1976. Print.

Descharnes, Robert and Gilles Néret. *Salvador Dalí: The Paintings*. Trans. Michael Hulse. Cologne: TASCHEN GmbH, 1993. Print.

Descharnes, Robert. *The World of Salvador Dalí*. Trans. Albert Field, and Haakon Chevalier. London: Macmillan, 1972. Print.

Diego, Estrella de. "Del leve paso por la celebridad. Breve historia de Andy Warhol y Salvador Dalí." *Arte y Parte*, no. 21. Santander: June-July 1999. 22–36. Print.

———. *Querida Gala: Las vidas ocultas de Gala Dalí*. Madrid: Espasa, 2003. Print.

Dufrêne, Thierry. *Salvador Dalí: double image double vie*. Vanves Cedex: Éditions Hazan, 2012. Print.

Éluard, Paul. *Letters to Gala*. Trans. Jesse Browner. New York: Paragon House, 1989. Print.

Etherington-Smith, Meredith. *The Persistence of Memory: A Biography of Dalí*. New York, Random House, 1993. Print.

Finkelstein, Nat. "Dinner with Dalí & Meeting Marcel." *Étant donné*, no. 5. Paris: 2003. 76–89. Print.

Gibson, Ian. *The Shameful Life of Salvador Dalí*. London: Faber and Faber Limited, 1997. Print.

Gómez de la Serna, Ramón. *Dalí*. Trans. Nicholas Fry, and Elisabeth Evans. Edison, NJ: The Wellfleet Press, 1988. Print.

Gómez de Liaño, Ignacio. *El camino de Dalí (Diario personal, 1978–1989)*. Madrid: Ediciones Siruela, 2004. Print.

Grenier, Catherine. *Salvador Dalí: L'invention de soi*. Paris: Flammarion, 2011. Print.

Hughes, Robert. "Baby Dalí: An exhibition shows that the young Salvador Dalí thought he could do anything, and he almost could." *TIME*. New York: July 4, 1994. 68. Print.

Ingram, Catherine. *This is Dalí*. London: Laurence King Publishing, 2014. Print.

King, Elliott H. *Dalí, Surrealism and Cinema*. Harpenden, Herts: Kamera Books, 2007. Print. kamerabooks.co.uk/dali.

Koons, Jeff. "Who paints bread better than Dalí?," *Tate Etc.*, issue 3. London: Spring 2005. Web. http://www.tate.org.uk/context-comment/articles/who-paints-bread-better-dali (last accessed on April 12, 2016).

Lake, Charlton. *In Quest of Dalí*. New York: G. P. Putnam's Sons, 1969. Print.

Lear, Amanda. *Je ne suis pas du tout celle que vous croyez...* Paris: Hors Collection, 2009. Print.

———. *Mon Dalí*. Paris: Michel Lafon, 2004. Print.

———. *My Life with Dalí*. London: Virgin Books Ltd., 1985. Print.

Lehmann, Detlef. *Die göttlichen Düfte: Salvador Dalí und seine Parfums*. Berlin, Paris, New York: Marco, 2004. Print.

Les Cahiers du Musée national d'art moderne, No. 121. Paris: Fall 2012. Print.

Lester, Peter. "Amanda Lear: Dalí's Muse." *Andy Warhol's Interview*. New York: January 1974. 26–27. Print.

Llongueras, Lluís. *Mi Dalí particular*. Barcelona: 1989. Print.

———. *Todo Dalí*. Barcelona: Ediciones Prensa y Video S.L., 2003. Print.

"Mao Tsé-toung illustré par Dalí." *Le Figaro*. Paris: February 28, 1967. Print.

"Marvelous & Fantastic." *TIME*. New York: December 14, 1936. 60–62. Print.

Mas Peinado, Ricard. *Dalí: Leben und Werk*. Trans. Annette Durner, Fritz Rückert, and Susan Elaine Gildersleeve. Petersberg: Michael Imhof Verlag, 2004. Print.

Maurer Queipo, Isabel, and Nanette Rißler-Pipka, eds. *Dalís Medienspiele: Falsche Fährten und paranoische Selbstinszenierungen in den Künsten*. Bielefeld: transcript Verlag, 2007. Print.

McGirk, Tim. *Wicked Lady: Salvador Dalí's Muse*. London, Sydney, Auckland, Johannesburg: Hutchinson, 1989. Print.

Mekas, Jonas. "The performance years." *Tate Etc.*, issue 10. London: Summer 2007. Web. http://www.tate.org.uk/context-comment/articles/performance-years (last accessed on April 12, 2016).

Michaud, Michael Gregg. "A Walk On The Surreal Side With Holly Woodlawn." *The Salvador Collector's Quarterly*, Vol. 2 No. 1. Pacific Palisades: The Salvador Dalí Gallery, 1992. 8. Print.

———. "Dalí Realizes Unreality with Pandora." *The Salvador Collector's Quarterly*. Pacific Palisades: The Salvador Dalí Gallery, Summer 1991. 5. Print.

———. "Dinner with Dalí, from Soup to Beans or Conquest of the Average." *The Salvador Collector's Quarterly*, Vol. 2 No. 2. Pacific Palisades: The Salvador Dalí Gallery, 1992. 6. Print.

———. "The Night Dalí Fell In Love With Pandora's Cranium." *The Salvador Collector's Quarterly*. Pacific Palisades: The Salvador Dalí Gallery, Fall 1991. 6. Print.

Miravitlles, Jaume. *Més gent que he conegut*. Barcelona: Destino, 1981. Print.

Montua, Gabriel. *Dalís 20. Jahrhundert: Die westliche Kunst zwischen Politik, Markt und Medien*. Berlin, Boston: De Gruyter, 2015. Print.

Moore, Peter. *Flagrant Dalí*. Trans. Nicolas Idier. Paris: Bernard Grasset, 2009. Print.

Morse, A. Reynolds. *A. Reynolds Morse Journals*. Washington: Smithsonian Archives of American Art, 1973. Microfilm.

Millet, Catherine. *Dalí and Me*. Trans. Trista Selous. Zurich: Scheidegger & Spiess, 2008. Print.

Nuridsany, Michel. *Dalí*. Paris: Flammarion, 2004. Print.

Orwell, George. *Dickens, Dalí & Others*. New York: Reynal & Hitchcock, 1946. Print.

Otte, Torsten. *Salvador Dalí: Eine Biographie mit Selbstzeugnissen des Künstlers*. Würzburg: Königshausen & Neumann, 2006. Print.

Pérez Andújar, Javier. *Salvador Dalí: A la conquista de lo irracional*. Madrid, México, Buenos Aires, San Juan, Santiago: Algaba Ediciones, 2003. Print.

Pitxot, Antoni. *Sobre Dalí: Conversaciones con Fernando Huici March*. Barcelona: Editorial Planeta, 2014. Print.

Pitxot, Antoni, and Montse Aguer. *Port Lligat Salvador Dalí House-Museum*. Barcelona: Editorial Escudo de Oro, S.A., 1998. Print.

Pitxot, Antoni, and Josep Playà. *Gala Dalí's Castle*. Barcelona: Editorial Escudo de Oro, S.A., 1998. Print.

Pitxot, Antoni, Montse Aguer, and Jordi Puig. *House-Museum Gala Dalí Castle Púbol*. Trans. Steve Cedar. Menorca: Triangle Postals, SL, 2011. Print.

———. *Salvador Dalí House-Museum Port Lligat – Cadaqués*. Trans. Steve Cedar. Menorca: Triangle Postals, SL, 2008. Print.

———. *The Dalí Theatre-Museum in Figueres*. Trans. Steve Cedar. Menorca: Triangle Postals, SL, 2005. Print.

Puignau, Emilio. *Vivencias con Salvador Dalí*. Barcelona: Editorial Juventud, 1995. Print.

Puyplat, Lisa, Adrian La Salvia, and Herbert Heinzelmann, eds. *Salvador Dalí: Facetten eines Jahrhundertkünstlers*. Würzburg: Königshausen & Neumann, 2005. Print.

Robinson, Ruth. "Dalí and His Art Preview at Hartford Gallery." *New York Times*, New York: December 18, 1965. Print.

Rogerson, Mark. *The Dalí Scandal*. London: Victor Gollancz Ltd., 1987. Print.

Romero, Luis. *Dedálico Dalí*. Barcelona: Ediciones B, 1989. Print.

Ross, Michael Elsohn. *Salvador Dalí and the Surrealists*. Chicago: Chicago Review Press, 2003. Print.

Rubio, José Luis. "El útimo show de Dalí." *Cambio 16*. Madrid: December 16, 1979. 87–95. Print.

Sánchez Vidal, Agustín. *Buñuel, Lorca, Dalí: El engima sin fin*. Barcelona: Planeta, 1996. Print.

San Martín, Francisco Javier. *Dalí-Duchamp: Una fraternidad oculta*. Madrid: Alianza Editorial, 2004. Print.

Saurat, Marie-France. "Le miracle Dalí." *Paris Match*, No. 2533. Paris: November 2, 1984. 92–95. Print.

Schaffner, Ingrid. *Salvador Dalí's Dream of Venus*. New York: Princeton Architectural Press, 2002. Print.

Secrest, Meryle. *Salvador Dalí: A Biography*. New York: Dutton, 1986. Print.

Shanes, Eric. *Dalí: Die Meisterwerke*. Trans. Karl-Heinz Ebnet. Zug: Swan, 1991. Print.

Ste. Croix, Philip de, ed. *In the Company of Dalí: The Photographs of Robert Whitaker*. Kent: Touchstone Books Ltd, 2006. Print.

Steiner, Paul. "Magical Meeting of Two Minds." *Journal*. Lorain, Ohio: December 19, 1970. Print.

———. "Salvador Dalí Gives His View of Mia Farrow." *Commonwealth Reporter*. Fond Du Lac, Wis.: October 16, 1970. Print.

Swing, Raymond Gram. "Nativity of a New World." *Esquire*. Chicago: December 1942. 40–43. Print.

Taylor, Michael R., ed. *The Dalí Renaissance: New Perspectives on His Life and Art after 1940. An International Symposium*. Philadelphia: Philadelphia Museum of Art, 2008. Print. Used with permission.

Tharrats, Joan Josep. *Cent anys de pintura a Cadaqués*. Barcelona: Parsifal Ediciones, 2007. Print.

Thurlow, Clifford. *Sex, Surrealism, Dalí and Me: The Memoirs of Carlos Lozano*. Penryn, Cornwall: Razor Books, 2000. Print.

Tusquets Blanca, Oscar. *Dalí y otros amigos*. Barcelona: RqueR editorial, 2003. Print.

Wernick, Robert. "Dalí's Dollars." *LIFE*. New York: July 24, 1970. 48–55. Print.

Zalman, Sandra. "Dalí, Margitte, and Surrealism's Legacy, New York c. 1965." *Journal of Surrealism and the Americas*. 6:1. Tempe, Arizona: 2012. 24–28. Print.

Andy Warhol

Andy Warhol: "Giant" Size. London, New York: Phaidon Press, 2003. Print.

Andy Warhol: Transcript of David Bailey's ATV Documentary. London: Bailey Litchfield/Matthew Miller Dunbar Ltd., 1972. Print.

"ANDY WARHOL, un fenómeno cultural y sociógico." *Hierro*. Bilbao: January 19, 1983. Print.

Antonio, Emile de, and Mitch Tuchman. *Painters Painting*. New York: Abbeville Press, 1984. Print.

Archerd, Army. "Just For Variety." *Daily Variety*. Hollywood, CA: November 20, 1968. Print.

Aronson, Steven M. L. "Possession Obsession." *House & Garden*. Beverly Hills: December 1987. 186–196. Print.

"art in view." *Andy Warhol's Interview*. New York: April 1973. 17. Print.

"Barbara Feldon + Andy Warhol = Pop Fashions." *TV Guide*. Vol. 14, No. 10. Radnor, PA: March 5, 1966. 23–27. Print.

Bianchi, Paolo, and Christoph Doswald. *Gegenspieler: Andy Warhol – Joseph Beuys*. Frankfurt am Main: Fischer Taschenbuch Verlag, 2000. Print.

Bockris, Victor. *Warhol*. London, Sydney, Ackland, Johannesburg: Frederick Muller, 1989. Print.

Bockris, Victor, and Gerard Malanga. *up-tight: The Velvet Underground Story*. New York: Cooper Square Press, 2003. Print.

Bourdon, David. *Warhol*. New York: Harry N. Abrams, Inc., Publishers, 1989. Print.

———. *Warhol*. Trans. Manfred Allié. Cologne: DuMont, 1989. German edition. Print.

Bradshaw, Kate. "Warhol exhibit coming to Dalí Museum in St. Pete." *TBO*. Tampa: November 7, 2013. Web. http://www.tbo.com/pinellas-county/warhol-exhibit-coming-to-dali-museum-in-st-petersburg-20131107/ (last accessed on April 6, 2016).

Brown, Mick. "Broken Lives." *Telegraph Magazine*. London: November 16, 1996. 32–41. Print. © Mick Brown – *Telegraph Magazine* 16th November 1996.

Candela, Ana. "Andy Warhol: un espectáculo casi pop." *Cinco Días*. Madrid: January 19, 1983. Print.

Colacello, Bob. *Holy Terror: Andy Warhol Close up*. New York: HarperCollins Publishers, 1990. Print.

———. "OUT." *Andy Warhol's Interview*. New York: March 1975. 40-41. Print.

———. "OUT." *Andy Warhol's Interview*. New York: May 1975. 41. Print.

Coplans, John. *Andy Warhol*. New York: New York Graphic Society Ltd., 1970. Print.

"Crazy Golden Slippers." *LIFE*. New York: January 21, 1957. 12-13. Print.

Crimp, Douglas. *"One Kind of Movie": The Films of Andy Warhol*. London: The Mitt Press, Cambridge, 2012. Print.

Crone, Rainer. *Andy Warhol*. Stuttgart: Verlag Gerd Hatje, 1970. Print.

Daggett Dillenberger, Jane. *The Religious Art of Andy Warhol*. New York: Continuum, 1998. Print.

DeRogatis, Jim. *The Velvet Underground: An Illustrated History of a Walk on the Wild Side*. Minneapolis, MN: Voyageur Press, 2009. Print.

"En su muestra madrileña, Andy Warhol reconoce que se repite a sí mismo." *El Correo Catalán*. Barcelona: January 19, 1983. Print.

Finkelstein, Nat. *ANDY WARHOL: 'Oh this is fabulous' – The silver age at the Factory 1964–1967*. Rotterdam: Bébert editions, 1989. Print.

Galella, Ron. *Warhol by Galella: That's Great!*. New York: The Monacelli Press, Inc., 2008. Print.

Geldzahler, Henry, and Robert Rosenblum. *Andy Warhol: Portraits*. London: Anthony d'Offay Gallery London in association with Thames and Hudson, 1993. Print. © 1993 Anthony d'Offay Gallery, London. Reprinted by kind permission of Thames & Hudson Ltd., London.

Glueck, Grace. "What Happened? Nothing." *New York Times*. New York: April 11, 1965. Print.

Golden, Reuel, ed. *Andy Warhol: Polaroids 1958–1987*. Cologne: TASCHEN, 2015. Print.

Goldsmith, Kenneth, ed. *I'll Be Your Mirror: The Selected Andy Warhol Interviews 1962–1987*. Introduction by Reva Wolf. Afterword by Wayne Koestenbaum. New York: Carroll & Graf Publishers, 2004. Print.

Gross, Michael Joseph. "Factory Boys." *New York*. New York: October 7, 2007. Web. http://nymag.com/arts/art/season2007/38966/ (last accessed on April 8, 2016).

Guilbert, Cécile. *Warhol Spirit*. Paris: Grasset, 2008.

Guiles, Fred Lawrence. *Loner at the Ball: The Life of Andy Warhol*. London, New York, Toronto, Sydney, Auckland: Bantam Press, 1989. Print.

Highberger, Craig B. *Superstar in a Housedress: The Life and Legend of Jackie Curtis*. New York: Chamerlain Bros., 2005. Print.

Hohenberg, Christophe von, and Charlie Scheips; *Andy Warhol: The Day the Factory Died*; Empire Editions, LLC, New York; 2006.

Hughes, Robert. "Man for the Machine." *TIME*. New York: May 17, 1971. 42-43. Print.

Ingram, Catherine. *This is Warhol*. London: Laurence King Publishing, 2014. Print.

Johnson, Catherine. *Thank you Andy Warhol*. New York, London: Glitterati Incorporated, 2012. Print.

Kornbluth, Jesse. *Pre-Pop Warhol*. New York: Panache Press, 1988. Print.

Liebs, Holger, and Jason Schmidt. "Buon Giorno!." *Monopol*. Berlin: July 2011. 64-73. Print.

Lüthy, Michael. *Andy Warhol: Thirty Are Better Than One*. Frankfurt am Main, Leipzig: Insel Verlag, 1995. Print.

Makos, Christopher. *Andy Warhol by Christopher Makos*. Milan: Charta, 2002. Print.

———. *Andy Warhol China 1982*. New York: Timezone 8 Limited, 2007. Print.

———. *Warhol Makos: A personal photographic memoir*. London: Virgin, 1988. Print.

———. *Warhol / Makos In Context*; Brooklyn, NY: powerHouse Books, 2006. Print.

Malanga, Gerard. *ARCHIVING WARHOL: An Illustrated History by Gerard Malanga*. New York: Creation Books, 2002. Print.

McCabe, David, and David Dalton. *A Year in the Life of Andy Warhol*. London, New York: Phaidon Press, 2003. Print.

Nemeczek, Alfred. "God bless you." *art*, No. 2. Hamburg: February 2007. 72-79. Print.

Newton, Jeremiah, Francesca Passalacqua, and D. E. Hardy. *My Face for the World to See: the Diaries, Letters and Drawings of Candy Darling, Andy Warhol Superstar*. Honolulu, Hardy Marks Publications, 1997. Print.

"New York Small Talk." *Andy Warhol's Interview*. New York: February 1974. 29-30. Print.

Nuridsany, Michel. *Warhol*. Paris: Flammarion, 2001. Print.

O'Connor, John, and Benjamin Liu. *Unseen Warhol*. New York: Rizzoli, 1996. Print.

O'Sullivan Shorr, Catherine. *Andy Warhol's Factory People: Book I – Welcome to the Silver Factory*. Planet Group Entertainment: 2014. Print.

———. *Andy Warhol's Factory People: Book III – Your 15 Minutes Are Up*. Planet Group Entertainment: 2014. Print.

Patalas, Enno. *Andy Warhol und seine Filme: Eine Dokumentation*. Munich: Wilhelm Heyne Verlag, 1971. Print.

Prekop, Rudo, and Micha Cihlář. *Andy Warhol and Czechoslovakia*. Řevnice: Arbor vitae, 2011. Print.

Ratcliff, Carter. *Andy Warhol*. New York, London, Paris: Abbeville Press, 1983. Print.

Shanes, Eric. *Warhol: The Masterworks*. London: Studio Editions, 1991. Print.

Sherman, Tony, and David Dalton. *Pop: The Genius of Andy Warhol*. New York: Harper, 2009. Print.

Shore, Stephen, and Lynne Tillman: *The Velvet Years: Warhol's Factory 1965–67*. New York: Thunder's Mouth Press, 1995. Print.

"Small Talk." *Andy Warhol's Interview*. New York: May 1973. 46-47. Print.

Smith, Patrick S. *Andy Warhol's Art and Films*. Ann Arbor, Michigan: UMI Research Press, 1986. Print.

———. *Warhol: Conversations about the Artist*. Ann Arbor, Michigan: UMI Research Press, 1988. Print.

Stein, Jean, and George Plimpton. *Edie: An American Biography*. New York: Alfred A. Knopf, 1982. Print.

Tavel, Ronald. *Andy Warhol's Ridiculous Screenplays*. Silverton, OR: Fast Books, 2015. Print.

The Andy Warhol Museum. *Andy Warhol: 365 Takes*. London: Thames & Hudson, 2004. Print.

"The Slice-of-Cake School." *TIME*. New York: May 11, 1962. 52-55. Print.

Ultra Violet. *Famous For 15 Minutes: My Years with Andy Warhol*. San Diego, New York, London: Harcourt Brace Jovanovich, 1988. Print.

Watson, Steven. *Factory Made: Warhol and the Sixties*. New York: Pantheon Books, 2003. Print.

Weinraub, Bernard. "Mothers." *Esquire*. New York: November 1966. 96-101, 158. Print.

Wilcock, John. *The Autobiography and Sex Life of Andy Warhol*. New York: Trela Media, LLC, 2010. Print.

Winsten, Archer. "Andy Warhol at Cinematheque." *New York Post*. New York: February 9, 1966. Print.

Woodlawn, Holly, and Jeffrey Copeland. *A Low Life in High Heels: The Holly Woodlawn Story*. New York: St. Martin's Press, 1991. Print.

Woronov, Mary. *Swimming Underground: My Years in the Warhol Factory*. London: Serpent's Tail, 2000. Print.

———. *Swimming Underground: my time at andy warhol's factory*. Montaldo Publishing. 2013. E-book.

Others

André, Michael. "Surrealism in Art." *ARTnews*. New York: April 1975. 91. Print.

Arnold, Steven. unpublished autobiography.

Ashley, April, and Douglas Thompson. *The First Lady*. London: John Blake Publishing, 2006. Print.

Banchoff, Thomas F. *Beyond the Third Dimension*. New York: Scientific American Library, 1990. Print.

Beard, Nejma, and David Fahey, eds. *Peter Beard*. Cologne: TASCHEN GmbH, 2008. Print.

Berkow, Ira. "Whitey Ford Switches From Pitcher to Pitchman." *Post & Times Star*. Cincinnati, Ohio: April 12, 1969. Print.

Blume, Lesley M. M. *It Happened Here*. New York: Thornwillow Press, 2011. Print.

Bonanos, Christopher. *Instant: The Story of Polaroid*. New York: Princeton Architectural Press, 2012. Print.

Bond, Jack. *Mad Jack*. unpublished autobiography.

Bonk, Ecke, ed. *Die grosse Schachtel: de ou par Marcel Duchamp ou Rrose Sélavy. Inventar einer Edition*. Munich: Schirmer/Mosel, 1998. Print.

Braudy, Susan. *This Crazy Thing Called Love: The Golden World and Fatal Marriage of Ann and Billy Woodward*. New York: New York, 1992. Print.

Breton, André. *Surrealism and Painting*. Trans. Simon Watson Taylor. Boston: MFA Publications, 2002. Print.

Buñuel, Luis. *My Last Breath*. Trans. Abigail Israel. London: Jonathan Cape Ltd, 1984. Print.

Cerwin, Herbert. *In Search of Something*. Los Angeles: Sherbourne Press, 1966. Print.

Cooper, Alice, Keith Zimmerman, and Kent Zimmerman. *Alice Cooper, Golf Monster*. London: Aurum, 2007. Print.

Crosby, Caresse. *The Passionate Years*. New York: The Dial Press, 1953. New York. Print.

Danicke, Sandra. "Revolution in Himbeerrot." *art*, No. 6. Hamburg: June 2008. 34-41. Print.

Dever, Joseph X. "Gotha G-Round." *New York World Telegram & Sun*. New York: April 6, 1965. Print.
Dougherty, Philip H. "Braniff Launches New Ad Campaign." *Star*. San Juan, Puerto Rico: February 18, 1969. Print.
Fallowell, Duncan, and April Ashley. *April Ashley's Odyssey*. London: Jonathan Cape, 1982. Print.
Farrow, Mia. *What Falls Away: A Memoir*. New York, London, Toronto, Sydney, Auckland: Doubleday, 1997. Print.
Fisher, Marc. *Something in the Air*. New York: Random House, 2007. Print.
Fuchs, Ernst. *Phantastisches Leben: Erinnerungen*. Berlin: Kindler Verlag GmbH, 2001. Print.
Garner, Philippe, and David Alan Mellor. *The Essential Cecil Beaton: Photographien 1920–1970*. Munich: Schirmer/Mosel, 2012. Print.
Gateau, Jean-Charles. *Paul Éluard oder Der sehende Bruder: Biographie ohne Maske*. Trans. Roswitha Litzka. Berlin: edition q, 1994. Print.
Gavzer, Bernard. "Tribute to Marilyn Monroe." *Post*. Chattanooga, Tenn: December 11, 1967. Print.
Gibson, Ian. *Federico García Lorca: A Life*. New York: Pantheon Books, 1989. Print.
Giorno, John. *You Got to Burn to Shine*. London, New York: High Risk Books/Serpent's Tail, 1994. Print.
Goll, Claire. *La poursuite du vent*. Paris: Olivier Orban, 1976. Print.
Haag, Romy. *Eine Frau und mehr*. Berlin: Quadriga, 1999. Print.
Habarta, Gerhard. *Ernst Fuchs: Das Einhorn zwischen den Brüsten der Sphinx*. Graz, Vienna, Cologne: Styria, 2001. Print.
Hahn, Otto. "Entretien avec Marcel Duchamp." Étant donné, no. 3. Paris: 2001. 116–125. Print.
———. "Passport No. G255300." *art and artists*. New York: July 1966. 6–11. Print.
Halsman, Philippe. *Halsman Sight and Insight*. New York: Doubleday, 1972. Print.
Halsman, Philippe, and Yvonne Halsman. *Halsman At Work*. New York: Harry N. Abrams, 1989. Print.
Harrison, Martin. *David Bailey Locations: The 1970s Archive*. London: Thames & Hudson, 2003. Print.
Haslam, Nicholas. *Redeeming Features: A Memoir*. New York: Alfred A. Knopf, 2009. Print.
Hirschberg, Lynn. "To The Manor Born." *The New York Times*. New York: August 19, 2001. Print.
Hughes, Robert. *Nothing If Not Critical: Selected Essays on Art and Artists*. New York: Penguin Books, 1992. Print.
"It was 'smile time' at the Polo Ground." *Broadcasting*. Washington, D.C.: April 22, 1963. Print.
James, Edward. *Swans Reflecting Elephants: My Early Years*. Edited by George Melly. London: Weidenfeld and Nicolson, 1982. Print.
James, Ted. "The Overnight Success." *Cosmopolitan*. New York: January 1966. 14–15. Print.
Jean, Marcel. *Geschichte des Surrealismus*. Trans. Karl Schmitz-Moormann. Cologne: Verlag M. DuMont Schauberg, 1961. Print.
Jodorowsky, Alexandro. "Dune – Le film que vous ne verrez jamais." Supplément au *Métal Hurlant*, No. 107. Paris: 1985. Print.
Koons, Jeff. *Conversations with Norman Rosenthal*. London: Thames & Hudson, 2014. Print.
La révolution surréaliste. Paris: Éditions Jean-Michel Place, 1975. Print.
Lautréamont, Comte de. *Les Chants de Maldoror*. Trans. Guy Wernham. New York: New Directions Publishing Corporation, 1966. Print.
Levy, Julien. *Memoir of an Art Gallery*. New York: G. P. Putnam's Sons, 1977. Print.
Lilly, Doris. "Doris Lilly's Party Line." *New York Post*. New York: February 8, 1967. Print.
Lois, George, and Bill Pitts. *The Art of Advertising: George Lois on Mass Communication*. New York: Harry N. Abrams, Inc., 1977. Print.
Lommel, Ulli. *Zärtlichkeit der Wölfe*. Munich: belleville, 2012. Print.
Loney, G. M. "OH NO! THE COCKETTES!" *Interview*. Vol. II No. 2. New York, 1971. 7. Print.
Lyons, Leonard. "The Lyons Den." *New York Post*. New York: May 5, 1965. Print.
Madoff, Steven Henry, ed. *Pop Art: A Critical History*. Berkeley, Los Angeles, London: University of California Press, 1997. Print.
Marcadé, Bernard. *Marcel Duchamp*. Paris: Flammarion, 2007. Print.
MacGraw, Ali. *Moving Pictures*. New York, Toronto, London, Sydney, Auckland: Bantam Books, 1991. Print.
Man Ray. *Self-Portrait*. Boston: Little, Brown and Company, 1988. Print.

Moore, Gene, and Jay Hyams. *My Time at Tiffany's*. New York: St. Martin's Press, 1990. Print.
Morella, Joe, and Edward Z. Epstein. *Paulette: The Adventurous Life of Paulette Goddard*. New York: St. Martin's Press, 1985. Print.
Morgan, Bill. *The Works of Allen Ginsberg 1941–1994: A Descriptive Bibliography*. Westport, Connecticut, London: Greenwood Press, 1995. Print.
Morris, Bob. "A Debutante Grows Up." *The New York Times*. New York: August 17, 2012. Print.
Osterwold, Tilman. *Pop Art*. Cologne: TASCHEN, 1989. Print.
Pellicer, Raynal. *Photobooth: The Art of the Automatic Portrait*; Abrams, New York, 2010. Print.
"People." *TIME*. Chicago: September 6, 1954. 32. Print.
"People." *TIME*. New York: December 15, 1967. 45. Print.
Polizzotti, Mark. *Revolution des Geistes: Das Leben André Bretons*. Trans. Jörg Trobitius. Munich, Vienna: Carl Hanser Verlag, 1996. Print.
Reed, Lou. *Pass Thru Fire: The Collected Lyrics / Alle Song*. Trans. Manfred Allié. Frankfurt am Main: S. Fischer Verlag, 2006. Print.
Reynolds, Jim. "Potassa: The Great Pretender." *Interview*. New York: April 1977. 32–33. Print.
Richardson, John. *Sacred Monsters, Sacred Masters*. London: Jonathan Cape, 2001. Print.
Rohwer, Jörn Jakob, and Vera Lehndorff. *Veruschka: Mein Leben*. Cologne: DuMont Buchverlag, 2011. Print.
Rose, Sir Francis. *Saying Life: The Memoirs of Sir Francis Rose*. London: Casssell, 1961. Print.
Rosenquist, James, and David Dalton. *Painting Below Zero: Notes on a Life in Art*. New York: Alfred A. Knopf, 2009. Print.
Salk, Susanna. *C.Z. Guest: American Style Icon*. New York: Rizzoli, 2013. Print.
Schjeldahl, Peter. "Marilyn: Still Being Exploited?" *New York Times*. New York: December 17, 1967. Print.
Spies, Werner, ed. *Max Ernst: Retrospektive 1979*. Munich: Prestel, 1979. Print.
Spoto, Donald. *Marilyn Monroe: The Biography*. London: Chatto & Windus, 1993. Print.
Stein, Danielle. "Portrait of a Lady." *W*. New York: December 2007. Web. http://www.wmagazine.com/people/insiders/2007/12/sao_schlumberger (last accessed on April 12, 2016).
Swift, Harry. "Inside Alice." *Rolling Stone*, No. 134, San Francisco: May 10, 1973. 36–42. Print.
Tinkerbelle. "Amanda Lear." *Interview*. New York: March 1978. 32–33. Print.
Tomkins, Calvin. *Marcel Duchamp: Eine Biographie*. Trans. Jörg Trobitius. Munich, Vienna: Carl Hanser Verlag, 1999. Print.
"Trotting to the Bank." *Newsweek*. New York: January 17, 1966. Print.
"U.S.A. Gentes." *La Vanguardia Española*. Barcelona: April 27, 1973. 26. Print.
Venosa, Robert. *Noospheres*. Petaluma, California: Pomegranate Artbooks; 1991. Print.
Webb, Constance. *Not Without Love: Memoirs*. Hanover, London: Dartmouth College, University Press of New England, Hanover, 2003. Print.
Weiermair, Peter, ed. *Steven Arnold: "Exotic Tableaux."* Kilchberg/Zurich: Edition Stemmle, 1996. Print.
Wilcock, John. *Manhattan Memories: an autobiography*. Raleigh, NC: lulu.com, 2009. Print.

5
**Interviews with
the Author**

Jade Albert: e-mail on June 30, 2011.
April Ashley: telephone conversation on July 30, 2011.
Marc Balet: conversation on December 3, 2012 in New York.
Prof. Thomas Banchoff: telephone conversation on May 26, 2010.
François-Marie Banier: e-mail on October 24, 2011.
Benedetta Barzini: e-mail on May 23, 2011; e-mail on May 24, 2011; e-mail on June 16, 2012; e-mail on July 29, 2012; e-mail on September 14, 2012.
Peter Beard: Skype conversation on September 24, 2010.
Dr. Frances F.L. Beatty: conversation on June 27, 2012 in New York.
Candice Bergen: e-mail from Alex McCann on July 6, 2012.
Brigid Berlin: conversation on December 4, 2012 in New York.
Bruno Bischofberger: e-mail from Silvia Sokalski on September 2, 2009.
Victor Bockris: e-mail on July 16, 2010; e-mail on September 9, 2015; e-mail on September 12, 2015.
Jack Bond: e-mail on June 19, 2012; conversation on July 27, 2012 in London; e-mail on February 9, 2016.

Lee Brooks: conversation on November 13, 2011 in San Francisco.
Stephen Bruce: telephone conversation on July 6, 2011.
Jean Jacques Bugat: conversation on December 29, 2013 in Paris.
Baron Roger de Cabrol: conversation on December 5, 2012 in New York.
Howard R. Carr: telephone conversation on January 10, 2013.
Neke Carson: conversation on December 6, 2012 in New York.
Sally Chamberlain: e-mails on October 24, 2015.
Wynn Chamberlain: telephone conversation on August 26, 2011.
Bettina Cirone: telephone conversation on August 11, 2014.
Bob Colacello: telephone conversation on September 22, 2010; conversation on June 26, 2012 in New York; e-mail on September 11, 2013.
Leslie Curtis: telephone conversation on April 27, 2013.
Ronnie Cutrone: telephone conversation on July 8, 2012.
Pierre Dinand: e-mail on April 18, 2012; e-mail on April 20, 2012; e-mail on September 7, 2012; e-mail on September 8, 2012; conversation on March 1, 2013 in Paris.
Manuel Donato Díez: conversation on March 20, 2013 in Nordstemmen.
Suzan Etkin: telephone conversation on July 26, 2010.
Jeff Fenholt: e-mail on May 31, 2010.
Suzannah Fleming: e-mail on November 25, 2011; e-mail on December 22, 2011; e-mail on December 23, 2011; e-mail on December 25, 2011; e-mail on December 28, 2011; e-mail on December 29, 2011; conversation on July 20, 2012 in London; e-mail on June 16, 2015.
Vincent Fremont: conversation on June 28, 2012 in New York; e-mail on April 16, 2015. © Vincent Fremont. All rights reserved.
Edgar Froese: e-mail on November 30, 2011.
Prof. Ernst Fuchs: conversation on May 13, 2010 in Klagenfurt; conversation on May 14, 2010 in Klagenfurt.
Ron Galella: e-mail from Anthony Miller on March 11, 2016.
Vito Giallo: telephone conversation on May 25, 2010.
John Giorno: conversation on March 13, 2011 in Besançon; e-mail on July 2, 2011.
Cornelia Guest: telephone conversation on January 3, 2013.
Jonathan Guinness, 3rd Baron Moyne: conversation on December 17, 2014 in London.
Bruce Gowers: telephone conversation on February 27, 2013.
Pat Hackett: conversation on December 4, 2012 in New York; e-mail on August 12, 2013.
Irene Halsman: telephone conversation on February 9, 2015.
Nicholas Haslam: conversation on July 20, 2012 in London.
Robert Heide: conversation on December 6, 2012 in New York.
Catherine Hesketh: telephone conversation on August 27, 2012.
Jane Holzer: e-mail on September 9, 2015; e-mail on September 13, 2015.
Lynn Karlin: e-mail on May 2, 2013.
Ivan C. Karp: e-mail on February 25, 2010; e-mail on March 2, 2010.
Leonard Kessler: letter in August 2011.
Udo Kier: telephone conversation on January 7, 2011.
Sally Kirkland: telephone conversation on December 16, 2012.
Bernd Klüser: conversation on April 30, 2010 in Munich.
Lady Anne Lambton: telephone conversation on August 11, 2012.
Amanda Lear: telephone conversation on March 13, 2010.
Vera von Lehndorff: telephone conversation on January 6, 2012.
Dorothy Lichtenstein: e-mail from Dr. Jack Cowart on May 12, 2010.
Benjamin Liu: conversation on November 30, 2012 in New York.
Lluís Llongueras: e-mail on February 2, 2010; e-mail on September 19, 2012.
Roxanne Lowit: telephone conversation on July 24, 2012.
Christopher Makos: e-mail on July 25, 2009; conversation on June 28, 2012 in New York.
Gerard Malanga: e-mail on September 24, 2009; e-mail on September 27, 2009; conversation on July 2, 2012 in Hudson, NY; e-mail on March 21, 2013; e-mail on March 2, 2015; e-mail on March 9, 2016. © Gerard Malanga.
Louis Markoya: e-mail on May 17, 2010; e-mail on November 30, 2011; e-mail on August 15, 2012; e-mail on March 10, 2016; e-mail on March 11, 2016; e-mail on March 12, 2016; e-mail on March 23, 2016.
Dr. Erich Marx: conversation on April 13, 2011 in Berlin.
George Mason: e-mail on June 8, 2011; e-mail on June 22, 2011; e-mail on July 26, 2012; e-mail on August 23, 2012; e-mail on February 4, 2016; e-mail on March 23, 2016.
Hans Mayer: conversation on March 11, 2011 in Düsseldorf.
David McCabe: telephone conversation on June 14, 2010.
Taylor Mead: telephone conversation on June 2, 2010.
Jonas Mekas: e-mail on July 31, 2011.
Heiner Meyer: conversation on February 16, 2011 in Bielefeld.
Sylvia Miles: conversation on July 1, 2012 in New York.
Mario Montez: e-mail from Marc Siegel on February 13, 2010.
Malcom Morley: e-mail from Andrew Lee on February 23, 2016.
Chris Murray: e-mail on November 15, 2012; e-mail on September 19, 2013; e-mail on October 2, 2013.
Billy Name: e-mail on July 2, 2009; e-mail on August 9, 2010; e-mail on August 13, 2012; e-mail on August 14, 2012.

Jeremiah Newton: telephone conversation on August 8, 2010; e-mail on September 23, 2013.
Ivy Nicholson: telephone conversation on November 20, 2009; telephone conversation on December 10, 2013.
Glenn O'Brien: e-mail on December 21, 2011.
Yoko Ono: e-mail from Amanda Season Keeley on Sept. 1, 2010.
Pandora: letter in August 2009; e-mail on November 19, 2009; letter on August 15, 2010; e-mail on May 31, 2011; conversation on November 20, 2011 in Mariposa, California; conversation on November 21, 2011 in Mariposa, California; e-mail on August 9, 2013; e-mail on August 19, 2015; e-mail on January 27, 2016.
Philip Pearlstein: telephone conversation on April 13, 2010.
Elsa Peretti: telephone conversation on October 2, 2015.
Antoni Pitxot: telephone conversation on August 5, 2009; conversation on September 5, 2009 in Cadaqués; letter on August 30, 2012.
Roger Prigent: conversation on June 27, 2012 in New York.
Asha Puthli: e-mail on January 2, 2012.
John Reinhold: telephone conversation on May 26, 2010.
Nick Rhodes: conversation on December 15, 2014 in London.
Allan Rich: telephone conversation on April 25, 2013.
Sir John Richardson: conversation on July 3, 2012 in New York.
James Rosenquist: e-mail on March 30, 2010.
William Rothlein: telephone conversation on October 23, 2011; telephone conversation on February 3, 2015; e-mail on September 1, 2015.
Chris Royer: telephone conversation on October 7, 2013.
Jörg Schellmann: conversation on April 30, 2010 in Munich.
Ingeborg Princess zu Schleswig-Holstein: conversation on June 30, 2011 in Hamburg.
Denise Sandell: telephone conversation on November 27, 2011; conversation on July 3, 2012 in New York; e-mail on December 5, 2015.
Folker Skulima: telephone conversation on September 17, 2009; telephone conversation on June 29, 2011; conversation on February 26, 2011 in Berlin.
Walter Steding: telephone conversation on January 12, 2013.
Jon Stevens: telephone conversation on December 16, 2011.
Harold Stevenson: telephone conversation on February 8, 2011; telephone conversation on July 3, 2015.
Michael Ward Stout: telephone conversation on June 9, 2010.
Dr. Elizabeth Teissier-Hynek: telephone conversation on October 21, 2015.
Nena Thurman: e-mail on September 21, 2011; telephone conversation on July 11, 2012.
Penelope Tree: e-mail on June 9, 2010.
Ultra Violet: telephone conversation on August 11, 2008; conversation on October 18, 2008 in New York; e-mail on April 17, 2009; conversation on October 18, 2009 in New York.
Santi Visalli: Skype conversation on July 9, 2012.
Monique van Vooren: telephone conversation on June 8, 2012; e-mail on July 23, 2015.
Viva: e-mail on April 17, 2012; e-mail on April 18, 2012.
Geneviève Waïte: telephone conversation on March 2, 2012.
Louis Waldon: telephone conversation on October 2, 2013.
Shelley Wanger: telephone conversation on July 23, 2012; conversation on December 3, 2012 in New York.
James Warhola: e-mail on September 13, 2011; conversation on December 2, 2012 in New York.
Paul Warhola: conversation on November 27, 2012 in Pittsburgh.
Paul C. Warhola: telephone conversation on June 28, 2013.
Horst Weber von Beeren: telephone conversation on June 22, 2011; conversation on September 16, 2011 in Düsseldorf; conversation on December 7, 2012 in New York; e-mail on February 10, 2013; e-mail on April 11, 2013; e-mail on May 13, 2013; e-mail on December 22, 2013; e-mail on April 28, 2015; e-mail on November 25, 2015; conversation on January 2, 2016 in Berlin.
Paul Weiss: telephone conversation on March 30, 2015.
Susan Whitaker: telephone conversation on April 18, 2012.
John Wilcock: e-mail on October 14, 2013; e-mail on October 15, 2013.
Gigi Williams: telephone conversation on May 5, 2014.
William S. Wilson: conversation on December 7, 2012 in New York.
Peter Wise: conversation on June 28, 2012 in New York.
Holly Woodlawn: e-mail from Craig Highberger on March 9, 2010.
Jamie Wyeth: telephone conversation on April 3, 2013.
Susi Wyss: conversation on October 25, 2013 in Paris.

**6
Online
Sources**

Andy Warhol Films: Newspapers Adverts 1964-1974. https://warholfilmads.wordpress.com/1966-2/ (last accessed on April 16, 2016).

"A Surrealist Parisian Dinner Party chez Madame Rothschild, 1972." Messy Nessy Chic, August 27, 2013. http://www.messynessychic.com/2013/08/27/a-surrealist-parisian-dinner-party-chez-madame-rothschild-1972/ (last accessed on April 13, 2016).

Bullock, Michael. "The Precious Moments Are Really Precious: How Victor Hugo Changed My Life." August 19, 2011. http://keepthelightsonfilm.com/archives/gay-new-york/victor-hugo-changed-my-life (last accessed on April 8, 2016).

Clark, Ron. "Harold Stevenson: A Brief History of an American Artist." 2009. http://www.ronclarkstudio.com/harold-stevensonb.html (last accessed on April 12, 2016).

Dalíplanet. http://daliplanet.blogsome.com/2008/06/28/the-st-regis-hotel/ (last accessed on November 29, 2011).

Davenport, Tawsha Brinkley. "Harold Stevenson Interview." http://www.warholstars.org/articles/haroldstevenson.html (last accessed on April 12, 2016).

Girst, Thomas. "Two Minds on a Single Wavelength." *toutfait.* December 1999. http://www.toutfait.com/issues/issue_1/Interviews/interview_tphillips.HTM (last accessed on April 8, 2016).

"Ivy Nicholson: Warhol's Superstar." http://www.speciousspecies.net/nicholson.htm (last accessed on April 5, 2016).

jonasmekas.com. http://jonasmekas.com/40/film.php?film=3 (last accessed on March 6, 2016).

Le petit dimanche illustré. http://www.ina.fr/video/CPF88004673/salvador-dali-video.html (last accessed on April 11, 2016).

Montes-Baquer, José. http://u2r2h-documents.blogspot.de/2007/07/download-impression-de-la-haute.html (last accessed on April 6, 2016).

oscars.org. http://aaspeechesdb.oscars.org/link/050-4/ (last accessed on April 12, 2016).

Planetentertainmentgroup. http://planetgroupentertainment.squarespace.com/the-louis-walden-interview/ (last accessed on January 25, 2016).

Saturday Night Live Scripts. http://snltranscripts.jt.org/81/81awarhol.phtml (last accessed on April 8, 2016).

"When Warhol Met Dalí." Phaidon. http://de.phaidon.com/agenda/art/picture-galleries/2011/october/24/when-warhol-met-dali/?idx=1 (last accessed on April 12, 2016).

7
Documentaries

Andy Warhol. Directed by Kim Evans. London: London Weekend Television "South Bank Show," 1987.

Andy Warhol: A Life at the Edge. Produced by Jeff Swimmer. New York: CBS News Productions, 1998.

Dalí in New York. Directed and produced by Jack Bond. London: BBC, 1965.

Gala. Directed by Silvia Munt. Barcelona: Ovideo; 2003.

Jodorowsky's Dune. Directed by Frank Pavich. Amsterdam: City Film; Paris: Camera One; New York: Endless Picnic, 2013.

Le divin Dalí. Directed by Gérard Thomas d'Hoste. Perpignan: Trabucaire, 1989.

Pie in the Sky: The Brigid Berlin Story. Directed and produced by Vincent Fremont and Shelly Dunn Fremont. New York: Vincent Fremont Enterprises, 1999.

The Fame and Shame of Salvador Dalí. Directed and produced by Mike Dibb. London: BBC, 1996.

Salvador Dali. Directed and produced by Gabriella Polletta. London: ITN Factual Ltd. for A & E Television Network, 2004.

Split: Portrait of a Drag Queen. Directed by Ellen Fisher Turk and Andrew Weeks. Charlottesville, VA: Water Bearer Films, 1993.

8
Television Programs

I've Got a Secret, February 25, 1963. New York: CBS.

The Merv Griffin Show, December 30, 1965. New York: Westinghouse Broadcasting.

9
Other Documents

Letter from A. Reynolds Morse to Andy Warhol on April 17, 1973. Archives of the Andy Warhol Museum, Pittsburgh.

Alphabetical Index

Image Credits

© 2016, ProLitteris, Zurich for the works by Peter Beard, Oriol
Maspons i Casades, Eric Schaal
© Salvador Dalí, Fundació Gala-Salvador Dalí / 2016, ProLitter-
is, Zurich for the works by Salvador Dalí
All Andy Warhol Artworks © The Andy Warhol Foundation for
the Visual Arts, Inc. / 2016, ProLitteris, Zurich

no. 1: © Víctor Mira
no. 2, 3, 11, 14, 15, 29, 30: © KEYSTONE/MAGNUM
PHOTOS/Philippe Halsman
no. 4, 16: © Robert Whitaker/Getty Images
no. 5: © J. Paul Getty Trust. Getty Research Institute, Los Angeles (2014.R20)
no. 6: © Botti/Stills/Gamma
no. 7: © KEYSTONE/MAGNUM PHOTOS/Burt Glinn
no. 8: © Woodfin Camp/The LIFE Images Collection/Getty
Images. Photo by Ken Heyman/Woodfin Camp
no. 9: © Ron Galella Collection
no. 10: © The Cecil Beaton Studio Archive at Sotheby's
no. 13: © Roxanne Lowit
no. 17: © The Estate of Nat Finkelstein
no. 18, 19: © 2016 The Andy Warhol Museum, Pittsburgh, PA,
a museum of Carnegie Institute.
no. 20: © The Village Voice
no. 21, 22: © *Interview* Magazine
no. 25: photo © Bridgeman Images
no. 26: © Peter Beard. Courtesy of Peter Beard Studio, New
York and Art + Commerce
no. 27: photo © MMK Museum für Moderne Kunst Frankfurt am Main, Ehemalige Sammlung Karl Ströher,
Darmstadt, photographer: Axel Schneider, Frankfurt
am Main
no. 31: photo © Christie's Images / Bridgeman Images
no. 32: photo © 2016. Image copyright The Metropolitan
Museum of Art/Art Resource/Scala, Florence.
no. 34: Photograph Courtesy of Sotheby's, Inc. © 2008
no. 36: photo © Christopher Makos 1981, makostudio.com
no. 37: photo by Eric Schaal ©Fundació Gala-Salvador Dalí,
Figueres, 2016
no. 38: © Paul Weiss
no. 39: © Billy Name / Lid Images
no. 40: © Chamberlain Family Collection
no. 41, 42: © David McCabe
no. 43, 44: © David Bailey
no. 45: Photo Robert Descharnes © Descharnes & Descharnes
sarl 2016
no. 46, 47, 48, 49: © AWF/ARS
no. 50, 51, 52: © Condé Nast Archive/Corbis
no. 53, 54, 55: © Jade Albert
no. 56: © Enrique Sabater
no. 57: photo © Torsten Otte

Despite best efforts, we have not been able to identify the holders of copyright and printing rights for all the illustrations.
Copyright holders not mentioned in the credits are asked to
substantiate their claims, and recompense will be made according to standard practice.

<table>
<tr><td>Concept and text</td><td>Torsten Otte</td></tr>
<tr><td>Graphic Design</td><td>2×Goldstein+Fronczek</td></tr>
<tr><td>Translations</td><td>Lynne Kolar-Thompson</td></tr>
<tr><td>Copyediting</td><td>Lisa Rosenblatt</td></tr>
<tr><td>Proofreading</td><td>Charlotte Eckler</td></tr>
<tr><td>Lithographs, printing and binding</td><td></td></tr>
<tr><td></td><td>Graphicom, Vicenza, Italy</td></tr>
</table>

Front Cover
Dalí Kissing Andy, New York 1978,
photo: Christopher Makos 1978, www.makostudio.com

Verlag Scheidegger & Spiess AG
Niederdorfstrasse 54   8001 Zürich   Switzerland
www.scheidegger-spiess.ch